St Augustine
AND THE CONVERSION OF ENGLAND

St Augustine

AND THE CONVERSION OF ENGLAND

EDITED BY RICHARD GAMESON

SUTTON PUBLISHING

First published in the United Kingdom in 1999 by
Sutton Publishing Limited · Phoenix Mill
Thrupp · Stroud · Gloucestershire · GL5 2BU

Copyright © The Contributors, 1999

All rights reserved. No part of this publication may be reproduced, stored in a retrieval system, or transmitted, in any form, or by any means, electronic, mechanical, photocopying, recording or otherwise, without the prior permission of the publisher and copyright holders.

British Library Cataloguing in Publication Data
A catalogue record for this book is available from the British Library

ISBN 0-7509-2087-4

Typeset in 11/15 pt Ehrhardt.
Typesetting and origination by
Sutton Publishing Limited.
Printed in Great Britain by
Redwood, Trowbridge, Wiltshire.

Contents

List of Contributors		vii
Foreword by the Dean of Canterbury		ix
Preface		x
Acknowledgements		xi
Abbreviations		xii
1	*Augustine of Canterbury: Context and Achievement* RICHARD GAMESON	1
2	*Augustine and Gregory the Great* R.A. MARKUS	41
3	*England and the Continent in the Sixth and Seventh Centuries: the Question of Logistics* STÉPHANE LEBECQ	50
4	*Augustine and Gaul* IAN WOOD	68
5	*The Archaeology of Conversion on the Continent in the Sixth and Seventh Centuries: Some Observations and Comparisons with Anglo-Saxon England* SIMON BURNELL and EDWARD JAMES	83
6	*The British Church and the Mission of Augustine* CLARE STANCLIFFE	107

7	*The Reception of Christianity at the Anglo-Saxon Royal Courts* BARBARA YORKE	152
8	*Questioning Ritual Purity: The Influence of Gregory the Great's Answers to Augustine's Queries about Childbirth, Menstruation and Sexuality* ROB MEENS	174
9	*The Gregorian Tradition in Early England* ANTON SCHARER	187
10	*The Architecture of the Augustinian Mission* ERIC CAMBRIDGE	202
11	*The* Biblia Gregoriana MILDRED BUDNY	237
12	*The Gospels of St Augustine* RICHARD MARSDEN	285
13	*The Earliest Books of Christian Kent* RICHARD GAMESON	313
14	*In Gregory's Shadow? The Pre-Conquest Cult of St Augustine* ALAN THACKER	374
15	Goscelin's *Life of Augustine of Canterbury* FIONA GAMESON	391
16	*The Early History of Saint Augustine's Abbey, Canterbury* RICHARD EMMS	410
General Index		429
Index of Manuscripts		435

List of Contributors

Mildred Budny, who specialises in the study of Anglo-Saxon manuscripts, is Director of the Research Group on Manuscript Evidence, based at Princeton. Her publications include *Insular, Anglo-Saxon and Early Anglo-Norman Manuscript Art at Corpus Christi College, Cambridge*, 2 vols (1997).

Simon Burnell has lectured at the Universities of Exeter, Berne and Zurich as well as working in various museums. He specialises in Merovingian archaeology and history, and has published most recently *Die reformierte Kirche von Sissach BL: mittelalterliche Kirchenbauten und merowingerzeitliche 'Stiftergräber'* (1998).

Eric Cambridge, who practises as a solicitor, holds an honorary research fellowship in the Departments of Archaeology and History, University of Durham. He has recently contributed to and co-edited *Oswald: Northumbrian King to European Saint* (1995).

Richard Emms, a retired schoolmaster, has a long-standing research interest in the history of Saint Augustine's Abbey and its manuscripts, on which he has published several articles.

Fiona Gameson, who teaches part-time at the University of Kent, specialises in Old English poetry, on which topic she has published several articles.

Richard Gameson is Reader in Medieval History at the University of Kent. He specialises in early manuscripts and cultural history. His most recent book is *The Manuscripts of Early Norman England* (1999).

Edward James is Professor of History at the University of Reading and Director of the Graduate Centre for Medieval Studies. His *Britain in the First Millennium* will be published in 2000, and is to be followed by a study of Gregory of Tours.

Stéphane Lebecq is Professor of Medieval History at the University of Lille III. His publications include *Les origines franques: Ve–IXe siècle* (1990). His *L'éveil de l'Occident (Ve–Xe siècle)* will be published in 2000.

Robert A. Markus is Professor Emeritus at the University of Nottingham and a Fellow of the British Academy. His most recent book is *Gregory the Great and his World* (1997).

Richard Marsden lectures in Old English and Anglo-Saxon Studies in the School of English Studies, University of Nottingham. He has published widely on medieval language and literature, and the history of the Latin Bible.

Rob Meens lectures in the History Department, University of Utrecht. A specialist in early medieval culture and religious history, his publications include *Het tripartite boeteboek. Overlevering en betekenis van vroegmiddeleeuwse biechtvoorschriften* (1994).

Anton Scharer is Associate Professor of Medieval History at the University of Vienna. His publications include *Die angelsächsische Königsurkunde im 7. und 8. Jahrhundert* (1982), and *Herrschaft und Repräsentation: Studien zur Hofkultur König Alfreds des Grossen* (at press).

Clare Stancliffe is Honorary Lecturer and Fellow at the University of Durham. Her recent publications include work on Columbanus and (as co-editor and contributor) *Oswald: Northumbrian King to European Saint* (1995).

Alan Thacker is Deputy Editor of the Victoria County History, and is based at the University of London's Institute of Historical Research. Recent and imminent publications include articles on the cult of Gregory the Great and on the saint as patron of the state in the early Middle Ages, and a volume of essays on medieval archaeology, art and architecture in Chester.

Ian Wood is Professor of Early Medieval History at the University of Leeds. In addition to numerous articles, he is the author of *The Merovingian Kingdoms 450–751* (1994) and *Gregory of Tours* (1994).

Barbara Yorke is Reader in the Department of History and Archaeology, King Alfred's College, Winchester. Her publications include *Kings and Kingdoms of Early Anglo-Saxon England* (1990) and *Wessex in the Early Middle Ages* (1995).

Dean and Chapter of Canterbury

Foreword

The fourteen-hundredth anniversary of the mission of St Augustine to re-convert England to Christianity in 1997 was marked by a number of significant events which focused on Canterbury Cathedral, Saint Augustine's Abbey, and the University of Kent at Canterbury. On St Augustine's Day, a National Ecumenical Service, in the presence of His Royal Highness the Prince of Wales, was held in the cathedral, and on the following day there was a Roman Catholic Mass in the ruins of Saint Augustine's Abbey, attended by some five thousand people, who afterwards processed to the cathedral for Vespers sung by the Benedictine monastic communities of England. English Heritage marked the occasion by opening a museum and visitor interpretation centre at Saint Augustine's Abbey; the Friends of Canterbury Cathedral sponsored three special academic lectures; and numerous exhibitions, pilgrimages and religious services were held throughout the year. Central to the celebrations was the academic conference at the University of Kent at Canterbury, organised by Dr Richard Gameson and sponsored by the university and the Dean and Chapter. This present volume contains the proceedings of that conference, which some seventy scholars from across the world attended. The papers form a significant contribution to the study of the Augustinian mission and the conversion of England, and it is a privilege to have been associated both with the conference and the addition to scholarship which it marked.

JOHN A. SIMPSON
Dean of Canterbury

Preface

The present volume originated in a conference held at the University of Kent in September 1997 as part of the celebrations commemorating the fourteen-hundreth anniversary of the arrival of St Augustine in England. It was sponsored by the School of History of the University of Kent, and the Dean and Chapter of Canterbury. In planning and realising the event, I received invaluable help from a steering committee comprising Richard Emms, Fiona Gameson, Margaret Sparks and Michael Stansfield, and we were supported by Jackie Waller and Sian Dixon of the School of History. It is impossible to imagine more agreeable and efficient colleagues.

Half in jest it was quipped at the last steering meeting that, if for any reason speakers dropped out or failed to produce a text, it would be incumbent upon members of the committee to fill the resulting gaps. A glance at the page of contents will reveal that, in the event, three of us were thus obligated. Now, while it might be considered an editor's duty to make good at least one such shortfall, members of another steering committee could reasonably have regarded themselves as exempt from such duty. It is a tribute to the affability, efficiency and scholarship of Richard Emms and Fiona Gameson that they accepted their 'commissions' at very late stages and carried them out so successfully.

It is a pleasure to pay tribute to Sutton Publishing, who have been sympathetic, supportive, and professional throughout the long business of turning the proceedings of the conference into this book. Equally, I wish to record my thanks to Christine Gameson, who, as ever, provided valuable help with the proofs; to Dr Ghazwan Butrous, who initiated and arranged the production of pl. I and figs 1.4–5; and to Paul Bennett and the Canterbury Archaeological Trust for their work on pl. II. Grateful acknowledgement is also made to the St Augustine's Foundation, Canterbury, for providing a subvention which permitted the inclusion of the colour plates. Finally, it is not invidious to single out one person for special thanks when such thanks are fully deserved, and I wish to record my particular gratitude for the staunch support I have received at every stage of my long involvement with St Augustine from Fiona Gameson.

RICHARD GAMESON
The Feast of Augustine of Canterbury, 1999

Acknowledgements

Grateful acknowledgement is here made to the libraries, museums and individuals who supplied artwork and photographs, and kindly granted permission for the material to be reproduced. The photographs of manuscripts at Corpus Christi College and Trinity Hall, Cambridge, and Worcester Cathedral reproduced in Chapters 11 and 16 were taken by Mildred Budny. Figs 11.1–2 were prepared by Leslie French and Mildred Budny. The artwork and photographs that are not credited below were by Richard Gameson.

Avranches, Bibliothèque municipale: fig. 13.24; Bibliothèque nationale de France: figs 1.10, 9.3, 13.25–8 and 30; Bodleian Library: figs 12.3–5, 13.5, 9–10, 12; British Library: pls VI–VIII, figs 9.1, 11.3–5, 11.7, 13.6–7, 13–14, 22–3, 15.1, 16.4; British Museum: figs 3.5, 7.1–2; M. Budny: pl. V, figs 11.1–2, 11.6, 8–10, 16, 16.3; S. Burnell: figs 5.1–4; G. Butrous: pl. I, figs 1.3–4; E. Cambridge: figs 10.1–10, 12–13; Cambridge University Library (the Syndics) fig. 11.13; Corpus Christi College, Cambridge (the Master and Fellows): pls IV, V, figs 11.10, 16, 12.1–2, 13.3, 16.3; Devizes Museum: fig. 7.4; J.P. Getty Museum: fig. 11.15; Istituto Fotografico Editoriale Antella, Florence: 11.12; Kungl. Bibliotek, Stockholm: figs 13.15–19, 21; S. Lebecq: fig. 3.4; National Museums & Galleries on Merseyside: pl. III; Society of Antiquaries: fig. 10.11; Trinity Hall, Cambridge (the Master and Fellows): figs 11.8–9; Troyes, Bibliothèque municipale: fig. 13.1–2; University of Kent, Photographic Service: fig. 1.5; I. Wood: fig. 4.1; Worcester Cathedral (the Dean and Chapter): fig. 11.6.

Abbreviations

Arch Cant	*Archaeologia Cantiana*
ArchJ	*Archaeologia Journal*
ASE	*Anglo-Saxon England* (Cambridge, 1972+)
ASSAH	*Anglo-Saxon Studies in Archaeology and History*
BAR	British Archaeological Reports
BL	British Library, London
BnF	Bibliothèque nationale de France, Paris
BodL	Bodleian Library, Oxford
CBA	Council for British Archaeology
CC	Corpus Christianorum (Turnhout)
CCCC	Corpus Christi College, Cambridge
CCSL	*Corpus Christianorum Series Latina*
CLA	E.A. Lowe, *Codices Latini Antiquiores: a Palaeographical Guide to Latin Manuscripts Prior to the Ninth Century*, 11 vols plus Supplement (Oxford, 1934–71), 2nd edn of vol. II (Oxford, 1972)
EEMF	Early English Manuscripts in Facsimile (Copenhagen)
EHR	*English Historical Review*
HBS	Henry Bradshaw Society
HE	*Bede's Ecclesiastical History of the English People*, eds B. Colgrave and R.A.B. Mynors (Oxford, 1969)
JBAA	*Journal of the British Archaeological Association*
JEH	*Journal of Ecclesiastical History*
MGH	Monumenta Germaniae Historica (Berlin, Hanover, Munich)
PL	*Patrologia Latina*, ed. J.-P. Migne, 221 vols (Paris, 1844–64)
RS	Rolls Series
SCH	*Studies in Church History*
TRHS	*Transactions of the Royal Historical Society*

CHAPTER 1
Augustine of Canterbury: Context and Achievement

Richard Gameson

In 596 the kingdoms of which 'England' was then composed were without exception pagan; a century later all were officially Christian (cf. fig. 1.1). There can be no doubt that the conversion of the Anglo-Saxons to Christianity was the single most important development in their history during this period: not only did it represent a major change in the system of belief and attendant religious custom, it also affected numerous other aspects of life (and death) – not to mention redefining England's relations with her neighbours. Henceforth England was spiritually, and hence culturally, increasingly in alignment with the countries of the old Roman Empire rather than with the northern Germanic realms beyond the Rhine. While much pertaining to the conversion of the Anglo-Saxons is unknown and unknowable, it is clear that the arrival of the Roman missionary, Augustine, in Canterbury in 597 represented a decisive stage in the process, and that this thereby marked a watershed in the history of England. Who then was Augustine; what was his context; what did he accomplish; and what were its implications?

At one level we are relatively well informed about Augustine: indeed we know more about his activities than those of most other figures of the early Anglo-Saxon period. Bede, whose magisterial *Ecclesiastical History of the English People* completed in 731 is our principal narrative source for early English history, devotes no fewer than fourteen chapters to Augustine and the mission that he led, while other chapters dealing with his immediate successors fill out the picture. Moreover, since, as Bede himself tells us, his leading source and helper in this work as a whole was Albinus, who was abbot of Saint Augustine's Abbey, Canterbury from 709–33, we can assume that the northern scholar had access to the best information about Augustine that was then available. Bede described Albinus's activities in this respect as follows:

1.1. The main kingdoms of Britain in the seventh century (including the location of selected towns and sites). (Gameson)

[He] carefully ascertained from written records or from the old traditions all that the disciples of St Gregory had done in the kingdom of Kent or in the neighbouring kingdoms. He passed on to me whatever seemed worth remembering through Nothhelm a godly priest of the church in London, either in writing or by word of mouth. Afterwards, Nothhelm went to Rome and got permission from the present Pope Gregory [II] to search through the archives of the holy Roman church and there found some letters of Gregory [I] and of other popes. On the advice of Father Albinus, he brought these to us on his return to be included in our *History*.

On the other hand, Bede was writing nearly 130 years after Augustine's death, and as the extract from his Preface quoted above makes clear, he is at best merely a secondary source for the time and events in question, being dependent on the material Albinus supplied. Moreover, the early communities at Canterbury do not seem to have been especially energetic in preserving Augustine's memory; and the dynamic Archbishop Theodore who contributed to revitalising the Anglo-Saxon church in the late seventh century (and whose protégé Albinus had been) promoted instead the cult of Gregory.[1] Indeed, the English as a whole preferred to see Gregory I as the founder of their church: it was not unflattering that the great Pope had taken a personal interest in their conversion. Symptomatic of this emphasis is the fact that, while no independent biography of Augustine was written until after the Norman Conquest (and was then, incidentally, the work of a Flemish scholar not an Englishman),[2] around 700 an anonymous Anglo-Saxon at Whitby composed a life of Gregory, which is, in fact, the earliest biography of that pontiff. Furthermore, in addition to any inherent bias in the material supplied by Albinus, Bede was himself a great admirer of Gregory, and took pains to stress the Pope's role in his account of the mission. And as the other main sources for the events – namely the papal letters and the *Libellus responsionum* (Gregory's replies to Augustine's questions), both of which Bede quotes extensively – were written by Gregory himself, Augustine has come down to us very much in the Pope's shadow.[3] Moreover, because of the wealth of information about Gregory, his shadow is a very long one.[4]

Modern accounts of the conversion of England, following Bede, have tended to stress the importance of Gregory on the one hand, and on the other of the Irish missionaries, notably Aidan, who were primarily active in Northumbria. By and large, Bede describes the exploits of the Irish with a warmth and colour that is lacking from his account of Augustine – the result of greater personal knowledge and of easier access to oral traditions. And while recent work has helped us better to perceive the possible contribution made by Frankia, and to appreciate more clearly the complex factors that may have led individual Anglo-Saxon kings to convert, less effort has been made to re-evaluate Augustine's achievement. This is what is attempted here. Bede's chapters, whatever their limitations, are the touchstone for our knowledge of Augustine; and our account necessarily follows them closely, while trying where possible to tease out their broader implications and to make allowance for their imbalances.

Bede's narrative of the Augustinian mission begins two-thirds of the way through the first book of his *Ecclesiastical History*. The previous twenty-two chapters provide a description of the British Isles, followed by an account of its history from the invasion by Julius Caesar to the eve of the mission. We learn of various Roman interventions in British affairs, and of the rise of British Christianity. Then, against a backdrop of the collapse of the Roman Empire, we are told how with the withdrawal of the Romans from England, the Britons were harried first by the Irish and the Scots, and then by the Saxons. These last, Bede recounts, were first summoned as mercenaries by the British King Vortigern, but then decided to conquer the country for themselves. Vague allusions to the troubled subsequent history of the Britons are interwoven with details of the activities of St Germanus of Auxerre in Britain. Concluding with the observation that among their many crimes the Britons never tried to convert the Anglo-Saxons, Bede then turns his back on the former; henceforth he focuses on the latter, setting the scene for the mission in resounding prose:

> Nevertheless God in his goodness did not reject the people whom he foreknew; but he had appointed much worthier heralds of the truth to bring this people to the faith.

In reality Bede knew pitifully little about England in the period from 411 to 596. He made the best use of what was available to him – essentially Gildas's *De excidio Britanniae*, and Constantius of Lyons's *Life of St Germanus of Auxerre* – but this was a woefully inadequate basis for the history of a tumultuous period which is still deeply obscure. On the other hand, some of what he says does give a useful impression, and three points in particular may be highlighted.

First, there is no doubt that this was a time of fairly continuous wars, struggles and ultimately acculturation between the Britons and their various 'neighbours', during which the Angles, Saxons, and Jutes, invaders from northern Germany, the low countries and southern Scandinavia, came to predominate in the area that broadly corresponds to England. And, although the details are irrecoverable, it is evident – as Bede's subsequent observations underline – that the main Anglo-Saxon kingdoms had taken shape by the late sixth century.

Secondly, what Bede says about the origins and settlement patterns of the Angles, Saxons, and Jutes seems to be fundamentally correct, albeit susceptible to refinement in detail. As archaeological evidence tends to confirm, the Angles settled in the north and the east, the Saxons in the south, while the Jutes occupied Kent, southern Hampshire and the Isle of Wight. The remaining areas (namely western, upland Britain) remained under the domination of the Britons.

Thirdly, Bede shows clearly that the Britons in the west retained their christian faith, and he portrays the continuity of their church with that of late Roman Britain – something which modern research has confirmed and amplified. The British church appears very infrequently in Bede's subsequent narrative; but when it does – such as for the two fateful meetings with Augustine – it is clear that it was a major, organised force with thriving communities (notably that at Bangor-is-Coed). And there is little doubt that the reality was far more impressive than Bede and the exceptionally depleted Welsh written sources suggest.[5] What is altogether more difficult to discern is the extent to which a British church and christian belief may also have survived further to the east in lowland Britain, where the Anglo-Saxons were dominant. All that one can say is that while there were doubtless pockets of British Christianity in Anglo-Saxon England in the sixth century, above all in the west, these are likely to have become progressively weaker the further one moved towards the south-east. The evidence one can cite in relation to Canterbury itself – namely the existence of a conceivably christian structure which the Frankish princess Bertha could take over for her church, and the possible vestiges of a cult of a martyr Sixtus, whose traditions had been forgotten – do not suggest the survival of a significant British christian community in the region: quite the reverse in fact.

Bede's attitude towards and presentation of the Britons, whom he censures for not having converted the Anglo-Saxons, has often come in for criticism. The dim view that he took of them was based on inadequate evidence; and he artificially accentuated the rift between the British and the Irish, while underplaying the divisions within the Anglo-Saxons themselves.[6] It is reasonably argued that because Bede believed that they had neglected their duty in this respect, and since he wished to highlight the Roman and Irish missions, he plays down the role of the Britons in the conversion of the Anglo-Saxons. In certain areas, such as the West Midlands where Anglo-Saxon and independent British communities were in closer contact, it is likely that some veneer of Christianity had thereby percolated to the English inhabitants before 597. Yet we may reasonably doubt whether the dominant invaders, whose primary requirement of a god seems to have been that he should provide success in the present life, will have seen much benefit in adopting the religion of the people they had conquered. Bede's culpability in this respect should not, therefore, be overstated. True, he presents the conversion of the Anglo-Saxons as an essentially self-contained story, unrelated to the previous christian traditions of Britain as a whole, which it was not. However, he does imply that the Anglo-Saxons rubbed shoulders with British Christians; and there is no doubt that the Anglo-Saxon kingdoms were indeed predominantly and 'officially' pagan in 596, as he says.

The 'worthier heralds of the truth' who are to convert the Anglo-Saxons are, of course, Pope Gregory the Great and Augustine, who take the stage in Book I, chapter 23. Bede provides a biographical appreciation of Gregory at a later point in his work, commemorating the Pope's death (604); the importance of this chapter is emphasised by its position at the very beginning of Book II (cf. fig. 9.2). Here Gregory's special status for the English, as Bede perceived it, is clearly articulated:

> We can and should by rights call him our apostle, for although he held the most important see in the whole world and was head of churches which had long been converted to the true faith, yet he made our nation, until then enslaved to idols into a church of Christ.

Bede's encomium of Gregory, a striking image of the model churchman *par excellence*, highlights three complementary aspects of his achievement. First there was the circumstance that he had to balance the requirements of spirituality with those of temporal responsibility, striving never to let the latter overwhelm the former, but rather to be informed by them. Secondly, there was the canon of his writings and their value; and thirdly, of course, the fact that he initiated the conversion of the English. Bede illustrates this last point with reference to the 'traditional' story – about which he evidently had reservations – that Gregory was inspired to undertake the task personally by an encounter with English slave boys in the market place in Rome (a tale also recounted in the Whitby *Life* of the Pope).

That Gregory's essentially monastic type of spirituality, his literary output, and his concern for the English should have seemed particularly worth highlighting to the learned English monk, Bede, is hardly surprising. Nevertheless, this is but a partial view, and there are many other aspects of the Pope's activities that Bede either does not present or glosses over. These include Gregory's heavy political responsibilities in Italy (the climax of which was his defence of Rome against the Lombards); his development of the status of the see of Rome within the remains of the old Roman Empire; his reorganisation of the papal estates; and his manifold attempts to oversee, raise the standard of, and expand the christian community in the West as a whole. As part of the last, he sent a mission to Sardinia in 594 to convert its pagans, and laboured to reform the church in Gaul.

If the former provides a precedent for his sending Augustine to England two years later, the latter endeavour in particular was to be intimately linked with the mission to the Anglo-Saxons. Consideration of the Pope's activities as a whole enables us to see the English mission in its true perspective – as one concern among many, and one which, as the evidence of his surviving correspondence underlines, only occupied a small proportion of his time and energy.

It is uncertain how much Gregory actually knew about the situation in England on the eve of the mission; and the exact circumstances that led to his bid to convert the Anglo-Saxons are matters of speculation. The traditional English explanation for the Pope's interest in the project, which is first recorded in the Whitby *Life* of *c.* 700, was that it was triggered by his encounter with some Anglo-Saxon slaves in Rome – and, although the form in which the story has come down to us is clearly the result of oral or literary artifice,[7] there is nothing implausible about such a meeting. Be that as it may, there is little doubt that Gregory saw the initiative in a Frankish context. Although the extent to which its timing related to the rapidly changing events in northern Gaul in the 590s and how exactly he envisaged the relationship between Gaul and England at the time are open questions, his knowledge of Frankish affairs from *c.* 595 should not be underestimated.[8] It is fairly clear that he did not conceive it in relation to the British church, which he seems hardly, if ever, to have considered.[9] Writing in 599, Gregory said that he had long had the mission in mind; and however much time is thereby implied, we know he was thinking of the English in the year before he dispatched Augustine, for in September 595 he had ordered Candidus (who was about to become rector of the Roman church's lands in Gaul) to use some of the income to purchase English slave boys who could be educated in monasteries. More intriguingly, the commendatory letters the Pope subsequently addressed to the rulers of Frankia allude to the fact that the English had apparently sought conversion, but the neighbouring bishops (and Frankish not British ones are almost certainly implied) had not responded. One might speculate that this apparent wish for conversion could have been connected with the presence of a christian Frank, Bertha, at the court of Kent; however, it is impossible to be certain. Similarly, while it is clear to us that Bertha provided a favourable context for a mission to Kent, it is an open question how much, if anything, Gregory knew of her. Suggestions that Augustine's mission was 'exploratory' or 'diplomatic' as opposed to proselytising pure and simple rest on assumptions about such imponderable issues. Whatever the truth, the venture is broadly intelligible in the context of the expansive view Gregory took of his responsibilities, of his missionary frame of mind, and of his concern for the spiritual health of the West as a whole, all of which was given urgency by his

1.2. Rome: Circus Maximus (foreground), Domus Augustana and (extreme right) S Gregorio (S Andreae in clivo Scauri). (Gameson)

belief that time was short since the end of the world was nigh (something to which he was to allude when writing to King Æthelberht of Kent). Bringing the Anglo-Saxons into the church fits into his broad conception of pastoral care, and sits comfortably alongside his wish to consolidate the church in Italy and to raise its standards in Gaul.[10]

As we have seen, both through the accident of the source materials that were available to him and through his own deliberate design, Bede stresses the Pope's commanding hand throughout his narrative of the mission. While at one level, given that it was his initiative and he was its ultimate authority, this is reasonable, nevertheless, it is all too easy to forget how little Gregory actually did once his envoys had left Rome, and correspondingly that the practical responsibilities and dangers fell squarely on Augustine's shoulders. Bede tells us almost nothing about Augustine himself and his background apart from the basic fact that he was 'a servant of God' (*servu[s] Dei*), and (subsequently) that Gregory intended to have him consecrated as bishop of the new church in England if the mission were favourably received. Little can now be done to fill in the picture. Apart from the fact that by 596 he was prior (*praepositus*) of Gregory's own monastery of Saint Andrew's on the Coelian hill in Rome (fig. 1.2 and cf. 10.4b), Augustine's early life is obscure; and given the lack of further information on this point in the *Life* of the saint that was written for the community of Saint Augustine's Abbey at the end of the eleventh century, it would seem that no further traditions had been preserved at Canterbury. In his letters to third parties, Gregory praised Augustine 'who was brought up under a monastic Rule and is filled with the knowledge of the holy scriptures and endowed with good works through the grace of God'; and we can presume that as prior of Saint Andrew's he had proven himself competent in practical matters as well as deeply spiritual, and hence the mission was entrusted to him. Moreover, he was well placed to be unable to refuse the Pope's command! The circumstances surrounding the eventual selection of Theodore of Tarsus to the see of Canterbury in 667 – the previous nominee, Hadrian, having turned down the 'honour' – imply that even by the late seventh century a 'posting' to the English church was not perceived as very desirable. How much less appealing and more sinister, then, must have seemed the task of trying to initiate the conversion of the country.

Bede provides no information about Augustine's journey from Italy (something which was tangential to his main concern), merely recording that the party 'got cold feet' *en route* and wanted to abort the project.

> They began to contemplate returning home rather than going to a barbarous, fierce and unbelieving nation whose language they did not even understand.

Augustine, we are informed, was delegated to go back to Gregory to request the official abandonment of the mission; however the Pope was adamant that it should continue. In order to stress his key role at this critical juncture, Bede quotes the letter Gregory sent to the missionary monks. In essence it offered spiritual encouragement rather than practical advice. Not addressing the missionaries' concern about the barbarous nature of the English, Gregory informed them that they should persevere because of the inherent worthiness of the task, stressing the potential spiritual rewards. Now while (with Bede) we may admire Gregory's determination and purity of thought, we might also compare the situation of the missionaries to that of the hapless police in Gilbert and Sullivan's *Pirates of Penzance* who are 'encouraged' in their task of apprehending the pirates with the words 'go to death and glory'! If the state of the missionaries was genuinely as anxious and negative as Bede implies, one may doubt that Gregory's words offered them much real consolation. However, the Pope also made Augustine their abbot with correspondingly absolute authority over them, and ordered them to obey him. If the event was a crisis in Augustine's leadership and resolve, the fact that, after having his authority strengthened, he was evidently willing and able to lead the party onwards, shows that it was

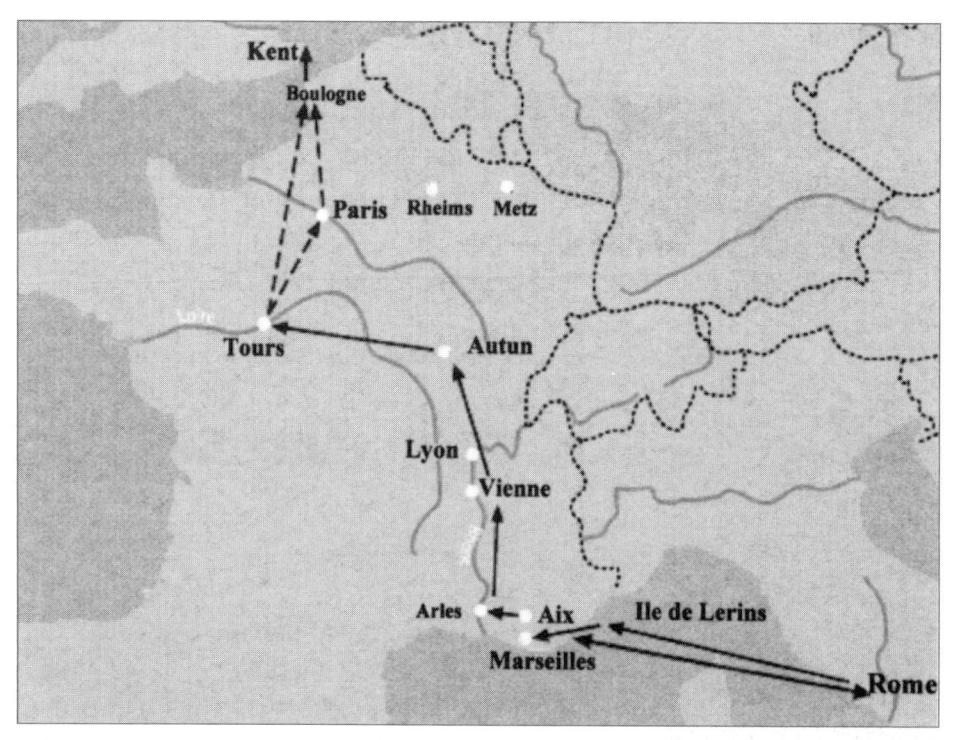

1.3. Schematic impression of Augustine's possible route from Rome to Kent. (Butrous; Gameson)

surmounted. More generally, however, it suggests that the Pope had not made adequate preparations before launching his mission, a contention supported by subsequent events, for it was only after this debacle that Gregory seems to have taken certain essential practical steps – including trying to remedy the problem of the language barrier. Gregory then, rather belatedly one feels, attempted to smooth the missionaries' path by equipping them with presents and commendatory letters (one of which Bede quotes) addressed to various Gallic ecclesiastics, as well as to the Frankish rulers Theoderic, Theodebert and Brunhild. In the letters destined for these rulers, he mentioned Augustine's need for interpreters; and as Bede alludes to Frankish interpreters 'acquired at the command of Gregory' landing in Kent with the Italian missionaries (and it is typical, incidentally, that he here lauds the Pope for what was in reality a tardy attempt to remedy a major oversight), it would appear that such help was forthcoming.

These letters enable us to perceive something of the route Gregory envisaged Augustine taking from southern France to Kent (cf. fig. 1.3). As on the one hand, the record is incomplete, while on the other hand there is no guarantee that Augustine actually went to all the places specified, one cannot put too much

1.4. The main roads of Roman Gaul (towns that Augustine visited or possibly visited are highlighted). (Butrous; Gameson)

weight on it; nevertheless such details as we have are worth rehearsing. At an uncertain point during the first half of 596 the party had travelled to southern France, presumably by boat – thereby circumnavigating the hostile Lombards in northern Italy – reaching the island monastic community of Lérins, and had then journeyed on to Aix-en-Provence. It was here apparently that the confidence of the group evaporated, and Augustine went back to Rome. Gregory's letters (all dated July 596) suggest that, after Augustine's return to Aix (perhaps via Marseille), the group then went to Arles, Vienne and Lyon, implying that the Pope envisaged the missionaries moving up the Rhône, presumably following the Roman roads (fig. 1.4). The next places for which addressees exist are Autun in central France, and Tours to the west – again major Roman roads linked the two. Syagrius of Autun was subsequently rewarded with a pallium for the (unspecified) aid he had afforded to the mission. Although hardly on the most direct route to England, a visit to Tours could have seemed spiritually as well as politically important. It was the cult centre of St Martin (d. 397), a pioneer of monasticism, a bishop who had been concerned for the conversion of rural Gaul, and an enormously popular miracle-working saint. In addition, Bertha, the Frankish queen of Kent, had close family connections with Tours: it was within the kingdom that had been ruled, albeit briefly, by her father, King Charibert (561–7); more significantly, her mother, Ingoberga, had been a friend of Bishop Gregory of Tours (d. 594) and a benefactor to two churches there; while her sister, Berthefled, had been a nun in the town. It may thus have seemed a likely source of information about Kent, and a potential way of ensuring a favourable reception there.

The church of Saint Martin's that Augustine could have visited in 596 was only a generation old for, as Gregory of Tours records, it had been rebuilt following a fire in 558. This makes the general point that these places were still major urban centres; and while one cannot be precise over the state of their various buildings at the end of the sixth century and the extent to which old Roman amenities were functioning, town life, with its various adjuncts such as building in stone, undoubtedly continued. The antique and Late Antique remains that still dominate Arles, for instance, remain very impressive (fig. 1.5).

No letters addressed to specific ecclesiastics based further north than Tours have come down to us, and Augustine's route thereafter is, in consequence, even more uncertain. Nevertheless, we can reasonably assume that the party followed one of the Roman routes northwards. Gregory noted subsequently (in a letter of 598 to Eulogius of Alexandria) that the bishop of the 'Germans' had made Augustine a bishop and had brought him to the English. While the exact implications of this are unclear, it would seem to imply that he had received significant support from the church in north-eastern Gaul; moreover, it shows that he had been made a bishop by Gallic ecclesiastics before the end of 597. In the circumstances it seems more likely that he was consecrated *en route* than that he returned to Provence for ordination within a few months of first arriving in Kent, as Bede's account (which is certainly flawed in detail) requires us to believe.

That Bede, focusing on the English, should not have tried to chronicle Augustine's journey is unsurprising; however, he thereby significantly diminishes his readers' perception of the range of activities and responsibilities of the missionaries. Gregory clearly intended to take advantage of his emissary's voyage north to communicate with, and to monitor Gaul, and to attempt to bring it a

1.5. Arles, aerial view. (Photographic Service, UKC)

little more under papal influence (the extant correspondence suggests that hitherto his contacts had essentially been limited to Provence, and the court of Queen Brunhild). Thus while the letters addressed to Gallic churchmen were designed to solicit their support for Augustine, they also urged them to be respectful of the temporalities of the church. (Similarly, the letters Gregory gave to the reinforcements of 601 targeted simony within the Gallic church.)

As noted above, Gregory also sent presents and wrote to the young brothers Theoderic and Theodebert II, the kings of Burgundy (596–613) and Austrasia (596–612) respectively, and to their formidable grandmother, Brunhild, trying to enlist their support. Following the death of King Guntram in 593 and Childebert II in 596, the titular rulers of Frankish Gaul – Theoderic and Theodebert (Childebert's sons) along with Chlothar II (who held Neustria) – were all minors.[11] The Pope evidently and correctly identified Queen Brunhild as the most important force in the kingdom at the time. She was then at the zenith of her long and colourful career, ruling for her grandsons; and despite the atrocities for which she is (in)famous, she was undoubtedly a pious woman. Moreover, she may have perceived political advantages in supporting Augustine: it was a way of enhancing her newly acquired position of regent, and perhaps in the longer term a means of expanding the influence of her family at the expense of its rivals in Neustria (namely the young Chlothar and his dying mother, Fredegund).[12]

While Gregory asked the churchmen to give Augustine a favourable welcome and to aid him in general terms, he specifically asked these rulers to protect the missionary and to ensure his safe passage – a point which underlines the difficulties and dangers of the journey itself. In addition, as we have seen, the letters mentioned Augustine's need of priests to act as interpreters: whether through common ancestry or continued contacts some inhabitants of northern France presumably spoke a dialect of Saxon or Frisian. Gregory also took the opportunity to criticise the (presumably) Gallic churchmen who had not responded to the Anglo-Saxons' own wish for Christianity. It is debatable whether this was designed to 'butter up' the state at the expense of the church, or to flatter Brunhild and her grandsons by implicit criticism of the previous political regime in the north. Be that as it may, the queen's support was secured; and although we do not know what she did, Brunhild was credited by Gregory with having made a particularly vital contribution to the success of the venture. The missionaries thus arrived under the aegis of the powerful if volatile neighbouring state with which south-east England already had close ties – as coins, jewellery and, above all, the marriage of Æthelberht show.

We do not know where in northern France Augustine, his Italian companions, and their Frankish interpreters embarked for England. The port that Bede highlighted as the nearest for travellers between England and the continent was *Gessoriacum* (Boulogne), the major alternative being Quentovic, a little to the south (near modern Etaples) (cf. fig. 3.1). We know that there was some maritime activity in the region *c.* 600; and the circumstance that the area had seen strong Saxon settlement is likely to have encouraged intercourse across the Channel.[13] Bede records that the group landed on Thanet, which was at the time an island separated from the mainland by the Wantsum Channel (pl. I; fig. 3.1). It is not possible – despite valiant efforts in the nineteenth century – to establish where on Thanet Augustine first set foot, but Ebbsfleet and Stonor are the most obvious possibilities. For what it is worth, English tradition as embodied in the *Anglo-Saxon Chronicle* credited Hengest and Horsa (the reputed leaders of the first wave of fifth-century Anglo-Saxon invaders) with having landed at the former. Nor can Richborough (*Rutupiae*), the Roman settlement which had latterly become one of the forts of the Saxon shore, be discounted for, although it is not actually on Thanet, it commanded the southern entry to the Wantsum Channel (fig. 1.6). Moreover, in his general description of Britain, Bede highlights it as the nearest port to the continent, implying that by the eighth century at least there was a well-established shipping route from there to Boulogne.

1.6. Richborough (the main port of entry to Roman Britain), showing mid-third-century triple ditches and the late third-century walls. (Gameson)

The company which landed was, according to Bede, some forty in number. Augustine, we are told, then sent word of his mission to King Æthelberht of Kent, whose capital was nearby Canterbury, the former Roman town of *Durovernum*. The latter ordered the group to remain on Thanet, supplying them with provisions, while he decided how to respond.

Æthelberht was, Bede tells us, a particularly powerful king whose influence then extended to the Humber, implying that most of the other Anglo-Saxon kingdoms were under his overlordship. Subsequent details broadly confirm this, showing that he exercised direct control over Essex, had some power over East Anglia, and was also influential in the West Midlands. There is a degree of confusion concerning when he had succeeded his father Eormenric; however, if, as seems likely, Bede was mistaken over the dates of his reign, he may only have become king *c.* 585–90 – a decade *after* he had married Bertha. Kent's temporary pre-eminence in the late sixth century was undoubtedly due at least in part to its position as 'gateway' to the continent: the density of Frankish and other continental goods in Kentish graves attests to the advantages it enjoyed in this respect, and to its relative economic strength at the time. Correspondingly, the opulence of the finest Kentish jewellery of late sixth- and early seventh-century date provides striking testimony to the kingdom's prosperity (pl. IIIc). Now it is undeniably the case that Æthelberht's wealth provided a favourable context for the mission; and Bede notes on several different occasions how the king supported the missionaries materially. Merely feeding a party of forty represented a major burden; and one wonders whether at an earlier date, with a more primitive economy, the Anglo-Saxons could easily have supported the considerable expense of a large, non-productive, hierarchical christian church conceived according to the Roman model.

An important side effect of Kent's interaction with the continent in the later sixth century was the circumstance that it undoubtedly had some acquaintance with the religion of its powerful Frankish neighbours. The clearest evidence for this is, of course, the fact that Æthelberht had a Frankish wife who was a practising Christian. Indeed Bede specifically acknowledges that some familiarity with the religion had reached the king through her. Bertha's political importance should not be overestimated. She was the daughter of King Charibert I who had ruled western Gaul, including Paris, from 561–7, and of Ingoberga, his first wife. On Charibert's death, his territory was broken up between his brothers Sigibert I (561–75), Guntram (561–92) and Chilperic I, the last of whom dominated the territories bordering the English Channel from his base at Soissons until his assassination in 584. In such circumstances it seems unlikely that the marriage of Bertha to a prince of Kent represented an attempt to extend Frankish hegemony over southern England; nor will it have been particularly advantageous politically (as opposed to in terms of prestige) for Kent. Indeed, as power passed to her uncles, moving to Kent might have represented a distinguished and safe form of exile for a princess of a defunct line. Bertha's religious importance, on the other hand, should not be underestimated. One of the conditions of the marriage – negotiated by whom, one wonders – was that she should have freedom of worship; and she was accompanied to Kent by her own chaplain. The fact that Liudhard, the individual in question, was a bishop (and an otherwise unattested one) implies that he was envisaged as having more than merely private responsibilities. (The parallel circumstances a generation later when the christian Kentish princess Æthelburh travelled north to be the bride of Edwin of Northumbria with guaranteed freedom of worship are suggestive here: she was accompanied by the Roman missionary Paulinus, who was consecrated bishop beforehand with the express intention of initiating a church in the northern kingdom.) As the marriage of Æthelberht and Bertha seems to have happened before 580 when Gregory of Tours alluded to it,[14] there had been a christian group at the Kentish court for over fifteen years by the time Augustine came. On the other hand, assuming that Æthelberht did not succeed to the throne until

1.7. St Martin's Church, Canterbury: chancel, south side. (Gameson)

c. 585–90,[15] then Bertha and her entourage had not enjoyed a particularly powerful position until fairly shortly before the arrival of the Roman mission. Be that as it may, there can be no doubt that the presence of a high-status christian community in Canterbury in 597 contributed both to the warm reception Augustine appears to have received, and to the rapid success he seems to have enjoyed. Writing in 601, Pope Gregory praised Bertha for the assistance she had afforded Augustine, implying that she had helped to predispose her husband towards the new faith – which was surely the case.

Bertha had been granted an old Roman church, St Martin's, which presumably she restored, drawing on the expertise of Gallic masons. Parts of the structure she inherited or remade survive in the chancel of the present church (fig. 1.7). The dedication to St Martin (which Bede records) is most likely to have been due to Bertha. This new chapel associated with the Kentish court must have been equipped with the basic accoutrements of the christian faith: vessels and textiles, along with some manuscripts; and if there is more than flattery and convention in Gregory's description of Bertha as 'learned in letters', the holding of books may have extended beyond the bare minimum. Further evidence of the presence of a high-status christian community in Canterbury at this time and its impact on material culture is provided by the enigmatic 'Liudhard medalet' (pls IIIa and b). This coin pendant has a double-barred (or 'patriarchal') cross design on one side, while on the other there is a simple bust portrait in profile, accompanied by an inscription in mirror writing which, when reversed, reads 'LEVARDUS EPS' ('Bishop Liudhard'). Whether made in Gaul or Kent (and the balance of the evidence favours the latter possibility), the object shows how christian culture had begun to impinge on Kent before the arrival of Augustine.

Given that Æthelberht had a christian wife, one might approach the next part of Bede's narrative with circumspection. He informs us that the king came to Thanet, and summoned Augustine to meet him in the open air – in order to avoid the danger of being overpowered by his magic indoors. It is not difficult to understand why such a detail should have appealed to Bede, for it both stresses the numinism of the missionaries, and underlines the extent to which the king was at this point sunk in superstition. However, it might be doubted that someone who was married to a Christian would really have held such views. Nevertheless, the story need not necessarily be rejected, for it is possible that at this preliminary stage Æthelberht had not yet identified these Italian-led missionaries as representatives of his wife's religion. If all the news that had reached him was that a large party of foreigners had arrived and that they wished to discuss matters of religion, then precautions were undoubtedly sensible.

Bede presents a striking image of the appearance of the missionaries before Æthelberht: they came bearing a silver cross and an icon of Christ painted on a panel. The latter advertised the traditions of narrative visual imagery that were integral to Christianity but alien to the Anglo-Saxons, whose native art was aniconic and essentially decorative (cf. pl. IIIc). Concerning the possible appearance of the image, one could do worse than consider the head of Christ in the mosaic over the triumphal arch of San Lorenzo fuori le Mura, Rome, a work commissioned by Pope Pelagius II (579–90), Gregory the Great's predecessor (fig. 1.8).

1.8. Head of Christ, triumphal arch mosaic, San Lorenzo fuori le Mura, Rome. (Gameson)

Æthelberht was, we are told, favourably impressed by the character and the preaching of the missionaries – which presumably echoed the beliefs of his wife – however, he did not himself convert, being, Bede says, reluctant to abandon his ancestral beliefs and traditions. Such a response, articulating the fact that a change of religion involved transformations in culture with major implications for one's relationship with one's followers and family – alive and dead – seems fundamentally plausible; and it doubtless typifies the natural caution that first greeted any call to convert.[16] What the missionaries may have perceived as a largely spiritual issue – abandoning one religion for another (or rather: leaving an abhorrent delusion for the true faith) – was from the point of view of an Anglo-Saxon king equally if not more a matter of culture, tradition, and family, not to mention power and politics. The Anglo-Saxon king was more than just a warrior-ruler with a central role in society: in addition he seems to have had a sacral, almost totemic status. Anglo-Saxon kings traced their ancestry to pagan gods, notably Woden, and seem to have held a role approaching that of mediator between their people and the gods on whose good offices the prosperity of the kingdom depended. Consequently, being a semi-religious figure as well as a political leader and warlord, the king had great authority to introduce new religious customs. But conversely, since the responsibility for the well-being of his people, material and spiritual, as dispensed by the gods, rested squarely upon his shoulders, he had to have very good reasons for introducing radical changes and abandoning traditional beliefs. Moreover, as plentiful incidents from seventh-century history underline, on these crucial issues the king had to move in harmony with his nobles, and with regard to the broader political implications of change. In such circumstances a false step could, quite literally, be fatal. These are aspects that Bede invariably plays down or glosses over in his account of events.

Whatever his initial reflections on such matters, Æthelberht seems to have regarded the missionaries as foreign dignitaries, and treated them as such. He proceeded to give them a base in Canterbury, along with provisions, and granted them some freedom to preach – the material resources, the security, and the provisional mandate essential for the success of the mission. It is interesting to note how, before his official conversion, the king was prepared to devote resources to the missionaries which, given their number, must have been considerable. Whatever he believed personally, he was then temporarily in the situation of materially supporting two religions, paganism and Christianity. Bede ends this chapter of his story by recounting the missionaries' triumphant liturgical procession into Canterbury: Roman Christianity had (re)established an official bridgehead in southern England.

What exactly were the 'ancestral beliefs' to which Æthelberht temporarily continued to adhere, Bede does not say. Indeed he was not in general forthcoming about Anglo-Saxon paganism: if he knew much more than he recorded, he doubtless felt that it was worthless to preserve such information – a view shared by other ecclesiastics, who were by definition the arbiters of what was written down and hence preserved. In consequence, our knowledge of what it was that the Anglo-Saxons had to be converted *from* is sadly limited – a major handicap for any attempt to assess the changes involved.[17] This should not, however, lead us to underestimate the importance of the systems of belief in question, which were clearly integral to the cultural and political as well as to the religious identity of Anglo-Saxon society. Bede does, it is true, make reference to idols and idolatry and to heathen temples at various locations in England: he notes, for instance, that Kent was the first kingdom in which idols were officially outlawed – something which happened under King Eorconberht (640–64). And the existence of substantial structures dedicated to heathen worship is seemingly confirmed by a couple of Gregory's letters – written after he had received first-hand reports of the situation in England – one urging Æthelberht to destroy pagan shrines, the other suggesting that the missionaries might cleanse and convert them to christian use. Identifiable traces of such pagan cult buildings have, however, proven remarkably elusive in the archaeological record, with the possible exception of one at Yeavering. Funerary customs – inhumation and cremation, not to mention the more exotic bed and ship burials (cf. fig. 3.5) – show that the Anglo-Saxons made decisions about their dead, but they fall short of articulating their concept of the afterlife. It is clear that they were polytheistic; and the evidence of place names reveals that the gods they revered included the well-known germanic ones, Tiw, Thor, Friya and Woden. Persuading them to accept another god was probably not, then, too difficult; but ensuring that they rejected all the old ones and became monotheistic was altogether more challenging. Bede is rather arch about this latter process; and the potentially relevant archaeological evidence can also require careful handling.[18] Sources written well into the christian era preserve the fact that the leading Anglo-Saxon dynasties still traced their pedigrees back to gods, with whom presumptively they had a special relationship; and the history of the conversion period itself shows that, whatever the Anglo-Saxons did or did not believe, they certainly expected a deity to protect and support his followers in the present life. Gods were judged, and venerated or rejected accordingly. Evangelists were consequently at pains to stress the superior efficacy of the christian God in this respect. If their message of peace was not always easily reconciled with this, the greater sophistication of their material culture added some weight to their claims.

Æthelberht may have been impressed by Augustine, but the king's capital, Canterbury, will not have impressed the missionary: quite the reverse in fact (pl. II).

Although the town had been relatively prosperous in the fourth century, and some urban activity had continued into the fifth, there is little doubt that the old Roman centre was in ruins by the late sixth century. The prospect that greeted Augustine is likely to have consisted of small-scale wooden structures scattered across the decayed and overgrown vestiges of a walled Roman town, whose urban facilities, such as bath houses, had long since ceased to function. The contrast between this and the cities such as Arles that he had probably visited *en route* – not to mention with Rome itself – can hardly be overstated (cf. figs 1.2 and 3); and whatever prejudices Augustine may have had about the 'barbaric' nature of the society to which he had been sent, they are likely to have been confirmed by the delapidated and primitive state of the Kentish capital. However, as a Roman bishop, he needed a town for his see, and a semi-derelict one was better than nothing.

The missionaries first operated from St Martin's, which, as Bertha's chapel, was already a usable christian structure and, presumably, the centre of at least a small community of believers (fig. 1.7). Bede, writing not least for his own generation and probably lacking more specific information, stressed the apostolic simplicity and the purity of the way of life of the missionaries, which made patent their spirituality. One is tempted to observe that, as new arrivals without official status, such 'apostolic simplicity' was *de rigueur*. This preliminary phase lasted, he says, until Æthelberht himself converted. Thereafter the king granted the missionaries other dwelling places; and they were able with greater liberty to preach and to build or restore churches.

Bede is vague about when Æthelberht converted, and laconic concerning why he did so. He seems to imply that the conversion occurred at an early stage, but gives no date. However, it seems fairly clear from Gregory's letter to Æthelberht in 601 that he had adopted the faith by then, and circumstantial evidence suggests that he had probably been baptised before the end of 597. In a letter to Eulogius, bishop of Alexandria written in 598, Gregory noted that more than 10,000 Anglo-Saxons had been baptised at Christmas of the previous year. Although reliance cannot be placed on the figure itself, there is no reason to doubt that a large number of people had indeed embraced the new faith then; and the obvious catalyst for such a development would have been the conversion of the king himself – for it is inconceivable that Æthelberht would have considered transferring his allegiance to the new religion without first securing the agreement and participation of his retinue and leading nobles. That this was indeed the royal approach to such a situation is underlined by the case of King Edwin of Northumbria (d. 633), which Bede describes in detail: despite mysterious portents, miraculous delivery from an assassination attempt, material success against his enemies, and a christian wife, all of which inclined him towards Christianity, Edwin still hesitated until he had assured himself that his council as a whole was in favour of the move. The fact that Æthelberht did not, according to Bede, force anyone to convert suggests that he was alive to the perils of introducing fundamental changes in religion and culture, and correspondingly appreciated the advantages of a *laissez-faire* approach to the matter of his subjects' beliefs and customs. Wholesale imposition of change would almost certainly have met resistance; and one is reminded of how when the Icelanders officially embraced Christianity at the *althing* (general assembly) of 999/1000 (the prime motive being, reputedly, to maintain political and social cohesion), provision was made for individuals to continue pagan practices in private if they so wished. When Bede praises Æthelberht for this policy on the grounds that conversion was properly a matter of individual conscience, he is making a virtue of what the king doubtless saw as a necessity. And it seems fairly clear that where he could exert himself – namely at royal level – Æthelberht did so, ensuring that the rulers of the neighbouring kingdoms, Sæbert of Essex (d. 616x17) and Rædwald of East Anglia (d. 616x27) were baptised. Significantly, once back in his own kingdom and with his political power in the ascendant, the latter seems merely to have 'lumped' the christian God alongside the pagan ones, reputedly having altars for both cults in one temple.

Bede, who believed that embracing Christianity was self-evidently the right decision for all but the bad and the mad (and the former, he tries to persuade his readers, were likely to join the latter as a consequence of their folly on this point), gives but two reasons for Æthelberht's conversion. The king was impressed by the pure lifestyle of the missionaries, and by their miracles. While the former characteristic *may* have underlined their spirituality, one might doubt that it was sufficient in itself to sway a king who was almost certainly predisposed to believe that religion should represent and convey power. Miracles, on the other hand, whatever they may have been – and the emissaries of a more sophisticated and materially superior culture may well have been able to accomplish things which seemed extraordinary by sixth-century Anglo-Saxon standards – could indeed have been impressive.

Various other factors that probably played a part have already been noted, among which pride of place belongs to Bertha and Liudhard, and the attendant circumstance that Æthelberht and the Kentish court had had direct experience of Christianity well before the arrival of Augustine. (Kent, we may note in passing, was the first of a number of Anglo-Saxon kingdoms whose courts received early exposure to the new faith through a christian royal bride.) The fact that Æthelberht was the most powerful king in England in 597 may have contributed to his decision, to the extent that it gave him a sense of freedom of manoeuvre, and that he could contemplate a radical change without the fear of reprisals from Anglo-Saxon neighbours; however, this should not be overstated since, conversely, the fact that he had achieved this status under the pagan gods might have weighed against change. The perceived prestige and superior material culture of the missionaries was doubtless a strong advertisement for their faith;[19] and it is relevant in this context to note the remarks of Bishop Daniel of Winchester (d. 745) when writing to the Anglo-Saxon missionary Boniface (d. 754). He listed various arguments that the latter might use to convert the pagan Germans; many of them are 'rational' – for example, demonstrating the logical fallacy of worshipping as gods, beings who were born like humans – but his final point is a particularly telling one: 'there must also often be brought before them the might of the christian world, in comparison with which those who still continue in the ancient false faith are few'. This raises a further issue which was possibly applicable to Æthelberht: it is conceivable that the option of accepting Christianity from a distant Rome seemed an attractive way of side-stepping any hint that adopting the religion of his neighbours on the other side of the Channel, the Franks, implied accepting their predominance. And one might advance a tentative parallel with Denmark four centuries later, where King Harald Bluetooth's 'personal conversion' in the 960s may have been, at least in part, a way of side-stepping the threat of domination in the name of religion from his powerful christian neighbour, Ottonian Germany. Yet this does not mean that one should minimise the importance of Frankish *example*, for the fact that Æthelberht will have wanted to avoid domination by his neighbours does not mean that he did not admire and envy their culture.

What the change meant for Æthelberht spiritually is irrecoverable, though the sincerity of his adherence to Christianity is beyond doubt, being demonstrated by the pains he took to ensure that he could be buried in a fitting christian context. Nor is it very clear how (or even if) he benefited from conversion politically and materially, beyond an enhanced ability to interact with a wider, continental world. For Augustine, however, the importance of the king's conversion was paramount: it gave him privileged, official status, and meant that henceforth he operated under the aegis of a powerful patron. Indeed, there is every reason to believe that the early success of the mission in Kent and its expansion in the south-east was a direct result of Æthelberht's support.

Whatever Augustine's hopes and fears may have been on his arrival, the mass baptisms of 597 along with the conversion of Æthelberht show that he enjoyed rapid initial success; and within four years the prospect was sufficiently promising for him to seek reinforcements from Rome. Bede says very little about the practicalities of establishing the new church, and how the missionaries dealt with the many problems they undoubtedly had to face: what Augustine did to consolidate his position and organise his church in the crucial years between 597 and 601 is thus left essentially unrecorded. The only information on such issues that Bede seems to have had – or at least chose to provide – came from the *Libellus responsionum*, the dossier of Augustine's questions to Gregory and the latter's replies (given in 601), which enjoyed considerable circulation in the early Middle Ages.[20] The questions had been transmitted from Canterbury to Rome by the priest Laurentius and the monk Peter, who were clearly key members of Augustine's team – the former was to be his successor as (arch)bishop of Canterbury, while the latter became the first abbot of SS Peter and Paul (Saint Augustine's Abbey).

Bede included a transcription of the *Libellus responsionum* in his work, thereby emphasising Gregory's continuing direction of the mission, and showing how from its earliest days the customs of the English church were in accord with Rome. An unfortunate side effect of its bulky presence, however, allied to Bede's generally understated presentation of Augustine, is that it can give the impression – and has sometimes been taken as evidence – that the missionary lacked initiative. However, it was hardly unreasonable, and certainly no sign of weakness for Augustine to seek guidance or reassurance from his mentor on certain issues. As a monk turned missionary, trying to plant his faith in a new society, he was inevitably encountering matters – such as marriage customs and sexuality – which were outside his former experience (and the enormous subsequent body of church legislation on a couple of these issues underlines their intractability). And there is no reason to assume that he would have been *au fait* with Gregory's thinking on them while he was in Rome.[21] Moreover, since he (perhaps unexpectedly) found himself alongside other Christians – Bertha's circle, and conceivably also some Britons – whose practices almost certainly differed in various respects from his own, a reinforced papal mandate for his traditions may have seemed useful. In point of fact, however, the argument for Augustine's dependence on Gregory can be turned on its head: the *Libellus responsionum* could equally be taken to show that the Pope had not really thought through the implications of his mission before dispatching it, and had not prepared his envoys adequately. Furthermore, if, as seems to be the case, this was all on which Augustine sought specific guidance from him, the amount he accomplished and dealt with on his own initiative – though not documented – was enormous. More generally, this may be taken as a microcosm of the relationship between the Pope and the missionary: the former may have had the vision and determination, but the heavy responsibility for implementing his dream and working it out in practice fell squarely on the latter.

Augustine's first question addressed fundamental issues of church organisation and the related matter of the apportionment of material resources. He enquired how Gregory thought bishops should live with their clergy, and the manner in which offerings to the church should be divided. The two issues were pertinent because being both a monk and a bishop, Augustine was in an unusual position – as the Pope acknowledged. Gregory's answer was direct: the missionary and his monastic entourage were to live communally, and therefore, although a bishop, Augustine would not need separate resources for himself. On the other hand, those in minor orders (as presumably some of the first Anglo-Saxon converts would be) could marry, live independently, and receive a stipend outside the community. Gregory impressed on Augustine the need to supervise such clerics very carefully, ensuring their spirituality remained intact, and that they chanted the psalms – the staple diet of the religious life – as appropriate. It is worth noting in passing that, assuming that Anglo-Saxon converts did indeed comprise some or most of the class in question, a precondition of achieving this was teaching them basic elements of the Latin language, a point to which we shall return.

Secondly, Augustine queried the liturgical differences between the Roman and the Gallic churches, a phenomenon that must have struck him on his long journey through Gaul, and which the presence of an enclave of the Gallic church in Canterbury itself, whose chapel he first shared – not to mention the Frankish clerics in his own party[22] – must have made a pressing issue. In the absence of adequate documentation from the sixth century or earlier, the extent and nature of the differences in question are impossible to reconstruct; however, there is no doubt that this period before the creation of normative liturgical books – the so-called 'Gregorian' sacramentary was a work of the seventh century, probably to be associated with Pope Honorius I (625–38) – was characterised by considerable diversity of practice, with individual offices and formulae being devised to meet local needs and tastes. Gregory's reply was a practical response to the realities of the situation: he encouraged Augustine to create a liturgy specifically for the English, drawing on such customs as he had encountered and judged to be good. Assuming Augustine followed this advice, we can credit him with significant liturgical activity; and presuming further that he committed his work to parchment, the resulting collection of texts would be the first book known to have been written in England.

The third question, how those who steal from churches should be punished, sheds clear light on the vulnerability of a new institution that was committed to pacificism in a violent society. Gregory's answer is a moral and philosophical rather than a practical one: it was the circumstances of the thief, not the nature of the act itself, that defined the severity of the crime. Concerning how the church might actually defend itself, the Pope was silent. In reality, it was King Æthelberht who safeguarded it. Bede comments approvingly in his epitaph for the king that his law had been designed 'to give protection to those whose coming and teaching he had welcomed'; and the very first clause of Æthelberht's law-code specifies the penalties that were incurred for theft of church property. Here, in contrast to Gregory's ruling, the degree of compensation is calculated according to the status of the individual whose property had been stolen, be he bishop, priest, deacon or cleric. It is interesting to note that the statute implies a fully developed church hierarchy, though whether this represented the automatic approach of Roman clerics, forward planning, or a reality at the time in question is open to debate. Considered as a whole, Æthelberht's law-code, with its elaborate itemisation of killings and maimings along with the appropriate reparations, provides graphic testimony to the harsh realities of the society in which Augustine and his fledgling church found themselves. The laws also suggest considerable licentiousness – something that Germanic society and christian church alike struggled (in vain) to eradicate.

The area of inter-personal relations was touched upon in Augustine's fourth and fifth questions, which concern marriage customs, and in particular the degree of affinity within which a union was permissible. The answer that Bede recorded for the fifth question – which caused St Boniface some consternation and for which authentication could not then be found in Rome – does not appear in the oldest copies of the *Libellus* itself, and is generally regarded as an interpolation. Be that as it may, as the closest degree of affinity that was therein permitted (and which had scandalised Boniface) was that of second cousins, this dubious, 'permissive' ruling reveals how the restrictive social teachings of the new church could present real difficulties for the Anglo-Saxons. For in a society of small, nucleated communities, some such marriages were almost inevitable. Furthermore, even though the reported answer is probably not a genuine Gregorian one, it nevertheless contains a revealing concession which undoubtedly illuminates the situation in England: many Anglo-Saxons had contracted such marriages when unbelievers, and these had to be accepted for the moment. This raises the general point that imposing any such regulations was going to be extremely difficult in the first instance, and flexibility and compromise (not to mention some failure) was inevitable. The crisis that arose in Kent after Æthelberht's death, when his son, Eadbald, married his stepmother, provides an extreme example of how christian teaching and Anglo-Saxon practice could be in conflict. Another, less clear-cut case appears when Bede justifies the death of King Sigibert of the East Saxons (d. 653x64) on the grounds that he had failed to shun an 'unlawfully' married retainer whom Bishop Cedd had condemned.

Augustine's sixth question, whether a bishop might be consecrated without other bishops present, was answered in the affirmative, owing to his special position at the time as the only holder of episcopal status in England. Gregory instructed him to consecrate other bishops; and thereafter the presence of three or four such would be mandatory for all consecrations to the episcopacy. Gregory's rhetorical question – 'For how often do bishops come from Gaul?' – which prepares the ground for his reply, presumes a negative response. Nevertheless, Gallic bishops were always clearly in his view. Not so their British counterparts – and it is revealing to note that it does not even seem to have occurred to Gregory that British bishops could have participated in episcopal consecrations in England – and this sets the scene for his answer to Augustine's next question.

Gregory's seventh reply outlined Augustine's relations with the bishops of Gaul and Britain. In the case of the former, the missionary was told that he had no authority to intervene in their affairs; however, Gregory envisaged him trying to raise the standards of the Gallic church by example. The implication here (as in the Pope's letter which is quoted by Bede in the next chapter) is that Augustine might sometimes be in Gaul. In striking contrast to this fairly lengthy and tactful part of the answer, Gregory's approach to the Britons was short, direct, and very different. He unhesitatingly committed to Augustine charge over all the bishops of Britain, adding unflatteringly that this was in order that 'the unlearned may be instructed, the weak strengthened by your counsel, and the perverse corrected by your authority'. A charitable reading of this extraordinary response would be that Gregory's dim view of British Christians was based on the isolated Britons whom the missionaries may have encountered in the south-east, and that it reflected a total lack of knowledge of the independent British church in the west.[23] It is not impossible that it indirectly reflects the aspirations towards the Britons of Æthelberht and Augustine – who had presumably supplied Gregory with at least some of the information on which he based his response. Nevertheless, the fact that Gregory had a more negative attitude towards the British church than did Augustine is implied by his reply to a question which Bede omitted. Having encountered a vestigial cult of a poorly attested Sixtus, Augustine sought relics of the Roman St Sixtus, seemingly to augment and validate the local cult. Gregory, however, was less conciliatory: he sent the missionary the relics he had requested, but instructed him to bury them separately from those of the British Sixtus, and to shut off the latter's tomb. The precise circumstances and thoughts that lie behind these replies are irrecoverable; however the dismissive and ignorant attitude to the venerable British church that they manifest doubtless contributed to the tension of the occasions when Augustine met its representatives.

Augustine's eighth and ninth queries related to issues of ritual purity: how soon after sexual intercourse or childbirth, for instance, people might enter a church.[24] Gregory's reflections on these questions were, by contemporary ecclesiastical standards, humane, rational and unpolemical; nevertheless, the christian church's deep antipathy to the pleasurable aspects of sexual intercourse had now reached the Anglo-Saxons:

> Fleshly copulation is lawful when it is for the sake of producing offspring, and not of desire; and the fleshly intercourse must be for the sake of producing children and not the satisfaction of vicious instincts. So if anyone approaches his wife, not carried away by lustful desire but only for the sake of getting children, such a man is by all means to be left to his own judgement both in the matter of entering the church, and of receiving the mystery of the Lord's body and blood; for one who is placed in the fire and yet cannot burn ought not to be hindered by us from receiving. But when it is not the love of getting children but desire which dominates in the act of coition, the couple have cause to lament.

Considered as a whole, the questions in the *Libellus responsionum* provide some insight into the range of activities in which Augustine was of necessity involved: organising and financing episcopal and monastic households; protecting the young church against violence and depredations; devising its liturgy; defining its relations with its neighbours; and working out the practical implications of its system of beliefs for the daily life of a new race. More generally, the clauses underline the extent to which the coming of Christianity involved social and not just religious changes, and was responsible not only for a new morality but also for a new dimension of taboos. The many English church council clauses devoted to these issues in subsequent centuries underline how much further thought they were to require, and how difficult it was to implement many such provisions satisfactorily. It is notable that, alongside these questions, Augustine made no enquiry about how to deal with paganism – entitling one to deduce that he felt that his existing approaches to this fundamental problem (whatever they were) were proving satisfactory. Nevertheless, Gregory was (rather belatedly) to forward advice on this point.

The *Libellus responsionum* was not the only thing to be dispatched from Rome in 601. Having received word of the encouraging progress of Augustine's work, Gregory sent reinforcements for the mission, among whom the leading figures were (according to Bede) Mellitus, Justus, Paulinus and Rufinianus. At the same time, he forwarded equipment in the form of sacred vessels, altar cloths and church ornaments, along with vestments, relics and a large number of manuscripts. While aspects of the *Libellus* addressed 'internal ritual', these items were essential for 'external ritual'. More generally, they remind us that the coming of Roman Christianity to England also implied the arrival of Mediterranean artefacts and art. We note from Gregory's letters that he sent presents to Æthelberht, which were presumably luxury items; and we know that Pope Boniface V (619–25) gave a golden robe and a garment from Ancyra to Edwin of Northumbria, while presenting a silver mirror and a gold and ivory comb to his Kentish wife, Æthelburh. Although their route of transmission to East Anglia is unknown, the set of Mediterranean silver bowls of sixth-century date – not to mention the much-discussed silver spoons, which possibly had baptismal associations – that were included in the Sutton Hoo ship burial provide tangible corroboration for the presence of such items in early seventh-century England.

The nature of the numerous books that Gregory sent to Augustine is unrecorded, but we can reasonably speculate that they comprised both volumes for use in services, and texts for reading. They may even have included a grand Bible.[25] Alongside the manuscripts that were doubtless imported by Augustine himself and the Frankish books that had presumably arrived with Bertha and Liudhard, these were the foundations of the earliest English libraries. A gospel book of later sixth-century date and Italian origin which was certainly in England at an early date and whose earliest documented provenance is Saint Augustine's Abbey, Canterbury, has a reasonable claim to be associated with the earliest phases of the Roman mission; and although we will never know for certain whether it had reached England by *c.* 600, it provides a useful example of the type of book that undoubtedly did (pls IV–V).[26] The traditions embodied in this volume, and the scribal practices we can reasonably impute to the Roman missionaries themselves, seem to have left a lasting imprint on south-eastern English book production. The earliest surviving Kentish volumes (none of which date from before the eighth century) show a strong debt to Italian models – with a certain admixture of Insular elements.[27] It is an interesting fact that, while Bede is often criticised for stressing the Roman and Irish contributions to the conversion of the English at the expense of the Frankish and British ones, the evidence of the oldest Anglo-Saxon manuscripts is wholly concordant with his emphasis.

More generally, the inclusion of books among the things that Bede describes as necessary for the worship and ministry of the church reminds us that literacy in Latin was a *sine qua non* of Christianity. The point is underlined by Willibald's description of the reinforcements for St Boniface's missionary work in Germany in the early eighth century:

an exceedingly large number of holy men came to his aid, among them readers, writers and learned men trained in the other arts.

Taking measures to ensure a continuing supply of adequately literate individuals must thus have been high on Augustine's list of priorities: it was a precondition of native converts being able to enter holy orders, and hence, quite simply, of the survival and growth of the church. Although the first certain evidence for the existence of a school at Canterbury dates from the 630s (when King Sigibert of East Anglia drew on its resources to establish a comparable establishment in his own kingdom), we can reasonably assume that some educational provision was put in place from the earliest stages. Similarly, we can safely presume that the young christian community rapidly took measures to ensure a local supply of writing materials – arranging the manufacture of parchment and ink. Although no locally made documents or books of such an early date have come down to us, we know that some writing must have gone on in England at this time: the liturgy that Gregory urged Augustine to draw up was presumably committed to writing, and the law-code of King Æthelberht (which, its rubric declares, was set down in Augustine's day) certainly was.

Along with the reinforcements, Gregory sent Augustine advice on the organisation of the church in England as a whole, recommending that it be headed by archbishoprics in London and York, each with twelve suffragan bishops. The circumstances that led the Pope to formulate this scheme are uncertain, but it is more likely to have been based on knowledge of Britain in late Roman times (when it was divided into two provinces with their capitals at London and York) than on contemporary information.[28] What is quite clear, however, is that such a plan, though reasonable in theory, was quite unrealistic in practice in 601, for it presupposed the conversion of all the Anglo-Saxon kingdoms, something that was to take the best part of a century to achieve even in name. The argument that the scheme was predicated on the knowledge of Æthelberht's dominant position in England *c.* 600, which raised hopes of the church's rapid expansion into other kingdoms, is patently flawed, since we are specifically told that his predominance only extended to the Humber, yet Gregory located not just a see but the second archbishopric in Northumbria. The driving force behind the plan is far less likely to have been calculations based on possible awareness of any hypothetical aspirations of Æthelberht than the Pope's implicit faith in such biblical texts as 'I can do all things through Christ who strengthens me' (Philippians 4:13), and 'If you have faith like a grain of mustard seed, you will say to this mountain "Move from here to there" and it will move; and nothing will be impossible to you' (Matthew 17:20; Luke 17:6).

How Augustine viewed the scheme and his chances of implementing it are unknown; he simply seems to have applied himself to realising what he could, to the best of his ability. If he did have reservations, he might have recalled the monastic philosophy made explicit in the sixty-eighth chapter of the *Rule of St Benedict* which explains that if a brother is set a truly impossible task yet his superior remains adamant that he should do it, he 'must understand that this is what is best for him, and let him lovingly trust in God's aid and so obey'. Augustine managed to establish sees at Rochester and London, areas that were then directly or indirectly controlled by Æthelberht, but he was not in a position to do more. Moreover, because his work was so firmly associated with Æthelberht whose principal centre was Canterbury, and since the see of London collapsed after that king's death and could not be restored by his son, Eadbald (ruled 616–40), Canterbury remained the centre of operations and became the southern archbishopric. The northern archbishopric collapsed in 633, when Paulinus fled from York following the death of the convert king, Edwin of Northumbria, at the hands of the pagan king, Penda of Mercia; and it was not to come definitively into existence until the second quarter of the eighth century. The numbers of bishops as a whole long remained much lower than Gregory had envisaged. All this clearly underlines the point that the founding of bishoprics could not be realised in the abstract; rather it was inseparable from the general expansion of Christianity, which was itself a piecemeal process that was intimately linked to the political geography of the country. And when a serious attempt was made to create a coherent ecclesiastical organisation for all England by Archbishop Theodore (669–90), he proceeded along rather different lines from those set out by Gregory.[29] Thus, far from blaming Augustine for not having managed to implement the Pope's overambitious scheme – it was unrealistic and unrealisable – we should rather be impressed that he managed to get as far as he did in such a short time.

Also in 601 Gregory wrote to Æthelberht and Bertha, exhorting them in their duties as christian rulers. He made the point, echoed by other missionaries and much stressed by Bede himself, that the christian king who discharged his duties appropriately could expect to prosper in the present world as well as in the next, underlining it with reference to the success and renown of Constantine the Great. Introducing the transcription of the letter to Æthelberht in his *Historia ecclesiastica* (he omits the one to Bertha), Bede commented that Gregory was anxious to glorify the king with temporal honours. Now, the technology of writing was a potent tool for perpetuating a reputation; and since in England it was an ecclesiastical monopoly, the new church effectively controlled how individual kings would be recorded – a small but not insignificant measure of power. Bede deployed it to great effect both implicitly – he suppressed via omission, for example, the enormous success of the great pagan king, Penda of Mercia (ruled 633–55) – and explicitly, as when he declared: 'So all those who compute the dates of kings have decided to abolish the memory of those perfidious kings [Osric and Eanfrith of Northumbria] and to assign this year to their successor, Oswald [d. 642], a man beloved of God.'

The particular duties Gregory envisaged Æthelberht discharging were fourfold: to suppress the worship of idols, to overthrow pagan buildings and shrines, to set a good example, and to listen to Augustine. It is clear that he was doing the last of these, and we can presume that, subject to the conventions of Anglo-Saxon kingship, he fulfilled the third. On the other hand, we know that he did not accomplish the first, for Bede subsequently tells us that it was only under King Earconbert (640–64) that the worship of idols was officially outlawed in Kent. As for the second, Gregory himself seems rapidly to have had second thoughts.

Shortly after writing to Æthelberht, the Pope sent another letter to the departing envoys with a different message. He had resolved, he said, that the English temples should not be destroyed, only the idols within them: rather they should be cleansed and then reused for christian services. Enforcement of orthodox Christianity by state compulsion was the norm in Late Antiquity, and Gregory seems initially to have assumed that Æthelberht could impose the faith in England in the same way. Subsequently he appears to have woken to the fact – which Æthelberht clearly perceived – that this was not feasible in the very different circumstances of Anglo-Saxon England. Gregory had realised, undoubtedly correctly, that, in the absence of a suitable force and context, people were more likely to accept the new religion if the transition was made as painless as possible – something to which continuity of the place of worship would undoubtedly contribute. Similarly, he advocated substituting christian celebrations for the pagan ones that were to be suppressed. Interesting as is the insight this gives into the Pope's outlook, it also usefully reminds us of the extent to which patterns of behaviour which Bede and other christian writers sharply distinguished as 'pagan' on the one hand and 'christian' on the other, actually overlapped. Adoption of Christianity inevitably implied an appreciable degree of religious syncretism, not only initially but for some time – and this is one of the reasons why 'conversion' as such can be difficult to pinpoint in the archaeological record.[30] One assumes that Augustine tried to implement these psychologically astute suggestions; evidence on the point is, however, lacking. Later Canterbury tradition, recorded by the late fourteenth-century chronicler, William Thorne, spuriously identified the early seventh-century chapel of St Pancras (located to the east of the complex of Saint Augustine's Abbey) as just such a church: there, it was claimed, Æthelberht had worshipped idols before the building was purified and rededicated by Augustine.

We know that Augustine did initiate the construction or reconstruction of a couple of buildings in Canterbury (fig. 1.9). For his cathedral he restored a church which was said to date back to Roman times, dedicating it to 'the holy Saviour, our Lord and God Jesus Christ', a dedication which echoed that of the Lateran basilica in Rome. Excavations in the nave of the present cathedral in 1993 brought to light small sections of walling that possibly belonged to the building in question. Associated with it he established an episcopal residence, implying some 'domestic' as well as ecclesiastical architecture. To the east of the town, outside the Roman walls, not far from St Martin's Augustine founded *de novo* a monastery, whose church was dedicated to SS Peter and Paul – echoing the dedications of the basilicas on the Vatican mount and on the road to Ostia in Rome that were associated with the bodies of the saints in question. Æthelberht helped with both projects; however, he seems to have taken a particular interest in the latter, being credited with its construction (presumably the financing thereof) and with providing a major endowment – a contribution which the community elaborated at the end of the eleventh century in forged charters (cf. fig. 15.1).[31] This enthusiasm presumably reflected the fact that the abbey church was also

1.9. Remains of Saint Augustine's Abbey, Canterbury, viewed from the south-east, with the cathedral in the distance. (Gameson)

designed as a necropolis, and was to receive the king's body as well as those of Augustine and the other early (arch)bishops of Canterbury (cf. figs 14.2–3). The circumstance that the ruler and his christian churchmen were to be buried together was a potent expression of the new spiritual alliance. Further royal investment followed; and the abbey complex was enlarged by Æthelberht's son, Eadbald, who sponsored a smaller chapel dedicated to Mary which was situated to the east of SS Peter and Paul. The other known building programmes associated with the first stage of the mission were located at Rochester and London, where episcopal churches dedicated to St Andrew and St Paul were established with Æthelberht's sponsorship. While no traces of the structure at London are known, excavations at Rochester in the late nineteenth century and again in 1998 brought to light the remains of a church whose form and material point to a seventh-century date, and which might have been that founded by Augustine and Æthelberht. The recent re-examination of the remains revealed that the church had been located on the site of an unidentified Roman structure.

The exiguous surviving evidence suggests that this first phase of building work may have owed more to the participation of Gallic masons than did subsequent ones, when Italian connections are more readily apparent.[32] Be that as it may, the return of building in stone to Anglo-Saxon England was a major event whose general significance should not be underrated. In addition to its practical advantages, such as security and durability, it was a forceful advertisement of the power and cultural sophistication of the new religion. The Anglo-Saxons described the ruins of the Roman buildings among which they lived as 'the work of giants' ('*enta geweorc*'): now, seemingly, the giants were returning to live with them.

While, as noted above, Pope Gregory unhesitatingly granted Augustine authority over the British church in the abstract, the realisation of this charge was far from easy. Apart from the considerable problem of the geographical distance between Wales and Kent, the objective observer can see that the missionary would have to give the Britons compelling reasons why, despite their own, venerable traditions, they should be subordinated to the new arrivals from Rome. Moreover, one further suspects that the fact that Augustine appeared under the aegis of the most powerful (and probably predatory) Anglo-Saxon king, is likely to have added to their reserve towards him. This is another case where Gregory's conceptions were out of touch with reality; yet Augustine, who had the Pope's mandate and doubtless did not see the issues in these terms, still tried to implement them. The events in question are probably to be dated to shortly after the missionary's receipt of Gregory's replies in 601.

Bede describes the sequence of events in considerable detail, with perceptible fluctuations in emphasis and effect that probably reflect the disparity of his sources

– Canterbury traditions on the one hand, British ones on the other – as well as his own views.[33] The story begins with a meeting between Augustine and the bishops 'of the neighbouring British kingdom' at a place known as 'Augustine's Oak' which was somewhere on the borders of the Hwicce and the West Saxons – roughly the area of modern Gloucestershire. The rendezvous had apparently been arranged with the help of Æthelberht – thus documenting his influence in two further neighbouring kingdoms, and underlining how his political power enabled the missionary to expand his field of operation. Bede's report of this meeting is very favourable to Augustine. His seemingly reasonable request that the Britons 'should preserve the catholic peace with him and undertake the joint labour of evangelising the heathen for the Lord's sake' is juxtaposed with the 'unorthodoxy' of the British churchmen, and with the fact that, despite Augustine's 'prayers, exhortations and rebukes', they preferred their idiosyncratic traditions to those of the universal church. Reasoning having failed, Augustine suggested that they resolve the matter via a direct appeal to God, looking to a sign in the form of a miracle as a way of discerning the relative spirituality of the different parties, a proposal to which the Britons reluctantly agreed. Augustine then successfully restored the sight of a blind man – the one specific miracle associated with him that Bede records – whereupon the British party acknowledged his spiritual standing, but said they could not commit themselves to his cause without the consent of their people as a whole. Consequently, a second meeting was resolved upon, to which a wider cross-section of British ecclesiastics came, including, we are told, seven bishops 'and many learned men, chiefly from their most famous monastery' Bangor-is-Coed – a rare case where Bede gives adequate insight into the extent of the British church.

The issues that are reported to have been addressed at this second conference were: the keeping of Easter, the nature of baptism, and whether the British would join Augustine in preaching to the Anglo-Saxons. Before the meeting, when wondering how they should respond to Augustine, the British party (typically) sought the advice of a hermit, who said they should follow the missionary if he were a humble man. In order to ascertain whether or not this was the case, they should let Augustine arrive first at the place of meeting; then, if he stood up when they approached, thus displaying his humility, he was worthy of their respect; but if he remained seated, then the reverse was evidently true. This plan was followed, and unhappily at the key moment Augustine remained seated: the British consequently refused to accede to his leadership, concluding that as he had not even shown them this initial courtesy, were they to be subject to him, he would surely despise them even more. Bede implies that a heated debate followed, which ended with Augustine prophesying that the British would be slaughtered by the Anglo-Saxons: 'if they would not preach the way of life to the English nation, they would one day suffer the vengeance of death at their hands'. This, Bede points out with some satisfaction, subsequently happened at the Battle of Chester (613x16) when King Æthelfrith of Northumbria 'made a great slaughter of that nation of heretics' including copious monks from Bangor who had been present, praying for the British troops. The modern reader might be inclined to see the tragedy as illuminating the political dimension as to why representatives of the British church, whose faith was sometimes directed to supporting their beleaguered christian kingdom against further aggression from their pagan neighbours, hesitated to subordinate themselves to a missionary who appeared with the backing of the most powerful Anglo-Saxon king.

Underlying this fruitless encounter we can discern several strands. On the one hand, since Gregory had already high-handedly entrusted the British bishops to his emissary's care, Augustine may have felt that their recognition of his leadership was a *fait accompli*; while the British, on the other hand, are not likely to have had much respect for the church of a distant nation that in the fifth century had abandoned them to the invading pagans, by whom they were still menaced. At the same time, the episode embodies a fundamental contrast between the Roman and British concepts of spirituality. Whereas the Roman church emphasised the dignity of the bishop, the British outlook was rather that christian authority rested less in an office than in the quality of truly and humbly following in the footsteps of Christ, the servant of all.

The modern response to the story – to see Augustine as proud and vengeful – is anachronistic. In a society that valued authority, the tale conveyed the fact that the Roman missionary had the mystical powers of healing and prophecy, not to mention innate *gravitas*. His prediction that the British would be slaughtered, and its fulfilment, illustrated his awesome prophetic abilities, and showed how divine power worked through him. Some of the stories of early British saints, which were likewise designed to underline their special relationship with God, show them to have been just as 'vengeful'. One thinks, for example, of the tale in the late eleventh-century *Life* of the early sixth-century Cadoc, wherein the saint cursed two of his disciples for having absent-mindedly left his book on the island of Holm, with the result that they drowned as they were trying to retrieve it! To be successful in early Anglo-Saxon England, Christianity had to be seen as a religion of supreme power which defended its followers. The story shows that Augustine, and by extension his religion, were clearly forces to be reckoned with; and if, as is possible, there were wider conflicts of authority between the Roman missionaries and British ecclesiastics, this was a clear demonstration of the divine mandate and spiritual superiority of the latter. (This fateful meeting did not, incidentally, mark the end of the Roman missionaries' interest in the British church, for Bede tells us that Augustine's successor, Laurentius, also tried to extend his pastoral care over them.)

Augustine's last recorded actions were his consecration of Mellitus and Justus in 604. Mellitus (one of the reinforcements sent from Rome in 601) was made bishop of London with a brief to preach to the East Saxons; Justus was ordained bishop of Rochester. As we have seen, both sees were established with the support of Æthelberht who, in addition to sponsoring cathedral churches, provided 'lands and possessions for the maintenance of the bishops' retinues'. Augustine also consecrated his own successor at Canterbury, thereby trying to avoid the potential crisis of a vacancy at this early stage. He chose Laurentius, one of the original missionaries who, it will be recalled, had been his emissary to Gregory in 601.

Bede then records Augustine's death, noting the date (26 May) but not the year; however, we know that it must have occurred between 604 and 609. As the abbey church of SS Peter and Paul was still under construction and had not been consecrated at the time in question, the body was first placed nearby. Subsequently, it was translated to the north *porticus* (chapel) of the finished church, the central altar of which was dedicated to Gregory. Augustine's resting place, together with those of the other early (arch)bishops who were subsequently buried alongside him in the same chapel, can still be located in the abbey ruins (cf. figs 14.2 and 3). It is possible that this clustering of episcopal burials echoed contemporary Roman practices; however, it does not seem to have represented an enshrinement.[34]

Historical circumstances then worked against the early development of a cult of Augustine, and the major figure who might have supported it, namely Archbishop Theodore, had good reasons for promoting Gregory instead.[35] It was not until the eighth century that a start appears to have been made, by which time specific facts seem to have been rather exiguous – as the circumstance that Bede did not apparently know the year of Augustine's death suggests. Nevertheless, by the ninth century the monastery of SS Peter and Paul was referred to as the *familia* of Augustine; and the missionary's cult developed further in the tenth and eleventh century with royal and episcopal support. According to medieval tradition, the abbey church was rededicated to SS Peter, Paul and Augustine in 978; and by this time, Augustine – as opposed to Gregory – was sometimes referred to as the Apostle of the English.

After the Norman Conquest the first Norman abbots of Saint Augustine's, Scotland and Wido, rebuilt the abbey church, sweeping away the accumulated earlier structures. Work began at the east, and the venerable bodies were, for the most part, temporarily rehoused in the western tower of the monastery. The climax of the enterprise came in 1091 with the translation of the bodies of Augustine and the other early archbishops to the new structure, a ceremony presided over by

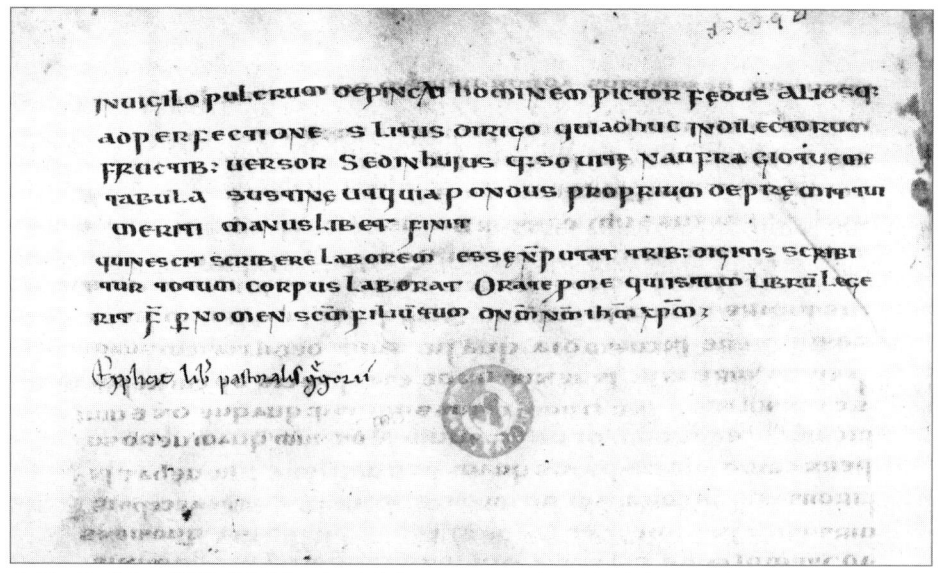

1.10. BnF, lat. 9561, fol. 81v. An eighth-century southern English copy of Ps.-Isidore, De ordine creaturarum *and Gregory the Great,* Regula pastoralis. *At the end of Gregory's text (seen here) the scribe added a colophon which reads: 'He who does not know how to write, does not think it is a labour. Writing is done with three fingers, but the whole body labours. Pray for me, whosoever may read this book. May it be so. In the name of your holy son, our Lord, Jesus Christ.' (Bibliothèque nationale de France)*

Bishop Gundulf of Rochester. The contemporary historian and hagiographer, Goscelin of Saint-Bertin, then a member of the community, reported that Augustine's corpse was well preserved; it was placed before the high altar for the celebration of Mass, and was then enclosed in its new shrine. Goscelin also wrote a *Life of St Augustine* and an account of his miracles, key parts of a series of works that celebrated the venerable Anglo-Saxon saints whose bodies were possessed by the abbey. With regard to the history of the mission, his *Life of Augustine* adds nothing of substance to the information provided by Bede and Gregory (which were, of course, the foundations of his own work); on the other hand, it is significant as a first serious attempt to emancipate Augustine somewhat from Gregory, and it sheds valuable light on how the saint was viewed by his own community at the end of the eleventh century. He appears as a miracle-working, apostolic bishop who took his mission the length and breadth of England.[36] A note added in the thirteenth century to the margin of the oldest extant copy of the text (in BL, Cotton Vespasian B. xx) shows that it was then being read in the refectory at Saint Augustine's Abbey on the saint's feast day.

Augustine was reburied in 1221 (doubtless in response to the translation of Thomas Becket's relics at the cathedral in the previous year); and as an early fifteenth-century drawing shows, he had pride of place at the east end of the abbey church. William Thorne, the abbey chronicler at the end of the fourteenth century, recorded that the head was enshrined in a separate reliquary made of precious metal and gems. Thus the body rested until the abbey was surrendered in 1538 at the dissolution of the monasteries. Although the shrine seems to have been temporarily saved from destruction by Edward Thwaites, lord of the manor of Easture and East Stour, who is believed to have removed it to Chilham church, nothing of it now remains.

What had Augustine achieved? He had carried through to a successful conclusion a difficult and dangerous mission, despite the initially inadequate preparations of its papal sponsor. In less than a decade he had planted Roman Christianity in south-east England; and, although following the death of Æthelberht the new church entered a period of crisis, a permanent bridgehead had nevertheless been established. Though there had been a christian community in Canterbury before Augustine's arrival, it had not been the official church of the kingdom. By the conversion of Æthelberht, Augustine managed to give Christianity the status of the authorised religion at the royal court that was then the most powerful in England, and the church was duly enshrined in law. In addition to Canterbury, Augustine established bishoprics at Rochester and London; thanks to Æthelberht, his work also reached the East Anglian court, and he had at least some contact with the Hwicce and the West Saxons.

As an integral part of this process, various social and cultural changes were introduced, whose impact can hardly be overestimated. New teachings and traditions began to govern marriage, birth, death, and sexual mores; while on the cultural side one thinks of the reintroduction of building in stone, the importation of Mediterranean art and artefacts, the introduction of books and, intimately related, of schooling in Latin. At a practical level, the arrival of Latin enabled England to communicate with a much wider area of Europe than had hitherto been the case – not to mention making the Anglo-Saxons an historic (as opposed to prehistoric) society.

The fact that Augustine did not manage to implement Gregory's design for the English church as a whole is hardly a fault, given that the scheme was idealistic rather than realistic; and it is clear that a substantial share of the blame for his failure to join forces with the British church in Wales should also be laid at the Pope's door.[37] Again, the circumstance that the church in the south temporarily collapsed on Æthelberht's death is not to be imputed to Augustine who had himself died a decade earlier. Indeed, it is a useful reminder that political factors wholly outside the control of the church were central to its success or failure – something that Gregory seems to have preferred not to recognise. In point of fact, the events in south-eastern England conform to a pattern that is well represented elsewhere, for most Anglo-Saxons kingdoms relapsed from Christianity after the first attempt at conversion; and it seems to have been rare for a whole royal family to have embraced the new faith at the initial encounter.[38] What is notable in the case of Kent after Augustine's mission is how brief was that period of apostasy.

Working far from home, in a country whose customs – not to mention its language – were very different from his own, Augustine made major strides in a very short time. He started the process of converting the Anglo-Saxons to Christianity – a watershed in the history of the country, whose effects have lasted to the present day. Contemporaries were in no doubt as to his achievement, which they summed up on his tomb thus:

> Here lies the most reverend Augustine, first archbishop of Canterbury, who was formerly sent hither by St Gregory bishop of Rome; being supported by God in the working of miracles, he led King Æthelberht and his nation from the worship of idols to faith in Christ and ended the days of his office in peace; he died on the 26th day of May during the reign of the same king.

Notes

1. See Alan Thacker, ch. 14 below.
2. See Fiona Gameson, ch. 15 below.
3. See further Anton Scharer and Alan Thacker, chs 9 and 14 below.
4. See further Robert Markus, ch. 2 below.
5. See Clare Stancliffe, ch. 6 below.
6. See further Clare Stancliffe, ch. 6 below.
7. Cf. Anton Scharer, ch. 9 below.
8. Cf. Ian Wood, ch. 4 below.
9. See Clare Stancliffe, ch. 6 below.
10. See further Robert Markus, ch. 2 below.
11. See further Ian Wood, ch. 4 below.
12. See further Ian Wood, ch. 4 below.
13. See further Stéphane Lebecq, ch. 3 below.
14. See Ian Wood, ch. 4 below.
15. See Ian Wood, ch. 4 below.
16. See further Barbara Yorke, ch. 7 below.
17. See further Barbara Yorke, ch. 7 below.
18. See further Simon Burnell and Edward James, ch. 5 below.
19. See further Barbara Yorke, ch. 7 below.
20. See further Rob Meens, ch. 8 below.
21. See further Robert Markus, ch. 2 below.
22. See further Ian Wood, ch. 4 below.
23. See further Clare Stancliffe, ch. 6 below.
24. See further Rob Meens, ch. 9 below.
25. See Mildred Budny, ch. 11 below.
26. See Richard Marsden, ch. 12 below.
27. See further Richard Gameson, ch. 13 below.
28. See further Clare Stancliffe, ch. 6 below.
29. See further Alan Thacker, ch. 14 below.
30. See further Simon Burnell and Edward James, ch. 5 below.
31. See Richard Emms, ch. 16 below.
32. See further Eric Cambridge, ch. 10 below.
33. See further Clare Stancliffe, ch. 6 below.
34. See further Alan Thacker, ch. 14 below.
35. See further Alan Thacker, ch. 14 below.
36. See further Fiona Gameson, ch. 15 below.
37. Cf. Clare Stancliffe, ch. 6 below.
38. Cf. Barbara Yorke, ch. 7 below.

CHAPTER 2

Augustine and Gregory the Great

R.A. Markus

In his *Life of Gregory the Great*, composed at the end of the seventh century or the very beginning of the eighth, the anonymous monk of Whitby wrote as follows:

> According to Gregory's opinion, when all the Apostles bring their own peoples with them and each individual teacher brings his own race to present them to the Lord in the Day of Judgement, he will bring us – that is the English people – instructed by him through God's grace . . .[1]

Gregory did indeed think that on that awesome day of reckoning each apostle would appear before the Judge with his flock, and he anxiously put the question to his fellow bishops:

> When so many shepherds appear with their flocks in the presence of the eternal Shepherd, what are we miserable men, who bear the name of shepherd, what are we then to say, returning to our Lord empty-handed at the end of our day's work?[2]

On that great day, we might wonder, will it be Gregory, or will it be Augustine that we will find ourselves queuing up behind? Although the definitive answer to that question will have to await the Day of Judgement itself, early English Christians, such as Bede and the anonymous monk of Whitby, as well as many others in later times, had no doubt. It was Gregory rather than Augustine who was 'their apostle', 'their master', 'their father' and so forth.[3] Augustine, although he was evidently rather more than a mere passive instrument, has by and large vanished in Gregory's shadow. To make Augustine visible in Gregory's shadow is one of the purposes of this volume as a whole; however, my brief is to deal with Augustine's Italian background; and that means Gregory the Great, and to that brief I propose to keep.

Gregory's shadow is, to be sure, a very large one; and not only because of his greatness, but also on account of the wealth of information at our disposal concerning him. The contrast with the comparative paucity of information about Augustine – essentially a few chapters in Bede's *Ecclesiastical History* – is very striking.

It could even be the case that in some respects we know more about Gregory than did Augustine. I have sometimes wondered, for instance, whether the questions Augustine put to Gregory in 601 (which are discussed in more detail below by Rob Meens) were quite as otiose as we are sometimes tempted to suppose. Anyone who has read through Gregory's surviving correspondence might well be in a position to guess his answers, for example, to questions about liturgical diversity, or about ritual purity. His replies are almost predictable; they certainly cohere with other things he wrote at one time or another.[4] This, however, may have been much less obvious to Augustine than to us. After all, although Augustine had been one of Gregory's monks, used, perhaps, to hearing Gregory discourse on Job or a gospel or some other biblical book, he is unlikely to have delved into the papal archives to read Gregory's letters to distant bishops. He may thus have known very little about Gregory's views on sex – not a subject in which Gregory shows much interest anyway – or on episcopal authority and ecclesiastical independence. His questions to Gregory need not then be taken to show lack of initiative or of imagination.

Gregory certainly expected Augustine, as he expected every bishop, to be a pastor. At the beginning of this chapter I quoted from a homily Gregory delivered to an assembly of bishops, early in his pontificate. On that occasion he was preaching on one of the New Testament's great missionary texts: Luke's account of the sending of the seventy (10:1–7): 'the harvest is plentiful, but the labourers are few'. Gregory's discourse is a statement of their – the preachers', the pastors', the bishops' – mission: to preach the Gospel and convert the people. He was, of course, speaking to Italian bishops, who were not likely or expected to go to distant lands of the heathen to convert them by their preaching. But Gregory knew of pockets of what he called pagans, infidels, idolaters and the like nearer home. He did not distinguish missionary from pastoral work; preaching to the unconverted was quite simply part of the bishop's pastoral care. In the same address to bishops, Gregory said:

> You see how the world is being ravaged by the sword; you see what blows are daily destroying the people. Whose sin but ours has brought this on us? Behold, towns are laid waste, fortified places overthrown, churches and monasteries wrecked, fields turned into wilderness . . . Multitudes have perished through our sin; through our neglect they have not been taught for [eternal] life. For what shall we

call the souls of men but the food of the Lord, created that they might be turned into His Body, that is to say, to the enlargement [*augmentum*] of His eternal Church? We should be the seasoning of this food; for, as I have said before, 'you are the salt of the earth' (Matthew 5:13) was said to the preachers being sent out.[5]

And just as he did not distinguish missionary from pastoral work in general, so Gregory did not generally distinguish between unbaptised infidels and baptised Christians who might have relapsed into the cult of idols, or continued to practise rites which were suspect as magic or witchcraft.[6] Conversion was for all sinners, baptised or not.[7] The boundaries between baptised but unsatisfactory Christians and unbaptised pagans were fluid, and Gregory had no great interest in defining them.[8] His pagans were rural backwoodsmen to be coerced into decent christian living and worship by their betters; and even when he had to imagine more distant pagans beyond the boundaries of the known world, such as the English, it was on this model he had to construct them. Bishops had an equal duty of preaching to convert both groups; and both groups equally needed to have salutary pressure applied to them.

To appreciate this, consider one of the precedents for Gregory's sending of Augustine to preach to the heathen English. In 594 Gregory, acutely dissatisfied with the archbishop of Caralis and many things in Sardinia, sent an Italian bishop, Felix, accompanied by one of his most trusted helpers, the monk Cyriacus,[9] to work on and with local landowners and other powerful men to convert local pagans to Christianity.[10] They were all asked to assist his emissaries in their work. Two years later Augustine was sent to the English. We do not know what instructions Gregory gave Augustine at this time; but the letters Gregory sent five years later, at the time of his first contact with the missionaries in 601, give us a clue: King Æthelberht was expected to act exactly as had been the great men of Sardinia. Even the language of the letter Gregory addressed to him recalls the language he had used seven years before to the dukes Zabarda and Hospito.[11] The only significant difference is that Æthelberht was invested with the additional grandeur of being told to model himself on Constantine,

> the most religious emperor who converted the Roman state [*rempublicam*] from the false worship of idols and subjected it along with himself to almighty God and our Lord Jesus Christ, turning to Him with all his heart together with the peoples subject to him . . .

So now let the king hasten to bring to the kings and peoples under his rule knowledge of the one God, the Father, Son and Holy Spirit.[12]

The pattern of Gregory's expectations is consistent; and, as the reference to Constantine makes explicit, it rested, ultimately, on the coercive régime of the christian Roman Empire. Since the time of Theodosius I at the end of the fourth century, the imposition of christian orthodoxy by compulsion had become the accepted norm. Gregory did not question this any more than did his contemporaries and predecessors. He only changed his mind about it when reflection on the situation in England brought home to him how unrealistic his expectations had been in this new situation. That reflection occasioned the revolutionary change in Gregory's missionary strategy with which we are familiar from that extraordinary letter he sent post-haste after the abbot Mellitus, 'somewhere in Frankia', a month after Mellitus had left Rome for England. That letter in effect countermanded the instructions Gregory had given for the destruction of the shrines when writing to the king some four weeks before.[13]

Gregory's ideas on missions and how to conduct them were fully crystallised long before he dispatched Augustine and his monks. A further dimension of these ideas needs underlining: in Gregory's address to the assembled bishops with which I began we caught an echo of his constant preoccupation with the speedy coming of the End. He had warned the bishops of their urgent duty in the apocalyptic language and imagery that he habitually employed, especially when rebuking pride, laziness, or complacency. It was the eleventh hour, the time was short, action was a matter of urgency.[14] Gregory's reminders of the imminent End served to focus attention and give direction to choice. It gave a seriousness to what human laziness would make trivial. It was in the same apocalyptic vein that he ended his letter to King Æthelbert: 'As the end of the world approaches ... be prepared.' There was nothing new here: the mission to the English was simply one of the many things waiting to be done before the End, and done soon.

I have been labouring the point that Gregory's intentions for Augustine's mission belonged to a cluster of ideas which were fully formed at the beginning of his pontificate, and were part of his conception of the duties of the pastoral office. Revolutionary and imaginative as it was, the sending of a mission really needs no special explanation. Unverifiable theories have been propounded to account for it, theories sometimes verging on the extravagant; and such theories have sometimes been allowed to obscure the simple and patent fact that the mission was quite simply a practical application of Gregory's concept of the pastoral office – a concept he had, as we know, meditated upon long and deeply.

When and why it took the specific shape of a mission to the English is a very secondary question, though one not without its own interest. In 599 Gregory said he had 'long contemplated' sending the mission.[15] How long was this 'long' is anybody's guess. However, it is hardly likely to go further back than the autumn of 595. In September that year Gregory wrote to his agent in charge of the Roman church's lands in Provence. He was instructed to use revenue from the lands which could not be transferred and spent in Rome to purchase 'clothes for the poor or English slave boys [*pueros Anglos*] aged seventeen or eighteen that they might be educated in monasteries'.[16] This is Gregory's first mention of English slaves in Gaul – though he had long had dealings with Provence, and knew about the slave trade that passed through it. Clearly, at this time the first thing that came into his mind was the old-established custom of his predecessors of buying clothes for the poor with their Provençal revenue.[17] The English slaves are a casually suggested alternative, which looks as if it had just occurred to him. He was thinking of the best use for bad money, rather than planning a mission to the English and recruiting for it. It could be, however, that the possibility of purchasing English slaves sparked off the idea.

At any rate, there is no need to invoke Gregory's worsening relations with the court and the patriarch of Constantinople to account for his interest in western Europe; and the case made for such a scenario is unconvincing.[18] If we look for a specific reason for Gregory's decision, it is more profitable to look West rather than East. Gregory may have heard rumours from Gaul, whether true or unfounded, that a missionary initiative might be welcomed by some in England – though a specific request from a party in England is unlikely.[19] He may also have shared the Byzantine view[20] that English kings were in some way subject to Frankish authority, and that Frankish kings and their clergy (who had hitherto neglected this duty)[21] would thus have an obligation to bring them to the christian faith. What is certain, though, is that he was interested in the Frankish church. He had been in contact with bishops in the Frankish kingdom since the first year of his pontificate. These contacts, however, were irregular, and confined to the south of the kingdom and the court of Queen Brunhild.[22] To be better informed about and to be able to influence the quality of the christian life of Frankish Catholics, Gregory had to develop more extensive relations with the Frankish church. The subsequent history of his concern for the Frankish and the English churches allows no doubt that he thought of the two churches in relation to one another.

When they set off, Augustine and his companions received from Gregory letters of recommendation – to the Frankish royal family, to the rector of the Roman church's patrimony in Gaul and local patrons there. But most important among them will have been the letters addressed to bishops on their route through Gaul, the abbot of Lérins, and perhaps others.[23] The missionaries were expected to make contacts in Gaul. Their success can be gauged by the greatly increased range of such contacts at the time Gregory sent reinforcements to England in 601. This time

2.1. Brescia, Museo Civico Cristiano, Diptych of Boethius: detail of the painting added to the inner face in the seventh century, showing SS Jerome, Augustine and Gregory. (After Hubert, Porcher and Volbach)

the letters of recommendation went to Vienne, Arles, Lyon, Toulon, Marseille, Châlon, Metz, Paris, Rouen, Angers and Gap as well as to the royal courts.[24] Gregory's contacts with Gaul had grown, and so had the range of his information, both in relation to the English, about whom he had known nothing five years before, and the Franks, about whom he had been a little better informed. Augustine's mission served not only to establish a foothold for Christianity among the Anglo-Saxons, but also to spur the Frankish church into action. In 596 Gregory had looked to the Frankish church for help. In 601 the new English church was expected to promote his cherished plans for the reform of the Frankish church. The two churches were to be associated in a partnership of christian renewal. That intention is likely to have shaped Gregory's plans from the start.

Others' contributions to this volume deal with the various aspects of Augustine's work, with Gregory's instructions to him, and – as far as we can trace them – the results. To sum up my overwhelming impression: Gregory's pastoral personality seems to me to be stamped over the whole enterprise. That, at least to my mind, fully accounts for his initiative in launching a mission, unprecedented by any previous pope. The mission 'to all nations' had been given reality, and was to bear ample fruit in the coming generations.[25] The roots of Gregory's initiative lie deep in the imperatives of his idea of the pastoral office. About the English heathen among whom Augustine was to work he knew nothing in 596; naturally, he imagined the situation Augustine was to enter on the model of what was familiar to him nearer home. He encouraged Augustine and his companions to venture into the unknown. The shape their mission was to take was determined by the ways in which Gregory, like his fellow bishops, approached the task of preaching to pagans and to ill-instructed Christians of less than acceptable manners. When eventually England turned out to be wildly different from what he had imagined, it took him no more than three or four weeks to break free of his old assumptions and to revise his missionary strategy in line with his new understanding. The timing and the immediate occasion of the mission are likely to have been determined by accident and contingency, especially the needs of the Frankish church; and we should always allow for inspired opportunism. Behind it all is the sense of urgency that inspired all Gregory's pastoral work, from advising a troubled community on electing a bishop,[26] to the conversion of the English. The latter was undertaken in the knowledge that God's mercy embraced even the English: for the heathen, too, were called to his kingdom. As Gregory once said, the heathen, too, were the *locus* of his mercy;[27] and as he never tired of insisting, God had sent his chosen preachers to the ends of the earth for the ministry of preaching.[28]

NOTES

1. Whitby *Life*, ch. 6. (*The earliest life of Gregory the Great, by an anonymous monk of Whitby*, ed. B. Colgrave (Lawrence, Kansas, 1968), p. 83). Colgrave (p. 143, n. 22) remarks on this passage: 'If the writer is quoting a definite passage from Gregory's writings, I have not been able to identify it.' He refers to Gregory's letter to Augustine quoted by Bede (*HE*, I, 23) in which Gregory expresses the hope that he might share in Augustine's reward for his labours.
2. *Homiliae xl in Evangelia* I.17.17 (*PL*, 76, 1075–312).
3. Bede, *HE*, II, 1, with Plummer's note (*Venerabilis Bedae Opera Historica*, ed. C. Plummer, 2 vols (Oxford, 1896), II, 67–8). See further the contributions by Alan Thacker and Fiona Gameson to the present volume.
4. See especially H. Chadwick, 'Gregory the

Great and the mission to the Anglo-Saxons', *Gregorio Magno e il suo tempo*, 2 vols (*Studia Ephemeridis Augustinianum*, 33–4, Roma, 1991), I, 199–212.
5. *Homiliae xl in Evangelia* I.17.16. For this and other material in this paper, see my *Gregory the Great and his world* (Cambridge, 1997), where I have dealt with the subject of this paper in greater detail.
6. Gregory made the distinction between baptised but unsatisfactory Christians and unbaptised pagans only once, in the case of Corsica: *Ep.* VIII.1 (though in *Ep.* V.38 he speaks of many *gentiles* who sacrifice to idols, of whom *some* are baptised. The letters are referred to in the edition by D. Norberg (*CC* 140 and 140A)); and he only once distinguished different ways of preaching to the two groups: *Moralia* XXIX.31.72 (ed. M. Adriaen) (*CC* 143, 143A and 143B).
7. On *'conuersio'* see C. Straw, *Gregory the Great. Perfection in imperfection* (Berkeley and Los Angeles, 1988), pp. 194–235, and C. Dagens, *Saint Grégoire le Grand. Culture et expérience chrétiennes* (Paris, 1977), pp. 247–346.
8. As I intend to show in another paper, I consider erroneous the view propounded by H.-D. Kahl, 'Die ersten Jahrhunderte des missionsgeschichtlichen Mittelalters. Bausteine für eine Phänomenologie bis ca. 1050', *Kirchengeschichte als Missionsgeschichte.* Band 2: *Die Kirche des frühen Mittelalters*, ed. K. Schäferdiek (Erster Halbband, München, 1978), 11–76, at p. 48.
9. Here referred to as *servus Dei*; he is probably identical with the abbot Cyriacus who was sent on difficult missions in Gaul and Spain.
10. *Epp.* IV.23 (to Sardinian landowners); 25 (to a *dux* Zabarda); 27 (to a *dux Barbaricinorum* Hospito). On the means of coercion cf. *Ep.* IX.205.
11. *Ep.* XI.37. In addition to the general likeness of Gregory's admonitions, note especially lines 9–11 and *Ep.* IV.27, lines 6–10 and lines 63–4; cf. *Ep.* IV.25, lines 10–11.
12. *Ep.* XI.37.
13. *Ep.* XI.56. On this, see my paper 'Gregory the Great and the origins of a papal missionary strategy', *SCH* 6 (1970), 29–38; reprinted in my *From Augustine to Gregory the Great* (London, 1983), XI.
14. E.g. *Homiliae xl in Evangelia* I.1.2. It is the 'eleventh hour': *Homiliae xl in Evangelia* I.19.2; I.4.5.
15. *Ep.* IX.222: *'diu cogitans'*.
16. *Ep.* VI.10. On the problem of currency convertibility, see P. Grierson, 'The *Patrimonum Petri in illis partibus* and the pseudo-imperial coinage in Frankish Gaul', *Revue belge de numismatique*, 105 (1959), 95–111.
17. Pelagius I, *Epp.* 4; 9 (eds P.M. Gassó and C.M. Batlle, Montserrat, 1956, 12, pp. 29–30).
18. I have criticised views of this type in detail in my 'Gregory the Great's Europe', *TRHS* 5th series 31 (1981), 21–36; esp. pp. 29–34 (repr. in *From Augustine to Gregory the Great*, XV).
19. *Ep.* VI.51.
20. Cf. Procopius, *Wars* VIII.20.10 (ed. H.B. Dewing, Cambridge, Mass. and London, 1928), 254. Cf. Ian Wood, 'Frankish hegemony in England', in M. Carver (ed.), *The Age of Sutton Hoo. The seventh century in North-Western Europe* (Woodbridge, 1992), pp. 235–41.
21. The *'sacerdotes e vicino'* of *Ep.* VI.51 are certainly Frankish clergy: cf. Ian Wood, 'The mission of Augustine of Canterbury to the English', *Speculum*, 69 (1994), 1–17.
22. He had only very recently been in touch with the see of Saintes: *Ep.* VI.50. The bearer of this letter, the priest Leuparicus, evidently had some link with the court of

Queen Brunhild: *Ep.* VI.58. The communication with Saintes seems thus to have been indirect, through the court.
23. *Epp.* VI.51; 52; 54; 55; 56; 57; 59; 60. Not all the letters may have been preserved. And in any case there were 'unofficial' contacts through Frankish clergy in Rome: cf. I. Wood, 'Augustine and Gaul' (ch. 4 below).
24. *Epp.* XI.34, 38, 40, 41, 42, 45, 47, 48, 50, 51.
25. Fritze, W., '*Universalis gentium confessio*. Formeln, Träger und Wege universalmissionarischen Denkens im 7. Jahrhundert', *Frühmittelalterliche Studien*, 3 (1969), 78–130.
26. *Ep.* III.29.
27. *Moralia* XXVII.34.58: '*locus autem misericordiae Dei est ipsa gentilitas*'.
28. *Moralia* IX.9.10; XXVII.11.19–21; XXVIII.6.15 and XXIX.25.50; *Homiliae in Evangelia* I.4.1; I.19.1; II.29.2. etc.

CHAPTER 3

England and the Continent in the Sixth and Seventh Centuries: the Question of Logistics

Stéphane Lebecq

The nature of the relations between England and the continent in the sixth and seventh centuries is an enormous issue; to treat it adequately would require a work on the scale of Wilhelm Levison's masterpiece dealing with the question in the eighth century.[1] Needless to say, such an approach is impossible in the present context. What I wish to do here is to study one very important aspect of these relations – indeed, the precondition for them – thereby describing the material background to the mission of St Augustine. Our subject is the practicalities that made links between Britain and the continent possible, and the logistics of their operation, at the time of 'the coming of Christianity to Anglo-Saxon England' – to borrow the title of Henry Mayr-Harting's famous book.[2]

When Bede, in his *Historia ecclesiastica*, mentions Augustine's journey from Rome to Britain in 596–7, he tells us nothing about the saint's itinerary across Gaul, nothing about his place of embarkation, and nothing about the conditions of his crossing. The only detail he gives is that Augustine landed on the banks of the *fluvius Uantsumu* (the Wantsum Channel), namely the channel that formerly separated *Cantia* (Kent) from *Tanatos insula* (the Isle of Thanet).[3] One has thus to turn to a variety of other written sources dating from the seventh century and the beginning of the eighth to get more precise information about the conditions in which missionaries used to travel between Britain and the continent – that is concerning embarkation and landing places, the chartering of ships, and the hazards of the crossing.

It is a striking fact that sixth-century sources are almost completely silent on these matters, whereas seventh- and eighth-century ones with relevant information are altogether more plentiful. Now, this contrast in quantity and quality of information is not simply a result of the vagaries of the sources, but seems also to echo a genuine contrast in the circumstances themselves. For if we take account of archaeological and numismatic evidence as well as written sources, we find that maritime exchanges seem to have been fairly *ad hoc* and disorganised until about AD 600, after which point, around the beginning of the seventh century, they seem to have become more orderly and organised – we then see ports with permanent infrastructures, not to mention regular sailing routes, and professional sea-going merchants.

Let us now consider in more detail the period between the decline of the Roman Empire and *c.* 600. With the exception of a few late and doubtful allusions in saints' lives to relations between the Atlantic seaboard of Gaul and the distant Celtic regions of north-western Europe,[4] the written sources of the sixth century tell us nothing about any maritime traffic between Gaul and the British Isles. The most important Roman ports in the region (see fig. 3.1) – *Gesoriacum/Bononia* (Boulogne) and *Iuliobona* (Lillebonne) in northern Gaul, and *Dubris* (Dover) and *Rutupiae* (Richborough) in Kent[5] – cease to be mentioned; and, if the name of an

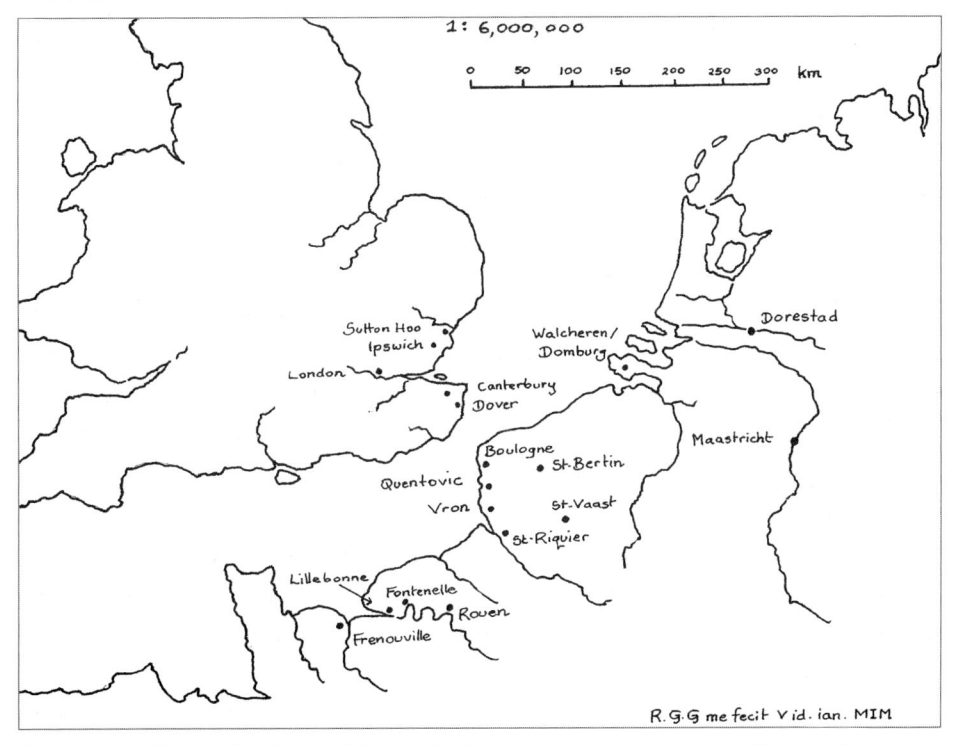

3.1. *Map of England and her neighbours in the sixth to seventh centuries.* (Gameson)

ancient city on a waterway like *Rotomagus* (Rouen) still appears, it is no longer referred to as a port.[6]

When trying to explain the decline of cross-Channel traffic after the heyday of the Roman Empire and hence the silence of the sources, the *Libri historiarum* of Gregory of Tours (d. 594) would seem to offer some guidance. One thinks in particular of Gregory's account of the raid of the *Danus rex Chlochilaichus* on the northern shores of Gaul around 525.[7] The maritime migrations and the concomitant piracy which had by then been rampant for two centuries undoubtedly made peaceful communications between the British Isles and the continent more difficult. This does not, of course, mean that all types of relations ceased to exist. On the contrary, the migrations during the fifth century resulted in the settlement of maritime peoples not only in the east and south of Britain, but also on continental shores, notably in the Boulonnais, the Bessin and the lower valley of the Loire (where Saxon settlement has long been recognised thanks to documentary and place-name evidence),[8] and in the Ponthieu and the Caen areas (as some recent cemetery excavations have shown).[9]

Such excavations (at Vron and Nouvion in Ponthieu; at Frenouville, Saint-Martin-de-Fontenay and elsewhere in Normandy) revealed an interesting distinction between the material culture of the first generations of settlers (the fourth century and the first half of the fifth), and that of their successors. Some of the objects that were buried with the former group came from northern Germany, such as certain kinds of tall conical bronze brooches (the so-called tutulus brooches) and crossbow brooches;[10] while objects that were interred with the latter group were similar to those that have been discovered in the south of England, especially in Kent and the Isle of Wight, such as disc brooches, button brooches, and some hand-made cremation urns. Correspondingly, contemporary graves in southeastern England include some material that originated on the continent.[11]

The contacts attested by such material imply certain practicalities to support them – men, ships, landing places, and even perhaps the implements of commerce. Unfortunately archaeological evidence to confirm this is in rather short supply: it is limited to the scales that were found in some tombs, particularly in Kent.[12] Written evidence is similarly lacking, except perhaps in relation to ships. For in his *De Excidio Britanniae*, the sixth-century British writer Gildas not only mentions the Celtic *currucae* (the famous curagh or skin-boats), but also the Saxon *tribus ut lingua eius [saxonum] exprimitur, cyulis, nostra longis navibus* – 'three keels, as they call long boats in their language'.[13] We thus learn that in the sixth century the Anglo-Saxons had ships that they called '*cyul*' and which would later be called '*ceol*' – a word that is etymologically related to the modern English keel. The ships to which the term refers were probably long,

3.2. The Nydam boat. (Gameson)

clinker-built, wooden vessels akin to the famous example from Nydam in Schleswig-Holstein, dating from *c.* 400 (fig. 3.2).[14] During the fifth and sixth centuries, these boats were propelled only by rowing, as is shown both by Sidonius Apollinaris's testimony about the Saxon pirates along the shores of Gaul in the second half of the fifth century ('You will see among them as many rowers [*remiges*] as pirates'),[15] and by the comments of Procopius on the ships of the Germans of the lower Rhine and those of the Anglo-Saxons: 'There were no supernumeraries in this fleet, for all the men rowed with their own hands. Nor do the islanders have sails; they always navigate by rowing along.'[16]

These ships had a symmetrical profile from stem to stern. They also had a relatively flat bottom, with the result that they could be beached almost anywhere.[17] Potential landing places were therefore numerous, particularly in the sandy shores of the southern coasts bordering the North Sea. And it is presumably because the maritime traffic was, in consequence, fairly widely scattered that it is so difficult to identify real trading ports between the end of the third century when Roman harbours started to decline, and the beginning of the seventh when a genuine revival of port activity took place. Nevertheless, the vestiges of some small trading posts that operated in this period can still be discerned. This is perhaps the case at Benouville (on the Orne estuary, near Caen), where a considerable quantity of imported material has been found, also appearing, moreover, in the nearby cemeteries.[18]

Be that as it may, none of the peoples that had newly settled in these seaboard regions minted coins. If they needed coinage, they presumably used Roman currency such as the gold *solidus*, or the gold *triens* or *tremissis*, which were being reproduced by Frankish moneyers in Gaul.[19] However, it is far from certain that they actually needed it: for according to Philip Grierson, intercourse between the inhabitants of Northern Europe at this date was scattered and episodic, exchange of goods being principally effected via barter and gift-giving, practices which were often part of diplomatic, matrimonial and social customs rather than commercial transactions.[20] Concordant with this, the few continental coins which reached Britain during this period seem, for the most part, to have been used as ornaments.

Such was the background against which the wedding between Æthelberht of Kent and Bertha, the daughter of King Charibert of Paris, took place in the late sixth century.[21] And this is probably also part of the context for, and helps to explain the heterogeneous nature of the grave goods that were found in the famous ship burial at Sutton Hoo (mound one). The items in question were gathered around 625–30, and were probably for the funeral of King Rædwald of East Anglia rather than for that of his son Sigibert, who had a Frankish name and who spent a long period of exile in Gaul.[22] Alongside the material of Eastern, Scandinavian and Rhenish origin which was found in mound one, the burial also included a hoard of thirty-seven *trientes*, each originating from a different Gallic mint. Now, however this be interpreted in detail, considered as a whole it undoubtedly highlights the artificiality of such a collection. These grave goods thus make the Sutton Hoo ship burial one of the best illustrations of this period of peaceful but not yet truly commercial exchanges between England and the continent. Nevertheless, it is also one of the last examples of such intercourse – for around the year 600 things began to change.

After *c.* 600 we seem to enter a new era: there are many signs that maritime exchanges were becoming more organized. In the first place, genuine ports began to appear on both sides of the Channel. In written sources, such places were called *emporium*, *portus* or, most commonly, *vicus*, a word that has left its legacy in the many place names ending in -*wik*, -*wijk*, and (especially in England) -*wich*. All these ports were to become the starting points of regular shipping lines. Secondly, coins began to be minted on a regular basis in the countries bordering the North Sea, and currency started to play an important part in the process of exchange – thereby suggesting that an organized trade was taking shape.

At the very end of the sixth century, the Frisians began to mint a series of gold *tremisses* or *trientes*, which were originally imitations of Maastricht *trientes* (so-called because they represented a third of the ancient *solidus*) and which are known as *Dronrijp Type* coins.[23] Soon afterwards, the Anglo-Saxons began in their turn to mint coins. The first of these gold *thrymsas*, as they were called in English, were struck in Kent, probably in Canterbury, around 600; but coining remained sporadic until *c.* 630. There was then an increase in minting activity, principally in Kent and London, and certain coins were struck by royal authority (some of them bear the name of Eadbald, who succeeded Æthelberht and was king of Kent between 616 and 640).[24] The coincidence in date between the appearance of the first Frisian minting and the first Anglo-Saxon one is suggestive. It seems to imply that intercourse between the area around the mouth of the Rhine on the one hand and south-eastern England on the other was growing in importance. One cannot simply regard this new minting activity as a symbol of prestige and power for the authorities who ordered it;[25] there must be a further explanation – namely the practical necessities for a growing trade between England and the continent. That this was indeed the case is indicated by the fact that several mints were established at port sites, and moreover by the circumstance that many coins that had been minted at other locations have been found in these places. English coins appear at continental ports and vice versa.[26]

The revival of port activity involved both old places and new ones. The old sites were often the *suburbia* of Roman cities, especially those in protected estuary locations. Examples include Rouen, where coins were minted from the end of the sixth century onwards,[27] and *Lundonia* (London), which was in 604, according to Bede, an *emporium* frequented by *multi populi terra marique venientes* ('many people coming by land and sea')[28] – something which has been confirmed by the excavations in the Strand (outside the city walls).[29] Certainly this was the part of the town that was to be called *Lundenwich* (i.e. the *wik* (port) of London) in the eighth-century *Life of St Boniface*,[30] reflecting the new fashion in names for ports of this generation. For around 600 ports also began to appear in new locations. The earliest ones to be identified by archaeology are Walcheren/Domburg on the Isle of Walcheren in Dutch Zeeland (namely the area where the Rhine, the Meuse and the Scheldt converge into the sea), and Gipeswic/Ipswich in Suffolk. At Walcheren/Domburg, archaeologists discovered – though not, unfortunately, within the context of scientific excavation – wooden structures, a considerable quantity of pottery and metal artefacts, and many coins, the earliest of which came from northern Gaul, while the later ones were of English origin.[31] At Ipswich, which was scientifically excavated, Keith Wade found not only many local ceramics, but also an important quantity of ceramics which had been imported from the Rhineland, from the region of the Meuse and from Flanders.[32] This might suggest that Ipswich had close links with Walcheren, and that a regular shipping line existed between the two locations. If so, this would be the first such line that we are able to identify.

What is most striking about all these changes which seem to have taken place at the end of the sixth and the beginning of the seventh centuries, is that they appear simultaneously on the continent and in Britain: it thus looks as if all the countries bordering on the North Sea were entering a new era. How can this be explained? Several interrelated factors can be adduced. In the first place, it was during the sixth century that, after a hundred and fifty years of migrations and piracy, the maritime peoples finally began to 'settle down'.[33] Consequently, contacts between peoples of Germanic origin, united by a common cultural heritage, could henceforth multiply more easily. Secondly, during the last quarter of the sixth century there was an upsurge in diplomatic and matrimonial links between the élites – particularly the royal families – of the continental world and the Anglo-Saxon one,[34] a process which was enhanced by the growth in religious ties that followed from the coming of Christianity to Anglo-Saxon England. Thirdly, in order to reinforce their authority and to benefit from the intensification of exchanges, kings tried to exert control over the developing network of communications, and the measures they used – promoting the establishment of ports, appointing personnel there, setting up customs offices, and claiming the right to mint coins – further enhanced their growth.[35]

Yet this was just a beginning: what happened around 600 was merely the first sign of more considerable changes. Written sources bear witness to the intensification of relations across the North Sea during the seventh century and the beginning of the eighth: the material in question is mainly hagiographical, relating the travels of missionaries between Britain and the continent. At the same time ports and shipping lines began to proliferate. In Kent, for instance, ports multiplied around Canterbury during the seventh century (see fig. 3.3). One thinks of Fordwich (whose existence is attested by a royal diploma of 675), Sandwich (documented in the *Life of St Wilfrid*), Sarre (mentioned in eighth-century texts, and also known from the cemetery which was excavated in the nineteenth century), not to mention the north-east *surburbium* of Canterbury itself (where a *wic* (port) was recently identified on the river Stour).[36] In Northumbria, *Eboracum* (York) had a couple of merchant suburbs which interacted with the Rhineland. One was around Coppergate; the other, excavated more recently, around Fishergate at the confluence of the rivers Ouse and Foss.[37] This was perhaps the eighth-century Frisian district to which the *Life of St Liudger* refers,[38] and the place referred to in the *Anglo-Saxon Chronicle* as '*Eoforwic*'[39] – a form of name paralleling '*Lundenwich*' which, as noted earlier, designated the port of London. In Wessex,

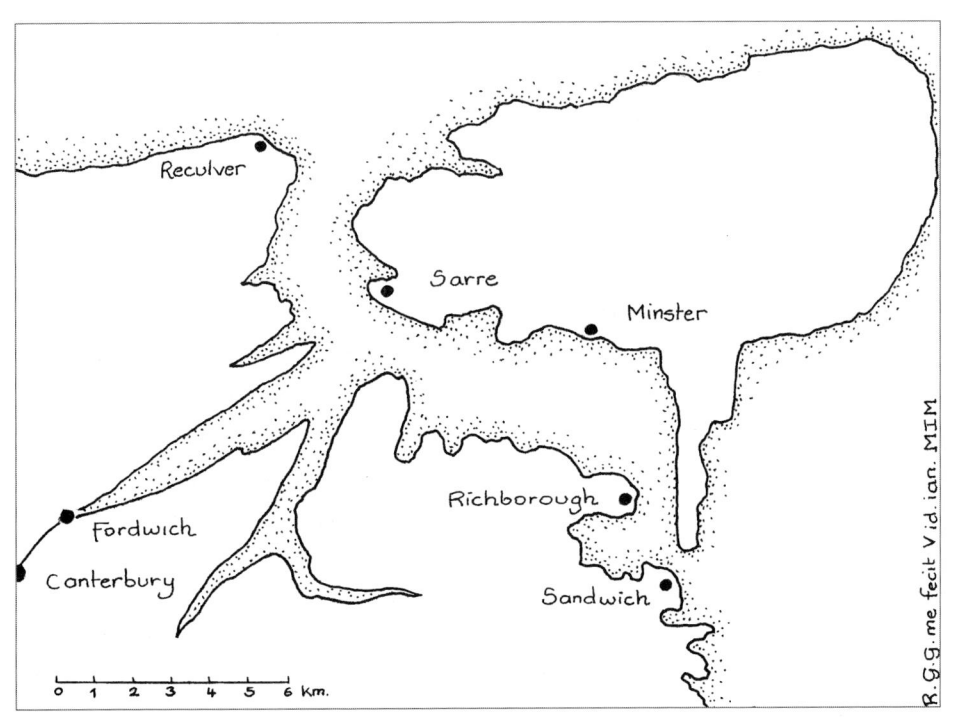

3.3. Canterbury and its ports, c. 600. (Gameson)

the port of Hamwi(c)h (latterly Southampton) began to develop at the beginning of the eighth century, intimately connected with the royal residence at nearby Winchester.[40] Crossing the Channel to Ponthieu, one of the maritime borders of Neustria, we find Quentovic developing in the Canche estuary during the seventh century (fig. 3.4). Although the first written evidence for this port appears in late seventh-century English sources, numismatic evidence suggests it emerged at an earlier date. One of the coins found in the Sutton Hoo purse was struck on the river *QVANTIA* (the Canche), while one of the coins in the Crondall hoard, which was hidden around 640, was minted in *WIC IN PONTIO* (Wic en Ponthieu, namely Quentovic).[41] The history of Dorestad, on the Rhine delta at the borders of Frisia and Austrasia, is almost exactly the same:[42] although the earliest written references date from the end of the seventh century, the first known coins were minted around 630–40, while the excavations directed by W.A.van Es and W.J.H.Verwers show an important development from around 675.[43]

At the same time, regular shipping lines developed between these different sites, and these were habitually used by missionaries, monks, and bishops. In 664, for example, Wilfrid, coming from northern Gaul, landed at Sandwich;[44] in 668 Archbishop Theodore sailed from Quentovic to Canterbury;[45] while in 678,

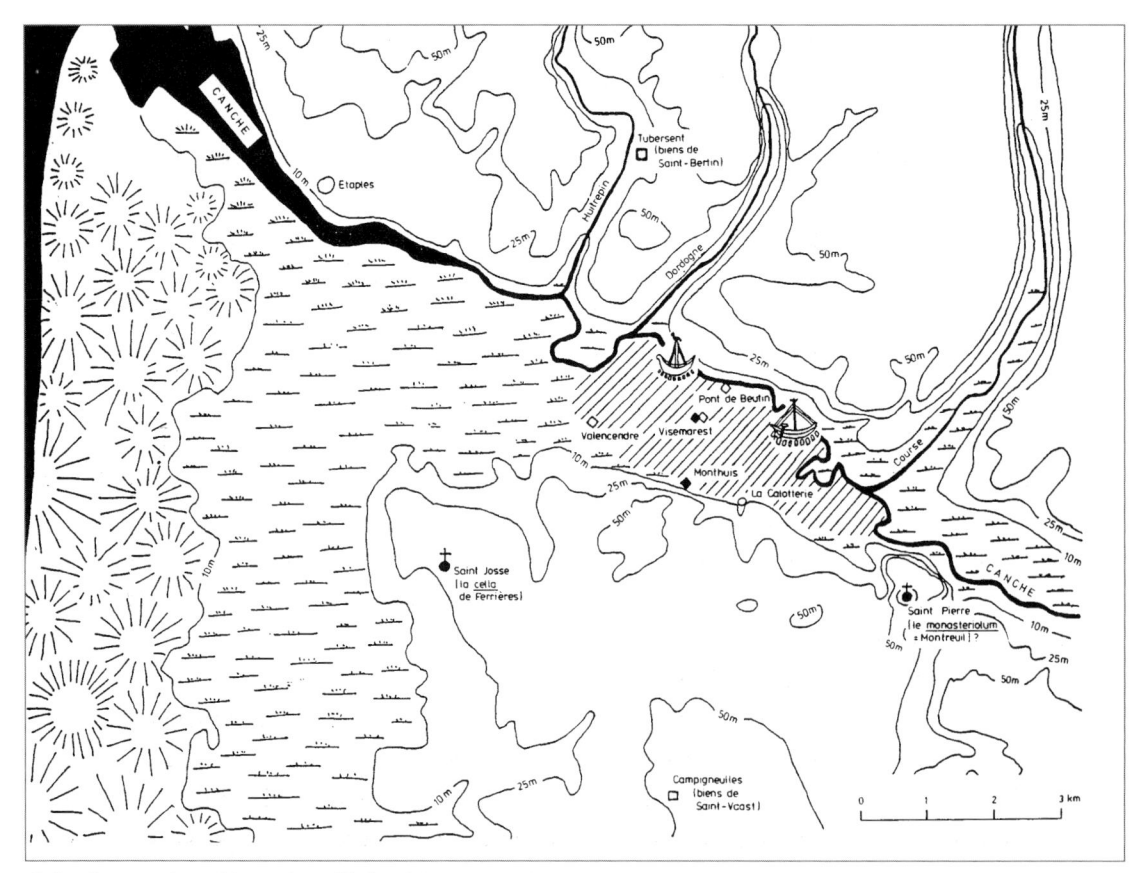

3.4. Quentovic and its setting. (Lebecq)

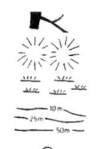

�ororsymbol	Waterways and Channel coast	▫	Existing village where there were abbey properties in the ninth century
	Area of sand dunes	♦ (with cross)	Ecclesiastical property of the former *vicus*
	Marsh or flood plain	♦	Place with a toponym in – vis (=*vicus*)
	Gradient	◇	Situation of archaeological finds
○	Existing town	▨	Maxim extension of the area of activity of the former *vicus*
○	Existing village		

Wilfrid, again wanting to travel from Britain to Rome, hoped to disembark at Quentovic in order to attain what his biographer identified as the *via rectissima* ('the most direct route') between England and the holy see; however, he was diverted to Frisia, possibly to Dorestad.[46] In 716, Boniface found in *Lundenwich* a ship to *Dorstet* (Dorestad);[47] in 718, again in *Lundenwich*, he found a boat to *Cuentawich* (Quentovic);[48] while in 720, his companion, Willibald, crossed the Channel from the *mercimonium que dicitur Hamwih* ('the entrepot (or port) which is called Hamwih [Southampton]') to the *urbs que vocatur Rotum, ubi fuit mercimonia* ('town which is called Rouen, where there was a trading place (or port)').[49] As a final example we may cite Alcuin's voyage across the North Sea from *Eboracum* to Dorestad in 780.[50]

The general pattern of the main shipping routes is now becoming evident, and may be summarised as follows. 'Lines' ran from the main ports of eastern and south-eastern England, (namely York, Ipswich and London) to Walcheren/Domburg and Dorestad, which functioned as the gateways to Frisia, Austrasia and the Rhineland; they ran from the south-eastern ports of England (i.e. London and the satellites of Canterbury) to Quentovic, which served as the gateway to northern Gaul, especially Neustria; and from the southern English ports, especially Hamwih, to Normandy and the Seine valley.

Everywhere, archaeology confirms the intensity of these relations. One thinks, for instance, of the quantity of the Frisian or Rhenish material that has been found in York, Ispwich, and London;[51] or of the abundance of Seine valley ceramics which has been discovered at Hamwih.[52] The kings, who wished to profit from this trade, appointed officers to collect the tax they imposed on it: on the continent they were called *procuratores* or *ministeriales*,[53] while in England they were called *wic-gerefa* ('wic-reeves'), as we read in the law-code of Hlothere of Kent (d. 685).[54] The contacts between England, especially the south-east, and the continent, particularly Frisia and the Lower Rhine area, became so close in the last quarter of the seventh century that there was a simultaneous monetary revolution in these two countries: around 670–80 the Anglo-Saxons and the Frisians both stopped minting golden coins, and began to strike the little silver coins that historians used to call *sceattas*, but which were in fact pennies or deniers.[55] Together, they spread these new coins, first in the area of their mutual interest, and then throughout the Western world: less than one century later, all the Western kingdoms minted silver coins. There is no better illustration of the close economic relations between England and the continent at the end of the seventh century and the beginning of the eighth.

Not only did the sea routes between England and the continent multiply during the seventh and eighth centuries, but the nature of the ships themselves changed: in particular, increasing numbers of continental and Anglo-Saxon ships had a sail. Whether this was true of the boat at Sutton Hoo (fig. 3.5) is disputed, but it was surely the case for the ships represented on the coins from Quentovic and Dorestad (fig. 3.6).[56] The sails in question were merely single square ones; nevertheless they changed both the proportions of the boats (i.e. the ratio between their length and their width) and the conditions of navigation. The use of a sail meant that the crew could be less numerous, and it made crossings easier, faster and cheaper. Moreover, it enabled a larger cargo to be carried, and more passengers to be embarked.[57]

The point may be illustrated with reference to the embarkation of Boniface in 716, and that of Willibald in 720. In chapter four of the life of the former, we read: 'When the sailors (*nautae*) were about to embark [from *Lundenwich*] on their return home, Boniface asked permission of the shipmaster (*nauclerius*) to go on board, and after paying his fare he set sail and came with favourable winds (*prospero ventorum flatu*) to Dorstet'.[58] Chapter three of the latter's life informs us: 'Taking with them the necessary money for the journey and accompanied by a band of friends, [Willibald and his companions] came to a place, which was known by the ancient name of *Hamel-ea-mutha*, near the port (*mercimonium*) of Hamwih. Shortly afterwards they embarked on a ship. When the captain (*nauclerius*) of the swift sailing ship had taken their fares, they sailed, with the west wind blowing (*circio flante*) and a high sea running, amidst the shouting of sailors and the creaking of oars (*remigiis crepitantis*) . . .'[59]

In conclusion, let us consider the case of St Augustine himself. Taking into account all the evidence, such as it is (and the reader will remember that it is much more plentiful and precise for the period after the Augustinian mission than for the era before it), can we divine the circumstances and conditions in which Augustine crossed the Channel in 597? Needless to say, this is a difficult issue. Henry Mayr-Harting thought that Augustine may have embarked in Tours, because the last known letter of introduction he carried from

3.5. The Sutton Hoo ship. (© Copyright The British Museum)

3.6. Coins from Quentovic and Dorestad, showing boats: a. Denier of Charlemagne struck at Quentovic; b. Denier of Louis the Pious struck at Dorestad. (Lebecq)

Pope Gregory the Great was addressed to the bishop of that town: 'They would probably find it easiest to take a boat from Tours to Kent because of the close trading and political links between the two'.[60] However, I very much doubt that this was the case. At the time in question nobody would have taken the risk of such a long sea voyage, if he had had the possibility of a shorter crossing. And Augustine might reasonably have expected to have been made welcome further north in Gaul, both in Neustria (roughly the equivalent of the north-west of modern France (except Brittany), plus western Belgium) and in Austrasia (the kingdom to the east of this). Queen Bertha of Kent had been born in the former,[61] while Pope Gregory supplied letters of introduction to the kings of the latter, Theodebert II and Theoderich II, not to mention Queen Brunhild.[62] Consequently, I believe that Augustine took the road northwards (perhaps from Tours – if he passed through that town). But did he take the Meuse or the Rhine route leading to Walcheren/Domburg, whose port was just beginning to develop, or the route through Ponthieu? If I had to choose, I should prefer the second solution[63] for three reasons. First, even if the port of Quentovic had not yet come into being at this early date, some maritime activity was beginning on the banks of the river Canche. Indeed, thanks to one of the thirty-seven coins in the Sutton Hoo hoard which bears the inscription *QVANTIA*,[64] we know that coins were minted on the shores of the river Canche around the year 600, possibly for commercial purposes. Secondly, as noted earlier, all the country around the river Canche, from the Boulonnais to the Ponthieu was occupied by Saxon settlements, which could have created a favourable environment for the missionaries. Thirdly, as Stephen of Ripon observed in relation to Wilfrid's voyage in 678, the *via rectissima* between England and the continent passed through Quentovic.[65]

So it is possible that Augustine and his forty companions embarked in this area, on boats which more probably resembled the Nydam ship of *c.* 400 than the vessels represented on the later coins of Quentovic (*c.* 800). If this were the case, it is possible that they did not have to pay a fare for crossing, but may instead have had to row with the crew!

NOTES

1. W. Levison, *England and the Continent in the Eighth Century* (Oxford, 1946).
2. H. Mayr-Harting, *The Coming of Christianity to Anglo-Saxon England* (London, 1972).
3. *HE*, I, 25.
4. See A. Lewis, 'Le commerce et la navigation sur les côtes atlantiques de la Gaule du Ve au XIe siècle', *Le Moyen Age*, 59 (1953), 249–98; E.G. Bowen, *Britain and the Western Seaways* (London, 1972); E.G. Bowen, *Saints, Seaways and Settlements in the Celtic Lands* (Cardiff, 1977), esp. pp. 160–90; E. James, 'Ireland and Western Gaul in the Merovingian Period', in D. Whitelock et al. (eds), *Ireland in Early Medieval Europe* (Cambridge, 1983), pp. 362–86; P. Johanek 'Der Aussenhandel des Frankenreiches der Merowingerzeit nach Norden und Osten im Spiegel Schriftquellen', in K. Düwel, H. Jankuhn, H. Siems and D. Timpe (eds), *Der Handel des frühen Mittelalters, Untersuchungen zu Handel und Verkehr der vor- und frühgeschichtlichen Zeit in Mittel- und Nordeuropa*, III (Göttingen, 1985), 214–54, esp. pp. 227–9; Stéphane Lebecq, 'La Neustrie et la mer', in Hartmut Atsma (ed.), *La Neustrie. Les pays au nord de la Loire de 650 à 850*, 2 vols (Sigmaringen, 1989), I, 405–40, esp. p. 412.
5. Some of them had been included in the late Roman defences of the *Litus Saxonicum*. See S. Johnson, *The Roman Forts of the Saxon Shore* (London, 1976), esp. pp. 48–53 (Richborough and Dover); and D.E. Johnston (ed.), *The Saxon Shore*, CBA Research Report no. 18 (London, 1977), esp. the papers by B. Philp ('Dover', pp. 20–1) and C. Seillier ('Boulogne and coastal defences in the 4th and 5th centuries', pp. 35–8).
6. N. Gauthier, 'Rouen pendant le haut Moyen Age (650–850)', in Atsma (ed.), *La Neustrie, II*, 1–20, esp. p. 3.
7. Gregory of Tours, *Historiarum Libri Decem*, III, 3, ed. R. Buchner, *Ausgewählte Quellen zur Deutschen Geschichte des Mittelalters* (Berlin, 1967), I, p. 143.
8. Gregory of Tours, *Historiarum Libri Decem*, II, 18–19 (Loire) and X, 9 (Bessin, around Bayeux), ed. Buchner I, p. 100 and II, p. 589. For the Saxon place names in the Boulonnais, see M. Gysseling, *Toponymisch Woordenboek van België, Nederland, Noord-Frankrijk en West-Duitsland (voor 1226)*, 2 vols (Tongeren, 1960). Still useful is the older account by F. Lot, 'Les migrations saxonnes en Gaule et en Grande-Bretagne', *Revue Historique*, 119 (1915), 1–40.
9. For the Caen area, see C. Pilet, 'Quelques témoignages de la présence anglo-saxonne dans le Calvados, Basse-Normandie (France)', *Frühmittelalterliche Studien*, 13 (1979), 357–81; and C. Lorren, 'Des

Saxons en Basse-Normandie au VIe? A propos de quelques découvertes archéologiques funéraires faites récemment dans la basse vallée de l'Orne', *Studien zur Sachsenforschung*, 2 (1980), 232–59. For the Ponthieu, see D. Piton, *La nécropole de Nouvion-en-Ponthieu* (Berck-sur-Mer, 1985); and C. Seillier, 'Développement topographique et caractères généraux de la nécropole de Vron (Somme)', *Archéologie Médiévale*, 16 (1986), 7–32. More generally, see Stéphane Lebecq, 'The Economy of the Northern Seas (from the fifth to the eighth century)', in *The New Cambridge Medieval History of Europe*, vol. I (Cambridge, forthcoming).

10. E. James, *The Franks* (Oxford, 1988), pp. 46–8.

11. See above, n. 9. For more synthetic approaches, see M. Welch, 'Contacts across the Channel between the fifth and seventh centuries: a review of the archaeological evidence', *Studien zur Sachsenforschung*, 7 (1991), 261–70; and Lebecq, 'Economy of the Northern Seas'. For the cemeteries on the Isle of Wight, see C.J. Arnold, *The Anglo-Saxon Cemeteries of the Isle of Wight* (London, 1982); for those in Kent, see the example of Finglesham: S. Chadwick Hawkes, 'The Anglo-Saxon Cemetery at Finglesham, Kent: a reconsideration', in *Medieval Archaeology*, 2 (19), 1–71; or her summary in J. Campbell (ed.), *The Anglo-Saxons* (Oxford, 1982), pp. 24–5. For discussion of V. Evison's opinion about the Frankish presence in south-east England, see James, *The Franks*, pp. 116–17.

12. H. Steuer, 'Gewichtsgeldwirtschaften im frühgeschichtlichen Europe. Feinwaagen und Gewichte als Quellen zur Währungsgeschichte', in K. Düwel, H. Jankuhn, H. Siems and D. Timpe (eds), *Der Handel der Karolinger- und Wikingerzeit, Untersuchungen zu Handel und Verkehr der vor- und frühgeschichtlichen Zeit in Mittel- und Nordeuropa*, IV (Göttingen, 1987), pp. 405–527, esp. pp. 447, 520. See C.J. Arnold, *An Archaeology of the early Anglo-Saxon Kingdoms* (London, 1988), pp. 59–61; and R. Hodges, *The Anglo-Saxon Achievement* (London, 1989), p. 55.

13. Gildas, *The Ruin of Britain and Other Documents*, chs 19 and 23, ed. M.Winterbottom (Chichester, 1978), pp. 19, 94 (*curucae*), and pp. 26, 97 (*cyulae*).

14. See for instance H. Jankuhn, *Nydam und Thorsberg. Moorfunde der Eisenzeit*, 12th edn (Neumünster, 1979), pp. 31–7; or Ole Crumlin-Pedersen, 'The boats and ships of the Angles and Jutes', in S. McGrail (ed.), *Maritime Celts, Frisians and Saxons*, CBA Research Report 71 (London, 1990), 98–116, esp. 105–11.

15. Sidoine Apollinaire, *Epistolae*, VIII, 6 (ch. 13), ed. and trans. A. Loyen, vol. III (Paris, 1970), p. 96. I do not agree with J. Haywood, *Dark Age Naval Power: a Reassessment of Frankish and Anglo-Saxon Seafaring Activity* (London, 1991), p. 71, who, quoting another passage of the same epistola (VIII, 6 (ch. 15), ed. Loyen, p. 97) emphasizes the ability of the fifth-century Saxons to sail; in my opinion the reference to the Saxons who leave '*de continenti in patriam vela laxantes*' (ch. 15) is more rhetorical than the precise reference to the '*remiges [Saxones]*' whom he could see along the Atlantic shores of Gaul (ch. 13).

16. Procopius, *History of the Wars*, VIII, 29, ed. and trans. H.B. Dewing, 7 vols (London, 1954), V, p. 261.

17. See, for instance, D. Ellmers, *Frühmittelalterliche Handelsschiffahrt in Mittel- und Nordeuropa*. (Neumünster, 1972); or S. McGrail, *Ancient Boats in North West Europe. The archaeology of water transport to AD 1500*, (London, 1987).

18. See C. Pilet et al., 'Les nécropoles de Giverville (Calvados) (fin Ve-fin VIIe

siècles après J.C.)', *Archéologie Médiévale*, 20 (1990), 3–140, esp. pp. 33–5; and idem, 'Le village de Sannerville, Lirose (fin de la période gauloise-VIIe siècle après J.C.)', *Archéologie Médiévale*, 22 (1992), 1–190, esp. 37, 39–40.

19. Philip Grierson and Mark Blackburn, *Medieval European Coinage*, 1: *The Early Middle Ages 5th–10th centuries* (Cambridge, 1986), *passim*.

20. Philip Grierson, 'Commerce in the Dark Ages: a critique of the evidence', *TRHS*, 5th series, 9 (1959), 123–40; and idem, 'La fonction sociale de la monnaie en Angleterre aux VIIe-VIIIe siècles' in *Moneta e Scambi nell'alto Medioevo = Settimana di studio del Centro Italiano di studi sull'alto Medioevo*, 8 (1961), 455–84. Both are repr. in his *Dark Age Numismatics, Selected Studies* (London, 1979).

21. *HE*, I, 25, pp. 72–4. For the context of the wedding, see Ian Wood, *The Merovingian North Sea* (Alingsas, 1983), esp. pp. 15–16.

22. R. Bruce-Mitford (ed.), *The Sutton Hoo Ship Burial*, I: *Excavations, background, the ship, dating and inventory* (London, 1975); A. Care Evans, *The Sutton Hoo Ship Burial* (London, 1986). Most scholars identify the dead man with King Rædwald of East Anglia; for an alternative view see Ian Wood, 'The Franks and Sutton Hoo', in I. Wood and N. Lund (eds), *People and Places in Northern Europe (500–1600): Essays in honour of Peter Hayes Sawyer* (Woodbridge, 1991), pp. 1–14.

23. Stéphane Lebecq, *Marchands et Navigateurs Frisons du haut Moyen Age* (Lille, 1983), I, pp. 50–4.

24. Grierson and Blackburn, *Medieval European Coinage*, 1, pp. 155–64; or, for a convenient summary, D.M. Metcalf, 'Anglo-Saxon Coins 1: Seventh to Ninth Centuries', in Campbell (ed.), *The Anglo-Saxons*, pp. 62–3.

25. I do not agree with the radical point of view of Philip Grierson (see above, n. 20) about the social rather than commercial significance of coinage during the Dark Ages. Cf. Arnold, *Archaeology of Early Anglo-Saxon Kingdoms*, pp. 58–9.

26. The first coins were struck in the Quentovic area *c.* 600 ('*QVANTIA*', in the Sutton Hoo hoard, for which see above, n. 22); while the first coins were struck in Canterbury or London in the first half of the seventh century (see Grierson and Blackburn, *Medieval European Coinage*, pp. 159–62).

27. J. Lafaurie, 'Trouvailles de monnaies franques et mérovingiennes en Seine-Maritime (Ve–VIIIe siècles), in Nancy Gauthier (ed.), *Histoire et numismatique en Haute-Normandie, Cahiers des Annales de Normandie* (Caen, 1980) 93–107, esp. p. 95.

28. *HE*, II, 3, p. 142.

29. Alan Vince, *Saxon London: an Archaeological Investigation* (London, 1990); and idem, 'The Development of Saxon London', in idem (ed.), *Aspects of Saxon and Norman London 2*, London and Middlesex Archaeological Society Special Paper 12 (1991), pp. 409–35.

30. Willibald, *Vita Bonifatii*, chs 4 and 5: *Die Briefe des Bonifatius. Willibalds Leben des Bonifatius*, ed. R. Rau, *Ausgewählte Quellen zur Deutschen Geschichte des Mittelalters*, IV b (Darmstadt, 1968), pp. 476, 480.

31. P.A. Henderikx, 'Walcheren van de 6e tot de 12e Eeuw: Nederzettingsgeschiedenis in fragmenten', *Archief van het Koninklijk Zeeuwsch Genootschap der Wetenschappen* (1993), 113–56; and Stéphane Lebecq, 'L'emporium protomédiéval de Walcheren-Domburg: une mise en perspective', in J.-M. Duvosquel and E. Thoen (eds), *Peasants and Townsmen in Medieval Europe. Studia in honorem Adriaan Verhulst*, (Gent, 1995), pp. 73–90.

32. Keith Wade, 'Ipswich', in R. Hodges and B. Hobley (eds), *The Rebirth of Towns in the*

West (AD 700–1050), CBA Research Reports 68 (London, 1988), 93–100; Hodges, *The Anglo-Saxon Achievement*, pp. 97–101.

33. Lucien Musset, *Les Invasions: les vagues germaniques*, 3rd edn with additions by Stéphane Lebecq (Paris, 1994).

34. Wood, *Merovingian North Sea*, and *The Merovingian Kingdoms (450–751)* (London, 1994), esp. pp. 176–9.

35. P. Sawyer, 'Kings and Merchants', in Peter Sawyer and Ian Wood (eds), *Early Medieval Kingship*, (Leeds, 1977), pp. 139–58; idem, 'Wics, Kings and Vikings', in Thorsten Anderson and Karl Inge Sandred (eds), *The Vikings*, Proceedings of the Symposium of the Faculty of Arts of Uppsala University (Uppsala, 1978), 23–31; Stéphane Lebecq, 'Première esquisse d'une économie médiévale', in P. Contamine et al., 'L'économie médiévale', 2nd edn (Paris, 1997), pp. 49–80, esp. pp. 75–6.

36. On Kentish ports in general, see Tim Tatton-Brown, 'The Towns of Kent', in J. Haslam (ed.), *Anglo-Saxon Towns in Southern England* (Chichester, 1984), pp. 1–36, esp. pp. 16–22; idem, 'The Anglo-Saxon Towns of Kent', in Della Hooke (ed.), *Anglo-Saxon Settlements* (Oxford, 1988), pp. 213–32; and Hodges, *Anglo-Saxon Achievement*, pp. 92–4. About Fordwich see P. Sawyer, *Anglo-Saxon Charters: An annotated list and Bibliography*, (London, 1968), no. 7, p. 72. On Sandwich, see *The Life of Bishop Wilfrid by Eddius Stephanus*, ed. and trans. by B. Colgrave, pb edn (Cambridge, 1985), ch. 13, p. 28. For Sarre, see Arnold, *Archaeology of Early Anglo-Saxon Kingdoms*, pp. 20, 59–63, 70, 148–50. For the early Anglo-Saxon port of Canterbury, see Tim Tatton-Brown, *Canterbury. History and Guide* (Stroud, 1994), p. 13; and on its later (eighth- to tenth-century) development see M. Lyle, *Canterbury* (London, 1994), pp. 46–7.

37. R. Hall, 'York (700–1050)', in Hodges and Hobley, *The Rebirth of Towns*, pp. 125–32, esp. pp. 129–30; R. Hall, *The English Heritage Book of York* (London, 1996), pp. 36–7. For more general accounts, see Hodges, *Anglo-Saxon Achievement*, p. 102, and N.G. Higham, *Northumbria (AD 350–1100)* (Stroud, 1993), pp. 168–9.

38. Altfrid *Vita sancti Liudgeri*, I, 11–12: *Die Vitae sancti Liudgeri*, ed. W. Diekamp, Geschichtsquellen des Bistums Münster (1881), pp. 16–17.

39. Cf., for example, D. Dumville and S. Keynes (eds), *The Anglo-Saxon Chronicle, IV: MS B (Cotton Tiberius A VI, British Library)*, ed. S. Taylor (Cambridge, 1983), p. 20 (anno. 643) and p. 34 (anno. 868).

40. M. Brisbane, 'Hamwic (Saxon Southampton): an eighth-century port and production centre', in Hodges and Hobley (eds), *The Rebirth of Towns*, pp. 101–8; and the important thesis of Richard Hodges, *The Hamwih pottery: the local and imported wares from 30 years' excavations at Middle Saxon Southampton and their European context*, CBA Research Report 37 (London, 1981).

41. For a mainly historical approach: Stéphane Lebecq, 'Quentovic: un état de la question', *Studien zur Sachsenforschung*, 8 (1993), 73–82. For a numismatical approach: V. Zedelius, 'Zur Münzprägung von Quentovic', *Studien zur Sachsenforschung*, 7 (1990), 367–77. For an archaeological approach: D. Hill, K. Maude, J. Warburton and M. Worthington, 'Quentovic defined', *Antiquity*, 64 (1990), 51–8.

42. Lebecq, 'Pour une histoire parallèle de Quentovic et Dorestad', in Jean-Marie Duvosquel and Alain Dierkens (eds), *Villes et campagnes au Moyen Age, Mélanges Georges Despy* (Liège, 1991), pp. 415–28.

43. Lebecq, *Marchands et Navigateurs Frisons,* esp. pp. 149–60. For an archaeological approach: W.A. van Es and W.J.H. Verwers, *Excavations at Dorestad I. The Harbour: Hoogstraat 1,* 2 vols (Amerfoort, 1980); W.J.H. Verwers, 'Dorestad: A Carolingian Town?' in Hodges and Hobley (eds), *The Rebirth of Towns,* pp. 52–6; W.A. van Es, 'Dorestad centred', in J.C. Besteman, J.M. Bos and H.A. Heidinga (eds), *Medieval Archaeology in the Netherlands: Studies presented to H.H. Van Regteren Altena* (Assen and Maastricht, 1990), pp. 151–82; W.A. van Es and W.A.M. Hessing (eds), *Romeinen, Friezen en Franken in het hart van Nederland: Van Traiectum tot Dorestad (50 v.C.–900 n.C.)* (Den Haag, 1994). About the first coinage of Dorestad, A.N. Zadoks-Josephus-Jitta, 'De eerste muntslag te Duurstede', *Jaarboek voor Munt- en Penningkunde,* 48 (1961), 1–14.
44. See *Vita Wilfridi* ch. 13: *Life of Wilfrid,* ed. Colgrave, p. 28.
45. *HE,* IV, 1, pp. 331–2.
46. *Vita Wilfridi,* chs 25 and 26, ed. Colgrave; and *HE,* V, 19, p. 522.
47. Willibald, *Vita Bonifatii,* ed. Rau, ch. 4, p. 476.
48. Ibid., ch. 5, p. 480.
49. *Vita Willibaldi* by a nun of Heidenheim (= Hugeburc), ch. 3., ed. O. Holder-Egger, MGH, *Scriptores,* 15 (1), (Hannover, 1887), p. 91.
50. *Alcuini carmina* no. 4, ed. E. Duemmler, MGH, *Poetae Latini Aevi Carolini,* vol. 1, (Berlin, 1881), pp. 220–22; French trans. in Lebecq, *Marchands et Navigateurs Frisons,* II, p. 22.
51. For York, see above n. 37; for Ipswich, n. 32; for London, n. 29.
52. See above n. 40. The kilns where the most important part of the imported ceramics found in Hamwih were produced have recently been discovered and excavated in La Londe, near Rouen: see R. Hodges, 'The eighth century pottery industry at La Londe, near Rouen, and its implications for cross-Channel trade with Hamwih, Anglo-Saxon Southampton', *Antiquity,* 65 (1991); and N. Roy, 'Un atelier de poterie du haut Moyen Age en forêt de La Londe, près de Rouen (Seine-Maritime). Etat de la recherche', in D. Piton (ed.), *La céramique du Ve au Xe siècle dans l'Europe du haut Moyen Age,* = n° 'hors-série' of *Nord-Ouest Archéologie,* (Arras, 1993), pp. 341–54.
53. For Dorestad, see Lebecq, *Marchands et Navigateurs Frisons,* I, pp. 158–9; for Quentovic, see idem, 'Quentovic' and 'Quentovic et Dorestad'.
54. *Cyninges wicgerefan* are mentioned twice in the law-code of King Hlothere (673–85), chs 16 and 16.2: *Die Gesetze der Angelsachsen,* ed. F. Liebermann, 3 vols (Halle, 1903–16), I, p. 11; and *English Historical Documents,* I, c. 500–1042, ed. D. Whitelock, 2nd edn (London, 1979), p. 395.
55. On this weighty question, see D. Hill and D.M. Metcalf (eds), *Sceattas in England and on the Continent,* BAR Brit. Ser. 128 (Oxford, 1984); and Grierson and Blackburn, *Medieval European Coinage,* esp. pp. 138–54, 164–89.
56. About the problem of the sail on the Sutton Hoo ship, see A. Care Evans, 'The Ship', in Bruce-Mitford (ed.), *The Sutton Hoo Ship Burial,* I, pp. 345–435; or ead., *The Sutton Hoo Ship Burial,* p. 27. On the diffusion of sailing in the northern seas during the seventh and eighth centuries, and the coin evidence, see Lebecq, *Marchands and Navigateurs Frisons,* I, pp. 177–81; and, for a different point of view, Haywood, *Dark Age Naval Power.*
57. On the capability of the square sail, see Thomas Gillmer, 'The Capability of the single square sail rig: a technical assessment', and Arne Emil Christensen,

'Viking Age rigging, a survey of sources and theories', both in S. McGrail (ed.), *Medieval Ships and Harbours in Northern Europe*, BAR Internat. Ser. 66 (Oxford, 1979), respectively pp. 167–82, 183–93; and S. McGrail, *Ancient Boats in North West Europe*, pp. 218–25. About the impact of rigging on the crews, see Stéphane Lebecq, 'Pour une histoire des équipages (mers du Nord, Ve-XIe siècles)' in A. Lottin, J.-C. Hocquet and Stéphane Lebecq (eds), *Les Hommes et la mer dans l'Europe du Nord-Ouest de l'Antiquité à nos jours*, n° 1 'hors-série', *Revue du Nord* (Lille, 1986), pp. 233–56.

58. Willibald, *Vita Bonifatii*, ch. 4; ed. R. Rau, p. 476; English translation, C.H. Talbot, *The Anglo-Saxon Missionaries in Germany* (London, 1954), p. 35.

59. *Vita Willibaldi* by Hugeburc, ch. 3; ed. O. Holder-Egger, p. 91; English trans., Talbot, *Anglo-Saxon Missionaries*, p. 156.

60. Mayr-Harting, *Coming of Christianity*, p. 61.

61. See above, n. 21.

62. For these letters of recommendation sent by Gregory the Great (*Epistolae* VI, 51 and 58), see R.A. Markus, *Gregory the Great and his World* (Cambridge, 1997), pp. 177–8 (and n. 63).

63. I thank Ian Wood for the suggestion that because Augustine was equipped with more letters of recommendation addressed to Austrasian personalities than to Neustrian ones, he may have embarked in the Rhine delta area. However, we know that some years later, Pope Gregory sent other letters to the bishops of Paris and Rouen, and to King Chlothar of Paris (cf. Markus, *Gregory the Great*, p. 180 and n. 74). Consequently I think the question remains open.

64. See above, nn. 22, 26.

65. See above, n. 46.

CHAPTER 4
Augustine and Gaul

Ian Wood

Gaul features significantly in the documentation for Augustine's mission.[1] The vast majority of letters written by Pope Gregory in support of Augustine in 596 and 601 are addressed to Gallic clerics and members of the Frankish royal family. Indeed, we know as much about Augustine's journey through Gaul and the support he received from the Merovingians as about his actual mission in Kent. From Gregory's letters we can trace Augustine's journey to Lérins and Aix, where he seems to have turned back to ask the Pope to abort the enterprise, leaving his companions, I would suggest, in the care of Bishop Protadius, who had previously been Gregory's *vicedominus* in Gaul.[2] Gregory, however, made him continue onwards through Marseille, Arles, Vienne, and thence to Tours and Autun (though in which order he visited these last two cities is not clear). Finally Augustine is known to have gone to the courts of the young kings, Theudebert II and Theuderic II, in Austrasia and Burgundy respectively, as well as to the regent, the dowager queen Brunhild, before continuing to England in 597.

These letters reveal to us not only Augustine's route, but also his search for support for the mission from members of the Gallic episcopate and from the ruling dynasty of Frankia, the Merovingian family, for Gregory's letters of introduction solicit more than hospitality for his emissary. Moreover, quite apart from seeking help for the English mission itself, the Pope also took advantage of Augustine's journey to deal with other papal concerns; and hand in hand with requests for support for Augustine, Gregory's letters also appealed on behalf of the papacy's Gallic agent, the new *vicedominus* Candidus. Thus in 596 Gregory used Augustine to strengthen the papacy's position in Frankia, just as he would use the reinforcing mission of 601, led by Laurentius and Mellitus, to attack the simony of the Gallic church.[3] Over and above its concern with the christianisation of the English, Augustine's mission was, therefore, intended to have an impact upon the Frankish church, bringing it more into line with what Gregory regarded as being acceptable ecclesiastical standards.

These are significant points for the history of the Merovingian church. Here, however, I shall largely limit myself to matters relating to the christianisation of Kent, and its context in the politics of the 590s. With regard to these last issues, we may add the information of Gregory's letters for the years from 597 to 601[4] to those of 596.[5] While the correspondence of 596 illustrates Augustine's search for support from the Gallic clergy and from the Merovingian family, the Pope's subsequent letters show that the mission actually received help from Theudebert II, Theuderic II and from their relative, the king of Neustria, Chlothar II; and more importantly that it was also backed by Brunhild and her favoured bishop, Syagrius of Autun. Syagrius, alone among the Frankish clergy, was awarded the *pallium* for his role in the English mission,[6] while Brunhild was seen as offering more support to Augustine than anyone.[7] In short, Gregory's letters show that it was essentially the courts of the Merovingian rulers – or to be more precise that it was largely, though not entirely, Brunhild – that provided backing for Augustine. Moreover, Syagrius apart, the Gallic clergy in general appear to have done little to aid the venture, and Syagrius can reasonably be seen as acting in tandem with the queen dowager.[8]

In writing to numerous bishops of Gaul and to the courts of the Merovingians, Gregory was taking advantage of Augustine's mission to further the cause of Candidus and to attack the problem of simony. In writing to the Merovingians themselves, however, Gregory was also showing his awareness of the political position of Kent in relation to Frankish Gaul. From the beginning of the sixth century Merovingian monarchs had made some claims of hegemony over England, and by the middle of the century those claims were being represented in Constantinople – though what they amounted to outside the rhetoric of diplomacy we cannot tell.[9] In line with what the Frankish kings were claiming, Gregory, when addressing the Merovingians, saw the English as subjects of Theudebert II, Theuderic II and Chlothar II[10] – and regardless of actual political realities, it is important to recognise that the Pope understood the English mission as being directed to a people who were thought in certain quarters to be in some way under Frankish jurisdiction. It is also important, in assessing the relations between Merovingian Gaul and the kingdom of Kent, to note that Gregory believed that the Gallic church had actually failed to evangelise the English, despite requests from England for Gallic missionaries: for there can be no doubt that the '*sacerdotes e vicino*' ('priests from the vicinity') who, according to Gregory, had refused to help christianise the English,[11] were Gallic and not British.

The issues that I have sketched so far have been covered at much greater length elsewhere.[12] My aim here is not to repeat the general points that have and can be made about Augustine, Kent and the Merovingians, but rather to spend some time in looking at the detailed political and chronological implications of our sources. Gregory's letters are not merely important for what they reveal about Augustine, his journey and the support he received: they are also crucial for reconstructing the internal history of the Merovingian kingdom itself. It should be remembered that Gregory of Tours' priceless *Histories* come to an end in 591, although the historian himself lived on until 594. His narrative was taken up around 660 by Fredegar,[13] whose knowledge of the 590s was weak, to say the least. The chronology of his account of Brunhild's regency, in particular, is hard to square with the information of the Pope's *Register*. It is Pope Gregory's letters relating to Augustine's mission, and not Fredegar's *Chronicle*, which allow us to infer something of the detailed background of Merovingian politics, which was crucial to the early years of the English church, and which can be seen as a vital force at least up to 614 when Bishop Justus of Rochester and Abbot Peter of Dover attended a council of the Frankish church in Paris. In short, my intention is to use the interface between Frankish and Kentish history to bring some precision to events on both sides of the Channel.

I shall begin the exercise, however, not in the 590s, but a quarter of a century earlier, with the history of Bertha's marriage to Æthelberht. The role of Bertha and her chaplain Liudhard in the history of Augustine's mission is almost impossible to assess: even Gregory's letter to the queen is difficult to evaluate.[14] Did the Pope think that she had not done enough to further the cause of Christianity? Or was his letter intended to encourage rather than criticise? The tone of his address is by no means easy to gauge. Although the comments that follow do not solve the problem of understanding the role of Bertha and her bishop Liudhard in the christianisation of Kent, they may at least help to provide some parameters within which that role should be understood.

Bertha was the daughter of Charibert I, who ruled between 561 and 567 over a kingdom based on Paris, and of the king's first wife Ingoberga. Gregory of Tours refers on two occasions to the princess: on the first occasion he says simply that Charibert and Ingoberga had a daughter who married a man from Kent;[15] on the second occasion, referring to Ingoberga's death in 589, he records that her daughter had married the son of a king of Kent.[16] These two pieces of information are important for Kentish chronology. Gregory of Tours knew that Bertha had married a Kentish prince, and he seems to have thought that Æthelberht's father was still alive at the time of writing. Since Gregory was very closely associated with Ingoberga, and even drew up her will, we can be fairly certain that he would have known of Æthelberht's accession, if it had happened before 589. Bede's chronology of Æthelberht's reign, the beginning of which he ascribes to 561,[17] thus falls to the ground. From the contemporary witness of Gregory of Tours it is necessary to conclude that Æthelberht became king of Kent at some point after 589; far from being a ruler who was pagan for the vast majority of his reign, until external challenges made him think again – which is a picture that some have seen in Bede's narrative[18] – Æthelberht in 596 was a relatively new king, whose embracing of Christianity came early in his reign.

Although Gregory of Tours does not give any indication of the date of Bertha's marriage to Æthelberht, we can deduce that it happened before 580, since Gregory appears to have written the fourth book of his *Histories*, which includes the first reference to Bertha's marriage, at some point between 576 and the end of the decade.[19] Bertha was, therefore, a christian princess in the court of a pagan king of Kent for at least a decade, and probably for more than fifteen years, before her husband ascended the Kentish throne. Far from being a queen who had failed to promote Christianity despite her position, Bertha was for most of her life in Kent no more than the wife of a prince, whose pagan father Eormenric continued to rule and doubtless to promote the existing religion of his family and followers.

We may infer a little more than this. Bertha's mother Ingoberga was Charibert's first wife. He was to marry at least two other women, and possibly a third, before his death in 567.[20] Unless we place the marriage of Bertha and Æthelberht very early in Charibert's reign, we must conclude that the princess is unlikely to have married until after her mother, Ingoberga, had been discarded by her father, and, indeed, that she may not have married before the king himself was dead. Since Charibert left no son when he died, his line of the family ceased to provide kings for the Merovingian throne: after 567 his daughter could not even look to a brother or half-brother for support; her nearest male relatives were uncles and cousins. It is most likely to have been her uncles who married her off, and one might look to Venantius Fortunatus's comments on the subservience of Saxons and Jutes at the time of Chilperic I to find a context for the marriage.[21] Bertha was not, therefore, a princess of much status at the time of her marriage, and Æthelberht was no more than the heir to a kingdom over which the Merovingians claimed hegemony. He was a minor prince in the world of Frankish politics, and he was married to a princess with few expectations.

It is possible to say a little more about the influences which may have weighed on the princess. Her father, Charibert, is most notable in the pages of Gregory of Tours for his uxoriousness; and although Venantius Fortunatus presents him in a rather better light, as a pious and cultivated king, who showed considerable care for the widow and female offspring of his uncle Childebert I,[22] one might note that the poet makes no comment on the king's concern for his own wives or his daughter. Rather more important is the information in Gregory of Tours' two comments on Ingoberga.

Ingoberga's first appearance in Gregory's *Histories* is as a jealous wife, determined to stop Charibert's marital infidelities by drawing his attention to the fact that the women he was chasing were the daughters of a woolworker. The result of her actions, however, was that the king discarded Ingoberga rather than the new objects of his lust![23] She makes her second and last appearance shortly before her death, when she summoned Gregory to help her draw up a will, in which she gave benefactions to the cathedral and St Martin's at Tours, and to the cathedral of Le Mans. On this occasion Gregory praises her wisdom.[24] Both times that he mentions the queen he refers to her daughter, which would seem to be significant, for Gregory is not in the habit of introducing characters or even of reminding the reader of family relationships for no apparent reason. Although he says next to nothing about Bertha, Gregory seems to have thought that she was worth a mention each time he referred to her mother. Quite why he did so is not immediately obvious, but his interest in the princess is worth bearing in mind.

Also significant in Gregory's comments is Ingoberga's clear attachment to the cult of Martin. According to Bede, before Augustine's arrival Bertha worshipped in a church dedicated to St Martin in Canterbury.[25] Furthermore, Bertha and Æthelberht were buried in a chapel with the same dedication in Augustine's monastery of SS Peter and Paul.[26] This commitment on the part of Ingoberga and Bertha to the cult of Martin is more remarkable than one might think. Although Gregory of Tours encourages us to assume that Martin was the dominant saint in Gaul, there were plenty of rival cults, and on the whole the Merovingian family seems to have been attached to other saints, among them Marcellus at Chalon-sur-Saône, Medard at Soissons and Denis, Genovefa, Germanus and Vincent in Paris. We should probably see in the Martin dedications at Canterbury the particular religious affiliations of Bertha and, behind her, of Ingoberga.

One might also wonder whether Augustine's own journey to Tours was prompted by the knowledge that Bertha had connections with the city. Augustine seems to have made a detour to visit the shrine of St Martin in 596:[27] Tours is out on a limb in relation to all the other cities to whose bishops the missionary is known to have had a letter of introduction. Of course Augustine may have wished to visit the metropolitan city of Tours, and he may have wished to see the shrine of a saint whom he may have seen as a role model, not least because Martin is depicted in a number of chapters of Sulpicius Severus's *Vita* as a major missionary.[28] On the other hand, Augustine may have known that Bertha's mother had lived in the city until 589. In the very year of the old queen's death, Gregory of Tours' deacon Agiulf had travelled to Rome, where he received relics from the

THE FAMILY CONNECTIONS OF BERTHA

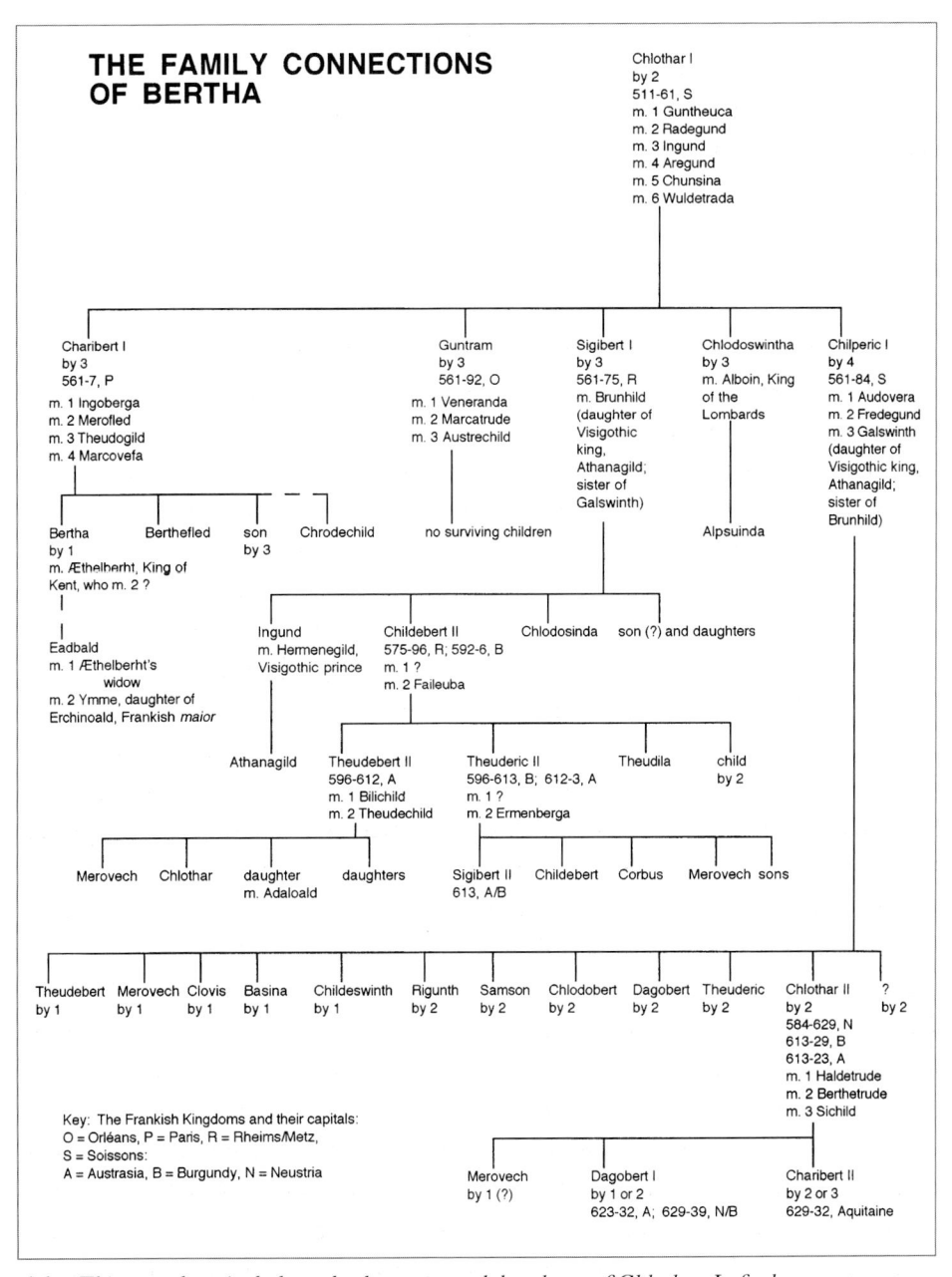

Chlothar I
by 2
511-61, S
m. 1 Guntheuca
m. 2 Radegund
m. 3 Ingund
m. 4 Aregund
m. 5 Chunsina
m. 6 Wuldetrada

Charibert I
by 3
561-7, P
m. 1 Ingoberga
m. 2 Merofled
m. 3 Theudogild
m. 4 Marcovefa

- Bertha — by 1 — m. Æthelberht, King of Kent, who m. 2 ?
  - Eadbald
    m. 1 Æthelberht's widow
    m. 2 Ymme, daughter of Erchinoald, Frankish *maior*
- Berthefled
- son — by 3
- Chrodechild

Guntram
by 3
561-92, O
m. 1 Veneranda
m. 2 Marcatrude
m. 3 Austrechild

— no surviving children

Sigibert I
by 3
561-75, R
m. Brunhild (daughter of Visigothic king, Athanagild; sister of Galswinth)

- Ingund
  m. Hermenegild, Visigothic prince
  - Athanagild
- Childebert II
  575-96, R; 592-6, B
  m. 1 ?
  m. 2 Faileuba
  - Theudebert II
    596-612, A
    m. 1 Bilichild
    m. 2 Theudechild
    - Merovech
    - Chlothar
    - daughter m. Adaloald
    - daughters
  - Theuderic II
    596-613, B; 612-3, A
    m. 1 ?
    m. 2 Ermenberga
    - Sigibert II 613, A/B
    - Childebert
    - Corbus
    - Merovech
    - sons
  - Theudila
  - child — by 2
- Chlodosinda
- son (?) and daughters

Chlodoswintha
by 3
m. Alboin, King of the Lombards

Chilperic I
by 4
561-84, S
m. 1 Audovera
m. 2 Fredegund
m. 3 Galswinth (daughter of Visigothic king, Athanagild; sister of Brunhild)

- Alpsuinda

- Theudebert by 1
- Merovech by 1
- Clovis by 1
- Basina by 1
- Childeswinth by 1
- Rigunth by 2
- Samson by 2
- Chlodobert by 2
- Dagobert by 2
- Theuderic by 2
- Chlothar II by 2
  584-629, N
  613-29, B
  613-23, A
  m. 1 Haldetrude
  m. 2 Berthetrude
  m. 3 Sichild
  - Merovech by 1 (?)
  - Dagobert I by 1 or 2
    623-32, A; 629-39, N/B
  - Charibert II by 2 or 3
    629-32, Aquitaine
- ? by 2

Key: The Frankish Kingdoms and their capitals:
O = Orléans, P = Paris, R = Rheims/Metz,
S = Soissons;
A = Austrasia, B = Burgundy, N = Neustria

4.1. This genealogy includes only those sons and daughters of Chlothar I of relevance to conversion history. A more complete Merovingian genealogy may be found in Ian Wood, The Merovingian Kingdoms 450–751, *pp. 343–9.*

future Pope Gregory.[29] He was to stay on to witness the papal election. During his lengthy stay in Rome, which involved at least one meeting with Gregory, he may well have passed on information relating to Ingoberga and Bertha. Even if Augustine did not know of Bertha's association with the city before he set out from Rome, he may have profited from his visit to Tours by learning something of the queen of Kent. That Bertha had been in contact with the shrine of St Martin might be implied by Gregory of Tours' repeated comment on the marriage of the princess to the son of the Kentish king. Indeed, it might be the explanation for Gregory's interest in the matter.

The connections between Bertha, Ingoberga, Tours and Augustine might amount to nothing more than chance. It may well be that the missionary did not know of Bertha's contacts with the city until after his arrival in Kent. Such a reading might seem logical in the light of what is often assumed about contacts between Rome and the Merovingian kingdom – that they were infrequent and insignificant. If we look carefully at the implications of Gregory's correspondence with the Merovingian court, however, we may wish to conclude that, on the contrary, the Pope was remarkably well informed about Frankish affairs, and that we have to reckon with an enormous amount of communication over and above what is revealed directly by the papal *Register*. This is not to say that all exchanges of information depended on official delegations: the presence of Gregory of Tours' deacon Agiulf in Rome in 589–90 is enough to show that there were unofficial channels for information to pass through. Some issues, however, the Pope must have learnt about and responded to at an official level, despite their absence in his surviving letters. Gregory's ability to cope with the political developments within Frankia in the 590s seems to require official contact beyond what his letters prove.

The 590s saw a remarkable amount of political change at the top of the Merovingian kingdom. In 593 Guntram, who had held kingly office since 561, died.[30] Three years later his nephew, Childebert II, who had added Guntram's kingdom to that of his own father Sigibert I, followed him to the grave.[31] This left the kingdom of the Franks in the hands of three minors: Childebert's sons Theudebert II and Theuderic II, who were kings respectively in Austrasia (east Frankia) and Burgundy, and another nephew of Guntram, Chlothar II, who had been king of Neustria (west Frankia) since 584. The picture was further complicated in that Chlothar's mother, Fredegund, who appears to have acted as his regent, is said by Fredegar to have died in 597.[32] Meanwhile, Brunhild, the grandmother of Theudebert and Theuderic, acted as regent in Austrasia and Burgundy.

According to Fredegar, Brunhild was driven out of Austrasia in 599 (or perhaps 600), and took refuge in Burgundy with her second grandson,

Theuderic II.[33] The Austrasian attack on the queen can plausibly be linked to the coming of age and marriage of Theudebert II.[34] On the other hand, Fredegar's account of Brunhild's exile, which involves her being discovered by a poor man, whom she subsequently elevated to the bishopric of Auxerre, is fanciful, to say the least. The bishop of Auxerre, Desiderius, was certainly not a man of lowly origin.[35] Moreover, Fredegar's account might be seen as being in conflict with Gregory's letters, which do not imply any major change in Brunhild's position before 602 at the earliest – though the Pope might have passed discreetly over a palace coup which excluded Brunhild from the regency of the kingdom of one of her sons.

Certainly it is unlikely that the apparent conflict between Fredegar and the papal *Register* reflects any lack of information at Gregory's fingertips, given the direct contact between the Pope and the English mission. Furthermore, there is clear evidence that Gregory had precise and immediate knowledge of the fast changing situation in the mid-590s. In 595 the Pope wrote to Childebert, sending the king a relic of St Peter.[36] Childebert was still alive on 1 March 596, when he presided over a great council at Cologne.[37] By July, however, he was dead; nevertheless the Pope already knew that he should address letters of recommendation for Augustine not to Childebert, but to the dead king's sons, Theudebert and Theuderic, even though they can have been on the throne for less than five months.[38] Moreover, the fact that, in recommending Augustine, Gregory makes no attempt to commiserate with the boys over their father's death would seem to imply that he had already sent his condolences. While the Frankish political scene was changing rapidly, Gregory was somehow – perhaps through Candidus – keeping abreast of those changes.

As we have seen, Gregory sent Augustine to Gaul in 596 with letters of recommendation not only to Theudebert and Theuderic, but also to Brunhild, with whom he had already corresponded in 595 over the appointment of Candidus as *vicedominus*.[39] Gregory seems to have sized up the queen regent remarkably well.[40] He already knew she was cultured and pious – later he would grant privileges at her request for a *xenodochium* and a monastery which she founded in Autun, and for a nunnery founded by her close ally Bishop Syagrius.[41] Gregory may also have known enough about Brunhild to reckon that her political ambitions, to which we shall return, would play into his hands. Certainly she responded energetically to his appeal for help in supporting the English mission, apparently throwing herself into the enterprise with more enthusiasm than anyone.[42]

While Gregory's *Register* contains letters written in 596 to Brunhild, Theudebert, Theuderic and the leading bishops of their kingdoms (Austrasia and Burgundy), it contains no letter of that year written to Fredegund or her son

Chlothar II or indeed to any of the bishops of his kingdom (Neustria). This raises a considerable problem. Can we conclude from the silence of the *Register* that there were no such letters? Since Bede copied into his *Ecclesiastical History* letters of the Pope which have not survived in Gregory's collection, the silence of the *Register* is not on its own proof of anything. Further, Bede's evidence apart, we have seen reasons for thinking that there were other letters, now lost, addressed to Merovingian kings. Moreover, in 601 Gregory did write to Chlothar II, praising his support for Augustine's mission.[43]

Yet there may still be reason for thinking that in 596 Gregory did ignore Chlothar and, more significantly, his mother Fredegund. According to Fredegar the old queen died in 597. Although some of Fredegar's chronology for this period is probably inexact, Fredegund had certainly survived into the 590s, since Gregory of Tours makes no mention of her death. And she must have been a good age: she was the first wife and first love of Chilperic I, who had ruled from 561 to 584.[44] Therefore Fredegar's placing of her death is unlikely to be far wrong. Pope Gregory might thus have avoided writing to Chlothar and his mother because he was aware that he would get little support from an old dowager who was known to be on her deathbed. Further, she may well have been regarded as a dangerous ally by churchmen ever since her supposed involvement in the murder of Bishop Praetextatus of Rouen.[45] It is, consequently, possible to see why Gregory might not have written to Fredegund or Chlothar II in 596, even though he was to write to the young king five years later. Thus, there may indeed have been no letters to Fredegund or her son in 596 – and the absence of letters to any of their bishops would seem to confirm the Pope's avoidance of contact with Neustria.

Whether or not Gregory was making calculated choices about which Merovingian to write to, there is every reason to suppose that individual Merovingians made deliberate political calculations when it came to a question of their own involvement in the mission – which is not to say that piety played no part in their actions. Here it is worth considering the position of Brunhild, who was undoubtedly a woman of considerable piety, as is most apparent from her work with Bishop Syagrius at Autun, mentioned earlier. On the death of Childebert in 596 she became regent for her two grandsons. Her position is likely to have been shaky, although not perhaps as shaky as Fredegar implies. She certainly had a tussle to establish herself as regent for her son Childebert after the death of her husband, Sigibert I, in 575.[46] She was to run into considerable hostility at the Austrasian court of Theudebert after 601, if not in 599. Further, after Childebert's death in 596 she might have been concerned that the king's widow Faileuba would take over the regency, and that she herself would lose her position as queen regent. The arrival of Augustine in the summer of that same year thus gave Brunhild a useful opportunity to enhance her authority. She could show her piety in backing the mission, while at the same time strengthening Merovingian hegemony in England, to the benefit of her own prestige. The recent death of Childebert and Brunhild's determination to survive may help to explain why the queen dowager threw herself into support for the mission in 596, even though, according to Pope Gregory, the Frankish church had only recently failed to respond to English requests for missionaries.

But rivals in Austrasia and Burgundy were not the only threat to Brunhild's position. Although the view that she and Fredegund had effectively been involved in a vendetta ever since the latter's supposed involvement in Sigibert's death in 575 is scarcely supported by Gregory of Tours, it is clear that there was considerable enmity between Brunhild and her descendants on the one hand and Fredegund and her son on the other. While Chlothar belonged to an older generation than that of Brunhild's grandchildren, all three boys were approximately the same age. In 596 Chlothar was still only twelve years old,[47] and his mother, Fredegund, who had been his chief protector was dying. The kingdom of Neustria, over which he ruled, essentially comprised the lands north of the Loire: most of the rest of the Frankish kingdom was in the hands of Brunhild's grandsons, and they were putting pressure on their cousin. In 600 – and again we should not put too much credence in the precise date – Chlothar's kingdom is said by Fredegar to have been reduced to 'twelve cantons between the Seine, the Oise and the sea'.[48] Beyond the sea lay the English coast. Brunhild might have calculated that if England belonged not so much to a Frankish hegemony as to a specifically Austrasian or Burgundian one, then Chlothar would be even more squeezed. In short, Brunhild's championing of Augustine's mission can be seen to have had a very precise political context.

Pope Gregory saw Brunhild as one of the key figures in the success of the mission, and her piety is beyond question; nevertheless, it is an open question whether she would have been so involved had the political circumstances not made involvement in Kent so attractive. The Merovingian church had, after all, not responded to an initial English request for missionaries.[49] The precise chronology of the mission is, as we have seen, significant for understanding exactly why it should receive backing, which was apparently crucial, from Brunhild and her closest supporter Syagrius: Frankish politics made involvement in Kent a very attractive proposition after Childebert's death in 596. Further, if this reading is correct, Gregory's letters in support of Augustine provide an important source for understanding events in Gaul in the later 590s – when Fredegar is arguably at his least reliable.

Brunhild is one key to the success of Augustine's mission and, I would suggest, her involvement has as much to do with Frankish politics as with the dowager's own piety. Within a very short period, however, Chlothar II and his advisers appear to have realised the political importance for the Franks of the English mission. In 601 Gregory wrote to Chlothar, much as he wrote to Brunhild and her grandsons, thanking him for supporting Augustine.[50] This letter of thanks comes from the year following that to which Fredegar ascribed Chlothar's confinement to the twelve cantons between the Seine, the Oise and the sea. Despite the pressure on him at home at that moment, Chlothar, or his supporters, had seen fit to cultivate the English mission. No doubt they saw what Brunhild had seen – that influence in Kent was a potential tool in the struggle between Austrasia and Burgundy on the one hand and Neustria on the other. Connections across the Channel could constrain or give Chlothar some freedom of manoeuvre in his conflicts with Theudebert and Theuderic.

In the event it would be Chlothar who won out. Gradually rivalry between Theudebert and Theuderic themselves came to be more significant than the brothers' hostility to Chlothar – not least because Theudebert had driven his grandmother out of Austrasia. The result was a civil war in 612 in which Theudebert and his descendants were exterminated. Then, by sheer chance, the following year Theuderic died, leaving his offspring and Brunhild at the mercy of Chlothar. The fate of the old queen, displayed on a camel and then tied to the tail of an unbroken horse, to be torn apart, is well known.[51] Chlothar's triumph was marked by concurrent religious and secular councils held in Paris in 614.[52] In the light of what had happened fifteen years previously, it seems significant that Bishop Justus of Rochester and Peter of Dover, the first abbot of SS Peter and Paul (Saint Augustine's Abbey), Canterbury, should attend and sign the proceedings of the ecclesiastical council of Paris. The Merovingians and their church had remained important for the Kentish church, but after 613 the centre of Frankish influence shifted, as indeed had the relationship between Canterbury and the Merovingian church. While Pope Gregory had used Augustine to keep a check on the Frankish church, by 614 it was Paris which was providing guidance for the church of Kent – and there is much to be said for the idea that it was Frankish models associated with Chlothar which underlay Æthelberht's law-code, with its opening concerns for the safety of the church.[53] Not surprisingly it was to Gaul that Mellitus and Justus fled during the Kentish apostasy that followed the death of Æthelberht in 616.[54] Moreover, it was on a crossing to Gaul that Peter of Dover was drowned.[55] For a generation after 596 the Kentish church was closely tied to that of the Merovingians – and after 613 those ties linked Canterbury not with the court of Brunhild, but with that of Chlothar.

The earliest contacts of the Merovingian church with that of Kent deserve a little more consideration. Although Bede presents the Franks as contributing no more than interpreters to Augustine's mission,[56] Gregory had actually asked Theudebert and Theuderic for clerical support.[57] In the light of the Pope's subsequent thanks, we may guess that some Frankish clergy did indeed accompany Augustine to Kent.[58] Unfortunately, although we do hear of the presence of named Frankish and Burgundian clerics in England at a slightly later date (men such as Felix, Agilbert, Leutherius and Richarius),[59] no named Frankish cleric is mentioned among Augustine's companions.

Some trace of the involvement of Frankish clergy, however, might be seen in the *Responsiones* of Gregory. As preserved in the question-and-answer recension of the text which was transmitted by Bede, the second of these replies is supposedly an answer to Augustine's enquiry: 'Even though the faith is one are there varying customs in the churches? And is there one form of mass in the Holy Roman Church and another in the Gaulish churches?'[60] Clearly Augustine cannot have asked this question as it stands for, having travelled through Gaul, he must have known the variety of liturgical practice better than the Pope himself.[61] Yet the response, which may well be authentic advice from Gregory, does imply that the question of varying liturgies had cropped up in Kent. One obvious source for the presence of liturgical practice other than that brought by Augustine himself would be Bertha's mysterious chaplain and bishop, Liudhard, who was sufficiently important to have been commemorated on the medallion which survives in the St Martin's hoard (pl. III a–b). Another would be the presence of Frankish clerics with their own service books among Augustine's missionary party. Such a service book might have provided Augustine with the anthem which he and his companions supposedly used as they first entered Canterbury, for the antiphon '*Deprecamur te, Domine*' appears from liturgical and manuscript evidence to have been of Gallic and not of Roman origin – however, it is far from clear that Bede's account of the arrival of the missionaries in the city is in any sense an actual description of what happened.[62]

The greater part of Bede's narrative is concerned to highlight Pope Gregory and his envoy, Augustine, as the real begetters of Christianity in Æthelberht's kingdom. Nevertheless, in recording the *Responsiones* of Gregory even Bede gives us some evidence of Frankish influence on the early Kentish church – an insight he provides only because he thought he was recording Gregory's own words. In general it is from the Pope's *Register* that our information on the significance of Gaul for Augustine's mission must be drawn; for the most part Bede is studiously silent about Frankish influence. What a comparison of Pope Gregory's letters and the historical narratives of the Merovingians highlight above all is not general influences, but specific circumstances. We will not understand the mission of Augustine unless we recognise the very precise context in which it took place: a Pope keen on mission, who had not long been elevated to the see of St Peter; a relatively new king and queen on the throne of Kent; a novel political constellation in Frankia following the deaths of Childebert II and Fredegund; and rivalry between Brunhild and the supporters of her nephew Chlothar II. Whether or not Gregory himself appreciated the complexities of Frankish politics before he sent Augustine north – and there is some evidence in his letters that he was not clueless on the matter – those complexities played into his hands; and the Frankish church, which had done nothing when the English appealed for '*sacerdotes e vicino*' earlier in the decade, finally offered some significant help, not least because Brunhild and then Chlothar could see the benefits of so doing.

NOTES

1. For further coverage of this issue see I.N. Wood, 'The Mission of Augustine of Canterbury to the English', *Speculum*, 69 (1994), 1–17; R.A. Markus, 'The Chronology of the Gregorian Mission to England: Bede's narrative and Gregory's correspondence', *JEH*, 14 (1963), 16–30; and R.A. Markus, 'Gregory the Great and a papal missionary strategy', *SCH*, 6 (1970), 29–38: both these last pieces are reprinted in his *From Augustine to Gregory the Great* (London, 1983), as nos X and XI. In addition see now R.A. Markus, *Gregory the Great and his World* (Cambridge, 1997), esp. pp. 177–87. I.N. Wood, 'Augustine's Journey', *Canterbury Cathedral Chronicle*, 92 (1998), 28–44, is essentially a companion piece to the present article, and deals in greater detail with some of the views expressed here.
2. See Wood, 'Augustine's Journey', 31–2.
3. See Wood, 'Augustine's Journey', 29–30, 32.
4. Gregory I, *Register*, VIII, 4, 29: IX, 213, 222: XI, 34, 35, 36, 37, 38, 39, 40, 41, 42, 45, 47, 48, 50, 51, 56, 56a, eds Paul Ewald and Ludo M. Hartmann, MGH, Epistolae 1 and 2 (Berlin, 1887–99).
5. Gregory I, *Register*, VI, 49, 50, 50a, 51, 52, 53, 54, 56, 57.
6. See Wood, 'Augustine's Journey', 39.
7. Gregory I, *Register*, XI, 48; Wood, 'The Mission of Augustine of Canterbury', 6–7.
8. See further Wood, 'The Mission of Augustine of Canterbury' and 'Augustine's Journey'.
9. Wood, 'Frankish hegemony in England', in M. Carver (ed.), *The Age of Sutton Hoo* (Woodbridge, 1992), pp. 235–41.
10. Gregory, *Register*, VI, 49; XI, 51.
11. Gregory, *Register*, VI, 49; with Wood, 'The Mission of Augustine of Canterbury', 8.
12. Wood, 'The Mission of Augustine of Canterbury' and 'Augustine's Journey'.
13. W. Goffart, 'The Fredegar Problem Reconsidered', *Speculum*, 38 (1963), 206–41, repr. in W. Goffart, *Rome's Fall and After* (London, 1989), pp. 319–54; I.N. Wood, 'Fredegar's Fables', in A. Scharer and G. Scheibelreiter (eds), *Historiographie im frühen Mittelalter* (Vienna, 1994), pp. 359–66.
14. Gregory, *Register*, XI, 34.
15. Gregory of Tours, *Libri Historiarum*, IV, 26, eds B. Krusch and W. Levison, MGH,

Scriptores Rerum Merovingicarum 1, 1 (Hannover, 1951).
16. Gregory of Tours, *Libri Historiarum*, IX, 25.
17. *HE*, II, 5.
18. For example, H. Mayr-Harting, *The Coming of Christianity to Anglo-Saxon England*, 3rd edn (London, 1991), pp. 63–6.
19. I.N. Wood, *Gregory of Tours* (Bangor, 1994), p. 3.
20. Gregory of Tours, *Libri Historiarum*, IV, 26.
21. Venantius Fortunatus, *Carm.* IX, 1, ed. F. Leo, MGH, Auctores Antiquissimi 4, 1 (Berlin, 1881): l. 20: '*transit et Oceanum fulgida fama sopho*' ('your dazzling reputation for wisdom has crossed even the Ocean'); l. 73: '*quem Geta, Vasco tremunt, Danus, Euthio, Saxo, Britannus*' ('You inspire fear in the Goths, the Basques, the Danes, the Jutes, the Saxons and the Britons'); trans. J. George, *Venantius Fortunatus: Personal and Political Poems* (Liverpool, 1995), pp. 74, 77. The panegyric to Chilperic was written in 580.
22. Venantius Fortunatus, *Carm.* VI, 2.
23. Gregory of Tours, *Libri Historiarum*, IV, 26.
24. Gregory of Tours, *Libri Historiarum*, IX, 26.
25. *HE*, I, 26.
26. *HE*, II, 5.
27. Gregory, *Register*, VI, 50.
28. Sulpicius Severus, *Vita Martini*, 13–15, ed. J. Fontaine, Sources Chrétiennes, 133–5 (Paris, 1967–9).
29. Gregory of Tours, *Libri Historiarum*, X, 1.
30. Fredegar, IV, 14, ed. J.M. Wallace-Hadrill, *The Fourth Book of the Chronicle of Fredegar* (London, 1960).
31. Fredegar, IV, 16.
32. Fredegar, IV, 17.
33. Fredegar, IV, 19.
34. J.L. Nelson, 'Queens as Jezebels: Brunhild and Balthild in Merovingian History', in *Medieval Women*, ed. D. Baker, *SCH*, Subsidia vol. 1 (Oxford, 1978), pp. 43–4, repr. in J.L. Nelson, *Politics and Ritual in Early Medieval Europe* (London, 1986), p. 15.
35. Wallace-Hadrill, *The Fourth Book of the Chronicle of Fredegar*, p. 13, n. 1.
36. Gregory, *Register*, VI, 6: see also V, 60.
37. *Pactus Legis Salicae*, capitulary VI, 3, ed. K.A. Eckhardt, MGH, Leges Nationum Germanicarum 4, 1 (Hannover, 1962).
38. Gregory, *Register*, VI, 49.
39. Gregory, *Register*, VI, 5.
40. On Gregory and Brunhild, see J. Richards, *Consul of God* (London, 1980), pp. 213–14.
41. See Gregory, *Register*, XIII, 7, 11, 12, 13; see Nelson, 'Queens as Jezebels: Brunhild and Balthild in Merovingian History', 55 (in *Medieval Women*); 26 (in *Politics and Ritual*).
42. Gregory, *Register*, XI, 48.
43. Gregory, *Register*, XI, 51.
44. Gregory of Tours, *Libri Historiarum*, IV, 28.
45. Gregory of Tours, *Libri Historiarum*, VIII, 31.
46. For Brunhild see Nelson, 'Queens as Jezebels'; also I.N. Wood, *The Merovingian Kingdoms 450–751* (London, 1994), pp. 126–36.
47. For Chlothar's birth, Gregory of Tours, *Libri Historiarum*, VI, 41.
48. Fredegar, IV, 20.
49. Gregory, *Register*, VI, 49.
50. Gregory, *Register*, XI, 51.
51. Fredegar, IV, 37–42.
52. Paris V, ed. J. Gaudemet and B. Basdevant, *Les canons de conciles mérovingiens* (VIe–VIIe siècles), 2 vols, Sources Chrétiennes, 353–4 (Paris, 1989), II, pp. 506–25; *Capitularia Merowingica*, 9, ed. A. Boretius, MGH, Capitularia Regum Francorum I (Hannover, 1883).
53. This idea is being explored in detail in forthcoming work by Patrick Wormald.
54. *HE*, II, 5.

55. *HE*, I, 33.
56. *HE*, I, 25.
57. Gregory, *Register*, VI, 49.
58. Wood, 'Augustine's Journey', 29.
59. *HE*, II, 15; III 7, 18: see I.N. Wood, 'The Franks and Sutton Hoo', in I.N. Wood and N. Lund (eds), *People and Places in Northern Europe 500–1600: Essays in honour of Peter Hayes Sawyer* (Woodbridge, 1991), pp. 8–12.
60. *HE*, I, 27. Other recensions deal with the same point in different form. On the different versions, and their authenticity, see especially P. Meyvaert, 'Bede's text of the "Libellus Responsionum" of Gregory the Great to Augustine of Canterbury', in eds P. Clemoes and K. Hughes, *England before the Conquest: Studies in primary sources presented to Dorothy Whitelock* (Cambridge, 1971), pp. 15–33.
61. One should also note the near certainty that Augustine had come across British liturgical practices: R. Meens, 'A background to Augustine's mission to Anglo-Saxon England', *ASE*, 23 (1994), 5–17. These, however, were clearly not at issue in the second of Gregory's responses, which is explicitly concerned with Gallic practices.
62. Wood, 'Augustine's Journey', 36–8.

CHAPTER 5

The Archaeology of Conversion on the Continent in the Sixth and Seventh Centuries

Some Observations and Comparisons with Anglo-Saxon England

Simon Burnell and Edward James

During the sixth and seventh centuries, and by AD 750 at the latest, most Germanic peoples on the continent and in England had been converted to Catholic Christianity; the only exceptions were the Saxons and Danes on the continent along with the other inhabitants of Scandinavia. Our chapter will consider the archaeological evidence for this process, and will be concerned mainly with the conversion of the Franks, Alamans and Bavarians. Since the latter two were subject peoples living on the south-eastern margins of the Merovingian dominions, this offers the opportunity of observing a process of primary and secondary conversion within a single large territorial-political entity. The Franks converted first, from the late fifth century onwards; under their immense influence, the Alamans and Bavarians also gradually came to adopt Christianity; within each people there is evidence of a progressive diffusion of Christianity among élites from the 'core' to the 'periphery'. There is also scope for interesting comparisons with the dynamics of conversion in Anglo-Saxon England (as distinct from studying the role of Anglo-Saxons in the continental missions from the end of the seventh century), an approach which hitherto has been neglected – in keeping with the general and incomprehensible rarity of discourse between Anglo-Saxon and Merovingian archaeology. We know from Bede that the step-by-step conversion of the Anglo-Saxon kingdoms in the seventh century had as much to do with power politics and peer pressure as it did with missionary activity in the purest sense. For the Merovingian kingdoms there exists no such systematic and detailed written history of the conversion process; indeed, such is the paucity of written material for Alamannia and Bavaria that even their political history in the seventh century is extremely fragmentary and obscure. However, this is offset by a very rich archaeology of christianisation – particularly in these south-eastern territories – which is dominated by the most unambiguous and directly relevant form of evidence, namely secular, rural churches whose origins can be dated by the furnished graves associated with them. In these regions, monastic foundations (which were of crucial importance in the conversion of Anglo-Saxon England) were late arrivals, a circumstance which provides a first pointer to significant differences in the respective dynamics of conversion. In other respects there may be parallels between the two areas, and not merely in the shared and perennial debate about the interpretation and implications of 'christian' artefacts. In both England and Germany, recent research has challenged the assumption of a uniform and one-sided pattern to the conversion process, drawing attention to possible archaeological evidence for pagan resistance to conversion, or of different, competing or regionally demarcated christianising influences.

In discussing the archaeology of conversion we are largely talking about the archaeology of Christianity and of christianisation; but it is worth starting with the archaeology of paganism. Indeed, the two are impossible to separate: interpretations of the christian character of a particular site or artefact are, by definition, making a comment about the perceived character of paganism as well as of Christianity. This is where a number of errors have arisen in the treatment of the subject, among both archaeologists and historians. Perhaps the most significant misunderstanding in the whole discussion of the topic in the past has been the assumption that either paganism or Christianity is easy to detect and to define. Of course, we are familiar with Germanic mythology, and can assume that elements of what we know from Snorri Sturluson's *Prose Edda* of the thirteenth century might be applicable to the Germans of the sixth and seventh centuries.[1] We know from place names, for instance, that Woden, Thor and Tiu were the principal gods of the Anglo-Saxons: so the *names* at least correspond to Snorri's myths. We are well informed about christian mythology too, from the New Testament and from the tales of the martyrs and saints. But we know precious little about the ordinary beliefs of lay people, particularly the ordinary beliefs of lay people in the areas settled by Franks, Alamans, Bavarians and, for that matter, Anglo-Saxons – that is, in areas which had already been exposed to Christianity by earlier Roman occupation, and were subsequently settled by peoples who themselves may have 'experienced' Christianity while outside the frontiers of *Romanitas* and *Christianitas*. Can an archaeologist or historian really hope to have an understanding of the different levels of syncretism which might have been involved? And when we are dealing with religious syncretism, are labels like 'pagan' and 'christian' necessarily apt, let alone easy to assign?

What is no longer tenable, for example, is what Heli Roosens asserts in his 1985 study of christianisation as reflected in the Merovingian cemeteries of Belgium:

> The indication of christianisation is often only a simple sign of the cross, or nothing more than a cruciform arrangement of decorative elements. In reality, clothing accessories are not utilitarian objects; they are intended to attract attention because of the meaning of the decoration. The rather low proportion of christian symbols certainly does not eclipse the much larger number of pagan symbols. I attach a real importance to pagan symbolism, as to christian symbolism, such as it manifests itself for example on the inlaid silver ornament of the seventh century. This style develops certain motifs from Germanic mythology, in the form of interlaced animals, such as the eagle, the wolf, the boar and others, some of which are difficult to identify.[2]

The sort of decoration, in other words, that one finds on such well-known examples of 'pagan' art as the Lichfield Gospels or the Book of Kells! And, to make another obvious point, the presence of a christian, or indeed a pagan, object in a grave says nothing for certain about the religious affiliation of the person with whom it was buried, or of those who carried out the burial. An object might have been acquired and valued on account of its intrinsic material worth, or prestige value as an exotic import or a novelty in the experience of the owner; an iconography or decoration symbolising religious beliefs not shared by the owner – even assuming that it was understood – would hardly have been likely to outweigh such considerations. A famous case in point is the probable liturgical ewer found in the rich grave 319 of a Frankish nobleman and contemporary of Clovis in the cemetery of Lavoye in north-eastern France.[3]

Another error is that, even if the use of syncretism is recognised, the whole area of experience which christians and pagans shared is ignored. To bring together everything that twentieth-century sceptics might regard as 'superstitious' into the category 'religion' is a serious mistake. In an age when the natural world was more thoroughly interwoven with people's daily lives and experience than is the case in our own, it is hardly surprising that images from the natural world were incorporated in (pagan) religious symbolism; but, by the same token, such images would be likely to have become staple elements of the artistic tradition, quite possibly for their own sake and without reference to religion. A belief in the magical and healing properties of stones and other natural objects, for instance, was held in common by Christians and pagans; and it is possible that the customs and rituals connected with burial were another area of shared practice and tradition.

The problems surrounding burial are central to the question of differentiating between Christian and pagan in the archaeological record; or, rather, they have in the past been seen to be central to this question. In fact, certain venerable beliefs regarding the supposed diagnostic value of burial orientation, or the presence or absence of grave goods *per se*, appear to be dying very hard in certain quarters: in discussing this subject at the present time, one is still as likely to present a revelation to some archaeologists as to risk insulting the intelligence of others. It is fair to say that, in general, continental archaeologists, especially in the German-speaking areas corresponding to the eastern fringes of the Merovingian dominions, have long had a more sophisticated and cautious attitude towards such issues than Anglo-Saxon archaeologists. One reason for this may be that, in contrast to England, these outlying Merovingian territories do not even have a rough historical *terminus post quem* for the advent of Christianity, as there is in England, to give rise to the temptation to construct interpretative frameworks in the light of supposed historical chronology. There is no equivalent to the arrival of St Augustine, with its convenient date of 597. A brief article which appeared in *The Times* on 31 December 1997 offered little encouragement to anyone inclined to despair at the persistence of certain simplistic interpretations in Anglo-Saxon cemetery archaeology, even allowing for possible journalistic naivety and over-simplification. Under the heading 'Grave mystery' it read:

> Archaeologists are trying to find out why some of the graves found at a Saxon dig in Southampton point the wrong way. Four are Christian burials, aligned east to west. But another is the opposite way round and a sixth faces north. One theory is that they are earlier pagan burials.

More generally, it is still not unusual to find Anglo-Saxon archaeologists talking about 'pagan cemeteries'.

From the end of the fifth century it became increasingly common in the Germanic world to bury the dead fully dressed, often including weapons in the case of men, and accompanied by pots and other vessels, as well as other items of personal equipment. (The use of the word 'Germanic' is of course highly problematical, as is the implication that burial fully dressed is in origin an ethnic custom.) This custom is evidenced throughout the Germanic world, from northern Italy and Bavaria in the south to Anglo-Saxon England in the north. Towards the end of the seventh century, in most parts of the Germanic world outside Scandinavia, the custom began to dwindle, and in the eighth century it vanished altogether in those areas of the Germanic world which had once been within the boundaries of the Roman Empire.

Now, to connect the origins of the custom of burying with grave goods with religion is nonsensical. It begins in Frankia among the aristocracy during the very generation in which the Frankish aristocracy converted to Christianity. Thus for the Franks, one could argue that if the practice were in any way connected with religion, then it would appear to signify Christianity, not paganism. Indeed, some of the most spectacular examples, graves filled with weapons, precious metals, pottery, glass and bronze vessels, as well as food offerings, have been found under cathedrals, such as that of Cologne, or abbey churches like Saint-Denis.[4] Countless examples of the imitation of this royal model are now known, spreading progressively eastwards in the course of the sixth and seventh centuries, in rural church burials in provincial Frankia and in Alamannia and Bavaria.[5] Yet sites in England with the same type of burial are customarily described as 'pagan cemeteries'. Such a designation relies on a range of assumptions about the nature of religious life and the process of conversion which are ultimately drawn from historical sources. Despite their frequent protestations about the importance of maintaining their disciplinary independence, early medieval archaeologists often fail to exercise sufficient caution in their use of such material. Are we still so ready to assume now that there were no Christians in Anglo-Saxon England before the well-known date of 597, for instance? In fact, we know that there were at least two, namely Queen Bertha and her chaplain, Bishop Liudhard, and they would surely have been accompanied to Kent by a wider retinue of servants and companions, who were presumably also Christians. Is it not likely that at least some Christians are represented among the burials in East Kentish cemeteries whose material culture reveals strong Frankish influence, and which date from before the end of the sixth century?

The practice of associating the end of the custom of furnished burials with changes in religion is perhaps more plausible. It need not necessarily be a direct result of conversion, of course, but might relate to changing clerical ideas about burial, or even to a more profound degree of christianisation. In his much-quoted article on Merovingian burial customs and religious beliefs, Bailey Young says:

> The persistence of burial with grave-goods during the Merovingian period confirms the traditional discontinuity between high culture and popular

culture, which was very apparent in the Roman period. The mass of the Franks remained for a long time close to the popular mentality; the Church took more than two centuries to 'convert' them to more rational conceptions.

And he concludes:

Is the disappearance of the traditional Merovingian cemetery around 700 the result of an evolution in the popular religious mentality? This would be a dangerous conclusion. It signifies rather that the long evolution of burial *ad sanctos* had borne fruit, and that the Church was ready to assume the full responsibility which had hitherto belonged to the family.[6]

One could take issue with several things here – in addition to the comment that the church somehow offered a 'more rational' solution than did the popular mentality. The most significant point to flag, in our opinion, is that the struggle the church was having to convert people to 'more rational' methods of burial is one that is almost entirely happening in the imagination of the modern scholar. There is precious little evidence from the sixth and seventh centuries – one might almost say 'none' – that the church was at all concerned with how burial took place. It was concerned, at least when it legislated, to make sure that only suitable people were buried in churches, but it did not legislate for what happened outside them. Gregory of Tours was moved to comment on the theft of rich grave goods from the grave of a woman recently buried under a church in Metz, but it was the desecration of the dead that horrified him, not the style of the initial burial.[7] Moving away from the Merovingian heartland of Gaul to the bishopric of Constance in Alamannia (probably founded in the early seventh century), it is difficult to imagine the see interfering in burial customs, even if from the outset it had been able to oversee its improbably huge territorial jurisdiction, which is doubtful. Such interference might have risked antagonising the local nobility who were busy studding the landscape with proprietary churches in which they could receive lavish burial. From the start such churches might also have had some relevance for the christianisation of the ordinary population, if the tied priests or noble 'chaplains' had been encouraged by their lords to go out and instruct a wider audience, in effect foreshadowing some of the pastoral functions of the later parish priests.

Some of the problems in the history of early medieval burial customs have never really been confronted, least of all on a Europe-wide basis. Can the same 'religious' explanations really be valid for phenomena in England and Frankia, when, in terms of conversion history, some parts of England lagged behind its continental neighbour by nearly two centuries (according to the normally accepted dates for the adoption of Christianity)? It is also by no means obvious that anything was happening in the Merovingian church around the year 700 that could have affected burial practices, as was implied by Bailey Young. Indeed, this pre-dated by more than two generations the Carolingian ecclesiastical reforms that did begin to regulate christian practices. Even an author who seeks – no doubt rightly – to highlight the Merovingian foundations of certain aspects of the Carolingian Renaissance, has to concede that:

> By 741 the Frankish Church was ripe for reform. The bleak assessment of the state of the Frankish Church in the early 740s given by St Boniface in his letters must be taken seriously, even when allowance has been made for regional variations (the problems in the German lands are likely to have been worse) and political antagonisms. According to Boniface the reputation of Frankish clergy, bishops and priests, as adulterers was notorious. Because no councils had been held for such a long time, Pope Zacharias said, many who call themselves priests hardly know what the priesthood is.[8]

In such a climate, it seems unlikely that the church would have had the moral authority or even the inclination to direct the populace in the adoption of 'more rational' burial customs.

No discussion of the archaeology of the conversion of Anglo-Saxon England would be complete without reference to the problem of the 'Final Phase' cemeteries, which has recently been reviewed by Andy Boddington.[9] According to the conventional model developed since the time of Lethbridge and Leeds in the 1930s, these seventh- to early eighth-century cemeteries have been interpreted as new christian cemeteries originating under the influence of the church. They tend to be small and to have more consistently oriented graves and a proportionately low incidence of grave goods – but with those that do occur not infrequently being of explicitly christian character – and occasionally they are observed to originate when neighbouring, older cemeteries were abandoned. Although Boddington is right to remind us that there would probably have been more than one factor behind the appearance of these cemeteries and their distinctive characteristics, there could still have been one main reason, and the explanation of changing religious beliefs or practices should not be too readily discarded.

Comparison with equivalent continental evidence, which Boddington did not attempt, may be helpful in exploring this question. On the continent it is not uncommon to find new, generally smaller, cemeteries springing up throughout the seventh century, often with a clear spatial relationship to older, previously established ones; and nowhere is this phenomenon better represented than in the *Separatfriedhöfe* of the Alamannic and Bavarian regions.[10] However, these smaller seventh-century cemeteries characteristically contain a much higher proportion of richly furnished graves (including a vastly higher incidence of horse burials) than the ordinary row-grave cemeteries; and it is widely acknowledged that the phenomenon has a purely social explanation, relating to a growing self-awareness of economic power and social prestige within the community (with a concomitant desire for segregation), and to the earliest origins of hereditary nobility. By contrast, the sobriety and modesty of the grave furnishings in the English 'Final Phase' cemeteries sit uneasily with this analogy (even allowing for the new, Mediterranean-influenced female dress fashions of the period), thus leading one back to a religious rather than a purely social or economic explanation. Paradoxical as it may seem, this is merely reinforced by the fact that one class of 'Final Phase' graves could be very rich. In this particular type, the characteristically small size of 'Final Phase' cemeteries tails off into small groups of burials or wholly isolated, single burials, which at the same time contain some of the most explicitly 'christian' grave goods. To turn around the words of Boddington – for whom the supposed absence of rich graves of the correct date which fulfil the other 'Final Phase' criteria was an obstacle to a religious explanation of the phenomenon as a whole – the model *can* 'take account of the very rich graves of that period'. It was misleading of him to hold up Sutton Hoo and Taplow as examples of such graves: these are graves of the first quarter of the seventh century (with Taplow possibly being even earlier). For greater chronological relevance, he ought to have been pointing to the rich, isolated barrow burials of the Wiltshire Downs and the Peak District, such as Roundway Down, Swallowcliffe Down, Benty Grange and Winster Moor (White Low), which date from further into the seventh century and often display a curious combination of intrinsically christian artefacts or symbols with a grave-form that one tends to think of as quintessentially 'pagan'.[11] It may be, then, that in England the dynamics of conversion were such that from an early stage the church was able to establish an infrastructure of local pastoral care and supervision, and really could influence burial practices, in a way that the Frankish church could not.[12] (After all, we should not forget that by the early eighth century the English church was already in a position to dispatch personnel to help remedy the problems of the Frankish church!) Against such a background, the rich 'Final Phase' burials could represent people who found themselves in a quandary: good Christians, yes, and possibly even influential benefactors of the church, but still desiring to uphold and demonstrate their social distinction in death. To this extent the analogy with the Merovingian *Separatfriedhöfe* remains helpful.

It is especially appropriate to compare and contrast the conversion process and its archaeology in Merovingian Alamannia and Bavaria with Anglo-Saxon England, because in all three areas the major developments were unfolding during the seventh century. Between them was situated the Merovingian heartland of Gaul, where conversion began earlier and has a fairly straightforward 'official' history. Clovis famously converted to Catholic Christianity, perhaps in the year 496, but possibly ten or more years later; his aristocracy and others soon followed suit. Although Gregory of Tours does mention the survival of pagan worship, for example in Trier some two generations after Clovis, there is very little indication in Gregory's *Histories* or in his other works that paganism was perceived as a problem in the Frankish kingdoms in the late sixth century. Gregory seems to see Arian Christians and Jews as far more of a religious threat than paganism; but then, of course, he was living in the highly Romanised west, and not in the more heavily Germanised north-eastern provinces of Gaul. Missionaries such as Amandus began evangelising those regions only in the seventh century, and their work is associated with the spread of rural monasticism in the tradition of Benedict and Columbanus.

Although, as has already been mentioned, Alamannia and Bavaria had no historic watershed comparable to the year 597 to form preconceptions about the onset and course of conversion, there are historical traditions of late missionary activity which have hitherto tended to straightjacket perceptions of the process. In Alamannia, Pirmin is the first well-documented 'missionary' figure, being responsible for founding the monastery of Reichenau in 724; but this does not necessarily mean that he was the first missionary in that region. Indeed, he spent only a short time in a very restricted part of Alamannia, being rapidly expelled by Duke Theudebald as a partisan of Charles Martel. It is a similar story with regard to the succession of traditional 'Apostles of the Bavarians', Emmeram, Rupert, Corbinian and Boniface, commencing with Emmeram no earlier than about 680. Moreover, the long-held view that Christianity only came very late to Bavaria found encouragement in the fact that a diocesan structure was only established there by Boniface in 739, after Duke Theodo had unsuccessfully petitioned the Pope for such a structure in around 715. However, once one looks beyond the traditions about these saints enshrined in the popular piety of the Baroque period, and analyses the historical sources more critically, it becomes clear that they were all highly political figures with complex agendas – in the sense of being agents of, or refugees from, the Pippinids or Carolingians of Frankia at a time when the Alamannic and Bavarian duchies were seeking greater autonomy. Their work in Bavaria was much more concerned with restoration and reorganisation than with heroic, primary missionary endeavour in the manner of St Augustine of

Canterbury (which is not to deny Boniface's role in just such endeavour in other missionary fields).[13] In any case, the traditional historical view tends to assume that what might be termed 'purposeful expeditionary missions' constitute the only possible model for the process of conversion and christianisation. Yet common sense suggests that this is unlikely within a single, if sprawling, political entity such as the Merovingian kingdom of Austrasia. Here an alternative model might be christianisation by osmosis, mediated by a cosmopolitan aristocracy with complex networks of association and interest extending over great distances.

Because Theodelinda, the daughter of the Bavarian duke, was a Catholic when she married the Lombard king Authari in 589, it is assumed that her family, the Agilolfings, were christian also; and there is hazy evidence of earlier seventh-century missions, of Columbanus and Gallus in Alamannia, and of Eustasius of Luxeuil in Bavaria. But it is first and foremost archaeological evidence which shows that the picture of the conversion found in the historical sources simply cannot be taken at face value. Before embarking on a more detailed discussion of a range of such evidence from Alamannia and Bavaria, we may briefly cite two cases concerning actual church buildings in one of Boniface's other spheres of action, in Hesse, which makes the point very clearly. Excavations at Fulda – the monastery that Boniface founded allegedly in a wilderness – have revealed a pre-monastic manorial or 'palace' complex of stone buildings, now confirmed as including a church, which may date from as early as the mid-seventh century.[14] And recent excavations beneath the cathedral of Frankfurt-am-Main have exposed the earliest stone church, which is dated by a very richly furnished young girl's burial of the late seventh century; yet there is no indication from any *historical* source that Frankfurt was a place of importance before the reign of Charlemagne, let alone that it was the seat of an eastern Frankish, christian aristocratic family before the end of the seventh century.[15]

The identification and interpretation of 'christian' artefacts are issues which Anglo-Saxon and Merovingian archaeology have in common. In some ways Anglo-Saxon archaeology is privileged in this regard: seventh-century Alamannic and Bavarian archaeology has little to compare with such explicitly christian objects as the cross on the Benty Grange helmet, the pendant or pectoral crosses from Desborough, Winster Moor, Ixworth, Wilton, Milton Regis and St Cuthbert's tomb, or for that matter St Cuthbert's coffin itself.[16] While acknowledging the methodological importance of the distinction between the *intrinsically* christian character of an object, and what other aspects of its composition, origins and functional context might suggest about its perceived significance for its owner, the fact that the English examples cited above were evidently designed for prominent display leaves little doubt that their owners were signifying their christian allegiance. In Alamannic and Bavarian archaeology, by contrast, it is frequently a matter of dispute whether or not an iconography is 'christian', while those symbols which are intrinsically christian often occur in a low-key or almost incidental way in the decoration of objects. Among the more explicit and important evidence are some pendant crosses (including a homogeneous group in the native metalworking tradition of silver-inlaid iron, and a Byzantine import found in situ in a young girl's grave in the exclusive *Separatfriedhof* at Friedberg near Augsburg);[17] and four examples of Latin inscriptions incorporated in the inlaid decoration of locally manufactured belt-pieces, two of which are definitely christian in content, being excerpts from psalms.[18] Yet the fact that such motifs occur in serially manufactured, widely distributed indigenous artefacts, whose find-contexts are poorly recorded, makes it difficult to bring such evidence into connection with the religious allegiances of specific individuals or communities. Heinrich Müller-Karpe has summed up the interpretative limits of the mass of the artefactual evidence as follows:

> It must remain an open question whether individual Christian symbols or images on costume, jewellery, utensils and weapons were consciously employed as visible testimony of a religious affiliation, that is, as a direct expression of Christian belief, or whether such an application of Christian symbols proceeded without that understanding of their significance and meaning which had given rise to them in the first place. The question of the status of a Christian sign is difficult to answer in individual cases: the possibilities range from genuine evidence of a religious awareness, through a superficial commemorative and decorative use, to one as an amulet with magical properties. As far as archaeological-historical studies are concerned, the most that can be said is that . . . the Christian objects in seventh-century Alamannic and Bavarian graves bear witness to a not inconsiderable diffusion of Christianity among these peoples by that time.[19]

The gold foil crosses (*Goldblattkreuze*) hold a special place among the Merovingian evidence for Christianity, not only on account of their intrinsically christian symbolism, but also because they offer the rare possibility of insights into the psychology of their use and of the way contemporaries responded to them. Beyond their well-known use in Lombard Italy, gold foil crosses are most commonly found in eastern Alamannia and, to a lesser extent, in Bavaria. They were locally made and not imported from Italy, as is evident from their different repertoire of forms and from the *ad hoc* use of various readily available objects to produce their decoration, instead of purpose-made dies as in Italy.[20] The first

5.1. Examples of gold foil crosses found lying in the head area of early to mid-seventh century male and female (child) burials in Alamannia and Bavaria. 1. Giengen an der Brenz (Kreis Heidenheim), grave 26; 2. Staubing (Kreis Kelheim), grave 76. (Scale: grave-plans c. 1:30, crosses 1:2.) Source: 1. After P. Paulsen and H. Schach-Dörges, Das alamannische Gräberfeld von Giengen an der Brenz *(Stuttgart, 1978), Tafel 2, 63. 2. After T. Fischer,* Das bajuwarische Reihengräberfeld von Staubing *(Kallmünz/Opf., 1993), Tafel 31. (Burnell)*

important point to note is that they were manufactured specially for funerary purposes (being far too fragile for any practical use by the living), which brings basic christian symbolism into direct association with ritual connected with death and burial. Sewn onto cloth backings, if not directly onto the clothing of the deceased, the crosses were most frequently placed over the face, although some cases feature two or more crosses in different positions on the body (fig. 5.1). The most natural interpretation of this usage is that, however much it might have been tinged with traditional superstition and belief in magical powers, it had an apotropaic purpose in a spirit of christian reverence. Further important, indirect evidence comes from the reaction of grave-robbers to gold foil crosses: in spite of their intrinsic value, they frequently refrained from touching them, and would even be deterred from disturbing the entire part of a grave in which they lay, notwithstanding the presence of other valuable objects. The most stunning evidence for this comes from the recent excavation of an aristocratic *Separatfriedhof* at Lauchheim in north-eastern Alamannia, which yielded consistent dendro-dates of around 700 from timber grave structures. The male grave 25 contained no fewer than five gold foil crosses laid out over the upper body, and while the lower part of the body area had been robbed, a complete drinking service of bronze and glass vessels located by the right shoulder of the deceased had been spared. Grave 27 similarly contained five gold foil crosses, which had been left behind by robbers who had otherwise completely ransacked the burial. Robbery proceeding from the foot end of the female grave 24 had ceased abruptly at the upper body, where a spectacular (and, in the Merovingian archaeological record, hitherto unique) jewelled gold brooch in the form of an equal-armed cross was left undisturbed.[21] The same phenomenon had long since been observed in eastern Frankish and western Alamannic contexts in relation to the later seventh-century 'bracteate-brooches' (the allegorical christian symbolism of whose iconography has been much debated).

Recently Horst-Wolfgang Böhme has suggested that the broadly discrete and mutually exclusive distributions of bracteate-brooches and gold foil crosses within Alamannia might represent two different and competing missionary currents: the first emanating from the Frankish hinterland of the upper and middle Rhine, with its several bishoprics located on the west bank of the river, and the second with a southern, Italian source. He further proposes that, within the distribution area of gold foil crosses, graves that contain them, and church burials in which they are rarely found (see below), symbolise a religious-ideological dichotomy with overtones of political-cultural allegiance.[22] While we should be wary of accepting such ingeniously tidy explanations of archaeological distribution patterns, it is very clear that there was a cultural divide between the west and the east of

Bavaria, which also encompasses the archaeology of Christianity, and which finds a ready explanation in the documentary and onomastic evidence for a very strong, continuing Romanic tradition in the east. This situation, and indeed the very suggestion of a dichotomy within Alamannia in the context of christianisation, inevitably recalls the duality of, and the tensions between, the Roman and 'Celtic' traditions, which are a central aspect of the seventh-century conversion history of Anglo-Saxon England. For England, it has also been suggested that archaeology provides evidence of self-conscious pagan resistance to Christianity and its political 'baggage'. Martin Carver sees Sutton Hoo as 'a theatre in which the longest running theme is the defiant pagan politics of an arriviste [East Anglian] monarchy' striving for as long as it can to hold off 'Christianity, the adoption of which reaches beyond the tonsure and the church to fealty to the Franks and their imperial echoes'.[23] One possible interpretation of the total cremation barrow burial of Asthall in Oxfordshire is that it represents 'an act of "transculturation", that is the incorporation of elite Anglian burial fashions in order to resist external domination', in the context of a small, independent polity threatened by more powerful, nouveaux-Christian neighbours.[24] Similarly, the localised existence of rich barrow burials of around 700, in close proximity to contemporary or earlier church burials in the area of Zurich in Alamannia and Regensburg in Bavaria, has been seen as evidence of a politically motivated pagan reaction at a time of renewed Frankish assertiveness, although nowadays it should perhaps more properly be viewed as a phenomenon analogous to the rich, isolated 'Final Phase' burials in England.

Where the Merovingian archaeology of conversion and christianisation has a huge advantage over the Anglo-Saxon is in the field of church archaeology. Since the early 1960s, excavations have taken place in hundreds of ordinary parish churches in southern Germany and Switzerland, in advance of renovations and the installation of improved under-floor heating systems, and in very many cases the exposed building-sequence has been found to begin with a church that is securely dated to the seventh century by associated furnished and frequently very rich graves, the so-called 'founder-graves' (*Stiftergräber*) (fig. 5.2).[25] This label should be understood as a term of convenience and not necessarily literally, since it has become apparent that the burials in individual churches can reflect various patterns of demographic selectivity or they may be chronologically sporadic, loosening the personal connection with the actual act of foundation (and because, most interestingly, some of the burials are those of clerics). Despite such nuances, the graves constitute extremely valuable dating evidence for structural remains which more than anything else reveal the practice of Christianity to have been rooted in the landscape; while at the same time they provide rich insights into the social context and dynamics of

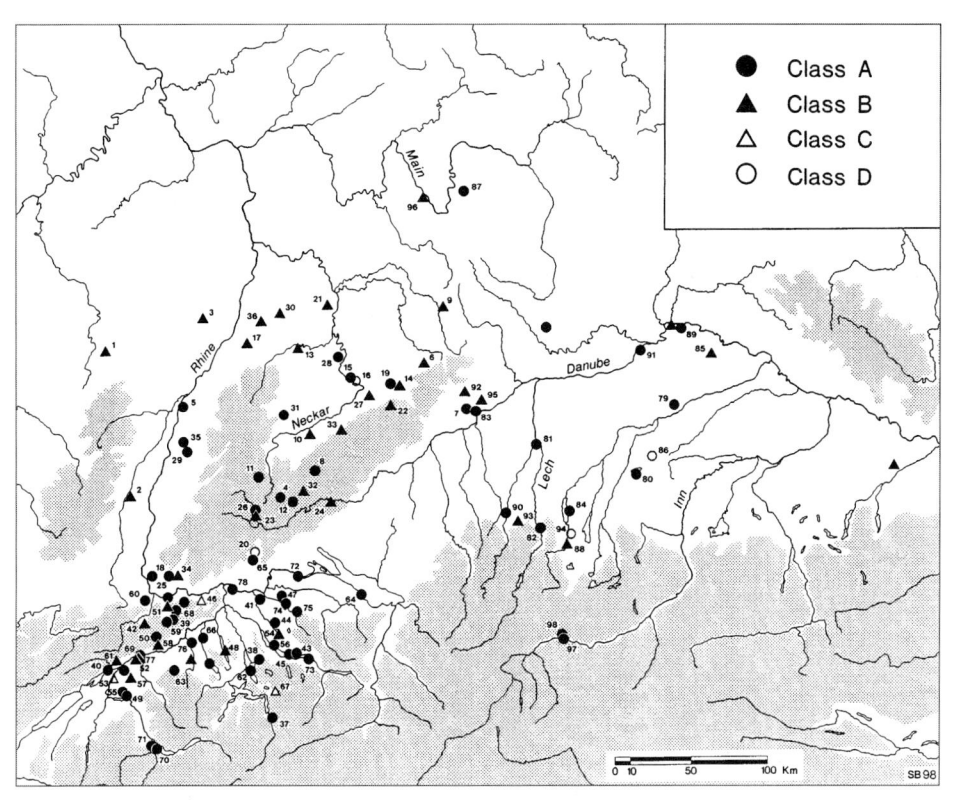

5.2. *Map showing the overall distribution of Merovingian to early Carolingian church 'founders' graves' sites in Alamannia and Bavaria. The site numbers refer to the Catalogue in Burnell,* Merovingian to Early Carolingian Churches, *vol. 3; unnumbered sites are more recently recorded or published finds. The classes refer to the quality of the evidence for contemporaneity of graves and an earliest church, from A (positive evidence of contemporaneity) to C (positive evidence for overbuilding of graves by earliest church); Class D finds are open field sites where graves are associated with an abandoned (usually post-hole) structure not conclusively identified as a church. (Burnell)*

christianisation. These are the burials of more or less 'noble' family members in or beside proprietary churches, and, whatever imponderables may attach to the general evidence for Christianity from graves and artefacts, there can be little doubt that these people were baptised Christians. The well-dated church-plan typologies constructed on this evidence also mean that other primary phase churches which happen not to have founder-graves can be broadly dated within the same parameters. The result is that, for the Alamannic area alone, literally scores of non-monastic church buildings, of both stone and timber construction, are known archaeologically from the period *c.* 600–750 (fig. 5.3).

The first founder-graves identified and described by Paul Reinecke early this century happened to be of relatively late date (*c.* 700), which seemed to accord

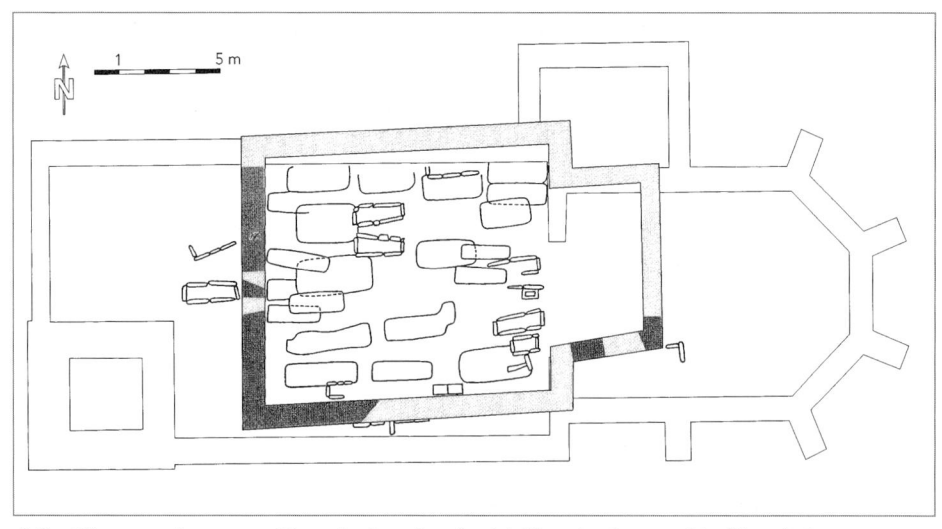

5.3. *The seventh-century Merovingian church with 'founders' graves' in Sissach (canton Basel-Land, Switzerland: no. 68 on figs 2 and 4). This find is unusual in featuring such a large assemblage of well-furnished and undisturbed burials.* Source: After S. Burnell, Die reformierte Kirche von Sissach BL: mittelalterliche Kirchenbauten und merowingerzeitliche 'Stiftergräber' *(Liestal, 1998), Abbildung 1. (Burnell)*

well with the 'historical' traditions of late missionary activity and conversion in Alamannia and Bavaria, and served to reinforce this interpretative model. Evidence which seemed to conflict with this model was conveniently ignored or explained away by various means. The dogma, in general discussions of the subject, of the *Stiftergräber der Zeit um 700* ('founder-graves of the period around 700'), persisted until 1974, when Rainer Christlein conducted a systematic review of the evidence in the light of more modern dating, and was able to show that there were in fact different chronological horizons represented by such finds within Alamannia and Bavaria, with the earliest going back to the beginning of the seventh century.[26] Since then, research in this important area has truly taken off: the list of finds is steadily being augmented (even if the rate of discoveries has somewhat slowed in the last ten years), and well-defined patterns in the spread of such sites have been recognised. Having already appeared and spread within Frankia in the course of the sixth century, founder-graves make their first tentative appearance in Alamannia in the first quarter of the seventh century, with strong evidence of Frankish influence. There is a handful of finds of this date from churches dedicated to St Martin in Inner Alamannia around the middle Neckar, and a larger cluster in the Romanic-Alamannic border area of the north-western Swiss Jura; while of great interest are sites with a Late Antique infrastructural heritage at Zurzach on the Rhine in northern Switzerland (not far from the former episcopal seat at Vindonissa-Windisch) and at Augsburg on the eastern border of Alamannia, both featuring the graves of Burgundian-Frankish or Romanic clerics alongside those of indigenous laypeople. This type of burial, with its distinctive accoutrement of bone or bronze reliquary buckles, wooden staffs, large knives and writing implements, was first recorded from a church at Saint-Quentin in Picardy, in northern France.[27] Among the middle Neckar cluster of founder-grave sites from the earliest phase, there are similar clerics' graves from Gruibingen and Pfullingen.[28] This evocative evidence bears witness to early missions, or more simply to the deployment of personnel as part of wider administrative initiatives, which find no explicit mention in historical sources. German historians have begun to link it with an intensive policy of bringing Alamannia into closer political integration pursued under the vigorous Frankish kings Chlothar II (613–29) and Dagobert I (623/29–39), which emerges dimly but consistently from a mosaic of later sources and traditions, including those of the foundation of the bishoprics of Constance and Augsburg.[29] Augsburg, Constance and Zurzach, along with bishops' seats situated along the left bank of the Rhine at Augst-Basel, Strasbourg and Speyer, appear to ring Inner Alamannia and to be strategically placed to exert influence over it. The cluster of middle Neckar sites, which appear to be more 'out on a limb' at this time, may represent direct implantations of Franco-Alamannic lordship around an important stage of the cross-country route between Speyer and Augsburg, at opposite ends of the peripheral 'ring' of ecclesiastical-administrative bridgeheads (fig. 5.4). Finally, at a distinctly early site for the Swiss midlands, at Zofingen just east of the River Aare, there is the burial of a woman with an unusual and exquisite suite of gold jewellery; she probably originated from Burgundian-Frankish court circles, and was involved in the foundation of a church with the tell-tale dedication to St Maurice in the years around 600, when Alamannic Switzerland was briefly annexed to the kingdom of Burgundy.

In the middle third of the seventh century both Inner Alamannia and Alamannic Switzerland 'fill out' with founder-grave sites; and to the same horizon belongs the earliest evidence from Merovingian Bavaria, that is, from east of the Lech. Highly significant for a model of christianisation as inextricably bound up with political integration and lordship is the fact that the two earliest and richest sites belong to élite social contexts (as attested by slightly later documentary evidence). These are Aschheim near Munich, the site of a ducal vill in whose church St Emmeram himself was temporarily buried around 685 before his translation to Regensburg, as well as the venue for a synod in the mid-eighth century; and Herrsching, a site which has plausibly

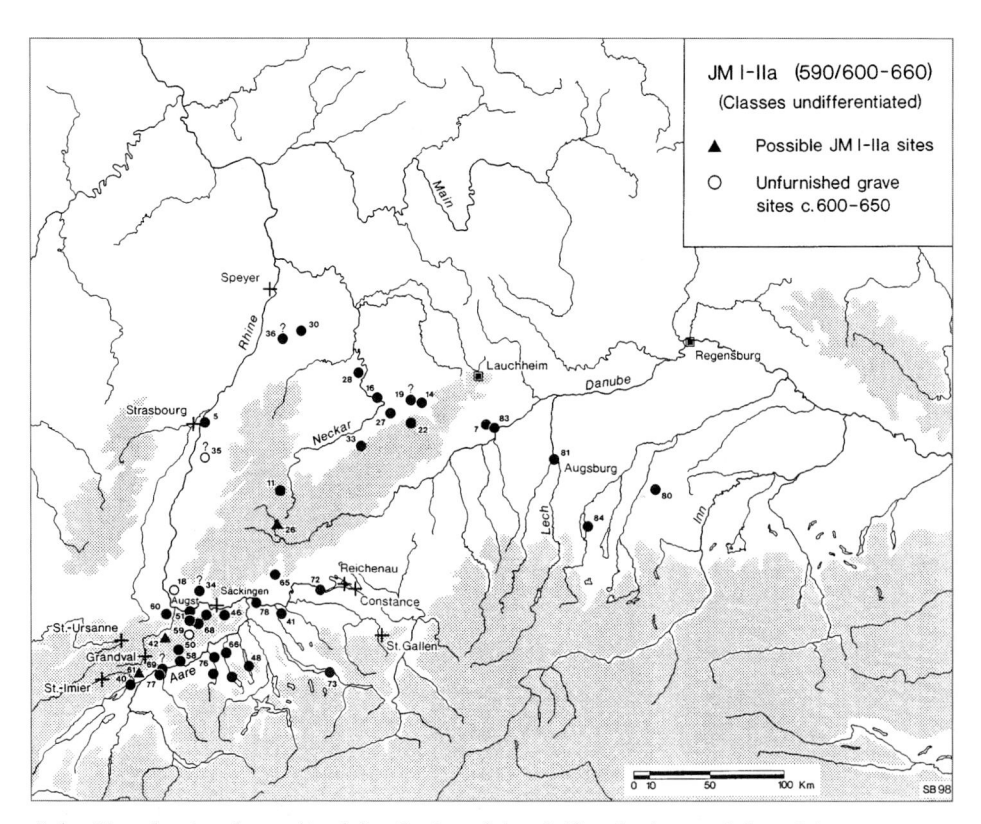

5.4. *Map showing the combined distribution of church 'founders' graves' sites of the chronological phases* Jüngere Merowingerzeit *(JM) I (590/600–620/40) and IIa (620/40–c. 660) in Alamannia and Bavaria. Numbered sites referred to in the text: Aschheim (80), Augsburg (81), Dunningen (11), Gruibingen (22), Herrsching (84), Kornwestheim (28), Pfullingen (33), Zofingen (76), Zurzach (78); also located by name are other sites mentioned in the text. (Burnell)*

been linked through eighth-century charter evidence to the Huosi, whose special status as the foremost Bavarian noble family after the Agilolfing dukes is enshrined in the *Lex Baiuvariorum*. On this basis it could be surmised that the christianisation of the Bavarian upper class begins a 'generation' later than that of its Alamannic counterparts. It is true, however, that the founder-grave sites in Bavaria are altogether fewer and less dense than in Alamannia (not least because, almost certainly for cultural-historical reasons, they are – with a single possible exception at Wels in Upper Austria – absent from the whole eastern half of the country), and that the majority originated in the later seventh century. The late missionary traditions may thus find some resonance in prime archaeological evidence after all. Recently this possibility has been strikingly reinforced by the find of a rich female burial dating from around 700 in a masonry grave chamber on the site of the church of St Emmeram in

Regensburg itself. The church, traditionally erected over the final resting place of Emmeram and originally dedicated to St George, has been found to have been built in an existing, rather unexceptional seventh-century cemetery. However, although there is no clearly contemporaneous relationship of the rich grave to early building remains, the burial is on a different alignment from the confirmed pre-church cemetery, while its outstanding character and distinctly late date suggest *prima facie* an association with a new departure in the status and function of the site.[30]

Besides mentioning more recent individual finds, it is only proper to highlight some new developments in the research of founder-graves in the decade since completion of the Oxford doctoral thesis on the subject which was respectively written and supervised by the authors of this chapter. In recent years it has become fashionable to view church burials as but one expression of the increasing tendency during the seventh century towards the separation and segregation of élite burials for social reasons: that is, as the ultimate stage in the observed progression from reserved burial precinct within a general cemetery, through the *Separatfriedhof*, a stone's throw away from the general cemetery, to one in splendid isolation (including the barrow groups).[31] A theoretical implication of this might be to undermine the finer dating value of church-associated graves, because a church might have existed for some considerable yet indeterminate time before it assumed a new significance as an exclusive burial place. In fact it is less likely that a chronological decoupling of the two vital components of such finds – church and aristocratic burial – need be a significant methodological concern, and more likely that the aristocratic proprietary burial churches were founded with a complex combination of religious and prestige motives: in other words, that the churches would not have been founded without the intention of also using them for aristocratic burial. Nevertheless, it is quite right in principle to stress the continuum of open *Separatfriedhöfe* and burial churches, if only because the 'retrospective founder-grave' has come increasingly to be recognised. The long-delayed, fuller publication of several sites excavated as long ago as the mid-1960s has revealed several places where a church was only built subsequently over a grave or small group of graves – in effect a *Separatfriedhof*. Unfortunately this seems to apply to Dunningen and Kornwestheim, two churches dedicated to St Martin which we had in the doctoral thesis ascribed to the mid-seventh-century 'filling-out' phase in Inner Alamannia, an area where integrity of the archaeological evidence is particularly valued because of the complete historical obscurity. In some such cases the time lapse may be so small as to make no difference – where stratigraphic observations suggest that a church was erected immediately or very soon over a burial, as the ultimate grave marker (as may be the case at Herrsching) – but in others it may be more significant. The recognition of this possible sequence at least bears out our methodological caution in the doctoral thesis in qualitatively classifying the sites according to the certainty of the relationship of graves to a contemporary church, evidence for which was often lacking from older or partial church excavations, or incidental finds (see fig. 5.2). At the time this caution was based more on positive observations from sites in the Rhineland and Belgium, such as Grobbendonk and the famous one at Morken, while in the meantime clear examples have also become available from our main study area.

The Merovingian archaeological phenomenon of church founder-graves has no equivalent in Anglo-Saxon archaeology. Indeed, the number of non-monastic church buildings dating from the seventh to the early eighth century known in England from archaeological or standing remains is pitifully small by comparison (although it should be said that the best English examples, such as Escomb (Co. Durham), are incomparably better preserved than those on the continent).[32] Of these, many belong in nothing less than a royal context: one thinks of St Martin's in Canterbury built around Roman remains (cf. fig. 1.5), the simple timber church of the latest phase at Yeavering, and the stone Old Minster church at Winchester. Apparently anonymous, rural sites like Nazeingbury in Essex, with its succession of two timber churches including a pair of prominently situated but unfurnished graves in the chancel of the earlier one,[33] and Cowage Farm near Foxley in Wiltshire, with an apsidal church within an enclosure as part of a manorial-type settlement,[34] might seem to correspond most closely in character to the late Merovingian churches under discussion; however, since the discovery of new documentary evidence, Nazeingbury may not be so anonymous after all, and may in fact represent an East Saxon royal nunnery, while a monastic status has also been suggested for Cowage Farm. It remains something of a puzzle, then, as to where the recently converted Anglo-Saxon sub-royal élite was being buried, inasmuch as they cannot all be accounted for by the isolated, rich 'Final Phase' burials of the mid- to later seventh century.

The key to understanding this puzzle, and the contrast with the archaeological picture from the eastern Merovingian provinces, probably lies in the importance of monasteries in the Anglo-Saxon conversion process. This is something that comes across vividly in Bede's account and in saints' Lives, as well as in early charter evidence, and is also reflected in the high proportion of monastic or quasi-monastic sites in the archaeological record of the earliest churches. The fluid definition of monastic functions and institutions in early Christian England means that there may have been even more 'monastic' (including 'minster'?)

churches with which members of the upper classes could associate themselves as benefactors – as the *princeps* Frithuric was associated with Breedon some time after 675 – and thereby earn the right to be buried in them.[35] It would probably not have been deemed appropriate for such burial to take place in an ostentatious, 'pagan' manner, even if there had been some traditional hankering for it, which would make them less visible archaeologically. While for the Alamannic and Bavarian nobility christianisation offered new opportunities for a yet more fiercely élitist expression of their status in death through an even more prestigious, private setting, for many of their Anglo-Saxon counterparts it may have meant entrusting their way of death to a 'public' institution which espoused principles of austerity and humility.

The English option was, in any case, not available to the Alamannic and Bavarian nobility of the later Merovingian period, because monasticism arrived late in these areas. Chronological synchronism between historical monastic foundations (in the Columbanian tradition) and the archaeologically dated evidence of founder-graves is closest in the Romanic Jura region of north-western Switzerland, where Moutier-Grandval (founded in around 635), Saint-Imier and Saint-Ursanne are situated; and it is noteworthy that the subject of the most believable of several more or less dubious monastic foundation traditions specifically linked to Alamannic missions in South Baden – namely Säckingen, allegedly founded by St Fridolin in around 640 – lies 'offshore' from this region on an island in the Rhine east of Basel. Thereafter, as one moves east the chronological displacement progressively increases in favour of the founder-graves (in Alamannia, St Gallen founded in 719 and Reichenau in 724), until in Bavaria there is a quite startling time lag, with the first monasteries not founded until the mid-eighth century. The reasons for this last phenomenon are not altogether clear, but may be connected with the long-delayed formal ecclesiastical organisation of the country. In contrast to Anglo-Saxon England, it seems that in Alamannia and Bavaria the christianisation of the aristocracy was the prerequisite for monastic foundations, not their first fruits. Ian Wood has evoked a certain symmetry between the peripheral Merovingian duchies and the Anglo-Saxon kingdoms in the age of Dagobert I, in terms of their size and importance, and has assembled evidence of this powerful Frankish king's 'concern to be involved in the christianisation of England' as 'an aspect of the extension of Frankish hegemony during his reign',[36] in a way which mirrors the growing recognition by German scholars of Dagobert's deliberate 'Alamannic policy'. But whatever the symmetry and parallels of the general background to the process, archaeological evidence strongly suggests important differences in the dynamics of conversion in the two areas.

Notes

1. There is a useful summary in J. Graham-Campbell, *The Viking World*, 2nd edn (London, 1990), pp. 178–82.
2. H. Roosens, 'Reflets de Christianisation dans les cimetières mérovingiens', *Les Etudes Classiques*, 53 (1985), 111–35, at p. 118: trans. by Edward James.
3. R. Joffroy, *Le cimetière de Lavoye (Meuse): nécropole mérovingienne* (Paris, 1974), pp. 95–100 and pl. 32.
4. J. Werner, 'Frankish Royal Tombs in the Cathedrals of Cologne and Saint-Denis', *Antiquity*, 38 (1964), 201–16.
5. S.P. Burnell, 'Merovingian to Early Carolingian Churches and their Founder-Graves in Southern Germany and Switzerland: The Impact of Christianity on the Alamans and the Bavarians', 4 vols (unpubl. D.Phil. thesis, Univ. of Oxford, 1988); H.W. Böhme, 'Adel und Kirche bei den Alamannen der Merowingerzeit', *Germania*, 74 (1996), 477–507.
6. B. Young, 'Paganisme, christianisation et rites funéraires mérovingiens', *Archéologie Médiévale*, 7 (1977), 5–81 at pp. 65, 66: trans. Edward James. Bailey K. Young's unpublished Philadelphia thesis ('Merovingian Funeral Rites and the Evolution of Christianity', University of Pennsylvania, 1978) remains an important study.
7. *Historiarum Libri Decem*, VIII.21, ed. R. Buchner, 2 vols (Darmstadt, 1974), II. 190–1: trans. in L. Thorpe (ed.), *History of the Franks* (Harmondsworth, 1974), p. 453.
8. G. Brown, 'Introduction: The Carolingian Renaissance', *Carolingian Culture: Emulation and Innovation*, ed. R. McKitterick (Cambridge, 1994), pp. 1–51 at p. 11.
9. A. Boddington, 'Models of Burial, Settlement and Worship. The Final Phase Reviewed', *Anglo-Saxon Cemeteries: A Reappraisal*, ed. E. Southworth (Stroud, 1990), pp. 177–99.
10. R. Christlein, 'Besitzabstufungen zur Merowingerzeit im Spiegel reicher Grabfunde aus West- und Süddeutschland', *Jahrbuch des Römisch-Germanischen Zentralmuseums Mainz*, 20 (1973), 147–80.
11. H. Geake, *The Use of Grave-Goods in Conversion Period England*, BAR Brit. Ser. 261 (Oxford, 1997), *passim*; G. Speake, *A Saxon Bed Burial on Swallowcliffe Down* (London, 1989).
12. A. Thacker, 'Monks, Preaching and Pastoral Care in Early Anglo-Saxon England', *Pastoral Care Before The Parish*, eds J. Blair and R. Sharpe (Leicester, 1992), pp. 137–70.
13. As examples of the extensive literature on this subject, F. Prinz, 'Arbeo von Freising und die Agilulfinger', *Zeitschrift für Bayerische Landesgeschichte*, 29 (1996), 580–90; H. Wolfram, 'Der heilige Rupert und die antikarolingische Adelsopposition', *Mitteilungen des Instituts für Oesterreichische Geschichtsforschung*, 80 (1972), 4–34.
14. H. Hahn, 'Eihloha. Sturm und das Kloster Fulda', *Fuldaer Geschichtsblätter*, 56 (1980), 50–82; H. Hahn, 'Fulda. Domplatz-Bereich', *Hessen im Frühmittelalter. Archäologie und Kunst*, Exhibition catalogue: Museum für Vor-und Frühgeschichte, Frankfurt am Main, ed. H. Roth and E. Wamers (Sigmaringen, 1984), pp. 300–7, esp. 303–4.
15. *Die Franken, Wegbereiter Europas. Vor 1500 Jahren: König Chlodwig und seine Erben*, Exhibition Catalogue: Reiss-Museum, Mannheim, ed. A. Wieczoreck et al. (Mainz, 1996), pp. 940–1.
16. Most of these pendant or pectoral crosses are described and illustrated in R. Jessup, *Anglo-Saxon Jewellery* (Aylesbury, 1974);

see also S.C. Hawkes and L.R.A. Grove, 'Finds From a Seventh Century Anglo-Saxon Cemetery at Milton Regis', *Arch Cant*, 78 (1963), 22–38, esp. pp. 29–33 with fig. 2:3. For Cuthbert's coffin, see E. Kitzinger, 'The coffin-reliquary', in C.F. Battiscombe (ed.), *The Relics of Saint Cuthbert* (Oxford, 1956), pp. 202–304.

17. H. Müller-Karpe, 'Der alamannische Kreuzanhänger von Pfahlheim (Kr. Aalen)', *Fundberichte aus Schwaben*, N.F.19 (1971), 338–41; R. Christlein, *Die Alamannen. Archäologie eines lebendigen Volkes* (Stuttgart/Aalen, 1978), p. 120, fig. 97.

18. H. Oomen, 'Lateinisch-christliche Inschriften aus alamannischen Gräbern', *Zeitschrift für Württembergische Landesgeschichte*, 30 (1971), 404–7; Christlein, *Die Alamannen*, pl. 100.

19. Müller-Karpe, 'Der alamannische Kreuzanhänger', at p. 340: trans. Simon Burnell.

20. For the most up-to-date gazetteer of Alamannic gold foil crosses, with good illustrations: W. Müller and M. Knaut, *Heiden und Christen: Archäologische Funde zum frühen Christentum in Südwestdeutschland* (Stuttgart, 1987), pp. 33–51.

21. I. Stork, 'Zeugnisse des Christentums in Fürstengräbern von Lauchheim', *Archäologie in Deutschland* (4–1993), 28–30.

22. Böhme, 'Adel und Kirche bei den Alamannen', pp. 494–500.

23. M. Carver, 'The Anglo-Saxon Cemetery at Sutton Hoo: An Interim Report', *The Age of Sutton Hoo: The Seventh Century in North-Western Europe*, ed. M.O.H. Carver (Woodbridge, 1992), pp. 343–71 at p. 365.

24. T.M. Dickinson and G. Speake, 'The Seventh-Century Cremation Burial in Asthall Barrow, Oxfordshire: A Reassessment', in *The Age of Sutton Hoo*, ed. Carver, pp. 95–130 at p. 123.

25. Burnell, 'Merovingian to Early Carolingian Churches'; Böhme, 'Adel und Kirche bei den Alamannen'.

26. R. Christlein, 'Merowingerzeitliche Grabfunde unter der Pfarrkirche St. Dionysius zu Dettingen, Kr. Tübingen, und verwandte Denkmäler in Süddeutschland', *Fundberichte aus Baden-Württemberg*, 1 (1974), 573–96.

27. A. France-Lanord, 'Die Gürtelgarnitur von Saint-Quentin', *Germania*, 39 (1961), 412–20.

28. D. Quast, 'Merowingerzeitliche Funde aus der Martinskirche in Pfullingen', *Fundberichte aus Baden-Württemberg*, 19/1 (1994), 591–660 (incl. excursus on Gruibingen).

29. H. Keller, 'Fränkische Herrschaft und alemannisches Herzogtum im 6. und 7. Jahrhundert', *Zeitschrift für die Geschichte des Oberrheins*, 124 (1976), 1–30; I. Eberl, 'Dagobert I und Alemannien. Studien zu den Dagobertüberlieferungen im alemannischen Raum', *Zeitschrift für Württembergische Landesgeschichte*, 42 (1983), 7–51.

30. U. Osterhaus and E. Wintergerst, 'Die Ausgrabungen bei St. Emmeram in Regensburg: Ein Vorbericht', *Bayerische Vorgeschichtsblätter*, 58 (1993), 271–303; U. Osterhaus, 'Eine Adelsbestattung vom Ende des 7. Jahrhunderts im Kloster St. Emmeram in Regensburg', *Das Archäologische Jahr in Bayern*, 1992 (1993), 136–8.

31. A. Burzler, 'Archäologische Beiträge zum Nobilifizierungsprozess in der jüngeren Merowingerzeit' (unpubl. dissertation, Univ. of Munich, 1991); H.W. Böhme, 'Adelsgräber im Frankenreich: Archäologische Zeugnisse zur Herausbildung einer Herrenschicht unter den merowingischen Königen', *Jahrbuch des Römisch-Germanischen Zentralmuseums Mainz*, 40 (1993),

397–534; Böhme, 'Adel und Kirche bei den Alamannen'.
32. E. Fernie, *The Architecture of the Anglo-Saxons* (London, 1983), pp. 32–63.
33. P.J. Huggins, 'Excavation of Belgic and Romano-British Farm with Middle Saxon Cemetery and Churches at Nazeingbury, Essex, 1975–6', *Essex Archaeology and History*, 10 (1978), 29–117; K. Bascombe, 'Two Charters of King Suebred of Essex', *An Essex Tribute: Essays Presented to F.G. Emmison*, ed. K. Neale (London, 1987), pp. 85–96.
34. J. Hinchcliffe, 'An Early Medieval Settlement at Cowage Farm, Foxley, near Malmesbury', *ArchJ*, 143 (1986), 240–59.
35. S. Foot, 'Anglo-Saxon Minsters: A Review of Terminology', *Pastoral Care*, eds Blair and Sharpe, pp. 212–25. For Breedon, see A. Dornier, 'The Anglo-Saxon Monastery at Breedon-on-the-Hill, Leicestershire', *Mercian Studies*, ed. A. Dornier (Leicester, 1977), pp. 155–68.
36. I. Wood, 'Frankish Hegemony in England', *The Age of Sutton Hoo*, ed. Carver, pp. 235–41 at p. 240.

CHAPTER 6

The British Church and the Mission of Augustine[1]

Clare Stancliffe

> Why did Roman Britain fail to follow the example of other provinces in the West and preserve a powerful and episcopally-led Christian Church, so that despite the destruction wrought by the barbarian invasions the continuity between Roman province and Germanic kingdom could be maintained? Why, alone among the western provinces, did Catholic Christianity have to be replanted in an almost wholly pagan environment whence all records of previous Christianisation appear to have perished?[2]

This quotation from a recent article by W.H.C. Frend makes a fitting start to a chapter on the British church at the time of Augustine's arrival, and this for two reasons. First, the basic question which Frend poses (even if we should wish to modify its wording) is of fundamental importance; it is therefore helpful to be aware of it from the outset, and to let it lie at the back of our minds until the moment that it is faced directly, later in this chapter. A second reason for beginning with this quotation is because its phrasing implies an attitude which is still all too widespread: 'why did Roman Britain *fail* . . .' implies that, somehow, the fact that the English church looks back to Augustine and not to the pre-existing British church is in some way the 'fault' of the British church. Such an assumption probably derives, albeit unconsciously, from Bede's *Ecclesiastical History*; and indeed it is all the more insidious because it is so unconsciously derived.

It is therefore essential for us to recognise that our direct sources for the British church around the sixth to seventh centuries are minimal, scrappy and inadequate, the result of chance survival; and that Bede's account, which we are in no position to dispense with, was written a century later, and so with hindsight, and with a particular view of the British church which may well have distorted the reality as it was in Augustine's day. Two passages in particular reveal Bede's animus against the British church. The first is his story of how the pagan king of Bernicia, Æthelfrith, slaughtered some 1,200 defenceless monks from the seemingly exemplary British monastery of Bangor. Bede writes with apparent equanimity of how this fulfilled Augustine's threat made to the British, when they had declined to accept his terms for cooperating with him in the conversion of the Anglo-Saxons, to the effect that if they would not accept peace with their brethren, they would suffer vengeance from their enemies. The second passage comes right at the end of his *History* when he is summarising the state of Britain at the time of writing. After commenting favourably on the Picts and the Irish living in Britain, he continues: 'Though, for the most part, the Britons oppose the English through their inbred hatred, and the whole state of the Catholic church by their incorrect Easter and their evil customs, yet being opposed by the power of God and man alike, they cannot obtain what they want in either respect.'[3]

This is not the place to examine Bede's handling of the Britons in any detail; but since we need to use his account, we must be aware of how his bias operated, and what underlay it. Although British and Irish Christianity around the year 600 were identical,[4] it suited Bede's purpose in imposing a pattern on the story of how the island of Britain came to a true acceptance of Christianity to drive a wedge between the Irish and the British: because the Irish had the charity to preach to the Anglo-Saxons, they could be cast as the heroes, who deserved to be converted to the true Easter by the Northumbrian Ecgberht. The British, on the other hand, are portrayed as inveterate sinners, always forsaking God, and even refusing to preach to the Anglo-Saxons; and for that reason they deserved to be replaced by the English.[5] It was thus axiomatic for the entire structure of Bede's *Ecclesiastical History*, and also for the justification of the Anglo-Saxons' seizure of land and power from the Britons, that the Britons had sinned and had refused to help to convert the Anglo-Saxons: 'indeed, to this day it is the custom of the Britons to despise the faith and religion of the English, and not to communicate with them in any respect more than with the pagans'.[6]

Bede, however, was writing with hindsight, as this quotation shows. How far was he justified in presenting 'the Britons' and 'the Anglo-Saxons' as two separate, coherent peoples, at enmity with each other right from the time of Augustine? Did the Britons really make no contribution to the conversion of any of the Anglo-Saxons? How securely founded was Bede's opinion of the British church at the time of Augustine's arrival? Fortunately, the survival of Gregory the Great's letters gives us a few strictly contemporary documents, which can shed light on the origins of at least some of Bede's assumptions. In his letter of July 596 to the Frankish kings Theuderic and Theudebert, Gregory writes:

We have seen in you much to make us suppose that you desire those subject to you to be completely converted to that faith in which indeed you, their kings and lords, are yourselves. And thus it has reached us that the English nation, by the compassion of God, eagerly desires to be converted to the Christian faith, but that the *sacerdotes e uicino* neglect it and refrain from kindling by their exhortation the desires of the English. On this account, therefore, we have arranged to send thither Augustine, the servant of God, the bearer of these presents . . . along with other servants of God. We have also enjoined them to take with them some *e uicino . . . presbyteros*, by means of whom they may be able to get to know the intentions of the English, and, as far as God may allow, assist them to their desires by their admonition.[7]

Now the fact that Augustine is to take Frankish priests – *e uicino . . . presbyteros* – with him as interpreters shows that the neighbouring bishops (*sacerdotes e uicino*) who had neglected the Anglo-Saxons must also have been *Frankish* bishops.[8] For Gregory, based in Rome, Kent lay just the other side of the English Channel from Frankia, and he conceived of Augustine's mission to the Anglo-Saxons in a Frankish context.[9] *Sacerdotes e uicino* was therefore for him a natural way of referring to Frankish bishops. Bede, however, was based in Northumbria. He clearly knew this papal letter to the kings (or the very similarly phrased one addressed to Queen Brunhild),[10] and I would suggest that we need look no further than this for the origin of his belief that the Britons never made any contribution to the conversion of the Anglo-Saxons. From an English perspective, it would be very easy to assume that the *sacerdotes e uicino* who had neglected the Anglo-Saxons before Augustine's arrival were the British bishops; and this would particularly have been the case for Bede, since he also knew, independently, of the story already referred to about how the British bishops refused a specific invitation to collaborate with Augustine in his mission to the Anglo-Saxons. We should therefore disregard Bede's general statement that the British had 'never' preached to the Anglo-Saxons[11] as being based on a false inference from one of Gregory's letters.

A similar misinterpretation may underlie Bede's comment, already quoted, about how the Britons 'to this day' despise the Christianity of the Anglo-Saxons, refusing to communicate with them any more than with pagans. The context for this remark is Cadwallon of Gwynedd's treatment of Northumbria following his victory over Edwin in 633.[12] This was Gwynedd's revenge for Æthelfrith's ferocious ravaging of the British over many years, and in particular for his slaughter of the British (including the monks of Bangor) at the battle of Chester;[13] Cadwallon's out and out hostility is understandable in this context. But the implication of Bede's wording, that thereafter the Britons consistently segregated themselves from the christian Anglo-Saxons, is manifestly wrong; for Bede himself includes the story of how Chad was consecrated to the Northumbrian bishopric *c.* 664 by Wine of the West Saxons together with two British bishops. What is more, this kind of cooperation is likely to have been normal at least in the Irish sphere of evangelisation since, as we have already seen, there was in reality no rift between their churches at this period.[14] The non-cooperation which Bede records probably stems once more from his readiness to generalise from individual events: this time from Cadwallon's treatment of Northumbrian Christianity in 633, and from the state of affairs which followed on from the synod of Whitby and the arrival of Archbishop Theodore, when both British and Irish churchmen found themselves treated as heretics.[15] In addition, it seems likely that Bede was influenced by his reading of Aldhelm's letter to Geraint, king of Dumnonia, which describes how the bishops of Dyfed (though not, apparently, elsewhere) refuse 'to celebrate the divine offices in church with us and to take courses of food at table for the sake of charity'.[16] Bede knew this letter to Geraint;[17] and Aldhelm's emphasis there on the all-important virtues of unity with the christian brethren and of charity, without which even the most perfect monastic discipline availed nothing, but with which 'many sins are forgiven', would appear to have left its mark on the monastic historian. For Bede could unblinkingly recount the vengeance wreaked on the Bangor monks, who in other respects lived exemplary lives, while he regarded the Irish possession of charity as the crucial virtue which differentiated them from the British.[18]

The irony of this is that the sixth-century British churchman, Gildas, had himself criticised the extreme ascetics within the British church, who 'prefer fasting to charity . . . their own contrivances to concord, the cell to the church'; and he had made clear his own preference for 'those who set themselves to do charity, which is the highest fulness of the law'.[19] Thus, historically, the lines of demarcation did not run between a purist British church on the one hand, and the Roman, Irish and Anglo-Saxon churches on the other, but rather *within* the British and Irish – and sometimes continental – churches;[20] and in origin, the grounds for refusing to communicate or to eat with others were because of their sinfulness, not because they came from a different christian tradition or country.[21]

We should further remember that Bede sought to play down internal divisions between the different Anglo-Saxon kingdoms, and rather present them as a single *gens Anglorum*, 'English people'; and one way of doing this was to emphasise the paschal controversy, which set off the 'English' on the one hand from the Britons and Irish on the other.[22] In reality, however, there was no monolithic grouping of all the Anglo-Saxon kingdoms on one side, and all the British ones on the other;

rather, we find alliances being made between particular kings for political reasons, which frequently run counter to such groupings. The most obvious of these is the alliance between the Anglo-Saxons of Mercia and the British of Gwynedd against Northumbria for much of the seventh century.

Now that we have sketched in these provisos about how we should regard Bede's account, let us turn to Gregory's decision to send Augustine's mission, and look at the way in which he envisaged Augustine relating to the British church. First, we need to ask what, if anything, Gregory knew of British Christianity before he received information on the subject from Augustine's party. The papacy had been responsible for commissioning Germanus of Auxerre to visit Britain and combat Pelagianism in 429, and had remained interested in the fortunes of Christianity in both Britain and Ireland (whither a first bishop had been dispatched in 431), at least up to the pontificate of Leo the Great, 440–61. Around that time, however, it apparently lost contact with both countries, presumably because of the Germanic invasions.[23] Whether any memory of these events survived at Rome to inspire Gregory is unknown. Britain had had trading contacts with the Mediterranean in the early sixth century, but not with Italy so much as with the east Mediterranean and north Africa; and in any case it was a thing of the past by Gregory's pontificate. By then, British trade was restricted to the Atlantic countries, particularly southwest Gaul.[24] The evidence of the transmission of books and ideas tells a similar story: Ireland and Britain remained in contact with Gaul, receiving, for instance, at least some of the sermons of Caesarius of Arles (d. 542) before *c.* 590.[25] Prior to Columbanus's continental career, however, our only evidence for sixth-century links with Rome comes from the (probably seventh-century) *Life of St Samson*, which portrays Irish pilgrims travelling back from Rome via western Britain.[26] The historicity of this pilgrimage, presumably set in the sixth century, is unknowable, but such pilgrimages may have taken place. There were certainly Britons in Gaul – and not just in Brittany – in the sixth century, and Gaul was in communication with Rome.[27]

There are two texts to which we can turn in the hope of gaining more precision on Gregory's own knowledge of the British church prior to Augustine's mission. The first occurs in Gregory's commentary on Job 36:30, expounding the greatness of God who rules the universe, spreads out the clouds, and sends his lightning to cover even the furthest parts of the sea. For Gregory, God has covered the furthest parts of the sea with clouds by extending the faith to the ends of the world, with the glittering miracles of preachers:

> For lo, [God] has already reached the hearts of almost all peoples; lo, he has joined in one faith the boundary of the east and of the west; lo, the tongue of

Britain, which had known nothing but barbarous gnashing of teeth, has now long since begun to shout aloud the Hebrew Alleluia in divine praises. Lo, the ocean, once swelling, now lies subservient before the feet of the saints. Its [presumably Britain's] barbarian movements, which earthly princes were unable to tame with the sword, are bound by the simple words of the *sacerdotes* (bishops/priests), through the fear of God; and he who as a heathen had had no qualms before ranks of warriors, now as a believer fears the words of the humble. For having received the heavenly words, and also been enlightened by miracles, he is filled with the power of divine knowledge . . .[28]

Now Bede took this passage to refer to the results of Augustine's mission, and most modern commentators have followed him.[29] There is, however, an insuperable obstacle[30] to this interpretation: Gregory said that he had completed his commentary on Job in 591, and in 595 he actually sent Leander of Seville a copy of the work, which, although missing some sections owing to the lack of a spare manuscript to hand, definitely included the relevant Book XXVII. Yet at that date Augustine had not even set off for England! Caught in this predicament, some modern scholars assume that the passage in question must have been a later addition to Gregory's text.[31] But, as its recent editor has pointed out, there is no indication in any of the manuscripts he has seen that there was any variation in the text at this point[32] – something which renders the revision hypothesis utterly implausible. Instead, I think we should follow those scholars who see this passage as one where Gregory is referring to the *British* church, which had indeed 'long since' imbibed Christianity.[33]

Further, the probable source of Gregory's knowledge lies to hand in Constantius's *Life of St Germanus*, which recounts that bishop's visit to Britain in the early fifth century. The reference to the shouting out of Alleluia matches Constantius's account of the Alleluia victory over Picts and Saxons;[34] the reference to the swelling ocean becoming subservient to the saints matches his account of the storm at sea that was calmed by Germanus;[35] the taming of the barbarian upheavals by the bishops' words again matches the Alleluia victory; and the final sentence referring to the neophyte both receiving verbal teaching and being enlightened by miracles also fits with Constantius's account.[36] Indeed, only the penultimate sentence does not fit: in reality, the Britons, who were converted, *had* previously feared their enemies, while there is no mention of the (perhaps fearless) Picts and Saxons being converted. This mismatch deters me from asserting straight out that the *Life of Germanus* was definitely the source whence Gregory derived his picture. None the less, I think it likely. This single mismatch might simply be due to an imperfectly remembered text and a desire to push further the image of the previous sentence concerning the power of God's word to reverse the military situation. What Gregory has recalled are the striking visual scenes conjured up by Constantius. Despite the absence of surviving early manuscripts of this *Life* from Italy, it was known at least at Pavia in the early sixth century;[37] and what is particularly telling is that whereas in any other scenario Gregory's comments appear as so much grandiloquent verbiage, once one sets them against Constantius's work Gregory can be seen to be alluding to specific incidents, and his words take on real meaning.

If we accept this passage of Gregory's *Moralia* as relating to Christianity in Britain before Augustine's arrival, it would suggest that Gregory's view was based on outdated information, gleaned from texts which related to the Roman and immediate post-Roman period. This is plausible. Gregory's world was above all a Mediterranean world; for instance, he was not concerned to differentiate between 'Frankia' and 'Germania'.[38] Indeed, it is salutary to be reminded that he was initially put in touch with bishops from *southern Gaul* only through the mediation and initiative of Jewish merchants.[39] Britain was far more distant in every sense; and it may well be that he had little idea of how extensive the Anglo-Saxon kingdoms were in Britain – at least until word reached him, perhaps via the Franks, that they were ripe for conversion. As regards the current state of Christianity among the British, Gregory was, we might think, largely ignorant.

Nevertheless, a second text implies that there was some knowledge of the British church in Gregory's circle before Augustine set out. The passage in question occurs in the letter which Bishops Laurentius, Mellitus and Justus sent to the Irish church some time during the episcopate of Augustine's successor, Laurentius (d. 619).

> The apostolic see . . . directed us to preach to the heathen in these western regions, and it was our lot to come to this island of Britain; before we knew them we held the holiness both of the Britons and of the Irish in great esteem, thinking that they walked according to the customs of the universal Church: but on becoming acquainted with the Britons, we still thought that the Irish would be better. But now we have learned from Bishop Dagan when he came to this island and from Abbot Columbanus when he came to Gaul that the Irish do not differ in any way from the Britons in their way of life . . .[40]

It is difficult to be precise over the length of the period during which the Roman bishops regarded the Britons as holy, particularly since Laurentius belonged to Augustine's original party which had set off in 596, whereas Mellitus and Justus formed part of the reinforcements sent in 601.[41] One possibility is that this period lasted right up to Augustine's meeting with the British bishops related by Bede. A second alternative would be to suggest that the occasion when they met Columbanus might have been in 601, as the party of reinforcements – which included the three signatories of this letter – made its way across Frankia. Although there is no evidence for their calling at Luxeuil, Columbanus was sometimes to be found at the royal court,[42] and the Roman missionaries would almost certainly have called at both the Burgundian and Austrasian courts on their journey.[43] This last scenario would imply that Augustine would already have discovered the British church's divergence from continental practices before 601. But in any case, the crucial point here is that at first, and so presumably in 596, Gregory's circle in Rome knew nothing against the British church, and indeed regarded its members as holy.

In view of this fact, it is odd to find no evidence of Gregory writing to the leaders of that church in 596 to commend Augustine's mission in the same way that he wrote at least eleven letters to bishops and rulers in Frankia. It is of course theoretically possible that Gregory did write such a letter(s), and that it has not survived: his correspondence that has come down to us is certainly incomplete.[44] However, the apparent absence of such a letter is all of a piece with Gregory's answers to Augustine's queries contained in the *Libellus Responsionum*, which I take to be a substantially genuine work of Gregory's sent to Augustine with the party of additional helpers in 601.[45] Here, Augustine had first asked about the problems of assembling three bishops for episcopal consecrations. Gregory's answer begins: 'In the church of the English, in which you find yourself to be still the only bishop, it is not possible for you to consecrate a bishop otherwise than alone. For when do bishops come from Gaul who might assist as witnesses at the consecration of a bishop?'[46] It is fascinating to see that, just as Gregory's letters of 596 betray a whole way of looking at the Anglo-Saxons as neighbours of the Franks, so this is still the case in 601, even after Laurentius and Peter had reported back to Gregory in Rome. It does not seem to have occurred to Gregory to seek actively to engage the British bishops in the project of converting the Anglo-Saxons right from the beginning of Augustine's mission.

This contrast between Gregory's attitude to the British bishops on the one hand and to the Gallic ones on the other becomes even clearer in his response to Augustine's next question, about how he should deal with the bishops of Gaul and Britain. The gist of Gregory's response is that Augustine has no authority over the Gallic bishops because Gregory has already granted the pallium to the bishop of Arles; and so if Augustine is aware of serious problems[47] among the Gallic episcopate, he should act diplomatically, consulting with the bishop of Arles, and persuading, coaxing, and setting a good example to the offending bishops. 'But we commit all the bishops of Britain to you, my brother, that the untaught may be taught, the weak strengthened by persuasion, and those who are wrong may be corrected by your authority.'[48] With the same batch of letters arrived that of 22 June 601 to Augustine, in which Gregory laid out his plans for 'the new church of the English'. It should have two metropolitan sees, at London and at York, each with twelve suffragan bishops. In the future, the senior metropolitan was to be whichever of the two had been in post longer, but for Augustine's own lifetime, he was to be the senior; and he was to supervise not only all the bishops ordained by himself and by the future metropolitan of York,

> but also, within the ultimate leadership of our Lord Jesus Christ, have subject to yourself all the bishops (*sacerdotes*) of Britain, so that from the words and life of your holiness they may receive a model of believing rightly and living well, and so, carrying out their office in faith and in their way of life, they may, when it please the Lord, attain the heavenly kingdom.[49]

This is a remarkable letter. Historians disagree over whether to see Gregory's blueprint as derived from a historical view of Roman Britain, which had in the third century been divided into two provinces with their capitals at London and York; or whether to assume that Gregory was *au fait* with the contemporary English scene, where a southern bretwalda had some kind of overlordship up to the Humber but not over the kingdoms to its north.[50] The problem with the latter view is why Gregory should have recommended that London, and not Canterbury, should be the metropolitan see: this did not match political reality *c.* 600. The former view would therefore seem more plausible. But if we then accept that Gregory was to some degree influenced by the administrative framework of Roman Britain, it becomes all the more noteworthy that he should see the church he is establishing under Augustine as 'the new church of the English' (*noua Anglorum ecclesia*), rather than thinking in terms of restoring the British church.

At this juncture, we need to try to discover what state the British church was in at the time of Augustine's arrival. At a very basic level, we can distinguish between the church in western Britain in areas that remained politically independent from the Anglo-Saxons and, on the other hand, the church under Anglo-Saxon domination (though obviously the Britons survived as a distinct entity to a far greater extent in more westerly Anglo-Saxon kingdoms, such as Wessex, than in eastern ones such as Kent). In 600, at least some of the independent British kingdoms of the west were still recognisably sub-Roman. They had not yet been restricted to those western and northern areas of Britain with unyielding rocks and poor soils typical of the highland zone. They were still trading overseas, particularly with Gaul, and may have continued to use Roman coinage on a restricted scale.[51] On a cultural plane, recent scholarship has revealed the skill and sophistication of Gildas's prose style, and this also presupposes that others had the ability to understand and appreciate this.[52] Gildas's prose left its mark on the mastery of Latin displayed by Columbanus;[53] and I think it is fair to assume that the *doctores* of Bangor-is-Coed, who were Columbanus's contemporaries, would have belonged to the same literary tradition. Indeed, they may well have composed their own works, for all that none has come down to us: the hazards of manuscript survival have dealt exceptionally harshly with the British/Welsh.[54] The British kingdoms of Dumnonia (roughly Devon and Cornwall), Dyfed, Gwynedd, and others within and bordering on what is now Wales had formerly belonged to a single Roman province, Britannia Prima; and Gildas's *De Excidio Britanniae*, written some sixty years before Augustine's arrival, suggests that the church in this area continued to have a sense of common identity – something which the involvement of Bangor-is-Coed monks in a synod held on the borders of the Hwicce and the West Saxons also implies.[55] Bishoprics were seemingly associated with different kingdoms – which is not to say that there was necessarily only one per kingdom.[56] At the same time, while monks appear to have been very few in number *c.* 540 when Gildas wrote his *De Excidio*, his apparently later *Fragments* implies that, by then, monasticism had grown in importance and diversity.[57] Indeed, according to Bede, by the early seventh century the monastery of Bangor-is-Coed had over two thousand monks, all of whom lived by the labour of their hands.[58] This must denote a very large number, even if Bede's figure is inflated. It is usually thought by modern scholars that the Welsh bishops retained control of territorial dioceses and of the monasteries within those dioceses, although some evidence in the *Life of St Samson* suggests that the actuality may have been less tidy.[59] There is no evidence of any metropolitan or archbishop at this period: the late Roman pattern whereby the bishop of the provincial capital became the metropolitan was probably disrupted by the Anglo-Saxon conquests, which by 600 included Cirencester as well as London, York and Lincoln.[60]

We must avoid the trap of assuming that, because we have so little evidence about the British church at this period, it necessarily follows that that church was unremarkable. We must also rid ourselves of the temptation to take Gildas's withering indictment as a fair representation of the British church *c.* 540; and, finally, we must guard against the assumption that nothing had changed since his day. On the contrary, there is some evidence to suggest that the worldly church which he had criticised so outspokenly had responded to his strictures. Gildas's

Fragments and other sources suggest, as we have seen, that there had been an ascetic renewal within the British church in the mid- and late sixth century.[61] There may still have been some worldly bishops, as in the days of the *De Excidio*, and as in contemporary Frankia. However, their worldliness had been challenged by the ascetic movement; and the story of how the British responded to Augustine suggests that by then, the bishops were receptive to the ascetic ideal and had found a way of including 'men of God' in their decision-making process.[62] The ascetic tradition was also responsible for other important innovations: both the penitential tradition and the distinctive Insular development of *peregrinatio* (an ascetic renunciation of one's homeland, the more readily to pursue one's pilgrimage through earth to heaven) seem to have originated with Britons.[63] Nor is there any reason to think of the British church as turned in on itself and isolated in the sixth century. Patrick's rather lonely work as a missionary in fifth-century Ireland paved the way for a large-scale input from British churchmen in the sixth century. Although their identity is largely unknown, the extent of their contribution is attested by the fact that the Irish learnt their Latin from teachers who spoke it with a distinctively British pronunciation, and adopted conventions of giving pet names from the British monks.[64] As regards links with the continent, we have already seen that the Insular churches continued to receive new works during the fifth and sixth centuries from Gaul. Perhaps it should be emphasised that they were not ignorant of the Easter tables produced in the mid-fifth century by Victorius of Aquitaine, and prescribed as normative for the Frankish church in 541. The Insular churches, however, preferred to retain their 84-year cycle. This was not an act of unthinking conservatism: the biblical texts, which provided the basic data which needed to be accommodated through complex computations, were themselves contradictory, and could be used to support different lunar limits for Easter. What is more, the Easter tables in use at Rome in the time of Pope Gregory appear to have been the very imperfect tables devised by Victorius, not the superior Alexandrian tables.[65] In these circumstances the British and Irish preference for retaining their 84-year cycle, which had a venerable past, is understandable.

If we turn now to consider the fate of the British church in Kent, it is immediately clear that we are dealing with something very different. Sparse as the evidence for the western British church may be, it at least exists, whereas further east there is, quite simply, virtually no direct evidence. Instead, we run up against a cluster of questions: how far was Kent christianised before the arrival of the Germanic settlers? Had Christianity reached the peasants, or was it restricted to the towns and the villa-owning aristocracy? The further question of what had happened to such christian communities as then existed is bound up with the way in which we conceive of Kent passing from British to Anglo-Saxon control. Was it violent or relatively peaceful? Should we be thinking of mass immigration and settlement, or of an incoming Germanic aristocracy taking control, and most of the British population remaining, but adopting the invaders' culture?

Our evidence for Christianity in Kent in Roman times comes from a limited number of places. In west Kent there is Lullingstone, an excavated Roman villa with a probable house church, together with the place name Eccles (derived from the Latin *ecclesia*, church), which lies between Rochester and Maidstone.[66] East Kent contains Richborough, a Roman shore fort where the remains of a baptistery have been identified, together with various christian portable objects;[67] Margate, which has also produced a portable find, a lamp with a chi-rho;[68] while from Canterbury itself, we have more extensive evidence. According to Bede, who was relatively well informed about the Augustinian mission to Kent through Abbot Albinus, both the extramural church of St Martin's and the intramural church given to Augustine and dedicated by him to the Saviour (Christ Church) were former Roman churches.[69] Modern scholarship, however, suggests that St Martin's may originally have been a Roman mausoleum, and so was not necessarily even christian in origin; while its dedication is likely to have been due to Bertha's Frankish bishop Liudhard, rather than inherited from the sub-Roman British church. For the intramural church, Bede may be correct, but there is no archaeological verification available.[70] In addition to these, it has been argued that other Canterbury churches may have had Roman origins.[71] The existence of Christianity in Canterbury in late Roman times is further confirmed by other archaeological finds: a potsherd with a chi-rho scratched on it has been found within 400 metres of St Martin's to the east of the city, while 200 metres outside the west wall a hoard of the early fifth century has been discovered which contained two objects with chi-rhos.[72]

But had Christianity penetrated beyond the villa, the Roman fort and the city to the rural population, where there is a greater likelihood of continuity between the Roman and Anglo-Saxon periods? There is no evidence from Kent; but other sites in south-east England have produced evidence of Christianity in rural areas – most helpfully, the lead tanks with chi-rho symbols.[73] It is therefore likely that Christianity was not restricted to the city, forts, and villas. Even so, given that the Anglo-Saxon takeover of Kent appears to have occurred within the fifth century,[74] the probability is that it occurred before much of the countryside had been effectively christianised.[75]

What, then, is the likelihood that British Christianity survived in Kent through the fifth and sixth centuries, to the time of Augustine's arrival? There is widespread agreement that some, at least, of the British population continued to live there under new leadership;[76] but there, agreement ends. One way of cutting through a swathe of uncertainties is to point out that, whether we think of the Anglo-Saxon takeover of Kent as involving considerable numbers of Anglo-Saxons who caused much disruption to the existing population, or whether we prefer to think in terms of acculturation, with relatively few incomers and the change visible in the archaeological record as being due rather to the native population adopting Anglo-Saxon culture, from the point of view of the church's fate, it makes little difference. Either way, the British church will have suffered severely. The former would be likely to disrupt the provision of priests, for unless a bishop survived, there would be no one to ordain priests or consecrate new churches. Christianity here paid a price for the focal role it assigned to bishops and to the sacerdotal dispensing of the sacraments. For although some christian teaching could be handed down in families, the necessity of having ordained ministers to administer the sacraments[77] meant that Christianity was badly placed to survive disruption. In the case of acculturation, we may assume that if Britons were abandoning their Romano-British culture and the Latin (and British) language(s), they would also have abandoned Christianity, identifiable as the religion of the Roman Empire. If they were unconverted or insecurely christianised in the first place, the transition would have been simple since pagan cults were not exclusive, and there was much common ground between Celtic and Germanic paganism.[78] Indeed, British paganism may well have influenced Anglo-Saxon paganism.

The general picture, then, is likely to have been one of disruption of the British church (which is not to say that no pockets of christian belief could have survived). Within Canterbury itself, although the city may never have been entirely deserted,[79] there is no evidence of the mingling of the two populations, and no grounds for thinking that a bishop's see would have continued: the archaeological evidence taken together with Bede's comments imply discontinuity here.[80] What is more, as Stenton long since remarked, Canterbury is ringed around by five sites of pagan worship which can still be identified from place names.[81] Perhaps we should set against this the fact that in north Kent as a whole, the survival rate of place names containing Latin elements is relatively high, implying contact of some kind between Latin speakers and the incoming Germanic speakers; but since most of the places concerned are so accessible to the continent by sea, the borrowing could have occurred long before the fifth-century invasions.[82] True, this seems inadequate to explain the names of some of the lesser places, such as Faversham and Eccles, and the latter in particular suggests that a christian community survived there into the Anglo-Saxon period.[83] Yet excavation at Eccles has so far revealed only seventh-century Anglo-Saxon burials in a former Roman villa. There thus appears to be a gap in the sequence.[84]

Recently, however, it has been suggested not just that some British Christians survived in the south-east, but even that there may have been bishops or priests among them. This has been inferred from Augustine's questions to Gregory as to whether menstruation, childbirth and sexual activity should debar lay people from entering church or receiving the sacraments for a certain time, after the analogy of Old Testament prohibitions. Such questions, it has been argued, would be more likely to be raised by existing Christians with a fair degree of biblical knowledge, rather than by the pagan Anglo-Saxons; and such Old Testament attitudes are known from Celtic penitential documents, prompting the suggestion that Augustine's questions had first arisen in those quarters.[85] The suggestion is a very interesting one, but remains speculative: it is far from clear that it was British-taught Anglo-Saxons who initiated these questions. First, it could well have been Augustine himself who was unsure of whether the Old Testament teaching should be taken literally or not; as a monk, he would not have encountered pastoral situations involving childbirth, menstruation and intercourse until he embarked on his mission.[86] Secondly, even if Augustine would not have encountered such a literal application of the Old Testament in Rome, he could well have done so in Frankia or, most plausibly of all, with Liudhard, Bertha's Frankish bishop. Caesarius of Arles had certainly regarded sexual intercourse and emissions during sleep as polluting occurrences which needed remedial action before a man was fit to receive communion, basing himself explicitly on Old Testament prescriptions. He further forbade married couples even to enter church for thirty days after their wedding, and he prohibited intercourse during Lent and on the days preceding Sundays and holy days, so that people would be in a fitting state of purity before approaching the altar. He also forbade intercourse while women were menstruating, again explicitly citing Leviticus.[87] Caesarius's sermons were widely and rapidly diffused, both within Frankia and beyond, even as far as Ireland; and they were probably responsible for the Old Testament-style attitudes towards matters of ritual purity that we find in the early Insular penitentials.[88] Of Augustine's ritual purity questions, the only one he raised which both figures in a Celtic text and had not previously been addressed by Caesarius concerns the prohibition on a woman entering church within a certain number of days after giving birth. But the earliest Irish text to contain this ruling, based on Leviticus 12, is the seventh-century penitential of Cummean, which post-dates Augustine's mission to England,[89] while other, similar questions raised by Augustine are not addressed anywhere.

What is surely of primary significance is the underlying attitude, namely that the purity taboos of the Old Testament should be applied literally, even in christian times. Caesarius's homilies were a very widely disseminated source of such views; and once churchmen had accepted his general premise, they could further elaborate on such matters for themselves, on the basis of the Old Testament. Thus in my opinion, if Augustine did not raise these questions with Pope Gregory unprompted, then the attitudes that led to his raising them are more likely to have derived from the Frankish church than from the British church. It is therefore unsafe to use this evidence as proof that Augustine encountered an organised British church with its own priests in south-east England.

The only solid evidence for British Christians surviving up to *c.* 600 within the area covered by Augustine's missionary work is that relating to St Sixtus.[90] It appears that, somewhere in the sphere of Augustine's mission, a (presumably British) christian community had kept alive the memory of a local martyr called Sixtus, although no information about his martyrdom had been handed down, nor did his burial place glitter with miracles. In these circumstances, Augustine had asked Gregory the Great for some relics of the Roman St Sixtus, an assured martyr and former pope. Augustine's caution about accepting a martyr's shrine attested only by local tradition, with no form of verification, is understandable, and can be paralleled elsewhere.[91] His intended means of bringing this local British cult site within the acceptable Roman fold can only be inferred from his request to Gregory for relics of St Sixtus. Probably he intended to add these to the existing relics.[92] This would have represented a compromise solution that on one level would have enabled local British Christians to continue to venerate their own St Sixtus, while simultaneously supplementing this uncertain cult with an assured, compatible, and potentially supplanting cult. Although Augustine fought shy of simply adopting the existing cult, preferring – quite literally – to 'Romanise' it, his was an ingenious solution which would have been considerably less high-handed than either outlawing the existing cult or replacing it with a totally unrelated one. Gregory, however, took a harder line. He sent Augustine the Sixtus relics requested, but told him to bury them 'separately' (i.e. not in the same tomb as the British St Sixtus); and he further ordered Augustine to shut off the British St Sixtus tomb totally, so as to prevent people from venerating 'uncertain' remains.

This is a most revealing incident. First, it confirms that pockets of British Christianity still existed in south-east England in 600. There is no reason to think that the British Christians venerating St Sixtus were unique: rather, it was only the incidental problem of a shrine with no assured record that prompted Augustine to consult Gregory, and so leave a trace in our written sources. Other places where British Christians carried on may well have gone unrecorded.[93] Secondly, the nature of the christian survival is worth noting. A saint's shrine could still be venerated simply by lay people visiting it, regardless of whether or not there were any clergy to celebrate the liturgy there. It is perhaps no fluke that the only other christian site in south-east Britain that we know continued as a frequented christian holy place from Roman to Anglo-Saxon times is another cult site, that of St Alban at St Albans. Bede's words imply that a church 'of wonderful workmanship', built there in Roman times, had survived to his day as a miracle-working shrine.[94] In neither case, however, can we conclude that British clergy and an ecclesiastical structure survived. Indeed, the St Sixtus evidence points in rather the opposite direction, since no one even of the older generation had ever heard their parents say anything about 'the course of his passion' (*passionis eius ordinem*).[95] Admittedly, it is unlikely that there would in any case have been a written *passio*; but if the clergy had continued at the site in an unbroken line, one might expect them to have said something about the saint at least once a year, at the patronal festival. Of course, this is not a conclusive argument for the absence of British clergy active in south-east England, but such indications as we have all point in the same direction. First, in addition to Bede's silence about the Roman missionaries encountering any British churchmen there, his story of Augustine journeying west to the border between the West Saxons and the Hwicce to meet British bishops and scholars[96] implies that there were no British bishops nearer to hand in south-east England; and if there were no bishops to ordain new recruits to the priesthood, there are unlikely to have been any priests either, for the reasons discussed above. Secondly, besides this inference one can also point to explicit evidence from another area. When the Anglo-Saxons advanced up into the Pennines around the 660s, the *Life of Wilfrid* records that the British clergy fled before the advance of the Anglo-Saxon warriors – and this despite the fact that by then, the Anglo-Saxons were (at least formally) Christians.[97] It is difficult to believe that British priests in Kent would have felt less apprehensive about the Anglo-Saxon conquests of the fifth century. Thus, as regards British Christianity in south-east England, we should probably think in terms of some pockets of survival at a popular level, but no active clergy or ecclesiastical structures remaining.

Important as the St Sixtus evidence is for its clues about the survival of British Christians in the south-east, it is equally revealing of Gregory the Great's attitude towards an unverifiable British martyr cult. If my interpretation of the evidence is correct, Gregory took a less sympathetic line towards the British St Sixtus shrine than Augustine himself had proposed: the British were to be prevented from honouring their own St Sixtus, with access to the tomb denied. This drastic measure, which rode roughshod over both the traditions and the sensibilities of the British, is all of a piece with Gregory's response to Augustine's seventh question where he committed all the British bishops to Augustine's care, seeing them as ignorant, weak in their faith, and wrong.[98]

We might, in fact, go further. Gregory's answers to Augustine's questions were sent via Laurentius and his companions in 601. Laurentius was one of Augustine's original company who had returned to Rome bringing news of Augustine's mission. By this date it is clear that Augustine had encountered some British Christians in south-east England: so much we can deduce from the request for relics of St Sixtus. These British communities are likely to have consisted of lay people, whose christian beliefs and practices had been informally handed down through the generations, probably without the regular ministrations of priests. In these circumstances, it is small wonder if the British Christians came across as ignorant, insecure, and wrong. Conversely, it seems unlikely that Augustine had yet met representatives of the British church in the independent British kingdoms of the west: given the need for a safe conduct across various other Anglo-Saxon kingdoms which were not directly ruled by Æthelberht, any such meeting would require careful planning; and I accept the common assumption that Augustine waited to get Gregory's reply to his question about how he should relate to the British bishops before embarking on the two meetings described by Bede.[99] A further telling point is that Augustine does not appear to have asked Gregory about different systems of dating Easter in the questions which he sent in 601. This again may suggest that he knew very little about the British church in the west at that time. This is surely relevant to the opinion that Gregory formed in 601 as to the worth of the British church and the British bishops. It is relatively easy for us to realise that the position of the British church in the independent British kingdoms of the west was quite different from that in the Anglo-Saxon kingdoms of the east; that the former could have bishops who were, by the standards of the early Middle Ages, adequately educated, and monastic scholars who may well have been very learned, whereas in areas where Anglo-Saxon settlement had disrupted the ecclesiastical structures and the provision of priests, such British communities as survived and retained their christian faith were likely to be ignorant and struggling. But Augustine and his fellow missionaries would so far have encountered only the latter; and, since they might as yet have known little or nothing of the clergy in the independent west, they may have reported back to Gregory in rather unfavourable terms about the British church without fully realising the need to distinguish between the two areas. That, in turn, would help to explain why Gregory took such a dismissive attitude towards the British church in the letters and replies which he wrote to Augustine in 601.

Augustine had told Gregory that his numbers were inadequate for the task of prosecuting the mission among the Anglo-Saxons as fully as the opportunities offered, and he was anxious to have more helpers.[100] This, together with the fact that he now had Gregory's instructions as to how he was to treat the British bishops, makes it likely that he sought to contact the British church in the independent west of Britain soon after receiving Gregory's replies to his various queries in 601. Bede's lengthy chapter about this contact and its aftermath is central to the issue of how the British church and Augustine related to each other; it is also one of the most complex chapters in the whole of the *Ecclesiastical History*. We will therefore begin by setting out what Bede tells us.

Bede's chapter falls into three parts which are marked by paragraph divisions in Mynors's text;[101] each part relates a separate incident, the first two presumably occurring fairly close in time to 601 (602–4?), the third one occurring *c.* 615.[102] Part one comprises Augustine's initial *colloquium* with bishops and scholars of the neighbouring British *prouincia*, which took place at 'Augustine's Oak', somewhere on the borders of the Hwicce and the West Saxons. The issues discussed were 'the catholic peace'; joining in the evangelisation of the Anglo-Saxons; and the date of Easter. When the British delegation persistently refused to give up their own traditions, Augustine 'proved' the rightness of his cause by a miracle. A blind man was produced. The British delegation was unable to heal him, but Augustine succeeded. At this, the Britons said that they understood that Augustine's way was the true one, but that they could not abandon their former customs without the agreement of their own people; they therefore asked for a second meeting, a synod with wider representation.

Part two of Bede's narrative is concerned with this second meeting and the British preparations for it. This meeting was, 'as they say', attended by seven British bishops and many scholars, particularly from the excellent monastery of Bangor, then ruled by Abbot Dinoot. These British representatives first consulted a holy anchorite as to whether or not they should abandon their own traditions at Augustine's bidding. The anchorite's advice was simple: 'If [Augustine] is a man of God, follow him.' They would know that he was indeed a man of God if he bore the marks of true humility, and rose to greet them. When they went to the meeting, however, Augustine stayed seated on his chair. He demanded that they adopt the Roman Easter, 'complete' the baptismal rite after Roman liturgical use, and join him in preaching the Gospel to the English. But the British rejected these requests, and told him that they would not accept him as their archbishop; for they felt that if they began to submit to his authority, then Augustine would cease to respect them. At this Augustine prophesied that if they would not have peace with their brothers and preach to the English, then one day they would suffer vengeance from them as enemies.

The third event narrated by Bede occurred several years after Augustine's death, and is the story of how Augustine's prophecy came true. Æthelfrith, king of Northumbria, was about to fight a battle against the Britons near Chester, but first he slaughtered some 1,200 monks of Bangor who had come to pray for a British victory – their guard, Brocmail, having fled with his soldiers. Thus Augustine's prophecy was fulfilled, namely that the British *perfidi* would suffer earthly death because they had spurned the proffer of eternal salvation.

If we turn now to analyse Bede's account, one striking feature is the fact that whereas part one is narrated straight, with no indication of its source or its reliability, parts two and three are peppered with phrasing suggestive of a less certain tradition, presumptively an oral one. At the beginning of part two, we read that seven British bishops and scholars came, *ut perhibent*, mostly from the monastery of Bangor, where Dinoot *narratur* to have been in charge. At the end of part two, Augustine *fertur* to have made his prophecy.[103] In part three, we are told that at Bangor *fertur* that there were so many monks that they were divided into seven sections, each with a superior, and no section having less than 300 men, all of whom lived by the work of their hands. A little further on, we read that *ferunt* that about 1,200 of those monks who had come to pray at the battle of Chester were killed, and only fifty escaped.[104]

A second point to make about Bede's overall narrative is that while part one contains information which could well have come solely from Roman/English sources, parts two and three contain information which must have originated with the British. This includes the proper names Dinoot (part two) and Brocmail (part three – note also 'Carlegion', the correct British name for Chester). We should also include here the story of how the British representatives sought the advice of an anchorite before meeting Augustine (part two),[105] and the details about the seven divisions in the monastery of Bangor, the numbers of Bangor monks, and their practice of manual labour (part three).

A third point to look at is the favourable or hostile presentation of people and institutions in Bede's account. In part one Augustine is presented as *sanctus pater* ('holy father'), who successfully performs a miracle where the British bishops have failed; he is then recognised as *uerus summae lucis praeco*,[106] who teaches 'the way of righteousness'. In part two, however, the Bangor scholars are *doctissimi* ('most learned'), and come *de nobilissimo eorum monasterio*.[107] The anchorite they consult is *sanctum ac prudentem* ('holy and sagacious'), and he gives what appears to be sound christian teaching. On this view, the implications of Augustine's failure to rise are that he is harsh and proud (*inmitis ac superbus*), and not 'a man of God.' However, towards the end of this section, that is contradicted in that Augustine is described as *uir Domini* when he threatens the Britons with vengeance; and this vengeance duly comes about *diuino agente iudicio*.[108] In part three, the Britons are referred to as a *gens perfida* or simply *perfidi*, and their army is *nefandae militiae copias*, while Augustine's prophecy is that of *sancti pontificis Augustini*.[109] On the other hand, the details of Bangor monastery, where all the monks perform manual labour, reflect well on the British side.

These points suggest that we should distinguish between, on the one hand, part one, and on the other hand, parts two and three. In part one, we see events uniformly from the Roman/English angle, there is nothing to suggest a British source, and the event is simply narrated as a factual narrative. All this implies that Bede's sole source of information for this section was Canterbury tradition, mediated to him through Abbot Albinus.[110] Parts two and three, however, share several features which distinguish them from part one: the relatively frequent use of expressions like *fertur*, 'it is said'; the proper names, Dinoot and Brocmail, and the details which could only have come from a British source; and, most intriguing of all, the fact that much of the time the British are sympathetically presented, though this is not consistently carried through. Manifestly Bede had access to a different source for these two parts. What was the nature of this source, and how was its information transmitted to Bede?

One type of evidence which has been pressed into service in an attempt to answer these questions is the spelling of the names Brocmail and Dinoot.[111] This was a period during which the British spoken language was evolving into Welsh, although the changes involved were often not represented contemporaneously in the spelling; the latter tended to keep to 'correct', traditional forms, even though these were now archaic when judged by the spoken norm. Thus the name Brocmail would have been pronounced with more of a 'ch' (as in Scottish 'lo*ch*') sound in the middle than with a hard 'c', even in 600. Bede's spelling therefore indicates either that he took it from a British *written* document, which kept the original spelling;[112] or, it has been suggested, it might be a spelling written down by the Roman missionaries in the early seventh century at a time when they had not yet learnt to represent the 'ch' sound by *spelling* it 'ch'.[113] Either way, however, we must be dealing with a written document. It has been further argued that the spelling 'Dinoot' suggests that this document was not written by the British, but by Anglo-Saxon or Italian missionaries, since in a British document we would expect to find a 'u' rather than an 'i' in the first syllable. It has therefore been suggested that Bede was drawing upon an early seventh-century document emanating from Canterbury.[114] This hypothesis presupposes something a little more complicated than simply a record of Augustine's two meetings with the British representatives, since at that time the ignoble behaviour of Brocmail still lay in the future. However, we know that Augustine's successor, Bishop Laurentius, wrote to the British church; and it is possible to envisage some such scenario as this letter being sent after the battle of Chester (rather than *c.* 610 as

Bede implies),[115] the letter-bearers reporting back what they had been told of the event from the British side, and a record being made of it at Canterbury.

There is, however, a serious flaw in this hypothesis: if either Bede, or Abbot Albinus in a letter to Bede, had been able to draw upon a Canterbury document of the early seventh century, this would have been an excellent source of reliable information; and Bede would have recognised it as such. If he had been sent the source, he might well have reproduced it verbatim, as he did with several of Gregory's letters. Even if all he had came to him mediated via Abbot Albinus, he would have regarded it highly; and this means that he certainly would not have prefaced information that he took from it with words like *fertur*. His normal practice appears to have been to use such expressions for hearsay or oral report which did not come down to him through a known line of witnesses or from reliable churchmen.[116]

We are faced, then, with a crux: the spelling of the proper names in sections two and three implies that Bede had a written source, and yet his own interjections of 'it is said' imply the opposite. Should we therefore suggest that Bede took the names of Brocmail and Dinoot from a written source,[117] but filled out the story on the basis of oral information? The problem here is that if we ascribe all information preceded by a word like *ferunt* to an oral source, we are forced to assume that the latter supplied all the details about the seven divisions within the monastery of Bangor, each consisting of at least 300 monks, together with the figure of 1,200 monks slain. This is not the sort of information which is usually handed down in popular oral tradition. Further, it seems rather artificial to separate out a written and an oral source and to envisage Bede having access to both, when both would appear to have contained information about Bangor and its involvement in the negotiations with Augustine and in the battle of Chester.

I would prefer to suggest that Bede was drawing on only one source, written (in Latin) by a Briton. We might think in terms of a letter, or perhaps a hagiographical text.[118] In this case one might argue that Bede prefaced information taken from this source with expressions like *fertur* because he viewed the British church of this period as schismatic, and therefore did not regard information emanating from it as having the same authority as information drawn from English writers (or pre-schismatic British ones, like Gildas). Some corroboration for such a hypothesis comes when we compare Bede's use of expressions such as *ferunt* in his biblical commentaries. In these, it is clear that such a usage is not restricted to traditions reaching him orally. For instance, Bede reproduces information derived from Pliny's *Natural History* with *ferunt*, 'they say'.[119] We cannot reach firm conclusions in the absence of a detailed study of Bede's use of such expressions; but, on the evidence available, the parallel treatment of a pagan classical author and a suggested British schismatic one appears plausible. If we accept this, the only drawback to the hypothesis that Bede had a written British source is the spelling of Dinoot with an 'i' in the first syllable, where we would have expected a 'u' if he was copying from a British source. However, although unusual, there are parallels for such a spelling.[120]

We have still to consider how Bede might have come into possession of a British source such as I am positing. A glance at a map of the places named by Bede in his *Ecclesiastical History* reveals how slight was his coverage west of the Pennines.[121] Indeed, Bangor and Chester appear rather isolated. There are, however, two possible lines of transmission, both for oral information and for texts. One option is to point out that Bangor-is-Coed lies just 12 miles north-east of Oswestry and, if we accept the identification of Oswestry with *Maserfelth*, where Oswald was killed, then we might envisage stories and texts being transmitted to Bede along the same channels as the miracle stories which took place at *Maserfelth*. These are likely to have reached Bede via the Mercian-founded monastery of Bardney, in Lindsey.[122] On the other hand, it is doubtful whether the inmates of Bardney would have had any interest in the monks of Bangor, and perhaps a more likely alternative would be for the material to have reached Bede via Malmesbury and Pehthelm. Malmesbury was founded by an Irishman before regular Anglo-Saxon contact with British monasteries was rendered difficult by the synod of Whitby (664) and the arrival of Archbishop Theodore (669).[123] Malmesbury also lies in the north-west of Wessex, close to the border with the Hwicce:[124] in other words, in the general vicinity of Augustine's Oak, where the first (and probably also the second) meeting between Augustine and the British church leaders took place. It is therefore easy to see why Malmesbury should have been interested in the negotiations; and Bede's detail that the place is 'up to this day' called Augustine's Oak[125] would fit nicely with information coming from this locality. Now Bede had a link with Malmesbury through Pehthelm, who had been a deacon and monk with Aldhelm 'for a long time', before becoming bishop of Whithorn.[126] Both through his link with Aldhelm (and probably Malmesbury),[127] and because of taking over a major British church at Whithorn, Pehthelm will have been interested in the British church and the issues which divided it from the Anglo-Saxons, and we know that he was Bede's informant for various miracle stories.[128] He therefore makes a plausible channel through which Bede could have derived information about the British monastery of Bangor, and its view of the meetings with Augustine.

I would envisage, therefore, Bede constructing this chapter on the basis both of Canterbury oral tradition, mediated to him through Abbot Albinus, and of information which he derived from a Latin document emanating from the British side – perhaps with additional oral information deriving from Pehthelm. Part one of Bede's chapter would have been derived from Canterbury tradition, which doubtless also made a contribution to part two as regards Augustine's demands. However, for parts two and three Bede was also able to obtain more detailed information from his British source. The presentation of the Britons as *perfidi* in the last part, however, was Bede's gloss: the attitude lying behind such terms can be discerned elsewhere in his work.[129] What, we might ask, was the origin of the prophetic threat of Augustine, and the interpretation of the battle of Chester as the fulfilment of that threat? Bede's wording, *uir Domini Augustinus* fertur *minitans praedixisse*,[130] implies that the prophecy came from the same source as the details about Bangor which are also introduced by such a word. Yet we can scarcely believe that the Britons themselves interpreted the slaughter of their monks at Chester as fulfilment of this prophecy. Two alternatives present themselves. One is that the story of Augustine's prophecy and its realization was a *popular* oral tradition among the Anglo-Saxons, either in the vicinity of Malmesbury or in Kent. (If the latter, we must assume that Albinus passed it on to Bede as such, distinct from the body of tradition which had come down via ecclesiastical channels.)[131] The second possibility is that Augustine's threat was indeed in Bede's British source, but that it was not there linked to the slaughter of the Bangor monks at the battle of Chester. On this scenario, it would have been Bede who imposed this interpretation. Almost certainly Bede will have been selective in his use of his British source, and he was well able to edit material so that it took on a meaning intended by him, but quite different from that which it had originally borne.[132]

We must in any case accept that this chapter is essentially Bede's presentation of how Augustine invited the British church to join the Roman mission, how it refused, and how divine judgement was passed on it for that refusal. We should probably view it as a set piece by Bede, comparable to that other carefully crafted set piece, his account of the synod of Whitby.[133] There, Bede gives both sides of the argument by assigning speeches to Colmán and Wilfrid. Here, also, we see the issues from both sides, with the British emphasis on holiness of life, over against the Roman position which saw Augustine as a figure representing the authority of the Catholic church, to which the British needed to conform.[134] Scholars are divided as to whether Bede portrays Augustine unsympathetically or not in part two of this chapter,[135] much as they are divided about his attitude to Wilfrid. I incline to the view that Bede accepted the rightness of Augustine's position with his head, but felt ambivalent about how he behaved towards the British delegation – an ambivalence which is reflected in his use (or retention) of favourable adjectives when describing the British anchorite, coupled with his failure to excuse or explain Augustine's behaviour.[136]

Whatever Bede's feelings, however, this chapter marks a turning point in his portrayal of the British church in the *Ecclesiastical History*.[137] Book II opens with a panegyrical account of Gregory the Great, hailing him as the one who converted the English from the power of Satan to the faith of Christ, and emphasising that Gregory's concern for conversion outweighed even his previous monastic perfection in the scale of virtue.[138] Chapter two demonstrates that while the British ranked highly as regards monastic perfection, their refusal to collaborate with Augustine in converting the Anglo-Saxons showed their lack of the crucial virtue of charity. It is almost as though Bede was deliberately taking a British monastery, which was acknowledged as excellent, and a hermit whose way of life was exemplary, to drive home the point that Aldhelm made in his letter to Geraint:

> For what profit the emoluments of good works, if they are performed outside the Catholic Church, even if someone should meticulously carry out the rules of practice of a rigid life according to monastic discipline, or with fixed purpose decline the companionship of mortals and pass a life of contemplative retirement away in some squalid wilderness?[139]

The crucial passage here is the phrase, 'outside the Catholic Church'. Towards the end of the letter Aldhelm returns to this theme, arguing that 'faith without works is dead', and therefore that believing aright, but keeping oneself apart from the Catholic church, was inadmissible: 'Surely the Catholic Faith and the harmony of brotherly love walk inseparably with even steps, as . . . [St Paul] elegantly attests: "And if I should have prophecy and should know all mysteries, if I should have all faith . . . and have not charity, it profiteth me nothing."'[140] Aldhelm's letter appears to have deeply influenced Bede, who at the beginning of his account of Augustine's meeting with the British churchmen represents Augustine asking them to share in the Catholic peace and common labour of evangelising the English, and who returns to the same themes at the end of part two after the Britons had rejected all Augustine's demands. Augustine threatened them with vengeance for refusing to be at peace with their brothers (in this context, Augustine and his companions), and for refusing to preach to the English.[141] Thus, to use Aldhelm's words, the Britons refused both the Catholic faith and the harmony of brotherly love when they rejected Augustine; and their accompanying refusal to preach to the Anglo-Saxons further shows that they lacked the one essential virtue of charity.[142] From this point of view, the Britons have put themselves in the wrong: they have shut themselves off from the Catholic church's overtures,[143] and have also demonstrated a lack of charity. So it is at this point that Bede begins to treat them as schismatic, labelling them as *perfidi* who were rightly visited by divine judgement.

We have clarified what Bede was doing in this chapter; it remains to ask whether he was representing historical events at all accurately, or whether the series of incidents recounted there is largely his imaginative reconstruction. Perhaps the most dubious episode is the healing of the blind man, both because its figural significance is so clear, and because precisely this form of 'proof' had been used by Bishop Germanus 170 years previously – a miracle story which Bede included in his *History*.[144] We have to remember, however, that Augustine received acclaim as a miracle-worker in his own day.[145] A second dubious feature is the use of the term archbishop, which is anachronistic for AD 600. Doubtless this was Bede's gloss; but in any case, Augustine's position in the English church as defined by Gregory amounted to much the same as the role of the later archbishop.[146]

Overall, there is a surprising number of indicators that Bede was not simply making up these events. We have already discussed the proper names Dinoot and Brocmail and the details of Bangor monastery, which Bede arguably drew from a written British source. From the same source, we may surmise, came the information that Augustine's meetings with the British involved *doctores* as well as bishops.[147] The category of *doctores*, or ecclesiastical scholars, is well known from Ireland, where they attended synods alongside bishops; and *doctores* also figure in the canons of a sixth-century British synod.[148] This detail is thus eminently plausible. At a more fundamental level, one might well wonder whether the episode of the British visit to the hermit originated as a story, rather than an actual event. But it is an intriguing fact that the Irish scholar, Cummian, addressed his treatise on the Easter question to Ségéne, abbot of Iona, and to Béccán, a hermit.[149] Even more intriguing, the line which the British hermit is reported as taking in Bede's *History* is precisely the same as the line which Columbanus was simultaneously taking in a letter to the Gallic bishops, when again the main issue was the Easter question. Columbanus insisted that both parties should practise true humility, and he quoted the same biblical passage as the British hermit, 'learn of me for I am meek and lowly of heart'.[150] As Columbanus put it in a later letter, 'among us it is not a man's station but his conduct that matters':[151] a statement which epitomises the gulf between the approach of the western churches to controversial issues, and that of Augustine. All this suggests that the story was not invented by Bede. He presumably found it in his British source; more than that, one cannot say.

The details of Augustine's demands to the British are a further pointer that Bede was drawing on existing material, not inventing his own account. At the second meeting, Augustine's demands included one that the British should 'complete' the rite of baptism according to Roman norms.[152] This requirement never surfaces again in later exhortations to (or disputes with) the British, and it is therefore unlikely to have been invented by Bede. Equally, we should note that the issue of the British tonsure is conspicuous by its absence.[153] In these two respects the issues at stake between Augustine and the British church differ from those addressed by Aldhelm a century later, and those which, at much the same time as Augustine, were causing problems between Columbanus's followers and the Frankish church.[154] This suggests that Bede was not simply generalising from the controversial issues that he knew of from a later period, but had access to information on the issues of *c*. 602. I would thus conclude that, although he was writing over a century after these events, Bede was reasonably well informed. I am therefore ready to accept that the two meetings between Augustine and the British bishops took place; and that Augustine's demands were much as Bede gives them: to join him in evangelising the Anglo-Saxons; to keep Easter according to the Roman calendar; to 'complete' their baptisms according to the Roman manner; and to accept his position as their ecclesiastical superior, as Gregory had directed.[155]

What of the Britons' reaction? Fortunately, as we have seen, we have grounds for thinking that Bede represents their response reasonably well. As far as we can tell from Bede's account, the evangelisation of the Anglo-Saxons was not a sticking point for them; and this is supported by the view of recent scholars that the Britons appear to have been responsible for converting the incoming Anglo-Saxons in the kingdoms of the Hwicce and the Magonsætan.[156] The problems on the British side at their first meeting with Augustine are rather represented as being due to their reluctance to give up their own traditions, particularly as regards the date of Easter; and, even when the delegates present had apparently been won over, they refused to commit their own church to such a major change on their own, without first consulting more widely.[157] All this is eminently plausible. Many of the Irish were similarly reluctant to give up their customary dating of Easter, which to them was hallowed by being the tradition followed by holy men to whom they looked back with reverence,[158] whereas Victorius's calculations (then probably followed by Gregory and Augustine) were regarded as recent, wrong, and resting on no such hallowed authority.[159] The need of the British to consult with those whom they were representing again looks plausible.[160] The British church, like the Irish church, presumably kept to the older pattern of taking major decisions communally, at synods, rather than following the leadership of someone placed at the top of a hierarchy.[161]

At the second meeting, the issues were, again, the Britons' reluctance to abandon their own traditions, together with their refusal to submit to Augustine's claim to authority over them; and it is clear that the latter was the root cause of their rejection of Augustine and his other demands. Naturally the Britons were reluctant to submit to the authority of one who came not solely as the representative of Pope Gregory, but also as the bishop of King Æthelberht, overlord of all the Anglo-Saxon peoples south of the Humber,[162] whose military power may have represented a threat to the independent British kingdoms in the west. The problem was compounded by the fact that Gregory had given Augustine full authority over all the British bishops, and had laid down provisions for his successor to have the pallium, apparently without doing anything to safeguard the rights of the British bishops. On top of this, it seems clear that the British church had a different approach towards authority within the church from the hierarchical view held by Gregory, and represented by Augustine. Many years ago Kathleen Hughes pointed to an interesting passage in Gildas's *De Excidio* which showed that Gildas took the text of Matthew 16, Jesus's commission of the keys to Peter, as applying to 'every holy bishop': not solely to the bishop of Rome.[163] Gildas, in the context of criticising the worldly bishops of his day, places the emphasis on the word 'holy'. This fits with the other pointers we have: with the story of the British delegation going to consult a holy anchorite; with Columbanus and Colmán's preference for a tradition which had been handed down to them by men of assured holiness;[164] and above all with Columbanus's insistence to the Pope that the latter was the key-bearer of the kingdom of heaven only as long as he kept the true faith; and that when there was a major problem, it should be resolved by a synod.[165] To this we should add the point, alluded to earlier, that in the Irish and (seemingly) British churches, representation at synods was not confined solely to bishops.[166] Further, if we turn to the letter which Columbanus sent to a synod of Gallic bishops *c.* 603, when he stood accused of his divergent dating of Easter, we see Columbanus ascribing ultimate authority in the church not to the bishops sitting in synod, but to Christ. He saw both the clergy (including bishops) and the monks as following parallel callings, under Christ; and the 'rules' they were to operate by as comprising the teaching of the New Testament.[167] 'If we all choose to be humble and poor for Christ's sake', then hatred and contention will have no place; rather, where there is diversity of practice, as now over the date of Easter, all should seek after the truth together.[168] In other words, the Easter question should be resolved jointly through the application of christian scholarship, and in an atmosphere of humility. The relevance of this to the British approach, as far as we can discern it through Bede's account, is obvious.

Equally obvious is the gulf that existed between this approach, and Gregory's instructions to Augustine as to how he should behave towards the British bishops. We should not automatically assume that it was impossible, c. 603, for Augustine and the British church to have reached some kind of accommodation. The Easter question clearly mattered: it would have been awkward for the British and Roman missionaries to have tried to evangelise the Anglo-Saxons jointly, if in some years the dates of Lent, Easter, and Whitsun had diverged. And the British scholars, like the Irish, would have argued for the rightness of their own practice – particularly when 'Roman' usage consisted of the very imperfect Victorian tables. But the advice of the hermit would appear to have been that they should be prepared to let go of such traditions provided that Augustine could be seen to bear the marks of a true follower of Christ, and that included humility. The fact that Augustine and his companions were monks meant that there was far more common ground between them and the British delegation than there was in Gaul between Columbanus and the Gallic bishops;[169] and the attempt to thrash out the issues at synods was probably the best approach available. Unfortunately, however, Gregory had advised Augustine to behave not with the humility of a monk, nor even with the tact of a brother bishop, as towards the simoniacal Gallic bishops, but, rather, with the authority of a superior.[170]

We may conclude that the request jointly to evangelise the Anglo-Saxons presented no problem for the Britons. The Easter question did, but on its own would probably not have posed an insuperable obstacle. The real problems lay elsewhere: in Gregory telling Augustine that, whereas he should behave towards the bishops of Gaul with tact, with the British bishops he was to assume the role of a superior who should teach the unlearned (*indocti* – those *uiri doctissimi* of Bangor?); strengthen the weak; and correct the *peruersi* (those calculating the date of Easter according to different principles?) with his authority.[171] It was the *combination* of this authority-centred approach, together with the fact that Augustine came as the bishop of an Anglo-Saxon king, that was so damaging: understandably, it made the British churchmen apprehensive that, once they admitted Augustine's authority, they would find themselves subject to a metropolitan whose see lay in the territory of another, potentially hostile, people.

This chapter has sought to clarify the relationship between the British church and the mission of Augustine by getting as close as our fragmentary sources allow to seeing how the relationship actually developed over the years following 596. In all this, a prerequisite for understanding what took place is to divest ourselves of hindsight: in particular of the knowledge that, in the event, the British did refuse to join Augustine's mission, and of all that followed from that. In this spirit of openness as to what might have transpired, let us return to the question posed by Frend in the quotation given at the beginning of this chapter: why did the church of Roman Britain not provide the basis and the framework for the Christianity of the Anglo-Saxons, in the way that (for instance) the church in Roman Gaul was able to provide them for the Frankish church?

There are three possible approaches that one might pursue, on their own or in combination, when seeking to answer this question. The first, which is followed by Frend himself, is to suggest that the Romano-British church was for some reason in a weaker position than the continental church when the barbarian invasions occurred in the fifth century. A second approach would be to argue that the actual barbarian invasions and their attendant circumstances differed in significant ways. For instance, that they were more violent in Britain, so involving less scope for fruitful intercourse between the invaders and the original inhabitants; or that the number of Germanic invaders was greater in Britain, or that they targeted the most romanised areas; or, conversely, that those invading Britain were less romanised, and so less receptive to a religion that had developed in the Roman Empire and in a Greco-Roman thought world. A third approach to the question of why the fortunes of the church were so different in Britain and on the continent would be to suggest that the disparity may not have been so significant at the time of the actual invasions, but rather that the crucial divergence occurred later: in northern Gaul, the church was eventually rebuilt and restored, whereas in Britain, the process of converting the incoming Anglo-Saxons followed a quite different path. The full explanation may well lie in a combination of all three approaches; but without prejudicing the contribution to be made by the others – the second, in particular, is surely important – I wish to focus now on the third approach; for it is this that is relevant to our understanding of the relationship between the Augustinian mission and the British church *c*. 600.

At a rather general level, one can point to parallels between the impact of the Franks on the church in northern Gaul, and that of the Anglo-Saxons in south-eastern and central Britain. If we look at the provinces of Belgica Secunda and Germania Secunda, we see that the fifth-century invasions dealt a serious blow to the church. Its diocesan structures were unable to survive in the *civitates* of Tournai, Thérouanne/Boulogne, and Arras, while the see of the *civitas Veromandorum* was withdrawn from Vermand to Noyon, and that of the *civitas Tungrorum* from Tongres to Maastricht. Throughout the *civitates* centred on Cambrai, Vermand/Noyon, Amiens, Beauvais and Rouen, rural paganism increased.[172] Also, the influx of Germanic-speaking peoples led to a permanent extension of their language, at the expense of Latin, down at least as far south as a horizontal east–west line running through a point some twenty kilometres north of Tournai, and perhaps originally further south than this. Thus while Clovis was converted *c.* 500, and those who followed him south were in time converted by the existing Gallic church, for the areas of denser Frankish settlement further north, it was only in the seventh century that missionaries made any significant progress in reconverting them. One thinks of the work of the Aquitanian missionary, Amandus, and of the role of 'Hiberno-Frankish' monasticism, such as the work of the bishops and monks connected with Luxeuil, who worked with the active encouragement of Dagobert I.

If we now turn to Britain, we will see that there are some parallels, and some differences. As in Gaul, we need to recognise different zones. In some areas to the west of the primary Anglo-Saxon settlements, we should probably be thinking in terms of relatively peaceful colonisation; and the likelihood that the invading Anglo-Saxons were converted by the existing British church in the kingdoms of the Hwicce and the Magonsætan, and probably also in parts of Wessex,[173] provides a parallel to the conversion of those Franks who moved south into areas where the Gallo-Roman church continued. On the other hand in south-east England, the area of Augustine's immediate mission, conditions may not have been wholly unlike those in, say, the former diocese of Tournai. Both areas were reconverted, from a very low christian base, in the course of the seventh century. There, however, the parallel ends. Because Frankia remained a reasonably coherent entity, missionaries from areas further south were both able and welcome to come and contribute to the christianisation of the north. In the sixth century the Austrasian kings, who also ruled part of Aquitaine, were able to draw upon churchmen from the latter to provide leadership for the church in the Rhineland, which had suffered seriously from the barbarian invasions.[174] Similarly, in the seventh century, the reunification of the whole of Frankia under Chlothar II and Dagobert I provided the conditions which enabled the missionary work in what is now northern France and southern Belgium to be carried out. In addition to contributing manpower, it is very significant that it was missionaries from the same kingdom, Frankia, who were able to do the necessary work. In the early Middle Ages, conversion could be used as a form of cultural imperialism, to bind the recipient into a filial, and so subordinate relationship to the donor.[175] Where the missionary work was internal to a single kingdom this problem was avoided.

The problem did, however, arise with the conversion of the Anglo-Saxons; for King Æthelberht had no area within his kingdom of Kent where the church had survived unscathed, in the way that the Merovingians could look to southern Gaul. Æthelberht was therefore forced to look elsewhere for missionaries. Whether he genuinely tried to get bishops from neighbouring Frankia before turning to the papacy for missionaries is unclear: although this is implied by Gregory's letter to kings Theuderic and Theudebert cited earlier,[176] several modern scholars suspect that he preferred to turn to the Pope rather than the neighbouring Frankish church in order to avoid being put in a position of subservience to the Merovingians.[177] In any case, the fact that Æthelberht's missionaries were sent from Rome overcame this difficulty. His church was thus enabled to be free standing, not placed under the aegis of a Merovingian metropolitan see – nor of a British bishop in the western part of Britain.

We can understand why Æthelberht would have wanted to avoid such a subordinate position for his church; but why did Gregory show no interest in trying to reconstitute the *ecclesia britannica*? The question is particularly puzzling since his letter to Augustine, which lays out his plans for two provinces with their metropolitan sees at London and York, does, as we have seen, hark back to the geography of Roman Britain. Yet that same letter makes it clear that what Gregory is there establishing is a *noua Anglorum ecclesia*: a new church of the English.[178] Further, Gregory also tells Augustine that he will not only have authority over any future bishop of York, but also over all British bishops. Thus, far from using the British church still remaining in western Britain as the framework into which Augustine's new Anglo-Saxon converts will be fitted, Gregory appears to be working the other way round: the British bishops will be subject to Augustine, who is envisaged by the Pope as becoming the metropolitan bishop of the see of London, located in Anglo-Saxon territory. It is not clear whether Gregory intended this arrangment to be permanent, or whether (as with Augustine's authority over York) this was simply an attempt to give Augustine full authority throughout Britain for his lifetime, without necessarily subordinating British bishops to a future bishop of London.

We can suggest some answers to the question of why Gregory acted like this, without showing any regard for the position of the existing British bishops. It would have been more palatable to King Æthelberht; and Augustine himself might well have desired such authority. With the wishes of both king and bishop coinciding, they would have been well placed to make representations to Gregory when messengers returned from Kent to Rome in 601. On top of this, if those same messengers painted a rather unflattering picture of the British church, Gregory might have felt that giving Augustine full authority was the best way to safeguard the nascent English church, while simultaneously reforming and regulating the British church where necessary. All of this makes particular sense if we realise that, *pace* popular Northumbrian tradition, the mission to England was probably not something which stemmed from a long-cherished plan held by Gregory to go out and reconvert a former Roman province;[179] rather, Gregory was simply responding to a report that such a mission was desired by at least some in Kent.[180] Thus, both the original intimation that missionaries would be welcome, and also the fuller information that reached Gregory once Augustine's mission was established in Kent, would have presented the missionary opportunity in an *Anglo-Saxon* context, not a British one. On top of this we must remember that Gregory knew little about the British church, and had only a limited amount of time to give to the Augustinian mission: witness the tiny proportion of his surviving correspondence which is dedicated to it. In view of all this we can see why Gregory simply reacted to requests coming from Kent, as a pastor. His concern was with saving souls, not with restoring lost Roman provinces.[181] This, in turn, largely explains why the Augustinian mission acted in a quite different way from the later, Byzantine-sponsored missions which were so successful at reconverting and Hellenising heavily barbarised areas in the eastern Mediterranean, like Greece.[182]

The fact that Gregory's actions can be understood and appreciated for what they did accomplish does nothing to lessen their unfortunate consequences as regards the British church. Gregory's failure here lay in his omitting to make direct contact with its leaders, and to work out a framework which would have been acceptable to them as well as to Augustine and Æthelberht. It is not impossible to envisage the bare bones of such a framework. Gregory might, for instance, have looked back to the provincial structure of fourth-century, not third-century Britain, and thought of an *ecclesia britannica* comprising two British provinces (one approximating to Britannia prima, plus a second province embracing all British areas north of the Mersey), in addition to his two Anglo-Saxon provinces of London and York; and the primacy could have rotated, going to the most senior metropolitan, as Gregory himself suggested should be the pattern. Such a scheme might have proved acceptable to all parties. It would have given the Britons safeguards, together with the chance to play an influential role in the development of Anglo-Saxon Christianity. On the Roman side, Gregory was remarkably accepting of the principle of diversity in unity[183] and, provided that the Britons had agreed to let go of their Easter calculations, he could have afforded to be generous on other matters. The Roman missionaries would thereby have gained a substantial body of helpers who had resources to hand, rather than relying only on support from the continent. As for Æthelberht, his assistance in enabling Augustine to meet the British church leaders shows that he must have been willing to accept additional missionaries from among the Britons; and provided that the position of his own bishops was not threatened, he would probably have acquiesced.

Would such a scheme, which might have involved rebuilding an *ecclesia britannica* rather than initiating an *Anglorum ecclesia*, have been possible? There is no *prima facie* reason why not. In 600 there was not a straightforward political polarisation between one British and one Anglo-Saxon kingdom, but rather a considerable number of smaller peoples who could and did forge alliances across the linguistic divide. Further, there was still scope for *imperium* or overkingship to pass from the Deiran Edwin to the Gwynedd king, Cadwallon: both, apparently, competing for rule over *Britain*, and laying both British and Anglo-Saxon peoples under tribute.[184] In addition, at this date there is no reason to think that the many kingdoms ruled by Germanic leaders and the various Angles, Saxons, Jutes and Frisians, who lie behind our modern shorthand of 'Anglo-Saxons', had any sense of common identity over against the Britons. On the continent, Germanic peoples showed themselves ready to ally with Rome and to attack other barbarian peoples, including fellow 'Germans', on Rome's behalf; and as soon as we have historical information on the various Anglo-Saxon peoples within Britain, we see them acting similarly. In particular, we should note the understanding between the Mercians and the Welsh throughout the seventh century, which left the former free to attack and subjugate many other Anglo-Saxon peoples.

On the British side the picture is certainly different, since they were aware of their common Roman past and their shared christian faith. Sometimes, at least, they saw the struggle between the Anglo-Saxons and themselves as one waged between 'them' and 'us'. The terms used by Gildas and the north-British section of the *Historia Brittonum* are revealing here: the British are Christians and *cives*, 'citizens', a very Roman way of expressing their identity, whereas the Anglo-Saxons are the 'enemy', 'hateful to God and man'.[185] This was not the only way that Britons conceived the relationship: some of them appear to have behaved pragmatically, turning against rival British leaders at critical points rather than presenting a united front against the Anglo-Saxons, and probably even allying with various Anglo-Saxon leaders when it suited them;[186] and of course, according to Gildas, the Saxons had originally been invited to Britain in order to fight as allies of the British against the Picts and the Irish.[187] However, although they did not always act upon it, we must recognise that the Britons did feel a common sense of their own identity. This was based not only on their former position in the Roman Empire and their opposition to the various barbarian raiders of Britain, but also on their continuing adherence to that empire's religion, Christianity. Their unselfconscious linkage of Roman citizenship and Christianity is illustrated in the fifth century by Patrick, in his letter directed to the soldiers of Coroticus. Here, Patrick expresses his reluctance to address them as 'fellow citizens or citizens of the holy Romans, but, rather, citizens of the demons', on account of their raid on his newly baptized converts.[188] The significance of this identification of Roman and Christian is that if those barbarians who had never been part of the Roman Empire adopted Christianity, it transformed their position in at least some people's eyes. This can be illustrated by the change in British attitudes to the Irish. In the fifth century the latter were perceived as raiding barbarians and enemies,[189] but by the end of the sixth century, when Christianity had become dominant in Ireland, the relationship was transformed: hostility had been replaced by mutual cooperation.[190]

If relations between the Britons and their erstwhile enemies to the west could be so transformed, why could the same not have happened with their enemies to the east, the Anglo-Saxons? As argued above, the British church leaders who met Augustine appear to have been willing to cooperate in converting the Anglo-Saxons, provided that they were treated as valued partners in a common cause, rather than subordinates lying under a metropolitan's authority; and provided, too, that they could feel confident that giving way on some matters would not have been the thin end of the wedge, leading to their incorporation into the 'new church of the English'.

Historians are not supposed to speculate about what might have been; yet, so inured are we to the millennium-old assumption that there has always been an 'English' identity over against a 'Welsh' identity,[191] that arguably we gain a more accurate insight into how things actually stood *c.* 600 by indulging ourselves a little in that direction. Over the past decades, we have learnt that national identities are forged, not inherited in the blood. Further, they can be forged between peoples of different origin, even those speaking a different language, as the example of Scotland shows. At the time of Augustine's mission, the Anglo-Saxons were not a coherent people with a sense of their own identity, and it might still have been possible to find a place for them as well as the Britons within the *ecclesia britannica*. Where that would have led, is anybody's guess. Note, however, that Gregory's assumption that the motley Anglo-Saxon kingdoms all formed part of a single *gens Anglorum*, or English people, appears to have lain at the root of establishing a common English identity.[192] A different approach might have led to a different outcome. Be that as it may, the mission which Gregory sent undoubtedly established a 'new church of the English'. By the same token, it drove several nails into the coffin of the *ecclesia britannica*.

Notes

1. .This chapter owes something to research undertaken, and an unpublished paper on 'Bede and the British' then given, during my tenure of an Isabel Fleck research fellowship at the History Department of Durham University, which I gratefully acknowledge.
2. W.H.C. Frend, 'Pagans, Christians, and "the Barbarian Conspiracy" of A.D. 367 in Roman Britain', *Britannia*, 23 (1992), 121–31, at p. 121.
3. *HE*, II, 2; and V, 23.
4. Letter of Laurentius, Mellitus and Justus to the Irish church, *apud* Bede, *HE*, II, 4,

quoted below, p. 113; and, on the Irish side, note that Columbanus refers to 'all the churches of *the whole west*', not simply of the Irish: Columbanus, ep. 2, 5; and cf. ep. 1, 5: *Sancti Columbani Opera*, ed. G.S.M. Walker (Dublin, 1957), pp. 8, 16.
5. For example, *HE*, I, 14–15, 22; II, 2. T.M. Charles-Edwards, 'Bede, the Irish and the Britons', *Celtica*, 15 (1983), 42–52; cf. H.E.J. Cowdrey, 'Bede and the "English People"', *Journal of Religious History*, 11 (1981), 501–23, at pp. 502–7; repr. as no. III in Cowdrey, *Popes, Monks and Crusaders* (London, 1984).
6. *HE*, II, 20.
7. Gregory I, ep. VI, 51: *S. Gregorii Magni Registrum Epistularum Libri I–XIV*, ed. D. Norberg, 2 vols, *CCSL* 149–149A (Turnhout, 1982), pp. 727–8; translation based on that of D. Whitelock, *English Historical Documents* I, *c. 500–1042*, 2nd edn (London, 1979), pp. 790–1.
8. *Venerabilis Bedae Opera Historica*, ed. C. Plummer, 2 vols (Oxford, 1896), II, p. 41; I. Wood, 'The Mission of Augustine of Canterbury to the English', *Speculum*, 69 (1994), 1–17 at pp. 6–9, who further suggests that the Frankish bishops who had earlier neglected the English might be bishops from Neustria, whereas it was the Burgundian/Austrasian kingdoms presided over by Brunhild which did most to support the mission. Cf. also below, p. 114.
9. Wood, 'The Mission', pp. 5–9; R.A. Markus, *Gregory the Great and his World* (Cambridge, 1997), pp. 177–87, esp. p. 185.
10. Cf. *HE*, I, 25; J.M. Wallace-Hadrill, *Bede's Ecclesiastical History of the English People: A Historical Commentary* (Oxford, 1988), pp. 33–4.
11. *HE*, I, 22.
12. *HE*, II, 20.
13. See *HE*, I, 34 and II, 2.
14. *HE*, III, 28; cf. above, n. 4.
15. Theodore, *Poenitentiale* I, v; II, ix; and cf. II, v, 11: *Councils and Ecclesiastical Documents relating to Great Britain and Ireland*, eds A.W. Haddan and W. Stubbs, 3 vols (Oxford, 1869–71), III, pp. 180–2, 197, 194.
16. Aldhelm, ep. 4; *Aldhelmi Opera*, ed. R. Ehwald: MGH, Auctores Antiquissimi 15, part ii (Berlin, 1914), pp. 480–6 at pp. 484–5. English trans. M. Lapidge and M. Herren, *Aldhelm: The Prose Works* (Ipswich, 1979), p. 158.
17. *HE*, V, 18: p. 514. Lapidge and Herren, *Aldhelm*, pp. 140–1, argue that despite Bede's wording here, Bede 'seemed to possess scant knowledge of the work'. Their arguments, however, are far from conclusive. (1) There is a plausible parallel for referring to such a work as a *liber* ('book'), not an *epistula* ('letter'): see M. Winterbottom, 'Columbanus and Gildas', *Vigiliae Christianae*, 30 (1976), 310–17 at pp. 310–11, n. 5. (2) There was no particular reason for Bede to say that it was addressed to Geraint. (3) Bede is correct in saying that the work was written at the command of a synod; and the slip of saying that it was requested by a synod *suae gentis* rather than of all Britain would be an easy one to make: authors frequently referred to texts without checking the precise wording. (4) Lapidge and Herren ignore the positive reasons for thinking that Bede knew this text, namely that Bede gives a value judgement on it (*egregium*), and (*pace* (3) above) an accurate account of it here; and that elsewhere in his *History* his ideas show a striking similarity to those expressed by Aldhelm, suggesting that this letter played a formative role for Bede: see my comments here, and below, p. 130.
18. Cf. Aldhelm, ep. 4, esp. pp. 481–2, 484–5, citing Luke 7:47, and Bede, *HE*, I, 22, II, 2

and III, 4, together with Charles-Edwards, 'Bede', pp. 44, 51–2; also below, pp. 130–1.

19. Gildas, *Fragmenta*, §3: *Gildas, The Ruin of Britain and Other Works*, ed. and trans. M. Winterbottom (London and Chichester, 1978), pp. 80–1, 144. Cf. also *Fragmenta*, §§1, 2 and 7. On the authenticity of the *Fragmenta*, see R. Sharpe, 'Gildas as a Father of the Church', *Gildas: New Approaches*, eds M. Lapidge and D. Dumville (Woodbridge, 1984), pp. 193–205.

20. Cf. with Aldhelm's ep. 4 that of Laurentius, Mellitus and Justus (cited by Bede, *HE*, II, 4), and, for a continental parallel, cf. Caesarius of Arles, sermon 42, 2: *Sancti Caesarii Arelatensis Sermones*, ed. G. Morin, 2 vols, *CCSL* 103–4 (Turnhout, 1953), I, pp. 185–6. Caesarius may have been untypical of the Gallic church, but was none the less influential on the Insular churches.

21. This is clear from Gildas, *Fragmenta*, ed. Winterbottom, §7; Columbanus, ep. 1, 6, ed. Walker; Jonas, *Vita Columbani Abbatis Discipulorumque eius*, I, 19: *Ionae Vitae Sanctorum Columbani, Vedastis, Iohannis*, ed. B. Krusch, Scriptores Rerum Germanicarum in usum scholarum ex MGH (Hannover, Leipzig, 1905), esp. pp. 189, 191; Bede, *HE*, III, 22, p. 284; and 'Fredegar', *Chron.* IV, c. 78: *The Fourth Book of the Chronicle of Fredegar*, ed. J.M. Wallace-Hadrill (London, etc. 1960), p. 66.

22. Cowdrey, 'Bede', esp. pp. 501–14.

23. T. M. Charles-Edwards, 'Palladius, Prosper, and Leo the Great: Mission and Primatial Authority', *Saint Patrick, A.D. 493–1993*, ed. D.N. Dumville (Woodbridge, 1993), pp. 1–12.

24. E. Campbell, 'The Archaeological Evidence for External Contacts: Imports, Trade and Economy in Celtic Britain A.D. 400–600', *External Contacts and the Economy of Late Roman and Post-Roman Britain*, ed. K.R. Dark (Woodbridge, 1996), pp. 83–96.

25. M. Curran, *The Antiphonary of Bangor and the Early Irish Monastic Liturgy* (Blackrock, Co. Dublin, 1984), p. 53; C. Stancliffe, 'The Thirteen Sermons attributed to Columbanus and the Question of their Authorship', *Columbanus: Studies on the Latin Writings*, ed. M. Lapidge (Woodbridge, 1997), pp. 93–199, esp. pp. 112–18, 176–7, 198.

26. *Vita Sancti Samsonis*, I, 37: *La Vie ancienne de saint Samson de Dol*, ed. P. Flobert (Paris, 1997), p. 200.

27. L. Fleuriot, *Les origines de la Bretagne* (Paris, 1980), pp. 149–56. J.M. Wallace-Hadrill, *The Frankish Church* (Oxford, 1983), pp. 110–22.

28. *Moralia in Iob*, XXVII, xi, 21: *S. Gregorii Magni Moralia in Iob*, ed. M. Adriaen, 3 vols, *CCSL* 143–143B (Turnhout, 1979–85), III, pp. 1345–6.

29. *HE*, II, 1, p. 130.

30. If not two obstacles: *iam dudum* most commonly refers to something in the distant past, hence my translation, 'long since'. This is scarcely compatible with the idea that Gregory added this passage when he heard of Augustine's very recent success.

31. See P. Meyvaert, 'The Enigma of Gregory the Great's *Dialogues*: A Response to Francis Clark', *JEH*, 39 (1988), 335–81, at pp. 348–51.

32. *Moralia*, ed. Adriaen, p. vi, n. 6, and p. 1346; cf. Meyvaert, 'The Enigma', p. 351, n. 61.

33. So W.H. Fritze, 'Universalis gentium conversio', *Frühmittelalterliche Studien*, 3 (1969), 78–130, at pp. 109–10.

34. Constantius, *Vita S. Germani* III, 18: *Constance de Lyon, Vie de saint Germain d'Auxerre*, ed. R. Borius, Sources Chrétiennes 112 (Paris, 1965), pp. 156–8. Apparently Ussher had already noted this

parallel: *Ven. Bedae Op. Hist.*,
ed. Plummer, II, p. 71.
35. Constantius, *Vita S. Germani*, ed. Borius, III, 13; cf. III, 18 and V, 25.
36. Ibid., III, 14–15.
37. *Vie*, ed. Borius, pp. 46–62, esp. p. 47.
38. J.M. Wallace-Hadrill, 'Rome and the Early English Church: Some Questions of Transmission', in his *Early Medieval History* (Oxford, 1975), pp. 115–37 at pp. 116–17.
39. Markus, *Gregory*, p. 170.
40. Cited from Bede, *HE*, II, 4.
41. So Bede, *HE*, I, 29. Gregory's letters of commendation, written in June 601, name only Laurentius (who had brought Gregory news from Kent) and Mellitus.
42. Jonas, *Vita Columbani*, ed. Krusch, I, 19, pp. 187–9. Jonas may have played down Columbanus's links with the Merovingians: I. Wood, 'The *Vita Columbani* and Merovingian Hagiography', *Peritia*, 1 (1982), 63–80 at pp. 70–80.
43. Cf. Gregory, ep. XI, nos. 46–50.
44. Meyvaert, 'The Enigma', p. 347.
45. P. Meyvaert, 'Le libellus responsionum à Augustin de Cantorbéry: une oeuvre authentique de saint Grégoire le Grand', *Grégoire le Grand*, eds J. Fontaine, R. Gillet and S. Pellistrandi (Paris, 1986), 543–9. See further the discussion of Rob Meens in the present volume.
46. Bede, *HE*, I, 27, p. 86.
47. *Vitia*, 'vices': *HE*, I, 27, question vii. *Vitia* could cover anything from venial sins like occasional drunkenness to serious sins like simony, but in context Gregory is likely to have been thinking of the latter: see Gregory, ep. XI, nos. 38 and 45, and cf. Markus, *Gregory*, pp. 171–4. Colgrave and Mynors's translation of 'faults' is quite inadequate.
48. Bede, *HE*, I, 27; cf. below, n. 98.
49. Gregory, ep. XI, 39: *CCSL* 140A, p. 935; cf. also *HE*, I, 29.

50. Cf. R.A. Markus, 'Gregory the Great and a Papal Missionary Strategy', reprinted in his *From Augustine to Gregory the Great* (London, 1983), no. XI at p. 33; and N. Brooks, *The Early History of the Church of Canterbury* (Leicester, 1984), p. 10.
51. See K.R. Dark, *Civitas to Kingdom: British Political Continuity 300–800* (Leicester, 1994), pp. 172–216; Campbell, 'Archaeological Evidence'.
52. M. Lapidge, 'Gildas's Education and the Latin Culture of Sub-Roman Britain', *Gildas*, eds Lapidge and Dumville, 27–50; N. Wright, 'Gildas's Prose Style and its Origins', ibid., pp. 107–28; G. Orlandi, '*Clausulae* in Gildas's *De Excidio Britanniae*', ibid., pp. 129–49.
F. Kerlouégan, *Le De Excidio Britanniae de Gildas: Les destinés de la culture latine dans l'Ile de Bretagne au VI siècle* (Paris, 1987), *passim*.
53. M. Winterbottom, 'Columbanus and Gildas', pp. 310–17; N. Wright, 'Columbanus's *Epistulae*', *Columbanus*, ed. Lapidge, pp. 29–92, esp. pp. 82–8.
54. P. Sims-Williams, 'The Uses of Writing in Early Medieval Wales', *Literacy in Medieval Celtic Societies*, ed. H. Pryce (Cambridge, 1998), 15–38.
55. Dark, *Civitas*, p. 262, n. 29. Cf. Bede, *HE*, II, 2. On the date of the *De Excidio*, see Stancliffe, 'Thirteen Sermons', pp. 177–81.
56. Gildas, *De Excidio Britonum*, 67,2: ed. Winterbottom, *Gildas, The Ruin*, p. 119; K. Hughes, 'The Celtic Church: Is This a Valid Concept?', *Cambridge Medieval Celtic Studies*, 1 (1981), 1–20; W. Davies, *An Early Welsh Microcosm* (London, 1978), pp. 139–63; but cf. T.M. Charles-Edwards, 'The Seven Bishop-houses of Dyfed', *The Bulletin of the Board of Celtic Studies*, 24 (1970–72), 247–62.
57. M.W. Herren, 'Gildas and Early British Monasticism', *Britain 400–600: Language*

and History, eds A. Bammesberger and A. Wollmann (Heidelberg, 1990), 65–78 (though I do not accept his early dating of Gildas: cf above, n. 55).
58. *HE*, II, 2; see the discussion below, pp. 124–32, esp. 125, 127.
59. Hughes, 'Celtic Church'; Davies, *Microcosm*, pp. 139–63; but cf. C. Stancliffe, 'Christianity Amongst the Britons and the Irish', *The New Cambridge Medieval History*, vol. 1, ed. P. Fouracre (Cambridge, forthcoming).
60. *The Anglo-Saxon Chronicle, s.a.* 577: *The Anglo-Saxon Chronicle*, ed. B. Thorpe, RS, 2 vols (London, 1861), I, pp. 32–3. For the late Roman period, see J.C. Mann, 'The Administration of Roman Britain', *Antiquity*, 35 (1961), 316–20; for the later, Welsh period, see W. Davies, *Wales in the Early Middle Ages* (Leicester, 1982), pp. 160–1; Davies, *Microcosm*, p. 149.
61. See Sharpe, 'Gildas', pp. 199–202.
62. *HE*, II, 2; cf. below, pp. 131, 133.
63. In addition to the obvious British texts edited in L. Bieler, *The Irish Penitentials* (Dublin, 1963), pp. 60–73, note that the 'Finnian' who produced the earliest penitential (*ibid*. pp. 74–95) is now generally thought to have been a Briton: D.N. Dumville, 'Gildas and Uinniau', *Gildas*, eds Lapidge and Dumville, pp. 207–14. For British *peregrinatio*, see *Vita S. Samsonis*, eds Flobert, I, 40, 45.
64. K. Jackson, 'Some Questions in Dispute, ii: Who Taught Whom to Write Irish and Welsh?', *Studia Celtica*, 8–9 (1973–4), 18–32 at pp. 18–19; D.N. Dumville, 'Some British Aspects of the Earliest Irish Christianity', *Irland und Europa: Die Kirche im Frühmittelalter*, eds P. Ní Chatháin and M. Richter (Stuttgart, 1984), pp. 16–24 at pp. 19–24. Cf. also R. Sharpe, 'Saint Mauchteus, *discipulus Patricii*', *Britain 400–600*, eds Bammesberger and Wollmann, pp. 85–93, esp. pp. 92–3; Sharpe, 'Gildas', pp. 196–202.
65. *Cummian's Letter De Controversia Paschali and the De Ratione Conputandi*, eds M. Walsh and D. Ó Cróinín (Toronto, 1988), pp. 18–22. T.M. Charles-Edwards, *Early Christian Ireland* (Cambridge, forthcoming), ch. 9. On the origins of the 84-year cycle, see D. McCarthy, 'The Origin of the *Latercus* Paschal Cycle of the Insular Celtic Churches', *Cambrian Medieval Celtic Studies*, 28 (1994), 25–49.
66. R. Morris, *The Church in British Archaeology* (London, 1983), p. 17; J.M.C. Toynbee, 'Pagan Motifs and Practices in Christian Art and Ritual in Roman Britain', *Christianity in Britain, 300–700*, eds M.W. Barley and R.P.C. Hanson (Leicester, 1968), pp. 177–92 at pp. 186–8; K. Cameron, 'Eccles in English Place-Names', *ibid.*, pp. 87–92, at p. 87; and cf. M. Gelling, *Signposts to the Past* (London, 1978), pp. 82–3. Cf. also below, n. 84.
67. P.D.C. Brown, 'The Church at Richborough', *Britannia*, 2 (1971), 225–31; C. Thomas, *Christianity in Roman Britain to AD 500* (London, 1981), pp. 89, 125, 126, 129, 131–2.
68. Thomas, *Christianity*, p. 126.
69. *HE*, I, 26 and 33; for Albinus's role, see *HE*, preface.
70. See R. Morris, *Churches in the Landscape* (London, 1989), pp. 17–25, for a good discussion of a complex subject.
71. So Thomas, *Christianity*, pp. 170–4, 194, on St Pancras, though his suggestion that this church was Bertha's 'St Martin's' seems implausible; see further Eric Cambridge's contribution to the present volume. For other churches, see Brooks, *Canterbury*, pp. 20–1.
72. Cf. Thomas, *Christianity*, pp. 89–90, 108, and 112, with Brooks, *Canterbury*, pp. 17–19.

73. See D. Watts, *Christians and Pagans in Roman Britain* (London, 1981), pp. 158–73.
74. S.C. Hawkes, 'Anglo-Saxon Kent, c. 425–725', *Archaeology in Kent to AD 1500*, ed. P.E. Leach (London, 1982), pp. 64–78, esp. pp. 70, 75.
75. Note the need for the majority of the soldiers led by Germanus in 429 to be baptized first: Constantius, *Vita S. Germani*, ed. Borius, III, 17. (The late Roman army was recruited principally from the peasantry.)
76. Literary sources are generally silent; but the provision in Æthelberht's law-code §26 for three classes of 'læt' with wergilds below that of a *ceorl* may well indicate the presence of Britons – cf. the laws of Ine, §32: *The Laws of the Earliest English Kings*, ed. F.L. Attenborough (Cambridge, 1922), pp. 6, 32.
77. Baptism could, in an emergency, be administered by a lay person; but even here, a bishop was required to confirm the recipient, so regularising the situation: F.E. Warren, *The Liturgy and Ritual of the Celtic Church*, 2nd edn, ed. J. Stevenson (Woodbridge, 1987), pp. xxiii–xxiv.
78. H.R. Ellis Davidson, *Myths and Symbols in Pagan Europe: Early Scandinavian and Celtic Religions* (Manchester, 1988), *passim*.
79. For a sceptical approach, see D.A. Brooks, 'The Case for Continuity in Fifth-Century Canterbury Re-examined', *Oxford Journal of Archaeology*, 7, i (1988), 99–114.
80. Bede's wording (*HE*, I, 26, 33, pp. 76, 114) implies that Augustine was building new churches or restoring derelict ones in all cases except St Martin's, where, as we have seen, the original building appears not to have been a church at all. Note also Bede's silence about a British church or bishop in Kent in Augustine's day.
81. F.M. Stenton, 'The Historical Bearing of Place-Name Studies: Anglo-Saxon Heathenism', reprinted in *Preparatory to Anglo-Saxon England*, ed. D.M. Stenton (Oxford, 1970), pp. 280–97 at pp. 283, 296–7.
82. Cf. Gelling, *Signposts*, pp. 60–86, and K.H. Jackson, *Language and History in Early Britain* (Edinburgh, 1953), p. 197; the latter is followed by E.A. Thompson, *Saint Germanus of Auxerre and the End of Roman Britain* (Woodbridge, 1984), pp. 52–3.
83. Gelling, *Signposts*, pp. 80–3; Brooks, *Canterbury*, p. 20.
84. Cf. J. Blair, 'Anglo-Saxon Minsters: A Topographical Review', *Pastoral Care Before the Parish*, eds J. Blair and R. Sharpe (Leicester, 1992), pp. 226–66 at pp. 240–1 and n. 62.
85. R. Meens, 'A Background to Augustine's Mission to Anglo-Saxon England', *ASE*, 23 (1994), pp. 5–17, esp. pp. 13, 17. See also his contribution to the present volume. Cf. Gregory's *Libellus Responsionum*, apud Bede, *HE*, I, 27, pp. 88–102.
86. Note that the more original forms of the *Libellus* leave open the possibility that it is Augustine, not the English, who is initiating the questions: see Meyvaert, 'Le libellus', p. 28.
87. Caesarius, serm. 44, §5, §3, §7: *CCSL* 103, pp. 196–9.
88. As above, n. 25; T.P. Oakley, 'Cultural Affinities of Early Ireland in the Penitentials', *Speculum*, 8 (1933), 489–500, esp. p. 494; T.P. Oakley, 'The Origins of Irish Penitential Discipline', *Catholic Historical Review*, 19 (1933–4), 320–32, esp. p. 328. The *Excerpta Quedam de Libro Dauidis* §8 (Bieler, *Irish Penitentials*, p. 70) ruling about nocturnal emissions is entirely unexceptional in a monastic context, as Cassian implies: see A. Demyttenaere, 'The Cleric, Women and the Stain', *Frauen in Spätantike und Frühmittelalter*, ed. W. Affeldt (Sigmaringen, 1990), 141–65 at

pp. 155–6. The *Penitentialis Vinniani* §48 (Bieler, *op. cit.* pp. 90–2) prohibitions on sexual intercourse at certain times agree with those in Caesarius, *serm.* 44, which is their probable source – as it is also of *Paenitentiale Cummeani* §30 (ibid., p. 116). Cf. Meens, 'Background', p. 10.

89. *Paenitentiale Cummeani* §31: *Irish Penitentials*, ed. Bieler, p. 116. This Cummean died *c.* 661, according to the Irish annals: *Cummian's Letter*, eds Walsh and Ó Cróinín, pp. 12–14.

90. The text of this question of Augustine, omitted in Bede's version, is printed by M. Deanesly and P. Grosjean, 'The Canterbury Edition of the Answers of Pope Gregory I to St Augustine', *JEH*, 10 (1959), 1–49 at pp. 28–9. See Brooks, *Canterbury*, p. 20. In a paper given at the 'Paganism to Christianity' conference in Oxford, in March 1997, Brooks suggested that the British St Sixtus cult might have been at St Osyth, Essex, since St Osyth's pre-Conquest name was *Cicc*, which might derive from Sixtus.

91. Cf. Martin of Tours' similar qualms: Sulpicius Severus, *Vita S. Martini*, c. 11: *Sulpice Sévère, Vie de Saint Martin*, vol. I, ed. J. Fontaine (Paris, 1967), p. 276. For a different approach, see I. Wood, *The Merovingian Kingdoms 450–751* (London and New York, 1994 (*recte* 1993)), pp. 74–5 (St Benignus cult).

92. I infer this both from the fact that Augustine was concerned to obtain relics of a saint of the same name; and also from the wording of Gregory's reply. In particular, Gregory's 'mihi *tamen* videtur' implies that he is telling Augustine to act differently from what Augustine had proposed: Deanesly and Grosjean, 'Canterbury Edition', pp. 28–9.

93. As, apparently, in Lincoln: M.J. Jones, 'St Paul in the Bail, Lincoln: Britain in Europe?', *Churches Built in Ancient Times*, ed. K. Painter (London, 1994), pp. 325–47.

94. *HE*, I, 7, p. 34; cf. W. Levison, 'St. Alban and St. Albans', *Antiquity*, 15 (1941), 337–59 at pp. 338–9, 350–1; M. Biddle, 'Archaeology, Architecture, and the Cult of Saints in Anglo-Saxon England', *The Anglo-Saxon Church. Papers . . . in Honour of Dr H.M. Taylor*, eds L.A.S. Butler and R.K. Morris (London, 1986), pp. 1–31 at pp. 10–16.

95. Deanesly and Grosjean, 'Canterbury Edition', pp. 28–9.

96. Bede, *HE*, II, 2, p. 134.

97. Stephanus, *Vita Sancti Wilfrithi*, 17: *The Life of Bishop Wilfrid by Eddius Stephanus*, ed. B. Colgrave (Cambridge, 1927), p. 36; cf. C. Stancliffe, 'Oswald, "Most Holy and Most Victorious King of the Northumbrians"', *Oswald: Northumbrian King to European Saint*, eds C. Stancliffe and E. Cambridge (Stamford, 1995), pp. 33–83 at pp. 77–8.

98. '*Ut indocti doceantur, infirmi persuasione roborentur, peruersi auctoritate corrigantur.*' *HE*, I, 27, p. 88.

99. Cf. *Ven. Bedae Op. Hist.*, ed. Plummer, II, p. 73; Wallace-Hadrill, *Commentary*, p. 52.

100. Gregory, ep. XI, 41.

101. *HE*, II, 2, pp. 134–42.

102. Cf. N.K. Chadwick, 'The Battle of Chester: A Study of Sources', *Celt and Saxon*, ed. N.K. Chadwick (Cambridge, 1964), pp. 167–85 at pp. 177–8.

103. *HE*, II, 2, p. 136, penultimate line; p. 138, line 2; p. 140, line 2.

104. *HE*, II, 2, p. 140, lines 16, 29.

105. Note also that the means chosen to test Augustine's humility, whether or not he rose to greet the British bishops, bears all the marks of originating in a British context: C.E. Stancliffe, 'Kings and Conversion: Some Comparisons between the Roman Mission to England and Patrick's to Ireland', *Frühmittelalterliche Studien*, 14 (1980), 59–94 at p. 93, n. 193.

106. 'A true herald of the most high light.' Bede's wording here picks up his reference at the end of *HE*, I, 22 to the *'digniores . . . praecones ueritatis'* – i.e. worthier heralds than the British.
107. 'From their most noble monastery.'
108. *Vir Domini*: 'a man of God'; *diuino agente iudicio*: 'through the workings of divine judgement'.
109. *Gens perfida*: 'faithless people'; *nefandae militiae copias*: 'the forces of the heinous host'; *sancti pontificis Augustini*: 'holy bishop Augustine'.
110. Cf. Bede, *HE*, preface.
111. For a lucid summary of the linguistic evidence, see T.M. Charles-Edwards *apud* Wallace-Hadrill, *Commentary*, pp. 218–19.
112. So Jackson, *Language and History*, p. 568; cf. later written examples on p. 464.
113. Charles-Edwards, *apud* Wallace-Hadrill, *Commentary*, p. 219.
114. Charles-Edwards, *apud* Wallace-Hadrill, *Commentary*, pp. 218–19.
115. *HE*, II, 4; cf. C. Cubitt, *Anglo-Saxon Church Councils c. 650–850* (London, 1995), pp. 248–9.
116. For example, Bede prefaces the origin legend portraying the Picts as coming from Scythia with 'ut perhibent' (*HE*, II, 1, p. 16), and, having prefaced his account of miracles at Oswald's death site with an introductory statement, 'multa . . . facta uirtutum miracula narrantur; sed nos duo tantum, quae a maioribus audiuimus, referre satis duximus', he introduces the second with 'ut ferunt' (*HE*, III, 9 and 10).
117. For example, from a fuller version of the Welsh and Irish annal entry recording the battle of Chester than any that has come down to us. For these annal entries, see Chadwick, 'Battle', pp. 171–5; and for the relationship of the different texts, K. Hughes, *Celtic Britain in the Early Middle Ages* (Woodbridge, 1980), pp. 68–70, 88–92.
118. We should not be deterred from positing the composition of such texts simply because of the dearth of *surviving* texts: cf. Sims-Williams, 'The Uses of Writing', pp. 20–7.
119. Bede, *In Cantica Canticorum* IV, v, 14: *Bedae Venerabilis Opera*, part II, *Opera Exegetica*, 2B, eds D. Hurst and J.E. Hudson, *CCSL* 119B (Turnhout, 1983), pp. 165–375, at p. 291, lines 766–7; cf. Pliny the Elder, *Naturalis Historia* VIII, v, 13; VIII, xii, 34; and cf. VIII, iv, 7: *Pline l'ancien: Histoire Naturelle livre VIII*, ed. A. Ernout (Paris, 1952), pp. 27, 35, and 25.
120. See Charles-Edwards, *apud* Wallace-Hadrill, *Commentary*, pp. 218–19, citing CIMESETLI; and P. Sims-Williams, 'The Emergence of Old Welsh, Cornish and Breton Orthography, 600–800: The Evidence of Archaic Old Welsh', *The Bulletin of the Board of Celtic Studies*, 38 (1991), 20–86 at p. 25, n. 1, and p. 49, n. 2, citing the parallel of Welsh *scipaur*, from Latin **scoparium*.
121. Morris, *Churches in the Landscape*, p. 11. This map, however, is incomplete: the 'Meuanias insulas' of *HE*, II, 5 and 9 are Anglesey and the Isle of Man.
122. C. Stancliffe, 'Where Was Oswald Killed?', *Oswald*, eds Stancliffe and Cambridge, 84–96, esp. pp. 94–5.
123. Lapidge and Herren, *Aldhelm: The Prose Works*, pp. 6–9. Their scepticism over Maildub, however, is unjustified: see A. Orchard, *The Poetic Art of Aldhelm* (Cambridge, 1994), pp. 2–5; P. Sims-Williams, *Religion and Literature in Western England 600–800* (Cambridge, 1990), pp. 108–9.
124. Sims-Williams, *Religion and Literature*, pp. 108–9 and map on pp. xiv–xv; B. Yorke, *Wessex in the Early Middle Ages* (London and New York, 1995), pp. 61–2.
125. *HE*, II, 2, p. 134.
126. *HE*, V, 18; V, 23.

127. From Bede's wording in *HE* V, 18, we cannot be certain that Pehthelm was with Aldhelm at Malmesbury, or only after the latter became bishop; but the 'multo tempore' and 'monachus' render it likely that he was with Aldhelm at Malmesbury for some time at least.

128. *HE*, V, 13 and 18. Note that Bede was careful to name his informant when including a miracle story, but generally not in other cases: D. Whitelock, 'Bede and his Teachers and Friends', *Famulus Christi*, ed. G. Bonner (London, 1976), pp. 19–39, at p. 30.

129. For example, *HE*, III, 1: 'reg[es] perfid[i]'; 'infandus Brettonum dux'. Cf. also above, n. 3.

130. 'Augustine, the man of God, *is said* to have threatened them and prophesied' (my italics).

131. See H. Mayr-Harting, *The Coming of Christianity to Anglo-Saxon England* (London, 1972), pp. 69–72, for the implausibility of the story reaching Bede via the latter.

132. If the British source was slanted in any way, rather than simply describing what had happened, one might conjecture that it would have presented Æthelfrith's death following so soon after his slaughter of the Bangor 'holy men' as due to the workings of divine vengeance: cf. *The Annals of Tigernach*, ed. W. Stokes, 2 vols (Felinfach, 1993, repr. from *Revue Celtique*), vol. I, p. 131.

133. *HE*, III, 25. Cf. R. Ray, 'The Triumph of Greco-Roman Rhetorical Assumptions in Pre-Carolingian Historiography', *The Inheritance of Historiography 350–900*, ed. C. Holdsworth and T.P. Wiseman (Exeter, 1986), pp. 67–84, esp. pp. 79–81.

134. See Stancliffe, 'Kings and Conversion', esp. pp. 93–4, and below.

135. The fullest interpretation and defence of Bede's portrayal of Augustine, arguing that Bede did not intend to cast him in an unfavourable light, is that of H. Vollrath, *Die Synoden Englands bis 1066* (Paderborn, etc. 1985), pp. 38–48, and cf. 409–10. It convinces me as I read it, but not when I return to Bede's text. As an example of the opposite view, see Mayr-Harting, *Coming*, pp. 171–2. Cf. also Wallace-Hadrill, *Commentary*, p. 54.

136. I agree with Vollrath (*Die Synoden Englands*, pp. 45–6) that one can defend Augustine's behaviour by reference to Gregory's insistence that a bishop should not show too much humility to those under him; but it is striking that Bede makes no such attempt.

137. Wallace-Hadrill suggested that *HE*, I, 22 (rather than *HE*, II, 2) marked such a turning point, whereas I would see Bede's comments there simply as a forerunner pointing to this chapter. With this proviso, however, Wallace-Hadrill's comments are very much to the point: *Commentary*, p. 30.

138. *HE*, II, 1, esp. pp. 122, 124, 130.

139. Ep. 4: *Aldhelmi Opera*, ed. Ehwald, p. 481; Lapidge and Herren, *Aldhelm*, pp. 155–6.

140. Ep. 4: *Aldhelmi Opera*, ed. Ehwald, p. 486; Lapidge and Herren, *Aldhelm*, p. 160.

141. *HE*, II, 2, pp. 134, 140.

142. See above, n. 18.

143. Cf. the opinion which Bede puts into Wilfrid's mouth at the synod of Whitby: it was pardonable for earlier Irish churchmen to follow their own practices before they knew any better, but once they had heard the Catholic church's teaching, then, if they refused to accept it, they sinned (*HE*, III, 25, at p. 306).

144. Constantius, *Vita S. Germani*, ed. Borius, III, 15; Bede, *HE*, I, 18. Cf. R.W. Hanning, *The Vision of History in Early Britain* (New York, 1966), pp. 80–1.

145. Gregory, ep. XI, 36; cf. Bede, *HE*, I, 31.

146. *HE*, II, 2, p. 138. The title belongs rather to the time of Theodore (*HE*, IV, 17, at

p. 384: Council of Hatfield; see also Charles-Edwards, *Early Christian Ireland*, ch. 10); but here, it is probably due to Bede, who calls Augustine 'archiepiscopus' in *HE*, II, 3.

147. *HE*, II, 2: 'episcopos siue doctores', p. 134; cf. also 'episcopi et plures uiri doctissimi'(p. 136).

148. *Sinodus Aquilonalis Britaniae*, §1: *Irish Penitentials*, ed. Bieler, p. 66. For *doctores* in Ireland, see Charles-Edwards, *Early Christian Ireland*, ch. 6, ii.

149. *Cummian's Letter*, ed. Walsh and Ó Cróinín, p. 56.

150. Columbanus, ep. 2, esp. §5: *Sancti Columbani Opera*, ed. Walker, pp. 14–16. Cf. Bede, *HE*, II, 2, p. 138.

151. 'Non . . . apud nos persona, sed ratio valet.' Ep. 5, §11.

152. *HE*, II, 2, p. 138. This sounds as though there was something odd about the British rite of confirmation, but Patrick's writings indicate that confirmation was practised, and give no hint of any irregularity: see his *Confessio* §38, §51: *Libri Epistolarum Sancti Patricii Episcopi*, ed. L. Bieler, 2 vols in 1 (Dublin, 1993), I, pp. 78, 86. See further Warren, *The Liturgy and Ritual*, ed. Stevenson, pp. xxiii–xxiv, liii–liv, 64–7; and S. McKillop, 'A Romano-British Baptismal Liturgy', *The Early Church in Western Britain and Ireland*, ed. S.M. Pearce, BAR Brit. Ser. 102 (Oxford, 1982), 35–48 (though Patrick's writings would seem to contradict her comment at the top of p. 43 re confirmation).

153. In about 602 the British tonsure may have been regarded as an allowable difference: cf. Bede, *HE*, II, 2, p. 138, and E. James, 'Bede and the Tonsure Question', *Peritia*, 3 (1984), 85–98, at pp. 97–8.

154. Aldhelm, Ep. 4: *Aldhelmi Opera*, ed. Ehwald, pp. 482–4. On the continent, the tonsure is first documented as a controversial issue at the synod of Mâcon (626 or 627): Jonas, *Vita Columbani*, ed. Krusch, II, 9.

155. I infer the last both from Gregory's response to Augustine, discussed above, p. 115; and from the Britons' reported response that 'they would not accept him as their archbishop' (*HE*, II, 2, pp. 138–9), albeit with the proviso that the use of the actual word, archiepiscopus, is anachronistic: see n. 146, above. The reality behind it, however, is not: see Gregory, ep. XI, 39 (*CCSL* 140A, p. 935).

156. Sims-Williams, *Religion and Literature*, pp. 55–86; S. Bassett, 'Church and Diocese in the West Midlands: The Transition from British to Anglo-Saxon Control', *Pastoral Care Before the Parish*, eds Blair and Sharpe, pp. 13–40.

157. *HE*, II, 2, p. 136, lines 4–6 and 23–5.

158. So Columbanus, ed. Walker, ep. 1, §§3–5, esp. §5 on Jerome; ep. 2, §7. Colmán spoke in the same terms at Whitby, according to Bede, *HE*, III, 25, p. 304.

159. *Cummian's Letter*, eds Walsh and Ó Cróinín, pp. 20–1; and, on their probable use by the papacy, ibid., p. 28.

160. Cf. the fact that Aidan was bound by the traditions of Iona, which had sent him: *HE*, III, 25, p. 296.

161. Cf. Columbanus's ep. 5 to Pope Boniface, esp. §§9–12, and the discussion below; and, for Ireland, Charles-Edwards, *Early Christian Ireland*, ch. 6.

162. *HE*, II, 5, p. 148.

163. Gildas, *De Excidio*, ed. Winterbottom, ch. 109, §§3–6, esp. §5: 'omni sancto sacerdoti'. K. Hughes, 'The Celtic Church and the Papacy', reprinted in Hughes, *Church and Society in Ireland A.D. 400–1200* (London, 1987), no. XV, pp. 8–9.

164. As n. 158.

165. Columbanus, ep. 5, §§11–12, §7; §§9, 10.

166. Bede's inclusion of *doctores* and *plures uiri doctissimi* alongside bishops in the British delegations that met Augustine (*HE*, II, 2,

pp. 134, 136) is our sole evidence from the British side. However, our evidence for the workings of the British church at this period is so minimal that the absence of corroboration elsewhere is not surprising; and what we do find in Bede fits neatly with evidence from Ireland (cf. n. 147 above).
167. Columbanus, ep. 2, §8; §§5–6. For further discussion, see C. Stancliffe, 'Jonas' *Life of Columbanus and his Disciples*', *Studies in Irish Hagiography*, eds J. Carey, M. Herbert and P. Ó Riain (Dublin, forthcoming).
168. Columbanus, ep. 2, §5.
169. Gregory's natural ally against the corruption and simony of the Gallic bishops would have been not Brunhild and Syagrius of Autun, but rather Columbanus. They were united both on the evils of simony, and on the merits of seeking reform through regular councils: cf. Columbanus (ed. Walker), ep. 1, 6, and ep. 2, 2; and Markus, *Gregory*, pp. 171–4, and cf. p. 187.
170. *HE*, I, 27, p. 88. I am now readier to lay responsibility for Augustine's behaviour towards the British bishops on Gregory than I was in my 'Kings and Conversion', p. 93; cf. also above, pp. 121, 122, on St Sixtus's relics.
171. Bede, *HE*, I, 27, p. 88, discussed above.
172. E. Ewig and K. Schäferdiek, 'Christliche Expansion im Merowingerreich', *Kirchengeschichte als Missionsgeschichte*, vol. II, 1: *Die Kirche des früheren Mittelalters*, ed. K. Schäferdiek (Munich, 1978), pp. 116–45, esp. pp. 116–17, 127–8; L. Duchesne, *Fastes épiscopaux de l'ancienne Gaule*, vol. III: *Les provinces du nord et de l'est* (Paris, 1915), pp. 10–16 and *passim*.
173. Yorke, *Wessex*, pp. 177–81; cf. above, n. 156.
174. E. Ewig, 'L'Aquitaine et les Pays Rhénans au haut moyen age', reprinted in E. Ewig, *Spätantikes und fränkisches Gallien: gesammelte Schriften (1952–1973)*, ed. H. Atsma, vol. I (Munich, 1976), pp. 553–72, at pp. 559–62, 566.
175. A. Angenendt, 'The Conversion of the Anglo-Saxons Considered against the Background of the Early Medieval Mission', *Angli e Sassoni al di qua e al di là del mare: Settimane di Studio del Centro Italiano di Studi sull'alto medioevo*, 32 (Spoleto, 1986), II, 747–81.
176. Ep. VI, 51; see above, p. 109. Wood, 'The Mission', pp. 8–9, interprets this at face value; but one might conjecture that Æthelberht was not very earnest in soliciting Frankish help, and was perhaps more concerned to convince Pope Gregory that he should send missionaries direct from Rome rather than assign responsibility to Frankish bishops.
177. J.M. Wallace-Hadrill, *Early Germanic Kingship in England and on the Continent* (Oxford, 1971), p. 29, and cf. p. 45; taken further by Angenendt, 'The Conversion', pp. 779–81.
178. Gregory, ep. XI, 39; see above, p. 115.
179. Contra Mayr-Harting, *Coming*, pp. 57–61. For Northumbrian tradition, see *Vita S. Gregorii*, chs 9–11: *The Earliest Life of Gregory the Great by an Anonymous Monk of Whitby*, ed. B. Colgrave (1968, reprinted Cambridge, 1985), pp. 90–2; Bede, *HE*, II, 1, pp. 132–4.
180. Gregory, ep. VI, 51. Wood, 'The Mission', pp. 9–11; cf. T.F.X. Noble, 'Morbidity and Vitality in the History of the Early Medieval Papacy', *The Catholic Historical Review*, 81 (1995), 505–40 at pp. 537–8.
181. Cf. Wallace-Hadrill, 'Rome', pp. 116–17; Markus, *Gregory*, pp. 185–7.
182. Cf. D. Obolensky, *The Byzantine Commonwealth* (London, 1971; pb edn 1974), pp. 104, 111–13; A.P. Vlasto, *The Entry of the Slavs into Christendom* (Cambridge, 1970), pp. 5–12.

183. P. Meyvaert, 'Diversity within Unity, A Gregorian Theme', reprinted in his *Benedict, Gregory, Bede and Others* (London, 1977), no. VI.
184. See Stancliffe, 'Oswald', pp. 47–50.
185. Gildas, *De Excidio*, ed. Winterbottom, chs 22–6, esp. 23, §§1–2 and 26, §1; *Historia Brittonum*, ch. 63: *Nennius, British History and Welsh Annals*, ed. J. Morris (London and Chichester, 1980), p. 79.
186. *Historia Brittonum*, ch. 63; *Sinodus Luci Victorie* §4: *Irish Penitentials*, ed. Bieler, p. 68; cf. D.N. Dumville, 'The Chronology of *De Excidio Britanniae*, Book I', *Gildas*, eds Lapidge and Dumville, pp. 61–84 at pp. 81–2; Stancliffe, 'Oswald', pp. 37–9.
187. Gildas, *De Excidio*, chs 21–23.
188. Patrick, *Epistola ad Milites Corotici*, § 2: *Libri Epistolarum Sancti Patricii Epicopi*, ed. Bieler, I, p. 92. For the sixth century, cf. Gildas, *De Excidio*, chs 92, §3.
189. Patrick, *Confessio*, §46; cf. *Epistola*, §§10–11, §16.
190. Cf. Dumville, 'Some British Aspects', pp. 20–1; Sharpe, 'Gildas'; *Vita S. Samsonis*, ed. Flobert, I, 37–40.
191. Bede's *HE* is obviously prime evidence for the English side; for the Welsh, cf. J. Rowland's discussion of *Canu Heledd* in her *Early Welsh Saga Poetry* (Cambridge, 1990), pp. 120–41.
192. P. Wormald, 'Bede, the *Bretwaldas* and the Origins of the *Gens Anglorum*', *Ideal and Reality in Frankish and Anglo-Saxon Society: Studies Presented to J.M. Wallace-Hadrill*, ed. P. Wormald (Oxford, 1983), pp. 99–129, esp. pp. 123–6.

CHAPTER 7

The Reception of Christianity at the Anglo-Saxon Royal Courts

Barbara Yorke

Readers of Bede's *Ecclesiastical History of the English People* are left in no doubt of the centrality of the royal courts to the spread of Christianity in Anglo-Saxon England. In his accounts, missionaries concentrate their attentions upon the rulers and are only successful in establishing permanent bases if, and while, they have the support of the reigning monarchs. Missionaries were dependent on their royal patrons for legal protection, grants of land and other such basic requirements.[1] Those who fell foul of rulers had no choice but to leave their kingdoms.[2] Even bishoprics could be terminated by kings if they so desired in those early years, and church offices might be bought and sold as they saw fit.[3] The conventions of 'heroic' conversion narratives may have led Bede, or those who framed some of the accounts he used, to overemphasize the role of individual missionaries battling for the souls of particular kings; nevertheless, there can be no doubt that the attitude of the royal circle was crucial for the success or failure of the different missions. Modern historians have been particularly interested in how political motivations may have affected royal attitudes to conversion. There has been much discussion, for instance, of how the spread of Christianity was facilitated by overlords choosing to impose the new religion on their underkings as a means of reinforcing their power.[4] But equally important for understanding the process is an appreciation of what expectations the royal courts had of religion in general, and of their previous experiences in absorbing new cultural influences. These themes will be the focus of this chapter, and require the narrative of the conversion, provided in Bede's *Ecclesiastical History* and other written sources, to be 'read' in the light of archaeological evidence and the conversion experiences of other Germanic peoples. From this contextualisation of the process of conversion, there emerges the importance of a transition period in which kings and missionaries learnt what compromises would have to be made if Christianity was to be the new religion of the Anglo-Saxon kingdoms.

PAGANISM AND THE ANGLO-SAXON ROYAL HOUSES

Unfortunately for us, Bede did not include in his *Ecclesiastical History* an overview of the pre-christian religious practices of the Anglo-Saxons. One could hardly expect him to have considered such matters with the detachment of a modern observer – even if he had definite knowledge about them – and his dominant view was that the pre-christian beliefs were self-evidently inferior to those of the religion which supplanted them. To clinch the matter, he gave one of the main speeches signalling such inferiority to the pagan priest Coifi who is made to declare 'I frankly admit that, for my part, I have found that the religion which we have hitherto held has no virtue nor profit in it'.[5] Bede goes on to describe how Coifi desecrated the temple at Goodmanham whose altars he had previously consecrated. Another speech belittling aspects of pagan religious practice was given to King Oswiu of Northumbria who is made to explain to King Sigibert 'Sanctus' of the East Saxons, 'that objects made by the hands of men could not be gods'.[6]

The reliability of the few such insights which Bede does provide into the pre-christian religious practices of the Anglo-Saxons needs careful assessment in the light of other evidence for Germanic paganism.[7] He can be suspected of a tendency, found in other medieval christian writers, to portray Germanic paganism as a negative mirror-image of christian practice,[8] though each element of what he says has to be considered on its own merits. His statement that Coifi is said to have consecrated altars as a christian priest would have done is a case in point. The lack of archaeological evidence for temples of the type Bede appears to describe (apart from that believed to have been excavated at Yeavering)[9] has raised doubts about whether he provides a true reflection of pre-christian religious observances here. His evidence has not looked convincing alongside that from other Germanic areas in the early Middle Ages. In Scandinavia, for instance, there appears to be little evidence either for worship in temples or for a priestly caste; instead, essential public rituals seem to have been carried out by local leaders in their own halls.[10] It seems that the subject of Adam of Bremen's famous description of the temple at Uppsala in Sweden may in reality have been the substantial royal hall uncovered in recent excavations.[11] However, the validity of using later Scandinavian evidence to interpret Anglo-Saxon practice in the seventh century can be questioned, not least because it should not be assumed that what we term 'Anglo-Saxon' was a purely Germanic culture. Probably the bulk of the population in the Anglo-Saxon kingdoms was of Romano-British descent, and their customs and practices must have had some impact on the incomers. John Blair has made a particularly important contribution in this respect to the debate about Anglo-Saxon paganism, suggesting that the Anglo-Saxon temples known to Bede and his informants may have been influenced by, or in some cases may actually have been, Romano-British temples.[12] He also brings together an impressive body of archaeological evidence to show how the prehistoric ritual landscape was utilised in Anglo-Saxon England and influenced the layout of cemeteries and sometimes also secular buildings, as Brian Hope-Taylor had previously argued for Yeavering.[13] When Bede puts words into the mouth of Coifi we can be reasonably certain that he is inventing dialogue to express views he would have liked Coifi to have held; for it is inherently unlikely that a verbatim report of Edwin's meeting with his counsellors a hundred years earlier had survived. But when he reports that the shrine at Goodmanham had enclosures, or that pagan priests were not allowed to carry weapons or ride stallions,[14] no propagandist purpose is being served. What we seem to have here are examples of Bede's practice of evoking a familiar, physical world for his readers and listeners — as he did, for instance, when he described King Edwin's would-be assassin not as carrying just any old sword, but 'a short sword, double-edged and smeared with poison'.[15]

Analogy with the Scandinavian evidence may be of greater use in alerting us to the role of secular leaders in pagan ritual and, in particular, showing how significant these rituals could be in underpinning secular status.[16] Royal involvement in religious ritual would not have been a topic on which Bede would have wished to dwell. One of the aspects of correct kingly behaviour he wanted to instil in Anglo-Saxon rulers was that they should accept guidance from church leaders, and not interfere in ecclesiastical matters which they were not competent to judge — as, of course, they were inclined to do.[17] It would therefore not have been, as Bede would have seen it, in the interest of the Anglo-Saxon churches to remind rulers that their predecessors had once played an active role in religious ritual. It was much more to Bede's purpose to stress that ritual had always been the preserve of priests, and such preferences would also have fitted with what his reading of the Old Testament would have led him to expect. As often appears to have been the case with Bede, it is not that what he tells us is untrue, but rather that he does not show us the whole picture, with the result that the general impression is distorted. The glimpses of temples and priests he provides may be authentic remembrances of the pre-christian past, but it is also possible that he has ignored aspects of royal involvement in pagan ritual.[18]

But what Bede cannot disguise, even if he does not spell it out, is the importance of links with the pagan gods for Anglo-Saxon kings in the immediate pre-conversion period. As is well known, Anglo-Saxon kings claimed descent from the god Woden, though it was, of course, only possible to record this fact in writing after the introduction of Christianity. Bede traces the descent of the Kentish kings from Woden 'from whose stock the royal families of many kingdoms claimed their descent',[19] but does not describe him as a god. Bede and other christian leaders may have rationalised Woden as a validating ancestor who had mistakenly been interpreted as a god[20] but, given the known contacts in the seventh and eighth centuries between Anglo-Saxon kingdoms and Scandinavia, where worship of Odin was still a going concern, it is likely that Woden's divinity remained well known. Literate Christians may have recorded Woden in the Anglo-Saxon genealogies, but they are unlikely to have invented the idea of him as the progenitor of royal houses. That, before the introduction of Christianity, royal houses were using Woden to underpin their authority and to stress their unique fitness to rule because of divine descent, is supported not only by wider studies of sacral kingship in the early Middle Ages,[21] but also by iconography. The naked figures, carrying spears and wearing helmets on which two birds perch, represented on the Sutton Hoo helmet panels and the Finglesham buckle, have close parallels in Scandinavia, and have convincingly been linked to the cult of Odin/Woden.[22]

Of course, Woden was not the only god culted in the early medieval Germanic world, and he may not originally have enjoyed the dominance implied by his position in the genealogies of the Anglian collection.[23] The East Saxon kings preferred in their pedigrees to trace descent from Seaxneat, a god whose worship is recorded among the continental Saxons.[24] Other significant gods may be concealed in the origin legends of kingdoms where they seem to have been rationalised as founding heroes.[25] Hengist and Horsa may have been twin horse deities rather than flesh-and-blood leaders invited to Britain by Vortigern. Hengist's supposed son Oeric is given the *cognomen* Oisc, which appears to mean 'god', and so when the Kentish royal house described itself as 'Oiscingas', descendants of Oisc, they were making a declaration of their divine descent.[26] Further godly progenitors are likely to be concealed in the upper registers of the pedigrees from other kingdoms. Undoubtedly the scanty origin myths which have survived have done so in bowdlerised form, and it is to be suspected that they are pale shadows of fuller accounts which, like some surviving continental examples, demonstrated how the royal dynasty had both divine and human progenitors.[27]

Cultural Assimilation at the Anglo-Saxon Royal Courts

Descent from the gods was an integral part of being royal and was part of what made a king more than just a war leader. Concepts of divine descent may have come from long-established Germanic tradition,[28] and could have been adapted to suit a new environment once Anglo-Saxons had become a dominant political force in parts of Britain. The adoption of temples and prehistoric ritual sites may have been part of the same process.[29] If we look more broadly at ways in which 'symbols of power' were utilised in early Anglo-Saxon England we see an even more eclectic mix, an apparent willingness to combine elements from a variety of cultures. The Sutton Hoo helmet, whose iconography apparently declared its owner to be a follower of Woden, had as its ultimate progenitor a late Roman cavalry helmet.[30] In fact, the whole striking ensemble of the occupant of mound one at Sutton Hoo, including epaulettes, belt buckle and sword harness, was based upon ceremonial apparel of officials of the late Roman world (fig. 7.1).[31] Adoption of power symbols of the Roman world, such as the elaborate belt sets worn by officials, had a long tradition among the Germanic peoples who had

7.1. Epaulettes from the mound 1 Sutton Hoo ship burial; the form is late Roman, but the decoration, including interlaced animals, two pairs of boars and use of gold, garnets and cloisonné, reflects contemporary Germanic tastes. (© Copyright The British Museum)

contact with the Roman Empire either through employment as fighters or through long-distance trade. Such signifiers of power were part of the common currency of Germanic élites, as the parallels for aspects of the mound one Sutton Hoo burial in the Vendel culture of Sweden have demonstrated.[32] Gold and garnet jewellery, also a striking feature of the Sutton Hoo mound one burial, was widely adopted among Germanic élites in the sixth century.[33]

As occupiers of part of a former Roman province, Anglo-Saxon rulers were probably not unaware that they were, to borrow the title of the recent British Museum exhibition, 'the heirs of Rome'.[34] Not the least striking aspect of the ensemble from Sutton Hoo mound one are the items of silverware that would have come ultimately from Byzantium, the eastern rump of the former Roman Empire.[35] Similar items may have graced the tables of other early seventh-century Anglo-Saxon rulers. King Oswald of Northumbria, for instance, was apparently able to order that a large silver dish, which sounds like a close relation of the Anastasius dish from Sutton Hoo, be taken from his table and broken into pieces for the benefit of the poor (fig. 7.2).[36] Even the objects from Sutton Hoo mound one which are interpreted as royal regalia may have taken their forms from the late Roman or Byzantine world. The whetstone 'sceptre' may have been influenced by the staffs of office of late Roman consuls, perhaps via a consular diptych,[37] while the object which is interpreted as a standard may be based on a depiction on a Roman coin.[38] Bede makes the conscious use of such Roman symbols of power clear in his description of King Edwin being preceded in his journeys through Northumbia by 'the type of standard which the Romans called a *tufa* and the English call a *thuf*', as well as using *vexilla* in battle and a *signifer* in peacetime.[39] A case has been made for seeing Sutton Hoo mound one as the grave of someone who wished to depict himself as a ruler in the Roman tradition.[40] The late Roman associations of the assemblage are, indeed, striking, but some of the iconography and the form of burial (in a ship within a mound) can be read as more self-consciously Germanic ways of proclaiming élite status.[41] It is perhaps the eclecticism of the mound one burial which is most marked, a willingness to draw upon symbolism from a variety of different traditions and blend them together. Like the Frankish King Childeric (d. 481x2),[42] the man buried in mound one at Sutton Hoo wished to signal that he

7.2. *Silver dish with date stamp of the Emperor Anastasius (491–518) from the mound 1 Sutton Hoo ship burial. (© Copyright The British Museum)*

was both a traditional Germanic king and an heir of Rome.

A comparison with the grave of Childeric is apt because much of the knowledge of, and the artefacts from the late Roman and Byzantine world that reached the Anglo-Saxons would have done so via the Frankish court. The Byzantine silver objects from mound one at Sutton Hoo may not have been direct imports from Byzantium, but may have arrived as diplomatic gifts from the Frankish royal house to the East Anglian one.[43] The trade route for luxury items, like the so-called 'Coptic' bowls found in mound one at Sutton Hoo and in other high-status Anglo-Saxon burials, seems to have run up from the Mediterranean through Frankish territory.[44] Prestige objects manufactured in Frankia itself, such as glassware and pottery, were imported into Anglo-Saxon England, and much of the gold which came into England probably came in the form of Frankish coinage or Byzantine coin transmitted via Frankia.[45] Frankish craftsmanship and fashion were very influential in sixth- and seventh-century England. Kent, which had the closest contacts with Frankia in the sixth century, was the first area to adopt the status symbols of the Frankish royal court such as gold and garnet jewellery (pl. IIIc) or the crystal balls with accompanying perforated spoons which women wore suspended from the waist, but their employment seems to have been rapidly copied in other Anglo-Saxon kingdoms (fig. 7.3). Emulation of Frankish styles fostered a major change in female dress in the late sixth and early seventh century, whereby the 'peplos' gown, fastened by brooches on either shoulder, was replaced by necklaces, pendants and veils which stemmed ultimately from an imitation of Byzantine court dress (fig. 7.4).[46]

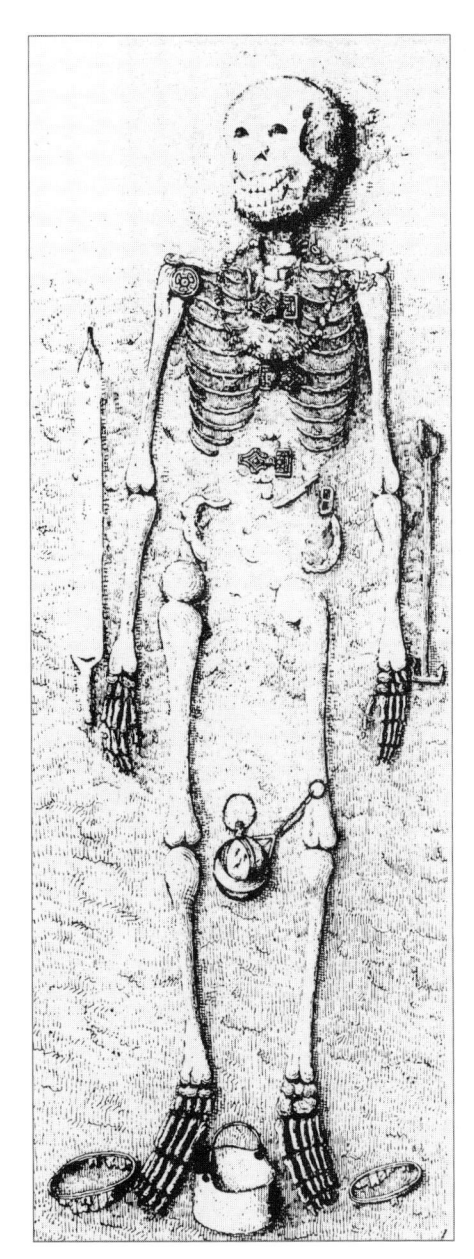

7.3. *Rich female burial of the late sixth century from Chessell Down cemetery, Isle of Wight, which includes crystal ball and brooches worn on the shoulder, the one on her left shoulder being a Frankish import. The burial has very close affinities with contemporary burials from Kent; the peoples of both Kent and the Isle of Wight are described by Bede as sharing a common Jutish identity. (C.R. Smith,* Collectanea Antiqua, *7 vols (1868), p. 6, pl. 28)*

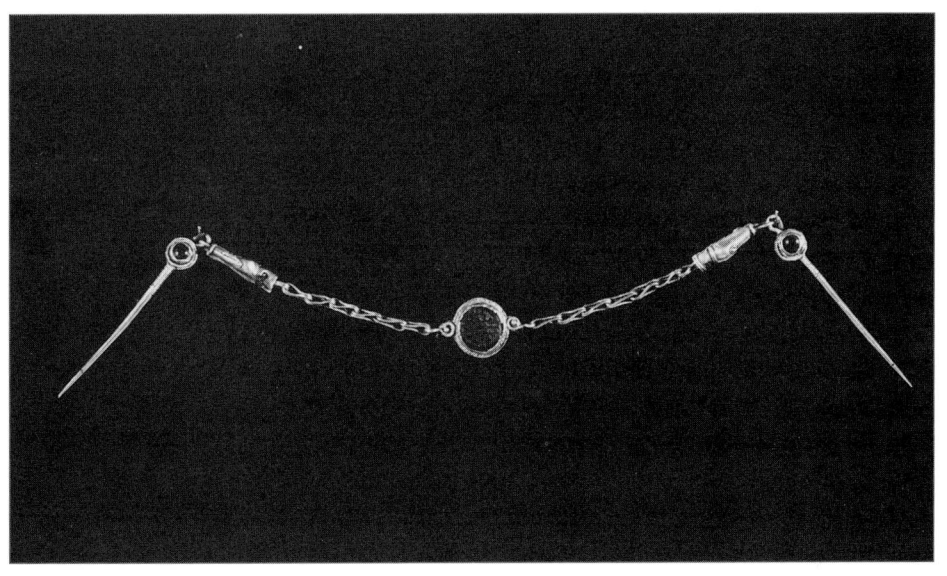

7.4. Pin-suite, probably for fastening a veil, from rich female burial of the seventh century in a barrow on Roundway Down (Wilts); the central blue glass stud is decorated with a cross and there are boars' head terminals at the end of the chains. (Devizes Museum)

THE CULTURAL ASSOCIATIONS OF CHRISTIANITY FOR THE ANGLO-SAXON ROYAL COURTS

The fact that Christianity implied links with the late Roman Empire and its continuation in Byzantium must have smoothed the way for its adoption by the Anglo-Saxon royal courts. Pope Gregory pointed out to Æthelberht of Kent that in converting to Christianity he was following in the steps of Constantine who had 'converted the Roman state from the false worship of idols',[47] while Pope Boniface reminded Edwin of Northumbria that 'the greatest empires and the powers of the world' recognised the christian God who was willing to extend his bounty to 'the frozen hearts of races even in the far corners of the earth'.[48] The popes backed their calls for support for Christianity with gifts of the types of object which Anglo-Saxon royalty seems to have been particularly eager to acquire from the Mediterranean lands. Edwin's wife Æthelburh received 'a silver mirror and an ivory comb adorned with gold' from Pope Boniface,[49] while Edwin himself received garments of silk and gold.[50] When the Anglo-Saxons in their turn wished to convert other Germanic peoples, they believed that they too would be impressed by the links between Christianity and the power and wealth of the Roman world. Bishop Daniel of Winchester (*c.* 705–44), perhaps drawing upon his own experiences in working among the West Saxons and the Jutes of Wight, advised Boniface to get his audience to reflect on the circumstance that while 'the

Christians possess fertile lands, and provinces fruitful in wine and oil and abounding in other riches, they have left to them, the pagans that is, with their gods, lands always frozen with cold'.[51] The prestige of personal connections with papacy was one which must have impressed Anglo-Saxon kings. King Oswiu of Northumbria was persuaded to accept the current methods used in Rome for calculating Easter because they would have had the approval of St Peter who had charge of the keys to heaven;[52] and a number of elderly or seriously ill Anglo-Saxon kings journeyed to Rome presumably in order to gain quicker admittance through St Peter's gates.[53]

But also important for the conversion of the Anglo-Saxon royal courts was the example and intervention of the Franks. To see Augustine and his mission as another commodity which travelled from the Mediterranean to Kent via Frankia might be a glib oversimplification, but one which nevertheless contains much truth.[54] There has been much debate recently about the role of the Franks in the conversion of Kent,[55] and although the accolade for Æthelberht's conversion belongs to St Augustine, credit should also be given for the foundation that had been laid by Bertha and Bishop Liudhard and the help accorded to the Gregorian mission by Frankish rulers and churchmen. According to Pope Gregory, the Frankish queen Brunhild had done more to aid the mission than anyone except God – apparently more than Augustine himself![56] One of her leading supporters, Syagrius of Autun, was rewarded with a pallium for the help he had provided.[57] Even allowing for the rhetoric of diplomatic language, the implication here is of more than just the provision of hospitality and interpreters.

The tenacity of the papal mission in the difficult period following Æthelberht's death[58] and the organisation that Canterbury provided for the emergent church, ensured that a large part of Gregory's blueprint for the Anglo-Saxon church was achieved. But much of the hard work of conversion in the south of England, particularly in East Anglia and Wessex, was carried out by Frankish missionaries who had little apparent contact with Canterbury.[59] Although it might appear that Frankish clergy had shown little interest in converting the Anglo-Saxons until Pope Gregory concerned himself with their spiritual welfare, the period of Frankish involvement can be seen to have coincided with a new enthusiasm for Christianity among aristocratic Franks stirred up by the activities of Columbanus (d. 615).[60] Many of the Franks who were most active in England had connections with religious houses founded or inspired by Columbanus, notably Agilbert and his nephew Leuthere who were both bishops in Wessex, and, in all probability, Felix, bishop of the East Angles.[61] Much as the Anglo-Saxon kings may have valued links with Rome, it seems to have been the leading aristocracy of northern Frankia who provided the role models for the Anglo-Saxon royal converts. One of the ways in which this can be most clearly seen is in the influence of the newly founded double monasteries of northern Frankia. East Anglian and Kentish princesses entered convents in northern Frankia,[62] and in the second half of the seventh century numerous 'double monasteries', based on Frankish prototypes were founded in Anglo-Saxon England.[63] Like earlier introductions from Frankia which became important royal status symbols, the trend began in the south-east of England and then spread rapidly so that by the end of the century every Anglo-Saxon royal family appears to have sponsored one or more of these foundations.[64]

THE COEXISTENCE OF PAGAN AND CHRISTIAN WORSHIP

Desire to enhance prestige by the associations Christianity could bring with the late Roman world and the Frankish royal courts would have figured among the incentives for Anglo-Saxon kings to convert to Christianity. However, we might expect these enticements to have been balanced by a reluctance to sever links with the old gods who helped to define what made a family 'royal'. And, indeed, an attraction to Christianity balanced by an unwillingness to give up the old gods is exactly what Bede's narrative appears to demonstrate. To give but one example, King Æthelberht is reported as saying to Augustine:

> The words and promises you bring are fair enough, but because they are new to us and doubtful, I cannot consent to accept them and forsake those beliefs which I and the whole English race have held so long.[65]

The question of at what point we can describe a kingdom as converted to Christianity depends upon the direction from which the issue is approached. Bede, who was inclined to take a positive view of such matters and was particularly concerned with tracing the institutional history of the Anglo-Saxon church, presented the first conversion of a province's king and the establishment of a bishopric as the defining point. He then interpreted any reversions to paganism as apostasy or some other aberration from a christian norm.[66] However, that is not the only way in which the reception of the new religion at the Anglo-Saxon royal courts can be understood. The first conversion of the king of the province might begin the process of the christianisation of the royal house, but that process could be said not to have been completed until the stage was reached when no more pagan kings ascended the throne and there were no more royally sponsored reversions to paganism. As is well known, most of the royal houses for which Bede provides information experienced apostasies or reversions to pagan worship at some point in the seventh century; and in the case of the East and

West Saxons, Christianity had to be reintroduced by new missions on more than one occasion. Although Sæbert of the East Saxons had been persuaded to convert to Christianity in 604,[67] the last reversion to paganism in the province occurred some sixty years later during the severe outbreak of plague in 663/4.[68] In Wessex the first king to be baptised was King Cynegils, in 635,[69] but it was apparently still possible for Cædwalla to succeed to the throne some fifty years later without having been baptised.[70] In the kingdoms of the East Angles, East Saxons, West Saxons, Northumbria and in Kent the reign of the first king to be baptised was followed by apostasy or reversion to paganism. The frequency with which this occurred led Professor Angenendt to propose that the eldest son was deliberately not baptised, but allowed to remain a pagan as a kind of insurance policy.[71] In Mercia, it would seem, the insurance policy worked in a different way: Penda of Mercia remained a pagan, but his eldest son Peada, sub-king of the Middle Angles, was allowed by him to convert to Christianity.[72] In fact, it was not just eldest sons who might remain unconverted. A more accurate way to characterise what occurred was that when the first king was converted only some of the royal family went to the baptismal font with him. Practice no doubt varied between kingdoms. Bede provides a long list of members of the Deiran royal house who were baptised in the reign of Edwin (616–33);[73] by contrast, it is apparent that after Sæbert of the East Saxons (d. 616x17) was baptised, not only did his three sons remain pagan, but so it would seem did more distant members of the royal house who subsequently inherited the throne.[74]

In assessing when the royal houses might be said to be fully converted to Christianity, we could also look for the point at which pagan altars and temples were destroyed – for until that happened we cannot assume that pagan worship was not continuing alongside Christianity. This, of course, is precisely what occurred in the well-known case of King Rædwald of the East Angles (d. 616x27) whom Bede castigated for maintaining two altars in his temple, one dedicated to the christian God and another on which he continued to offer sacrifices to his pagan deities.[75] The continued existence of pagan temples and 'idols', and so presumably the continuation of pagan ceremonies, was a major concern to the Gregorian mission. Pope Gregory wrote to King Æthelberht of Kent in 601 urging him to 'suppress the worship of idols; overthrow their buildings and shrines', implying that the conversion of the king did not automatically lead to the suppression of pagan practices within the kingdom.[76] In fact, Bede records that Æthelberht's grandson Eorconberht (640–64) was the first English king to order pagan worship to cease and all the idols to be destroyed.[77] Rædwald's temple evidently survived until about the same date, since Ealdwulf, future king of the East Angles, saw it when he was a boy, which probably means in the 640s.[78] So it would appear that the initial conversion of a king and the establishment of a bishopric did not imply that pagan worship ceased in a kingdom. In Kent, which could be regarded as the 'flagship' christian kingdom and the only one whose main see had an unbroken tradition, there was apparently a gap of about forty years between the first acceptance of Christianity and the order for pagan worship to cease.

The point at which paganism was finally abandoned may have been a more significant staging post for the Anglo-Saxon royal houses than is commonly appreciated. Although we have a specific reference to a royal order for the destruction of idols only for Kent, in most of the other kingdoms the transition to full acceptance of Christianity was marked in some significant way. In many of the kingdoms the last recorded pagan reign can be linked to the phenomenon of a reigning monarch abdicating in order to enter a religious community.[79] The earliest example is Sigibert of the East Angles (acc. 630 or 631) who succeeded the last pagan East Anglian ruler and may, if King Ealdwulf's testimony about Rædwald's temple can be so interpreted, have ordered the destruction of East Anglian shrines.[80] The East Saxon Sæbbi (acc. by 664) also resigned the throne to become a monk, though at a rather later point in his life than Sigibert.[81] Sæbbi had originally ruled jointly with Sigehere who reverted to paganism during the plague of 663/4 and is the last known pagan East Saxon ruler.[82] In Wessex King Centwine abdicated in 685 to enter a monastery and was succeeded by Cædwalla, the last West Saxon to come to the throne as a pagan.[83] The Mercian King Æthelred (acc. 675), who resigned his throne in 704 to enter the monastery of Bardney,[84] was slightly more distanced from the last Mercian pagan ruler, his father Penda, as his brother Wulfhere had reigned before him as a Christian, but he still belonged to the first generation of the Mercian royal house to be fully committed to the promotion of Christianity. The apparent willing abdication of a reigning monarch in order to enter a religious community is extremely unusual in early medieval Europe.[85] Its occurrence as royal houses were making their final commitment to the transition from paganism to Christianity is suggestive, as well as illustrative, of the type of competitive emulation which is so characteristic of the early Anglo-Saxon kingdoms.[86] These abdications mark the point at which the royal houses had finally fully accepted Christianity, and were a very public demonstration of that fact, albeit one that the church was quick to discourage. Although a genuine enthusiasm for the new religion may lie behind the abdications, there would have been a number of reasons why church leaders would have felt it undesirable to have rulers resigning their secular office to take up an ecclesiastical one.[87] Royal women, whether they had once been married or not, were the highest-ranking members of the royal house who were welcomed into monastic life. King Eorconberht, who ordered the destruction of the idols in Kent, did not enter a religious house in Kent himself, but sent his daughter Eorcengota to become a nun at Faremoutier-en-Brie where she was subsequently recognised as a saint.[88] By the end of the seventh century, all the Anglo-Saxon kingdoms contained royal nunneries, and the bloodline of most of the royal houses had been enhanced by the recognition of saintly kinswomen.[89] The best chance a king had of becoming a saint was to die in battle against a pagan. In Northumbria the successor to the last pagan rulers was Oswald (634–42) who seems to have been regarded as a saint soon after his death in battle,[90] and was the first of the Anglo-Saxon kings to be culted in this way.[91]

For those royal houses whose conversion Bede records in some detail, a hiatus can thus be recognised between the time of the first acceptance of Christianity and that of the formal abandonment of pagan worship which could be as long as forty to fifty years. No doubt there were others who followed Rædwald's practice of having altars to both christian and pagan gods.[92] After all, to practitioners of a polytheistic religion there was no particular problem in extending worship to include another deity. Scandinavians likewise assumed when Christianity was first introduced that it would be compatible with continuing pre-christian religious practices. According to the *Landnámabók* ('Book of Settlements') of the Icelanders, which in its earliest version probably dates back to the beginning of the twelfth century, Helgi inn Magri, one of the early settlers, was a believer in Christ, but would call on Thor for help when in trouble at sea. Thor is said to have shown him where to build his farm, but it was named after Christ.[93] Ari Thorgilsson, who claimed the son of the first native Icelandic bishop as his informant, recorded that when the Icelanders agreed formally to convert to Christianity, private worship of the gods was allowed to continue. Polytheism among the Scandinavians also allowed for rejection of a god who did not seem to be performing as a loyal adherent might expect. Egil Skalla-Grimsson bitterly rebuked Odin for betraying his trust in letting his son drown; but even more striking for parallels with seventh-century England is the account by the English priest Ælnoth of the rejection of Christianity in Sweden when it was discovered not to be effective in preventing times of hardship:

> The Svear and the Gotar, however, seem to honour the christian faith only when things go according to their wishes and luck is on their side; but if storm winds are against them, if the soil turns barren during drought or is flooded by heavy rainfalls, if an enemy threatens to attack with harrying and burning, then they persecute the christian faith that they claim to honour, and with threats and injustice against the faithful they seek to chase them out of the land.[94]

Bede portrays very similar pagan reactions in seventh-century England after defeat in battle or an outbreak of plague.

The polytheism of the Anglo-Saxons allowed an initial acceptance of Christianity to be achieved quite easily, but would also have encouraged the assumption that it could be integrated with existing religious practices. Easy acceptance might also mean easy rejection, especially if the christian God did not seem to provide a better solution than his pagan rivals for the problems of this world. Furthermore the Anglo-Saxon royal courts had already had experience of absorbing and combining different cultural influences. An object like the Benty Grange helmet, whose wearer would have received dual protection from its boar crest, with probable pagan connotations, and christian cross on the nose-piece, seems to capture the flavour of the first half of the seventh century when the royal courts thought they could draw support from both religions.[95] Of course, a degree of assimilation was the way forward, but both missionaries and kings had to recognise that there were certain areas where no compromise was possible.

THE PROCESS OF ASSIMILATION

The missionaries very quickly showed awareness that they would need to take the religious expectations of their 'audiences' into account. Once Pope Gregory had been informed of the true situation in England he changed his missionary strategy.[96] In a letter written to King Ætheberht of Kent on 22 June 601 he had urged him to suppress all signs of paganism and destroy pagan temples,[97] but by 18 July in the same year he wrote to Mellitus that he had 'after long deliberation' decided on a shift in strategy and was instead authorising a degree of syncretism through which the Anglo-Saxons could be lured into acceptance of Christianity by associating it with familiar religious observances.[98] Rather than destroying temples, Mellitus was advised to convert them into churches. Of all the missionary groups, the Italians probably found it most difficult to know how far they could temper christian expectations to take account of Anglo-Saxon traditional practices. Augustine's famous series of questions to Gregory suggests how difficult he found the task of adapting basic christian precepts to situations for which his previous training had ill-prepared him.[99] The faithful imposition by his successors of Gregory's ruling that a man could not legally marry his stepmother nearly finished the mission altogether, when King Eadbald took exception to their attempts to interfere with his marital arrangements.[100] Not only was this undue interference in an act which probably had an important symbolic significance for continuity from one reign to another,[101] but it was probably also a matter which he would not have expected to come under the jurisdiction of priests.

Irish and Frankish missionaries may have had a surer feel for what Germanic kings, who had been newly introduced to Christianity, would or would not find acceptable. Aidan's granting away of the 'royal horse' he had been given by King Oswine can be seen as an action nicely calculated to have an immediate impact on his Northumbrian audience.[102] The king was initially angered that Aidan had thus disposed of a horse he had specially chosen for him from the royal stud and which was accoutred with 'royal trappings'. 'Have we not many less valuable horses or other things which would have been good enough to give the poor?', Bede presents him as saying. To which Aidan promptly replied, 'Surely the son of a mare is not dearer to you than that son of God?' It was the immensity of Aidan's self-denial, the granting away of what others in Oswine's entourage would have loved to receive, that made an impression on his audience about a religion whose rewards could transcend those of earthly wealth. Whether this story about Aidan was apocryphal need not be an immediate concern. It makes the point that the missionaries soon became aware of the need to present Christianity to the Anglo-Saxons in ways to which they could relate.

But although the christian God and his adherents might on occasion impress by confounding the expectations of traditional Anglo-Saxon society, there was also the danger that the new religion might be thought to be inappropriate for its needs. The claim that certain marriage practices were unacceptable has already been cited as a major stumbling block, especially no doubt because of the implications for inheritance. One of the two royal princes who murdered Sigibert 'Sanctus' of the East Saxons had been excommunicated by Bishop Cedd because of what was deemed an unlawful marriage. But the main reason the assassins gave for the murder was 'that they were angry with the king and hated him because he was too ready to pardon his enemies, calmly forgiving them for the wrongs they had done him, as soon as they asked his pardon'.[103] Thus Sigibert had died, as Bede acknowledged, because 'he had devoutly observed the gospel precepts'. If asked to expatiate, the two murderers would no doubt have explained that there was no advantage for them in serving a king who showed as much favour to his enemies as to those who served him loyally. If Christianity was felt to be a religion that was too 'soft' for the rigours of a warrior society and unacceptable to the king's *comitatus*, that was a serious bar to its widespread adoption, and Bede swiftly moved on to say that Sigibert had died because he had disobeyed Cedd's order not to socialise with his excommunicated kinsman.

In their presentation of Christianity the missionaries seem to have tried to promote it as a religion that was compatible with the needs of a warrior society,[104] that is if we can accept the testimony of Bede's conversion narratives. Time and time again it was a victory in battle which is said to have persuaded a hesitant king to accept Christianity – and sometimes disappointment at a defeat which swayed matters the other way. Bede does not spell it out, but we can surely see here the christian God in competition with Woden.[105] It was vitally important that both the kings and their followers believed that the christian God could 'deliver' on the battlefield, and fortunately there were numerous examples from the Old Testament to show his effectiveness, as well as more recent examples like that of Constantine to dangle before them.[106]

If kings were obliged to concede that acceptance of Christianity meant the worship of only one god, the missionaries had to recognise that there could be no clean break with the pre-christian past which was so essential for validating the status of the royal houses. Radbod of Frisia drew back from conversion when he discovered that if he became a Christian he would not be able to join his pagan ancestors after death as they would be consigned to hell.[107] Links with the ancestors, whether real or acquired from the prehistoric past,[108] involved more than just sentiment for they were one of the means through which royal houses claimed their right to rule. The church found ways to accommodate them. As we have seen, Woden and other quasi-divine founders could be included, but also neutralised, in christianised genealogies and foundation accounts; literacy ensured that these accounts were then preserved for posterity. Bede could allow that a pagan king like Æthelfrith of Bernicia was part of the divine plan; though he was ignorant of Christianity, he 'might indeed be compared with Saul'.[109] A change in religion did not have to mean an immediate change in burial practice or place of burial. Not all converts seem to have followed Æthelbert of Kent in adopting burial in an annex to a church as the Frankish kings had done.[110] Burial of people of high status who were apparently christian continued in pre-christian burial grounds with provision of grave goods, which may have been felt to be more concerned with the display of status than with pagan customs. Eventually burial *ad sanctos*, some of whom might be their own ancestors, came to seem more desirable and as conferring the greater status.[111] Nor was it only the immediate pre-christian Germanic past which was incoporated; Anglo-Saxon kings could also continue to be associated with the Roman past. A Roman ruler might mingle with Germanic heroes in the upper reaches of a genealogy,[112] and an object like the Franks Casket demonstrates that Roman, Germanic and christian legend could all be acknowledged as contributing to the contemporary Anglo-Saxon world.[113]

Conclusion

The conversion of the Anglo-Saxon royal houses was a complex process which is only partially recorded for us in our main written source, Bede's *Ecclesiastical*

History. The advent of Christianity was such a significant break with the past for Bede, both because of the shift in religion and, more mundanely, because of the change in the sources available, that it is easy to overlook that the choice may not have been so obvious to the rulers to whom the good news came. The pressures applied by overlords were, of course, part of the equation through which individual kings decided to accept or reject Christianity, but the role of religion in early medieval society cannot be understood simply as a by-product of the political process. Although for christian writers like Bede one either was or was not a Christian, royal houses would initially have seen no particular bar to incorporating aspects of christian worship into existing religious practices and may have proceeded to do so for several decades. The issue became not would a king accept or reject Christianity, but could a way be found of accommodating it which would satisfy the needs of the royal courts without compromising the basic tenets of the christian religion. Christianity, being infinitely flexible, naturally rose to the challenge, and the advantages it could present to kings, not least in upholding royal authority on earth and promising eternal life after death, swayed royal opinion before any practical disadvantages, such as expectations of moral behaviour and of generous, permanent, gifts of lands, became overtly apparent.[114]

NOTES

1. *HE*, I, 25 and II, 5 for Æthelberht's provisioning and protection of the Augustinian mission, something which is also brought out in his law-code: *The Laws of the Earliest English Kings*, ed. F.L. Attenborough (Cambridge, 1922), pp. 2–17.
2. *HE*, II, 5 for expulsion of members of the Augustinian mission from the kingdom of the East Saxons.
3. *HE*, III, 7 for examples.
4. H. Mayr-Harting, *The Coming of Christianity to Anglo-Saxon England* (3rd edn, London, 1991), pp. 64–8; J. Campbell, 'Observations on the Conversion of England', *Essays in Anglo-Saxon History* (London, 1986), pp. 69–84, esp. pp. 74–7; D.P. Kirby, *The Earliest English Kings* (London, 1991); N. Higham, *The Convert Kings* (Manchester, 1997).
5. *HE*, II, 13.
6. *HE*, III, 22; see II, 10 for the same arguments in a letter from Pope Boniface to King Edwin of Northumbria.
7. R. Page, 'Anglo-Saxon Paganism: the Evidence of Bede', *Pagans and Christians. The Interplay between Christian Latin and Traditional Cultures in Early Medieval Europe*, eds T. Hosfra, L.A.T.R. Houwen and A.A. MacDonald, Germania Latina II (Groningen, 1995), pp. 99–130; I.N. Wood, 'Pagan Religions and Superstitions East of the Rhine from the Fifth to the Ninth Century', *After Empire. Towards an Ethnology of Europe's Barbarians*, ed. G. Ausenda (Woodbridge, 1995), pp. 253–79.
8. L.E. v. Padberg, 'Odin oder Christus? Loyalitäts- und Orientierungskonflikte in der frühmittelalterlichen Christianisierungsepoche', *Archiv für Kulturgeschichte*, 77 (1995), 249–78.

9. B. Hope-Taylor, *Yeavering: An Anglo-British Centre of Early Northumbria* (London, 1972), pp. 95–118.
10. O. Olsen, *Hørg, Hof og Kirke* (Copenhagen, 1966); idem, 'Is There a Relationship between Pagan and Christian Places of Worship in Scandinavia?', *The Anglo-Saxon Church*, eds L.A.S. Butler and R.K. Morris, CBA report 60 (London, 1986), pp. 126–30.
11. Adam von Bremen, *Hamburgische Kirchengeschichte*, ed. B. Schmeidler, Scriptores rerum Germanicarum (Hannover and Leipzig, 1917), p. 258; S. Brink, 'Political and Social Structures in Early Scandinavia. A Settlement-Historical Pre-study of the Central Place', *Tor*, 28 (1996), 235–81.
12. J. Blair, 'Anglo-Saxon Pagan Shrines and their Prototypes', *ASSAH*, 8 (1995), 1–28. However, there is some evidence for use of temples among the continental Germans in the eighth and ninth centuries; Wood, 'Pagan Religions and Superstitions', pp. 255–6.
13. Hope-Taylor, *Yeavering*, pp. 244–6. See also R. Bradley, 'Time Regained: the Creation of Continuity', *JBAA*, 140 (1987), 1–17.
14. Page suggests that Bede may be projecting ideals of Christian priesthood onto Coifi in this passage: 'Anglo-Saxon Paganism', pp. 111–21; but the likelihood of such priestly taboos having existed is supported in J. Hines, 'Religion: the Limits of Knowledge', *The Anglo-Saxons from the Migration Period to the Eighth Century. An Ethnographic Perspective*, ed. J. Hines (Woodbridge, 1997), pp. 375–401, at pp. 379–80.
15. *HE*, II, 9; presumably a seax is meant. Bede's attention to the details of artefacts and buildings can be compared to that of the *Beowulf* poet and presumably can be seen as a narrational device with which his audience would be familiar.
16. P. Meulengracht Sørensen, 'Håkon den Gode og guderne. Nogle bemærkninger om religion og centralmagt', *Fra Stamme til Stat in Danmark 2, Høvdingesamfund og Kongemagt*, eds P. Mortensen and B. Rasmussen (Århus, 1991), pp. 235–44; idem, 'Religions Old and New', *The Oxford Illustrated History of the Vikings*, ed. P. Sawyer (Oxford, 1997), pp. 202–24, esp. pp. 214–6. For public pagan ritual in Frisia, see Wood, 'Pagan Religions', pp. 261–2.
17. See, for instance, the unwillingness of Kings Ecgfrith and Aldfrith of Northumbria to accept the papal ruling that Bishop Wilfrid should be restored to his previous position in the Northumbrian church: *The Life of Bishop Wilfrid by Eddius Stephanus*, ed. B. Colgrave (Cambridge, 1927), pp. 70–1, 126–7.
18. Divination, for instance, seems to have been an important pagan ritual in which rulers might be involved: Wood, 'Pagan Religions', pp. 260–3. Pope Boniface in his letter to Queen Æthelburh praises her brother, King Eadbald of Kent, for resisting the lure of auguries as well as rejecting the worship of idols: *HE*, II, 11.
19. *HE*, I, 15.
20. That is the view expressed by Æthelweard: *The Chronicle of Æthelweard*, ed. A. Campbell (London, 1962), p. 7; E. John, 'The Point of Woden', *ASSAH*, 5 (1992), 127–34.
21. R. Wenskus, *Stammesbildung und Verfassung* (Köln, 1961); K. Hauck, 'Lebensnormen und Kultmythen in germanischen Stammes- und Herrschergenealogien', *Saeculum*, 6 (1955), 186–223.
22. R. Bruce-Mitford, *The Sutton Hoo Ship-Burial II: Arms, Armour and Regalia* (London, 1978), pp. 186–220; S. Jensen, 'Odin from Ribe', *Oldtidens Ausigt/Faces of the Past*, eds P. Kjærum and R.A. Olsen (Copenhagen, 1990).

23. D.N. Dumville, 'The Anglian Collection of Royal Genealogies and Regnal Lists', *ASE*, 5 (1976), 23–50; ibid., 'Kingship, Genealogies and Regnal Lists', *Early Medieval Kingship*, eds P. Sawyer and I.N. Woods (Leeds, 1977), pp. 72–104.
24. B.A.E. Yorke, 'The Kingdom of the East Saxons', *ASE*, 14 (1985), 1–36, at pp. 13–15.
25. H. Moisl, 'Anglo-Saxon Genealogies and Germanic Oral Tradition', *Journal of Medieval History*, 7 (1981), 215–48.
26. N. Brooks, 'The Creation and Early Structure of the Kingdom of Kent', *The Origins of Anglo-Saxon Kingdoms*, ed. S. Bassett (Leicester, 1989), pp. 55–74, esp. pp. 58–64.
27. For example, Fredegar's account of origins of the Merovingian dynasty: Moisl, 'Anglo-Saxon Genealogies', pp. 223–6. See also G. Steinsland, *Det Hellige Bryllup og Norrøn Kongeiolgi* (Oslo, 1991), for the descent of Norse kings from the unions of gods and giants.
28. O. Höfler, 'Der Sakralcharakter des germanischen Königtums', *Das Königtum, seine geistigen und rechtlichen Grundlagen*, ed. T. Mayer (Lindua-Konstanz, 1956), pp. 75–104; J.M. Wallace-Hadrill, *Early Germanic Kingship in England and on the Continent* (Oxford, 1971), pp. 7–16.
29. Bradley, 'Time Regained'.
30. Mitford, *Sutton Hoo II*, pp. 220–4.
31. *Op. cit., passim*; W. Filmer-Sankey. 'The "Roman Emperor" in the Sutton Hoo Ship Burial', *JBAA*, 149 (1996), 1–9; M. Archibald, M. Brown and L. Webster, 'Heirs of Rome: the Shaping of Britain AD 400–900', *The Transformation of the Roman World*, eds L. Webster and M. Brown (London, 1997), pp. 208–48, esp. pp. 222–3.
32. Bruce-Mitford, *Sutton Hoo II*, pp. 205–19; *Vendel Period Studies 2*, eds J.P. Lamm and H.-Å. Nordström (Stockholm, 1983); A. Care-Evans, *The Sutton Hoo Ship-Burial* (London, 1986), pp. 113–17.
33. B. Arrhenius, *Granatschmuck und Gemmen ans nordischen Funden des frühen Mittelalters* (Stockholm, 1971); Bruce-Mitford, *Sutton Hoo II*, pp. 597–603.
34. Webster and Brown, *Transformation of the Roman World*, pp. 220–4.
35. R. Bruce-Mitford, *The Sutton Hoo Ship-Burial III*, ed. A. Care-Evans, 2 vols (London, 1983), pp. 1–201.
36. *HE*, III, 6; distribution of such largesse to the poor was also appropriate behaviour for late Roman office-holders and seems to have been imitated by the Frankish kings, as perhaps Bede was aware – J. Campbell, 'The First Century of Christianity in England', in his *Essays in Anglo-Saxon History* (London, 1986), pp. 49–67, esp. pp. 54–5.
37. Bruce-Mitford, *Sutton Hoo II*, pp. 311–93.
38. *Op. cit.*, pp. 403–31.
39. *HE*, II, 16; M. Deanesley, 'Roman Traditionalist Influence Among the Anglo-Saxons', *EHR*, 58 (1943), 129–46, esp. pp. 136–42. Whether we should regard the Sutton Hoo standard as a *thuf* is, of course, another matter.
40. L. Webster, 'Death's Diplomacy: Sutton Hoo in the Light of Other Male Princely Burials', *Sutton Hoo Fifty Years After*, eds R. Farrell and C. Neuman de Vegvar, American Medieval Studies 2 (Miami, 1992), 75–82; Filmer-Sankey, 'The "Roman emperor"'.
41. J. Shepard, 'The Social Identity of the Individual in Isolated Barrows and Barrow Cemeteries in Anglo-Saxon England', *Space, Hierarchy and Society*, ed. B.C. Burham and J. Kingsbury, BAR Internat. Ser. 59 (Oxford, 1979), 47–79; R. van de Noort, 'The Context of Early Medieval Barrow Burial in Western Europe', *Antiquity*, 66 (1992), 66–73; O. Crumlin-Pedersen and B.M. Thye,

The Ship as Symbol in Prehistoric and Medieval Scandinavia (Copenhagen, 1995).

42. E. James, *The Franks* (Oxford, 1988), pp. 58–64; P. Périn and M. Kazanski, 'Das Grab Chiderichs I', *Die Franken Wegbereiter Europas* (Mainz, 1996), pp. 173–82.
43. I.N. Wood, 'The Franks and Sutton Hoo', *People and Places in Northern Europe 500–1600. Essays in Honour of Peter Sawyer*, eds I.N. Wood and N. Lund (Woodbridge, 1991), pp. 1–14. See also the contribution of Stéphane Lebecq to the present volume.
44. S. Chadwick Hawkes, 'Anglo-Saxon Kent c. 425–725', *Archaeology in Kent to AD 1500*, ed. P.E. Leach, CBA Research Report 48 (London, 1982), pp. 64–78, at pp. 76–7; J.W. Huggett, 'Imported Grave Goods and the Early Anglo-Saxon Economy', *Medieval Archaeology*, 32 (1988), 63–96.
45. Bruce-Mitford, *Sutton Hoo II*, pp. 611–14, 618–25.
46. G. Owen-Crocker, *Dress in Anglo-Saxon England* (Manchester, 1986), pp. 57–63, 85–101.
47. *HE*, I, 32.
48. *HE*, II, 10.
49. *HE*, II, 11.
50. *HE*, II, 10.
51. *English Historical Documents I, c. 500–1042*, ed. D. Whitelock, 2nd edn (London, 1979), pp. 795–7.
52. *HE*, III, 25.
53. C. Stancliffe, 'Kings who Opted Out', *Ideal and Reality in Frankish and Anglo-Saxon Society*, eds P. Wormald, D. Bullough and R. Collins (Oxford, 1983), 154–76; pilgrimage to Rome also became popular with royal and noble Anglo-Saxons who hoped to return home afterwards.
54. See maps of findspots of coptic bowls in Hawkes, 'Anglo-Saxon Kent', p. 77 and of Augustine's route to England in D. Hill, *An Atlas of Anglo-Saxon England* (Oxford, 1981), p. 146.
55. I.N. Wood, 'The Mission of Augustine of Canterbury to the English', *Speculum*, 69 (1994), 1–17; Higham, *Convert Kings*, pp. 62–90; and the contributions of Wood and Lebecq to this volume.
56. Gregory I, *Register*, eds P. Ehwald and L.M. Hartmann, MGH Epistolae 1 and 2 (Berlin, 1887–99), 11.48, as pointed out by Edward James in lectures at various conversion conferences in 1997.
57. Gregory, *Register*, 11.47, 48, 50, 51; Wood, 'Mission of Augustine', pp. 6–7.
58. *HE*, II, 6; see further below. Although Bede gives Archbishop Laurence the credit for turning Eadbald back to Christianity, it may be that his desire to make a Frankish marriage was responsible for his change of heart.
59. Campbell, 'First Century of Christianity', pp. 49–67.
60. F. Prinz, *Frühes Mönchtum in Frankenreich* (Munich, 1965); *Columbanus and Merovingian Monasticism*, eds H.B. Clarke and M. Brennan, BAR Internat. Ser. 113 (Oxford, 1981), *passim*; P.J. Geary, *Before France and Germany: The Creation and Transformation of the Merovingian World* (Oxford, 1988), pp. 171–6.
61. Campbell, 'First Century', pp. 57–9.
62. *HE*, III, 8.
63. M. Bateson, 'Origin and Early History of Double Monasteries', *TRHS*, 13 (1899), 137–98; D. Baltrusch-Schneider, 'Die angelsächsischen Doppelklöster', *Doppelklöster und andere Formen der Symbiose männlicher und weiblicher Religiosen im Mittelalter*, eds K. Elm and M. Parisse (Berlin, 1992), pp. 59–79.
64. B.A.E. Yorke, *Nunneries and the Anglo-Saxon Royal Houses* (forthcoming).
65. *HE*, I, 25.
66. The two pagan rulers who succeeded to Bernicia and Deira on the death of King

Edwin were, according to Bede, struck from the record by those who computed the reigns of kings and the year of their rule added to that of their successor Oswald (*HE*, III, 1). However, memory of them was evidently not obliterated altogether as Bede knew their names and details of their reigns.
67. *HE*, II, 3.
68. *HE*, III, 30.
69. *The Anglo-Saxon Chronicle*, eds and trans D. Whitelock, D.C. Douglas and S.I. Tucker (London, 1961), *sub anno* 635, p. 18.
70. *HE*, IV, 16.
71. A. Angenendt, 'The Conversion of the Anglo-Saxons Considered Against the Background of the Early Medieval Mission', *Angli e Sassoni al di qua e al di la del Mare, Spoleto Settimane di Studio*, 32 (1986), II, 747–81.
72. *HE*, III, 21.
73. *HE*, II, 14 and III, 1.
74. *HE*, II, 5 and Yorke 'Kingdom of the East Saxons', *passim*.
75. *HE*, II, 15.
76. *HE*, I, 32.
77. *HE*, III, 8. The first Kentish legislation actually to forbid certain pagan practices is that of Eorconberht's grandson Wihtred – Attenborough, *Laws*, pp. 24–31.
78. *HE*, II, 15; however, it is not clear whether the temple remained in use or not. Abandoned temples survived to be revived by King Sigehere of the East Saxons and his people in 663/4: *HE*, III, 30.
79. Stancliffe, 'Kings Who Opted Out'; S. Ridyard, 'Monk-kings and the Anglo-Saxon Hagiographic Tradition', *Haskins Society Journal*, 6 (1994), 13–27.
80. *HE*, II, 15 and III, 18.
81. *HE*, IV, 11.
82. *HE*, III, 30.
83. *Aldhelm: The Poetic Works*, eds M. Lapidge and J. Rosier (Woodbridge, 1985), pp. 40–1 and 47–9.
84. A. Thacker. 'Kings, Saints and Monasteries in Pre-Viking Mercia', *Midland History*, 10 (1985), 1–25, at pp. 1–4.
85. Stancliffe, 'Kings Who Opted Out'; as opposed to involuntary retirement used in Frankia from the sixth century as a means of removing political enemies. Similar 'political' retirements seem to have been found in Anglo-Saxon England from the eighth century, perhaps beginning with the forcible tonsure and (temporary) retirement of King Ceolwulf of Northumbria in 731.
86. Seen, for instance, in the rapid adoption among the kingdoms of such new forms of royal aggrandisement as nunneries and coinage. Desire to find out more about an innovation made in another kingdom, of course, helps to explain the sudden interest in Christianity once it had been accepted in Kent.
87. Ridyard, 'Monk-kings', 21–7.
88. *HE*, III, 8.
89. Yorke, *Nunneries and the Anglo-Saxon Royal Houses*.
90. A. Thacker, '*Membra Disjecta*: The Division of the Body and the Diffusion of the Cult', *Oswald. Northumbrian King to European Saint*, eds C. Stancliffe and E. Cambridge (Stamford, 1995), pp. 97–127, esp. pp. 97–107. However, Bede does not present Oswald as a martyr; see V.A. Gunn, 'Bede and the Martyrdom of St Oswald', *SCH*, 30, ed. D. Wood (Oxford, 1993), 57–66.
91. For the importance of royal saint-kings for conversion in Scandinavia, see Sørensen, 'Religions Old and New', pp. 128–33.
92. *HE*, II, 15.
93. Sørensen, 'Religions Old and New', p. 223.
94. Ibid., p. 221; the quotation comes from the *Life* of St Knut, written c. 1122.
95. R. Bruce-Mitford, 'The Benty Grange Helmet and Some Other Supposed Anglo-

Saxon Helmets', *Aspects of Anglo-Saxon Archaeology: Sutton Hoo and Other Discoveries* (London, 1974), 223–52.
96. R.A. Markus, 'Gregory the Great and a Papal Missionary Strategy', *SCH*, 6 (Cambridge, 1970), 29–38.
97. *HE*, I, 32
98. *HE*, I, 30.
99. *HE*, I, 27.
100. *HE*, II, 5.
101. Wallace-Hadrill, *Early Germanic Kingship*, p. 92; P. Stafford, *Queens, Concubines and Dowagers. The King's Wife in the Early Middle Ages* (London, 1983), pp. 168–9.
102. *HE*, III, 5.
103. *HE*, II, 22.
104. P. Wormald, 'Bede, Beowulf and the Conversion of the Anglo-Saxon Aristocracy', *Bede and Anglo-Saxon England*, ed. R.T. Farrell, BAR 46 (Oxford, 1978), 32–95.
105. Padberg, 'Odin oder Christus?', pp. 249–78.
106. *HE*, I, 32.
107. Padberg, 'Odin oder Christus?', pp. 270–3; Wood, 'Pagan Religions', pp. 263–4.
108. Bradley, 'Time Regained'.
109. *HE*, I, 34.
110. D. Mauskopf Deliyannis, 'Church Burial in Anglo-Saxon England: the Prerogative of Kings', *Frühmittelalterliche Studien*, 29 (1995), 96–119.
111. D. Bullough, 'Burial, Community and Belief in the Early Medieval West', *Ideal and Reality in Frankish and Anglo-Saxon Society*, pp. 177–201; see also Simon Burnell and Edward James, ch. 5 above.
112. Deanesly, 'Roman Traditionalist Influence', 129–30; M. Hunter, 'The Sense of the Past in Anglo-Saxon England', *ASE*, 3 (1974), 29–50, esp. p. 39.
113. L. Webster, 'Stylistic Aspects of the Franks Casket', *The Vikings*, ed. R.T. Farrell (Chichester, 1982), pp. 20–31.
114. Versions of this chapter were delivered in 1997 to audiences at the British Museum, Rewley House (Oxford), the University of Reading and the International Medieval Conference at the University of Leeds. I am grateful to the organisers of all these occasions and to the feedback received. I would also like to thank Richard Gameson, in his role as editor of this volume, for suggesting improvements.

CHAPTER 8

Questioning Ritual Purity

The Influence of Gregory the Great's Answers to Augustine's Queries about Childbirth, Menstruation and Sexuality

Rob Meens

When Augustine came to England 1,400 years ago, he did not come into a country that was totally ignorant of Christianity. The king's wife, Bertha, was a Merovingian princess, who had been accompanied by a bishop named Liudhard to cater for her christian needs. They used a church to the east of Canterbury that was dedicated to St Martin and had according to Bede been built in Roman times. After his conversion, King Æthelberht helped Augustine and his companions to 'recover' (*recuperauit*) another Roman church that lay in the town of Canterbury.[1] So, christian churches not only still existed in Kent – though it is hard to say in what state – but people also still remembered that these buildings were, or had been churches.[2] The survival of the place name 'Eccles' in Kent, a name deriving from the Latin word for Church (*ecclesia*), but through the British *eclēs, suggests that British christian communities survived long enough for this christian name to be adopted by the English. Gregory the Great also sent relics of the martyr, Pope Sixtus II, to Augustine to replace a local cult of a martyr bearing the same name. Although Gregory does not specify the exact location of this cult, it proves that Augustine encountered existing christian cults in England.[3]

It seems that Augustine also encountered christian ecclesiastical customs. Based upon different conceptions of ritual purity, these varying customs clearly disturbed him. People in a state of bodily impurity were prohibited from entering church or receiving communion. Such bodily impurity was apparently inherent in three basic states of the human condition: giving birth, menstruation and sexual intercourse. It is evident from Augustine's correspondence that a woman could not enter church immediately after the delivery of a child, but had to wait for a certain time until she had become 'pure' again. This impurity apparently also affected the newly born child, for there was some doubt over how soon a new-born baby could be baptized. Menstruation caused impurity as well, and consequently a menstruating woman was not permitted to enter church or receive holy communion. These two things were likewise denied to a man who had had sexual intercourse with his wife. Nor could a man receive communion after a seminal emission in his sleep; and if he was a priest he was not allowed to celebrate Mass.

That Augustine felt disturbed by these issues is clear from the fact that he felt obliged to ask Pope Gregory the Great's advice on them. Gregory's answers to these requests make up a large part of the so-called *Libellus Responsionum*.[4] The authenticity of this 'booklet', in which Gregory answered several problems Augustine had encountered during his mission, has been seriously questioned, but it is now generally regarded as a genuine Gregorian document. It can be shown that the document already existed in several recensions by the time Bede included it in his *Historia ecclesiastica*.[5] In some crucial places it clearly reflects genuine Gregorian thought, and the questions of ritual purity were not, as had been thought, first introduced by Archbishop Theodore of Canterbury in the seventh century.[6] The problems raised by these issues show that the coming of Christianity not only affected the religious beliefs of the Anglo-Saxons, but also had implications for how people regarded the human body which affected their personal life. Gregory's answers came to enjoy a wide circulation in western Europe. The *Libellus Responsionum* still exists in about 200 medieval manuscripts[7] while, as we will see, its provisions were also included in a great number of medieval penitentials and collections of canon law. Its popularity shows the importance that was attached to such matters by medieval Christians.

In his reply, Gregory seems to criticize Augustine for not having dealt with these problems himself. Although Old Testament evidence can be found to support such notions of impurity as Augustine had encountered among the Anglo-Saxons, these scriptural passages are to be interpreted, so Gregory holds, not in a literal but in a spiritual sense. Gregory made an important distinction between the letter and the spirit, the outward and the inward, the Old Testament and the New, as is clear from his words: 'In the Old Testament it is the outward deeds that are observed, . . . in the New Testament careful heed is paid not so much to what is done outwardly as to what is thought inwardly'.[8] For Gregory it is the inner state that counts, not a bodily, outward state. The impurity in the cases mentioned above is, in his view, part of man's fallen nature, and should not, therefore, be considered a sin.[9]

Before having a closer look at the way Gregory's answers influenced views on bodily impurity during the Middle Ages, something should be said about the question of why Augustine felt obliged to refer such matters to the Pope.

THE BACKGROUND TO AUGUSTINE'S QUERIES

It has been thought that Augustine's questions on bodily pollution were triggered by pagan, Anglo-Saxon notions of purity and impurity; but if that were really the case, it seems peculiar that Augustine felt obliged to ask the Pope for advice. In responding to pagan custom surely his own authority would have sufficed. Moreover, it is revealing that these problems arose in connection with christian rituals, such as holy communion, baptism and entering a church. It seems more likely, therefore, that Augustine sought to reinforce his stance because he was confronted not by pagan Anglo-Saxons, but by christian ones who had been influenced by British ideas about the relationship between impurity and holiness. In other words Augustine's questions and Gregory's replies suggest that British Christianity had impinged on the Anglo-Saxons, even though Bede explicitly denies that they had undertaken any missionary activity.[10]

Ian Wood, however, has recently taken this argument a step further, while at the same time questioning some of its assumptions.[11] From studying the evidence for 'paganism' he suggests that several features of Anglo-Saxon heathen religion may have been indebted to Christianity. For example, while religious buildings are almost totally lacking among the Germanic peoples on the continent, apart from the Frisians, there is by contrast some evidence for the existence of Anglo-Saxon temples, even though their appearance is uncertain.[12] Wood suggests that the Anglo-Saxons and Frisians borrowed the idea of temples from the Roman world, and possibly from Late Antique Christianity, while adopting their physical remains. The concept of priests may also have been borrowed from the Roman, and possibly the christian, world. Yet, while it is possible that notions of sacral buildings and the concept of priesthood were adopted from Late Antique Christianity, this does not seem to be the case for the concept of ritual purity. Ideas of purity and impurity as we encounter them in the *Libellus Responsionum*, seem only to have developed in the British and Irish churches in the wake of the Anglo-Saxon invasions.

Gregory the Great does not specify in his answers whether he is dealing with ideas current among the Anglo-Saxons or among the British. I supposed Gregory referred to Anglo-Saxon attitudes because Augustine had asked: 'All these things the ignorant English need to know.' The textual transmission of the *Libellus* is, however, a complicated one. While it is now generally accepted that the text of the *responsiones* is genuinely Gregorian, Wood queries whether the particular questions might not have been added to the text at some later date. If Wood is right in assuming that the exact formulation of Augustine's questions is the result of some later editorial work, then there is no reason to assume that these matters refer to Anglo-Saxon customs. They might as well apply solely to customs within the British church. Although in general the *Libellus Responsionum* deals with problems of the English church, it is not impossible that problems related to the British church were also a matter of discussion between Augustine and Gregory, as is shown in the seventh question – how to deal with the bishops of Gaul and Britain. The bulk of the issues discussed in the *Libellus Responsionum*, however, relate to problems in the nascent Anglo-Saxon church. This includes the third question on the 'general issue of theft from churches', which was the first problem dealt with in the laws of Æthelberht.[13] So, though it is not impossible that answers eight and nine deal only with ecclesiastical customs from the British church, of which Augustine had gained some knowledge, it seems, nevertheless, more likely that such purity rules caused problems in the young church in Kent when British customs clashed with Roman ones.

In an earlier study I tried to chart the divergent attitudes in matters of ritual purity among the christian churches with which Augustine interacted. Ian Wood has now underlined the importance of making adequate allowance for the potentially great diversity within what is described by the one word 'paganism'.

The Future of Gregory's Answers

Athough Gregory the Great was held in great esteem, especially among the English,[14] his rulings in these matters of ritual purity, did not settle the question.[15] St Augustine's successor in the see of Canterbury in the later seventh century, the Greek monk Theodore of Tarsus, not only still encountered ideas about impurity that were apparently inspired by a literal interpretation of Old Testament rules, but actually endorsed some of these views himself.[16] Like the *Libellus Responsionum*, the penitential that bears his name has a complicated textual history; nevertheless in essence it goes back to his teachings. It prescribes a three-week penance for a woman who enters church during her period of 'impurity' after childbirth; and it is specified that this period of uncleanness lasted for forty days. Theodore also forbade women to enter church or to receive communion while menstruating, even if they were nuns. If they entered a church building in such an impure state and received communion, they had to fulfil a penance of three weeks.[17] It is a mystery why Theodore did not refer to Gregory's answers here. Given that they had been sent to Canterbury, why then was a distinguished holder of that archbishopric seemingly unaware of the Pope's rulings? Did Theodore not know the *Libellus Responsionum*, or did he simply ignore it? In 735 St Boniface, who was mainly interested in the document's privilege allowing the newly converted Anglo-Saxons to marry within the third degree of kinship, asked Nothelm of Canterbury to send him a copy of the *Libellus*, the authenticity of which he doubted. He had already asked in vain for it in Rome: it could not be found in the papal archives.[18] Unfortunately, we do not know whether Nothelm was able to comply with Boniface's wish, and consequently we remain unsure about the availability of the *Libellus* in Canterbury by the year 735. It would be a great help if we knew how Bede had come to know this text. Did he get it from Rome, from Canterbury, or somewhere else? Meyvaert hypothesised that Bede was acquainted with the *Libellus* by way of a manuscript which also contained the penitential of Theodore, a combination well known from later continental manuscripts. He further suggested that similar manuscripts might once have been fairly common in England too. Now, if this were indeed the case it would not be necessary to assume that Bede got his knowledge from Canterbury or Rome.[19] However, Bede shows no familiarity with Theodore's penitential, nor does he mention this text when praising Theodore's achievements in Canterbury.[20] Yet, we should bear in mind that composing a penitential text does not seem to have been considered worthy of mention in an early medieval biography: Jonas of Bobbio, for example, does not once refer to Columbanus compiling his penitential. We might even wonder what authorship means in the context of a penitential.[21] The question of whether or not Theodore is likely to have known the *Libellus* seems destined to remain open for the moment. However, it is difficult to believe that there was no copy extant at Canterbury in his day.

Be that as it may, Theodore did not, or chose not to, abide by Gregory's teachings. Instead, he endorsed a literal interpretation of the biblical precepts. There were probably two reasons for this: on the one hand, the enduring influence of Irish and possibly also British Christianity; and on the other, Theodore's Greek background. Greek attitudes seem, in general, to have been more in line with the Old Testament rules.

Gregory the Great or Theodore of Canterbury?

If we follow the subsequent history of Gregory's and Theodore's texts concerning these aspects of ritual purity, then it becomes clear that neither view prevailed over the other, and that correspondingly there was ample room for diversity in this field, a diversity to which Gregory the Great would not have objected.[22] Theodore's views are incorporated into a number of early medieval penitentials, some of which have come down to us in manuscripts that also contain the *Libellus Responsionum*. This did not come about by accident, but was rather a concious act of compilation. Consequently, the readers of some manuscripts encountered two different ways of treating these questions of ritual purity. That this did not remain unnoticed is clear from texts that deliberately oppose the two views. While the Theodorian canon forbidding menstruating women to enter a church was adopted in the *Paenitentiale Capitula Iudiciorum*, for instance, this text added that Pope Gregory allowed ingress to such women. Gregory's responses are also cited in two other penitentials, *Merseburgense A* and *Ps.-Gregorii*, implying that their compilers favoured his views. The same cannot be said, however, of all the scribes who actually copied *Merseburgense A* and *Ps.-Gregorii*, for in both cases, one of the extant manuscripts leaves out the Gregorian passages or alters them in such a way that it endorses instead a literal interpretation of the purity rules. How readers responded to manuscripts in which the conflicting rulings were presented remains unclear. If Gregory's personal prestige is likely to have added weight to his views, popular attitudes may have favoured the literal interpretation. Although the Carolingian moralist Jonas, bishop of Orléans (812–45) knew and used the *Libellus Responsionum*, he praised women who abstained from entering a church during menstruation. He insisted that people should enter church and receive holy communion with a pure mind and a clean body.[23]

Gregory's response concerning a period of purification after the birth of a child also entered the authoritative collection of authentic and inauthentic Carolingian capitularies assembled around the middle of the ninth century by the mysterious Benedictus Levita.[24] From Benedict's collection this response was adopted independently into two episcopal capitularies of the Carolingian era: that of Isaac, bishop of Langres (857–80) and that of Hérard, bishop of Tours (856–71?). Both allowed women to enter church immediately after delivery (*post partum statim*) if they wanted to express their gratitude to the Lord, although Hérard made an exception in the case of adulterers who were required to stay away from the holy building.[25]

Pope Nicolas I (858–67) cited Gregory's response when asked for advice by the Bulgarians. In his letter to the Bulgarians addressing a variety of questions about christian behaviour (indeed a document that resembles the *Libellus Responsionum*), Nicolas referred to Gregory's reply, in answer to a query concerning how long a woman should abstain from church after childbirth.[26] If this shows that Gregory's views were authoritative in Rome in the second half of the ninth century, it also reveals that issues of purity and childbirth remained problematic. It is uncertain whether such questions arose among the Bulgarians because of the activities of Greek missionaries or of Latin ones. However, since efforts to christianize the Bulgarians were also made from Bavaria, it is not impossible that Irish or Anglo-Saxon views spread to the Bulgarians via southeast Germany.

The evidence of his handbook for episcopal visitations, suggests that Regino of Prüm (*c.* 840–915) was unaware of Gregory's rulings, for he there cites an unnamed penitential, possibly the penitential now known as *P. mixtum Bedae-Egberti*, which forbade women from entering church after giving birth. Regino adopted the Old Testament distinction between the birth of a boy and that of a girl, decreeing an abstinence of thirty days in the former case and one of forty days in the latter.[27]

Burchard, bishop of Worms from 1000–25, cited Gregory's response in his influential collection of canon law known as the *Decretum*, when dealing with the question of whether a priest should sacrifice Mass after being 'defiled' during sleep.[28] However, he also included a canon prescribing a seven-day penance for receiving the Eucharist after such a nocturnal delusion.[29] When dealing with women, moreover, Burchard ignored Gregory's views, for he imposed a penance for women who entered church during menstruation. He does not follow Theodore's views here, but returns to the Old Testament view that the birth of a boy is less polluting than that of a girl – in the former case a woman should stay away from church for thirty-three days, in the latter twice as long. The penance prescribed by Burchard seems to be linked to the measure of pollution. The young mother has to do penance for as long as she should have stayed out of church.[30] Theodore's canon concerning the entry of menstruating women into church and of their taking communion (here attributed to a council from Mainz), is slightly changed in Burchard's *Decretum*. He speaks not of entering church or taking communion, but of 'offering' (*non offerant*). This seems to imply that women were allowed to enter church and, possibly, receive holy communion, but were not allowed to approach the altar.[31]

Burchard's canons were adopted by 'the best scholar in canon law in northern Europe before (...) Gratian': Bishop Ivo of Chartres (1091–1116).[32] This pupil of the later archbishop of Canterbury, Lanfranc of Bec, included Burchard's decision in his collection of canon law known as the *Decretum*, though according to the edition in the *Patrologia Latina*, the period of impurity after the birth of a girl lasted for fifty-six days instead of sixty-six. Whether this scribal error (which also occurred in Irish texts) is due to Ivo, his exemplar or to the modern edition is unclear.[33] The elaborate preface, that was attached to his *Panormia* as well as to the *Decretum*, shows that Ivo was sensitive to the problem of conflicting canons, or rather of different answers applied to similar problems occurring in different circumstances.[34] Yet, he rarely openly discussed such contradictions.[35] The fact that he does not discuss the differences of opinion between Gregory and Theodore seems, however, to be caused by the fact that Ivo was unaware of Theodore's penitential as well as of the *Libellus Responsionum*. Ivo's citation from the *Libellus* in his *Panormia* on the question of the purity of a priest after a nocturnal delusion is probably an indirect one derived from Burchard's *Decretum*.[36]

GRATIAN AND THE DECRETISTS

The *Libellus Responsionum* was known to 'the father of canon law', the Bolognese master Gratian.[37] When discussing natural law and its immutability in his *Concordance of discordant canons*, or simply the *Decretum* (*c.* 1140), he cites Gregory's work extensively, and does not once refer to Theodore's views. Instead he quotes the Old Testament canons concerning the impurity of women during menstruation and after delivery (Leviticus 12:2–5 and 15:19). 'Certain things are now conceded', so Gratian declared, 'which are contrary to what is prescribed in the Law.' 'A menstruating woman is held to be impure [*immunda*] by the law, but we do not forbid her to enter church immediately or to take part in the mysteries of sacred communion; nor is it prohibited that a mother or her child be baptized immediately after birth.'[38] The ease with which Gratian treats these issues, is concordant with his view that sexual abstinence during periods of impurity is only 'a secondary issue in the life of married persons.'[39]

Gratian's work was the basis for all subsequent teaching of canon law in the high and later Middle Ages. The *Decretum* was commented upon by later canonists, who are, therefore, known as Decretists. Yet Gratian's teaching concerning the topic of ritual purity was not adopted as such by the Decretists. Already within a few decades of Gratian, his pupil Paucapalea, when commenting upon the *Decretum*, observed the contradiction between Gregory's rulings and Theodore's.[40] Another Bolognese Decretist, Rufinus of Bologna, agreed with Gratian that the rulings for menstruating women, and women who had recently given birth, to stay away from Church belonged to the *ceremonalia* and not to the *moralia*, and were therefore not immutable. However, he came to a totally different solution. For him it was not the Old Testament rulings that were obsolete, but Gregory's teachings![41] Not only in Bologna, but also in the schools of Paris and Cologne, were Theodore's rulings known, though it is hard to tell as to how far they were actually observed.[42] It seems, therefore, that in the later period at least in some regions 'a contrary popular custom that was resistant to official ecclesiastical teaching' (as put forward by Gregory the Great, Nicolas I and Gratian) existed.[43] This popular custom is also attested by benediction formulas for women entering church after delivering a child, which we find from the end of the eleventh century onwards.[44] It is hard to establish the significance of such rituals for the women and men concerned, but it would be arrogant to dismiss such notions and rituals as a relic of superstitious beliefs, as Erasmus of Rotterdam did when discussing a passage from the *Libellus Responsionum*: 'It seems a relic from superstition when even the holy Gregory of the Roman Church prescribes that a man after having had intercourse with his wife should abstain a while from entering the temple and should only enter after washing himself.'[45]

Conclusion

One may conclude that Augustine's questions to Gregory the Great triggered a discussion about sexuality, human nature and impurity that lasted during the whole period we now call the Middle Ages. Gregory's views did not always have to yield to archaic views on sexuality and pollution, nor were his teachings invariably regarded as too permissive: his voice was therefore heard during the early medieval period.[46] The manuscript tradition of the *Libellus Responsionum* and the use made of this text by later authors clearly shows that Gregory's views did matter to medieval confessors and canon lawyers, in the earlier period as well as in the later. The tension between the inward and the outward, between inner conviction and ritualistic behaviour, already so apparent in Gregory's work, was, however, never completely resolved during the Middle Ages. A tendency to regard women and men in certain bodily states as impure and to bar them from the holy, apparently persisted throughout the period. Though the aspect of penance became less and less important in the course of the centuries, we have to wait for Erasmus for these ideas to be dismissed out of hand. Whether in this the humanist Erasmus was, indeed, wiser than Gregory the Great remains to be seen.

Notes

1. *HE*, I, 26 and 33, pp. 76, 114. The translation of *recuperare* with 'recovered', instead of 'restored' stems from N. Brooks, *The Early History of the Church of Canterbury: Christ Church from 597 to 1066* (Leicester, 1984), p. 50.
2. Brooks, *Early History*, p. 17. See also Clare Stancliffe, ch. 6 above.
3. The evidence for Romano-British continuity up to Augustine's arrival has been collected by Brooks, *Early History*, pp. 17–21.
4. Ed. L. Hartmann, MGH Epp. II, 2 (Berlin, 1895), pp. 332–43; this letter of

Gregory the Great was included in *HE*, I, 27, pp. 78–102 and for convenience's sake I will refer to the text as found in Bede. Its content is summarised in ch. 1 above.

5. P. Meyvaert, 'Bede's text of the *Libellus Responsionum* of Gregory the Great to Augustine of Canterbury', in P. Clemoes and K. Hughes (eds), *England before the Conquest: studies in primary sources presented to Dorothy Whitelock* (Cambridge, 1971), pp. 15–33; repr. in P. Meyvaert, *Benedict, Gregory, Bede and others* (London, 1977) as no. X.

6. P. Meyvaert, 'Diversity within Unity, a Gregorian Theme', *The Heythrop Journal*, 4 (1963), 141–62; repr. in Meyvaert, *Benedict, Gregory, Bede*, as no. VI; R. Kottje, *Studien zum Einfluss des Alten Testamentes auf Recht und Liturgie des früheren Mittelalters (6.–8. Jahrhundert)*, Bonner Historische Forschungen 23 (Bonn, 1970), pp. 112–4.

7. P. Meyvaert, 'Le *Libellus Responsionum* à Augustin de Cantorbéry: une oeuvre authentique de Saint Grégoire le Grand', in J. Fontaine et al. (eds), *Grégoire le Grand, Colloques internationaux du C.N.R.S. Chantilly, Centre culturel Les Fontaines, 15–19 septembre 1982* (Paris, 1986), pp. 543–9, esp. p. 543.

8. Resp. VIII, *HE*, I, 27, pp. 94–5: 'Sicut enim in Testamento ueteri exteriora opera obseruantur, ita in Testamento nouo non tam quod exterius agitur quam id quod interius cogitatur.'

9. This is in accordance with Gregory's normal reading of scripture, for which see now R. Markus, *Gregory the Great and his World* (Cambridge, 1997), pp. 45–7.

10. R. Meens, 'A Background to Augustine's mission to Anglo-Saxon England', *ASE*, 22 (1994), 5–17.

11. I. Wood, 'Some historical re-identifications and the christianisation of Kent' (forthcoming).

12. J. Blair, 'Anglo-Saxon Pagan Shrines and their Prototypes', *ASSAH*, 8 (1995), 1–28.

13. Ed. F. Liebermann, *Die Gesetze der Angelsachsen I: Text und Übersetzung* (Halle a.S., 1903), p. 3; citation from Wood, 'Some historical re-identifications'.

14. Cf. A. Scharer's contribution to this volume, ch. 9 below.

15. Much of this ground has been covered in the somewhat dated, but still fundamental study of P. Browe, *Beiträge zur Sexualethik des Mittelalters*, Breslauer Studien zur historischen Theologie (Breslau, 1932).

16. See R. Meens, 'Ritual purity and the influence of Gregory the Great in the early Middle Ages', *SCH*, 32 (Oxford, 1996), 31–43, esp. 35–6. For Theodore, see now B. Bischoff and M. Lapidge (eds), *Biblical Commentaries from the Canterbury School of Theodore and Hadrian* (Cambridge, 1994), esp. pp. 5–82, 133–89; and the studies in M. Lapidge (ed.), *Archbishop Theodore. Commemorative studies on his life and influence* (Cambridge, 1995).

17. *Paenitentiale Theodori, Discipulus Umbrensium* I, 14, 17–18, ed. P.W. Finsterwalder, *Die Canones Theodori Cantuariensis und ihre Überlieferungsformen* (Weimar, 1929) pp. 308–9; vgl. *Canones Gregorii* 125–6, op. cit., p. 265; *Canones Cottoniani* 106, op. cit., p. 278; *Capitula Dacheriana* 42 and 122, op. cit., pp. 243 and 249; *Canones Basilienses* 43a–b, ed. F.B. Asbach, *Das Poenitentiale Remense und der sogen. Excarpsus Cummeani: Überlieferung, Quellen und Entwicklung zweier kontinentaler Buflbücher aus der 1. Hälfte des 8. Jahrhunderts* (Regensburg, 1975), Anhang, p. 83. For the complicated history of Theodore's penitential, see R. Kottje, 'Paenitentiale Theodori', in *Handwörterbuch zur deutschen Rechtsgeschichte*, vol. 3 (Berlin, 1984), col. 1413–16, and T. Charles-Edwards, 'The penitential of Theodore and the

Iudicia Theodori', in Lapidge, (ed.), *Archbishop Theodore*, pp. 141–74.

18. Bonifatius, ep. 33, ed. R. Rau, *Briefe des Bonifatius. Willibalds Leben des Bonifatius. Nebst einigen zeitgenössischen Dokumenten*, Ausgewählte Quellen zur deutschen Geschichte des Mittelalters. Freiherr vom Stein-Gedächtnisausgabe, vol. IVb, (Darmstadt, 1968), p. 110.
19. Meyvaert, 'Bede's text of the *Libellus Responsionum*', p. 26.
20. *HE*, IV, 2, pp. 332–4.
21. See the complicated genesis of Columbanus's penitential, as sketched by T. Charles-Edwards, 'The penitential of Columbanus', in M. Lapidge (ed.), *Columbanus. Studies on the Latin Writings* (Woodbridge, 1997), pp. 217–39, which raises questions about what authorship means in such a case.
22. See Meens, 'Ritual purity'.
23. Jonas of Orléans, *De institutione laicali*, II, x–xi: *PL* 106, cols 186–8.
24. Benedictus Levita (II, 207), ed. F. Knust in G. Pertz (ed.) MGH, LL 2, 2 (Hannover, 1837), 83–4; vgl. E. Seckel, Studien zu Benedictus Levita VII, 2 *Neues Archiv*, 35 (1910), 105–91, pp. 168ff., and H. Fuhrmann, *Einfluß und Verbreitung der pseudoisidorischen Fälschungen. Von ihrem Auftauchen bis in die neuere Zeit*, Schriften der MGH 24,1 (Stuttgart, 1972), pp. 163–7.
25. Isaac of Langres, ch. XI, 18, ed. Rudolf Pokorny, Martina Stratmann, unter Mitwirkung von Wolf-Dieter Runge, *Capitula Episcoporum II*, MGH Capitula Episcoporum II (Hannover, 1995), p. 236; Herard ch. 60, ibid., p. 141.
26. Nicolas I to the Bulgars, ch. 68, MGH Epp 6, p. 591; for this letter see R.E. Sullivan, 'Khan Boris and the conversion of Bulgaria. A case-study of the impact of christianity on a barbarian society', *Studies in Medieval and Renaissance History*, 3 (1966), 53–139 and L. Heiser, *Die Responsa ad consulta Bulgarorum des Papstes Nikolaus (858–867)* (Trier, 1979).
27. Regino I, 339, ed. H. Wasserschleben, *Reginonis libri duo de synodalibus causis et disciplinis ecclesiasticis* (Leipzig, 1840), p. 160; for the version of the penitential attributed to Bede and Egbert used by Regino, see R. Haggenmüller, 'Zur Rezeption der Beda und Egbert zugeschriebenen Bußbücher', in H. Mordek (ed.), *Aus Archiven und Bibliotheken. Festschrift für Raymund Kottje zum 65. Geburtstag* (Frankfurt a.M., et alibi, 1992), pp. 149–59, esp. pp. 155–6; *P. mixtum* V, 1, edited as 'Poenitentiale Pseudo-Bedae' in H. Wasserschleben, *Die Bussordnungen der abendländischen Kirche* (Halle, 1851), p. 262: 'Uxor post natum sobolem abstineat se ab ecclesia, si filius est, dies XXX, si filia, XL dies'. For the penitentials attributed to Bede, see R. Haggenmüller, *Die Überlieferung der Beda und Egbert zugeschriebenen Bußbücher* (Frankfurt a.M., Bern, et alibi, 1991).
28. Book V, 42: *PL* 140, 759–61. For a discussion of edition of the *Decretum*, see H. Hoffmann and R. Pokorny, *Das Dekret des Bischofs Burchard von Worms. Textstufen – Frühe Verbreitung – Vorlagen*, MGH Hilfsmittel 12 (München, 1991).
29. *Decretum* V, 51: *PL* 140, 762.
30. Book XIX, 141: *PL* 140, 1010: *tot dies in pane et aqua poeniteat, quot ecclesia carere debuerat*; cf. XIX,5, op. cit., 959.
31. Book XIX,140: *PL* 140, 1010.
32. R. Southern, *Scholastic Humanism and the Unification of Europe I: Foundations* (Oxford, 1997), p. 252.
33. Ivo of Chartres, *Decretum*, XV, 150–1 and 163: *PL* 161, 891–3. For the problems in using the printed edition, see P. Landau, 'Das Dekret des Ivo von Chartres. Die handschriftliche Überlieferung im Vergleich zu den Editionen des 16. und 17.

Jahrhunderts', *Zeitschrift der Savigny-Stiftung für Rechtsgeschichte, Kan. Abt.*, 70 (1984), 1–44. For a reassessment of Ivonian authorship of the works traditionally attributed to him, see now R. Sommerville and B.C. Brasington, *Prefaces to Canon Law Books in Latin Christianity. Selected Translations, 500–1245* (New Haven and London, 1998), pp. 111–15.

34. The prologue has now been translated in Sommerville and Brasington, *Prefaces to Canon Law Books in Latin Christianity*, pp. 132–58. See B. Brasington, 'The prologue of Ivo of Chartres. A fresh consideration of the manuscripts', in S. Chodorow (ed.), *Proceedings of the Eighth International Congress of Medieval Canon Law* (Vatican City, 1992), pp. 3–22.

35. B. Brasington, 'Studies in the *Nachleben* of Ivo of Chartres: The Influence of his Prologue on several Panormia-Derivative Collections', in P. Landau and J. Mueller (eds), *Proceedings of the Ninth International Congress of Medieval Canon Law* (Vatican City, 1997), pp. 63–85, esp. p. 72.

36. *Panormia* I, 159: *PL* 161, 1082; cf. Burchard, V, 42.

37. About Gratian we know next to nothing: see the sceptical scrutiny of the evidence in J.T. Noonan Jr., 'Gratian slept here: The Changing Identity of the Father of the Systematic Study of Canon Law', *Traditio*, 35 (1979), 145–72.

38. D. 5, dict. ante. 1, ed. E. Friedberg, *Corpus Iuris Canonici*, vol. 1 (Leipzig, 1879), p. 7. This part has been translated in A. Thompson and J. Gordley, *Gratian. The treatise on laws (DD. 1–20) with the Ordinary Gloss*, Studies in Medieval and Early Modern Canon Law 2 (Washington DC, 1993), p. 16, who, basing themselves on the Roman edition of Gratian of 1582, probably rightly, add 'immediately' after 'enter church'.

39. J. Brundage, *Law, Sex, and Christian Society in Medieval Europe* (Chicago and London, 1987), p. 242.

40. Distinctio V, J.F. von Schulte (ed.), *Paucapalea, Summa über das Decretum Gratiani* (Giessen, 1890), p. 11, citing Isidore of Seville's Etymologies XI, 1, pp. 140–1, ed. W.M. Lindsay, *Isidori Hispalensis episcopi Etymologiarum sive Originum*, 2 vols (Oxford, 1911).

41. H. Singer (ed.), *Rufinus von Bologna (Magister Rufinus), Summa Decretorum* (Paderborn, 1902), pp. 16–19.

42. J.F. von Schulte (ed.), *Stephan von Doornick (Étienne de Tournai, Stephanus Tornacensis), Die Summa über das Decretum Gratiani* (Giessen, 1891), pp. 14–16; T.P. McLaughlin (ed.), *The Summa Parisiensis on the Decretum Gratiani* (Toronto, 1952), pp. xx–xxi and 5; A.J. de Groot (ed.), *Distinctiones 'Si mulier eadem hora' seu Monacenses*, Rechtshistorische reeks van het Gerard Noodt Instituut 36 (Nijmegen, 1996), p. 1. For the relation of the latter text with the school of Cologne, see S. Kuttner and E. Rathbone, 'Anglo-Norman Canonists of the Twelfth Century: An Introductory Study', *Traditio*, 7 (1951), 279–358.

43. P. Payer, *The Bridling of Desire. Views of Sex in the Later Middle Ages* (Toronto, 1993), p. 105.

44. A. Franz, *Die kirchlichen Benediktionen im Mittelalter*, 2 vols (Freiburg, 1909), II, pp. 223–9.

45. Erasmus, Ep. 916, ed. P.S. Allen, *Opus epistolarum Des. Erasmi Roterodami* III (Oxford, 1913) p. 487, lines 255–8: 'Ex qua superstitione relictum videtur, quod diuus etiam Gregorius Romanae ecclesiae vsu receptum praecipit obseruandum, vt vir qui cum vxore propria rem habuisset, abstineret aliquandiu ab ingressu templi, nec ingreditur nisi lotus . . .'; see also idem., *Enarrationes in Psalmos*, enarratio

psalmi XXXVIII, ed. *Opera omnia*, V, 3 (Amsterdam, 1996), p. 196, where Erasmus mentions Gregory's views when discussing earlier teachings of the church that have become obsolete; see also *Ad Notationes Eduardi Lei in marcum*, ed. J. Leclerc, *Desiderii Erasmi Roterodami opera omnia emendatiora et auctiora* . . . IX (Leiden, 1706), 145A. I owe these references to István Bejczy.

46. Gregory's influence is graciously ignored by A. Angenendt, *Das Frühmittelalter. Die abendländische Christenheit von 400 bis 900* (Stuttgart, Berlin and Cologne, 1990), p. 346; cf. A. Angenendt, '"Mit reinen Händen". Das Motiv der kultischen Reinheit in der abendländischen Askese', in G. Jenal (ed.), *Herrschaft, Kirche, Kultur. Beiträge zur Geschichte des Mittelalters. Festschrift für Friedrich Prinz zu seinem 65. Geburtstag*, Monographien zur Geschichte des Mittelalters 37 (Stuttgart, 1993), 297–316. See now his monumental study *Geschichte der Religiosität im Mittelalter* (Darmstadt, 1997), pp. 406–7.

CHAPTER 9

The Gregorian Tradition in Early England

Anton Scharer

The importance of Pope Gregory the Great for the development of Anglo-Saxon England was very considerable. His legacy stretched well beyond the immediate consequences of the mission of St Augustine which he instigated, and he was held in the highest regard by the English. The Gregorian tradition in early England was a rich one. I should perhaps state at the outset what I am not going to deal with: the transmission of Gregory the Great's writings in Anglo-Saxon England. The host to the conference[1] that lies behind the present volume has supplied some relevant data concerning the *Regula pastoralis* and the *Dialogi* in his admirable study on Alfred the Great and the destruction and production of christian books,[2] as had Sir Roger Mynors before him in the supplement volume to *Codices Latini Antiquiores*.[3] Nor could I sketch the influence of Gregory's writings on Anglo-Saxon authors. Such observations as I may make in these respects have no pretensions to be more than hints. What then is the focus of this investigation of Gregorian tradition in early England? My approach is at one and the same time more limited, yet broader than a definition of tradition as 'a statement, belief, custom etc. handed down by non written (especially oral) means from generation to generation'[4] would suggest. To view tradition as only that which had been preserved orally would be too narrow. Moreover, had it not been written down, we would have nothing to go by. Definitely included in my understanding of 'Gregorian tradition' is what the German term *'Nachleben'* ('after-life') denotes. And this in turn has much to do with the shaping of an 'image' of Gregory in collective memory and popular culture. We shall thus consider the disparate written evidence that has come down to us for the light it sheds on Anglo-Saxon perceptions of Pope Gregory and his importance.

The first substantial, though perhaps not the earliest, evidence[5] that bears on this question is provided by the *Liber beati et laudabilis viri Gregorii papae urbis*

Romae ('The Book of the blessed and praiseworthy man, Gregory, pope of the city of Rome') which was compiled in Whitby at the end of the seventh or the beginning of the eighth century.[6] Thus about a century lies between the earliest attempt at a biography of Gregory and the Pope's death (604). This medley of stories illustrating Gregory's life and the conversion of the English with a focus on the Northumbrians and especially on King Edwin was, in all likelihood, intended to promote the cult of Gregory the Great,[7] and in its wake to boost that of King Edwin and proclaim the transfer of the latter's relics to Whitby. This was perhaps an attempt to recover lost ground, since Queen Osthryth, Oswiu's daughter and hence Oswald's niece, and her husband King Æthelred of Mercia had taken the lead in establishing the cult of a saintly English king with the translation of Oswald's relics to Bardney in Lindsey *c.* 679.[8] That the resting places of Edwin were closely attached to the cult of Gregory is not only suggested by the Whitby *Liber beati Gregorii*, where it is stated that now Edwin's 'holy bones are honourably buried in the Church of St. Peter . . . together with other of our kings, on the south side of the altar which is dedicated to St. Gregory',[9] but also by Bede who noted that 'the head of King Edwin . . . was brought to York and afterwards placed in the church of St. Peter, which he himself had begun to build . . . It was placed in the chapel of the holy pope Gregory from whose disciples he himself had received the word of life'.[10]

In order to create a portrait of the Pope, the author of the *Liber beati Gregorii* strung together a number of anecdotes which, while they demonstrate Gregory's supernatural powers, show no development, no chronological sequence. Nevertheless they were vital elements in the 'image' of Gregory, and their subsequent influence was considerable.[11] The frequent references to narrative tradition in these stories[12] have led many commentators to assume that the legendary accounts were spread by way of mouth, and hence that the compiler of the *Life* relied to a large extent on oral tradition.[13] However, closer attention to the work suggests that the author was actually conscious that such stories were comparatively few in number[14] and attempted to remedy this deficiency by combing Gregory's writings for biographical information.[15] Thus we are led to the possibility, recently advanced in a fundamental reappraisal, that some of the other stories, hitherto attributed to oral tradition, may also derive from literary models.[16] And this obviously has implications for the famous episode of the 'fair-skinned and light-haired' Anglian youths in Rome interviewed by Gregory.[17]

The story runs as follows: '. . . [Gregory] asked what people they belonged to. . . . They answered, "The people we belong to are called Angles." "Angels of God," he replied. Then he asked further, "What is the name of the king of the people?" They said, "Aelli", whereupon he said, "Alleluia, God's praise must be heard there." Then he asked the name of their tribe, to which they answered, "Deire", and he replied, "They shall flee from the wrath of God to the faith.'"[18] Some elements of the tale could have been lifted from Gregory's writings,[19] in which case there would be reasonable grounds for crediting the anonymous Whitby writer with having put together and thus having created the story.[20]

Moreover the puns on *Angli* and *Aelli* are taken up again subsequently[21] as though to enhance the message of the story.[22] And one must add to this the author's statement, 'when all the Apostles bring their own peoples with them and each individual teacher brings his own race to present them to the Lord in the Day of Judgement, he [i.e. Gregory] will bring us – that is, the English people (*gentem Anglorum*) instructed by him through God's grace';[23] the account of the alleged missionary attempt by Gregory himself;[24] and the frequent references to Gregory as '*doctor noster sanctus Gregorius*' ('our teacher the holy Gregory'), '*noster magister*' ('our master'), '*apostolicus noster sanctus Gregorius*' ('our apostle, the holy Gregory'), or '*beatus noster apostolicus Gregorius*' ('our blessed apostle, Gregory').[25]

This evidence clearly ought to be, and partly has been interpreted as expressing a sense of community and collective identity.[26] Undoubtedly the aforementioned *Angli* are not in a limited sense the Angles who had settled in parts of Britain, but rather the English as a whole. Gregory the Great himself had always spoken of the *Angli*,[27] and this usage can also be observed in the *Liber beati Gregorii*, when for instance King Æthelberht of Kent is heralded as the first among the '*reges Anglorum*' ('kings of the English') to have received baptism.[28] Gregory the Great, to return to the legend again, had not given the Anglian youths a new name, as Woden had done in the case of the Longobards,[29] but he had charged the existing one spiritually. By having thus gained a providential role and having been raised to angelic levels, the name 'Angli' could be shared by a community which was greater and more extensive than just the Angles, a community which belonged together by conversion and shared a common hope of salvation.

At the roots of this community stood Gregory the Great; hence commitment to Gregory as master, teacher and spiritual patron was a way of, even perhaps a formula for, expressing this sense of collective fate and community – all the more so among those who may have felt misgivings about the likely political overtones of 'Angli' and the vested Northumbrian, specifically Deiran, interest in the story. Furthermore, it is relevant to note, how the spread of Christianity to Northumbria was perceived in a Gregorian perspective. There is no word about the Irish missionary effort in the work of the anonymous writer of Whitby, and although this remains notable in the context of a work which does treat certain aspects of the growth of Christianity in Northumbria, and which was written at a centre whose foundress, Hilda, had been under the tutelage of the great Irish missionary, Aidan, the subject of the *Life* was, of course, Gregory. More suggestive perhaps is the fact that whereas Gregory and Paulinus appear in the earliest layer of the Calendar that was written for St Willibrord,[30] a Yorkshireman who spent some twelve years in Ireland before embarking on his famous mission to Frisia, Aidan on the other hand only features among the later additions to it.[31] This overall impression is confirmed by Bede's major Chronicle attached to *De temporum ratione* where the Irish missionary effort is not mentioned.[32] When the record was 'put straight' in the *Ecclesiastical History*, Bede 'was anxious to set Lindisfarne in a Gregorian context'.[33]

The wish to appropriate Gregory the Great as the founding father of an imagined community, is not only voiced by the *Liber beati Gregorii*: it was also shared by somebody who, in all likelihood, would have objected to being addressed as an 'Angle', namely Aldhelm of Malmesbury (d. 709).[34] His testimony may in fact antedate that of the Whitby *Life of Gregory*. In the prose *De virginitate* ('On virginity'), Aldhelm remarked in a reference to book 31 of the *Moralia*: 'Gregory, pontiff of the apostolic see, from whom we (English) took the rudiments of faith and the sacraments of baptism'.[35] On another occasion, when dealing with Agatha and particularly with 'the most chaste virgin' Lucia, he referred to Gregory as 'our teacher and instructor';[36] and once more, this time in greater detail, he commented 'Gregory, the watchful shepherd and our teacher – [our], I say, (because it was he) who took away from our forebears the error of abominable paganism and granted them the rule of regenerative grace'.[37] Aldhelm dedicated his prose *De virginitate* to Hildilith, abbess of Barking in Essex, and to a number of her nuns.

By briefly focusing on Barking we may broaden the perspective of our investigation into, and our understanding of, 'Gregorian tradition'. Hildilith's predecessor as abbess of Barking was Æthelburh (d. after March 687?), sister of Bishop Earkonwald of London. She received a large grant from Hodilred (Æthelred), a member of the East Saxon royal family. The original document for the grant has survived (fig. 9.1),[38] and it is most likely to date from March 687.[39] The diploma was drafted in uncial script by two scribes:[40] the first, who wrote the best part of the charter breaking off in the *corroboratio*, worked around this time; the second, who added the bounds, a *benedictio* and the witness list, should be dated to the eighth century, probably the second half. This latter apparently copied an earlier authentic witness list (which may originally have been attached to the charter on a separate piece of parchment), and also supplied the bounds and a *benedictio* which point towards a mid-eighth-century date. As regards the formulae, they share some features with those of Gregory the Great's donation

9.1 Charter of Hodilred. British Library, Cott. Ch. Aug. II. 29. (British Library)

charter for his monastery of St Andreas in Clivo Scauri, dating from 587.[41] These parallels, which are most telling in the rather rare form of proem and in some of the *verba dispositiva*, should tentatively be interpreted as vestiges of 'Gregorian' influence.

Closely related in style to this East Saxon diploma are three further charters: first, a grant by Frithuwald, sub-king of Surrey, to Chertsey datable to 672x74,[42] which, although a 'forgery', derives from a genuine late seventh-century text; secondly, a forged grant of Frithuwald and Earkonwald for Chertsey[43] which draws on the previous document; and thirdly and finally, a grant by Cædwalla, king of the West Saxons, of sixty hides at Farnham to Cedde, Cisi and Criswa,[44] dated 688, but actually referring to 685x87.

The charters of Æthelred for Barking, Frithuwald for Chertsey, and Cædwalla to Cedde, Cisi and Criswa[45] do not share the same transmission,[46] but do have a common denominator in Bishop Earkonwald of London, who features in them as recipient, relative of the recipient, and prominent witness. He had founded the abbeys of Chertsey and Barking, and he claimed to have visited Rome,[47] on which occasion he could have procured the papal privilege for Chertsey[48] whose substance has been shown to be genuine.[49] Earkonwald, let me venture to speculate, could also have obtained in Rome a copy of Gregory the Great's charter for St Andreas in Clivo Scauri. If so, he would qualify as a precursor of Nothelm, who searched the papal archives in the early eighth century, forwarding relevant letters to Bede.[50]

The apparent influence of some formulae from Gregory's Roman grant on an East Saxon diploma and a group of related charters is perhaps an unexpected testimony to 'Gregorian tradition' and as such deserves further consideration. It leads one to wonder whether the choice of uncial for Hodilred's diploma to Barking is not only an indication that 'Italian' exemplars were followed, but was also motivated by the possible Gregorian connotations of the script. A note of caution has to be struck here, however. There is no mention of 'Gregorian script' in the sources, and the charter of Gregory the Great that apparently influenced Hodilred's grant stylistically would not itself, of course, have been drawn up in uncials, but rather in an altogether less formal hand, typical of Late Antique documentary production. In his review of E.A. Lowe's *English Uncial*, Bernhard Bischoff put forward the hypothesis of a Roman or continental 'script-province' ('*Schriftprovinz*') in southern and Midland England,[51] and he went on to remark that 'a very old, for southern England "apostolic" tradition of uncial script would make intelligible the remarkable fact of its appearance in the earliest Kentish and Mercian diplomas'.[52]

Even the 'cultivation' of uncial in Wearmouth–Jarrow was interpreted as an offshoot of southern English writing culture.[53] In the case of the *Codex Amiatinus* Bischoff pointed to a fragmentary copy of Augustine's *Speculum*, written in a fine rectilinear uncial, with rustic capitals for chapter headings as the model imitated by the Northumbrian scribes.[54] In *CLA*, E.A. Lowe assigned a seventh-century date to this manuscript, which may have belonged to the ancient stock of biblical and patristic fragments of Italian, mostly southern Italian in origin.[55] More recently it has been said to provide 'one of the best examples of Roman uncial'.[56] Thence one is led to Malcolm Parkes's characterization of the formal uncial used in the *Codex Amiatinus* as an imitation of Roman uncial.[57] As regards the motives for this deliberate choice of Roman models, let me quote from Parkes's perceptive analysis: 'Roman models inspired in Ceolfrid and his monks a particular kind of respect because of the place from which they had come, hence his scribes regarded the particular version of Uncial developed in Rome about the time of Gregory the Great as especially suitable for the script of Holy Writ.'[58] The high esteem and veneration in which Gregory was held at Wearmouth and Jarrow is also suggested by the fact that, apart from biblical texts, the only other work written there in formal uncial, the highest grade of script available, that has come down to us is a now fragmentary copy of Gregory's *Moralia in Iob*.[59]

We may take all this as encouragement to view the phenomenon of English uncial – at least its origins – within the context of Gregorian tradition, and to indulge in the speculation that the appearance of the diploma under discussion and the manuscripts just mentioned would have appealed because it implied

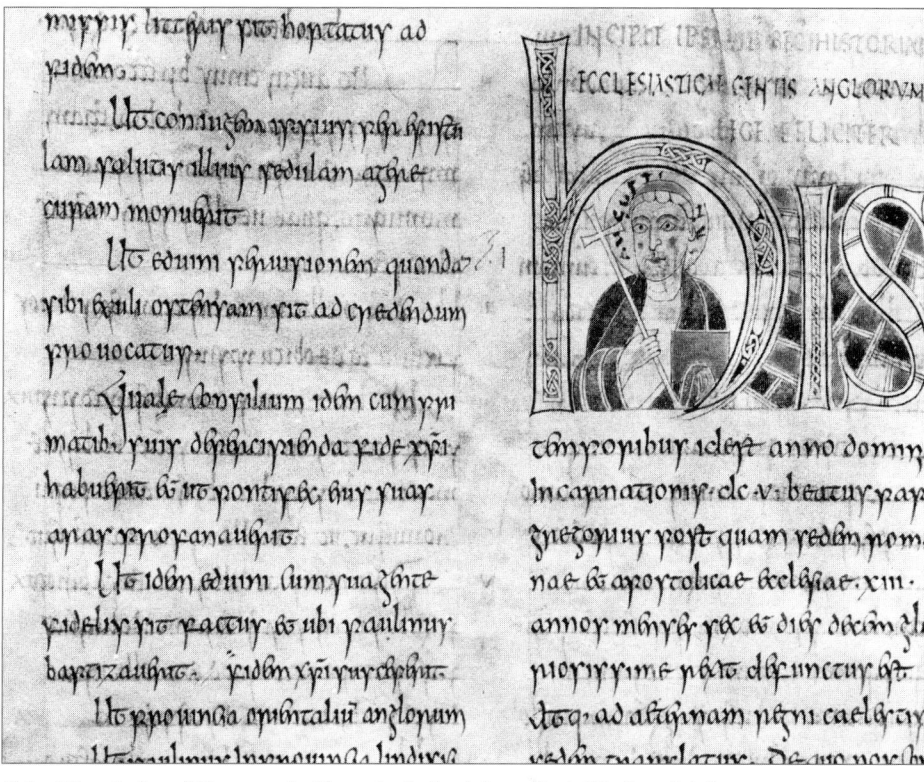

9.2 Historiation of Gregory the Great in the Incipit *to Book II of an eighth-century Northumbrian copy of Bede's* Historia ecclesiastica *(St Petersburg, Public Library, Lat. Q. v. I. 18, fol. 26v, detail). (After Voronova and Sterligov)*

commitment to Gregory as apostle, master and teacher, a message it could have conveyed even to an illiterate beholder. In this connection it seems appropriate to point to another, related piece of evidence: the large historiated initial in the oldest manuscript of Bede's *Historia ecclesiastica* which in all likelihood depicts Gregory the Great.[60] It occurs at the opening of the second book, thus underlining the special prominence that Bede wished to give 'to his biography of Gregory by placing it at the very outset of Book II' (fig. 9.2).[61]

By writing an ecclesiastical history, Bede gave pride of place in his account of the English people to their conversion and the growth of their church. Hence a community was envisaged – for which *Angli* served as the catchword[62] – which surpassed all political divisions, and at whose origins stood Gregory the Great and his missionaries. It is in Gregorian terms that the Irish missionary effort was fitted into the picture. Bede could obviously draw on much richer Gregorian material than the compiler of the Whitby *Life* – such as the letters conveyed to him via Canterbury. None the less he also included in his appreciation of Gregory a version of the story concerning the Anglian youths, as well as a mention of

Gregory's own attempt to start out on a mission to the English.[63] It hardly needs repeating that Gregory is also referred to with great poetic force as the 'apostle of the English'.[64] Bede's genius as an author, and the success and popularity of his *Historia ecclesiastica* propagated this sense of spiritual community, the terminology of which (namely *Angli*) went straight back to Gregory. And this brings me, in passing, to a fundamental but often neglected point, namely that Bede was, as Henry Mayr-Harting has so aptly put it, one 'of the greatest Gregorians in the early Middle Ages'.[65]

The cult of Gregory may have reached a climax in the early eighth century,[66] but there is no abatement in the tribute paid to him as teacher and as instigator of the conversion during the following century and a half; nor a perceptible break, or even a lull in Gregorian tradition in its more general form, although other figures, most notably Augustine of Canterbury himself, were promoted in the great Pope's wake. At the council of 'Clofesho', held in 747, canon 17 stipulated that the feasts of Pope Gregory (who is referred to as *'pater noster'*) and of Archbishop Augustine be celebrated, and that the name of Augustine, *'doctor noster'* ('our teacher'), be sung in the litany after that of Gregory the Great.[67] This explicit recognition of Augustine's role may on the one hand reflect the changed position of the church of Canterbury from the days of Theodore;[68] on the other hand it may be an indication of the impact of Bede's recently published *Historia ecclesiastica*. As a coda to this we may note that the oldest manuscript transmitting the acta of the council of 'Clofesho', namely London, BL, Cotton Otho A.I, of which only fragments survive, has a strong Gregorian flavour. This episcopal 'handbook' dating from the second half of the eighth century also included an abridgement of Gregory's *Regula pastoralis*.[69]

When Archbishop Cuthberht of Canterbury wrote to Bishop Lul of Mainz after the news of Boniface's martyrdom (5 June 754) had spread,[70] he mentioned that in a general synod of the English church[71] – in point of fact, Cuthberht seems to have been writing on behalf of the assembled clergy – it had been decided to celebrate the feast of Boniface and thus to join him as patron to the blessed Gregory and Augustine.[72] Given that church councils nurtured 'a sense of collective identity (and purpose) among the leaders of the church',[73] how better could they achieve this than by calling on Gregory? The frequent references to Gregory as 'our' teacher in, for instance, Archbishop Egbert of York's *Dialogus ecclesiasticae institutionis* (a kind of canon-law collection in dialogue form),[74] and in Alcuin's correspondence[75] cannot be examined in detail here. It suffices to observe that they served as a constant reminder to a predominantly English audience of the imagined founder of their 'community', thereby conveying a sense of belonging together, and of sharing the same destiny. They thus propagated an identity.

Moving on to the ninth-century evidence, let us first consider the Old English martyrology.[76] In its entry on Gregory the Great (12 March),[77] several familiar topics recur. Gregory is praised as 'the father of our learning, who had sent us baptism to Britain. He is our teacher and we are his disciples'. Then follow two of the legends which were first recorded in the Whitby *Liber beati Gregorii*: the incident of Gregory's tears and prayers rescuing the soul of the emperor Trajan from hell,[78] and the tale of the white dove inspiring Gregory with divine wisdom as he was writing (fig. 9.3).[79] This seems to show the continued currency in England of stories featuring Gregory which are likely to have appealed to a wide audience, and may well have been part of what we might term 'popular culture'.

9.3 *Image of Gregory being inspired by the white dove, in a Sacramentary fragment from Metz of 869, associated with the Court School of Charles the Bald (BnF, lat. 1141, fol. 3r). (Bibliothèque nationale de France)*

Knowledge of the martyrology was in all likelihood mediated to King Alfred's court by the king's Mercian helpers.

Let me conclude with one of the greatest 'Gregorians' after Bede, King Alfred the Great (871–99). At Alfred's behest, Werferth, bishop of Worcester, translated Gregory's *Dialogi* into English,[80] and the king himself translated the *Regula pastoralis*, one of the books he identified as 'most necessary for all men to know'.[81] However, Gregorian influence did not stop here; rather it permeated the court at large. Consider the picture that Asser drew of Alfred in his biography of the king. Some of the themes, such as the significance of suffering, betray a dependence on Gregory,[82] as does the following story. In his youth, fearing he could not control his carnal desires, Alfred had asked God for 'some illness which he would be able to tolerate – not, however, that God would make him unworthy and useless in worldly affairs' and 'after some time he contracted the disease of piles through God's gift'![83] Charlemagne's son Louis the Pious when faced with similar circumstances, i.e. fearing lest he be carried away by his desires, got married.[84]

The model for Alfred's behaviour (at least as it is presented by Asser) is St Benedict who, according to the account in Gregory's *Dialogi*, had on one occasion been tempted by such strong carnal desire that he threw himself into some thornbushes, the resultant bodily wounds healing his inner wounds.[85] But this is not quite the end of my tale.

The concern for the 'Angelcynn'[86] (the Old English equivalent to *'gens Anglorum'* or 'the nation of the English') shown by King Alfred and his court should also be seen within the same Gregorian context, because the concept of 'the English' as one distinct nation which goes back to Bede, the Whitby *Liber beati Gregorii*, and ultimately to Gregory himself, had now for the first time been transferred to the political sphere where it was used to describe and propagate a new identity. Alfred himself used the term in the prose preface to his translation of the *Regula pastoralis*, and in the introduction to his laws;[87] but arguably more significant was its deployment in the *Anglo-Saxon Chronicle* to describe a key event that took place in the year 886. After Alfred had occupied London 'all the English people ['Angelcyn'] that were not under subjection of the Danes submitted to him'.[88] This act of state, with which some sort of oath-taking is likely to have been associated,[89] took place in London. There are good reasons why this should have been so, considering the strategic role of the city and Alfred's earlier attempts to gain influence over it.[90] But recently Janet Nelson has persuasively argued that the importance Alfred attached to London may also have had something to do with the king's awareness that Gregory had intended London to be the metropolitan see.[91]

Concomitant with the promotion of 'Angelcynn', the concept of the English nation, by Alfred and his court are, it would seem, certain changes in the royal styles.[92] Alfred's predecessors had called themselves *Saxonum rex* ('King of the Saxons') or *Occidentalium Saxonum rex* ('King of the West Saxons') in their 'West Saxon' charters, and this practice is said to have continued into Alfred's reign[93] right to the early 880s. Then a change to *Angul Saxonum rex, Anglorum Saxonum rex* ('King of the Anglo-Saxons') and similar variants can be observed. Asser's usage seems to reflect this trend. Alfred's predecessors are invariably styled *Occidentalium Saxonum rex*, or on occasion *Saxonum rex*,[94] but Alfred generally features as *Angul-Saxonum rex*, and once, in the dedication, as *Anglorum Saxonum rex*.[95] Adding the 'Angles' to the royal title was a clear declaration of a momentous message. It must have meant more than simply giving expression to the newly gained authority over London and non-Viking Mercia: it most probably harked back to the all-embracing notion of *Angli* 'the English', the inheritance of Gregorian tradition.

NOTES

1. Whom I want to thank for his kind invitation and the many improvements to this chapter. He and his wife made this conference an intellectually stimulating and most enjoyable event. With a few exceptions, I have kept this chapter much as it was read in Canterbury. My debts to some splendid articles by Sarah Foot, Simon Keynes, Alan Thacker and Patrick Wormald will be obvious.
2. R. Gameson, 'Alfred the Great and the Destruction and Production of Christian Books', *Scriptorium*, 49 (1995), 180–210, at p. 203, n. 121.
3. *CLA* Supplement, p. 75. To which should now be added the following items: *CLA*, 1820, 1830, 1845, 1847, 1849, 1863, 1876 and 1884. Out of this total, three, namely *CLA*, 1820, 1847 and 1849, originated in an Anglo-Saxon ambiance. See B. Bischoff and V. Brown, 'Addenda to Codices Latini Antiquiores', *Mediaeval Studies*, 47 (1985), 317–66, at pp. 324, 339, 340–1, pls IIIa, XIIc and XIIIb; *idem* and J.J. John, 'Addenda to Codices Latini Antiquiores (II)', *Mediaeval Studies*, 54 (1992), 286–307.
4. *The New Shorter Oxford English Dictionary*, ed. L. Brown, 2 vols (Oxford, 1993), p. 3358.
5. See the reference to Aldhelm below.
6. *The Earliest Life of Gregory the Great by an Anonymous Monk of Whitby*, ed. B. Colgrave (Kansas, 1969, repr. Cambridge, 1985). Colgrave proposes a date between 704 and 714 (ibid., pp. 47–9); M. Lapidge, 'Anglo-Latin Literature' in his *Anglo-Latin Literature 600–899* (London, 1996), pp. 1–35 at p. 13 prefers 680–704.
7. Sian E. Mosford, 'A Critical Edition of the *Vita Gregorii magni* by an anonymous Member of the Community of Whitby' (University of Oxford, unpublished thesis, 1988), p. xxvi, suggests that the life may have been read on Gregory's feast day. In the last chapter of the *Life of Gregory*, ed. Colgrave, ch. 32, p. 138, there is also a reference to Gregory being invoked in the litany of saints; according to Edmund Bishop, *Liturgica Historica: Papers on the Liturgy and Religious Life of the Western Church* (Oxford, 1918), p. 146, this is the earliest attestation 'of the existence and use of a litany of saints'. See also *Anglo-Saxon Litanies of the Saints*, ed. M. Lapidge, HBS, 106 (London, 1991), p. 25. On all matters concerning the cult of Gregory the Great special mention must be made of the fine paper by A. Thacker, 'Memorializing Gregory the Great: the Origin and Transmission of a Papal Cult in the Seventh and Early Eighth Centuries', *Early Medieval Europe*, 7 (1998), 59–84.
8. Bede, *HE*, III, 11, pp. 244–50; J.M. Wallace-Hadrill, B*ede's Ecclesiastical History of the English People: A Historical Commentary* (Oxford, 1988), p. 103.
9. *Life of Gregory*, ed. Colgrave, ch. 19, pp. 104–5.
10. Bede, *HE*, II, 20, pp. 204–5.
11. See generally Colgrave's remarks, *Life of Gregory*, pp. 50–3, along with his commentary.
12. Of the various examples, it will suffice to cite the following, *Life of Gregory*, ed. Colgrave, ch. 20, p. 104: 'Nam antiquorum fertur esse narratio'; ch. 21, p. 108: 'Est et altera vetus relatio viri Dei istius fame'; ch. 29, p. 126: 'Quidam quoque de nostris dicunt narratum a Romanis'; ch. 32, p. 136: 'De fine vero huius vitae viri . . . minime audivimus'.
13. Most notable in this respect is C.E. Wright, *The Cultivation of Saga in Anglo-Saxon England* (Edinburgh, 1939), esp. pp. 46–8.

14. Expressed in the concern to explain the scarcity of miracles in theological terms: *Life of Gregory*, ed. Colgrave, chs 4, 5, 30, pp. 76–82, 128–134.
15. As perceptively noted by W. Berschin, *Biographie und Epochenstil im lateinischen Mittelalter II* (Stuttgart, 1988), pp. 262, esp. 265.
16. A point convincingly argued by Thacker, 'Memoralizing Gregory the Great'.
17. *Life of Gregory*, ed. Colgrave, ch. 9, p. 90.
18. Translation according to Colgrave, p. 91. Latin text (ibid. p. 90): '... cuius gentis fuissent, inquisivit.... Cumque responderent, "Anguli dicuntur, illi de quibus sumus," ille dixit, "Angeli Dei." Deinde dixit, "Rex gentis illius, quomodo nominatur?" Et dixerunt, "Aelli." Et ille ait, "Alleluia. Laus enim Dei esse debet illic." Tribus quoque illius nomen de qua erant proprie requisivit. Et dixerunt, "Deire". Et ille dixit, "De ira Dei confugientes ad fidem."'
19. Colgrave in *Life of Gregory*, p. 145, n. 43; M. Richter, 'Bede's Angli: Angles or English?', *Peritia*, 3 (1984), 99–114, at pp. 102–4, detecting three elements from Gregory, from which he concludes, however, 'that the story arose with Gregory' (p. 104); Mosford, 'Critical Edition of the *Vita Gregorii magni*', pp. xviii–xix.
20. For once H.S. Brechter, *Die Quellen zur Angelsachsenmission Gregors des Großen* (Münster, 1941), pp. 122 ff. and 156 appears to have been right.
21. *Life of Gregory*, ed. Colgrave, ch. 13, pp. 94–6.
22. And to graft Edwin on it: ibid., ch. 14, p. 96.
23. *Life of Gregory*, ed. Colgrave, ch. 6, pp. 82–3.
24. Ibid., ch. 10, p. 92.
25. Praef. and chs 3, 5, 13, 14, etc., pp. 72, 76, 80–82, 95–96, to give a few examples.
26. Thus, with regard to Bede's rendering of the story of the Anglian youths, the classic study by P. Wormald, 'Bede, the Bretwaldas and the Origins of the Gens Anglorum', *Ideal and Reality in Frankish and Anglo-Saxon Society: Studies Presented to J.M. Wallace-Hadrill*, ed. P. Wormald with D. Bullough and R. Collins (Oxford, 1983), pp. 99–129, esp. pp. 120–3.
27. Richter, 'Bede's Angli', p. 105; Wormald, 'Bede, Bretwaldas and Origins', p. 124.
28. *Life of Gregory*, ed. Colgrave, ch. 12, p. 94, and the editor's comment at p. 145.
29. *Origo gentis Langobardorum*, MGH Script. rer. Langobard., ed. G. Waitz (Hannover, 1878), ch. 1, p. 3; Paul the Deacon, *Historia Langobardorum*, MGH (as above), eds L. Bethmann and G. Waitz, I, 8, p. 52; Wormald, 'Bede, Bretwaldas and Origins', p. 124.
30. *The Calendar of St. Willibrord: From MS Paris. lat. 10837. A Facsimile with Transcription, Introduction, and Notes*, ed. H.A. Wilson, HBS, 55 (London, 1918), pl. III (= fol. 35v) and pl. X (= fol 39r); see also the editor's introduction, p. xxii, and Mosford, 'Critical Edition of the *Vita Gregorii magni*', p. xxvi, n. 56.
31. *The Calendar of St Willibrord*, pl. VIII (= fol. 38r).
32. A point made by Thacker, 'Memoralizing Gregory the Great', p. 80.
33. A. Thacker, 'Bede's Ideal of Reform', *Ideal and Reality in Frankish and Anglo-Saxon Society*, ed. Wormald, pp. 130–53, at p. 144. See also the illuminating remarks by H. Mayr-Harting, *The Coming of Christianity to Anglo-Saxon England*, 3rd edn (London, 1991), p. 6, with reference to idem, 'The Venerable Bede, the Rule of St. Benedict, and Social Class' (Jarrow Lecture, 1976), pp. 20–2.
34. Wormald, 'Bede, Bretwaldas and Origins', p. 123.

35. Aldhelm, *The Prose Works*, trans. M. Lapidge and M. Herren (Cambridge, 1979), p. 70. The original, Aldhelm, *De virginitate*, ch. 13: *Aldhelmi Opera*, ed. R. Ehwald, MGH Auctores Antiquissimi 15 (Berlin, 1919), p. 242, reads: 'Gregorius, sedis apostolicae praesul, a quo rudimenta fidei et baptismi sacramenta suscepimus'.
36. Aldhelm, *Prose Works*, p. 108, rendering Aldhelm, *De virginitate*, ch. 42, p. 293: 'praeceptor et pedagogus noster Gregorius'.
37. Aldhelm, *Prose Works*, p. 125, a translation of Aldhelm, *De virginitate*, ch. 55, p. 314: 'Gregorius, pervigil pastor et pedagogus noster – noster inquam, qui nostris parentibus errorem tetrae gentilitatis abstulit et regenerationis gratiae normam tradidit'.
38. BL, Cotton Ch. Augustus II. 29: P.H. Sawyer, *Anglo-Saxon Charters: An Annotated List and Bibliography* (London, 1968), no. 1171; for a facsimile see *Chartae Latinae Antiquiores III*, eds A. Bruckner and R. Marichal (Olten, 1963), no. 187; for comment see above all P. Chaplais, 'Some Early Anglo-Saxon Charters on Single Sheets: Originals or Copies?', *Journal of the Society of Archivists*, 3 (1965–9), 315–36, repr. *Prisca Munimenta: Studies in Archival and Administrative History Presented to Dr. A.E.J. Hollaender*, ed. F. Ranger (London, 1973), pp. 63–87, at pp. 78–83, and A. Scharer, *Die angelsächsische Königsurkunde im 7. und 8. Jahrhundert* (Vienna, 1982), pp. 129–41.
39. This obviously has implications (in regard to the *terminus post quem*) for the dating of Aldhelm's prose *De virginitate*: cf. Aldhelm, *Prose Works*, at pp. 13–15.
40. See the careful analysis by Chaplais, 'Early Anglo-Saxon Diplomas', pp. 82–3; and B. Bischoff's review of *ChLA*, parts III, IV and V, *Historische Zeitschrift*, 223 (1976), 689–96, at p. 691.
41. Appendix I in: Gregory the Great, *Registrum epistolarum*, eds P. Ewald and L.M. Hartmann, MGH Epist. 1 and 2, 2 vols (Berlin, 1891–99), II, pp. 437–9.
42. Sawyer, *Anglo-Saxon Charters*, no. 1165.
43. Sawyer, no. 1181.
44. Ibid., no. 235.
45. We exclude Sawyer, no. 1181, a grant of Frithuwald and Earkonwald for Chertsey, from the following discussion, as it is a later fabrication which does not draw on any authentic, first-hand material.
46. For details see Sawyer, *Anglo-Saxon Charters*, nos 1171, 1165 and 235.
47. In Sawyer no. 1246, a grant of privileges for Barking, dated 695. Though spurious, this need not invalidate the information about Earkonwald's visit to Rome.
48. *Cartularium Saxonicum: A Collection of Charters Relating to Anglo-Saxon History*, ed. W. de Gray Birch, vol. I (London, 1885), no. 56.
49. According to H.H. Anton, *Studien zu den Klosterprivilegien der Päpste im frühen Mittelalter unter Berücksichtigung der Privilegierung von St. Maurice d'Agaune* (Berlin, 1975), esp. pp. 65, n. 62 and 83 against earlier doubts.
50. Bede, *HE*, Praef., p. 4.
51. B. Bischoff, 'Anzeige von E.A. Lowe, English Uncial (Oxford 1960)', *Gnomon*, 34 (1962), 605–15, repr. in his *Mittelalterliche Studien: Ausgewählte Aufsätze zur Schriftkunde und Literaturgeschichte*, vol. II (Stuttgart, 1967), pp. 328–39, at p. 338.
52. A free rendering of the statement in Bischoff, 'Anzeige', p. 338: 'Eine sehr alte, für Südengland "apostolische" Tradition der Unziale würde die merkwürdige Tatsache begreiflich machen, daß das kentische und mercische Urkundenwesen sich bei seinem Auftreten ihrer bedient.'
53. Ibid. 'südenglische Schriftkultur'.
54. Paris, B.N. nouv. acq. lat. 1596: *CLA*, 686.
55. Bischoff, 'Anzeige', p. 331.

56. A. Petrucci, 'Book, Handwriting and School', in his *Writers and Readers in Medieval Italy: Studies in the History of Written Culture*, ed. and trans. C. Radding (New Haven, 1995), pp. 59–76, at p. 64.
57. M.B. Parkes, *The Scriptorium of Wearmouth–Jarrow* (Jarrow Lecture, 1982), repr. in his *Scribes, Scripts and Readers: Studies in the Communication, Presentation and Dissemination of Medieval Texts* (London, 1991), pp. 93–120, at p. 94.
58. Ibid. p. 118.
59. New Haven, Yale University, Beinecke Library, 516: *CLA*, 1849; see further n. 3 above, and Parkes, *Scriptorium of Wearmouth–Jarrow*, p. 95, n. 10.
60. St Petersburg, Public Library, Q. v. I. 18: *CLA*, 1621; J.J.G. Alexander, *Insular Manuscripts 6th to the 9th Century* (London, 1978), no. 19, pp. 47–8, pl. 84.
61. P. Meyvaert, 'Bede and Gregory the Great' (Jarrow Lecture, 1964), repr. in his *Benedict, Gregory, Bede and Others* (London, 1977), no. 8, p. 3.
62. From Patrick Wormald's papers on this and related topics, see most recently his 'The Venerable Bede and the "Church of the English"', *The English Religious Tradition and the Genius of Anglicanism*, ed. G. Rowell (Wantage, 1992), pp. 13–22, at pp. 20–3; also Richter, 'Bede's Angli', pp. 108–10, 113–14.
63. Bede, *HE*, II, 1, pp. 122–34.
64. See esp. the beginning of *HE*, II, 1, p. 123.
65. H. Mayr-Harting, 'Bede's Patristic Thinking as an Historian', *Historiographie im frühen Mittelalter*, ed. A. Scharer and G. Scheibelreiter (Vienna, 1994), pp. 367–74, at p. 367; idem, *Coming of Christianity*, p. 218.
66. Mosford, 'Critical Edition of the *Vita Gregorii magni*', p. xxvii; Thacker, 'Memorializing Gregory the Great', p. 79: 'The Gregorian cult reached its apogee in eighth-century England.'
67. *Councils and Ecclesiastical Documents Relating to Great Britain and Ireland*, ed. A.W. Haddan and W. Stubbs, vol. III (Oxford, 1871), p. 368; C. Cubitt, *Anglo-Saxon Church Councils c. 650–c. 850* (London, 1995), p. 151.
68. See Thacker, 'Memorializing Gregory the Great', esp. pp. 81–2 and his contribution to this volume, ch. 14 below.
69. On which see the fine article by S. Keynes, 'The Reconstruction of a Burnt Cottonian Manuscript: the Case of Cotton MS Otho A. I', *British Library Journal*, 22 (1996), 113–59; Scharer, *Königsurkunde*, pp. 188–95.
70. *Die Briefe des heiligen Bonifatius und Lullus*, ed. M. Tangl, MGH Epist. sel. 1 (Berlin, 1916), no. 111, pp. 238–43.
71. Ibid., p. 240: 'in generali synodo nostro'. On the synod see also Cubitt, *Anglo-Saxon Church Councils*, pp. 267–8.
72. *Briefe*, ed. Tangl, p. 240: 'utpote quem (sc. Bonifatium) specialiter nobis cum beato Gregorio et Augustino et patronum quaerimus et habere indubitanter credimus coram Christo domino'.
73. S. Keynes, 'The Councils of Clofesho' (Eleventh Brixworth Lecture, 1993, Vaughan Paper no. 38, 1994), p. 22.
74. *Councils and Ecclesiastical Documents*, ed. Haddan and Stubbs, vol. III, p. 411.
75. For example, Alcuin, *Epistolae*, ed. E. Duemmler, MGH Epist. IV, Karolini aevi II (Berlin, 1895), no. 124 (797), p. 182; no. 125 (797), p. 184; no. 128 (797), p. 189, and no. 279, p. 436. On the first of these letters see D.A. Bullough, 'What has Ingeld to do with Lindisfarne?', *ASE*, 22 (1993), 93–125.
76. *Das altenglische Martyrologium*, ed. Günter Kotzor, Bayerische Akademie der Wissenschaften, philosophisch-historische Klasse, Abhandlungen Neue Folge, Heft 88/1 and 2 (Munich, 1981), pp. 449*–454* on the date.
77. *Das altenglische Martyrologium*, ed. Kotzor, p. 32.

78. *Life of Gregory*, ed. Colgrave, ch. 29, pp. 126–8.
79. Ibid., ch. 26, pp. 120–2.
80. Asser, *De rebus gestis Aelfredi*, ed. W.H. Stevenson (Oxford, 1904), ch. 77, p. 62; S. Keynes and M. Lapidge, *Alfred the Great: Asser's Life of King Alfred and Other Contemporary Sources* (Harmondsworth, 1983), p. 92 and p. 123 for a translation of King Alfred's preface to the translation of the *Dialogi*.
81. Keynes and Lapidge, *Alfred the Great*, p. 126.
82. Anton Scharer, 'The Writing of History at King Alfred's Court', *Early Medieval Europe*, 5 (1996), 177–206, at pp. 187–9. I am unconvinced by the most recent attempt (as also by earlier attempts) to claim Asser's *Life of Alfred* as a later forgery (of the early eleventh century), thus to redate and re-attribute the work: Alfred P. Smyth, *King Alfred the Great* (Oxford, 1995), esp. pp. 149–367. On which see Simon Keynes, 'Review Article: On the Authenticity of Asser's Life of King Alfred', *JEH*, 47 (1996), 529–51, and Janet L. Nelson, 'Review Article: Waiting for Alfred', *Early Medieval Europe*, 7 (1998), 115–24.
83. Asser, *De rebus gestis Aelfredi*, ed. Stevenson, ch. 74, p. 56; the translation is that of Keynes and Lapidge, *Alfred*, pp. 89–90.
84. Astronomus, *Vita Hludowici imperatoris*, ed. E. Tremp, MGH Script. rer. Germ. in usum scholarum 64 (Hannover, 1995), ch. 8, pp. 306–8.
85. Gregory, *Dialogi*, ed. U. Moricca, Fonti per la storia d'Italia 57 (Rome, 1924), II, 2, pp. 78–9.
86. On which see the stimulating paper by Sarah Foot, 'The Making of Angelcynn: English Identity before the Norman Conquest', *TRHS*, 6th series 6 (1996), 25–49.
87. For the details see ibid., pp. 30–2.
88. *Two of the Saxon Chronicles Parallel*, eds C. Plummer and J. Earle, vol. I (Oxford, 1892), p. 80; the translation derives from *English Historical Documents I, c. 500–1042*, ed. D Whitelock, 2nd edn (London, 1979), p. 199.
89. Already convincingly suggested by Keynes and Lapidge, *Alfred the Great*, p. 38; and further developed in an important paper by S. Keynes, 'King Alfred and the Mercians'. I record my thanks to Dr Keynes for having sent me this paper prior to publication.
90. Which can be deduced from the numismatic evidence. See *Medieval European Coinage with a Catalogue of the Coins in the Fitzwilliam Museum, Cambridge: I The Early Middle Ages (5th–10th centuries)*, eds P. Grierson and M. Blackburn (Cambridge, 1986), pp. 310–14; M. Archibald in *The Making of England*, eds L. Webster and J. Backhouse (London, 1991), pp. 284–6; Keynes, 'King Alfred and the Mercians' and other contributions to *Kings, Currency and Alliances: History and Coinage of Southern England in the Ninth Century*, eds M. Blackburn and D.N. Dumville (Woodbridge, 1998).
91. J.L. Nelson, 'The Political Ideas of Alfred of Wessex', *Kings and Kingship in Medieval Europe*, ed. A.J. Duggan (London, 1993), pp. 125–58, at pp. 155–6. Cf. Bede, *HE*, I, 29, pp. 104–6 on Gregory's plan.
92. For what follows I heavily rely on S. Keynes, 'The West Saxon Charters of King Aethelwulf and his Sons', *EHR*, 109 (1994), 1109–49, at pp. 1147–9; idem, 'King Alfred and the Mercians'; and Nelson, 'Political Ideas of Alfred', pp. 154–5.
93. Keynes, 'Charters', p. 1147.
94. Asser, *De rebus gestis Aelfredi*, ed. Stevenson, p. 149, nn 2, 3.
95. Ibid., p. 149, n. 1.

CHAPTER 10

The Architecture of the Augustinian Mission[1]

Eric Cambridge

Compared to the often dramatic archaeological discoveries which have transformed our understanding of early medieval church building elsewhere in England over the last thirty years or so, the earliest churches of the south-east have received comparatively little attention. In part this may be due to the fact that, despite recent activity involving both the re-excavation of some sites,[2] and the exploration of others previously unexamined,[3] no major archaeological contribution to our knowledge of the earliest period – that is, up to *c.* AD 700 – has seen the light of day since the publication in 1927 of excavations at SS Peter and Paul, Canterbury, and at Reculver.[4] Such comparative quiescence might appear to suggest that the interpretation of the material we do have has become a reasonably well-settled matter. Even the differences of opinion about the continental sources of these buildings found in the most recent surveys reflect divergences of view which had already crystallized in the literature more than half a century earlier.[5]

It is the purpose of this chapter to focus upon three closely related aspects of the material evidence in respect of which the generally received view may be considered open to question. The first and fundamental issue is the extent to which it is in fact appropriate to treat the remains of the early churches of south-eastern England as an essentially homogeneous group. Admittedly, it is not difficult to make out a plausible *prima facie* case in favour of so doing, particularly when (as has generally been the case) the evidence is approached from an overtly Insular perspective, which tends to focus attention upon those features which are at once common to early churches in that region and rare or unknown elsewhere in England. To take only the most obvious example, where the form of the east end of churches from that area has been established archaeologically it is invariably apsidal, a form rarely encountered among demonstrably early churches elsewhere in England. The approach is reinforced by the widespread (and, though not strictly accurate, undoubtedly convenient) use of the shorthand term 'Kentish' for the group as a whole, an adjective which has arguably come to bear a significance beyond its strictly geographical reference.[6] Yet the inherent danger of implicitly reinforcing the similarities at the expense of the (potentially no less significant) differences between the various sites to which such an umbrella term is applied should be immediately apparent. The investigation of the other two aspects of the material remains which will be considered here, that is, the architectural sources of the early churches in the south-east and the historical context or contexts within which those sources were transmitted, must be regarded as essentially dependent upon the results of our initial enquiry into the degree of homogeneity exhibited by those buildings: the less the evidence is considered to favour the traditional, essentially homogeneous, interpretation, the less plausible it becomes to treat the issues of sources and contexts in terms of single rather than multiple questions. For example, the most recent discussions of the sources, polarised as they still are between Gaul and Northern Italy,[7] are nevertheless united in their assumption that there is a single answer to that question; similarly, discussions of the historical context of the transmission of those sources have tended to focus upon the earliest phases of Augustine's mission, an approach which has doubtless been reinforced by the circumstance that we happen to be rather better informed about those events than about much of the sequel. Nevertheless, the attempt to make due allowance for the unevenness of the sources is a duty incumbent upon architectural historians no less than archaeologists, particularly when the dated remains are known to span some three-quarters of a century, a period during which the mission churches and their native successors underwent several dramatic changes in fortune. Before any of these questions can be tackled, however, the nature and chronology of the surviving remains need to be reviewed: it is particularly important to be clear at the outset about what we do know with reasonable certainty and what we do not.

A particularly acute difficulty that needs to be faced at the outset is the more or less fragmentary extent of the surviving early remains at most sites. Even at places where substantial quantities of fabric do survive above ground, as at Bradwell-on-Sea and Minster-in-Sheppey, they mostly derive from those parts of the buildings which are least diagnostic from an architectural point of view. At other sites known only from excavation, such as Rochester and, most importantly, SS Peter and Paul at Canterbury, significant parts of the ground plans remain unrecovered (figs. 10.1a, 10.2a). At yet others, notably Lyminge, the quality of the nineteenth-century excavations is so suspect as to render any comment of doubtful value – a situation which could only be changed by undertaking extensive reinvestigation.[8] From this

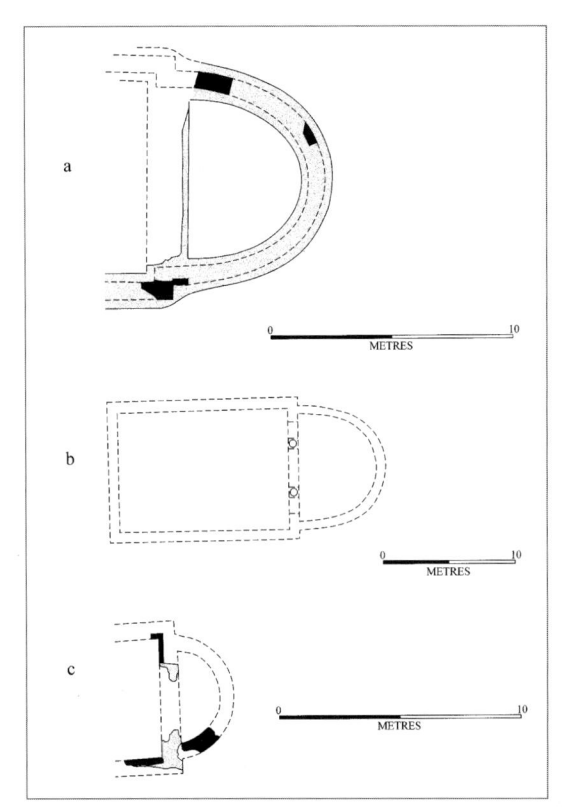

10.1. Conventions used throughout plans: solid black, wall; grey, foundation; dashed lines, hypothetical/uncertain; continuous lines, retained from earlier phase. a. Rochester, remains of church as excavated by Livett (after Livett, op. cit. in n. 10, pl. I); b. Rochester, church as reconstructed by Hope (after Hope, op. cit. in n. 10, pl. II); c. Ambérieu-en-Bugey (Ain), chapel of Saint-Germain d'Ambérieu, detail of east end (after PMCF, op. cit. in n. 5, I, figs on pp. 197–8).

perspective, it is understandable that the churches about which we happen to have the most complete overall information – St Pancras in Canterbury, Bradwell-on-Sea, and Reculver – have tended to be used as models in attempting to reconstruct the less complete remains at other sites.[9] Provided that its hypothetical basis is not overlooked, the process of reconstruction has an important and legitimate role to play in understanding and interpreting fragmentary remains at particular sites. What needs to be carefully distinguished from exercises of this kind, however, is the implicit reliance upon reconstructions of individual buildings to support generalisations about the structures as a group – i.e. using reconstructions as if they themselves constituted a source of primary evidence in defining the common characteristics of the sites. Even if the more obvious dangers of circularity of argument are avoided, there remains the hazard that reconstructions have an insidious tendency to imprint themselves on the mind in such a way as to reinforce the impression of group homogeneity when the evidence upon which they are based is in fact far from being clear-cut. Two examples will suffice to illustrate the problem.

The excavation of the early church at Rochester by Canon Livett in the 1880s revealed most of an apsidal foundation, slightly inset from the nave, with a broad foundation on the chord of the apse (fig. 10.1a).[10] Subsequent commentators, beginning with Hope, have suggested that the purpose of this foundation was probably to carry the columns of a triple arcade of the kind already known from Reculver (figs 10.1b, 10.2b, 10.10a), and later publications have generally shown the church so equipped.[11] But it must be emphasized that there is no archaeological evidence that the church possessed such a feature.[12] What is more, numerous churches throughout Late Antique Europe could be cited in which a foundation is found dividing nave from apse, presumably for reasons of structural stability (for example, fig. 10.1c); yet only in the context of interpreting the remains of early churches in south-east England is it alleged that such foundations were intended to support arcades – even though Reculver and St Pancras, Canterbury (in its modified form), are the only certain examples in the region. This is not to suggest that such an interpretation is impossible, but rather to assert that, in the absence of any positive proof that this was in fact its purpose, the evidence of the foundation from Rochester should properly be treated as entirely neutral and non-diagnostic on the point.

The second example concerns the way in which the fragmentary remains of the church of SS Peter and Paul at Canterbury have recently been interpreted by reference to Reculver.[13] The logical basis of this approach has been most systematically set out by Fernie, who argues that, since the surviving western parts of the former (fig. 10.2a) closely resemble the equivalent parts of the latter (fig. 10.2b), it is reasonable to infer that the destroyed eastern parts of SS Peter and Paul were also similar to those of Reculver.[14] This approach has been widely followed,[15] most recently by Gem, whose reconstructions of the churches of SS Peter and Paul and of St Mary at Canterbury follow (though with significant modifications) the reconstruction of Reculver first proposed by Harold Taylor in 1969.[16] It is worth pausing, however, to consider how close are those alleged resemblances in fact. They comprise: the location of doorways in north, south and west walls of the nave; the use of walls of similar width and materials; and the flanking of the west doorways by buttresses. Of these, the first is undoubtedly true but, in the absence of evidence as to how the doorways at other contemporary sites were disposed, it is difficult to know how much weight to attach to it. Again, the similarities in construction do not seem sufficiently distinctive to enable one to infer any particularly close relationship. Finally, the buttresses flanking the western doorways are in fact arguably quite different. First, those at Reculver form part of a systematic use of buttresses in the outer walls of the nave, which is not

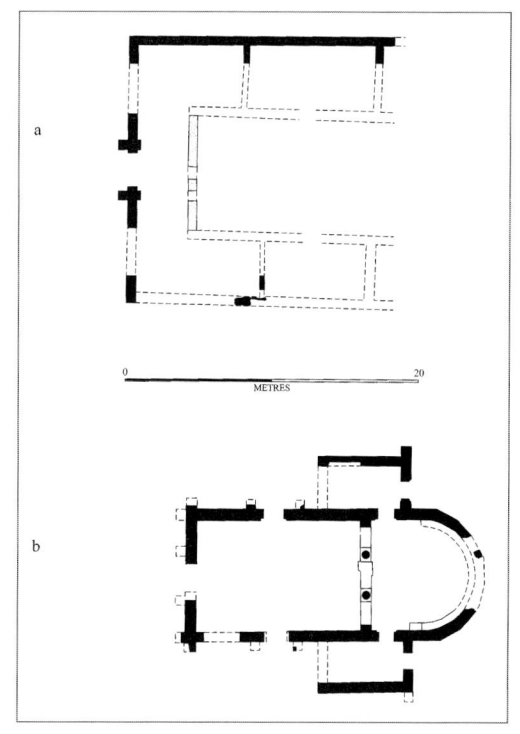

10.2. a. Canterbury, remains of church of SS Peter and Paul, earliest phase (after Saunders, op. cit. in n. 2, fig. 8, p. 45, with minor modifications from Gem, 'The Anglo-Saxon and Norman Churches', op. cit. in n. 5, fig. 35, p. 98); b. Reculver, remains of church, earliest phase according to Peers (after Peers, op. cit. in n. 4, fig. 4, p. 245).

apparently the case at SS Peter and Paul. Secondly, only at the latter does the buttressing extend inwards as well as outwards from the wall surface.[17] And thirdly, the contexts of the two associated doorways are quite distinct, that at Reculver being in the west wall of the nave proper, while the one at SS Peter and Paul was almost certainly the entry to an outer narthex.[18] What is actually known of the western parts of these two buildings thus seems to provide at best equivocal evidence that they were closely related to one another; it follows that this is an insecure basis from which to infer that the lost parts of SS Peter and Paul resembled those of Reculver to any significant degree or, indeed, at all.[19] This is not to deny the possibility that the eastern parts of these two churches *might* have been similar, but merely to point out that the alleged similarities between the parts that do survive are not sufficient to support that contention. The qualification is important, since the way in which we reconstruct the east end of SS Peter and Paul has profound implications for our understanding of the development of early church design in south-east England; for, if the above argument were to be accepted, it would imply that at least some of the distinctive features of the east end of Reculver were already present at one of the first churches to be erected by the Augustinian missionaries.

Examples of how fragmentary remains have been interpreted and reconstructed to conform to more complete examples from other sites in south-east England could be multiplied;[20] but perhaps the clearest indication of the extent to which this approach has become deeply embedded in the interpretative procedures of architectural historians is in the recent publication of the excavations beneath the nave of Canterbury Cathedral. Here the extremely fragmentary remains attributable on stratigraphic grounds to a post-Roman context are reconstructed (albeit explicitly acknowledging its hypothetical nature) by reference to the proportions of the ground plan of SS Peter and Paul, Canterbury (fig. 10.3a);[21] yet it will be recalled that fundamental aspects of the proportions of the latter, most notably the ratio of width to length of its nave, remain unknown (fig. 10.2a).[22] Further details, including a triple arcade at the junction of nave and chancel, preceded by an altar, are borrowed from Reculver.[23] The comparative ground plans selected and displayed alongside this reconstruction offer a powerful visual reinforcement of the impression of uniformity,[24] all being furnished with triple arcades (a feature only certainly attested at Reculver (fig. 10.2b) and St Pancras, Canterbury, as modified (fig. 10.13a)) and continuous surrounding *porticus* (only certainly attested as a primary feature at SS Peter and Paul, Canterbury (fig. 10.2a)).

Perhaps the most curious example of the power of the 'Kentish' construct to override the archaeological evidence is the reconstruction of the early medieval church of Saint

Martin at Angers published in 1953 by Forsyth. There the foundation dividing nave from chancel is reconstructed as if it were the foundation for a triple arcade of Reculver type (fig. 10.3b).[25] A recent re-evaluation has, however, concluded that there is no archaeological basis for this interpretation,[26] which has clearly been determined by a sideways glance at Reculver.[27] Quite apart from the lack of evidence, such a procedure entails making fundamental assumptions about the nature of the relationship between the architecture of south-east England and Merovingian Gaul which, as we shall see, are open to question.[28]

There are additional conceptual difficulties in the above approach which need to be confronted. The earliest phase of the remains at Reculver almost certainly dates from some seventy years after the time of St Augustine, the period to which the remains at Christ Church, Canterbury, are assigned by the excavators; a similar interval separates Reculver from SS Peter and Paul at Canterbury.[29] While the differences between the dates of these buildings are not in themselves fatal to the hypothesis that they might be related, the question of whether or not the forms of the early churches of this region changed significantly over time must be a matter for investigation rather than assumption – a point which the fact that a significant proportion of the remains are insecurely dated should not be allowed to obscure. Accordingly, the evidence for the dating of those remains is as clearly in need of critical re-evaluation as is that relating to their architectural characteristics.

Two principal categories of documentary evidence are available for attempting to date the remains of the early churches of south-east England: specific references from which the dates of individual structures may be inferred; and the general

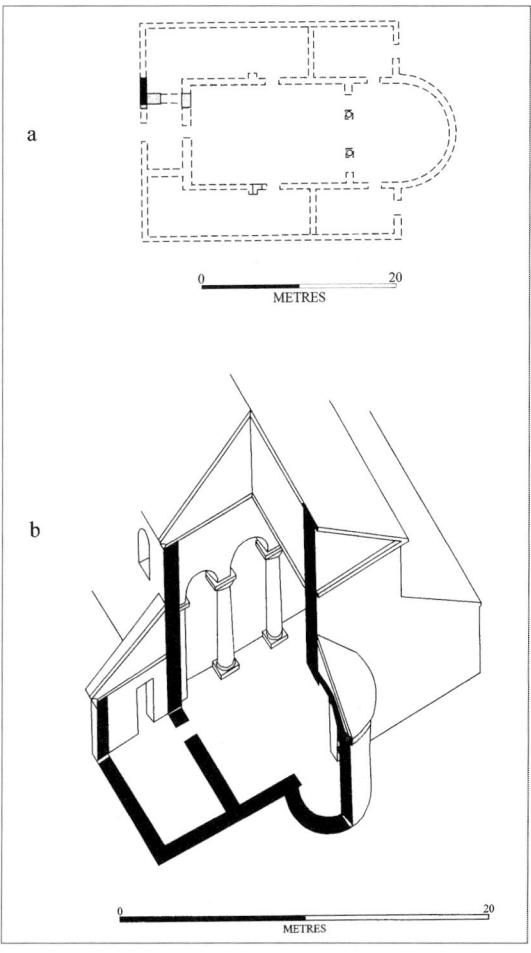

10.3. a. Canterbury, remains excavated beneath cathedral, earliest post-Roman phase, as reconstructed (after Blockley et al., op. cit. in n. 3, fig. 36, p. 98).
b. Angers (Maine-et-Loire), church of Saint-Martin, detail of reconstruction showing triple arcade (after Forsyth, op. cit. in n. 25, fig. 184).

historical context of the church itself as an institution. Though the latter can only indirectly increase our understanding of the material evidence, it has perhaps been given less consideration hitherto than it deserves, its particular importance in the present case being its potential for providing the only 'independent' means (i.e., one not based on architectural typology) by which those remains which are not specifically mentioned in the sources can be placed in any kind of temporal context.

Four churches in the south-east can certainly or probably be dated by specific documentary references. SS Peter and Paul, Canterbury, was incomplete at Augustine's death (604x609, probably shortly after 604) and was presumably complete when consecrated by his successor, Laurence, who died between 616 and 619.[30] The church of St Mary at Canterbury, immediately to the east of SS Peter and Paul, was built by King Eadbald of Kent (616x618–640) and, according to Bede, was dedicated by Archbishop Mellitus, who died in April 624.[31] To the extent that the apsidal remains located at Rochester may be identified with the church of St Andrew founded there by King Æthelberht (d. 616x618) in or shortly after 604, they may be regarded as securely dated.[32] Unfortunately, however, there are no features which positively confirm the identification,[33] while the nineteenth-century excavation also revealed fragmentary remains of adjacent structures to the south which remain undated and uninterpreted;[34] and even given the meagre resources of the see, it is not impossible that there was more than one church at the site in the early Middle Ages. Lastly, the traditional identification of the first phase of the excavated remains of the church at Reculver with the church for whose foundation King Ecgberht of Kent is recorded as having granted the site to the priest Bassa in 669 may still be sustainable, though must inevitably be regarded as provisional pending the publication of the re-excavation of 1969–70.[35]

At other sites the evidence is less precise: as at Minster-in-Sheppey, where the recorded foundation of the religious community between 664 and 679, probably c. 675–9,[36] only provides at best a *terminus post quem* for the actual construction of the church, substantial parts of which still survive.[37] In other cases the evidence is so weak as to be unreliable. For example, the remains at Lyminge have traditionally been associated with the monastery that was allegedly founded there c. 633.[38] But, as has already been noted, the site is so badly in need of re-examination that it would be inappropriate to make any such inference.[39] What is more, the reliability of the documentary evidence for the foundation of the monastery at so early a date has been doubted, and a point at the very end of the seventh century is now regarded as more likely.[40] Similarly, Bradwell-on-Sea is traditionally dated by association with the missionary activities of Cedd who, according to Bede, established a church there in or shortly after 653;[41] as Fernie points out, however, this falls short of dating the existing church, merely showing that it can hardly have been erected earlier than this.[42]

Documentary evidence thus permits the fragmentary remains of only one building, SS Peter and Paul in Canterbury, to be dated with confidence to the period 597–*c*. 618. In addition, it is possible that the surviving fragment of St Mary at Canterbury dates from around 624, and that parts of the church documented as having been erected at Rochester at the beginning of the seventh century were identified in the nineteenth-century excavations. There is no other building which can be regarded as even reasonably firmly dated until Reculver, and even there the dating depends on identifying the foundations excavated by Peers with a church presumed to have been erected shortly after the grant of the site in 669; Minster-in-Sheppey probably also dates to approximately the same period, or slightly later in the seventh century.

As noted above, besides the existence of specific references to some churches, and of particular historical contexts to which others might be assigned with more or less plausibility, the more general historical context within which the buildings were erected also needs to be considered. There are at least two aspects to this: the external circumstances of the mission; and its internal composition.

From a political standpoint, the close dependence of the mission, particularly in its early stages, upon the patronage of individual Kentish kings must have entailed a particular sensitivity to the changing political fortunes and attitudes of successive rulers. Throughout the period from the arrival of the first missionaries in 597 to the conversion of Eadbald, Æthelberht's son and successor, *c*. 624, there are no grounds for supposing that the mission extended beyond the episcopal churches closely associated with royal centres. The reverses of the later part of this period, involving the abandonment of the sees of London and Rochester (the latter temporarily, the former for perhaps half a century) and the flight of members of the mission to Gaul, were very probably even more severe than Bede's account (and presumably the Canterbury sources behind it) implies.[43] Kirby has argued cogently that the paganism of Eadbald may have been longer lasting than generally supposed; and as he married Æthelberht's widow (who was presumably therefore herself a lapsed Christian if not actually a pagan), the difficulties may have commenced immediately following Bertha's death rather than Æthelberht's.[44]

There is no clear evidence that the mission did more than mark time in the generation following Eadbald's conversion. The foundation of the church of St Mary at Canterbury, apparently as Eadbald's own burial church, suggests that its close dependence upon the ruling Kentish dynasty continued. This period must also have seen a significant shift in the composition of the mission, as its original members gradually became extinct and were replaced by the English recruits whom they had trained. When Archbishop Honorius, 'one of the disciples of Pope Gregory', died in the autumn of 653, it is difficult to believe that, if any others were still left, they can possibly have long survived him.[45]

It was apparently not until the third generation after the arrival of the mission, under Eadbald's successor, Eorconberht (640–64), that pagan practices were expressly outlawed and christian observance officially enjoined in Kent – though how effectively these precepts were implemented we cannot know.[46] It was also during this king's reign that the practice of sending royal women to train in Gallic nunneries is first certainly documented; and it is surely not coincidental that the foundation of royal nunneries or double monasteries in places other than the existing episcopal centres also probably began before Eorconberht's death. The latter process appears to have accelerated in the last third of the seventh century, and must have entailed a correspondingly marked increase in the demand for church building.[47]

It is worth underlining that the documentary evidence relating to individual buildings and what we know of the general historical context of the mission present a concordant picture. There is some evidence relating to the history of the early days of the mission in the south-east, and to the development of the church in that region in the second half of the seventh century; there is also evidence to enable us to attribute remains at specific sites (albeit with varying degrees of confidence) to each of those periods. In marked contrast, the intervening generation, from the 620s to the 650s or 660s, remains equally elusive whether approached in general historical terms or in terms of buildings which might be attributed to it. This situation should in itself be sufficient to give one considerable pause for thought before making facile connections between first and third generation remains. Exiguous in the extreme though the material evidence is, when it is approached free of any presumption in favour of homogeneity it at least raises the possibility that significant changes might have taken place in the period that intervened between the construction of these two groups of buildings. The slight insetting of the apse from the nave at Rochester, for example, is wholly unlike the treatment of that junction at Reculver, where the apse is the same width as the nave (figs 10.1a, 10.2b). Similarly, there is no sign at SS Peter and Paul, Canterbury (or, at any rate, in what now survives of it), of the systematic use of pilaster buttresses which is so characteristic of Reculver.[48] What happened in that middle generation, what (if any) remains can be attributed to it, and how these relate to the remains of the preceding and succeeding generations, are questions which therefore assume a fundamental importance if the development of early church building in the south east is to be properly understood.

In an attempt to establish what might have characterised the activities of the mission in the second quarter of the seventh century, and what their architectural implications might have been, it is worth looking more closely at the evidence relating to the one place in England where activity is most likely at this period, namely, the city of Canterbury itself (fig. 10.4a). It has frequently been remarked that the patron saints selected for the principal churches of the mission were probably intended to recall arrangements in and around the city of Rome. Thus the dedication of the cathedral to the Saviour echoes that of the papal cathedral in the Lateran, while that of the extra-mural monastery to SS Peter and Paul reflects the two great apostolic cults of Rome.[49] The process appears to have gone further, however. Levison long ago noted the specifically Roman connotations of the dedication of a *martyrium* in Canterbury to the Four Crowned Martyrs.[50] This dedication was always an extremely rare one in medieval Europe.[51] Bede's choice of the term *martyrium* here is also interesting. It appears very infrequently in the

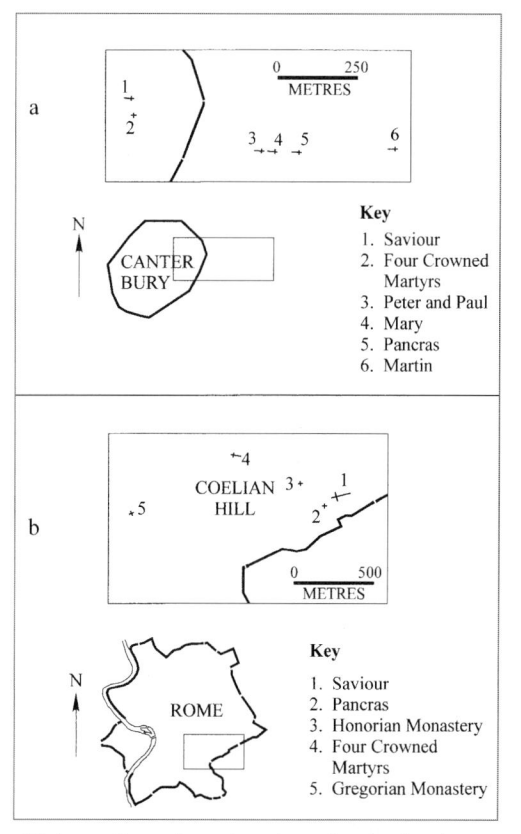

10.4. a. Canterbury, locations of early churches *(after* Topographical Maps of Canterbury, 2nd edn, Canterbury Archaeological Trust *(Canterbury, 1982)); b.* Rome, locations of selected early churches around Coelian Hill *(after map in C. Huelsen,* Le Chiese di Roma nel Medio Evo: Cataloghi ed Appunti *(Florence, 1928).*

Ecclesiastical History and then only to describe churches associated with major relics or holy places,[52] which strongly suggests that the prime function of the building in Canterbury was to house relics (at this date surely non-corporeal ones) of its dedicatees. Unlike the case of the Four Crowned Martyrs, the dedication of another church in the city to a Roman martyr, St Pancras, is not actually documented until the late Middle Ages;[53] nevertheless, its extreme rarity as a dedication in England and the Roman origin of the cult strongly suggest both that an association with the mission is in fact the most plausible context for it and that the structure originated as another such *martyrium* specifically built to house relics of that saint.

The *martyrium* of the Four Crowned Martyrs at Canterbury was apparently in existence by the pontificate of Archbishop Mellitus (619–24) who, according to the miracle reported by Bede, miraculously saved it from destruction by fire. It is far from certain, however, that this particular story can be relied upon to provide a *terminus ante quem* for the construction of the building, since there is a distinct possibility that the miracle was a Canterbury fabrication of later date.[54] With regard to the date of St Pancras, Gem has recently pointed out that the cult of that martyr is likely to have received a particular boost in the time of Pope Honorius I (625–38) who reconstructed the saint's martyrial basilica.[55] The same point may be made with respect to the *martyrium* of the Four Crowned Martyrs, since Honorius is also recorded as having rebuilt the church dedicated to them in Rome.[56] In any event, these dedications are probably best explained as reflections of the particular interests and contacts of the Italian missionaries: neither is likely, therefore, to be later than the mid-seventh century, by which time the original group must largely have been dead.[57]

One further consideration supports a specific association between these dedications and the Italian missionaries, and that is the possibility that the decision to represent those two particular martyrial cults at Canterbury might have been connected with their locations in Rome. Brooks has pointed to the fact that the church of the Four Crowned Martyrs in Rome was a neighbour of Gregory's monastery on the Coelian hill from which Augustine himself and at least some of the other missionaries had been recruited (fig. 10.4b).[58] What has not been previously noted is that there may also be a link with the cult of St Pancras in that same area, perhaps reflecting the tradition of the saint's baptism on the Coelian hill and perhaps also arising from the presence at the Lateran of his head (though it is not certain how early that relic came into its possession).[59] This is surely the most plausible explanation for why the only demonstrably early dedication to St Pancras in Rome, other than the extramural *basilica ad corpus* itself, is that of the church serving the oldest of the basilical monasteries attached to the Lateran.[60] It lay immediately south-west of the cathedral, and was thus another fairly close neighbour of Gregory's monastery (fig. 10.4b).[61] Two points need to be stressed here. First, there is the relatively close proximity of all these churches to one another amid a multiplicity of churches and cults both in and around the city. Secondly, there is the circumstance that, if their location in the same area of Rome is indeed significant, it strengthens the likelihood that their selection as dedications in Canterbury dates back to a period when the missionaries for whom those cults would have had a local significance in their Roman context were still alive.

If this is indeed the most likely context for the dedication of a church to St Pancras at Canterbury, it is still far from establishing that the remains of the structure which bore that dedication later in the Middle Ages were erected in the early seventh century and were associated with the martyr's cult from the outset.

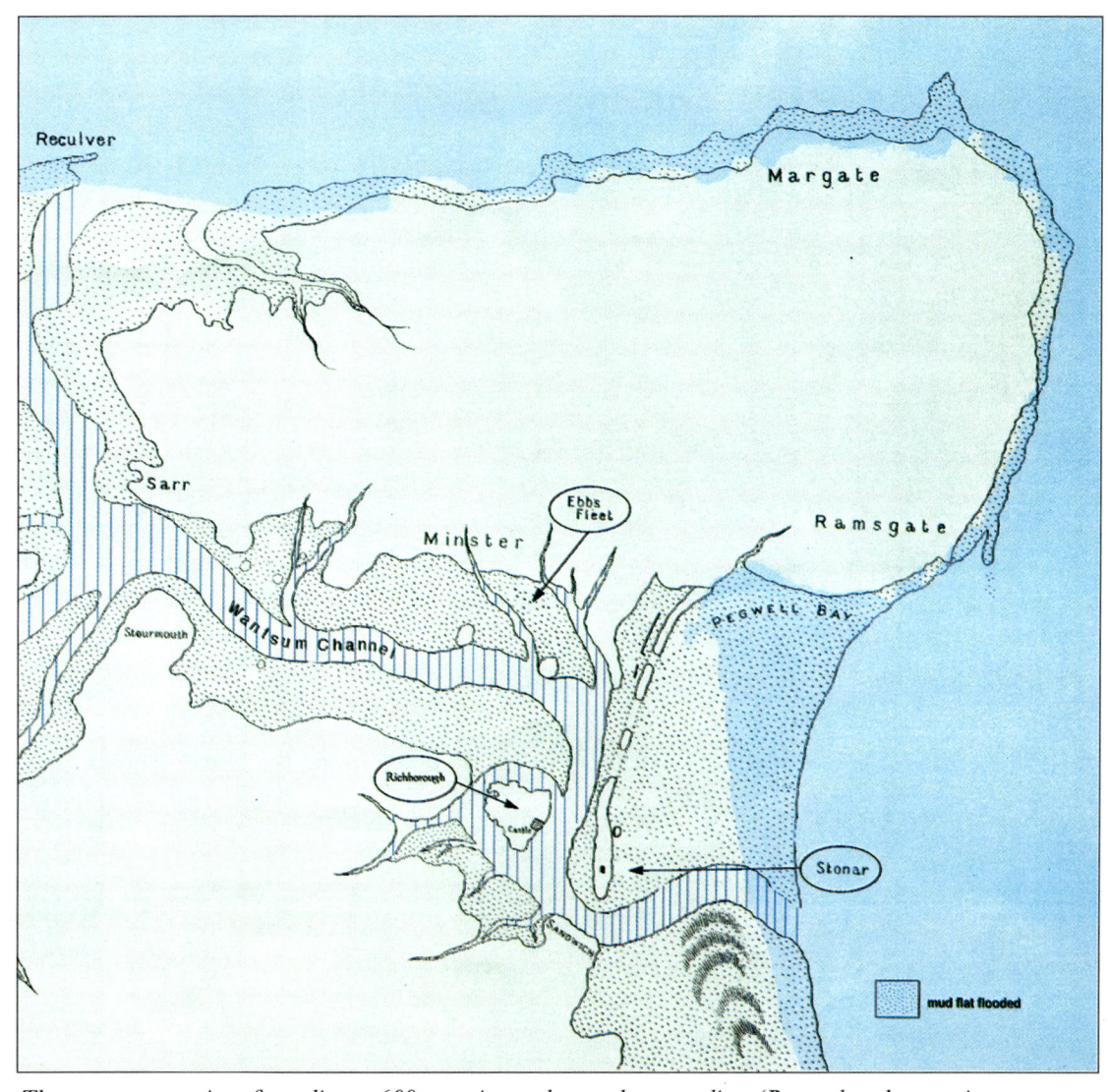

Thanet: reconstruction of coastline, c. 600, superimposed on modern coastline. (Research and conception: G. Butrous and R. Gameson; realisation: J. Phipps.)

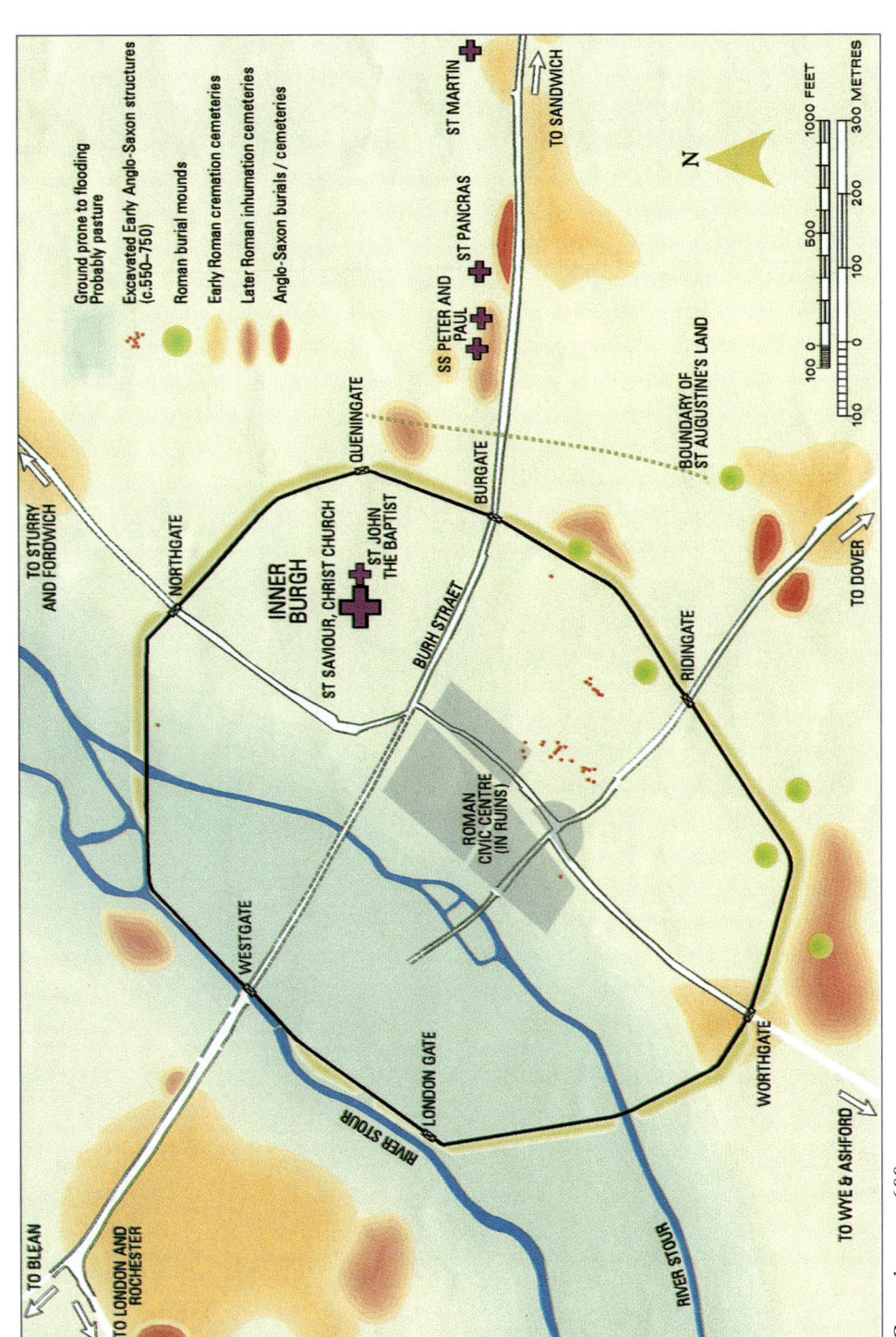

Canterbury, c. 600.

The Liudhard Medalet, obverse. (The Board of Trustees of the National Museums & Galleries on Merseyside)

The Liudhard Medalet, reverse. (The Board of Trustees of the National Museums & Galleries on Merseyside)

The Kingston Brooch. (The Board of Trustees of the National Museums & Galleries on Merseyside)

CCCC, MS 286, fol. 125r, The Gospels of St Augustine: the tailpiece illustration for Mark's gospel with scenes of Christ's Passion. (The Master and Fellows of Corpus Christi College, Cambridge)

CCCC, MS 286, fols 129v + 130r, The Gospels of St Augustine; portrait of St Augustine; incipit of Luke's gospel. (Mildred Budny; The Master & Fellows of Corpus Christi College, Cambridge)

HIC GABRIEL AN
GELVS ZACHARIE
SACERDOTI IN
TEMPLO ŌNI AP
PARVIT ALMVMQ
PRAE CVRSORĒ
MAGNI REGIS EI
NASCITVRVH·
PRAEDIXIT·

BL, Royal MS 1 E. vi, fol. 44r: the inscription for the frontispiece for Luke's gospel with the Annunciation to Zacharias. (British Library)

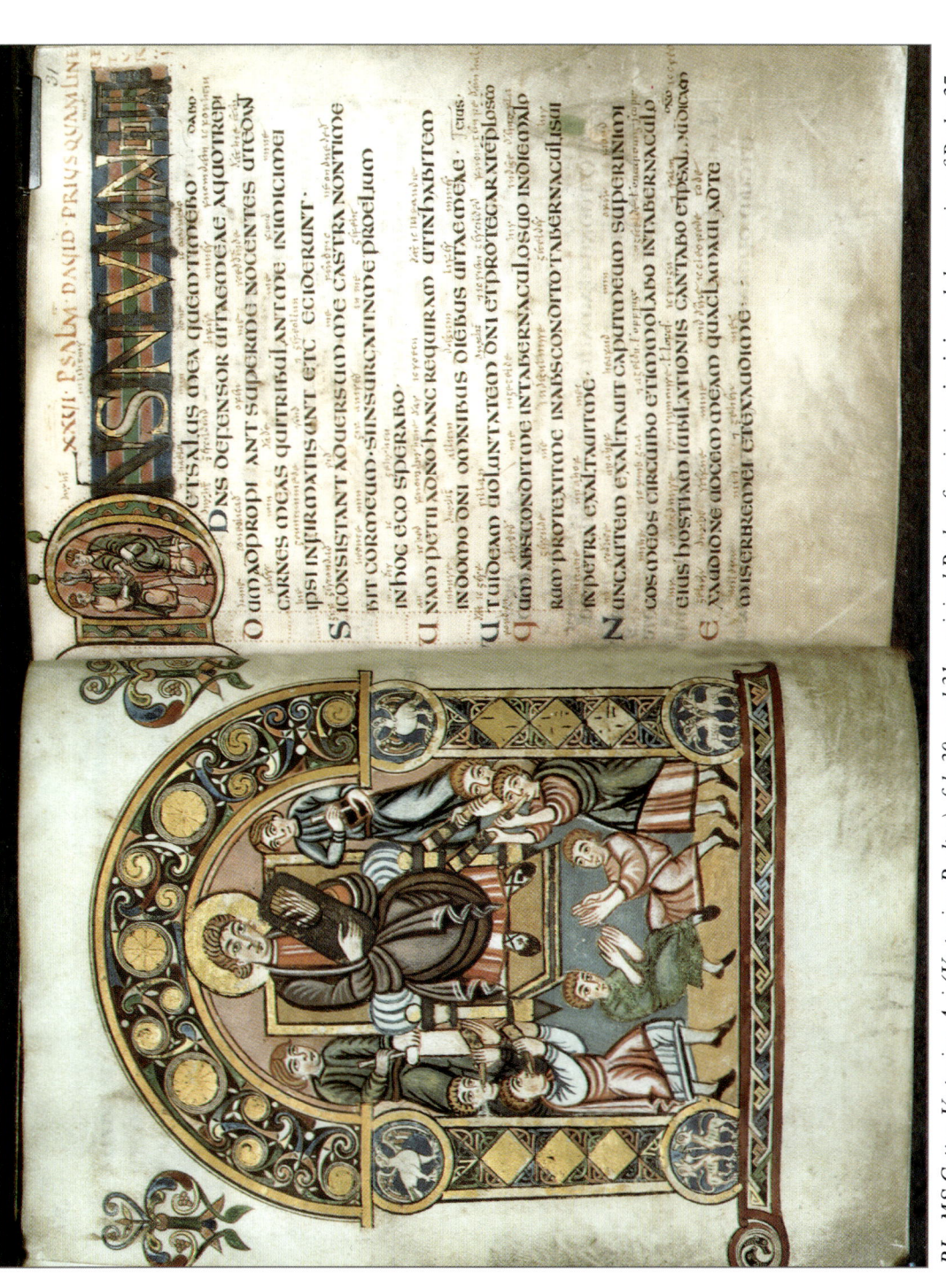

BL, MS Cotton Vespasian A. i (Vespasian Psalter), fols 30v and 31r: original Psalter frontispiece; incipit and the opening of Psalm 27. (British Library)

LII· IN FINEM PRO MELECH INTELLECTUS DAUID

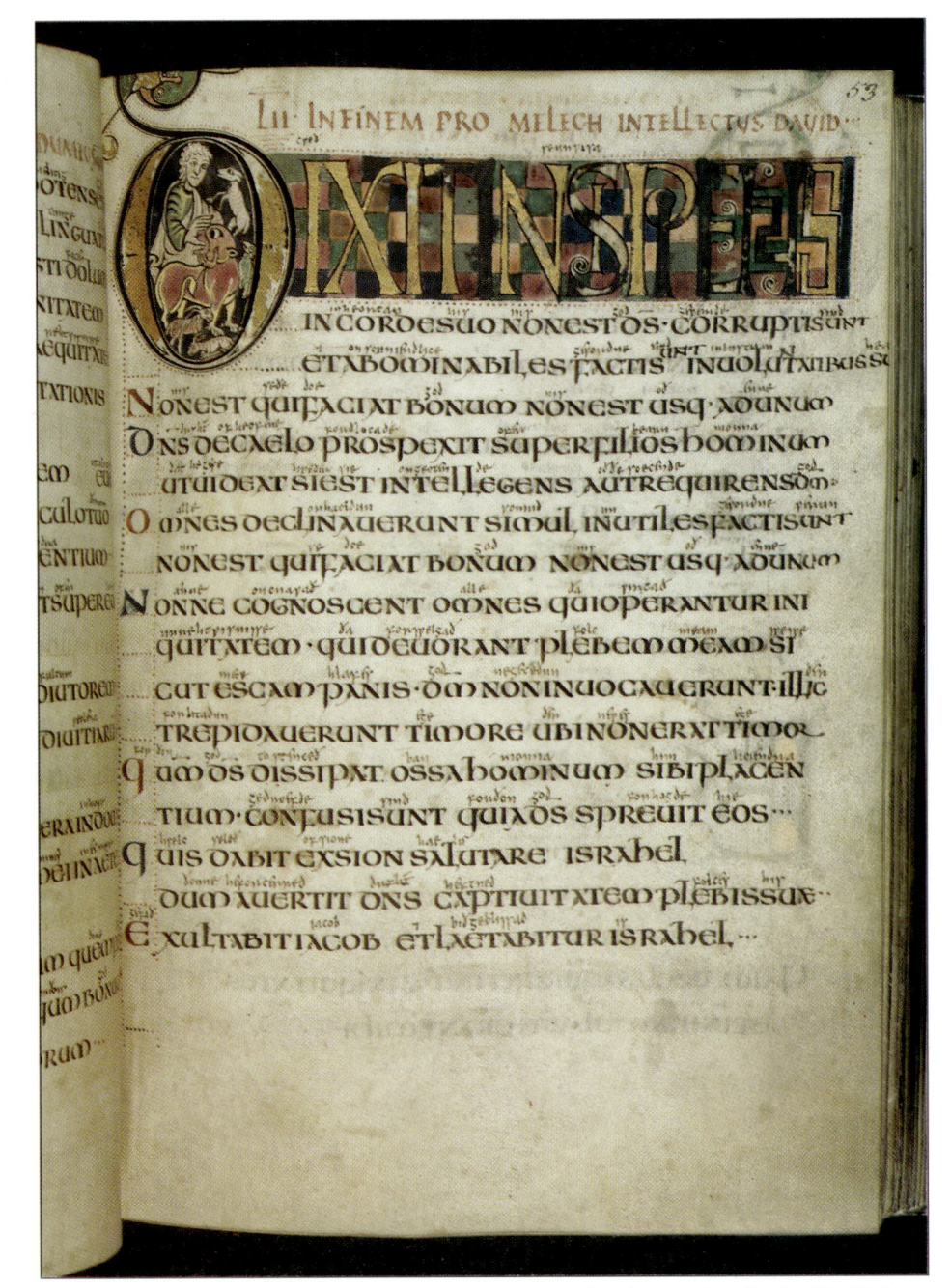

DIXIT INSIPIENS
IN CORDE SUO NON EST DS· CORRUPTI SUNT
ET ABOMINABILES FACTI SUNT IN UOLUTATIBUS
NON EST QUI FACIAT BONUM NON EST USQ· AD UNUM
DNS DE CAELO PROSPEXIT SUPER FILIOS HOMINUM
UT UIDEAT SI EST INTELLEGENS AUT REQUIRENS DM·
OMNES DECLINAUERUNT SIMUL· INUTILES FACTI SUNT
NON EST QUI FACIAT BONUM NON EST USQ· AD UNUM
NONNE COGNOSCENT OMNES QUI OPERANTUR INI
QUITATEM· QUI DEUORANT PLEBEM MEAM SI
CUT ESCAM PANIS· DM NON INUOCAUERUNT· ILLIC
TREPIDAUERUNT TIMORE UBI NON ERAT TIMOR
QUM DS DISSIPAT OSSA HOMINUM SIBI PLACEN
TIUM· CONFUSI SUNT QUIA DS SPREUIT EOS···
QUIS DABIT EX SION SALUTARE ISRAHEL·
DUM AUERTIT DNS CAPTIUITATEM PLEBIS SUAE··
EXULTABIT IACOB ET LAETABITUR ISRAHEL·...

BL, MS Cotton Vespasian A. i (Vespasian Psalter), fol. 53r: the incipit *of Psalm 52. (British Library)*

Unfortunately the interpretation of what survives at the site and of the succession of excavations to which it has been subjected is a complex and often obscure matter. What does seem clear is that the remains are of at least two main phases, though neither can be closely dated on purely archaeological grounds.[62] Indeed, the earlier has been claimed to be of Roman date by Thomas, a view which has found more ready acceptance among students of Roman Britain than their early medieval colleagues.[63] Thomas argues that this earlier phase building was the church frequented by Bertha and her chaplain and the one which was subsequently used by the missionaries on their arrival in 597, rather than (as is usually supposed, following Bede) the earliest (almost certainly Roman) parts of the church of St Martin, which lies further to the east (cf. fig. 1.7).[64] Such an identification is open to two objections, however. First, it arises from doubts about identifying Bertha's church with St Martin's; yet, as Brooks has pointed out, this is a matter which is very unlikely to have become confused in the traditions of the community at SS Peter and Paul, which was immediately adjacent to the site in question.[65] What is more, as Morris has shown, those doubts can largely be resolved without abandoning the traditional identification if one bears in mind the possibility that the earliest phase of St Martin need not have been built as a church, even though that is what Bede (presumably reflecting the belief current at Canterbury in his time) appears to have thought.[66] Secondly, Thomas's argument implies that the first phase of St Pancras is unlikely to date from later than the early fifth century; however, such a date is implausible for its associated architectural features, which (in the context of south-east England) are more realistically associated with a seventh-century date or later, a point reinforced by the lack of parallels between those features and other known Romano-British churches.[67]

Despite these uncertainties, if the hypothesis can at least be entertained that the earliest phase of St Pancras (fig. 10.5) can be interpreted as a *martyrium* erected to house relics of that saint at a time when his cult was being promoted at Rome and when it would still have been of interest to the missionaries in Canterbury, the characteristic features of that church would then be of particular importance as the only surviving product of the mission in the generation between the early period and the later seventh century. The identification of those features is unfortunately not without difficulties of its own, however. At least the pronounced stilting of the apse and its slight insetting from the nave can both be accepted as elements of the primary structure.[68] The shape of that apse has sometimes been claimed as polygonal rather than continuously curved,[69] but so little survived of its walling that this must be regarded as wholly uncertain. The use of pilaster buttresses is again certainly attested in phase one, most notably in

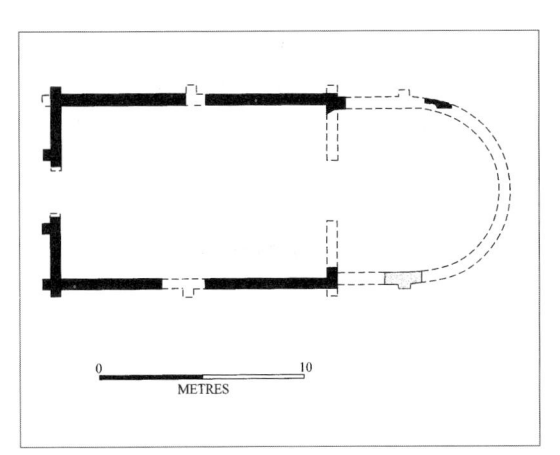

10.5. Canterbury, St Pancras, remains of church, earliest phase (after Hope, op. cit. in n. 72, p. 228 and fig. following p. 236, with some modifications adapted from Jenkins, op. cit. in n. 2).

the pairs clasping the western angles of the nave; the existence of a number of other pilaster buttresses is sometimes claimed, but once again this is best regarded as uncertain.[70] The final feature, the original form of the junction between nave and choir, requires more extended discussion.

Following his re-excavation of the church in the 1970s, Frank Jenkins considered that the junction between the nave and chancel had originally been in the form of a single arch flanked by short sections of solid walling, and that this was later modified by the piercing of the flanking walls to produce a triple arcade carried on four columns, the lower part of the southernmost of which still survives *in situ*.[71] The proportions of this arcade, with a comparatively wide central arch and much narrower flanking openings would, on Jenkins's interpretation, have been determined by the retention of the central arch from the earlier phase. The evidence for this is first the use of the yellow mortar characteristic of the earliest phase of the building in a fragment discovered in 1900, and probably to be interpreted as part of that original central arch;[72] and secondly the fact that the surviving column belongs stratigraphically to phase two.[73] Nothing is known of the shape or mortar composition of the masonry forming the heads of the flanking openings, however, leaving unanswered the question of whether these were also primary features or later insertions. The evidence relating to the base of this wall is similarly ambiguous, though Jenkins evidently observed that the areas to either side were treated differently from that in the centre in some way, and it seems clear that the four-column arrangement is a secondary modification. This evidence could be interpreted, with Jenkins, as indicating that the flanking openings were inserted into what had originally been solid walls, but it is equally consistent with the hypothesis that the original arrangement was three openings which were later underpinned when the original supports were removed and replaced by columns.[74]

Assuming that the chronological context proposed above for St Pancras can be accepted, and bearing in mind that, even if this be so, we have no way of knowing how typical of 'second generation' buildings its design was, what then are the wider implications of the features we have just examined? Since the evidence from buildings certainly or probably earlier is so exiguous, it is impossible to determine with confidence how far St Pancras might have represented a new departure. Nevertheless, such evidence as there is seems to underline its differences from, rather than its similarities to, 'first generation' structures. The slight insetting of the apse at Rochester provides the sole possible parallel, though this is, alas, too common a feature to justify inferring any connection between the two. Furthermore, if St Pancras did indeed have a pilaster buttress at the eastern end of its north and south nave walls, as suggested by Jenkins's plan,[75] a connection would be even less likely, since Rochester apparently lacked a buttress in the equivalent position (figs. 10.1a, 10.5). The apse at St Pancras is also much more stilted than at Rochester. Even allowing for the differences in plan and the fragmentary nature of the remains, comparison with what we know of SS Peter and Paul at Canterbury yields no grounds for supposing that its design had anything in common with that of St Pancras.

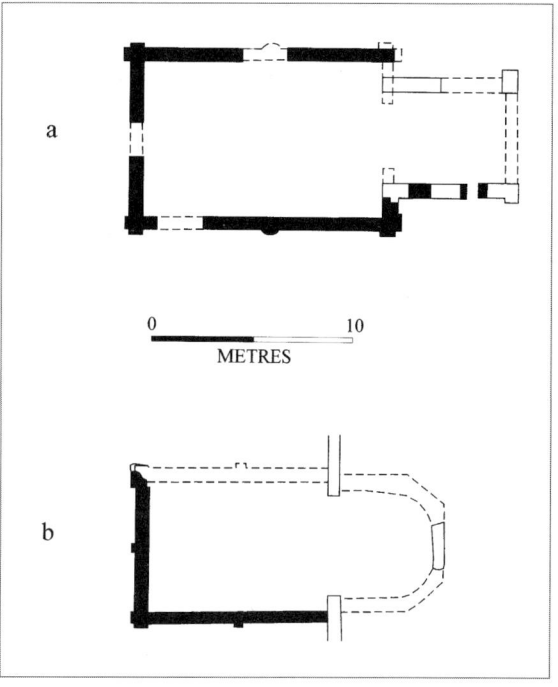

10.6. *a. Canterbury, St Martin (after plan by Canterbury Archaeological Trust); b. L'Isle Jourdain (Gers), excavated church (after PMCF, II, fig., p. 157).*

In contrast, a positive case can be made for links between St Pancras and 'third generation' buildings. At Reculver the resemblance is clearest in the use of pilaster buttresses and of an apse with pronounced stilting,[76] though unlike Reculver (and Bradwell), the apse at St Pancras is slightly inset from the nave (figs 10.2b, 10.5). In addition, it is conceivable that St Pancras might also have provided a precedent for the use of the triple arcade between nave and chancel found at Reculver.[77] Whether the same could have been true in relation to other features at Reculver, such as the externally polygonal apse or the forms of the surviving architectural details, is unknowable owing to the fragmentary state of the remains at St Pancras.[78]

If St Pancras is indeed an example of 'second generation' church building, and if, as appears to be the case, its stylistic affinity to buildings of the succeeding generation was significantly closer than to those of the generation which preceded it (though given the extremely fragmentary nature of the

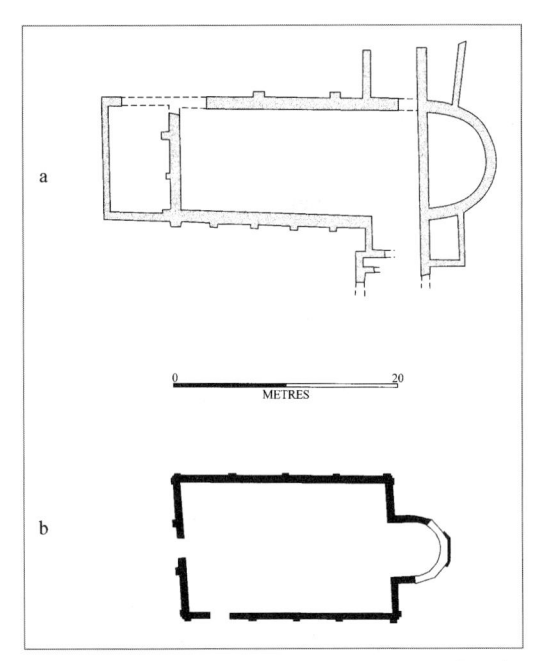

10.7. a. Doss Trento (Trentino), southern church of double church complex, after Jakobsen, Schaefer and Sennhauser (op. cit. in n. 125, II, p. 417); b. S. Michele, Santarcangelo di Romagna (Romagna), after Deichmann (op. cit. in n. 82, II(3), Ab. 31).

remains of the latter, it may well be that the disparity is more apparent than real), it follows that the most significant changes in the design of church building in the region are more likely to have taken place in or around the 620s than after the middle of the century. What remains to be seen is whether the apparent differences between 'first generation' buildings on the one hand and later buildings on the other, and in particular the suggestion that pilaster buttresses were absent from the former, might not only be potentially significant as chronological indicators but also as pointers to the continental origins of the architectural forms which define those differences.

The question of the architectural sources of the early churches of south-east England has generally been approached in terms of an opposition between Gallic influences and north Italian ones.[79] A possible historical context can be adduced in support of either hypothesis, the close dynastic, political, cultural and economic links between Kent and the adjacent areas of Merovingian Gaul being taken to support the former, the Italian origin of the missionaries themselves favouring the latter.[80] In evaluating these possible sources from an architectural viewpoint, however, it must be stressed at the outset that the feasibility of such an exercise is severely compromised by the exceptionally poor survival rate of Gallic buildings of the period, a problem particularly acute in northern and western Gaul, that is, the regions geographically closest to south-east England; consequently it is not only difficult to assess the extent to which English buildings resembled their Gallic counterparts, but also how much regional variation might have existed within Gaul itself which (if present) might enable those similarities with English buildings which can be identified to be related to a particular area. Further, it is clear from what does survive that some features will be more indicative than others of their place of origin. For example, small churches surrounded by a continuous envelope of *porticus*, as at SS Peter and Paul, Canterbury, are widely distributed in Late Antique Europe, which makes it difficult to identify a specific source on the grounds of the plan type alone.[81] Accordingly, the following analysis will confine itself to those features which appear to be most likely to reveal their region of origin. Four of these will be considered in turn: pilaster buttresses; externally polygonal apses; triple arcades dividing nave from chancel; and minor architectural details.

At first sight, so mundane a feature as the use of buttresses might not seem to offer a promising line of enquiry; in fact, however, their distribution in the Late Antique west is unexpectedly distinctive. Buttresses also have the additional advantage for our investigation that, as a feature which is as much a manifestation of building technique as of aesthetic preference, in those areas where they are used they will occur in major and minor buildings alike. Where, then, are they found? They appear at five sites in south-east England: SS Peter and Paul, St Pancras, and St Martin at Canterbury, Reculver and Bradwell. Pilaster buttresses punctuating lateral walls and occurring as pairs of clasping buttresses on external angles are ubiquitous in Ravenna, and can also be found in adjacent areas of northern Italy, the northern Adriatic, and the Alps.[82] In contrast, they are absent from surviving churches in contemporary Rome,[83] and are virtually unknown in early medieval Gaul, the single exception, at L'Isle Jourdain near Toulouse (fig. 10.6b), being dated by the excavators to the second half of the seventh century.[84] Unless future archaeological research reveals further and earlier Gallic examples of this feature, it appears upon present evidence that L'Isle Jourdain is more plausibly interpreted as a cousin than a parent of the English examples,[85] which seem most likely to have been derived directly from a source in Ravenna or the territories under its influence.[86]

What is attested in Gaul, however, but is apparently absent both from Rome and from Ravenna and associated regions, is the use of buttresses for the sole purpose of framing external entrances to *porticus*, projecting inwards as well as outwards from the surfaces of the adjacent walls. Examples are known from the outer *porticus* of Saint-Laurent de Choulans at Lyon (fig. 10.8a) and Saint-Blaise at Saint-Mitre-les-Remparts, and possibly also in the western entrance of the narthex at Saint-Barthélemy at Saint-Denis (fig. 10.8b).[87] The only possible example of such a feature in England occurs at SS Peter and Paul, Canterbury, where the narthex entrance buttressing appears to have been of this type (fig. 10.8c).[88] If correctly interpreted, this would be the sole architectural feature so far identified in the early churches of south-east England for which an exclusively Gallic source could be claimed.

Before considering the sources of externally polygonal apses, it must be remembered that the one at Reculver is the only certain example in south-east

England, as the semicircular foundations that survive elsewhere leave open the possibility that the now lost walling which rested upon them was either polygonal or semicircular.[89] It is therefore impossible to be certain exactly when the motif was introduced or how common it was. In order to set the Reculver apse in context, the general characteristics and distribution of this form in Late Antique Europe need to be considered briefly. The feature first appeared in the late fourth century. By the sixth century the version comprising three sides of an octagon had become most common in the eastern empire (at least in the areas most directly influenced by Constantinople), whereas the most frequently occurring type in the west was of five sides, the westernmost two joining the rest of the building at an obtuse angle.[90] Variants of the basic form, created by the use of more than five sides, by the addition of parallel western facets, or by both these features combined, also occur in the west. Ubiquitous in Ravenna,[91] which has by far the greatest concentration of polygonal apses, examples also occur (though not to the exclusion of non-polygonal types) in the northern Adriatic, northern Italy (but, with a single exception, conspicuously excluding Rome),[92] south-eastern Gaul,[93] and in adjacent areas of the Alps.

The Reculver apse, with its seven sides plus parallel western facets (fig. 10.10a),[94] cannot be precisely paralleled, but regular seven-sided forms occur in Ravenna in the upper storey of the apse of S Giovanni Evangelista, generally considered to be part of the original build of 424–34,[95] and at the Basilica Apostolorum (now S Francesco) of the third quarter of the fifth century (fig. 10.10b).[96] There is also a single example in Gaul, with extended western facets, at Saint-Pierre in Vienne, perhaps datable to the late fifth century (fig. 10.10c).[97] What makes the ultimate source of the Reculver apse more likely to lie in Ravenna or its hinterland than in Merovingian Gaul, however, is the fact that a continuous tradition of constructing externally polygonal

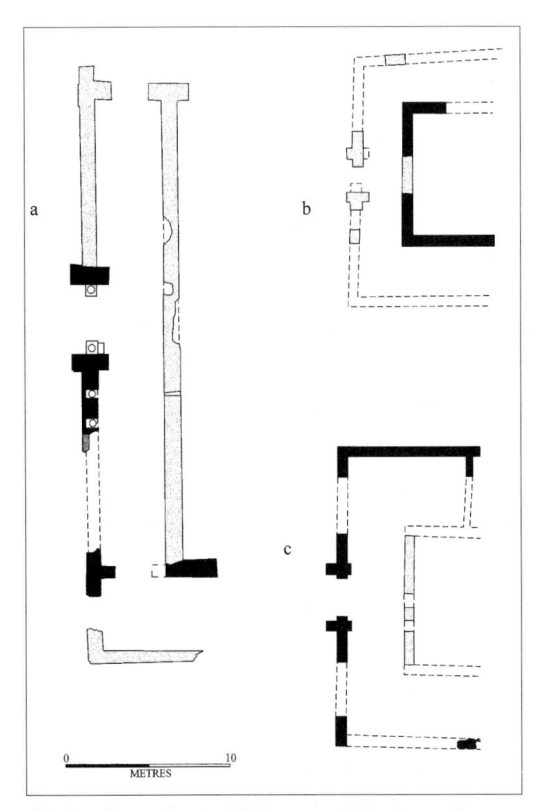

10.8. Canterbury, SS Peter and Paul, narthex entrance, and some possible Gallic comparanda: a. Lyon (Rhône), Saint-Laurent de Choulans, entrance of north porticus (after PMCF, I, figs on pp. 279–90); b. Saint-Denis (Seine-Saint-Denis), Saint-Barthélemy, narthex entrance (after PMCF, III, figs on pp. 203–4); c. Canterbury, SS Peter and Paul, narthex entrance (after Saunders, op. cit. in n. 2, fig. 8, p. 45).

apses can be demonstrated in the latter, at least into the late sixth and early seventh centuries,[98] whereas such forms seem always to have been comparatively uncommon in Gaul (where rectangular east ends appear to have been increasingly preferred, at least for minor churches) and are scarcely attested so late.[99]

Though evidence relating to the use of an arcade to separate nave and chancel in the churches of south-east England is slightly more secure than that for polygonal apses, the only certainly attested examples, at Reculver (figs 10.11–12) and Bradwell,[100] are certainly or probably part of third generation structures; and although, as we have seen, the presence of this feature *ab initio* at St Pancras, Canterbury is possible, this is far from certain.[101] Peers raised the possibility that

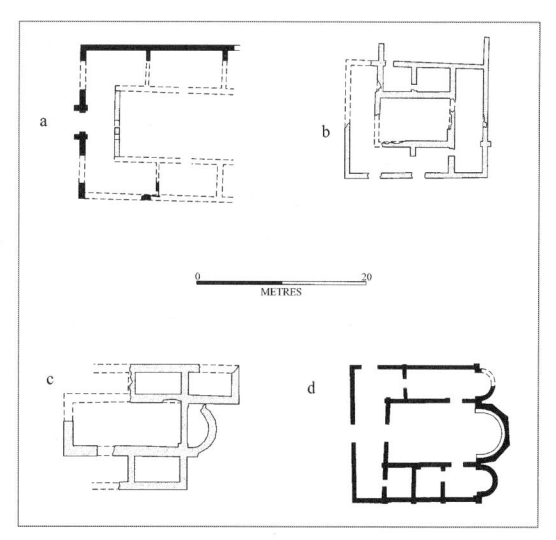

10.9. Churches surrounded by porticus*: a. Canterbury, remains of church of SS Peter and Paul, earliest phase (after Saunders, op. cit. in n. 2, fig. 8, p. 45); b. Seyssel (Haute-Savoie), Basilique D'Albigny-Condion (after* PMCF, *I, fig., p. 306); c. Veurey (Isère), Saint-Ours (after* PMCF, *I, figs on pp. 245–6); d. Muntajana (Istria), church (after Bratož, loc. cit. in n. 81).*

the use of this form may to some extent have been a consequence of other design choices, perhaps involving practical and structural considerations which are more difficult to discern given that we know so little about the elevations of the churches in question.[102] For example, it may have been the most appropriate solution in contexts where the height of a building in relation to its width, and the difference in height and width between the spaces east and west of the chancel wall, would combine to make a single span arch either uncomfortably wide, with disproportionately short jambs, or alternatively would entail an arch of normal proportions but much narrower span than the width of the adjacent spaces.[103] What is significant for present purposes is the choice of this particular method to overcome such design problems.

The use of triple arcades to divide lower subsidiary (and usually apsidal) spaces from larger volumes had a wide currency in Antique architecture and appears to have been well established in secular contexts before appearing in religious ones.[104] Such arcades do appear in specifically christian contexts, however, particularly in North Africa.[105] More directly relevant to the English examples is the fact that the form continued to be used in Late Antique contexts in northern Italy and the northern Adriatic. Clapham long ago pointed to its occurrence in the first-floor hall of the episcopal palace at Poreč in Istria (fig. 10.13c).[106] Here

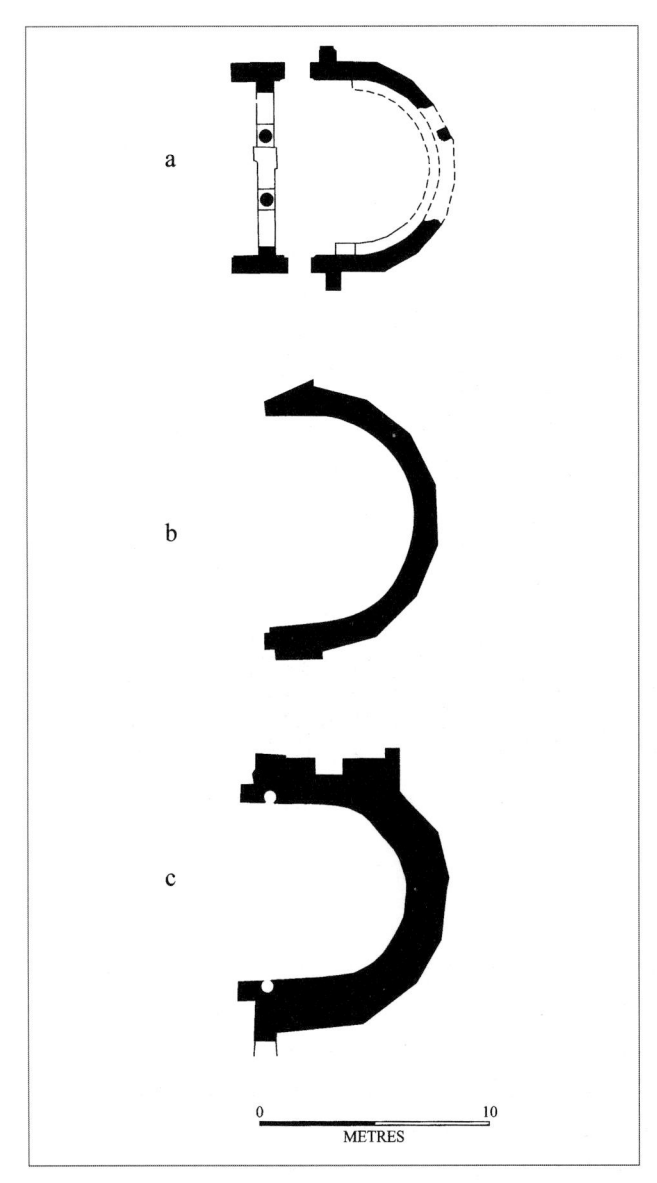

10.10. Polygonal apses: a. Reculver, chancel (after Peers, op. cit. in n. 4, fig. 4, p. 245); b. Ravenna (Romagna), Basilica Apostolorum (now S Francesco), apse (after Mazzotti, op. cit. in n. 96, plan preceding p. 97); c. Vienne (Isère), Saint-Pierre, apse (after PMCF, I, fig., p. 256).

the central opening is appreciably wider than the flanking ones. The form also occurs at the junctions between the lateral chambers and the ambulatory of S Michele Arcangelo at Perugia, the central arch again being significantly wider than the flanking ones (fig. 10.13b).[107] The surviving architectural details in the palace at Poreč, and in particular the use of decorative stucco on the soffit of the central arch of the triple arcade, suggest that it cannot be far removed in date from the adjacent basilica, reconstructed in the mid-sixth century.[108] The date of the church at Perugia is uncertain but, as has already been noted, the most recent analysis (pointing to the use of Ravennate features such as the externally polygonal eastern apse) suggests an early seventh-century date.[109] Given the ambiguous nature of the evidence from St Pancras, Canterbury,[110] it is difficult to assess the possible significance of the fact that, if the triple arcade were an original feature of that building, its form would have been closer than anything else attested in England to the examples at Poreč and Perugia, with a pronouncedly wider central arch (fig. 10.13a). No less significant from the point of view of determining the sources of the south-east English examples is the fact that the type apparently remains unattested in either contemporary Rome or Gaul.[111]

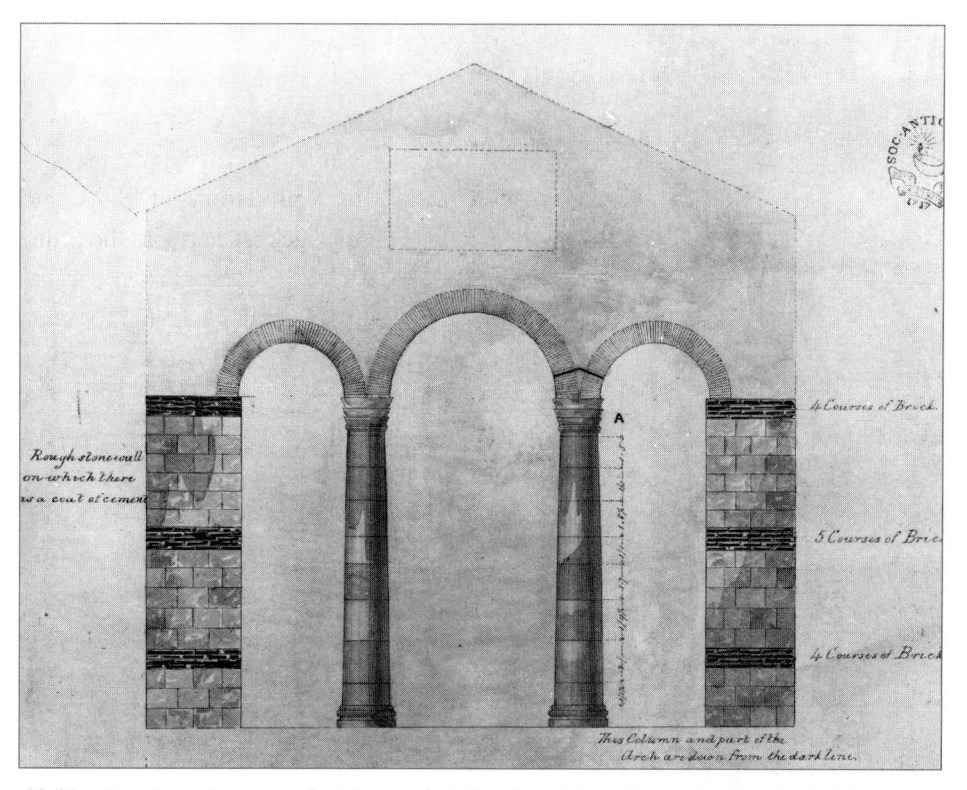

10.11. Reculver, elevation of triple arcade before demolition (drawn by Gandy; by kind permission of the Society of Antiquaries of London).

The state of preservation of the early churches in south-east England is in general so poor that hardly any examples of architectural details survive, the only exceptions being the single base from St Pancras (which belongs stratigraphically with the later phase of that church),[112] and the capitals (fig. 10.14b) and bases from the triple arcade at Reculver (figs 10.11–12). Blagg has argued persuasively that the ultimate prototypes of the Reculver capitals lie in the Late Antique Mediterranean zone, pointing to the likelihood that they derive from the trapezoidal shapes used occasionally for capitals and regularly for prominent impost blocks from the fifth century onwards in that region, Ravenna and its hinterland affording numerous examples of both.[113] Impost blocks of this form do also occur in late sixth- and early seventh-century Rome, for example, in the gallery capitals at S Lorenzo fuori le mura and S Agnese,[114] but the trapezoidal capital type appears to be unknown there, whereas it is attested at Ravenna, for instance, in the presbytery at S Vitale (fig. 10.14a).[115] Equally significant is the absence of any such forms from Gaul, where Corinthian-derived forms appear to be ubiquitous. Blagg also demonstrates the Mediterranean origin of the bases at both St Pancras and Reculver, again pointing to specific parallels in Ravenna.[116] What is less

10.12. Reculver, triple arcade during demolition, looking north-west (drawn by Baynes, engraved Adlard).

certain in this latter case, however, is whether or not these features are also absent from contemporary Rome and Gaul. Thus, while the evidence of the bases is not inconsistent with the hypothesis of a Ravennate or north Adriatic origin implied by the Reculver capital type, it cannot be used positively to support it.

The above discussion has been at pains to stress either that many of the features under consideration occur only at Reculver, or that it provides the only example which might be dated with any degree of confidence. This might be held to imply that they were not introduced into England until the probable date of Reculver's construction in the late seventh century. The fact that several of those features are also attested in Gaul might also make it possible to argue that, even if their ultimate origin in Ravenna or an area under its influence were accepted, they might have been transmitted to England via a Gallic intermediary. On the currently available evidence, however, several considerations combine to make this interpretation unlikely. First, the Gallic evidence needs to be seen in the general context of a region which had probably already developed its own distinctive building traditions in the late Roman period, traditions which continued to flourish in the late sixth and early seventh centuries. While individual Ravennate features do occur in Gaul, it seems reasonably clear that they are atypical of the Gallic architectural repertoire, at least as it has come down to us. Further, there are no examples of sites in Gaul at which Ravennate features occur in combination, whereas at Reculver the presence of several Ravennate features in the same building strongly suggests that its designer was directly familiar with that architectural tradition in some way. If this was indeed the case, it seems likely that the transmission to England would have occurred at a time when that tradition was still current in its original context: this, as we shall see, tends to suggest a date in the first rather than the second half of the seventh century. In contrast to the range of features pointing to Ravennate sources, the only evidence in south-east England of a feature apparently derived from a distinctively Gallic architectural milieu is the buttressing of the narthex doorway at SS Peter and Paul, Canterbury; further (and perhaps most surprisingly

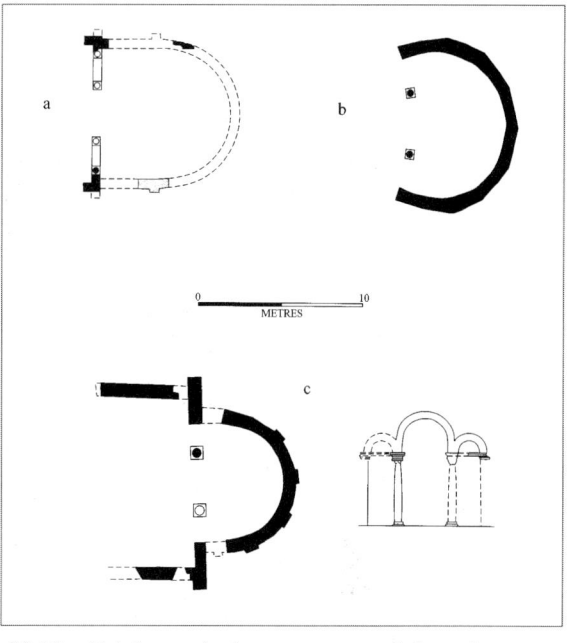

10.13. *Triple arcades between nave and chancel: a.* Canterbury, St Pancras, junction of nave and chancel, showing arcade as modified (after Hope, op. cit. in n. 72, fig. following p. 236); *b.* Perugia (Umbria), S Michele Arcangelo, apse and junction with ambulatory (after Scortecci, op. cit. in n. 98, fig. 5, p. 410); *c.* Poreč (Istria), first-floor audience hall of episcopal palace, apse and junction with main vessel, plan and reconstructed sketch elevation (after Prelog, op. cit. in n. 106, figs, pp. 15–16).

of all), there are no features which suggest a derivation from what we know of the architecture current at Rome itself.[117] The final issues which need to be considered are thus the historical circumstances which might explain the presence in south-east England on the one hand of features connected to the architectural traditions of Ravenna and perhaps also those of Gaul (though the evidential basis for the latter is undeniably slender), and the apparent absence of any derived from Rome on the other.

It is not difficult to envisage circumstances in which architectural contacts between south-east England and Merovingian Gaul might have been established. While the hypothesis that the mission received active support from Gaul has not been universally accepted, there can be no doubting the contacts that Augustine and his successors must have made there,[118] whether in passing through it on journeys to and from Rome, or during the exile of various of its members following the pagan reaction after Æthelberht's death.[119] Nor should the possible

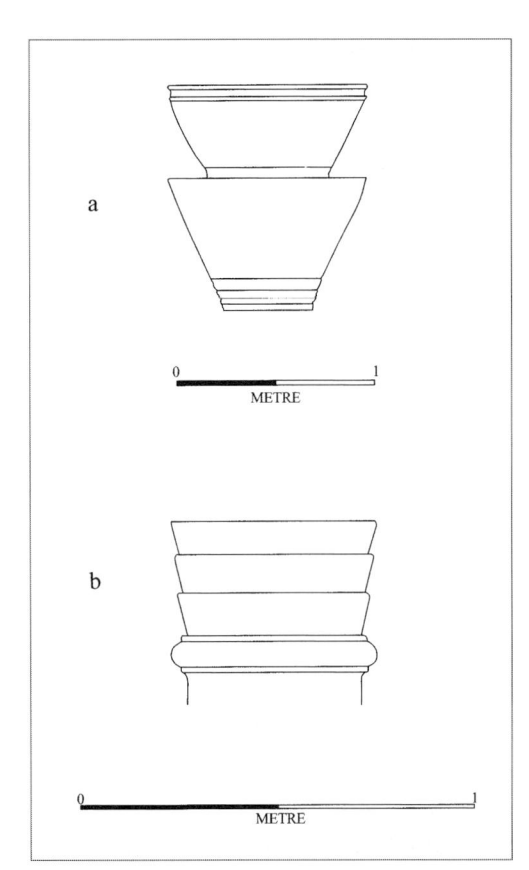

10.14. a. Ravenna (Romagna), profile of capital from south arcade of presbytery (after Deichmann, op. cit. in n. 82); b. Reculver, profile of capital from triple arcade (after Blagg, op. cit. in n. 113).

architectural implications of the dynastic and political links implied by the presence of Bertha in Kent be underestimated.[120] In contrast, the precise historical circumstances which might explain architectural contact specifically with northern Italy in the early seventh century are not so clear-cut. Neither Augustine's own arrival from Rome in 597 nor that of the reinforcements in 601 will adequately explain the phenomenon, for what evidence there is suggests that the relevant architectural contact only arose at a later date in the seventh century, in the mission's subsequent phases. What is more, the apparent preoccupation of the missionaries with specifically Roman cults might have led one to expect architectural connections with the city, whereas the above analysis points rather towards the exclusion of Rome in favour of links with northern Italy. In order to attempt to explain these seeming paradoxes, the history of the building industry in those areas in the late sixth and early seventh centuries needs to be considered briefly.

By far the most important single centre of Late Antique building activity in northern Italy and the northern Adriatic was, of course, the city of Ravenna itself, pre-eminent from its adoption as the imperial capital in the early fifth century, and retaining its dominance as successively the seat of Ostrogothic and Byzantine power. There the deep-rooted Late Antique phenomenon of conspicuous consumption manifested itself in architectural terms in an extended series of fifth- and sixth-century ecclesiastical building projects. But in the late sixth century that long-established pattern of patronage appears to have suffered a comparatively sudden, traumatic and (as things were to turn out) permanent disruption; the last major new building projects recorded at Ravenna date from the years 578–95,[121] and it is likely that the same pattern was repeated in the adjacent, less well-documented areas of northern Italy.[122] In contrast, at Rome itself, where documentation relating to building is again comparatively full, the series of works attributed to Pope Honorius I (624–38) (though not more precisely datable within the limits of his pontificate) implies that major projects continued to be undertaken there for a generation after they had ceased at Ravenna, continuing well into the second quarter of the seventh century, and petering out only around 640.[123]

The principal historical context of the sharp decline in building activity in northern Italy in the late sixth century is presumably to be sought in the impact of the Lombard invasions, beginning in earnest in 569 and resulting in significant territorial gains by the early seventh century.[124] In architectural terms the invasions arguably produced an initial stimulus in demand as the wealthier ecclesiastical patrons built accommodation for themselves at the places to which they had fled for refuge.[125] In the longer run, however, political instability, social disruption, and diversion of resources to meet the threat posed by the Lombards (whether in actively combating them or buying them off) appear to have combined to deal the building industry in the region a blow from which it was never to recover.

The implications of these events in northern Italy for our understanding of the presence of Ravennate features in the early churches of south-east England are twofold. First, they provide a context in the early seventh century, after the north Italian and northern Adriatic building industry had begun seriously to contract but before that process was so far advanced as to diminish significantly (and ultimately to extinguish) the number of trained builders available, in which it would have been easier to recruit masons to work in England than at any time before or since. In consequence, the architectural parallels between buildings in the two areas noted above might be plausibly interpreted as indicating direct links rather than coincidental parallels or indirect reflections.[126] Secondly, the delay in the collapse of the building industry in Rome itself where, as we have seen, it occurred a generation later than in the areas to the north and east, suggests a possible explanation for why the city's links with England are so elusive: this must have been a time when masons were still gainfully employed in Rome, while their less fortunate northern colleagues might in consequence have been more ready to offer their services to missionaries engaged in foreign parts.[127]

If we are prepared to accept the hypothesis that both Italian and Gallic masons might have been at work in south-east England in the early seventh century and, further, that the chronology of the English buildings suggests that any possible Gallic influence was confined to the initial phase, after which a reorientation towards Italianate sources took place, it may be worth speculating as to how such a sequence of events might have come about.

Slight though its evidential basis admittedly is, we have already seen that the only building which contains specific features which might be interpreted as pointing to the presence of Merovingian masons in south-east England is the church of SS Peter and Paul, Canterbury – and that is precisely where one would most expect, on historical grounds, to find it. Perhaps the most important personal need which King Æthelberht and Queen Bertha would have expected the mission to fulfil was the establishment of a community to pray for their souls and to care for their bodies' last resting place. Though, as already noted, the evidence of what we know of the plan of that church is not in itself diagnostic of its place of origin, the immediate inspiration for a church serving such a purpose was, arguably, a Merovingian one, mirroring (even if on a humbler scale) the royal dynastic funerary basilicas (sometimes, as here, combined with episcopal burials) with which Bertha would have been familiar from her homeland.[128] And it can hardly be doubted that the easiest place from which to acquire masons at relatively short notice, and the one to which Æthelberht and Bertha are most likely to have turned instinctively, was Gaul.

In contrast, the employment in the 'second generation' of north Italian masons might be seen as a consequence of the fact that the preference of the missionaries themselves was by then beginning to be permitted to assert itself. Once the initial pragmatism dictated by the twin constraints of lack of resources and dependence on the patronage of a Frankish queen and her consort were removed, the missionaries' own architectural inclinations arguably lay rather with the building traditions of their homeland, and entailed a decisive rejection of those of their Gallic neighbours. As we have seen, the situation in northern Italy itself suggests that the likeliest period for direct links with masons trained there would have been the first third of the seventh century, which tallies exactly with the period in which its Italian members are likely to have dominated the English mission. It would also, incidentally, support the hypothesis that Ravennate forms first appeared in England a generation earlier than the putative date of Reculver, the building in which most of them are first attested.[129] In so far as the architectural evidence can be held to imply a change in architectural sources, then, this might most plausibly be explained as the consequence of a shift away from direct and active royal patronage towards one in which the missionaries were permitted to exercise patronage on their own behalf.

In attempting to define the historical circumstances which determined the forms of the early churches of south-east England, it appears that the traditional preoccupation with the first phases of the Gregorian mission may have obscured the issue in two key respects: its possible initial espousal of Gallic forms, reflecting its early dependence on Merovingian patronage; and its subsequent rejection of these in favour of Italian ones, perhaps as a deliberate cultural statement, in a period when links with its homeland, though less well documented than in the days of Gregory and Augustine, were no less important. What became the characteristic architectural forms of the Augustinian mission may thus have owed more to the era of Honorius I (d. 638) than to that of his great predecessor. And whether by fortune or design, the adoption of those forms in south-east England ensured that the major branch of the Late Antique building tradition in the west enjoyed an unexpected afterlife in this most unlikely of locations for at least a generation after its effective demise in its original homeland. For, if the surviving putatively 'third generation' buildings in south-east England are in any sense typical, they suggest that it was the Ravennate influences which proved the more enduring. The forms in question imbued the ecclesiastical architecture of the region with a distinctively Late Antique character at a period (from the later seventh century onwards) when renewed contact with Gaul would otherwise have led one to expect Gallic influence to have predominated – as, indeed, in other areas of England it clearly did.[130]

However this may be – and its speculative nature must be frankly admitted – the above analysis has suggested that the early architecture of south-east England is intimately bound up with the chequered history of the Augustinian mission, and that its remains constitute a more complex and varied body of evidence than has hitherto been supposed. What is more, they have the potential to tell us much about the cultural orientation of both their secular and ecclesiastical patrons, and about the changing relations between the two, in the century after Augustine first set foot among the English.

Addendum

A recent fundamental reassessment of early medieval building in Rome came to my attention too late to be taken into account here: R. Coates-Stephens, 'Dark Age Architecture in Rome', *Papers of the British School at Rome*, 65 (1997), 177–232. The (hitherto neglected) evidence that it assembles for church building in Rome in the period *c*. 640–*c*. 730 is not, however, sufficient in my view to warrant any significant departure from the hypothesis that there was a severe recession in church building in the city during that period (and particularly in the generation following the death of Honorius I). I am most grateful to Professor T.F.X. Noble for drawing my attention to this reference.

NOTES

1. An earlier version of this chapter was delivered at a conference in Oxford on 16 March 1997; I am most grateful to the Oxford University Department of External Studies for their kind invitation on that occasion. The following have generously provided information and assistance: Richard Bailey; Rosemary Cramp; Colin Clarkson; Jane Cunningham; Richard Gameson; David Salmon; Andrew Saunders; John Schofield; and the Inter-Library loans section of the University Library, Durham. I am particularly indebted to the representative of the Croatian Ministry of Culture who kindly arranged access to the episcopal palace at Poreč, and to Allan Williams and Tony Liddel for their wise advice upon, and generous assistance with, the layout and drawing of the figures.

2. A.D. Saunders, 'Excavations in the Church of St Augustine's Abbey, Canterbury 1955–58', *Medieval Archaeology*, 22 (1978), 25–63. It is a matter of very considerable regret that the re-excavations of two key sites have never been properly published: the late Frank Jenkins produced only a short interim report on his activities at St Pancras, Canterbury (F. Jenkins, 'Preliminary Report on the Excavations at the Church of St. Pancras at Canterbury', *Canterbury Archaeology* (1975–6), 4–5); while the re-investigation of Reculver by B.J. Philp has received only the briefest of printed notices (D.M. Wilson and D.G. Hurst, 'Medieval Britain in 1969', *Medieval Archaeology*, 14 (1970), 155–208, at p. 161). I am grateful to Rosemary Cramp for drawing my attention to the latter reference.

3. K. Blockley, M. Sparks, and T. Tatton-Brown, *Canterbury Cathedral Nave: Archaeology, History and Architecture*, The Archaeology of Canterbury, new series, 1 (Canterbury, 1997).

4. C.R. Peers and A.W. Clapham, 'St. Augustine's Abbey Church, Canterbury, before the Norman Conquest', *Archaeologia*, 77 (1927), 201–18; C.R. Peers, 'Reculver: its Saxon Church and Cross', *Archaeologia*, 77 (1927), 241–56.

5. E.C. Fernie, *The Architecture of the Anglo-Saxons* (London, 1983) (hereafter: Fernie, *AAS*), ch. 3; cf. A.W. Clapham, *English Romanesque Architecture Before the Conquest* (London, 1930), pp. 28–33; R.D.H. Gem, 'The Anglo-Saxon and Norman Churches', *St Augustine's Abbey Canterbury*, ed. R.D.H. Gem (London, 1997), pp. 90–122, cf. Peers and Clapham, 'St. Augustine's Abbey,' pp. 207, 210. In 1901, Peers (though apparently considering Gaul a likelier source than Rome) was much more equivocal (C.R. Peers, 'On Saxon Churches of the St. Pancras Type', *ArchJ*, 58 (1901), 402–34, at p. 431). An opportunity to reassess this question has been provided by the recent completion of the publication of the French corpus of pre-Carolingian churches: *Les Premiers Monuments Chrétiens de la France*, 3 vols (Paris, 1995–8, hereafter: *PMCF*).

6. For example, Clapham, *English Romanesque Architecture*, pp. 17ff.; one of the sites, Bradwell-on-Sea, is, of course, in Essex.

7. See Fernie, *AAS*, and Gem, 'Anglo-Saxon and Norman Churches'.

8. H.M. Taylor, 'Lyminge Churches', *ArchJ*, 126 (1969), 257–60, at pp. 258–9; *idem* (with J. Taylor), *Anglo-Saxon Architecture*, 3 vols (Cambridge, 1965–78), III, pp. 785, 1082; Fernie, *AAS*, p. 39.

9. Peers, 'Churches of the St. Pancras Type'; for Taylor's reconstruction of Reculver, see H.M. Taylor, 'Reculver Church', *ArchJ*,

126 (1969), 225–7, at p. 226, fig. 15, the caption expressly indicating reliance on a range of buildings, the appropriateness of which (with the exception of Bradwell) is open to question; for the use made of it subsequently, see below, pp. 205–6.

10. G.M. Livett, 'Foundations of the Saxon Cathedral Church at Rochester', *Arch Cant*, 18 (1889), 261–78, at pp. 263–5, 268, pl. I, fig. 6 on pl. II; subsequent sondages allegedly establishing the dimensions of the nave (W.H. St J. Hope, 'The Architectural history of the Cathedral Church and Monastery of St. Andrew at Rochester', *Arch Cant*, 23 (1898), 194–328, at p. 212) have never been verified archaeologically.

11. Beginning with Hope, 'Rochester', pl. II.

12. Taylor, *Anglo-Saxon Architecture*, III, p. 785.

13. No resemblance seems to have been noted by Peers, despite his involvement with the almost simultaneous excavation and publication of both sites (Peers, 'Reculver'; Peers and Clapham, 'St. Augustine's Abbey'). Taylor seems to have been the first to allege a similarity between SS Peter and Paul and the *first* phase at Reculver (Taylor, 'Reculver Church', p. 227).

14. Fernie, *AAS*, p. 37.

15. Including by the present writer: E. Cambridge, 'Reculver Abbey', *The Dictionary of Art*, ed. J. Turner, 34 vols (London and New York, 1996), XXVI, pp. 66–7, at p. 67.

16. R.D.H. Gem, 'Reconstructions of St Augustine's Abbey, Canterbury, in the Anglo-Saxon Period', *St Dunstan, his Life, Times and Cult*, eds N.L. Ramsay, M.J. Sparks and T.W.T. Tatton-Brown (Woodbridge, 1992), pp. 57–73, at pp. 59–61, fig. 5; Gem, 'Anglo-Saxon and Norman Churches', pp. 97–9, fig. 37; Taylor, 'Reculver Church', p. 226, fig. 15 (on which, see above, note 9).

17. The outer buttresses have been interpreted as a later addition (though see below, n. 88).

18. For the likelihood that the narthex was outside rather than inside the main volume of the nave, see Gem, 'Reconstructions', p. 59; for the possible significance of this distinction, see above, pp. 217, 226.

19. Perhaps the fact that, following the addition of an envelope of *porticus*, the western parts of Reculver subsequently came to resemble those of SS Peter and Paul much more closely than they did as first designed, has reinforced the tendency to regard the two as related from the outset.

20. Most notably Lyminge (see above, n. 8).

21. Blockley et al., *Canterbury Cathedral Nave*, p. 99, at p. 95.

22. The statement that most of the Kentish churches '. . . are of similar size and proportions to one another' (Blockley et al., *Canterbury Cathedral Nave*, p. 98) has no basis in archaeological fact; further, it conceals the potentially significant fact that only the naves of St Pancras and St Martin at Canterbury are closely similar in both respects (figs 10.5, 10.6a).

23. Blockley et al., *Canterbury Cathedral Nave*, p. 95.

24. Ibid., p. 98, fig. 36.

25. G.H. Forsyth, *The Church of St. Martin at Angers: the Architectural History of the Site from the Roman Empire to the French Revolution* (Princeton, NJ, 1953), pp. 28–9, fig. 184.

26. *PMCF*, II, 235 ('. . . purement hypothétique').

27. Forsyth, *Church of St. Martin at Angers*, p. 57 and n. 26 (which expressly acknowledges reliance on Reculver).

28. See below, pp. 216–23.

29. For Reculver and SS Peter and Paul, see below, p. 208; for Christ Church, Blockley et al., *Canterbury Cathedral Nave*, p. 100.

30. *HE*, I, 33, pp. 114–15; *HE*, II, 3, pp. 142–5. For the problems of dating the pontificates of the early archbishops, see

E.B. Fryde, D.E. Greenway, S. Porter, and I. Roy (eds), *Handbook of British Chronology*, 3rd edn (London, 1986), p. 213; D.P. Kirby, *The Earliest English Kings* (London, 1991), p. 39. The location of some of the archiepiscopal burials (for which, see Gem, 'Anglo-Saxon and Norman Churches', pp. 100–1, fig. 38) confirms the identity of the building beyond doubt.

31. *HE*, II, 6, pp. 156–7; if (which is far from certain) Bede's attribution of its dedication to Mellitus is reliable, it must have taken place before he died in May 624; in any event, Kirby's argument that Eadbald's conversion was delayed until *c.* 624 implies that the dedication is most unlikely to be earlier (Kirby, *Kings*, pp. 40–1).

32. *HE*, II, 3, pp. 142–3.

33. In particular, no traces were located which might be identified with structures corresponding to either: (a), the *secretarium* in which Paulinus was buried, probably in 646 (*HE*, III, 14, pp. 256–7; Kirby, *Kings*, p. 107, n. 2), Colgrave's suggestion (*HE*, p. 132, n. 1) that the term refers to the sanctuary of the church being unlikely in the light of the avoidance by the missionaries of burial inside churches (Fernie, *AAS*, p. 42), as evidenced at SS Peter and Paul Canterbury; or (b), the '*porticus* of St Paul within the church of St Andrew' built by bishop Tobias, who died in 726, as his burial place (*HE*, V, 23, pp. 556–7).

34. Hope, 'Rochester', pp. 214–15, pl. II; see now A. Ward, 'Boley Hill, Rochester: repaving project', *Kent Archaeological Society Newsletter*, 43 (1999), 1–4, at p. 4, suggesting a Roman date. I am most grateful to the editor for drawing my attention to this reference.

35. *Anglo-Saxon Chronicle* 'A'/'E', *s.a.* 669: *Two of the Saxon Chronicles Parallel*, eds C. Plummer and J. Earle, 2 vols (Oxford, 1892), I, pp. 34–5. As Taylor first pointed out, the identification depends partly on the failure to locate any earlier christian remains on the site (Taylor, 'Reculver Church', p. 227); the excavations of 1969 by Philp did locate earlier structural remains underlying the present church (see above, n. 2), but their date and function remain as yet uncertain.

36. K.P. Witney, 'The Kentish Royal Saints: an Enquiry into the Facts behind the Legends', *Arch Cant*, 101 (1985), 1–21, at pp. 10–12.

37. Fernie, *AAS*, p. 39.

38. Clapham, *English Romanesque Architecture*, p. 21.

39. See above, n. 8.

40. Witney, 'Kentish Royal Saints', pp. 2–5.

41. *HE*, III, 22, pp. 282–5, followed by Clapham, *English Romanesque Architecture*, p. 22; and Gem, 'Anglo-Saxon and Norman Churches', p. 107.

42. Fernie, *AAS*, p. 38, suggesting a date after the accession of Archbishop Theodore in 669. Another possible context is in the late 680s or early 690s, when Kent was temporarily subject to East Saxon overlordship: see B. Yorke, 'The Kingdom of the East Saxons', *ASE*, 14 (1985), 1–36, at pp. 20–1, 29–30.

43. *HE*, II, 5–6, pp. 151–7.

44. See above, n. 31.

45. *HE*, V, 19, pp. 518–19; *HE*, III, 20, pp. 276–7.

46. *HE*, III, 8, pp. 236–7.

47. Witney, 'Kentish Royal Saints'; see above, p. 208.

48. Admittedly, the destruction of key areas of the remains at Canterbury where pilaster buttresses might have been expected to occur (most notably the western angles of the nave (fig. 10.2a)), makes it uncertain as to whether they were a feature of the building or not; they are, however, absent from the external walling. Indeed, the only surviving buttressing, framing the narthex

49. N.P. Brooks, *The Early History of the Church of Canterbury: Christ Church from 597 to 1066* (Leicester, 1984), pp. 91–2, who speculates that the relationship between these two might have mirrored that of the monasteries attached to the major Roman basilicas, the monks of which assisted with the performance of the liturgy. Those monasteries are, however, significantly closer to the basilicas they served than would be the case at Canterbury (cf. below, n. 61).
50. W. Levison, *England and the Continent in the Eighth Century* (Oxford, 1946) p. 36.
51. The Bollandist fathers knew of only one other, a chapel in the region of ancient Pannonia, the province from which the martyrs originally hailed (*Acta Sanctorum quotquot Toto Orbe coluntur vel a Catholicis Scriptoribus celebrantur* . . . (Antwerp and Brussels, 1643–), Novembris, III, p. 762).
52. P.F. Jones, *A Concordance to the Historia Ecclesiastica of Bede* (Cambridge, Mass., 1929), p. 310, s.v. *martyrium*.
53. In the late fourteenth-century chronicle of William Thorne ('Chronica Guill: Thorne Monachi S. Augustini Cant. de rebus gestis Abbatum Sancti Augustini Cantuariae', *Historiae Anglicanae Scriptores X* . . ., ed. R. Twysden (London, 1652), cols 1753–2202, ch. 5, s.a. 598 (at col. 1760)).
54. *HE*, II, 7, pp. 156–9. J.M. Wallace-Hadrill, *Bede's* Ecclesiastical History of the English People: *a Historical Commentary* (Oxford, 1988), p. 62, notes the close resemblance between the miracle attributed to Mellitus and one attributed in Gregory the Great's *Dialogues* to Marcellinus, Bishop of Ancona, without, however, going on to impugn the authenticity of the Bedan text. Nevertheless, there must be a distinct suspicion that the story is a learned Canterbury fabrication, derived from the Gregorian text, in an attempt to flesh out the (evidently rather scant) records at Canterbury relating to the early archbishops. As Kirby has recently pointed out, exactly the same may be said of the story of the scourging of Archbishop Laurence (*HE*, II, 6, pp. 154–6; Kirby, *Kings*, p. 38). The point of the reference to the *martyrium* would presumably therefore be to add authenticating local detail to the Mellitus miracle; the reliability of its association with the archbishop, however (and consequently the date of the building), must remain in serious doubt.
55. Gem, 'Anglo-Saxon and Norman Churches', p. 101; *Le Liber Pontificalis: Texte, Introduction et Commentaire*, ed. L. Duchesne, 3 vols (Paris, 1886–1957) I, p. 324.
56. *Liber Pontificalis*, ed. Duchesne, I, p. 324. (Corporeal relics of the martyrs were not placed in it until the mid-ninth century.)
57. See above, p. 210 and n. 45.
58. Brooks, *Church of Canterbury*, p. 34.
59. *Acta Sanctorum*, Maii, III, p. 21 (baptism), p. 18 (head relic).
60. It was probably in existence long before its first mention, in 593–4 (G. Ferrari, *Early Roman Monasteries: Notes for the History of the Monasteries and Convents at Rome from the V through the X Century* (Vatican City, 1957), p. 245). Its dedication to St Pancras (jointly with SS John the Baptist and the Evangelist) is first recorded in 731 x 741; again, there is no reason to suppose that it is not much older (ibid., pp. 242, 252). Note that the dedication is sometimes referred to as being to St Pancras alone (ibid., p. 253).
61. Ferrari, *Early Roman Monasteries*, and plan II.
62. The excavator's view was that the interval separating the two phases was

comparatively long (Jenkins, 'St. Pancras', p. 4).

63. For example, D. Watts, *Christians and Pagans in Roman Britain* (London and New York, 1991), p. 111, and references there cited; compare Fernie, *AAS*, p. 37, and Gem, 'Anglo-Saxon and Norman Churches', pp. 101–3.

64. C. Thomas, *Christianity in Roman Britain to AD 500* (London, 1981), pp. 170–4.

65. Brooks, *Church of Canterbury*, ch. 2, p. 333, n. 8.

66. R. Morris, *Churches in the Landscape* (London, 1989), pp. 20–5; *HE*, I, 26, pp. 76–7.

67. In particular, pilaster buttresses are most unlikely to pre-date the fifth century, which makes a late Roman context highly unlikely in Britain (see above, p. 217). The juxtaposition of the plan of St Pancras with other demonstrably Roman buildings by Watts arguably serves to emphasise the differences rather than the similarities (Watts, *Christians and Pagans*, p. 145, fig. 17).

68. Jenkins's text and plans are inconsistent as to whether any of the *porticus* formed part of the original build, the plan (Jenkins, 'St. Pancras', at p. 5, followed by Gem, 'Anglo-Saxon and Norman Churches', p. 101) indicating that the south chancel *porticus* is primary, while the text (at p. 4) explicitly states that it is secondary. Presumably the latter is to be preferred.

69. Thomas, *Christianity in Roman Britain*, p. 173, fig. 34.

70. Jenkins, 'St. Pancras', fig. on p. 5; for example, H.M. and J. Taylor, *Anglo-Saxon Architecture*, I, pp. 146–7, fig. 64.

71. Jenkins, 'St. Pancras', p. 4.

72. W.H. St J. Hope, 'Excavations at St. Austin's Abbey, Canterbury, I – The Chapel of St Pancras', *Arch Cant*, 25 (1902), 222–37, at p. 231, pl. following p. 232.

73. Jenkins, 'St. Pancras'.

74. Ineffectively, to judge by the (apparently early) blocking walls inserted into the flanking openings: Hope, 'Chapel of St Pancras', pp. 231–2, pl. following p. 230.

75. Jenkins, 'St. Pancras', fig. on p. 5; see above, nn. 68, 70.

76. The apse at Bradwell is only very slightly stilted, implying that, while the presence of stilting suggests a comparatively late date, the contrary does not necessarily follow.

77. See above, pp. 219–20.

78. See above, pp. 217–19, 221.

79. See above, p. 202, n. 5.

80. See above, pp. 223–5.

81. It occurs, for example, at Muntajana in Istria (R. Bratoz, 'The Development of the Early Christian Research in Slovenia and Istria between 1976 and 1986', *Actes du XIe Congrès International d'Archéologie Chrétienne*, 3 vols (Vatican City, 1989), II, 2345–88, at p. 2372, fig. 6), and at Veurey and Seyssel in Gaul (respectively *PMCF*, I, 245–7, 304–7): see fig. 10.9.

82. For Ravenna, see F.W. Deichmann, *Ravenna: Hauptstadt des Spätantiken Abendlandes*, 3 vols in 6 (Wiesbaden, 1958–89), II (3), pp. 253–4; for north Italian and Istrian examples, see respectively figs 10.7, 10.9d.

83. The absence of these feature from churches such as S Lorenzo and S Agnese, datable respectively to 579–90 and 625–38 is especially significant (see R. Krautheimer et al., *Corpus Basilicarum Christianarum Romae*, 5 vols (Vatican City, 1937–77), II, esp. pp. 125–7, fig. 122, plan II; I, pp. 19–35, plans IV, VI).

84. *PMCF*, II, pp. 155–9, plan on p. 157.

85. See below, n. 126.

86. At St Martin, Canterbury (Gem, 'Anglo-Saxon and Norman Churches', pp. 93–5, figs 30–32) and Bradwell (Clapham, *English Romanesque Architecture*, pl. 2), the only two English examples where the elevation

of the pilaster buttresses is known, they stop short of eaves level (only rising about halfway up the walls in the case of Bradwell) and are finished off with sloping tops. Further, the buttress in the centre of the south wall of the nave at St Martin's is semicircular rather than rectangular (fig. 10.6a). There appear to be no continental parallels for either feature; equally, there is no knowing how typical of the English series these were.

87. Saint-Laurent de Choulans (where it is clearly a later insertion into the wall of the north *porticus*), *PMCF*, I, 278–82, esp. pp. 280 (plan), 282 (reconstruction); Saint-Blaise, *PMCF*, I, 147–50, esp. p. 148 (plan); Saint-Barthélemy, *PMCF*, III, 201–5, comparison between the earlier and more recent reconstructed ground plans (respectively *Naissance des Arts Chrétiens, Atlas des Monuments Paléochrétiens de la France* (Paris, 1991), p. 212c and *PMCF*, III, 204) implying that the interpretation in the former of a foundation as belonging to a southern internally projecting buttress has subsequently been withdrawn, the latter also presenting the whole feature as secondary: for the evidence, see the stone by stone plan in *PMCF*, III, 203. Compare also the buttresses of the gallery west of the principal church of the complex at Digne (*PMCF*, I, 69–80, fig. 2 on p. 72).

88. See above, p. 206 and n. 17. The north external narthex buttress of SS Peter and Paul, upon re-excavation in the late 1950s, 'appeared to be butt-jointed to the main wall' (Saunders, 'Excavations' (*op. cit.* in n. 2), p. 48). This has led to it being interpreted as a later addition (Gem, 'Anglo-Saxon and Norman Churches', p. 98, fig. 35). Comparison with the stone by stone drawing of the external narthex buttresses at Saint-Barthélemy at Saint-Denis, however, where the northern one appears to be butt-jointed externally but the southern not (*PMCF*, III, plan on p. 203) suggests that this may be a feature indicative of structural technique rather than chronological sequence. Note that, if the Canterbury example is a primary feature of the design, it is the only closely datable example in the whole group.

89. Peers, 'Reculver', p. 249.

90. The junction of the polygonal section with the rest of the building may be effected by the addition of parallel western facets (often of differing length to those of the apse proper), or by extending the westernmost polygonal facets.

91. Deichmann, *Ravenna*, II (3), pp. 254–6.

92. S Giovanni a Porta Latina, probably of the mid-sixth century (Krautheimer, *Corpus*, I, pp. 313–14, fig. 165). Krautheimer's initial view that this church was associated with Ravenna (loc. cit.) was later revised in favour of a derivation from eastern sources (R. Krautheimer, *Early Christian and Byzantine Architecture*, 4th edn, eds R. Krautheimer and S. Curcic (New Haven and London, 1986), p. 275.)

93. N. Duval, 'L'architecture cultuelle', *Naissance des Arts Chrétiens*, pp. 186–219, at p. 209.

94. Fernie describes it as 'nine sides of a regular 16-sided polygon' (Fernie, *AAS*, p. 35). The facts that the westernmost angles are slightly sharper, and the parallel western facets distinctly longer, than the others, both argue against this analysis.

95. Deichmann, *Ravenna*, II (1), pp. 98–100, followed by Krautheimer, *Early Christian and Byzantine Architecture*, p. 185. The awkward relationship of the upper section to the three blocked windows below suggests that it might have been a later (if still comparatively early) addition, however.

96. M. Mazzotti, 'Pavimenti Neoniani nella Basilica Apostolorum di Ravenna', *Rivista di Archeologia Cristiana*, 45 (1969), 97–105,

folding plan preceding p. 97. Deichmann, *Ravenna*, II (2), pp. 308–18.
97. *PMCF*, I, pp. 254–66, at pp. 256 (plan), 265 (date).
98. For example, S Michele Arcangelo at Perugia, recently re-dated to the beginning of the seventh century (D. Scortecci, 'Riflessioni sulla Cronologia del Tempio Perugino di San Michele Arcangelo', *Rivista di Archeologia Cristiana*, 67 (2) (1991), 405–28, at pp. 427–8), and see below, p. 220.
99. Only two examples of polygonal apses considered to date from later than *c*. 500 are recorded in the Gallic corpus: that of the second phase of Saint Just at Lyon, a typically Ravennate pentagonal form, assigned probably to the sixth century (*PMCF*, I, pp. 271–7, at pp. 275–6 (plan), 277 (date – though note that Duval would prefer to place it in a fifth-century context); and that of Civaux, which is of five sides plus long parallel western facets, dated to the sixth or seventh centuries (*PMCF*, II, 272–7, at p. 276 (date), 277 (plan). The latter is, however, polygonal internally as well as externally, like the three-sided apses added successively to the east end of Saint-Bertrand-de-Comminges at unknown dates (*PMCF*, II, 177–89, at p. 182 (plan), 187–8 (date). The latter examples suggest that a later, distinctively Gallic, tradition of constructing apses developed (see Duval above, n. 93), though what (if any) relation it bore to its Late Antique antecedents in the region it is impossible to say.
100. The arcade at Bradwell may have been double rather than triple: H.M. Carter, *The Fort of Othona and the Chapel of St. Peter-on-the-Wall, Bradwell-on-Sea, Essex* (Chelmsford, 1966), p. 18, fig. on p. 19, Gem, 'Anglo-Saxon and Norman Churches', p. 107; contrast, however, Fernie, *AAS*, p. 38. The matter has not been definitively established archaeologically.
101. See above, p. 214.
102. Peers, 'Churches of the St. Pancras Type', p. 431.
103. Together with the fact that the evidence at Bradwell indicates that the apse there was certainly lower than the nave (*Royal Commission on Historical Monuments (England). An Inventory of the Historical Monuments in Essex*, IV (London, 1923), p. 15, pl. facing p. 17), this consideration makes Gem's recent reconstruction of SS Peter and Paul with a lower apse (Gem, 'Anglo-Saxon and Norman Churches', p. 99, fig. 37) more plausible in this respect than his earlier one in which the apse was shown as equal in height to the nave (Gem, 'Reconstructions', p. 60, fig. 5).
104. For example, the building underlying the church of S Pietro in Vincoli at Rome (Krautheimer, *Corpus*, III, pp. 190–1, fig. 158).
105. For example, at Sabratha (J.B. Ward-Perkins and R. Goodchild, 'The Christian Antiquities of Tripolitania', *Archaeologia*, 95 (1953), 1–82, at pp. 7–18, 63–4, figs 29–30); Fernie, *AAS*, p. 41.
106. Clapham, *English Romanesque Architecture*, p. 31; M. Prelog, *Eufrazijeva Bazilika u Poreču* (Zagreb and Poreč, 1994), figs on pp. 15, 16.
107. Scortecci, 'Riflessioni', figs 5, 12. A similar arcade was inserted into the church of S Stefano, Verona, possibly in the seventh century (P. Verzone (trans. P. Waley), *From Theodoric to Charlemagne: A history of the Dark Ages in the West* (London, 1968), p. 48, fig. 20).
108. Krautheimer, *Early Christian and Byzantine Architecture*, pp. 278–80.
109. See above, n. 98. The term 'Ravennate feature' is used here as a shorthand term to describe elements typical of the architecture of that city in Late Antiquity,

even though these may have originated elsewhere, and generally had a wider distribution than Ravenna itself.

110. See above, p. 214.
111. For the reinterpretation of the alleged example at Saint-Martin, Angers, see above, p. 207, nn. 25–7.
112. Jenkins, 'St. Pancras', p. 4. (Its present context does not rule out the possibility that it was reused from the earlier phase, however.)
113. T.F.C. Blagg, 'Some Roman Architectural Traditions in the Early Saxon Churches of Kent', *Collectanea Historica: Essays in Memory of Stuart Rigold*, ed. A. Detsicas (Maidstone, 1981), pp. 51–3, at p. 52, fig. 7B.
114. (S. Lorenzo): Krautheimer, *Corpus*, II, figs 36–9; (S. Agnese), ibid., I, figs 18–19.
115. Krautheimer, *Early Christian and Byzantine Architecture*, pl. 189.
116. Blagg, 'Roman Architectural Traditions', pp. 52–3, fig. 7C.
117. The apparent absence of pilaster buttresses at SS Peter and Paul would of itself be consistent with a Gallic or a Roman origin; it is only the form of the narthex entrance buttressing which argues in favour of the former (see above, pp. 206, 217).
118. I. Wood, 'The Mission of Augustine of Canterbury to the English', *Speculum*, 69 (1994), 1–16, at pp. 6–10; Gem, 'Anglo-Saxon and Norman Churches', pp. 91–3; see also Ian Wood, ch. 4 above.
119. Mellitus is recorded as having attended a synod in Rome in 610 (*HE*, II, 4); on the flight to Gaul, see *HE*, II, 5.
120. On Bertha and the native impetus behind the mission, see Wood, 'Mission', pp. 10–11.
121. References conveniently collected in B. Ward-Perkins, *From Classical Antiquity to the Middle Ages: Urban Public Building in Northern and Central Italy AD 300–850* (Oxford, 1984), appendix 2, pp. 241–4. Given the interest of the author of the primary documentary source, Agnellus, in ecclesiastical building works, his silence after this period (paralleled by a comparable lacuna in the archaeological evidence) can hardly fail to be significant.
122. The situation in Istria appears to have been less catastrophic (Bratož, 'Early Christian Research in Slovenia and Istria', pp. 2377–9), though the transfer of relics from Istria (and Dalmatia) to Rome by Pope John IV (640–2) suggests that any recovery in the early seventh century was short-lived (*Liber Pontificalis*, ed. Duchesne, I, p. 330).
123. Ward-Perkins, *From Classical Antiquity to the Middle Ages*, appendix 2, pp. 236–41. The end of large-scale building was no doubt accelerated by the sack of the papal treasury in the summer of 640 (*Liber Pontificalis*, ed. Duchesne, I, pp. 328–9). As at Ravenna, the interest of the *Liber Pontificalis* in (admittedly primarily papal) building works makes the sharp decline in the number of references after *c.* 640 significant.
124. For a concise recent summary, see N. Christie, *The Lombards: The Ancient Longobards* (Oxford and Cambridge, Mass., 1995), pp. 73–91, fig. 6 on p. 74.
125. For example, by the bishop of Trento at Doss Trento around 570 (W. Jakobsen, L. Schaefer, and H.R. Sennhauser, *Vorromanische Kirchenbauten*, II, *Nachtragsband* (Munich, 1991), pp. 417–18); and the patriarch of Aquileia at Grado between 571 and 586 (G. Cuscito, *Grado e le sue Basiliche Paleocristiane* (Bologna, 1992), p. 5).
126. The Ravennate features at L'Isle Jourdain (see above, p. 217) might then be interpreted as a parallel example of the diaspora of north Italian masons into southern Gaul.
127. The impression of what characterised the architectural output of Rome in the

generations around 600 may be significantly distorted by the loss of evidence, particularly as regards smaller churches. On the other hand, if Ravennate features such as polygonal apses and pilaster buttresses were an established part of the mainstream Roman building tradition, they would be expected to occur in major as well as minor buildings, so their absence from the former suggests that the Roman tradition really was distinctively different (see above, pp. 217–22, and n. 83). While the possibility cannot be ruled out that, by the early seventh century, some patrons of smaller churches were commissioning masons trained in the Ravennate tradition, it may be significant that the only surviving example of an externally polygonal apse at Rome, at S Giovanni a Porta Latina, is now considered to reflect eastern rather than Ravennate sources (see above, n. 92).

128. Particularly in the church the monastery of Sainte-Croix-et-Saint-Vincent (now Saint-Germain-des-Prés) in Paris (K.H. Krüger, *Königsgrabkirchen der Franken, Angelsachsen und Langobarden bis zur Mitte des 8. Jahrhunderts: Ein Historischer Katalog* (Munich, 1971), pp. 454–7, 463–5; *PMCF*, III, pp. 165–71). Given that the few known Gallic examples of subdivided *porticus* (as opposed to the usual continuous type) occur in the same region of south-eastern Gaul, around Lyon and Vienne, as do most of the examples of the buttressing comparable to the narthex doorway at SS Peter and Paul, it may be worth speculating whether there might be a specific architectural link with that region, then part of the Burgundian kingdom. If so, frequent contact would have been established in travelling to and from Rome. It should also be noted, in the light of Wood's hypothesis regarding Brunhild's active backing of the mission, that this was an area under her direct control until her death in 613 (E. James, *The Origins of France from Clovis to the Capetians, 500–1000* (London and Basingstoke, 1982), p. 138).

129. See above, pp. 208; 222–3.

130. For example, in Wessex (Fernie, *AAS*, p. 46, fig. 20) and Northumbria (ibid., pp. 56–8). The possibility that other aspects of the design of Reculver not discussed here reflect late seventh-century influences, whether Gallic or otherwise, should certainly not be ruled out.

CHAPTER 11

The *Biblia Gregoriana*

Mildred Budny

INTRODUCTION: THE BIBLE AS RELIC OF GREGORY'S APOSTOLIC MISSION TO ENGLAND

The *Biblia Gregoriana* (the 'Bible of Gregory the Great') was one of the chief treasures of Saint Augustine's Abbey, Canterbury. This manuscript stands in first place in both the late fifteenth-century catalogue of the abbey library and the early fifteenth-century list by Thomas of Elmham of the Gregorian books venerated at the abbey (fig. 11.9). It was a magnificent large-format Late Antique Bible in Latin, mainly in the Vulgate version of Saint Jerome. It was written in stately script, most probably uncial, and equipped both with a number of purple leaves and with a very large cycle of illustrations. Such a manuscript would have been prized anywhere, but it had a special significance at the abbey founded by Gregory's missionary Augustine. Although Augustine dedicated the abbey to the apostolic saints Peter and Paul, it had been known principally by his name since at least the tenth century.[1]

The *Biblia Gregoriana* apparently no longer survives, alas, but it has left multiple traces in records and monuments in England spanning many centuries. They extend from the early Anglo-Saxon period to the Stuart age.

THE 'ROYAL BIBLE' OF SAINT AUGUSTINE'S ABBEY

Major traces of the relic reside in the ninth-century 'Royal Bible' made at Saint Augustine's Abbey. Now fragmentary, this book is mostly preserved in London as Royal MS 1 E. vi in the Old Royal collection (whence derives its modern name), with a leaf apiece in Canterbury and Oxford.[2] Insofar as they now stand, with trimmed margins, the large-format leaves measure at the most $c.$ 471 × 348 mm.

Only seventy-nine leaves survive of the original total of more than one thousand. They preserve most of the four gospels, some prefatory texts for them and part of the Acts of the Apostles. The text is a rendition of the Vulgate version with an admixture of Old Latin and Insular readings. The London portion

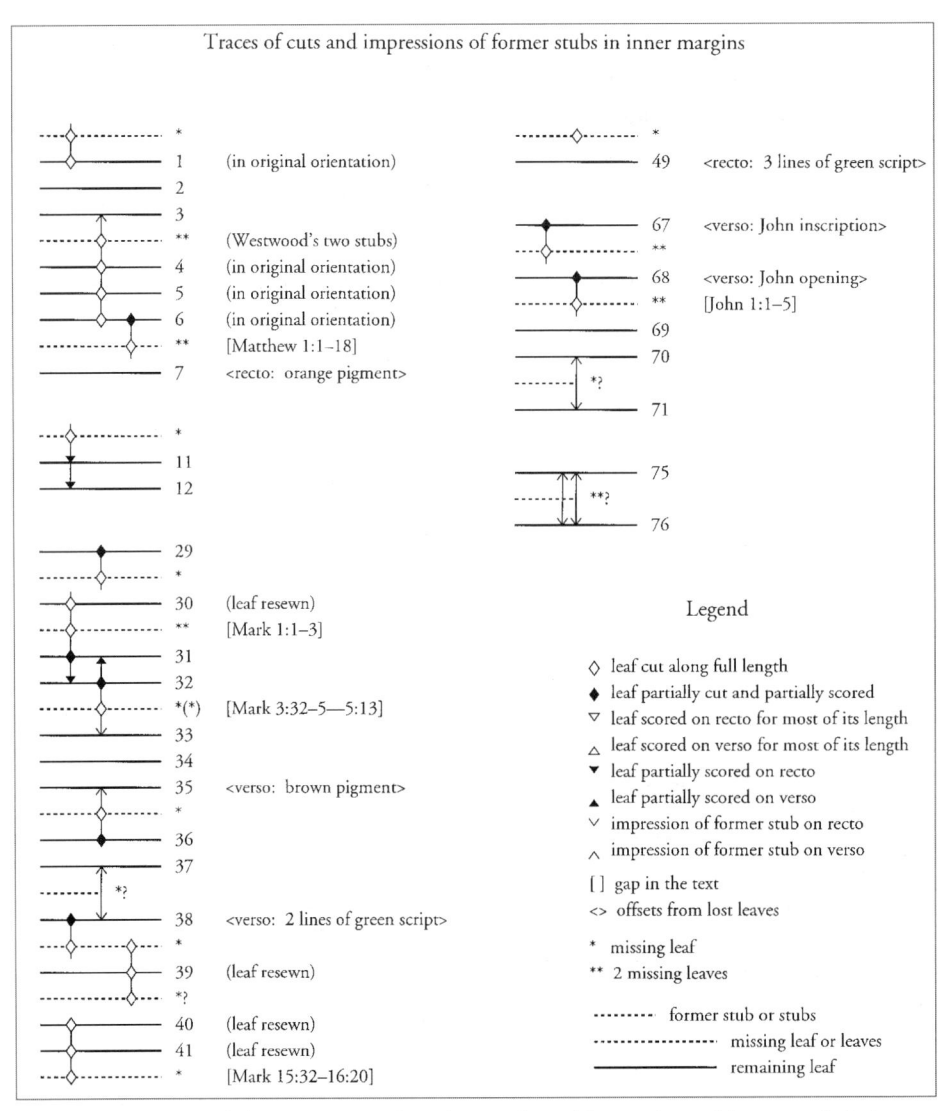

Traces of cuts and impressions of former stubs in inner margins

— 1	(in original orientation)	— 49 <recto: 3 lines of green script>
— 2		
— 3		— 67 <verso: John inscription>
**	(Westwood's two stubs)	**
— 4	(in original orientation)	— 68 <verso: John opening>
— 5	(in original orientation)	** [John 1:1–5]
— 6	(in original orientation)	— 69
**	[Matthew 1:1–18]	— 70
— 7	<recto: orange pigment>	*?
		— 71
— 11		— 75
— 12		**?
		— 76
— 29		
*		**Legend**
— 30	(leaf resewn)	
**	[Mark 1:1–3]	◇ leaf cut along full length
— 31		◆ leaf partially cut and partially scored
— 32		▽ leaf scored on recto for most of its length
*(*)	[Mark 3:32–5—5:13]	△ leaf scored on verso for most of its length
— 33		▼ leaf partially scored on recto
— 34		▲ leaf partially scored on verso
— 35	<verso: brown pigment>	∨ impression of former stub on recto
*		∧ impression of former stub on verso
— 36		[ ] gap in the text
— 37		<> offsets from lost leaves
*?		* missing leaf
— 38	<verso: 2 lines of green script>	** 2 missing leaves
*		
— 39	(leaf resewn)	·········· former stub or stubs
*?		············ missing leaf or leaves
— 40	(leaf resewn)	———— remaining leaf
— 41	(leaf resewn)	
*	[Mark 15:32–16:20]	

11.1. BL, Royal MS 1 E. vi: traces of cutting marks and impressions of former stubs in inner margins. (Budny)

(fols 1–77) and the Canterbury leaf (an unnumbered fol. '78') contain the bulk of the gospels, presented in the standard Vulgate order of Matthew, Mark, Luke and John. A pair of added front endleaves, probably of thirteenth-century date, accompanies the London portion (fols i–ii). The gospel text has a few gaps at several points because of missing leaves (figs 11.1–2) and it breaks off abruptly about one-third of the way through John, within 12:34 on the Canterbury leaf.[3] The Oxford leaf contains the text of Acts from within 18:28 to within 20:12. To judge by the usual rate of script by the main scribe (who wrote most of the surviving pages), the portion of Acts preceding the Oxford leaf would have occupied some thirteen leaves of script, while the missing portion of John would have spanned some six leaves. If the manuscript followed the standard Vulgate order, Acts would have followed the gospels directly.[4]

The gospel prefatory texts appear in the London portion. Jerome's prologue beginning 'The new work' (*Novum opus*), which occupies fol. 2r–v, introduces the gospel unit as a whole. Describing his approach to the work, it has the form of a dedicatory epistle which Jerome wrote in Rome in 383 to his patron Pope Damasus

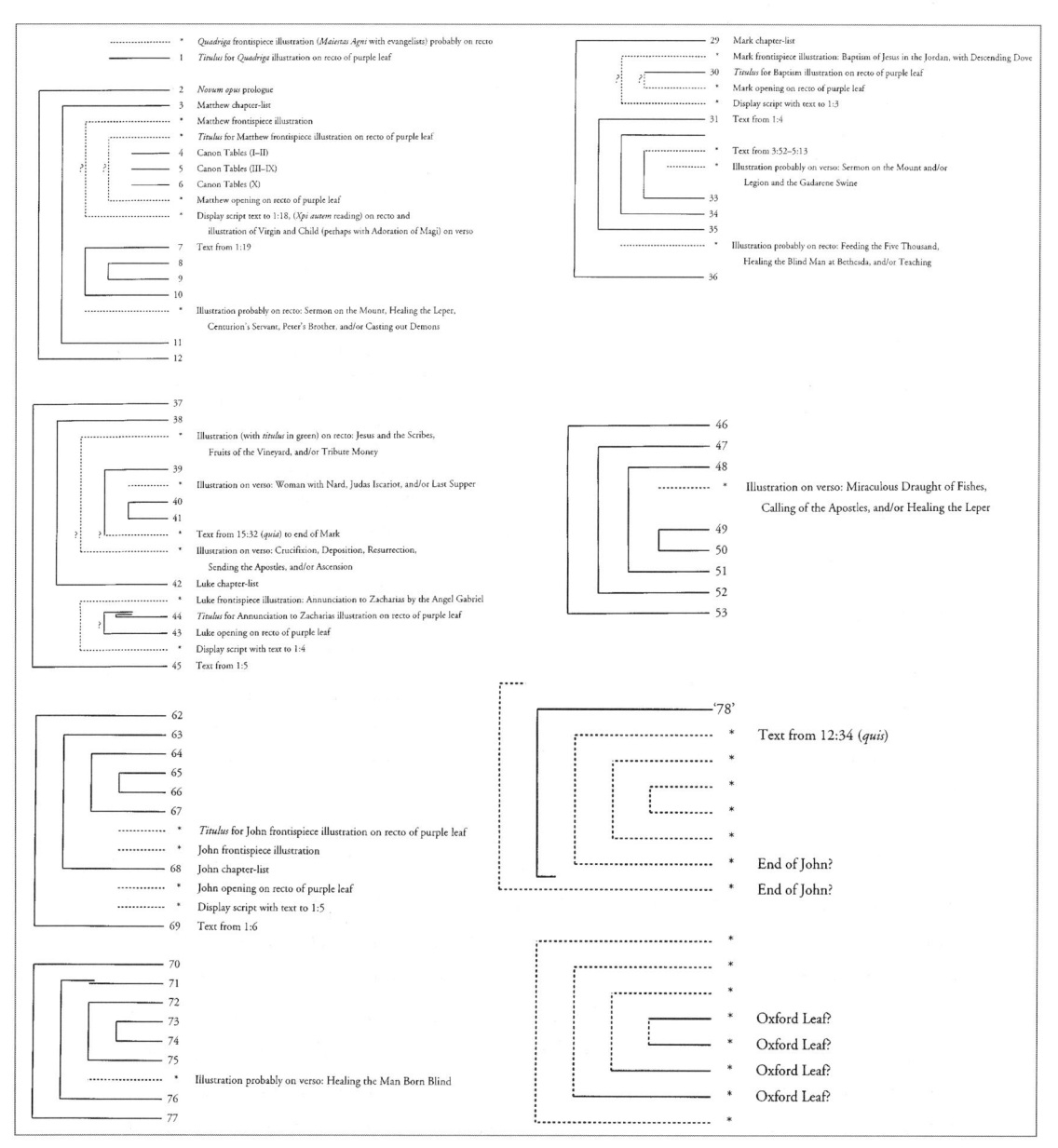

*	*Quadriga* frontispiece illustration (*Maiestas Agni* with evangelists) probably on recto
1	*Titulus* for *Quadriga* illustration on recto of purple leaf
2	*Novum opus* prologue
3	Matthew chapter-list
*	Matthew frontispiece illustration
*	*Titulus* for Matthew frontispiece illustration on recto of purple leaf
4	Canon Tables (I–II)
5	Canon Tables (III–IX)
6	Canon Tables (X)
*	Matthew opening on recto of purple leaf
*	Display script text to 1:18, (*Xpi autem* reading) on recto and illustration of Virgin and Child (perhaps with Adoration of Magi) on verso
7	Text from 1:19
8	
9	
10	
*	Illustration probably on recto: Sermon on the Mount, Healing the Leper, Centurion's Servant, Peter's Brother, and/or Casting out Demons
11	
12	
37	
38	
*	Illustration (with *titulus* in green) on recto: Jesus and the Scribes, Fruits of the Vineyard, and/or Tribute Money
39	
*	Illustration on verso: Woman with Nard, Judas Iscariot, and/or Last Supper
40	
41	
*	Text from 15:32 (*quia*) to end of Mark
*	Illustration on verso: Crucifixion, Deposition, Resurrection, Sending the Apostles, and/or Ascension
42	Luke chapter-list
*	Luke frontispiece illustration: Annunciation to Zacharias by the Angel Gabriel
44	*Titulus* for Annunciation to Zacharias illustration on recto of purple leaf
43	Luke opening on recto of purple leaf
*	Display script with text to 1:4
45	Text from 1:5
62	
63	
64	
65	
66	
67	
*	*Titulus* for John frontispiece illustration on recto of purple leaf
*	John frontispiece illustration
68	John chapter-list
*	John opening on recto of purple leaf
*	Display script with text to 1:5
69	Text from 1:6
70	
71	
72	
73	
74	
75	
*	Illustration probably on verso: Healing the Man Born Blind
76	
77	

29	Mark chapter-list
*	Mark frontispiece illustration: Baptism of Jesus in the Jordan, with Descending Dove
30	*Titulus* for Baptism illustration on recto of purple leaf
*	Mark opening on recto of purple leaf
*	Display script with text to 1:3
31	Text from 1:4
*	Text from 3:52–5:13
*	Illustration probably on verso: Sermon on the Mount and/or Legion and the Gadarene Swine
33	
34	
35	
*	Illustration probably on recto: Feeding the Five Thousand, Healing the Blind Man at Bethesda, and/or Teaching
36	
46	
47	
48	
*	Illustration on verso: Miraculous Draught of Fishes, Calling of the Apostles, and/or Healing the Leper
49	
50	
51	
52	
53	
'78'	
*	Text from 12:34 (*quis*)
*	
*	
*	
*	End of John?
*	End of John?
*	
*	
*	Oxford Leaf?
*	Oxford Leaf?
*	Oxford Leaf?
*	Oxford Leaf?
*	

11.2. BL, Royal MS 1 E. vi: the quires and their contents reconstructed. (Budny)

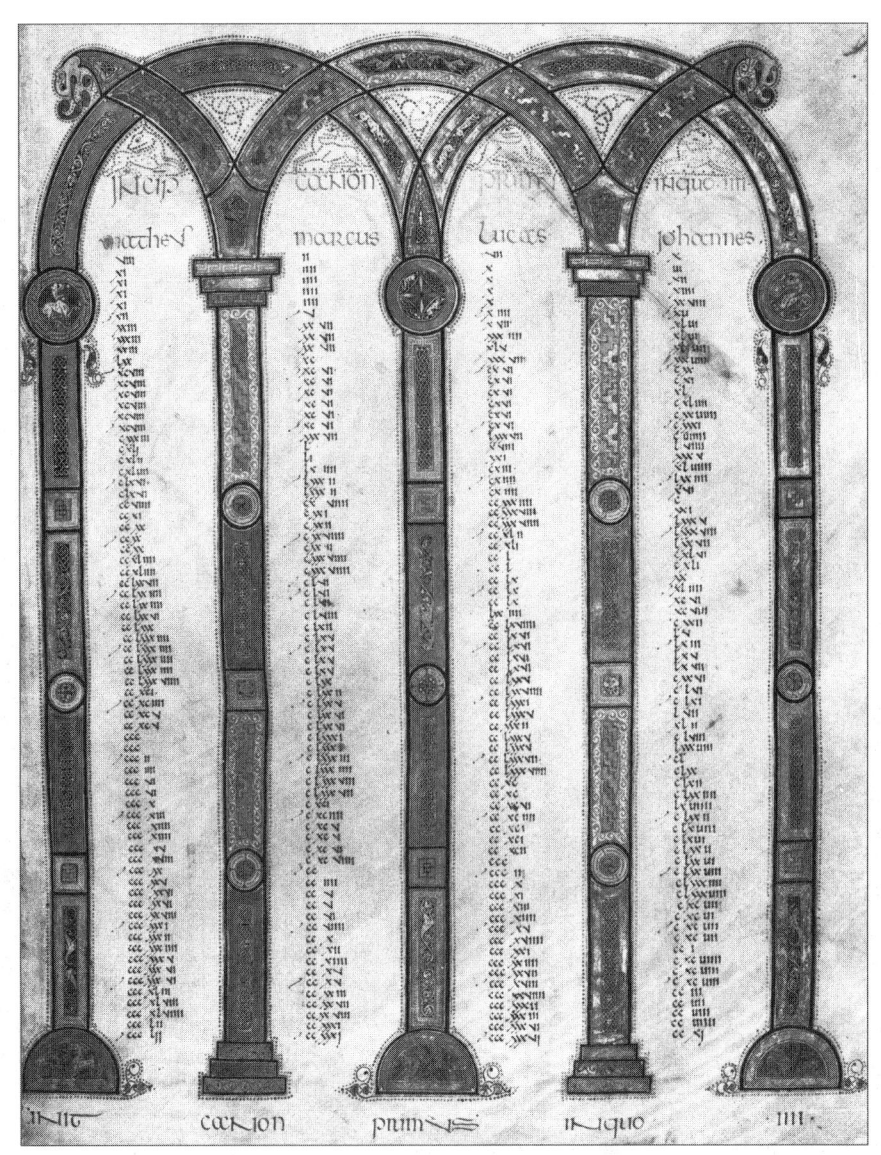

11.3. BL, Royal MS 1 E. vi (Royal Bible), fol. 4r: Eusebian Canon I and its arcade. (British Library)

(366–84).[5] There is a full set of ten Eusebian canon tables on fols 4r–6r. Devised for the Greek gospels by Eusebius, bishop of Caesarea (d. c. 340), and adopted by Jerome for his Vulgate version, the canons list concordant passages between gospels and then cite passages unique to individual gospels.[6] The set spans five pages, enclosed within majestic arcades, whose colors and patterns alternate in complexly balanced sequences (fig. 11.3).[7] Each gospel is preceded by its chapter list on a leaf to itself (fols 3, 29, 42, 68), usually with a blank verso, except for Luke's. The lists,

11.4. BL, Royal MS 1 E. vi, fol. 43r: opening page of Luke's gospel with the opening words within a monumental arcade. (British Library)

which give brief summaries of the contents respectively in 28, 13, 20 and 14 chapters, belong to an 'old' group which Donatien De Bruyne labelled as Group B (*Breviatus* or 'abridged').[8] The text of a gospel opens magnificently, with its first words enclosed within a full-page decorative arcade (fig. 11.4).

The main text, including the prologue and chapter lists, is written in two columns per page, normally of forty-two lines per column (fig. 11.5). The biblical texts are

11.5. BL, Royal MS 1 E. vi, fol. 28v: last page of Mark's gospel and its concluding title. (British Library)

arranged partly *per cola et commata* (in phrases or sense units), according with Jerome's layout for the Vulgate, and partly in paragraphs. Mostly the text is written in an extraordinarily elaborate form of Anglo-Saxon hybrid minuscule, mixed – most remarkably – with other grades of script, including capitals, uncials and monograms (figs 11.5, 7). Such elements are generally used at line-endings and run-overs, not only to save space, it seems, but also to display virtuosity.

The surviving portions exhibit the work of five scribes, of whom one was the master ('Scribe I'). Besides all the inscriptions, rubrications, prefatory texts, canon tables and quire numerals, he wrote almost all the gospel texts (except for a few parts of Matthew and Luke by 'Scribes II–IV') and the vast majority of the corrections, both in his own sections and those of other scribes. He also executed all the decorated arcades and the figural illustrations. His hand in the rubrications and some corrections on the Oxford leaf (mostly written by 'Scribe V') establishes that it formed part of the same manuscript, despite certain differences in format and textual family between it and the other portions. This master's work displays an astonishing range of scripts, from monumental capitals to informal minuscules, frequently mixed with each other. His extensive activity as the main scribe, rubricator, corrector, teacher and artist (figs 11.3–5 and 7; pl. VI) implies that he served as overseer of the whole, as would have befitted his formidable range of skills.

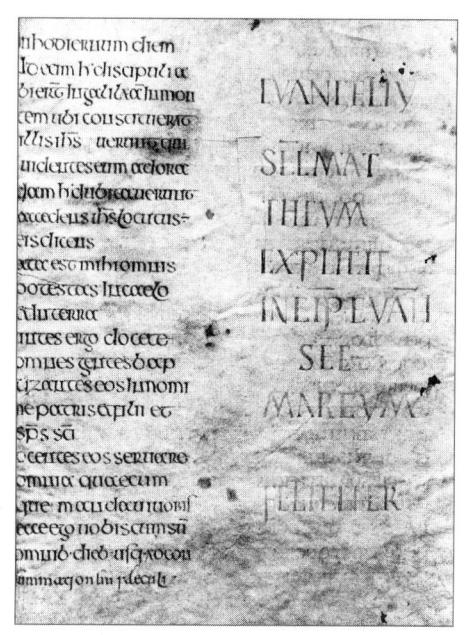

11.6. Worcester, Cathedral Library, Additional MS 1 (Part of the Worcester–Oxford Gospels), fol. 1v: last page of Mark's gospel and its concluding title. (Budny; D & C of Worcester)

His script makes it possible to locate the place of origin of the manuscript. His hand appears in other manuscripts, including some made or owned by Saint Augustine's Abbey. Among them is the eighth-century Vespasian Psalter (pls VII–VIII; figs 13.13–14).[9] To it this scribe added almost all of the continuous interlinear Old English gloss, renowned as a major early witness to the language.[10] The gloss uses the same virtuoso script as most of this scribe's corrections in the Royal Bible: an informal, rapid, but still stunningly calligraphic, Anglo-Saxon current minuscule, mixed – of course – with other forms.

The Royal Bible contains some purple-dyed leaves (pl. VI; fig. 11.4), which place it firmly in the rich Mediterranean tradition of purple codices.[11] Such books stem from the venerable antique tradition of purple as *the* senatorial, regal or imperial colour, produced by an extremely expensive dyestuff obtained from the shellfish murex. In a christian book, it accords homage to Christ the King. There survive many examples or fragments of Late Antique 'empurpled books' (*codices purpurei*), aptly written in gold and silver, in various mediterranean languages. Some, moreover, are illustrated, as with the sixth-century Vienna Genesis, Rosanno Gospels and Sinope Gospels, all in Greek and all apparently made in Syria.[12] Among surviving Anglo-Saxon manuscripts, very few contain purple-dyed leaves, although various others have purple-painted leaves or parts thereof, which merely imitate the effect of true riches appropriate to the genre.[13]

Four surviving leaves of the Royal Bible are purple. They comprise the leaf which opens Luke's gospel (fol. 43) and the three leaves which carry monumental full-page inscriptions (fols 1, 30, 44). The inscriptions serve as titles for the frontispiece illustrations respectively for the gospel unit as a whole and for the gospels of Mark and Luke (pl. VI). The opening page for Luke frames the first two words of the gospel, *Quoniam quidem* ('Forasmuch as many'), within an elaborate arcade (fig. 11.4). All the purple leaves are richly embellished with metallic gold and silver pigment. In their original design, only one side of each purple leaf carried an image or inscription, leaving the other side blank. This sumptuous, expansive effect gives the impression of dazzling riches to spare.

The remarkable titles offer elaborate, evocative guides to their scenes.[14] The title for the Luke frontispiece illustration (pl. VI) describes an image of the Annunciation to Zacharias the priest by the angel Gabriel:

Hic Gabriel angelus Zachariæ sacerdoti in templo domini apparuit almumque praecursorem magni regis ei nasciturum praedixit.

(Here the angel Gabriel appeared to Zacharias the priest in the temple of the Lord and prophesied that a holy [*or* blessed] precursor of the great king was about to be born to him.)

The title for the Mark frontispiece illustration describes an image of the Baptism of Christ in the River Jordan:

Hic Iesus baptizatus est ab Iohanne in Iordane cœlis apertis spiritu sancto in specie columba discendente super eum uoceque paterna filius altithroni vocicatus [est].

(Here Jesus is [*or* was] baptised by John in the Jordan, with the heavens being opened and the Holy Spirit descending in the form of a dove above him, and by the Father's voice is [*or* was] called Son of Him Enthroned on High.)

The title for the frontispiece for the gospel unit describes an image of the *Maiestas Agni* ('Majesty of the Lamb') accompanied by a *quadriga* ('team of four') comprising four *proceres* ('princely' *or* 'noble ones'), evidently the evangelists themselves:

Haec est speciosa quadriga luciflua animae spiritus gratia per os agni dei inlustrata in quo quattuor proceres consona uoce magnalia dei ca[ntant or *-nentes].*

(This is the resplendent *quadriga*, light-flowing by the grace of the Holy Spirit, illuminated through the mouth of the Lamb of God, [and] in which the four leaders, with harmonious voice, celebrate [*or* are celebrating] in song the miracles of God.)[15]

The opening word *Hic* or *Haec* for each inscription points to an accompanying image of its subject, demonstrating that it served as an explanatory *titulus* ('title' or 'label') for an illustration.

The word *proceres* appears to rule out the possibility that the first inscription served as a metaphorical title page, referring to the gospels themselves, rather than as such a *titulus*. It also apparently indicates that the image of the *Maiestas Agni* included the evangelists rather than – or in addition to – their symbols, which figure instead much more frequently in extant early medieval representations of the subject. Examples of frontispieces with the same subject – but with the evangelist symbols and prophets surrounding the Lamb – and in the same position, preceding the gospel unit, appear in both medium and large format in some Carolingian manuscripts made at the Abbey of Saint Martin at Tours during the time of Abbot Adalhard (834–43), as in the Gospels of Saint Gauzelin and the Bamberg Bible.[16]

Originally the manuscript had numerous purple leaves, carrying the other gospel openings and the *tituli* for the frontispiece illustrations. They and many undyed leaves have been cut out and lost, including all the frontispiece illustrations and the illustrations interspersed within the text. Leaves or parts thereof with text have also been cut out, including the inscriptions for the Matthew and John frontispieces, the last line of the *Quadriga* inscription and the concluding title for the Mark chapter list. Presumably such components were removed as samples, models or souvenirs.

There remain, however, multiple traces of their former presence (fig. 11.1).[17] Some leaves carry offsets of pigment which has migrated, through rubbing or corrosion, from elements formerly adjacent. Offsets from both the *titulus* and gospel opening for John show a remarkable consistency with the survivors (pl. VI; fig. 11.4), even to the number of lines and the structure of the arcade; such consistency is unusual for early Anglo-Saxon manuscripts. Some leaves retain

11.7. BL, Royal MS 1 E. vi, fol. 14r, lower portion: page of text within Matthew 12. (British Library)

cutting marks in the form of slits or scores made by knifepoint in excising leaves from the bound book; the directions of the cuts perhaps indicate which side of the removed leaf carried the (more) desired element. A few leaves have impressions of former stubs, some of which resulted from the cuts. Two such stubs, one purple and one undyed, between fols 3 and 4 (presumably from the Matthew *titulus* and frontispiece) were reported by J.O. Westwood[18] before their removal without notice in the nineteenth-century rebinding. During that rebinding, some leaves (including three of the four remaining purple leaves) were also silently shifted from their original orientations by being inverted, reversed, or refolded with new gutters – alterations which complicate the process of detecting the original structures. In combination, all these clues enable us to reconstruct the lost elements, including some subjects for the illustrations.

The surviving figural illustrations indicate the high standard achieved by the master artist. The arcade opening Luke's gospel (fig. 11.4) contains the part-length figures of a bull in the tympanum and Christ in the medallion at the top, forming an *imago clipeata* ('image depicted in a shield-formed surface').[19] The superb classicising style of these images points to a truly exceptional Late Antique exemplar, which far surpassed in skill those reflected in most other extant Anglo-Saxon biblical illustrations.[20] For example, the style and features of the medallion figure in the Royal Bible closely resemble the meticulous classicism achieved in such painted works from the Late Antique world as the sixth-century icon of Christ, shown half-length and nearly life-size, preserved in the Monastery of Saint Catherine on Mount Sinai and made probably at Constantinople (fig. 11.8).[21] The resemblance extends to many features, from the rim of the nimbus and the intense stare of the eyes, through the form of the purple mantle, to the Greek form of blessing and the closed book held upright against the chest. Although larger and more elaborately painted, the subtly rendered image in the icon belongs firmly to the type of Late Antique tradition of painting from which the figure in the Royal Bible stemmed, as well as to much the same type of figure itself.

Likewise, the meticulous execution of the winged bull far surpasses most early medieval representations of evangelist symbols, including those Carolingian versions which exhibit a

11.8. Mount Sinai, Monastery of Saint Catherine, Icon of Christ as Pantocrator (after K. Weitzmann).

comparable classicism, as with the *Maiestas Christi* ('Majesty of Christ') frontispiece in the Xanten Gospels of *c*. 800.[22] The detailed rendering of the bull's wings in the Royal Bible has few close relatives and no peers among early medieval representations in manuscripts or any other media. Comparable command of detail to that in the Royal Bible appears, however, in some notable earlier mediterranean renditions, as on the base of the Roman column, dating to 161–9, of the Emperor Antoninus Pius.[23] Its ascending Genius in the image of imperial apotheosis, carved in relief, has spread wings replete with alula, webbed vanes and rachides, but they are depicted with only primary feathers, instead of both primary and secondary as in the Royal Bible. Comparably skilled ornithological precision appears in the set of naturalistic images of birds in smaller scale illustrating an ornithological treatise in the Vienna Dioscurides, a copy of scientific treatises in Greek made in Constantinople shortly before 512 for the imperial princess Juliana Anicia.[24]

By their detailed classicism, the wings as well as the rest of the bull in the Royal Bible attest to a Late Antique model of great skill and precision. Many signs amply point to the *Biblia Gregoriana* as that exemplar.

THE DISAPPEARANCE OR MIGRATION OF THE GREGORIAN BIBLE AFTER THE ENGLISH REFORMATION

That venerable Bible was last recorded as surviving in the time of King James I (1603–25), according to *A Petition Apologeticall* presented to him by the Lay Catholics of England in July 1604. Printed in secret in England, the petition pointed to 'the very originall Bible, the selfe same *numero* which S. *Gregory* sent in with our Apostle S. *Augustine*, being as yet reserued by Gods especiall prouidence as a *Testimony*, that what Scriptures we haue, we had them from *Rome*'.[25] As part of his reply to the petition in 1606, Matthew Sutcliffe appropriately queried '*Where?*' and retorted, 'as *if uue had in* England *no Bibles, but* Gregories *Bible: or as if* Gregory *uuer the author of the Bible*'.[26] The expert palaeographer Humfrey Wanley recorded in 1705 that he had looked for that manuscript, but in vain.[27]

Perhaps it has simply gone into hiding along with Catholic recusants; and it, or its remnant(s), is no longer recognised as such. The pious rescue of sacred books by Catholics or Catholic sympathisers in the aftermath of the English Reformation is discernible in other cases, including from Saint Augustine's Abbey.[28] The *Biblia Gregoriana* could have been a prime target for such rescue, keeping it safe from viewers less able to appreciate its stature as relic, until such time as it might re-emerge.

THE THREE WEARMOUTH–JARROW BIBLES AND THEIR REMNANTS

We might take hope from the piecemeal recovery of dispersed leaves and scraps, reused as binding material, from one or both of the sister Bibles to the *Codex Amiatinus*.[29] Only the latter survives in full – apart from its original binding – of the three large-format single-volume Bibles known to have been produced at the double monastery of Wearmouth–Jarrow in Northumbria for its Abbot Ceolfrid (d. 716). The commission and production of his three Bibles are recorded in two versions of the 'Lives of the Abbots' (*Historia Abbatum*) of that monastery by one or two of its monks, including one version compiled after 715 by Bede (673–735).[30] Both versions record Ceolfrid's substantial contributions to the collection of books and mention in particular the 'three full Bibles' (*tres pandectes*). He gave one to each church of his monastery and took one with him as a gift for the see of Saint Peter when he set out for Rome on his final journey.[31]

The *Codex Amiatinus*, the one which Ceolfrid took to the continent, extends to 1,030 leaves measuring *c.* 505 × 340 mm and comprising 131 quires or gatherings. Written apparently by seven scribes, it contains a few pages of illustrations, variously part page, full page and double page. Placed at the beginning of each Testament, they include images of the *Maiestas Christi* accompanied by angels, evangelist symbols and apparently the evangelists (fol. 796v); the Old Testament scribe Ezra at work before an opened book cupboard which contains the multiple volumes of a full Bible (fol. Vr); the Three Persons of the Trinity at the top of diagrams which show the order and divisions of the Books of the Bible according respectively to both Pope Hilarus and Epiphanius of Cyprus, to Jerome and to Augustine of Hippo (fols VIIr, VIr, 8r); and a bird's eye view of the Tabernacle in the desert and its utensils, as described in Exodus 25:30 (fols IIv–IIIr).

The book also contains two purple leaves, each with contents on both sides. They present full-page pairs respectively of arcades enclosing a prologue and a contents list for the Bible (fol. Vr–v); and of diagrams relating to the Books of the Bible (fol. VIIr–v), in which their two-fold division according to Hilarus and Epiphanius is backed by a five-fold account of the Books of the Pentateuch, with extracts from Jerome introducing each one. Those two leaves are only painted, not dyed, and so the book forms a poor cousin to true purple codices.

Fragments survive from one or both of Ceolfrid's other Bibles. Discovered in stages in divers locations ranging from Newcastle upon Tyne to Dorset, they are the Greenwell leaf, the Middleton leaves and the Bankes leaf.[32] Written in double columns in stately uncial of Wearmouth–Jarrow type, they contain portions of the Old Testament, with parts of Books III–IV Kings written by one scribe and a leaf from the Apocryphal Book of Ecclesiasticus written by another scribe, using a somewhat different layout and ruling. The text on all the fragments received a set of chapter numbers in the late thirteenth century or the early fourteenth. The set accords with the influential system of numeration developed in the thirteenth century by theologians at the University of Paris (and still in widespread use). Decorated with pen flourishes in red pigment, these numbers were added by a single hand in the portions of Kings and perhaps by a different hand, more skilled, on the Ecclesiasticus leaf. Their presence attests to the use and survival of the Bible more or less intact to that date. Apparently the leaves from Kings, at least, formed part of the Bible reputed to have been given to Worcester by Offa, King of Mercia (757–96). Their find-places and the Worcester connections in the several fragments associated with them imply that one of Ceolfrid's Bibles made its way to Worcester as Offa's gift or purported gift.[33]

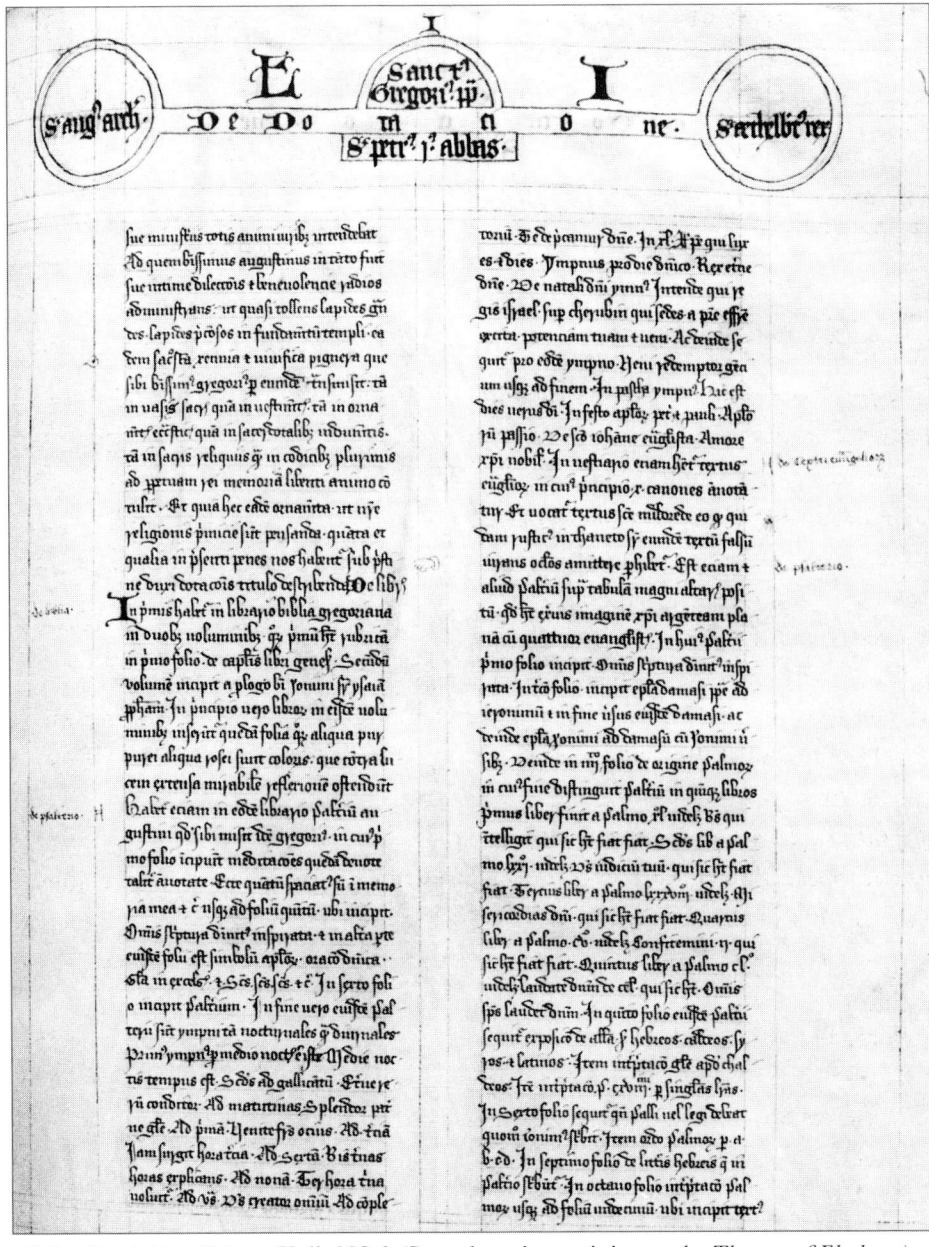

*11.9. Cambridge, Trinity Hall, MS 1 (*Speculum Augustinianum *by Thomas of Elmham), fol. 19r: chapter* De libris, *opening with the* Biblia Gregoriana. *(Budny; Master and Fellows of Trinity Hall)*

The records and traces of the *Biblia Gregoriana* are similarly scattered but, in combination, they make it possible to reconstruct much of the original state and grandeur of the book. Long ignored or misunderstood, these clues could enable us to recognize any remnants for what they are, should they come to light.

THE GREGORIAN BOOKS OF SAINT AUGUSTINE'S ABBEY AS RECORDED BY THOMAS OF ELMHAM

The monk Thomas of Elmham (1364– at least 1426) described the *Biblia Gregoriana* in his chronicle of Saint Augustine's Abbey, entitled the 'Augustinian Mirror' (*Speculum Augustinianum*) and composed between 1414 and 1418. His text survives at Trinity Hall, Cambridge, in a single large-format, luxurious medieval copy, probably made under his supervision.[34] Elmham described eight Gregorian books, kept in the vestry and the library, in his chapter entitled 'On the Books' (*De Libris*), which begins on fol. 19, column a. There (fig. 11.9) he called them 'the earliest of the books of all the English Church' (*primitiae librorum totius ecclesiae Anglicanae*). The full-page coloured drawing of the interior of the abbey church illustrates six of them on the high altar (fig. 11.10), where they are labelled as 'books sent by Gregory to Augustine' (*libri missi a Gregorii ad Augustinum*).

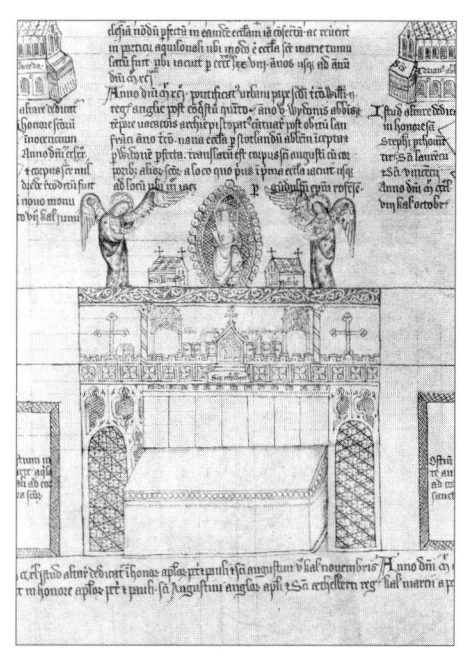

11.10. Cambridge, Trinity Hall MS 1, fol. 77v, detail: high altar of Saint Augustine's Abbey, with the 'books sent by Gregory to Augustine'. (Budny; Trinity Hall)

Some books in Elmham's account survive. At least one psalter and probably both gospel books survive to greater or lesser extents, albeit dispersed in several different collections and minus the bindings described by Elmham.

THE VESPASIAN PSALTER: THE SECOND GREGORIAN PSALTER

It has long been recognized that 'the second psalter' (*aliud Psalterium*) in Elmham's list, described as being kept on the high altar and therefore presumably one of those in his illustration (fig. 11.10), is the Vespasian Psalter.[35] This luxurious manuscript was made at the abbey in about the second quarter of the eighth century and given an Old English gloss there in about the second quarter of the ninth by the master scribe of the Royal Bible, so it could not have been truly Gregorian. However, its stately English uncial script (pls VII–VIII; figs 13.13–14) and its splendid illustrations in classicising style, which appear in the frontispiece and the historiated initials, might easily have led it to be mistaken for a genuinely Roman product.

THE GREGORIAN GOSPEL BOOKS: THE GOSPELS OF SAINT AUGUSTINE OF CANTERBURY AND THE CAMBRIDGE–LONDON GOSPELS

Recently both gospel books in Elmham's list have also been identified. Both survive in fragmentary form in Cambridge, although the second has other *membra disiecta* ('dispersed components') in London.

The first, 'the text of the gospels' (*Textus Evangeliorum*) kept in the library and known as 'the Text of Saint Mildred' (*Textus Sanctae Mildredae*), is most probably the Gospels of Saint Augustine of Canterbury.[36] This manuscript comprises an illustrated Late Antique gospel book in the Vulgate version, with prefatory texts. It was made in Italy, perhaps at Rome, in the sixth century. It retains the text of all four gospels, along with the chapter lists and prefaces for each, although it now starts abruptly within the chapter list for Matthew. Its losses include leaves at the front and back of individual gospels, with frontispiece and tailpiece illustrations. There survive the tailpiece illustration for Mark's gospel, with a full-page cycle of scenes from Christ's Passion (pl. IV), and the frontispiece illustration for Luke's gospel, with a full-page depiction of the evangelist accompanied both by his symbol, the bull, and by a cycle of scenes from the gospel (pl. V).

Various additions attest to the English provenance of the manuscript from an early date. Added texts which stand on some originally blank pages within the initial core and on some added endleaves attest to ownership by Saint Augustine's Abbey from at least the tenth century to the thirteenth. They comprise charters, grants and a list of relics pertaining to the abbey. Among them are two Anglo-Saxon records, copied into the book respectively in the tenth century (cf. fig. 16.3) and the late tenth century or early eleventh.[37] Written in English uncial, probably Kentish, of the late seventh century or first half of the eighth, numerous additions to the original text and illustrations, including titles for all the gospel scenes, attest to the arrival of the manuscript in England in the early Anglo-Saxon period.[38]

Elmham's second Gregorian gospel book, called 'the other text of the Gospels' (*alius Textus Evangeliorum*) and kept in the library, is most probably the Cambridge–London Gospels, an Insular gospel book from Northumbria. Reduced to remnants, it is divided between Corpus Christi College in Cambridge and the British Library in London, with a portion from the Cotton collection and

11.11. CCCC, MS 197B (part of the Cambridge–London Gospels), fol. 1r: frontispiece for John's gospel with the evangelist symbol and Matthew Parker's inscription attributing the book to Archbishop Augustine. (Budny; The Master and Fellows of Corpus Christi College, Cambridge)

apparently also another one from the Old Royal collection.[39] The Cotton portion, badly damaged by fire in 1731, retains parts of the gospels of Matthew and Mark, with prefatory texts, in scraps of 109 or 110 leaves. The Corpus portion contains thirty-six leaves from the gospels of Luke and John. The Royal portion comprises two leaves concluding a set of Eusebian canon tables.

This manuscript retains its frontispieces for both Mark and John, albeit damaged to various extents. They present monumental images of the evangelists' symbols. The frontispiece for John (fig. 11.11), which now opens the Cambridge portion, depicts a stately eagle poised in flight within a band-like frame with cruciform elements. Across the top of its page, a sixteenth-century inscription restates the belief that the book had been owned by Archbishop Augustine: 'This book was at one time sent by Pope Gregory to Archbishop Augustine' (*Hic liber olim missus a Gregorio papa ad Augustinum archiepiscopum*). The inscription was written by Matthew Parker, archbishop of Canterbury (1559–75), who owned the portion and had it rebound. Sir Robert Cotton (1571–1631) recorded a similar attribution for his own portion of the same manuscript: 'a book once of Augustine, apostle of the English' (*Liber quondam Augustini Anglorum Apostoli*).[40] There is no evidence that either owner was aware of the survival of other portions. Their equivalent Augustinian attributions for the book must derive from earlier sources, most likely drawing upon the practice of Saint Augustine's Abbey, whose terms reported by Elmham closely resemble Parker's phrasing.

Like the Vespasian Psalter, the Cambridge–London Gospels is an eighth-century Anglo-Saxon product, and could not have belonged to Augustine, except posthumously. The attributions for both books show that the abbey was not above confecting or confusing relics of its founder and his papal patron.

The Gospels of Saint Augustine of Canterbury, however, probably has legitimate claim to its Gregorian and Augustinian attribution. Such legitimacy arises in combination from the sixth-century date and Italian origin of the book and its signs of early English ownership, evidenced in the many entries in English uncial script of the late seventh century or first half of the eighth.

THE GREGORIAN BIBLE VERSUS THE ROYAL BIBLE

Similar authenticity pertains to the *Biblia Gregoriana*. Elmham described it in his chapter (fig. 11.9) thus:

In primis habetur in librario biblia gregoriana in duobus voluminibus quorum primum habet rubricam in primo folio de capitulis libri Geneseos. Secundum volumen incipit a prologo beati Ieronymi super Ysaiam prophetam. In principio vero librorum in eisdem voluminibus inseruntur quaedam folia quorum aliqua purpurei aliqua rosei sunt coloris quae contra lucem extensa mirabilem reflexionem ostendunt.

(First, there is kept in the library the Gregorian Bible in two volumes, of which the first has on the first leaf the heading 'Of the Chapters of the Books of

Genesis'. The second volume begins with the Preface of Saint Jerome on the Prophet Isaiah. Moreover, at the beginnings of the books in these volumes, there are inserted certain leaves, of which some are purple, others of a rose colour, which, [when] extended against the light, display a marvellous reflection.)

In the nineteenth century, Westwood believed that this description perfectly applied to the Royal Bible of Saint Augustine's Abbey, which likewise contains purple leaves inserted at the front of some books, as for Luke (pl. VI; fig. 11.4). Those leaves vary in hue from deep purple to rose, depending on the different dye baths and extents of exposure over time. Westwood's belief that the Royal Bible was the *Biblia Gregoriana* derived from the presence of purple leaves, the Saint Augustine's Abbey ownership inscription and the high quire numeration. Recognising that 'the writing and ornaments' make it 'clear that it is not of Continental origin', as entailed by the Gregorian association, Westwood supposed that the Royal Bible might have been made 'in the time of St Augustine' and might 'actually have belonged to him'. Westwood reckoned that 'the noble size and appearance of the two volumes' of the *Biblia Gregoriana* 'might easily have endured a monkish writer in the fifteenth century to have erroneously identified those two volumes with the . . . copy of the Bible' held to have been sent by Gregory to Augustine.[41] The identification persisted for some time, albeit with certain qualifications or reservations.[42]

Often the fragmentary survival of the Royal Bible has led to the conclusion that this large-format manuscript comprised only the gospels, but the high quire numeration establishes beyond doubt that originally it formed a full Bible. Written by the main scribe, that numeration survives only in the London portion (as in fig. 11.5). Placed in the lower margin at the back of each quire, it now starts with *LXXX* at the beginning of the gospels (fol. 12v) and runs consecutively through to *LXXXVIII* (fol. 77v), albeit with some corrections by the same scribe to produce the consistent series. At the same rate of script, earlier portions of the Bible would have fitted comfortably into the preceding seventy-nine quires.

Yet the Royal Bible cannot be the *Biblia Gregoriana*, because the Royal Bible had been dismembered and partly reused for binding material – as attested by the single leaves in Canterbury and Oxford – by the thirteenth century, when the abbey library inscriptions were entered upon surviving portions.[43] The inscriptions on the Oxford leaf and in the Royal portion include both the library pressmark and a declaration of ownership by the abbey in the standard simple – and early – form 'Book of Saint Augustine of Canterbury' (*Liber Sancti Augustini Cantuariensis*), which identifies the monastery simply by its patron saint, in accordance with widespread medieval practice in many regions.[44] The library inscriptions on the

Oxford leaf, which contains part of the Acts of the Apostles, pertain not to that text but to a tenth-century copy of the *Life of Saint Gregory the Pope* (*Vita Sancti Gregorii Pontificis*) by John the Deacon (active in the ninth century), for which the large leaf, folded in half, then served as the front endleaves.[45]

Entered upon an added front endleaf (fol. ii[r]), the library inscriptions in Royal 1 E. vi apparently describe *it* as a despoiled fragment of the gospels. Their first of three lines states:

> *Quatuor evangelia nuda* [with this word cancelled by a horizontal line in the same ink as the line of script] *vetera cum A*.
>
> ([*Bare* or *despoiled*] *old gospel book with* [*the letter-mark*] A.)

Letter-marks occur on a few of the surviving bindings of books from the abbey library; they were also entered in the library inscriptions as well as in the library catalogue. The inscription on the Oxford leaf records the letter-mark *B* for the *Vita Sancti Gregorii* which it accompanied. The badly rubbed and abraded Canterbury leaf, which served to cover some unknown material as a folder or loose wrapper, carries the traces of a letter-mark *D* followed by a title.

The unusual use of the word *nuda* for the gospel fragment almost certainly refers to the already spoliated state of the volume, which pre-dated the inscription by several centuries, rather than to an unbound or unglossed state.[46] The cancellation of the word here might reflect a change of mind about how to describe the volume, as *nuda* could imply that it was not worth preserving, while the retained word *vetera* is more neutral. It also might imply that the inscription, which would have corresponded to an inventory or library list, was being drafted or revised directly here.

The middle line of the library inscription in the London portion records the pressmark, which has undergone several stages of alteration through erasure and addition. Now it reads: *Distinctio III Gradus I* ('Section *or* Compartment III, Shelf I'), transformed by permutations from *Di. III Ga. III* > *Di. I Ga. III* (or *Di. I Ga. I*) > *Di. III Ga. I*. The stages may reflect not only scribal error but also some re-classification or re-shelving, as seems the case with the alterations of some other extant pressmarks in abbey books, including on the Oxford leaf. Both the abbey library catalogue and the final forms of pressmarks in extant books from the library show that the pressmarks

> *Di. I Ga. I* (as well as *Di. II* and others) marked the Bibles;
> *Di. I Ga. III* marked individual books of the Old Testament, one of the gospel books (no. 192) and some other books of the New Testament;

Di. III Ga. I marked most of the gospel books and the books of the individual gospels; and

Di. III Ga. III marked some volumes of the Acts of the Apostles and some commentaries on books of the Bible.[47]

The pressmarks *Di. III Ga. III* and *Di. I Ga. III* would thus seem to be sheer scribal error in Royal 1 E. vi, given the inscription by the same hand describing the contents as a gospel book, but the alteration(s) of the pressmark and the order of writing the different parts of the inscriptions might reflect some confusion or hesitation as to whether this volume belonged among the gospel books or the Bibles. The final form places the volume among the majority of gospel books. At an earlier stage, it might have had the pressmark of the ninth gospel book in the catalogue. For a time it might have had the presssmark of the Bibles and was shelved among them, perhaps on account of its size, although by then it lacked the other parts of the Bible.

Neither the London portion of the Royal Bible nor the *Vita Sancti Gregorii* containing the Oxford leaf appears in the surviving library catalogue for Saint Augustine's Abbey, made in the late fifteenth century.[48] The catalogue, incomplete in many respects and evidently unfinished, omitted numerous books known to have belonged to the library.[49] The absence of these two volumes from the catalogue, like others including the Vespasian Psalter, could mean that by then they had been mislaid or discarded or had already left the abbey. Had one or another of them been stored elsewhere at the abbey or lent out at the time the catalogue was compiled, this state might have been noted in the – incomplete – register at the front. Neither manuscript, however, shows any trace of late medieval consultation, although they both contain the marks of earlier use.

None of the *membra* of the Royal Bible can be shown to correspond exactly to any of the books in the other late lists of manuscripts which belonged to the abbey. The first is Elmham's early fifteenth-century list of the eight Gregorian books. The others are two short lists of select manuscripts, including two volumes of the gospels, which John Leland saw among the treasures of the abbey soon after 1533–4, when he was commissioned King's Antiquary, and before the dissolution of the abbey in July 1538, when its deed of surrender was signed.[50] The signs are that when Elmham and Leland drew up their lists, Royal 1 E. vi was relegated to the library shelves and disregarded, if it had not already left the library. After the dissolution the abbey library, one of the most extensive in England, was widely dispersed in various ways and stages; very many books were lost.[51]

The next known owner of Royal 1 E. vi was John Lord Lumley (*c.* 1534–1609), who acquired it before 1596, when the catalogue of his collection was prepared,[52] and from whom it passed into the Royal collection, thence into the British Museum and Library. The Canterbury and Oxford leaves took different routes from the abbey to enter their different present homes.

Accompanying the tenth-century *Vita Sancti Gregorii*, the Oxford leaf came into the hands of the noted book collector Thomas Allen (1540–1632),[53] who gave the volume, along with eighteen other manuscripts, to the Bodleian Library upon its foundation in 1601.[54] As one of the sixteen saints' *Lives* which he owned, and moreover as the biography of Pope Gregory the Great, it accords well with what is known of the Catholic Allen's 'interests and religious sympathies'.[55] His gift of the volume to Bodley may have had special significance for him, in keeping with his hope for a special college in England for Catholic gentlemen. Similar aspirations for a Catholic resurgence underpin the presentation by the antiquary Robert Hare (d. 1611) to Trinity Hall of its manuscript of Elmham's chronicle (figs 11.8–9), only until such time – as recorded on its fol. 1r – when Saint Augustine's Abbey might be refounded, when the book should revert to the abbey.[56]

Among the surviving portions of the Royal Bible, the Canterbury leaf, as a cover or wrapper [*cum*] D, moved least of all. Like many books from Saint Augustine's Abbey, and probably along with most of them not long after the dissolution, it went to Canterbury Cathedral; most of the property of the abbey was handed over to the archbishop. At the cathedral, perhaps in stages, the leaf was removed from the wrapped contents and placed in a series of boxes in the library, whence it was recovered and identified as part of the same manuscript as the London portion.[57] Apparently encouraged by this discovery, the palaeographer E.A. Lowe attributed the Oxford leaf also to the same book.[58]

The library inscriptions on the remnants demonstrate that, more than a century before Elmham's description, their portions of the gospels and Acts had become separated from the rest of the Royal Bible. The early binding marks at its front demonstrate that, earlier still, the gospel portion began – or completely filled – one of the volumes, whereas the second volume of the *Biblia Gregoriana* began with Isaiah. By the time of the *Apologetic Petition* of 1604, Royal 1 E. vi had reached Lumley's collection and been catalogued as part of it.

Like the surviving parts of the original three Wearmouth–Jarrow pandects, the recognition of the various remnants of the Royal Bible, dispersed in different collections after subjection to spoliation and reuse in divers ways, has proceeded piecemeal. Likewise, the recognition of its identity as a Bible, moreover as one different from the *Biblia Gregoriana*, has taken some time. All these stages have paved the way to discerning its power as a witness to its venerable model.

The Royal Bible and the Worcester–Oxford Gospels as Reflections of the *Biblia Gregoriana*

Although not the Gregorian Bible, the Royal Bible nevertheless preserves many of the Late Antique features of that book. For example, the monumental *tituli* for frontispieces as well as the rubricated title at the end of Matthew's gospel (pl. VI; fig. 11.5) have a blend of monumental capitals most remarkable for an Anglo-Saxon manuscript.[59] The title, which concludes Matthew's gospel and introduces the next gospel as well, takes no notice of the intervening chapter list, which occupies fol. 29r. Laid out in six lines of large ornate script in metallic red pigment, the title states: 'The gospel according to Matthew ends. The gospel according to Mark begins auspiciously.' (*Evangelium secundum Mattheum explicit. Incipit evangelium secundum Marcum feliciter*). The wording harks back, as Patrick McGurk sensitively observed, to an early stage in the transmission of the Latin Bible.[60]

Both the same wording and a strikingly similar blend of monumental capitals occurs in the fragmentary Worcester–Oxford Gospels (fig. 11.6), now preserved in only four fragmentary leaves, with one in Oxford and the others at Worcester.[61] The leaves contain one leaf apiece from Matthew (28:5–20), Mark (10:26–42) and John (16:26–17:13), as well as one with the Mark chapter list. The master scribe of the Royal Bible also contributed to this manuscript (as its 'Scribe B'), at an earlier stage in his career. His work appears on the badly damaged Oxford leaf, which contains the remnants of John.

The titles at the end of Matthew in both manuscripts share the same layout in the right-hand column of a page, either on its own in the Worcester version or following the last tapered lines of the gospel text in the Royal Bible. In both cases, the letters stretch between alternate rulings and leave equivalent interlines between them. The two versions share many of the same letter forms. The principal difference between them consists of the greater use of flourishes in the Royal Bible.

In having only the chapter lists before the individual gospels and no prefaces for them or lists of the Hebrew names pertaining to them, the Royal Bible corresponds to few extant manuscripts. Among them is this gospel book,[62] which apparently shared the same exemplar.

A full collation of their texts, insofar as they jointly survive, shows that they both copied the same exemplar and not one another.[63] The portion of John on the Oxford leaf does not survive in the Royal Bible, whereas the surviving parts at Worcester are matched within Scribe I's realm in the Royal Bible. The very few variations between their versions are due principally to intervention by the two different scribes as they copied the same exemplar. The principal differences concern spellings and the contrast between a few abbreviations in the one manuscript where the other has the word written out in full. Such would most likely have derived from the individual scribe's choice as he went along whether to abbreviate or not. Those choices often depended upon how close the scribe was to the end of a line, where abbreviations cluster to save space. More significantly, however, the Worcester chapter list keeps to the chapter divisions, while the Royal version lapses from them. Moreover, the reading *para* for *parabola* in chapter 10 of the Worcester list probably derives from scribal omission; the reading in the Royal Bible could not have derived from it.

Their early Latin exemplar had certain variants pointing to Greek contacts. For example, the John chapter list in the Royal Bible has some readings (*ac dicit* for *Hac dicit* in chapter V; *praedicationem* for *per dedicationem* and *oblis* for *et houili* in chapter VIII) which match or resemble those apparently found only in sixth-century Italian witnesses: the *Codex Oxoniensis* and the *Codex Foro-Juliensis*.[64] The apparently unique addition of *dicens* after *paenitentiam* in Matthew 11:20 occurs in a verse which also contains an Old Latin reading (*eo quod non egerint* for the standard Vulgate *quia non egissent*).[65] The addition of *et recumberet* after *leprosi* in Matthew 26:6 apparently has no extant match.[66] The reading *crederitis* for *creditis* in John 4:48, which Wordsworth and White cited as unique among Latin manuscripts, corresponds to the reading πιστεύσητε found in many Greek codices.[67]

Similar relationships with early Latin witnesses closely linked with Greek pertain to the text of Acts on the Oxford leaf of the Royal Bible. For example, its apparently unique addition of *ubique* after *quaslibet* in 9:11 may represent an early reading, like *magna diana* (corrected from *de-*) *est* in 19:28, which corresponds only to the bilingual Greek–Latin/Latin–Greek witnesses in the *Codex Bezae* and the Laudian manuscript of Acts.[68] The former was written in the early fifth century, perhaps in the eastern Mediterranean, and the latter in the sixth or seventh century, probably in Sardinia. A similar unusual stature pertains to the corrected reading *magna est diana* in 19:34 of the Royal Bible, to which, alongside these two bilingual witnesses, are added Spanish witnesses such as the ninth-century La Cava Bible.[69]

From their shared exemplar both the Royal Bible and the Worcester–Oxford Gospels most probably derive the remarkably plentiful uncial intrusions in their minuscule text script. The Worcester–Oxford Gospels, made in the late eighth or early ninth century, perhaps at Saint Augustine's Abbey, offers the earliest evidence of the influence of the *Biblia Gregoriana* in England.

The Evidence of the Abbey Library Catalogue

The late fifteenth-century library catalogue of Saint Augustine's Abbey adds more information for the reconstruction of Gregory's Bible. The first two items in its list of books, at the top of fol. 1r, column a, are the 'First part' and 'Second part' of the 'Bible of Saint Gregory' (*Prima pars* and *Secunda pars* of the *biblie sancti Gregorii*).[70] Both items have the pressmark *Distinctio I Gradus I*, assigned to all the full Bibles in the abbey library. The opening words of the second leaf of this Bible are recorded as '*in doctrina* within the prologue' (*in prohemio in doctrina*) for volume I and as '*non feram*' for volume II. The opening page of the register at the front of the catalogue, which begins on a separately numbered fol. 1r and reports the location of various books, states that both volumes were kept in the vestry – a change from the library in Elmham's time.

The words *non feram* occur in Isaiah 1:13, not in Old Latin versions[71] but in the Vulgate version. The prologue mentioned by Elmham and the amount of Vulgate text of Isaiah to this point span respectively thirty-two long lines and nearly one and a half columns of lines laid out *per cola et commata* in the standard Vulgate edition.[72] Thus the first leaf of volume II would have contained – possibly spread out with headings, initials, display script and so on – rather less text than a standard full leaf of the Royal Bible, written in a formal hybrid minuscule. The latter usually corresponds to about five columns in the Vulgate edition, while its text of the *Novum opus* prologue, which occupies fifty-nine long lines in the edition, nearly fills an entire leaf.[73] The Isaiah leaf of the *Biblia Gregoriana* would have had about three-quarters or five-eighths of the standard amount in the Royal Bible, in effect slightly more than three columns out of four on a full leaf written by its main scribe.

The amount in the *Biblia Gregoriana* contrasts even more with the text span per leaf in Carolingian or later Bibles, written in compacted scripts. Samples among ninth-century Carolingian Bibles in their two extant formats demonstrate the range. In the large-format Moutier-Grandval Bible, made at the Abbey of Saint Martin at Tours probably *c.* 840 and laid out in double columns, the Isaiah preface occupies the recto of one leaf, but does not fill it, leaving the lower half of the second column blank; and the verso carries the text of Isaiah to 1:31, with an expansive opening title, initial and uncial display script at the top.[74] Among the medium-format Bibles made for Theodulf, bishop of Orléans (d. 821), and written in much smaller script in triple columns, one leaf in the London Theodulf Bible carries the Isaiah preface and text to 5:29.[75] The sample in the former Bible corresponds to more than four columns in the Vulgate edition and in the latter to more than eleven.

Instead, the amount in the *Biblia Gregoriana* corresponds very closely to Bibles written in larger, spacious scripts, notably uncial. The large-format Wearmouth–Jarrow Bibles, written in uncial and laid out *per cola et commata* in double columns, carry about the same amount as the sample for its volume II. For example, the Greenwell leaf from the Ceolfrid/Offa Bible corresponds to nearly four columns in the edition, while a leaf from the *Codex Amiatinus* usually spans about three and a half to four columns.

Such comparisons with surviving early Bibles make it clear that, although the fifteenth-century descriptions do not report its size, the Gregorian Bible must have been a large Bible with a stately script. Its main script was most probably uncial, as reflected in the Worcester–Oxford Gospels and the Royal Bible (figs 11.5–7). Its titles most probably contained impressive monumental capitals, as reflected in theirs (figs 11.5–6; pl. VI).

The testimony of these two witnesses also indicates, apart from lapses, that it was laid out for the most part *per cola et commata* and in *scriptura continua* ('uninterrupted writing' without spaces between words), as customary for Late Antique texts. Their other early symptoms include the tapered last columns (as in fig. 11.5), the form of citation marks at the left of lines (as in fig. 11.7), the differentiation between sizes of scripts for the prefatory and gospel texts, the austere restriction of gospel prefaces only to *Novum opus* and the chapter lists, the rarity of headings and the sparsity of numbering for the chapter lists and text divisions alike.[76] Both Anglo-Saxon manuscripts offer much evidence about the character of Gregory's Bible, but their own precarious survival as fragments means that their collective testimony pertains mainly to parts of its New Testament.

THE OLD TESTAMENT PORTION

The Old Testament filled all of the first volume and some of the second. Elmham and the catalogue reveal that volume I began with the Genesis chapter list and its second leaf started part-way through one of Jerome's prefaces. The phrase *in doctrina* does not occur in any of the usual Bible prefaces except for Jerome's 'Epistle to Paulinus the Priest' (*Epistola ad Paulinum presbyterum*, number LIII among his epistles), beginning 'Brother Ambrosius' (*Frater Ambrosius*).[77] This text uses the phrase twice (lines 57 and 74 in print, although for the second case some witnesses use *ad doctrinam*).[78] It also once (lines 122–3) has the phrase *in doctrinam* ('in regard to teaching *or* doctrine'), which could have been recorded as *in doctrina* ('in the capacity of teaching') by a cataloguer, especially if abbreviated with a suspended final -*m* in the manuscript; at least two manuscripts have *in doctrina* here as well.[79] As a result, we cannot be completely sure of the text span for the first leaf of volume I, so we must make do with the known span for volume II.

The epistle *Frater Ambrosius* appears as a Bible preface in many manuscripts, but the Gregorian Bible is potentially the earliest witness to such use. The epistle became the customary first text in biblical manuscripts, but its earliest surviving occurrences as such a preface date from the late eighth century, beginning with the Theodulf Bibles. However, the *Codex Amiatinus* has extracts from it, both in its Pentateuch diagram (fol. VIIv) and at its beginnings of each of the twelve Minor Prophets after the first, Hosea; it it also places these Books in the order prescribed by the epistle: Hosea, Joel, Amos, Obadiah, Jonah, Micah, Nahum, Habakkuk, Sephaniah, Haggai, Zechariah and Malachi.[80] The same approach to the Minor Prophets appears also in the seventh-century single-volume Léon Bible, now fragmentary and doubly or trebly palimpsested.[81] Such extracts show that Jerome's epistle was considered appropriate for Bibles already from an early period in divers regions. Given the survival pattern for the epistle as a Bible preface as such, Bonifatius Fischer thought that the *Biblia Gregoriana* would have been a ninth-century product, most probably yet another of the many Bibles produced at Tours under the Anglo-Saxon Alcuin (abbot from 796–804) and his successors.[82] As such, it would constitute 'yet another Turonian Bible' (*noch eine turonische Bibel*) to add to the known list.[83] The conjectured presence of this epistle as a preface, however, need not entail a Carolingian date, as the Carolingian versions could have copied earlier manuscripts in this respect as they did in many others.[84]

Similarly, the heading recorded by Elmham for the Genesis chapter list, *De Capitulis Libri Geneseos*, is very rare among extant manuscripts, both Vulgate and pre-Vulgate. It apparently has no exact parallel. The headings closest in form occur in one family of pre-Vulgate chapter lists, identified by Henri Quentin as [Group] I, Series Λ, *Forma* a.[85] It consists of eighty-two chapters and begins: 'Of the first day, on which light was created' (*De die primo in quo lux facta est*). To the family belong some ninth-century Carolingian Bibles and twelfth-century Bibles of the Alcuinian recension, which have the heading: 'The Chapters of the Book of Genesis begin' (*Incipiunt capitula libri geneseos*).

As for the second volume, among the reported variants of the opening title to Jerome's preface to Isaiah, the closest version by far to Elmham's account (*secundum volumen incipit a prologo beati Ieronymi super Ysaiam prophetam*) occurs in an early thirteenth-century glossed Bible from Christ Church, Canterbury, now in Paris. Partly hidden in the tightly bound book, its title reads: *[In]cipit prologus beati [Hie]ronimi presbyteri [super] ysiam prophetam.*[86] Perhaps this manuscript reflects the *Biblia Gregoriana* itself, like some other books from Canterbury.

THE NEW TESTAMENT AND ITS ACCOMPANIMENTS

Components of the New Testament portion can be discerned in the remnants of the Royal Bible and other progeny. They range from the prefatory texts, through the manner of opening major books, to a formidable cycle of illustrations.

THE EUSEBIAN CANON ARCADES

Important signs appear in the canon arcades of the Royal Bible. They present the Eusebian tables of concordances of gospel passages within five majestic full-page arcades.[87] The large format enables the long lists of numerals of the full set of ten canons to fit on to a few pages, while in a medium-format Latin gospel book they take twelve or seventeen, in the standard longer or shorter versions. The layout here resembles other Bibles of the early medieval period, especially the *Codex Amiatinus*[88] and the two earliest Tours Bibles, made during the time of Alcuin and preserved at Sankt Gallen and Monza.[89] The former uses seven pages and much plainer arcades, while the latter pair uses four pages of decorated arcades. All their frameworks combine the *M*-type of multiple arches, in two major bays, with an infrastructure of subsidiary arcades also of *m*-type, in two or more bays. The *Mm*-type contrasts with the more customary *Nm*-type used, for example, in the later Tours Bibles as well as many gospel books, with a single major arch enclosing multiple subsidiary arcades.[90] Similar combinations of *M*- and *m*-types appear in two sixth-century Greek manuscripts in medium format: a fragment of canon tables in London and a gospel book in Vienna, of which the former was probably made in Constantinople and the latter in Ravenna.[91]

The *Mm*-type evidently represents an early form, whose application in large-format Bibles seems traceable through the Royal Bible back to an earlier stage than the *Codex Amiatinus* and the earliest Tours Bibles. In those Northumbrian and Turonian cases, it appears without much variation in each series. In the Royal Bible, however, not only does the series exhibit extensive variations, but also the variations closely fit the structures and lengths of the different canons, so as to establish a hierarchical series of portals toward the gospels. The first arcade (fig. 11.3) represents an interlaced variation, apparently unique, of the *M*-type and an unusual *N*-type with flanks. The last arcade presents a highly unusual modification of the *Mm*-type, with an atrophied middle pillar, apparently paralleled only in a ninth-century Greek gospel book in Athos.[92] In its varied forms, the extraordinary set of canon arcades in the Royal Bible evidently points to an exceptional early model with Greek contacts.

The decoration of the arcades in the Royal Bible also includes some Late Antique motifs unusual for Anglo-Saxon manuscripts, although its rendition of the motifs accords with ninth-century Anglo-Saxon fashion, as seen in royal and other imposing jewellery.[93] Notable are the frontal beasts' masks and the hybrid creatures whose tongues or tails extend as scrolling stems, which in turn have animal heads for buds or fruits. Such creatures abound in mediterranean ornament, ranging from sculptures to mosaics.[94]

THE FRONTISPIECE ILLUSTRATIONS

The lost illustrations of both the Royal Bible and its model must have closely resembled such rare images as the four full-page New Testament illustrations of uncertain early date on a pair of leaves now bound at the end of the tenth-century Armenian Etchmiadzin Gospels.[95] Now lacking the text which originally accompanied them, the illustrations apparently emanated from the Armenian sphere before the Arab invasion of 640. They depict the Annunciation to Zacharias, the Annunciation to the Virgin Mary, the Adoration of the Magi and the Baptism of Christ (fig. 11.14). The text of the Mark *titulus* in the Royal Bible implies a scene in the same tradition as its Baptism illustration, with opened heavens, descending dove and paternal blessing. Similarly, features of its Annunciation to Zacharias match the Luke *titulus* (pl. VI). The rest of the set could indicate which images accompanied the lost Matthew and John *tituli*, as well as what elements they may have possessed in their rendition. These rare survivors afford a glimpse of some frontispieces which apparently once graced our Bibles.

THE GOSPEL INITIAL PAGES

So, too, the Luke arcade in the Royal Bible (fig. 11.4) owes much to monumental mediterranean splendour. At one and the same time, the image in the book functions as a portal and leads the beholder to the gospel text within; and the gospel text leads the contemplator to Christ in heaven. The ensemble is richly resonant, resembling the mosaic-filled apse of a magnificent Italo-Byzantine church, notably Sant'Apollinare in Classe outside Ravenna, consecrated by Archbishop Maximian in 549 (fig. 11.12).[96] Across the top of its triumphal arch mosaic, evangelist symbols emerge in pairs from clouds at either side of the central *imago clipeata* of Christ, robed in imperial purple. The luxurious and stately arcade in the Royal Bible evokes such architectural structures, illuminated with polychrome ornamental and figural motifs, inlaid with porphyry, steeped with triumphal imagery and centred upon the contents and message of the gospel.

11.12. Ravenna, Sant'Apollinare in Classe: apse. (Instituto Fotografico Editoriale Antella, Florence)

11.13. Cambridge University Library, MS Ll. 1. 10 (Book of Cerne), fol. 21v: evangelist Luke and his symbol the bull. (Syndic of Cambridge University Library)

Although the Royal Bible retains only its opening page for Luke, the other members of its original gospel set are echoed in the rather clumsy copies in the nearly contemporary Book of Cerne, made in Mercia.[97] This medium-format prayerbook, intended for private devotional practice, includes a series of extracts from the passion narrative of each gospel.

The frontispiece to its extracts from Luke on fol. 21v (fig. 11.13) manifestly borrows the arcade, figures and lettering of the Royal Bible, albeit with some maladjustments. Not only does it forego the sumptuous purple background and simplify both the arcade and the rendering of the figures, but also it transforms the human figure into the evangelist Luke – with poised pen and book – whom it emphatically identifies by inscription. The awkward transition between the forequarters and hindquarters of the bull readily attests to its adaptation from part-length models. Many of the bull's features, such as the hairs at the top of the head, the improperly foreshortened (or shrivelled) foreleg at the right and the eye peculiarly tilted at the side of the head, exactly match those of the bull in the Royal Bible. These correspondences point to the Royal Bible in particular – or its identical twin – as the model.

The three other frontispieces for gospel extracts in the Book of Cerne, which occupy fols 2v, 12v and 31v, presumably also preserve awkward traces of the Late Antique model superbly emulated in the Royal Bible. They depict Matthew and his angel, Mark and his bull and John and his eagle.[98] They help to show how that model influenced works in various centres, directly or indirectly, in early Anglo-Saxon England.

THE INTRA-TEXTUAL ILLUSTRATIONS IN THE GOSPELS AND OTHER BOOKS OF THE BIBLE

Several witnesses imply that the Gregorian Bible possessed a very large cycle of intra-textual illustrations, either full page or part page. The sources include the

Royal Bible and other illustrated manuscripts from or perhaps from Canterbury, with Late Antique symptoms.

THE ROYAL BIBLE AND THE GETTY GOSPEL LECTIONARY OF C. 1000

From the surviving remains of the Royal Bible, we know that the gospel portion of the book alone had a very large amount of illustrations, occupying at least seventeen or eighteen leaves (figs 11.1–2, 4). The principal evidence comprises the cutting marks, traces of former stubs and offsets of pigment left by lost leaves, as well as their locations within the manuscript.[99] Some of these features attest to losses where there are no textual gaps. For some of them, the offsets of pigment or titles part-way down a page and/or the directions of the cutting marks imply illustrations which formerly faced certain pages, as with fols 7r and 10v. Sometimes, however, the evidence is insufficient to indicate which side (or page) of the lost leaf carried illustrations. Moreover, the leaves perhaps had illustrations on both sides, so that it is necessary to consider the text upon the entire opening at the point of loss. It is also uncertain whether every illustrated page contained a single illustration or a set of illustrations, and the practice may have varied between pages.

Candidates for their subjects or groups of subjects can be narrowed down. To judge by its textual location, the illustration(s) facing fol. 7r probably depicted the Virgin and Child, perhaps with an Adoration of the Magi; the pattern of offsets suggests a composition with a haloed central figure. The second illustrated leaf in Matthew perhaps depicted the Sermon on the Mount, Healing the Leper, Centurion's Servant, Peter's Brother, Casting out Demons or a combination of these episodes (facing fol. 10v). Luke and John had at least one illustrated leaf each. The former perhaps depicted the Miraculous Draught of Fishes, the Calling of the Apostles and/or Healing the Leper (facing fol. 49r); and the latter perhaps Healing the Man Born Blind (facing fol. 76r). Others may have been lost from within the last third of John which no longer survives. Mark's gospel had at least four illustrated leaves and perhaps a fifth (between fols 37 and 38). Its first perhaps depicted the Sermon on the Mount and/or Legion and the Gaderene Swine (facing fol. 33r); the second perhaps the Feeding of the Five Thousand, Healing the Blind Man at Bethesda and/or Teaching (facing fol. 35v); the penultimate perhaps Jesus and the Scribes, the Fruits of the Vineyard, and/or the Tribute Money (facing fol. 38v); and the last perhaps the Crucifixion, Deposition, Resurrection, Sending the Apostles and/or the Ascension (before or after the lost last leaf of text, which followed fol. 41).[100]

11.14. Erevan, Matenadaran MS 2374 (Etchmadzin Gospels), fol. 229v: baptism of Christ (after Der Nersessian). (Budny)

Some conjectured subjects are rare, as with the miracle of the Gadarene Swine. This episode is depicted, with Late Antique symptoms (fig. 11.15), in a fragmentary Anglo-Saxon gospel lectionary made *c.* 1000, perhaps at Canterbury to judge by its script.[101] Its two surviving leaves carry the text of Matthew 8:23–8 on one page and three full-page illustrations on the others. Unusually, the latter serve as full-page illustrations interleaved within the text, like those lost from the Royal Bible. Moreover, they similarly illustrate unusual scenes, one or more of which the Royal Bible probably shared. They respectively depict Christ healing the two Demoniacs at Gerasa and the Gadarene Swine (fol. 1v); Christ sitting on a mound, flanked by three figures and probably teaching (fol. 2r); and Christ instructing Peter on the tribute money and Peter fishing (fol. 2v). Both the imagery and the rendering point to Early Christian models.

The scale of illustration discernible in the surviving portions of the Royal Bible far exceeds the standards of any early medieval competitor among Bibles. Its scale may well have extended to the rest of the book.

Early Christian Cycles in Greek Manuscripts

It seems likely that other major Books of the Bible were treated similarly, so that they would have had many illustrations within the text as well as the frontispieces accompanied by full-page inscriptions on purple leaves. To gauge the extent, we must refer to Late Antique and related manuscripts with very large cycles. Examples include the Vienna Genesis and the Cotton Genesis, both in Greek.[102] Originally they contained some 192 and 330 illustrations respectively – the former on purple leaves.

The Illustrated Old English Hexateuch of Saint Augustine's Abbey

Closer to home is the illustrated eleventh-century Old English Hexateuch, made at Saint Augustine's Abbey.[103] Containing a vernacular version of parts of the first six books of the Old Testament, it has nearly four hundred illustrations, with blanks left for many more. Some illustrations, as with the Building of Babel on fol. 19r, notably exhibit Late Antique features.[104]

In this manuscript, some illustrations were made by the same artist who added a Mark evangelist portrait to fol. 30v of the Royal Bible, on the verso of the purple leaf with the Mark inscription.[105] The portrait was painted upon the leaf after it – along with others – had been completely severed from its place in a cutting operation for intended despoliation, which left a stub; and after it had been recovered and resewn to that stub. The sequence of events is established by the traces of pigment belonging to the portrait which overlie part of the stitching. Perhaps the portrait was entered as a trial upon an available purple expanse.

11.15. Los Angeles, The J. Paul Getty Museum, Getty MS 9 (Getty Gospel Lectionary), fol. 1v: the Gadarene Swine. (J. Paul Getty Museum)

This artist was responsible, in part or in whole, for illustrations on fols 68v–69v, 113v and 142r in the Old English Hexateuch.[106] They prove that at least one of the makers of that manuscript had direct access to the Royal Bible. Such links could indicate that at least parts of the Old Testament cycle in the Hexateuch derived, directly or indirectly, from the *Biblia Gregoriana* of the abbey.

The Eadwine Psalter of Christ Church, Canterbury

Further traces of that Bible probably reside in the four illustrated leaves detached from the Eadwine Psalter, made at Christ Church Cathedral Priory in the mid-twelfth century, perhaps *c.* 1147.[107] These leaves have more biblical scenes, both Old and New Testament, than any surviving Ottonian manuscript.

Each leaf contains multiple scenes within the panels of a full-page, grid-like, upright rectangular frame. Usually, apart from one verso largely devoted to the Tree of Jesse, each side or page contains twelve rectangular compartments in four rows of three across. Often the compartments subdivide horizontally into two or even three tiers, sometimes with further vertical subdivisions, giving scope for very many scenes per page. They include such gospel scenes as the Adoration of the Magi, Healing the Leper, Stilling the Storm, Curing the Demoniac, Disputing with the Pharisees, Feeding the Five Thousand, Walking on Water, Judas receiving the Silver, the Last Supper, Christ in the Hall of Judgement, the Mocking and Scourging of Christ and other Passion scenes. The gospel illustrations alone amount to about 150 scenes. The Old Testament illustrations, which occupy most of one leaf, include scenes devoted to Moses, Joshua, Saul and David, ranging from Pharoah Enthroned to David perhaps Entering Jerusalem.

The scale of illustration on the four leaves could well reflect the illustrious Gregorian Bible. *Mutatis mutandis*, despite their differences in scale and in style, they probably afford a fair indication of the lost gospel illustations both in that Bible and in the Royal Bible. Further work may reveal traces in other manuscripts, too, from Canterbury and elsewhere, now that the model has been identified.[108]

The Parallel Case of the Gospels of Saint Augustine of Canterbury

The repeated consultation over the centuries of an Early Christian manuscript at Canterbury by artists seeking models and inspiration for their own works has an important parallel in the sixth-century Gospels of Saint Augustine, another major treasure of Saint Augustine's Abbey (pls IV–V). This book appears to have been used repeatedly during the medieval period as a source of pictorial models executed in divers media. Among them are the eleventh-century Bayeux Tapestry, perhaps designed at the abbey; some late Romanesque or early Gothic thirteenth-century stained-glass windows at Christ Church Cathedral; and various manuscript illuminations from the abbey and Christ Church alike.[109]

Conclusion: The Import and Impact of the Gregorian Bible

The *Biblia Gregoriana* was evidently a major source of inspiration and subject of veneration at medieval Canterbury. The various reports concerning it and its divers progeny among surviving books enable us to glimpse its stature as a large-format two-volume Latin Bible, in which the text was predominantly Vulgate, with prefatory material. It was written probably in uncial. It was very extensively illustrated and provided with resplendent purple leaves at the beginning of some books. It apparently had a superb and unusual set of Eusebian canon arcades. All its elements are compatible with what can be surmised of luxurious Bible manuscripts in the Late Antique period. Gregory might well have sent, or Augustine have obtained, such a Bible for the new English church.

The medieval tradition might well be correct. The Worcester–Oxford Gospels (fig. 11.6) show that it was in England and being used as a model already in the late eighth or early ninth century; it could have been there long before.

Parts of its text, titles and other features are preserved in both the Worcester–Oxford Gospels and the Royal Bible (pl. VI; figs 11.3–7). Both these manuscripts shared the same imposing early Latin exemplar, which had numerous elements reflecting Greek contacts. Those elements range from unusual variant readings to the exceptional canon arcades. Although the text of the Royal Bible in both Acts and the gospels exhibits marked Insular intrusions (notably in spelling), which the Gregorian Bible would not have contained, many of its variants not attributable to Insular intervention could derive from it. Given the varying patterns of Latin Bible texts in sixth-century manuscripts, it is by no means certain that Gregory's Bible would have had to be pure Vulgate.

Both the Ravennate character of the extant illustrations in the Royal Bible (fig. 11.4) and the eastern mediterranean elements in illustrations of related manuscripts indicate that the decoration in that Bible had a distinct Greek accent. After all, Gregory the Great had important contacts with Contantinople, notably through his period there as papal apocrisarius and his correspondence with the Byzantine court as Pope.[110] Moreover, many works from sixth-century Italy, not least Ravenna, exhibit marked Byzantine features; some may have been made by Byzantine artists.[111]

Given Gregory's practical views on the proper methods of converting and instructing the English by degrees, and given his fond regard for the English mission, which he himself had considered undertaking, Gregory may indeed have seen fit to send in support of that mission a Bible fit for a king, richly decked with purple leaves and illustrations.[112] To Theodolinda, queen of the Lombards, Gregory presented in 603 a magnificent gospel book with a richly bejewelled gold cover, which survives at Monza.[113] A superb Gregorian Bible for the English mission would have formed a worthy accompaniment to 'the silver cross and the image [*imaginem*] of the Lord Saviour painted upon a panel [*in tabula depictam*]' which, as Bede recorded, Augustine and his comrades carried when they went to meet Æthelberht I, king of Kent (d. 616), on the fateful day when the king gave them 'a dwelling in the city of Canterbury ... the chief city of all his dominions'.[114]

In reporting that Gregory also sent 'many books' along with all the other requisites 'for the worship and service of the Church',[115] Bede did not feel the need to identify them. In this respect, he perhaps followed his acknowledged direct source for Canterbury matters, his friend Albinus, eighth abbot of Saint Augustine's (708–32). Other Anglo-Saxon sources later than Bede specify some books – Gregory's 'Rule of the Pastor' (*Regula Pastoralis*) and his antiphonary and missal – sent by Gregory with or to Augustine,[116] but none mentions a Bible. Presumably it was too obvious.

The first surviving mention of the *Biblia Gregoriana* appears in the thirteenth-century chronicle of the abbey by Thomas Sprott, who apparently flourished *c.* 1270. In the late fourteenth century, the monk William Thorne copied Sprott's report almost verbatim in his own chronicle of the abbey, which extends to the year 1397. Commenting upon relics given by Augustine to his monastery, Sprott observed that 'many remain up to now' (*multa manent usque ad huc*). He enumerated some of them (such as Aaron's rod and the Virgin's hair) and added:

habemus eciam bibliam sancti Gregorii et evangelia eiusdam et eciam quasdam capas veteres que ad huc vocantur Gregoriane que omnia idem Gregorius misit beato Augustino una cum pallio per Laurentium presbyterium et Petrum monachum huius monasterii primum Abbatem.

(We also have the Bible of Saint Gregory and the gospel book of the same and certain old copes, which to this day are called Gregory's, all of which the same Gregory sent to the blessed Augustine, together with the pallium, via Laurence the priest and Peter the monk, the first abbot of this monastery).[117]

In the early fifteenth century, Thomas of Elmham described a larger set of Gregorian books, for which he also provided an illustration on the high altar of the abbey church (figs 11.9–10). The set included the *Biblia Gregoriana* and two gospel books. It apparently included not only some books wrongly reattributed to so early an origin, as must have been the case with the Vespasian Psalter (pls VII–VIII; figs 13.13–14) and was apparently the case with the Cambridge–London Gospels (fig. 11.1), but also some items newly rediscovered. Such items perhaps came from some other centre(s) in response to the search by the abbey to extend its group of Gregorian relics. Not all the set, however, necessarily comprised posthumous accretions to the sainted founder of the monastery and his papal patron. This distinction is

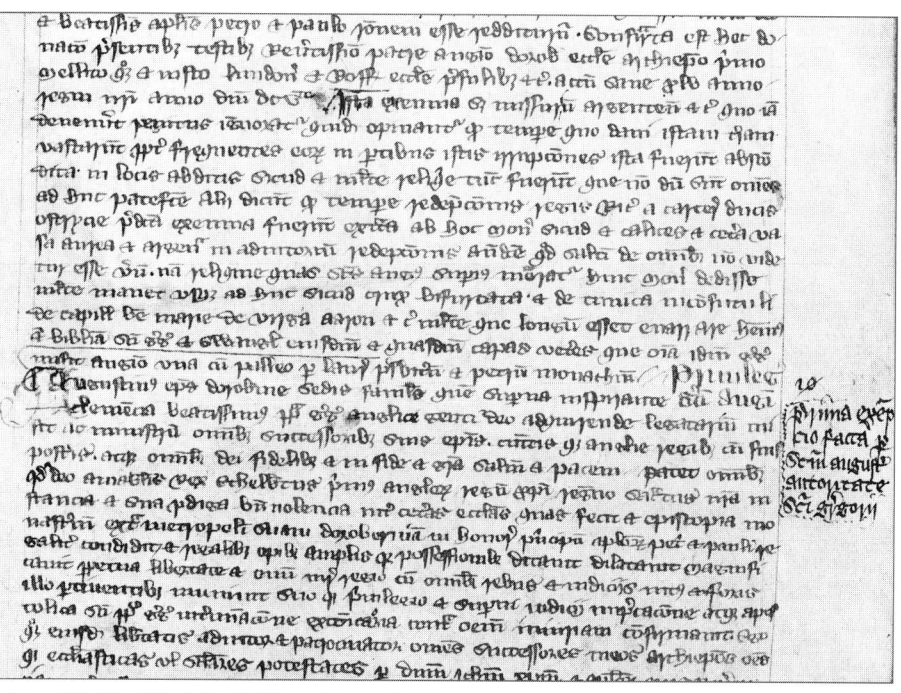

11.16. *CCCC, MS 189 (William Thorne's* Chronicle of Saint Augustine's Abbey*), fol. 47r: passage reporting the* Biblia Gregoriana, *highlighted by Matthew Parker's underlining and* indicatorium *in the margin. (Budny; The Master and Fellows of Corpus Christi College, Cambridge)*

demonstrated by the apparent presence in the list of the sixth-century Gospels of Saint Augustine of Canterbury and by the *Biblia Gregoriana*, insofar as it can be conjured back from the past through its traces.

The copy of Thorne's chronicle owned by Archbishop Matthew Parker contains Parker's own drawing of a hand – a *maniculum* or *indicatorium* – pointing to this very passage, which he also underlined in the same red crayon (fig. 11.16).[118] These marks show the first Elizabethan archbishop of Canterbury taking note of a major book relic of his earliest predecessor in office. This record is poignant, given Parker's major rôle in the early modern recovery of medieval English sources, not least to show the independence of the English church throughout its history. It is poignant also that the very same period of upheaval and reformation in English religious life and culture proved decisive in driving Gregory's Bible to destruction, or at least underground for safety.

The fate of the Royal Bible seems also ironic. Its emulation of the *Biblia Gregoriana* might go far to account for its dismemberment at the abbey which made it. Perhaps it received such treatment precisely because it was not that Bible, alongside which it could have come to be seen as superfluous, inferior and expendable, despite its magnificent materials and expert skill. Once the taste for the distinctive ninth-century Anglo-Saxon script and ornament had passed out of fashion, the Royal Bible could have offered no match for the Bible venerated as Gregory's gift and Augustine's relic.

This very fact perhaps saved the Royal Bible – relegated in pieces to the library cupboards – from total destruction, whereas the treasured *Biblia Gregoriana* has disappeared. All the same, we might be grateful for the small mercies, which have preserved some potent, majestic and tantalising traces of that superlative monument of Gregory's mission. Perhaps one day it will return to our midst.[119]

NOTES

1. The history of the abbey is reported in W. Thorne, *De Rebus Gestis Abbatum S. Augustini Cantuariae*, ed. R. Twysden, *Historiae Anglicanae Scriptores X* (London, 1652), cols 1788–91, trans. A.H. Davis, *William Thorne's Chronicle of Saint Augustine's Abbey, Canterbury, now Rendered into English* (Oxford, 1934); *Historia Monasterii S. Augustini Cantuariensis by Thomas of Elmham, Formerly Monk and Treasurer of that Foundation*, ed. C. Hardwick (London, 1858); N. Brooks, *The Early History of the Church of Canterbury: Christ Church from 597 to 1066* (Leicester, 1984); R. Emms, 'The Historical Traditions of St Augustine's Abbey, Canterbury', in *Canterbury and the Norman Conquest*, eds R. Eales and R. Sharpe (London, 1995), pp. 159–68; *Charters of St Augustine's Abbey, Canterbury, and Minster-in-Thanet*, ed. S.E. Kelly (Oxford, 1995); *English Heritage Book of St Augustine's Abbey, Canterbury*, ed. R. Gem (London, 1997); and Richard Emms, ch. 16 below.

2. BL, Royal MS 1 E. vi + Canterbury, Cathedral Library and Archives, Add. MS 16 + BodL, MS Lat. Bibl. b. 2 (P). The *membra disiecta* are listed as *CLA*, II, nos 212 + 244; and Supplement, p. 5 and no. 214. Their character as a Bible was identified by P. McGurk, 'An Anglo-Saxon Bible Fragment of the Late Eighth Century: Royal 1 E. VI', *Journal of the Warburg and Courtauld Institutes*, 25 (1962), 18–34. A detailed examination of the manuscript as a whole appears in M.O. Budny, 'British Library Manuscript Royal 1 E. VI: The Anatomy of an Anglo-Saxon Bible Fragment' (unpublished Ph.D. thesis, University of London, 1984). Brief accounts appear, for example, in J.J.G. Alexander, *Insular Manuscripts, 6th to the 9th Century* (London, 1978), no. 32; *The Making of England: Anglo-Saxon Art and Culture*, eds L. Webster and J. Backhouse (London, 1991), no. 171; S. Heslop and J. Mitchell, 'The Arts and Learning', in Gem, *St Augustine's Abbey*, pp. 67–89, at pp. 72–5; and Richard Marsden, ch. 12 below.

3. The gaps occur for Matthew 1:1–18; Mark 1:1–3; Mark 3:52–5:15; Mark 15:32–16:20; Luke 1:1 (*multi*) to 1:4; and John 1:1–5. Given the layout for surviving parts, the losses amount to two leaves apiece at the beginnings of Matthew, Mark and John; and one leaf apiece in the midst and at the end of Mark.

4. The standard edition is *Biblia Sacra iuxta Vulgatam versionem*, eds R. Weber, B. Fischer, J. Gribomont et al., 2nd edn, 2 vols (Stuttgart, 1975).

5. F. Stegmüller, *Repertorium Biblicum Medii Aevi* (Madrid, 1940–80), I: *Initia Biblica. Apocrypha. Prologi*, no. 595. The text of the prologue is printed, for example, in Weber, *Biblia Sacra*, II, pp. 1515–16. Its appearance in the Royal Bible is reproduced in Budny, 'Anatomy', pls 6–7.

6. The genre is surveyed in C. Nordenfalk, *Die Bucherornamentik der Spätantike*, I: *Die spätantiken Kanontafeln* (Göteborg, 1938). An important variant is assessed in *idem*, 'The Apostolic Canon Tables', *Gazette des Beaux-Arts*, series 6, 62 (1963), 17–34. The creative deployment in the Royal Bible of the genre and that variant is assessed in Budny, 'Anatomy', pp. 458–97, 547–633.

7. The first arcade is reproduced in colour in R. Gameson, *Saint Augustine of Canterbury* (Canterbury, 1997), back cover. The second two arcades are reproduced in colour in Budny, 'Anatomy', pl. 23, with all five reproduced in monochrome in pls 1–5.

8. D. De Bruyne, 'Notes sur la Bible de Tours au IXe', *Göttingische gelehrte Anzeigen*, 93 (1931), 352–9, at p. 355; and P. McGurk, *Latin Gospel Books from A.D. 400 to A.D. 800* (Paris, 1962), pp. 26–7.

9. BL, Cotton MS Vespasian A. i. Alexander, *Insular Manuscripts*, no. 29; Webster and Backhouse, *Making of England*, no. 153 and Richard Gameson, ch. 13 below; facsimile in: D.H. Wright, *The Vespasian Psalter: British Museum Cotton Vespasian A. I*. EEMF, 14 (Copenhagen, 1967).

10. The language is assessed, for example, in A. Campbell, 'The Glosses', in Wright, *Vespasian Psalter*, pp. 81–92; C.J.E. Ball, 'The Language of the Vespasian Psalter Gloss: Two Caveats', *Review of English Studies*, n. s. 21 (1970), 462–5; and P. Pulsiano, 'The Originality of the Old English Gloss of the *Vespasian Psalter* and its Relation to the Gloss of the *Junius Psalter*', *ASE*, 25 (1996), 37–62. The text is printed in *The Vespasian Psalter*, ed. S.M. Kuhn (Ann Arbor, 1965). The hand of the gloss is identified in Budny, 'Anatomy', pp. 777–80.

11. This tradition is surveyed, for example, in W. Wattenbach, *Das Schriftwesen im Mittelalter*, 3rd edn (Graz, 1958), pp. 248–51; and H. Roosen-Runge, *Farbgebung und Technik frühmittelalterlicher Buchmalerei. Studien zu den Traktaten 'Mappae Clavicula' und 'Heraclius'*, 2 vols (Berlin, 1967), II, pp. 25–31, 34–7.

12. Vienna, Österreichische Nationalbibliothek, Cod. theol. gr. 31; Rossano, Biblioteca Arcivescovile, s.n.; and BnF, MS suppl. gr. 1286. These manuscripts are *Age of Spirituality: Late Antique and Early Christian Art, Third to Seventh Century*, ed. K. Weitzmann (New York, 1977), nos 410, 442–3. They are reproduced in facsimile in H. Gerstinger, *Die Wiener Genesis. Farblichtdruckfaksimile der greichischen Bilderbibel aus dem 6. Jahrhundert n. Chr. Cod. Vindob. theol. graec. 31* (Vienna, 1931); A. Muñoz, *Il codice purpureo di Rossano e il frammento Sinopense* (Rome, 1907); and A. Grabar, *Les Peintures de l'Evangéliare de Sinope (Bibliothèque nationale, Suppl. gr. 1286) reproduites en fac-similé* (Paris, 1948).

13. Anglo-Saxon cases with purple-painted leaves or part leaves include Alexander, *Insular Manuscripts*, nos 7, 21, 66; and Elżbieta Temple, *Anglo-Saxon Manuscripts, 900–1066* (London, 1976), nos 19.ii, 56; her no. 55 with a purple-dyed leaf constitutes the Royal Bible (the added illustration on fol. 30v).

14. Thus they belong to the corpus reported by E.C. Teviotdale, 'Latin Verse Inscriptions in Anglo-Saxon Art', *Gesta*, 35:2 (1996), 99–110, with the *tituli* in the Royal Bible and some major relatives cited in n. 3 on p. 107.

15. The probable reconstruction and meaning of this inscription are assessed in

Budny, 'Anatomy', pp. 511–16, 518–22, 528–35.

16. Nancy, Cathédrale, Trésor, s.n., fol. 3v; and Bamberg, Staatliche Bibliothek, Misc. MS Bibl. 1, fol. 339v: reproduced in colour in J. Hubert, J. Porcher and W.F. Volbach, *Europe in the Dark Ages* (London, 1969), figs 120–1. They and related gospel frontispieces are considered, for example, by H.L. Kessler, *The Illustrated Bibles from Tours* (Princeton, 1977), pp. 36–58. Their relation to the one lost from the Royal Bible is evaluated in Budny, 'Anatomy', pp. 689–702.

17. The traces are reproduced in Budny, 'Anatomy', pls 8, 17, 20–1, 46; reconstructed in figs 4–7, 10b; and analysed on pp. 315–38, 442–5, 518, 704–6, 714–19.

18. J.O. Westwood, *Palaeographia Sacra Pictoria* (London, 1843–5), p. 1 accompanying pl. 21; and idem, *Fac-Similes of the Miniatures and Ornaments of Anglo-Saxon and Irish Manuscripts* (London, 1868), p. 40.

19. The identity of this figure, sometimes regarded as the evangelist, is assessed in Budny, 'Anatomy', pp. 432–42.

20. Many of these images are reproduced among the plates in Alexander, *Insular Manuscripts*; and Temple, *Anglo-Saxon Manuscripts*.

21. K. Weitzmann, *The Monastery of Saint Catherine at Mount Sinai: The Icons*, I: *From the Sixth to the Tenth Century* (Princeton, 1976), no. B.1 and pls. I–II.

22. Brussels, Bibliothèque Albert 1er, MS 18723, fol. 16v. W. Braunfels, *Die Welt der Karolinger und ihre Kunst* (Munich, 1968), p. 150 and pl. 175.

23. Vatican, Cortile della Pigna; L. Vogel, *The Column of Antoninus Pius* (Cambridge, Mass., 1973), pp. 36–7 and pls 3–6.

24. Vienna, Österreichische Nationalbibliothek, Cod. med. gr. 1, fol. 483v; K. Weitzmann, *Late Antique and Early Christian Book Illumination* (New York, 1977), pl. 20; see also pls 15–19. Facsimile in H. Gerstinger, *Dioscurides, Codex Vindobonensis Med. Gr. I der Österreichischen Nationalbibliothek*. Codices selecti, 12 (Graz, 1970).

25. *A Petition Apologeticall, presented to the Kinges most excellent Maiesty by the Lay Catholikes of England in Iuly last: The Coppie of the Banished Briestes Letter to the Lordes of his Maiesties . . . Privie Councell* [ed. J. Lecey] ('Doway', recte England, 1604), p. 17 (emphasis his). This text is reprinted in M. Sutcliffe, *A Briefe Examination, of A Certaine Peremptorie menacing and disleal petition presented, as is pretended, to the Kings most excellent Maiestie, By certaine Laye Papistes, calling themselves, the Lay Catholikes of England, and now lately Printed, and diuulged by a busie compagnion, called John Lecey* (London, 1606), p. 87 (emphasis his). It is also reprinted, but with modernised spelling and punctuation, in H. Wanley, *Librorum Vett. Septentrionalium, qui in Angliæ Biblioth. extant, Catalogum Historico-Criticus; nec non multorum* Vett. *Codd. Septentrionalium alibi extantium notitiam, cum totius operis sex Indicibus*: vol. II of G. Hickes, *Antiquæ Literaturæ Septentrionalis*, 2 vols (Oxford, 1705), p. 173; Westwood, *Palaeographia Sacra Pictoria*, p. 4 accompanying pl. 21; and idem, *Fac-Similes*, p. 40.

26. Sutcliffe, *Brief Examination*, p. 87, nn. 4–5.

27. Wanley, *Librorum Vett. Septentrionalium*, p. 4.

28. Cases are reported in A.G. Watson, 'Thomas Allen of Oxford and his Manuscripts', in *Medieval Scribes, Manuscripts & Libraries: Essays Presented to N.R. Ker*, eds M.B. Parkes and A.G. Watson (London, 1978), pp. 279–314; and further below.

29. Florence, Biblioteca Medicea Laurenziana, MS Amiatino I. D.H. Wright, 'Some Notes

on English Uncial', *Traditio*, 47 (1961), 441–56, at pp. 443–4; R.L.S. Bruce-Mitford, 'The Art of the Codex Amiatinus (Jarrow Lecture 1967)', *JBAA*, 3rd series 32 (1969), 1–25; Alexander, *Insular Manuscripts*, no. 7; K. Corsano, 'The First Quire of the Codex Amiatinus and the *Institutiones* of Cassiodorus', *Scriptorium*, 41 (1987), 3–34; R. Marsden, *The Text of the Old Testament in Anglo-Saxon England* (Cambridge, 1995), pp. 76–201; and P. Meyvaert, 'Bede, Cassiodorus, and the Codex Amiatinus', *Speculum*, 74 (1996), 827–83.

30. Both works are printed in *Venerabilis Baedae Opera Historica*, ed. C. Plummer, 2 vols (Oxford, 1896), I, pp. 364–87, 388–404. Their sequence of composition and the authorship of the anonymous work, perhaps an earlier version by Bede, are examined in J. McClure, 'Bede and the Life of Ceolfrid', *Peritia*, 3 (1984), 71–84; and J.M. Wallace-Hadrill, *Bede's Eccesiastical History of the English People: A Historical Commentary* (Oxford, 1988), p. 239.

31. Ch. 20 of the anonymous work and ch. 15 of Bede's acknowledged work. They are printed respectively in Plummer, *Baedae Opera Historica*, I, pp. 395, 379–80; and translated, for example, in Marsden, *Old Testament*, p. 86, nn. 51–2.

32. BL, Add. MSS 37777 (Greenwell leaf) + 45025 (Middleton leaves); and Loan MS 81 (Bankes leaf), owned by the National Trust, Kingston Lacy, Dorset. The find-places and piecemeal discovery of these fragments, reused as covers for documents of widely different dates, are reported in Webster and Backhouse, *Making of England*, nos 87a–c; and Marsden, *Old Testament*, pp. 43–4, 90–8, 107, 114, 123–9, 187, 190–201. The related provenance of the fragments and the shared character of their text, script, layout and additions imply that they all came from the same manuscript (at least the Greenwell and Middleton leaves) or group of Ceolfrith's manuscripts.

33. The evidence for this identification is reported in *Early Worcester MSS: Fragments of Four Books and a Charter of the Eighth Century belonging to Worcester Cathedral*, ed. C.H. Turner (Oxford, 1916), Appendices I–II, pp. xli–li; N.R. Ker, *Catalogue of Manuscripts Containing Anglo-Saxon* (Oxford, 1957), no. 29; idem, 'Hemming's Cartulary: A Description of the Two Worcester Cartularies in Cotton Tiberius A. XIII', in idem, *Books, Collectors and Libraries*, ed. A.G. Watson (London, 1985), pp. 31–59; and M. Budny, *Insular, Anglo-Saxon, and Early Anglo-Norman Manuscript Art at Corpus Christi College, Cambridge: An Illustrated Catalogue*, 2 vols (Kalamazoo, 1997), no. 41.

34. Cambridge, Trinity Hall, MS 1. M.R. James, *A Descriptive Catalogue of the Manuscripts in the Library of Trinity Hall* (Cambridge, 1907), no. 1. The text is printed in Hardwick, *Historia Monasterii S. Augustini Cantuariensis*.

35. The identification is demonstrated in Wright, *Vespasian Psalter*, pp. 37–41.

36. CCCC, 286. The identification is reported in Budny, *Manuscript Art*, no. 1. Cf. F. Wormald, *The Miniatures in the Gospels of St. Augustine (Corpus Christi College MS 286)* (Cambridge, 1954); repr. in idem, *Collected Writings*, eds J.J.G. Alexander, T.J. Brown and J. Gibbs, 2 vols (London, 1984–88), I, pp. 13–34; and Gameson, *Saint Augustine of Canterbury*, no. 1. See further Marsden and Gameson, chs 12 and 13 below.

37. These two records are *Anglo-Saxon Charters: An Annotated List and Bibliography*, ed. P.H. Sawyer (London, 1968), nos 1198, 1455; and Kelly, *Charters of St Augustine's Abbey*, nos 24, 31. See also Emms, ch. 16 below.

38. Detailed examination of these titles is reported in Budny, *Manuscript Art*, no. 1.
39. The portions are CCCC, 197B + BL, Cotton MS Otho C. v and apparently also Royal MS 7 C. xii, fols 2–3. Alexander, *Illuminated Manuscripts*, no. 12; G. Henderson, *From Durrow to Kells: The Insular Gospel Books, 650–800* (London, 1987), pp. 68–70; Webster and Backhouse, *Making of England*, nos 83a–c; and Budny, *Manuscript Art*, no. 3.
40. Cotton entered this attribution as a note to the entry for his portion in the earliest catalogue for his collection: BL, Harley MS 6018, item 185. Any similar attribution which may have stood in that portion itself has been lost, perhaps in the fire.
41. Westwood, *Palaeographica Sacra Pictoria*, p. 4 accompanying pl. 21 (see also p. 39); and *idem*, *Fac-Similes*, p. 40. Westwood reiterated his belief, for example, in *The Book of Kells: A Lecture* (Dublin, 1887), at pp. 7–8.
42. For example, E. Maunde Thompson and G.F. Warner, *Catalogue of Ancient Manuscripts in the British Museum*, II: *Latin* (Oxford, 1884), 22; H.J. White, 'Vulgate', in *A Dictionary of the Bible*, ed. J. Hastings et al., 5 vols (Edinburgh and New York, 1900–4), IV, pp. 873–90, at p. 887; and K. Sisam, 'Canterbury, Lichfield, and the Vespasian Psalter', *Review of English Studies*, n. s. 7:25 (1956), 1–7, at p. 7.
43. The inscriptions are reproduced in Budny, 'Anatomy', fig. 3 on p. 184 and pls. 33, 37, 38a, 39a; and described and analysed on pp. 200–14.
44. Such practice is reported in *Medieval Libraries of Great Britain: A List of Surviving Books*, ed. N.R. Ker, 2nd edn (London, 1964), pp. xvi–xvii.
45. BodL, Bodley MS 381. Removed from that volume in the late nineteenth century, the Oxford leaf now stands on its own, framed between sheets of glass and classed as Lat. Bibl. b. 2 (P). It is described in *A Summary Catalogue of Western Manuscripts in the Bodleian Library at Oxford*, ed. F. Madan et al., 7 vols (Oxford, 1895–1953), II, no. 2202; and Budny, 'Anatomy', pp. 167–79.
46. The range of meanings is surveyed, for example, in *A Latin Dictionary*, eds C.T. Lewis and C. Short (Oxford, 1879), s.v. 'nudus.' The meaning here is assessed in Budny, 'Anatomy', pp. 203–4.
47. They are listed in M.R. James, *The Ancient Libraries of Canterbury and Dover: The Catalogues of the Libraries of Christ Church Priory and St Augustine's Abbey at Canterbury* (Cambridge, 1903), pp. 197–213; and Ker, *Medieval Libraries*, pp. 40–7.
48. Dublin, Trinity College, MS D. 1. 19 (360): M.L. Colker, *Trinity College Library Dublin: Descriptive Catalogue of the Mediaeval and Renaissance Latin Manuscripts*, 2 vols (Aldershot, 1991), no. 360. Its text is printed, albeit with errors, in James, *Ancient Libraries*, pp. 200–406. The absence of Royal MS 1 E. vi and Bodley MS 381 from its list is assessed in Budny, 'Anatomy', pp. 215–19.
49. They are surveyed in James, *Ancient Libraries*, pp. lix–lv, 532; Ker, *Medieval Libraries*, pp. xiii, 40–7; and A.B. Emden, *Donors of Books to S[t] Augustine's Abbey, Canterbury* (Oxford, 1968), p. 1.
50. Leland's surviving notes on the abbey library were published on the one hand in *Commentarii de scriptoribus Britannicis, auctore Joanne Lelando Londinate*, ed. A. Hall, 2 vols (Oxford, 1709), II, pp. 299–301 (singling out for mention six manuscripts among the oldest in the library); and on the other hand in *Joannis Lelandi Antiquarii De Rebus Britannicis Collectanea ex Autographis*, ed. T. Hearne, 6 vols (Oxford, 1715), III, pp. 7–8 (listing nearly thirty texts). James, *Ancient Libraries*, pp. lxxvii–lxxx, 503–4, translated

51. The dissolution of the abbey and its aftermath are described, for example, by M. Sparks, 'The Abbey Site, 1538–1997', in Gem, *St Augustine's Abbey*, 143–61. The dispersal and destruction of the books are reported in James, *Ancient Libraries*, pp. lxxxi–lxxxii; and C.E. Wright, 'The Dispersal of the Libraries in the Sixteenth Century', *The English Library before 1700: Studies in its History*, eds F. Wormald and C.E. Wright (London, 1951), pp. 148–75.

    the one and repeated the other. Their testimony in relation to the Royal Bible is assessed in Budny, 'Anatomy', pp. 219–20.

52. The catalogue survives in a copy of 1609: Cambridge, Trinity College, MS O. 4. 38 (1268), with this gospel manuscript listed on fol. 21v (as no. 304). The catalogue is M.R. James, *The Western Manuscripts in the Library of Trinity College, Cambridge: A Descriptive Catalogue*, 3 vols (Cambridge, 1902), no. 1268. Its text is printed in *The Lumley Library: The Catalogue of 1609*, eds S. Jayne and F.R. Johnson (London, 1956); its fol. 21v is reproduced in Budny, 'Anatomy', pl. 41a.

53. Allen's life and book collection are surveyed in Watson, 'Thomas Allen and his Manuscripts'; M. Foster, 'Thomas Allen (1540–1632), Gloucester Hall and the Survival of Catholicism in Post-Reformation Oxford', *Oxoniensia*, 46 (1981), 98–128; *idem*, 'Thomas Allen, Gloucester Hall and the Bodleian Library', *The Downside Review*, 309 (1982), 116–37; and S. Keynes, 'The Reconstruction of a Burnt Cottonian Manuscript: The Case of Cotton MS. Otho A. I', *The British Library Journal*, 22:2 (1966), 113–60, at pp. 119–21.

54. Bodley MS 381 is no. 40 in the Register of Benefactors of the Bodleian Library, as noted by Madan et al., *Summary Catalogue*, II, no. 2202; and I, p. 80. The latter account (published in 1953) misleadingly lists the Oxford leaf as no. 41, whereas these two items came to Bodley as a unit.

55. Foster, 'Thomas Allen', p. 109.

56. The inscription is printed in full in James, *Manuscripts of Trinity Hall*, no. 1.

57. W. Urry, 'An Eighth-Century Fragment of the Gospels in the Chapter Library', *Friends of Canterbury Cathedral, Annual Report*, 21 (1948), 33–5.

58. *CLA*, II, nos 214 + 244, treated as distinct items in the 1st edn (1935).

59. The blend is assessed in McGurk, 'Anglo-Saxon Bible Fragment', pp. 20–1; and Budny, 'Anatomy', pp. 536–47.

60. McGurk, 'Anglo-Saxon Bible Fragment', p. 26.

61. Worcester, Cathedral Library, Add. MS 1 + BodL, MS Lat. Bibl. d. 1 (P); Turner, *Early Worcester MSS*, pls 7–14; *CLA*, II, nos 245, 262; McGurk, 'Anglo-Saxon Bible Fragment', pp. 27–32; Budny, 'Anatomy', pp. 86, 403–9, 764–9; and Marsden, ch. 12 below.

62. McGurk, *Latin Gospel Books*, pp. 110–13 (Appendices I and III, Group 4), nos 38, 43, 57, 61, 137.

63. The collation is reported in Budny, 'Anatomy', pp. 391–411.

64. BodL, MS Auct. D. 2. 14; and Cividale, Museo Archeologico, s.n. + Prague, Knihovna Metropolitní Kapitoly, Cim. 1 + Venice, San Marco, s.n. *Novum Testamentum Domini Nostri Iesu Christi latine secundum editionem sancti Hieronymi*, eds J. Wordsworth, H.J. White and H.F.D. Sparks, 5 vols (Oxford, 1889–1954), I, ad loc.; *CLA*, II, no. 230; and III, no. 285 + X, no. 285.

65. P. Sabatier, *Bibliorum Sacrorum Latinæ Versiones Antiquæ, seu Vetus Italica, et Cæteræ quænque in Codicibus MSS. & antiquorum libris reperiri potuerunt*, 3 vols (Paris, 1751), III, ad loc.

66. Wordsworth et al., *Novum Testamentum*, I, ad loc.

67. Ibid., ad loc.
68. Cambridge, University Library, MS Nn. 2. 41; and BodL, Laud MS gr. 35. Wordsworth et al., *Novum Testamentum*, III:i, ad loc. See *CLA*, II, nos 140, 251.
69. La Cava dei Tirreni, Biblioteca della Badia, MS memb. I. Wordsworth et al., *Novum Testamentum*, III:i, ad loc; cf. J. Williams, *Early Spanish Manuscript Illumination* (London, 1977), pls 1–2.
70. This page is reproduced in colour in J. Roebuck, *St Augustine's Abbey* (England, 1992), p. 6 (top left).
71. Cf. Sabatier, *Bibliorum Sacrorum Latinæ Versiones Antiquæ*, III, ad loc.
72. Weber et al., *Biblia Sacra*, II, pp. 1096–7.
73. Ibid., II, pp. 1515–16.
74. BL, Add. MS 10546. The manuscript is described and assessed in E.K. Rand, *A Survey of the Manuscripts of Tours: Studies in the Script of Tours*, 1, 2 vols (Cambridge, Mass., 1929), I, no. 77; *Die karolingischen Miniaturen*, ed. W. Koehler, I: *Die Schule von Tours*, 3 vols (Berlin, 1930–3), I, no. 311; Kessler, *Illustrated Bibles from Tours*; and J. Duft et al., *Die Bibel von Moutier-Grandval. British Museum Add. Ms. 10546* (Bern, 1971).
75. BL, Add. MS 24142. The Theodulf Bibles are considered in M. Vieillard-Troiekouroff, 'Les Bibles de Théodulphe et leur décor aniconique', in *Études ligériennes d'histoire et d'archéologie médiévales: Mémoires et exposés présentés à la semaine d'études médiévales de Saint-Benoît-sur-Loire du 3 au 10 juillet 1969*, ed. R. Louis (Auxerre, 1975), pp. 345–60; B. Fischer, 'Bibeltext und Bibelreform', in *Karl der Grosse: Lebenswerk und Nachleben*, ed. W. Braunfels, 4 vols (Düsseldorf, 1965–7), II, pp. 156–216, repr. in B. Fischer, *Lateinische Bibelhandschriften im frühen Mittelalter* (Freiburg, 1985), pp. 101–202; and E. Dahlhaus-Berg, *Nova antiquitas et antiqua novitas: Typologische Exegese und isidorianisches Geschichtsbild bei Theodulf von Orléans* (Cologne and Vienna, 1975), esp. pp. 61–76.
76. The import of these features is described by McGurk, 'Anglo-Saxon Bible Fragment', pp. 26–8; *idem*, 'Citation Marks in Early Latin Manuscripts', *Scriptorium*, 15 (1961), 3–13; and Budny, 'Anatomy', pp. 406–11. The citation marks are noted in *CLA*, II, no. 214.
77. S. Berger, *Histoire de la Vulgate pendant les premiers siècles du moyen âge* (Nancy, 1893), no. 1, with the manuscripts listed on pp. 337–8; and Stegmüller, *Repertorium Biblicum Medii Aevi*, I, no. 284. The text is printed, for example, in *Biblia Sacra, iuxta latinam vulgatam versionem ad codicum fidem, cura et studio monachorum Abbatiae pontificiae Sancti Hieronymi in Urbe O.S.B. edita*, ed. H. Quentin et al., 18 vols (Rome, 1926–94), I, pp. 3–37, with the manuscripts listed on p. 2.
78. Quentin et al., *Biblia Sacra*, I, pp. 10 (line 4), 11 (line 10).
79. Ibid., pp. 17 (line 5), 18 (line 1), with *in doctrina* reported for MSS *S* and *h*.
80. As noted on the one hand by B. Fischer, 'Codex Amiatinus und Cassiodor', *Biblische Zeitschrift*, N. F. 6 (1962), 57–79, at p. 71; and *idem*, 'Die Alcuin-Bibeln', in Duft et al., *Bibel* (1971), pp. 49–98, at p. 66; and on the other hand by P. Courcelle, *Late Latin Writers and their Greek Sources*, trans. H.E. Wedeck (Cambridge, Mass., 1969), p. 339. Fischer's articles are reprinted in *idem, Lateinische Bibelhandschriften*, pp. 9–34, 203–403. The Pentateuch diagram is reproduced in Bruce-Mitford, 'Art of the Codex Amiatinus,' pl. XII. Its use of Jerome's extracts is assessed in Corsano, 'First Quire of the Codex Amiatinus', pp. 30–1. Their use both in the diagram and for the Minor Prophets is assessed in

Marsden, *Old Testament*, pp. 36, 38, 122–3, 168–9.

81 Léon, Archivo catedralicio, MS 15. Quentin et al., *Biblia Sacra*, XVII, pp. xxv–xxv, 7–15. *CLA*, XI, no. 1636; Fischer, *Lateinische Bibelhandschriften*, pp. 70, 73–5, 77–8, 247; and P. McGurk, 'The Oldest Manuscripts of the Latin Bible', in *The Early Medieval Bible: Its Production, Decoration and Use*, ed. R. Gameson (Cambridge, 1994), pp. 1–23, at p. 7.

82 Letter to M. Budny of 26 April 1982. See also Fischer, 'Alcuin-Bibeln', pp. 59, 66–7.

83 The phrase derives from the title of C. Nordenfalk, 'Noch eine turonische Bilderbibel', in *Festschrift Bernhard Bischoff zu seinem 65. Geburtstag dargebracht von Freunden, Kollegen und Schülern*, eds J. Autenrieth and F. Brunhölzl (Stuttgart, 1971), pp. 153–63. The known corpus is surveyed in D. Ganz, 'Mass Production of Early Medieval Manuscripts: The Carolingian Bibles from Tours', in Gameson, *Early Medieval Bible*, pp. 53–62, with a list of members on pp. 61–2. Their recognition or discovery has continued to expand over the past decades, as cited in M. Budny, 'The Vivian Bible and Scribal, Editorial, and Organizational Marks in Medieval Books', in *Making the Medieval Book: Techniques of Production*, ed. L.L. Brownrigg (Los Altos Hills and London, 1995), pp. 199–239, at p. 235, n. 12.

84 See further Budny, 'Anatomy', pp. 227–9.

85 Quentin et al., *Biblia Sacra*, I, pp. 91–101.

86 Paris, Bibliothèque Mazarine, MS 5, fol. 186ra. Quentin et al., *Biblia Sacra*, I, p. 3, with the manuscript (assigned the siglum Ωm) described on pp. xlii–xliii; and in A. Moliner, *Catalogue des manuscrits de la Bibliothèque Mazarine* (Paris, 1885), I, 2–3.

87 A detailed study of their forms, decoration, and significance appears in Budny, 'Anatomy', pp. 547–633.

88 An example is reproduced in Bruce-Mitford, 'Art of the Codex Amiatinus,' pl. XVI (fol. 799r with Canons IV–V).

89 Sankt Gallen, Stiftsbibliothek, Cod. 75; and Monza, Biblioteca Capitolare, MS G. 1. Cf. Fischer, 'Alcuin Bibeln', pp. 7–8. Their arcades are analysed in Nordenfalk, *Spätantike Kanontafeln*, pp. 298–9; and idem, 'Beiträge zur Geschichte der turonischen Buchmalerei', *Acta Archaeologica*, 7 (1936), 281–304, at pp. 298–304. Examples are reproduced in Koehler, *Karolingische Miniaturen*, I, pls 1–2, 9–10.

90 The *M*-, *N*-, and combined *Nm*-types are described in Nordenfalk, *Spätantike Kanontafeln*, pp. 73–9, with the use of the latter in the Tours Bibles post-dating Alcuin reported on p. 299. The combined *Mm*-type is identified in Budny, 'Anatomy', pp. 566–9.

91 BL, Add. MS 5111, fols 10–11; and Vienna, Österreichische Nationalbibliothek, Cod. 847. Nordenfalk, *Spätantiken Kanontafeln*, pp. 127–46 and pls 1–4, 42–3; Weitzmann, *Age of Spirituality*, no. 441; and idem, *Book Illumination*, pl. 43.

92 Mount Athos, Lavra Cod. A.23. Nordenfalk, *Spätantiken Kanontafeln*, pl. 161.

93 The correspondence is demonstrated in D.M. Wilson, *Anglo-Saxon Art from the Seventh Century to the Norman Conquest* (London, 1984), pp. 94–6 and pls 103–6, 114–20; and Budny, 'Anatomy,' pp. 589–632, 757–60.

94 Such ornament is assessed, for example, in J.M.C. Toynbee and J.B. Ward-Perkins, 'Peopled Scrolls: A Hellenistic Motif in Imperial Art,' *Papers of the British School in Rome*, 18 (1950), 1–3; and C.M. Dauphin, '"Inhabited Scrolls" from the IVth to the VIIth Century A.D. in Asia Minor and the Eastern Provinces of the Byzantine Empire' (unpublished Ph.D. thesis, University of Edinburgh, 1974).

95. Erevan, Matenadaran MS 2374 (*olim* 229), fols 228r–229v. The gospel manuscript itself was made in 989 at the Monastery of Noravank', Siunik'. The four inserted illustrations are reproduced in colour in L.A. Dournovo, *Armenian Miniatures* (New York, 1961), pls on pp. 33, 35, 37, 39. Their character and probable date are assessed in S. Der Nersessian, 'The Date of the Initial Miniatures of the Etchmiadzin Gospel', *The Art Bulletin*, 15 (1933), 1–34, repr. in *idem, Byzantine and Armenian Studies* (Louvain, 1973), pp. 533–58; and T.F. Matthews, 'The Early Armenian Iconographic Program of the Éjmiacin Gospel Erevan, Matenadaran MS 2374 (*olim* 229)', in *East of Byzantium: Syria and Armenia in the Formative Period*, ed. N. Garsoïan (Dumbarton Oaks, 1982), pp. 199–215.

96. F.W. Deichmann, *Ravenna, Hauptstadt des Spätantiken Abendlandes* (Wiesbaden, 1969–76), I: *Geschichte und Monumente* (1969), pp. 257–78; II: *Kommentar* with *Plananhang*, 3 vols (1974–6), II, pp. 233–80; and III: *Frühchristliche Bauten und Mosaiken von Ravenna*, 2nd edn (1976), pp. 257–91 and pls 119–20, 226–7, 297, 301, 311.

97. Cambridge, University Library, MS Ll. 1. 10. Alexander, *Insular Manuscripts*, no. 66; Webster and Backhouse, *Making of England*, no. 165; and M.P. Brown, *The Book of Cerne: Prayer, Patronage, and Power in Ninth-Century England* (London and Toronto, 1996). The derivation of the image is analysed in Budny, 'Anatomy', esp. pp. 486–94.

98. All four frontispieces are reproduced in colour in Brown, *Book of Cerne*, pls Ia, IIa, IIIa, IVa.

99. They occur before fol. 7r (which carries Matthew 1:19–2:19); between fols 10v and 11r (which pages carry respectively Matthew 6:33–7:22 and 7:23–8:17); between 32v and 33r (Mark 3:5–32 and 3:32–5:40); between fols 35v and 36r (Mark 8:8–35 and 8:35–9:20); between fols 38v and 39r (Mark 11:27–12:21 and 12:21–13:3); perhaps between fols 37v and 38r (Mark 10:24–51 and 10:51–11:26); between fols 39v and 40r (Mark 13:3–32 and 13:33–14:22); between fols 41v (Mark 15:8–39) and 42r (the Luke chapter list); between fols 49r and 50r (Luke 5:1–18 and 5:18–6:21); and between fols 75v and 76r (John 8:28–54 and 8:54–9:23).

100. The leaf perhaps lost between fols 37 and 38 could have depicted Christ's Entry into Jerusalem, the Healing of the Blind Bartimæus and/or the Purging of the Temple.

101. Los Angeles, The J. Paul Getty Museum, MS 9 (*olim* Damme, Musée van Maerlant, s.n.), fol. 1v; Temple, *Anglo-Saxon Manuscripts*, no. 53; and J.J.G. Alexander, 'Some Aesthetic Principles in the Use of Colour in Anglo-Saxon Art', *ASE*, 4 (1975), 145–54, at pp. 151–2 and pl. VIII.

102. Vienna, Österreichische Nationalbibliothek, Cod. theol. grec. 31; and BL, Cotton MS Otho B. vi. The former is reproduced in Gerstinger, *Wiener Genesis*. The latter is assessed and reconstructed in K. Weitzmann and H.L. Kessler, *The Cotton Genesis: British Library Codex Cotton Otho B. VI* (Princeton, 1986); and J. Lowden, 'Concerning the Cotton Genesis and Other Illustrated Manuscripts of Genesis', *Gesta*, 31:1 (1992), 40–53.

103. BL, Cotton MS Claudius B. iv. Temple, *Anglo-Saxon Manuscripts*, no. 86; and *The Golden Age of Anglo-Saxon Art, 966–1066*, eds J. Backhouse, D.H. Turner and L. Webster (London, 1984), no. 157; facsimile in *The Old English Illustrated Hexateuch: British Museum Cotton Claudius B. iv*, eds C.R. Dodwell and P. Clemoes, EEMF, 18 (Copenhagen, 1974).

104. The Babel scene is reproduced in colour in A. Grabar and C. Nordenfalk, *Le Haut moyen âge du quatrième au onzième siècle* (Geneva, 1957), p. 189. Late Antique features in the cycle are considered, for example, in G. Henderson, 'Late-Antique Influences in Some English Mediaeval Illustrations of Genesis', *Journal of the Warburg and Courtauld Institutes*, 25 (1962), 172–98; *idem*, 'The Sources of the Genesis Cycle at Saint-Savin-sur-Gartempe', *JBAA*, 26 (1963), 11–26; *idem*, 'The Joshua Cycle in B.M. Cotton MS Claudius B. IV', ibid., 31 (1968), 38–95; and *idem*, 'The Programme of Illustrations in Bodleian MS Junius XI', in *Studies in Memory of David Talbot Rice*, eds G. Robertson and G. Henderson (Edinburgh, 1975), pp. 113–45. All four studies are reprinted in Henderson, *Studies in English Bible Illustration*, I (London, 1985), pp. 76–215.

105. Temple, *Anglo-Saxon Manuscripts*, pl. 172. The features of the portrait and the evidence and probable motivation for its installation after the despoliation are analysed in Budny, 'Anatomy', pp. 236–53.

106. This artist's surviving works are assessed in ibid., pp. 236–56; and Budny, *Manuscript Art*, no. 23.

107. Cambridge, Trinity College, MS R. 17. 1 (987) + New York, Pierpont Morgan Library, MSS M 724 + M 521 + BL, Add. MS 37472 (1) + Victoria and Albert Museum, MS 661. *The Canterbury Psalter*, ed. M.R. James (London, 1935); C.M. Kauffmann, *Romanesque Manuscripts, 1066–1190* (London, 1975), nos 66, 68; *English Romanesque Art, 1066–1200*, eds G. Zarnecki, J. Holt and T. Holland (London, 1984), nos 47–50, 62; and *The Eadwine Psalter: Text, Image, and Monastic Culture in Twelfth-Century Canterbury*, eds M. Gibson, T.A. Heslop and R.W. Pfaff (London and University Park, 1992).

108. The study merits application to a broad range of medieval English manuscripts with cycles of biblical illustration, whose Late Antique symptoms hitherto have appeared unexplainable in terms of known cycles, notably in the Cotton Genesis and its derivatives. The problem usually leads to conjectured lost models otherwise unknown, as reported, for example, in K.E. Haney, *The Winchester Psalter: An Iconographic Study* (Leicester, 1986), esp. pp. 73–7.

109. Such derivation is reported, for example, by N.P. Brooks and H.E. Walker, 'The Authority and Interpretation of the Bayeux Tapestry', *Proceedings of the Battle Conference on Anglo-Norman Studies*, I: 1978, ed. R. Allen Brown (Ipswich, 1979), 1–34, 191–9, at pp. 13–18; M.H. Caviness, *The Early Stained Glass of Canterbury Cathedral, circa 1175–1220* (Princeton, 1977), pp. 79, 119; *eadem, The Windows of Christ Church Cathedral, Canterbury* (London, 1981), pp. 131–2; and Budny, *Manuscript Art*, no. 1.

110. Accounts of Gregory's career, influences and impact appear, for example, in E.H. Fischer, 'Gregor der Grosse und Byzanz', *Zeitschrift der Savigny-Stiftung für Rechtsgeschichte*, 67: Kanonistische Abteilung, 36 (1950), 15–144; J. Richards, *Consul of God: The Life and Times of Gregory the Great* (London, 1980); and J. Herrin, *The Formation of Christendom* (Oxford, 1987), pp. 145–82.

111. Eastern Mediterranean influences in Ravenna in the sixth century are reported, for example, in O. von Simson, *Sacred Fortress: Byzantine Art and Statecraft in Ravenna* (Chicago, 1948); and C.O. Nordström, *Ravennastudien: Ideengeschichtliche und ikonographische Untersuchungen über die Mosaiken von Ravenna* (Uppsala, 1953).

112. Gregory's views concerning the stages of conversion and instruction required for the

English are reported, for example, in *HE*, I, 27, pp. 80–1. They are assessed, for example, in P. Meyvaert, *Bede and Gregory the Great* (Jarrow-on-Tyne, 1964); *idem*, 'Bede's Text of the *Libellus Responsionum* of Gregory the Great to Augustine of Canterbury', in *England Before the Conquest: Studies in Primary Sources presented to Dorothy Whitelock*, eds P. Clemoes and K. Hughes (Cambridge, 1971), pp. 15–33; H. Mayr-Harting, *The Coming of Christianity to Anglo-Saxon England*, 3rd edn (London, 1991); H. Chadwick, 'Gregory the Great and the Misison to the Anglo-Saxons', in *Gregorio Magno e il suo tempo*, I: *Studi Storici* (Rome, 1991), 199–212, at pp. 207–11; and I. Wood, 'The Mission of Augustine of Canterbury to the English', *Speculum*, 69 (1994), 1–17. Meyvaert's two articles are reprinted in *idem, Benedict, Gregory, Bede and Others* (London, 1977).

113. The front and back covers are reproduced in colour in Hubert et al., *Europe in the Dark Ages*, pl. 241. They are F. Steenbock, *Die kirchliche Prachteinband im frühen Mittelalter von den Anfängen bis zum Beginn der Gotik* (Berlin, 1965), no. 1.

114. *HE*, I, 25, pp. 74–5.

115. *HE*, I, 29, pp. 104–5.

116. Plummer, *Bedae Opera Historica*, II, 56–7, 70; D. Bullough, 'Roman Books and Carolingian *Renovatio*', *SCH*, 14 (1977), 23–50, at pp. 30–1; and Gameson, ch. 13 below.

117. BL, Cotton MS Tiberius A. ix, fol. 108v, lines 27–32. The other fourteenth-century copy – London, Lambeth Palace, MS 419 – omits the last word (fol. 112v, lines 30–6) and the two sixteenth-century transcripts do not include this passage. The surviving copies of Sprott's chronicle are described in Davis, *Thorne's Chronicle*, pp. xx–xxvii; and M.A.F. Borrie, 'The Thorne Chronicle', *British Museum Quarterly*, 31 (1967), 87–90, at p. 88.

118. CCCC, MS 189, fol. 47r, line 22. M.R. James, *A Descriptive Catalogue of the Manuscripts in the Library of Corpus Christi College, Cambridge*, 2 vols (Cambridge, 1912), no. 189. Such active attention by Parker to the texts of his manuscripts is reported in R.I. Page, *Matthew Parker and His Books: Sandars Lectures in Bibliography, 1990* (Kalamazoo, 1993). Parker's special interest in the early history of his see of Canterbury as reflected in his manuscripts is examined, for example, in Budny, *Manuscript Art*, I, pp. xliii, xliv and nos 3, 22.

119. For help in answering my queries about the *Biblia Gregoriana*, its traces, its probable character, its context and its possible survival, I particularly thank Bruce Barker-Benfield, Adelaide Bennett, Christopher de Hamel, Richard Emms, the late Bonifatius Fischer, Leslie French, David Ganz, Herbert Kessler, Alexei Lidov, Patrick McGurk, Robert Mathiesen, Paul Meyvaert, Tim Rogers, Dorothy Shepard, Margaret Sparks, Georgina Stoner, Nigel Wilkins and David Wright. David Ganz kindly proposed and presented this chapter for me at the conference at Canterbury in September 1997 commemorating St Augustine and his mission. Richard Gameson generously gave excellent editorial advice and encouragement in preparing the publication.

CHAPTER 12

The Gospels of St Augustine

Richard Marsden

Early historians of the Vulgate applied the resonant title Gospels of St Augustine to two gospel books of Italian origin but Anglo-Saxon provenance, one now in the Parker Library, Cambridge (CCCC, MS 286) and the other in the Bodleian Library, Oxford (MS Auct. D. 2. 14). Today only the former continues to be considered likely to deserve its title, but I shall take this opportunity to re-examine the textual history of both, for they are England's two earliest surviving gospel manuscripts and this gives them an unquestionable importance, not only in the early history of the Anglo-Saxon gospel book but in Vulgate history in general. Furthermore, no assessment of them has been made since the new text collations by Bonifatius Fischer became available, complementing the information in the first volume of the great critical edition of the Vulgate New Testament by Wordsworth and White.[1]

The older of the two gospel books is Corpus, which I designate X, following the convention of Wordsworth and White; in Fischer's newer and more comprehensive system it is styled Jx, where 'J' identifies 'x' as belonging to a large group of Italian manuscripts.[2] A small book (245 × 180 mm), now in a modern leather binding, it was written in Italy in the sixth century in an attractive round uncial, the text being spaciously set out, *per cola et commata* (figs 12.1–2). It begins imperfectly in the *capitula* to St Matthew's gospel and only two of the several full-page miniatures with which it was originally illustrated survive, one showing scenes from Christ's life and the other the evangelist Luke (pls IV–V).[3] X was given to Corpus by Archbishop Parker in 1575. The Oxford gospel book, siglum O [Jo], is a little larger than X (250 × 195 mm) and never carried illustrations. It too is imperfect, the head and tail having been lost, so that its text starts at Matthew 4:14 and ends at Jn 21:15.[4] This manuscript is also Italian in origin but is of a later date than X, probably in the first half of the seventh century. Like X, it is written in uncials but the interpretation of the script is more stylized (figs 12.3–5). In contrast with X, O's text is presented in continuous lines to begin with, but this lasts only until the end of the first gospel, after which the

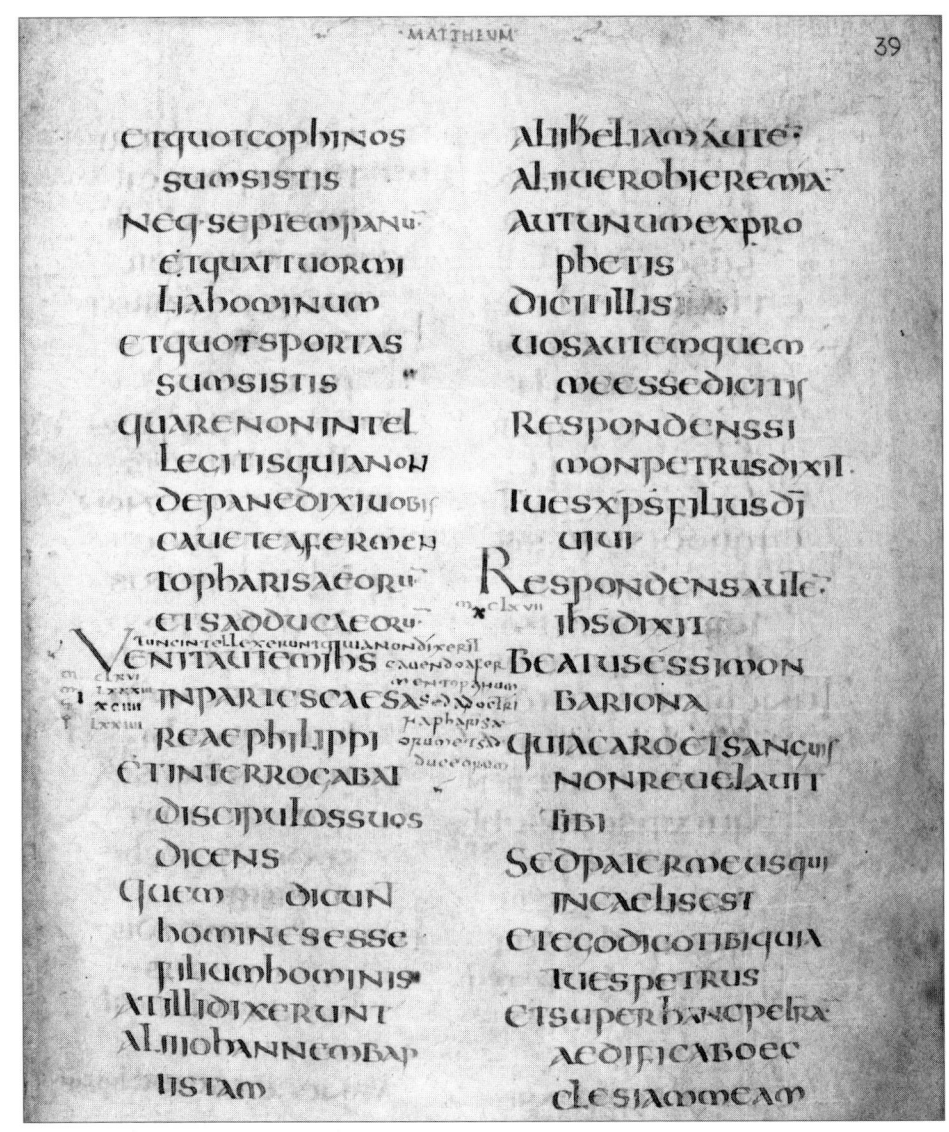

12.1. CCCC, 286, fol. 39r. Note the restitution of an omission (the whole of Matthew 16:12) in small uncials contemporary with the original. (The Master and Fellows of Corpus Christi College, Cambridge)

others are written *per cola et commata*. Even when complete, with around 200 folios, it would have been far thinner than the plump X, which had more than 265. O was given to the Bodleian Library by Sir Robert Cotton in 1603.

In what follows, I shall tackle a series of questions about our two manuscripts. Why were they associated with St Augustine and his mission, and with Canterbury? What are their respective textual genealogies and the relationship between them? Can any textual continuity be demonstrated between them and biblical manuscripts known or thought to have been copied at Canterbury; and

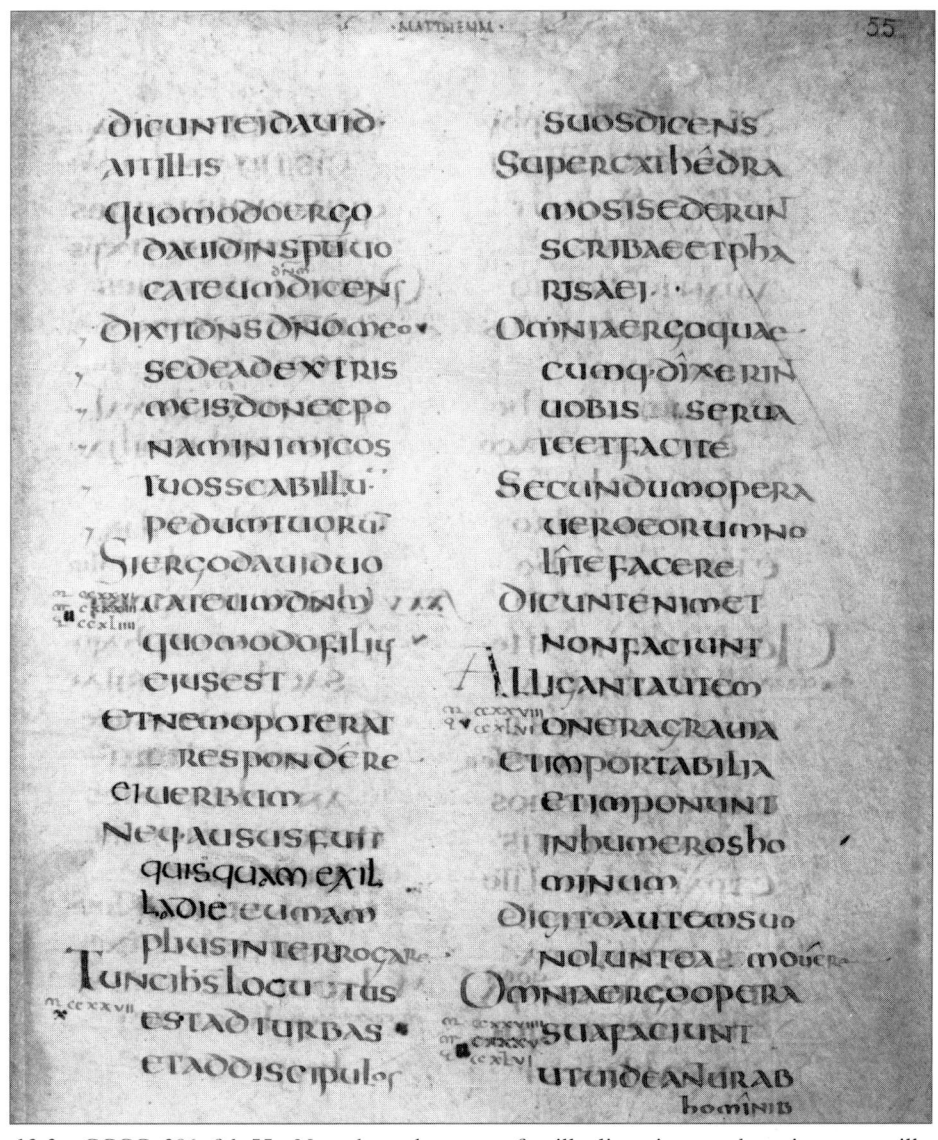

12.2. CCCC, 286, fol. 55r. Note the replacement of ex illa die quisquam *by* quisquam ex illa die *in Matthew 22:46. (The Master and Fellows of Corpus Christi College, Cambridge)*

did they have any wider influence on the subsequent history of the gospel text in Anglo-Saxon England? Finally, what is the significance of the considerable amount of emendation which both manuscripts subsequently underwent?

THE ASSOCIATION WITH ST AUGUSTINE

Two obvious historical facts lie behind the supposed association of our two Italian gospel books, X and O, with St Augustine. First, when Augustine and his fellow monks landed in Kent in 597 with the intention of evangelizing, they undoubtedly carried with them the wherewithal for such a mission. That must have meant at the very least a psalter and a gospel book, and probably other service books, for they could hardly otherwise have met in the church of St Martin, as Bede tells us they did, 'to chant the psalms, to pray, to say mass, to preach, and to baptize'.[5] Secondly, as again Bede reports, Gregory soon reinforced the mission by sending more monks and ministers, who carried with them 'all such things as were generally necessary for the worship and ministry of the church'. These included, along with sacred vessels, vestments and relics, 'very many manuscripts'.[6] Certainly X, copied some years before the mission, could have arrived with it or been one of the manuscripts sent soon afterwards. However, books probably continued to arrive periodically from Italy at least up to the time of Theodore and Hadrian in the closing decades of the seventh century, and so we should admit the possibility of a later arrival. Corrections in Anglo-Saxon scripts confirm that the gospel book was in England by the end of the seventh century or the beginning of the eighth.[7] It has excellent Canterbury credentials, too, in the form of added documents in Old English relating to Saint Augustine's Abbey, but these only prove that it was there by the beginning of the tenth century.[8] As for O, the Oxford manuscript, if it does indeed date from the early seventh-century, it is less likely to have been among the earliest books to reach England, but it could still have arrived during the first half of that century. Corrections and additions in Anglo-Saxon scripts show only that it was here by the end of the eighth century. Nothing directly connects it with Canterbury, however, and the evidence for its association with other centres is extremely tenuous. Lichfield has been suggested, because of a marginal liturgical entry in Anglo-Saxon script referring to St Chad; Bury St Edmunds, too, on the strength of an eleventh-century book-list bound with the gospel book and containing perhaps the name of an abbot of Bury.[9]

Earlier historians were much encouraged in their speculations about our two manuscripts by the chronicle of Thomas of Elmham, whose early fifteenth-century account of Saint Augustine's Abbey included a description of the monastery's books (cf. fig. 11.8).[10] Among these were two copies of the gospels, one kept in the vestry, the other in the library (items 3 and 5 in Thomas's list). Both had the ten Eusebian canon tables prefixed to them, wrote Thomas, and the former was said 'to be called the Text of St Mildred because a countryman in Thanet swore falsely upon it and, it is said, lost his eyes'.[11] Four of the eight items listed were said by Thomas to be placed on the high altar of the abbey church – a psalter (item 4), two books of passions, one of the apostles (item 6) and the other of the saints (item 7), and an exposition of the epistles and gospels (item 8). A diagram of the sanctuary which appears in the Cambridge manuscript of Thomas's chronicle shows books on the high altar and labels them '*libri missi a Gregorio ad Augustinum*' ('the books sent from Gregory to St Augustine') (cf. fig. 11.9).[12] The remaining two books on Thomas's list (items 1 and 2) were both kept in the library and were again linked directly with the Gregorian mission. The first was a two-volume Bible, the so-called *Biblia Gregoriana*, and the second was another psalter, the so-called *Psalterium Augustini*. The latter is assumed to be the surviving 'Vespasian Psalter' which, though long associated with the name of St Augustine, was in fact not copied until the early eighth century, probably at Saint Augustine's Abbey (pls VII–VIII).[13] The two-volume Bible is no longer extant, but it appears to have survived until the time of James I and, if Mildred Budny is right, it influenced the architecture of a later Canterbury Bible which does survive, though sadly incomplete, in BL, Royal 1. E. vi and a few other fragments.[14] Theoretically, both X and O could be either of the gospel books listed by Thomas (as items 3 and 5), but this is additionally likely in the case of X, which we have seen was certainly in Canterbury well before the fourteenth century. There is no proof, of course, for Thomas's labelling, along with his concluding comment that 'these were all the books of the early English Church', may do no more than state a tradition current in the fifteenth century.[15] The example of the *Psalterium Augustini*, written as we have seen a century after the Augustinian mission, offers a salutary warning. Yet the speculation that X, at least, belongs to the period of that mission, and was in some way associated with it, even if not from the very beginning, remains attractive.[16]

Origins and Relationship of X and O

The textual closeness of X and O has often been overstressed, with the stated or implied corollary that the two manuscripts may even have originated in the same centre.[17] It is true that the manuscripts agree consistently in a notable number of variants, but this appears far more significant when one views them in the context of Wordsworth's and White's limited collations than in those of Fischer. Among the latter's Italian manuscripts (J) – twenty-six of them, dating from the sixth to the ninth centuries, of which a majority originated in central or northern Italy – X and O (his Jx and Jo) frequently agree in their readings but never stand out as a pair against the others. Indeed, I have found no significant variants shared only by X and O, nor any consistent alignment of both with any specific group of the Italian witnesses. Furthermore, the considerable differences between the texts of the two gospel books cannot be ignored. In analyses of selected passages in the four gospels where significant variation occurs (comparatively rare though this may be), I have found that the agreements between X and O reached only a little more than 50 per cent overall. They are closest in John (with about 70 per cent of significant variants shared), and farthest apart in Matthew and Mark (around 40 per cent in each case). This analysis takes no account of much orthographical variation and differences in scribal convention – in, for instance, the method of suspending 'm' or marking omissions. The period which separates the copying of the two manuscripts – probably not much less than 50 years but not as many as 100 – means that an origin in the same copying centre is not ruled out, for scribes grow old and conventions change, but positive evidence in favour of this proposition is lacking and there is absolutely no reason to expect any.

The most we can say about X and O is that they both originated in Italy, probably within a couple of generations of each other, and that they belong in the same generally good Vulgate textual tradition that was being transmitted widely, with much variation, in central and northern Italy from the sixth to the ninth centuries. The Italian origin of both X and O was not always recognised, however. Samuel Berger, from the limited evidence available to him, concluded that both were Insular, full of 'Irish' readings, a view shared originally by White but treated with caution by Wordsworth and decisively refuted by Chapman.[18] The Wordsworth and White collations seemed to show that X and O belonged in the textual tradition represented by two other uncial Italian gospel books: BL, Harley 1775 (Z [Jz]) from the early sixth century,[19] and a manuscript now divided between Cividale, Prague, and Venice (J [Jj]), also from the sixth century and copied apparently in the north of Italy, probably in Aquilea.[20] A distinction was discernible, established in a wide range of variants, between this northern Italian textual tradition and the tradition witnessed by the gospel text which the *Codex Amiatinus* (A [Na]) and the Lindisfarne Gospels (Y [Ny]) share, and which is known to have originated in the Naples area.[21] Indeed, the manuscripts represented by Z (Harley 1775) and those represented by AY (Amiatinus-Lindisfarne) constituted for Wordsworth and White the schema of two main families of earlier gospel texts, all more or less free from interpolations, which Fischer later endorsed.[22] The AY family has on the whole the better text (that is, it is judged to be closer to Jerome's original). Connected with it are several other gospel texts produced in Northumbria, along with some others originating on the continent, including one completed in 547 for Victor of Capua[23] and, before correction, an early Theodulfian Bible copied in Orléans between 795 and 800.[24] Distinct from the two older families, Z and AY, is the important group of less 'pure' (i.e. more interpolated) so-called 'Irish-Northumbrian' manuscripts, whose main representatives are the Book of Armagh, Egerton 609, the Lichfield Gospels, the Book of Kells, and the MacRegol Gospels, the respective sigla of which, DELQR, have often been used to designate the group.[25] Although this schema remains a useful theoretical yardstick by which to assess Insular texts, its inadequacy as an accurate tool of analysis has become increasingly apparent as more collations have appeared. The schema is in fact at its most unsatisfactory in precisely that area where we need it most – in reference to the manuscripts which do not easily fit into the AY or DELQR groups. Not the least of the problems with the latter group (the members of which often vary widely among themselves) is the obvious one that its most characteristic readings are ultimately Italian, and their occurence in other Insular manuscripts may result from direct contact with Italian texts, rather than in response to members of DELQR.[26] Furthermore, there are a number of Italian gospel texts which share important characteristics of both the Z and the AY traditions.[27]

Close analysis of the texts of X and O confirms, then, that they belong securely in Fischer's J group of Italian manuscripts (encompassing Wordsworth's and White's Z). However, within that large group, where more than twenty gospel texts may be available for any one reading, no consistently clear relationships between our two manuscripts and other members emerge; indeed, as so often in gospel book studies, we find that the texts of the four gospels within a single manuscript have subtly different affiliations with other copies. Certainly Z [Jz] itself, Harley 1775, in general deserves its established place as one of the more important witnesses. In the readings which X and O share, it shows consistently high agreement with them in Matthew, Luke and John, though very little in Mark. In Matthew and John, the relevant variants are often also shared by Jl, a late eighth-century copy, perhaps from Lucca.[28] In Mark, the fragmentary sixth-century Italian Ja seems particularly close,[29] and it might have turned out to be more significant overall, if it were not for its poor state of preservation; almost nothing is available in Matthew and there are frequent large gaps elsewhere.[30] Similarly, Jq, a late sixth-century copy, probably from Perugia, prominently shares XO variants in Matthew but it is frequently unavailable in the other gospels.[31] The sixth- to seventh-century northern Italian copy, Jy, is almost as good a witness to the variants as Z in Matthew, and compares quite well in Mark and Luke, but is not available for parts of John.[32] Notable for its very poor showing of XO variants in all the gospels is J [Jj], the now-dispersed sixth-century gospel book, probably from Aquilea, discussed above and used extensively by Wordsworth and White. It is, however, unavailable for most of Mark.

When we consider X and O separately, and assess those many readings where they disagree, the picture is no clearer. In Matthew I have been unable to identify any one other Italian manuscript whose text is consistently and significantly closer throughout to that of one of our manuscripts rather than the other. In parallels with O's text of Mark, however, Ja and Jy are prominent, both of them independently witnessing a little more than half of its variants; and it is the same for Luke in Jy, though not in Ja. In John, on the other hand, it is Jz and Jl which appear to show some affinity with O.[33] Parallels for distinctive features of the text of X are even harder to find; indeed, one of its characteristics is a fair number of variants which are found in no other Italian manuscripts of the J group, nor often in copies from elsewhere. Only in Mark does X show distinct parallels with other J texts, namely Jg and Jk, which are both of northern Italian origin but widely apart in date, the former originating in the sixth century, the latter in the second half of the ninth.[34]

Chapman called X and O 'first cousins'.[35] I would prefer to describe the relationship as no closer than that of second or even third cousins, in a rather large and promiscuous family, the significance of whose 'shared' variants becomes less and less, the wider it spreads. All the manuscripts I have noted in connection with the texts of X and O were copied in northern or, in a few cases, central Italy, most of them in the sixth or seventh centuries, and X and O are simply unexceptional members of this group, though O is rather more in the 'mainstream' than the elder X, which is often idiosyncratic. Conceivably, further painstaking work with Fischer's collations may make it possible to draw an outline stemma for the J group, but it will remain tentative, for the earliest witnesses – one of which dates from as early as the first half of the fifth century – are incomplete and in some cases fragmentary.[36]

Most of the manuscripts under consideration have, in addition to their gospel text, lists of sometimes quite extended chapter headings prefacing each gospel, and these may also be considered in assessments of manuscript relationships. However, such *capitula* have their own textual traditions which, confusingly, have a transmission history more or less independent of the texts which they accompany. Perhaps because of their comparative brevity and lack of contentious material, variation within the text of *capitula* occurs less often than in the gospels themselves and so the former tend to retain their integrity for longer than the latter.[37] There is a distinctive *capitula* text which, with only small variations, the members of Wordsworth's and White's Z family share. Since Z itself (Harley 1775) does not have its *capitula*, and no comprehensive collations are available for the majority of other Italian manuscripts, we may call it the JXO series. Neither X nor O possesses its Matthew list complete. In the case of Luke (the only book where comparisons may be made), the JXO version of the *capitula* also appears in the Anglo-Saxon *Codex Bigotianus* (which I discuss below). In their prefaces, too, where comparisons may be made, X and O again are close, concurring generally with Z. However, in the Luke preface at least, they are not very close to *Bigotianus*.

The evidence that I have surveyed thus confirms that the texts of the Corpus Christi (X) and Oxford (O) gospel books are only distantly affiliated. As both originated in northern Italy within a period of two or three generations, it is not surprising that both belong within the J textual tradition, and this is confirmed by the form of their *capitula*, but no close affinities can be established between them and other surviving carriers of the tradition. This is a testimony to the large volume of biblical manuscripts (of which only a fraction survive) produced in Italy during the sixth and seventh centuries, and to the frequency of their export to England, before the focus of production moved into the more northerly parts of Europe, including England itself.

Textual Continuity with Known Canterbury Books

The short answer to the question whether there is any evidence of the influence of either of our two gospel books on manuscripts subsequently written (as far as we can tell) at Canterbury, and which might thus confirm the early presence there of X or O, must be 'no', but the story of Canterbury manuscripts is a difficult and incompletely known one. No manuscripts written in the seventh century in Kent or any other southern Anglo-Saxon kingdom are known to survive. Our earliest firm evidence for southern English book production comes from two books, both written in uncial, probably in Kent, during the early part of the eighth century. As I have already noted, it is likely that the Vespasian Psalter was made at Saint Augustine's Abbey, Canterbury, and it may be one of the psalters mentioned by Thomas of Elmham as one of the oldest Roman books at the abbey.[38] It is the first known witness anywhere to the *Romanum* text of the psalms, and it was presumably copied from a psalter that was brought from Rome either with the original mission or shortly thereafter. The other book is a copy of the Acts of the Apostles, which was at Saint Augustine's Abbey in the medieval period but which Richard Gameson has attributed to Minster.[39]

The only evidence for the gospel text at Canterbury during the first hundred years after the mission is indirect. Some of it comes from the activities of Theodore, archbishop of Canterbury 668–90, and Hadrian, abbot of SS Peter and Paul (subsequently Saint Augustine's Abbey), who between them established at Canterbury the school which was to receive such fulsome praise from Bede.[40] A record of instruction on the Bible given there by the masters is preserved in numerous scriptural glosses transmitted in an eleventh-century Italian manuscript, which is one of a complex series of related glossaries of the so-called 'Leiden family' preserved in continental manuscripts.[41] The glosses include lemmata which are presumably direct citations from the Bible manuscripts in use by Theodore and Hadrian. Unfortunately, the amount of quotation from the four gospels is small, but Patrick McGurk's analysis of the material, such as it is, shows a mixture of both Italian and Northumbrian influences on the text; there is no significant use of X or O variants.[42] In connection with Theodore, we can, alas, only speculate about the identity of a gospel book mentioned in the record of the Synod of Hatfield in 679. As transmitted by Bede, the record describes how Archbishop Theodore 'sat with the other reverend bishops of the island of Briton, having the most holy gospels before [them]'.[43]

A second potential source of textual evidence of the gospels is the extensive works of the most famous alumnus of the Canterbury school, Aldhelm, a prolific writer of both prose and poetry who became abbot of Malmesbury in 673 or 674 and bishop of Sherbourne in 706.[44] There are some hundred recognizable gospel references in his edited works, although in 80 per cent of them he gives wide paraphrases or allusions rather than direct citations.[45] In several cases Old Latin influence on the form of the text cited is apparent, but more frequent are variant readings which have no known parallels. In the cases where he cites Vulgate passages in which variation is well attested among the manuscripts, Aldhelm's versions suggest a mixture of both Italian and Northumbrian influence – rather as Theodore's lemmata do, though I have found no significant readings shared by the two writers. There is no hint that Aldhelm used a gospel text similar to that in X or O.

An important gospel book copied towards the mid- or later eighth century may be a product of Canterbury, though I can say little of the greatly puzzling *Codex Aureus* here.[46] Suffice it to note that its text of the gospels is heavily influenced by Old Latin variants. Why such a version of the gospels should have been copied at Canterbury (if it was) as late as the second half of the eighth century is not immediately obvious. Yet we might bear in mind the example of Wearmouth–Jarrow during the first half of the century, where we know that there was a stock of Old Latin manuscripts, as well as some Greek ones from which Bede cited often. In an age when the elucidation of the meaning of scripture was not yet tied strictly to its precise wording, Old Latin texts seem to have been happily accepted alongside the Vulgate for such purposes. As I have noted, at least parts of an Old Latin version of the gospels were apparently known to Aldhelm, though his citations (which may have been taken from unidentified patristic writings) differed from the text used in the *Codex Aureus*.[47] However, it was the Vulgate that was deliberately and persistently copied in the north and south for Bibles or part Bibles – with the exception of the *Codex Aureus*. According to Fischer, the Old Latin text of *Aureus* had been influenced by northern Italian or southern Gaulish traditions, rather than Roman, but there is really very little firm contemporary manuscript evidence to go on.[48] It hardly needs pointing out that the text of the *Codex Aureus* has no connection at all with that of our two Gospels of St Augustine. Nor, incidentally, was either affected by it during their respective phases of emendation, which I discuss below.

Chronologically, the next manuscript to consider is the early ninth-century Bible fragment, BL, Royal 1. E. vi (plus *membra disjecta*), which bears a fourteenth-century library inscription from Saint Augustine's Abbey and has been attributed to that house on art-historical grounds (cf. figs 11.3–5; pl. VI). The seventy-nine leaves that remain comprise the gospels and a fragment of Acts, but the large format (467 × 345 mm) and the evidence of the quire signatures leave little doubt that they were once part of a complete Bible.[49] As such, this is our only certain evidence for the production of complete Bibles in England between the *Codex Amiatinus* (copied before 716) and the late tenth-century Royal 1. E. vii + viii.[50] Written in half uncial and hybrid minuscule and including sumptuously decorated pages, the manuscript has been dated to the first half of the ninth century. It has been identified in the past with several items on Thomas of Elmham's list but especially the *Biblia Gregoriana*. This it cannot be, for that book was still intact in the early seventeenth century, whereas our Bible appears to have been broken up by the thirteenth. However, Mildred Budny has made a good case for Royal 1. E. vi having been modelled architecturally and decoratively on the *Biblia Gregoriana*.[51]

The text of Royal 1. E. vi has never been fully studied. From a cursory reading, it is easy to gain the impression (especially in parts of Matthew) of an even mix of northern Italian and the Irish-Northumbrian readings, with no significant influence from the AY (Amiatinus-Lindisfarne) tradition.[52] But the 'Irish-Northumbrian' variants are widely found in Italian manuscripts, and the character of Royal's text is as likely to have been formed before its ancestor manuscript or manuscripts reached England as thereafter. Hans Glunz unhelpfully identified the text as of the XO type.[53] X certainly shares some of Royal's significant variants, but only to the extent of about a quarter, with the figure higher (perhaps as high as half) in Luke. Parallels between Royal and O are fewer. Now that we have Fischer's collations for portions of each gospel, we can see that other manuscripts in the Italian tradition match Royal's text more or less consistently, though none shows evidence of a really close connection. Up to half of significant variants are in the seventh-century Vatican, Biblioteca Apostolica, Vatic. lat. 7223 [Xh/Jh] (produced in northern Italy or France),[54] except in Matthew, where the figure may be as low as a fifth. Here it is in fact Z (Harley 1775) and Perugia, Biblioteca Capitolare 2 [Jq] (*c*. 800, from Perugia itself)[55] which offer the most parallels; Z shares many variants in Mark and Luke also. These observations, provisional though they be, do not contradict Mildred

Budny's conjecture that Royal 1. E. vi preserves not only the architectural features of the *Biblia Gregoriana* but also its text.[56] That such was not necessarily the case is shown by the *Codex Amiatinus* and its sister Vulgate pandects, which were influenced by the *Codex grandior* of Cassiodorus in many ways but not by its text, which was in an Old Latin (specifically hexaplaric) version. However, the scanty reported evidence we have of the contents of the *Biblia Gregoriana* does indicate a Vulgate text.[57]

The most interesting thing about the text of Royal 1. E. vi is that it is almost exactly paralleled by that in another Anglo-Saxon manuscript, an occurrence unique among contemporary gospel books. The manuscript is Worcester Cathedral Library, Add. 1, which comprises three folios dating from the second half of the eighth century (fig. 11.6).[58] The text preserved is most of the last chapter of Matthew, the *capitula* for Mark, and part of Mark 10, and it is remarkably close to the corresponding sections of Royal 1. E. vi, even to the extent of sharing orthographical idiosyncrasies.[59] That there is a connection between them is not in doubt. Bearing in mind that, to judge from their palaeography, Royal was copied a couple of generations later than Worcester, the former might be a younger sister of the latter; at the very least they must have shared a grandmother. It is clear that a further gospel book fragment, BL, Lat. Bibl. d.1 (P), which contains parts of John 16–17, was written at the same centre as the Worcester leaves and was probably part of the same volume.[60] Its text ought to confirm the blood relationship but, alas, everything from the end of John 11 is wanting in the imperfect Royal manuscript, so that comparisons cannot be made. In view of the well-established fact that textual genealogy can vary considerably between, and even within, the gospels of a single gospel book, the consistency of the conjectured Worcester–Oxford volume in relation to Royal may be surmised but cannot be guaranteed.

OTHER ANGLO-SAXON GOSPEL BOOKS

If manuscripts fairly certainly produced at Canterbury offer no evidence of the textual influence of either X or O, what of gospel books made elsewhere in England (a surprising number of which, however, have also had alleged Canterbury connections)? The first positive signs of possible affiliation to have been discovered involve O and an eighth-century manuscript from Northumbria, the so-called 'Durham Gospels', a luxury manuscript which may have been written at Lindisfarne.[61] Christopher Verey concluded in his 1980 study that John and Mark 'almost certainly derived from a text akin to that found in O', and Luke quite possibly also.[62] More recently he has widened the nexus by demonstrating the remarkable closeness of the Durham text to that of the eighth-century Cambridge–London Gospels, which survive only in parts of Luke and John in Cambridge and in fire-damaged fragments of Mark in London (cf. fig. 11.10).[63] There is a third member of this newly identified text family, too – the eighth-century gospel book of which Durham, Cathedral Library A. II. 16 is a part.[64] Verey assumes that the distinctive text reached the three manuscripts in parallel from a single archetype, which he places in Northumbria, where he believes all three gospel books may have been produced. The archetype, he suggests, stemmed from an imported Italian book closely similar in text type to O, though he has not ruled out the possibility of a more direct line of descent from O to the Northumbrian family.[65]

The Cambridge–London Gospels have been associated with Canterbury at least since the sixteenth century, when both Archbishop Matthew Parker and Sir Robert Cotton (who owned the Cambridge and London portions, respectively) claimed they had once belonged to St Augustine, a connection recorded in a 1696 catalogue and inscribed on the first of the Cambridge leaves.[66] Janet Backhouse has noted that there is much evidence for the movement of books during the seventh and eighth centuries and that the Cambridge–London Gospels – along with the Echternach Gospels – was produced to less exacting standards than the Lindisfarne and Durham Gospels and could have been made by request for a centre outside Northumbria.[67] Thus the association with Canterbury is very possible and the identification of Cambridge–London as one of Thomas of Elmham's gospel books may then be correct.[68] Such movement between centres would help to explain the mixing of textual traditions which is apparent in the surviving gospel texts from Canterbury.

Much of the history of gospel transmission in Anglo-Saxon England, especially in Southumbria, has yet to be written. According to the list I compiled recently, there are seventy-six surviving manuscript witnesses to the gospels which were written in England, or imported and used here, up to *c.* 1100.[69] About a third of these consist of no more than odd leaves or fragments, but the rest are substantial, if not all complete. Many are as yet very little known. I have examined fifteen which may have been produced in the south of England before *c.* 900, to ascertain whether there is any evidence that the texts of either of our two Gospels of St Augustine may have had any direct or indirect influence on them.

An interesting example is the so-called *Codex Bigotianus*, whose provenance is Normandy but which appears to have been copied in England towards the end of the eighth century.[70] Its text was collated by Wordsworth and White for their edition of the Vulgate (B [Eb]) and a close reading of the evidence they present shows that, both in its *capitula* and in its main text, it belongs securely to the

Z family of Italian texts. There is no close affiliation with X and O, however. It is true that O shows the greatest number of agreements with B among Fischer's Italian (J) manuscripts, but these are often cancelled out by disagreements. In Matthew and Luke, it is notable that O, after correction (see below), agrees with a very high proportion of B's distinctive readings (as many as 90 per cent in passages of Matthew) but there are still enough disagreements to make any direct connection between B and corrected O implausible. B may simply be the descendant of yet another member of the spreading northern Italian family. Variants in Z itself frequently parallel those in B, especially in John.

Among the English gospel books of which there remain only fragments, three have been little studied and deserve brief comment here. None was collated by Wordsworth and White nor, more recently, by Fischer. In Prague, Universitní Knihovna, Roudnice VI. Fe. 50, there are two folios from Mark, carrying 14:3–21 and 14:62–15:10.[71] I have been unable as yet to examine more than a small part of one of the leaves, but here the text differs in no significant way from X or O, which means that they share several readings which distance them from most other members of the Italian J group. There are no characteristic AY or Irish-Northumbrian variants. Lowe posited an origin for the Prague fragments in southern England but no specific centre is indicated; certainly nothing would suggest Canterbury. Secondly, Brussels, Bibliothèque Royale, II. 436, is a single gospel book leaf with the text of Luke 11:10–29. The half-uncial script appears to be English, and of eighth-century date, but it does not point to a particular centre; the fragment was in the Liège area by the fifteenth century. Its text appears to be in the Italian tradition but no particularly close affiliation to X or O is evident.[72] Five folios containing portions of the text of Mark and Luke and the preface to John, now dispersed between St Petersburg and Avranches, constitute my third remnant.[73] Richard Gameson has now assigned it convincingly to Kent. He has noted some close textual correspondence with O in the parts he has examined,[74] but – as with all our remnants – the amount of text involved is too small for conclusions to be safely drawn from such evidence, and a general textual affiliation to Italian manuscripts is most likely.

Finally in this section, I turn to another little-understood English gospel book, the Barberini Gospels in the Vatican Library (Fischer's Ev).[75] Like *Bigotanus*, it is likely to have been copied in the second half of the eighth century, according to Lowe, who suggested an origin in Northumbria or Mercia. Michelle Brown has noted the presence of four scribes and suggested that two of them, whose writing style is more idiosyncratic than that of the other pair, were Mercian, under the supervision of Northumbrian scribes probably connected with Lindisfarne.[76] The text of the Barberini Gospels is another of those which have a misleading stratum of apparent 'Irish-Northumbrian' variants, despite their base being firmly in the northern Italian tradition. There is, however, no close relationship with X or O. Indeed, the interest of this text lies elsewhere, in its textual relationship with two manuscripts produced at the monastery at Echternach in the first half of the eighth century. The volumes in question, the Augsburg Gospels and the Maeseyck Gospels, are textually very close to each other and it is clear that either they shared an exemplar or one manuscript is a copy of the other.[77] Barberini shares over 90 per cent of its variant readings with this text.[78] Echternach was founded by the Anglo-Saxon Willibrord at the end of the seventh century, but he seems to have gone there directly from Ireland, where he had spent some years, and it is likely that the exemplar for Augsburg and Maeseyck came from Ireland. The source of Barberini's exemplar and the location in which it was copied are thus questions of the greatest interest.[79]

There remains much work to be done on the texts of Anglo-Saxon gospel books. It is possible that some further affiliations between these and the texts in X or O will be revealed, but the odds are that the pattern of textual relationships will remain largely ill-defined. The parallel between O and the archetype of three gospel books probably produced in Northumbria is a striking one, but probably tells us more about textual transmission in Italy than in England.

CORRECTIONS TO X AND O

Finally, I turn to a more concrete matter, the afterlife of our two Gospels of St Augustine – that is, the alterations their texts underwent after they had arrived in England. It is apparent that both gospel books continued to be actively used and carefully read for several centuries.

To begin with X, the manuscript had been fairly accurately copied, and certainly with more skill than O. A few major omissions resulting from homoeoteleuton were made good in a small uncial very like the main script, presumably (in Italy) very soon after copying (fig. 12.1).[80] On the other hand, most of the interventions in later hands are emendations. Most seem to have been made in the eighth or earlier ninth centuries, many in a thin-stroked, informal but tidy uncial.[81] It is notable that all the alterations to X, of whatever date and whatever kind, were done tidily, if not always with an eye for aesthetic proprieties. Wholesale emendation presupposes the careful comparison of the original text with another manuscript version, and the deliberate choice of alternative readings used by the latter, presumably because its text has been judged to represent a more accurate or authoritative tradition. The alterations in X are of little help in trying to identify such a specific tradition, however, for the readings introduced are often those most commonly found in Vulgate manuscripts. The process of emendation may simply have been perceived as one of normalisation. Very often the original readings had been shared by only a few other manuscripts, usually including Z. A few seem to have been unique to X, and these include a number of word-order inversions which were of little apparent consequence, so that the fact that they were nevertheless corrected attests to the care with which the manuscript must have been read through. Sometimes such alterations were made by the simple method of marking the words which were to be transposed with a slanting line over a dot, placed above the start of each of the words involved, and an example occurs in Matthew 11:10, where *hic est enim* is corrected to *hic enim est*. Yet, surprisingly, more often than not this simple and familiar method of correction was eschewed in favour of complete erasure and rewriting. I can think of no other biblical manuscript where this happens so consistently. In Matthew 22:46, for instance, X's original version of the account of Christ's encounter with the Pharisees went *neque ausus fuit ex illa die quisquam eum amplius interrogare* ('nor dared from that day anyone question him further'). This appears to have been the regular version in the Italian Z tradition, though rare elsewhere. The emender of X completely erased *ex illa die quisquam* and wrote afresh *quisquam ex illa die* (see fig. 12.2). This more widespread version, which keeps the pronoun adjacent to its verb (as in the Greek), is perhaps marginally clearer ('nor dared anyone from that day'), but the main impulse for such a fussy change presumably came from a perception of the greater authority of the alternative exemplar.

The fact that this revised version of Matthew 22:46 was used by members of the other important Italian family, AY, would not in itself be signifcant, for it could have been found in almost any Vulgate manuscript of the time (except most of those of the Z family). However, many of the other readings that were introduced into X, far less common than this one in Matthew 22:46, also concur with the AY tradition. Throughout the gospel book, in fact, emendations persistently bring the text into line with AY, and in some instances X's new reading is witnessed there alone.[82] There is an example in Luke 22:3, where the corrector has substituted AY's *uocatur* for the original *cognominabatur*, though the new verb scarcely affects the sense of the verse ('is called' for 'was surnamed').[83] Occasionally the new reading appears to be exclusive to A, such as the imperfect *ueniebant* ('they were coming') for the perfect *uenerunt* ('they came') in John 10:41. Nevertheless, despite the statistical strength of the AY tradition in relation to the emended readings in X, it must be emphasized that there are still many instances where the alterations go completely against it, or where patently non-AY readings have not been altered.[84] Clearly, then, the manuscript used for the emendation of X (assuming it was a single one) was not the immediate exemplar of the AY gospel text or a faithful copy of it, but merely one that was textually related to it. We need not assume that a gospel book written in England was involved; it might just as easily have been another Italian manuscript which had been brought to Canterbury, one strongly influenced by (or perhaps derived from a tradition feeding into) the Neapolitan tradition. More extensive research on X's alterations, based on Fischer's collations, may enable us to be more specific.

As for O, this manuscript, too, underwent extensive correction and emendation in recognizably Insular hands, most of it apparently during the eighth and ninth

12.3. BodL, Auct. D. 2. 14, fol. 7r. Matthew 9:18–33, including three tenth-century liturgical annotations. (Bodleian Library, University of Oxford)

centuries. In addition, there are three layers of liturgical or lectionary annotations, according to the analysis by Chapman. He noted six original seventh-century annotations in very small and neat uncials, a further thirty-three in a scrawled uncial, added in the seventh century but after the book had been bound, and then almost forty more by the corrector of most of Matthew, writing probably in the tenth century (see fig. 12.3).[85] All these annotations concur more or less with the texts of the Roman rite. Several scribes, in addition to Chapman's annotators, were involved in textual corrections or emendations in O, suggesting that these were effected over a considerable span of years. One scribe used a large and rather untidy cursive script, another a neatish uncial which mimics the original script, and a third, making some of the longer additions, a tidy minuscule. There are far more corrections in Matthew and the first two chapters of Mark (which have as many as six or eight per page) than in the later parts of the manuscript. These early pages look particularly untidy, for they have also been disfigured by marks which were added to divide the text into a sort of imposed *cola et commata* system, obviously for reading purposes.[86] There are further concentrations of such activity at the start and in the middle of Luke. Many corrections rectified the careless scribal errors, including omissions, which are characteristic of the original text of O;[87] others seem simply to be asserting alternative orthographical conventions.[88] There is, however, no consistency in the alterations, and no sign of a careful and systematic programme of correction and standardisation throughout the manuscript.

Many of the interventions in O are textual emendations of the sort we have seen in X, and a number were added as variants or glosses without erasure of the original reading. There is, however, no indication that a single source with an identifiable textual character provided a significant proportion of these new readings, as seems to be the case in X. Added variants characteristic of the AY tradition show up only occasionally in O. The 'Irish-Northumbrian' group – at least as it is represented by DEQ – seems to be rather more influential, but there is no consistency. Overall, the impression given is of a continual tinkering with the text over a considerable period of time, perhaps two centuries, using a variety of sources. Some of the emendations are minor, such as those involving non-essential pronouns,[89] but others are more interesting. In Matthew 5:24, O's original *relinque ibi munus tuum ad altare* ('leave there thy offering at the altar') was emended by the addition of *ante* above *ad*, not by the striking out of *ad*. Perhaps this was intended as a sort of clarifying gloss, stressing that one's offering is to be left 'before' the altar, as the Greek has it,[90] not upon it, which *ad* does not preclude; certainly *ante* is likely to have been Jerome's version and is in most manuscripts, though AY are notable exceptions. It is thus interesting to note the reverse process in X, which originally had *ante altare* here until the preposition was corrected to *ad*, presumably after comparison with the hypothetical manuscript described above, which often followed the AY tradition.

Another interesting addition to O comes in Luke 9:54, in the story of the Samaritans' refusal to accommodate Christ, which prompts John and James to ask whether they may call down fire from heaven to burn up the villagers. To the words *domine uis dicimus ut ignis descendat de caelo* ('Lord, do you wish us to command fire to come down from heaven?') have been added, in a neat minuscule, the words *sicut elias fecit* ('as Elijah did'), preceded by the abbreviation *al.* for *alia*, which announces that 'other' versions have what follows.[91] The added words derive from the Greek and are in a majority of the Old Latin versions of Luke, but among Wordsworth's and White's Vulgate manuscripts they are witnessed only by M [Fm], a northern Italian gospel book of the first half of the sixth century,[92] and an early eighth-century Theodulfian Bible, θm [Om].[93] There is no consistent link between corrected O and the text of M, whose text seems to stand as near to A as to Z,[94] but as a majority of O's emendations fall outside the passages covered by Fischer's recent collations, it is impossible to construct a coherent overall picture. Another gloss of Old Latin origin has been added to O in Matthew 6:16, where *exterminant* is given for *demoliuntur* (both meaning 'they destroy').[95] In this case, however, the variant had very wide circulation, for it is both in AY and in many Italian manuscripts, including B, Z and M. Similarly an Old Latin addition with wide circulation, *debitum*, has been added to *reddi* in Matthew 18:25 (see fig. 12.4). In Luke 22:27, the original text of O had already been expanded by two Old Latin additions, one of two words and the other of eight; the only other Vulgate manuscripts recorded by Wordsworth and White as having either of these additions are the Book of Kells (which, in the first case, expands the addition to fifteen words) and Egerton 609 (E [Be], which has only the second, in a slightly varying form). An emender has erased the shorter one, but the longer has been left untouched.[96]

Although both X and O, like so many Insular biblical manuscripts before the Conquest, underwent much correction and emendation after their arrival in England, spread over a considerable time, it is clear that the process in X was rather more focused and a large proportion of the emendations were made at one time, using apparently a specific source, a manuscript in some way connected with the AY textual tradition. I have noted already how carefully the alterations were always done; and there is no sign that X was ever used liturgically. All this is consistent with its being a particularly valued manuscript, kept in one centre. Conversely, O has the appearance of a book which passed through many hands and was much in demand, at least during some periods in its life, for practical purposes.

12.4. BodL, Auct. D. 2. 14, fol. 20v. Matthew 18:15–27, including tenth-century liturgical annotation, plus an addition in Matthew 18:25 (reddi + debitum: *an Old Latin reading, found in AY, Kells and others, and also added in X*). (Bodleian Library, University of Oxford)

Conclusions

As is so often the way in textual criticism of the Latin Bible, this brief account of the two manuscripts alleged at one time to be the Gospels of St Augustine has offered generalisations and many negatives. Both the books were written in Italy and subsequently came to England, and in the case of X, Corpus Christi 286, we

12.5. BodL, Auct. D. 2. 14, fol. 31r. Matthew 25:1–16. Note addition of originally omitted Matthew 25: 16ᵇ–25ᵃ at foot of page. (Bodleian Library, University of Oxford)

know for certain that it was at Canterbury during the Anglo-Saxon period. It is eminently possible (though it cannot be proved) that the manuscript arrived with St Augustine himself in 597. Whatever the truth of this matter, X is by far the earliest biblical manuscript used in England to have survived and thus forms a cornerstone for the study of the Anglo-Saxon Bible text. And O, BL, Auct. D. 2. 14, cannot be far behind, if it arrived before the last quarter of the seventh century, which is very likely.[97] Without X and O, our knowledge of the gospel text in Anglo-Saxon England would thus be even more unbalanced than it is, and our picture of an Italian textual invasion in the south, complementing the invasion which carried the AY tradition to the north (which I believe remains a valid one despite the complexity of mixing into which the textual history then falls) would be largely obscured. Between them, our two manuscripts show us just how, over a comparatively short time, Bible texts become altered, old textual traditions become diluted, and new ones arise. The hints in the *Codex Bigotianus* (insubstantial though they be) that part of its text might derive from the corrected version of O illustrate one of the possible sources of complexity. The invaluable presence of X and O inevitably draws our attention to the many absences, for it is clear that they are just small pieces of a larger mosaic. The virtual impossibility of drawing lines of connection between even the manuscripts which remain highlights how many others there must have been – more undoubtedly brought to England from Italy (to both the north and the south) and many more copied in England and distributed during the seventh and eighth centuries. Finally, however, the Gospels of St Augustine are not only the foundation of the history of the Anglo-Saxon Bible but of English Christianity itself and they will remain, whatever textual critics may do with them, an eloquent symbol of Augustine's mission.

NOTES

1. Fischer, *Die lateinischen Evangelien bis zum 10. Jahrhundert I. Varianten zu Matthäus, II. Varianten zu Markus, III. Varianten zu Lukas,* and *IV. Varianten zu Johannes*, Vetus Latina: Aus der Geschichte der lateinischen Bibel 13, 15, 17 and 18 (Freiburg, 1988–91); and *Nouum Testamentum Domini nostri Iesu Christi latine secundum editionem sancti Hieronymi*, eds J. Wordsworth and H.J. White, 3 vols (Oxford, 1889–1954): I *Quattuor Euangelia* (1889–98). Fischer's material poses two problems, however: its sheer density (for it aims to include all extant manuscripts) and its inevitable restriction to only a few short sections of each gospel.

2. Hereafter, when citing gospel manuscripts, I give Fischer's sigla in square brackets after those of Wordsworth and White, where these exist (and in these cases Fischer uses the earlier letter in lower-case). On X, see *CLA*, II, no. 126; M.R. James, *A Descriptive Catalogue of the Manuscripts in the Library of Corpus Christi College, Cambridge*, 2 vols (Cambridge, 1909–12), pp. 52–6; P. McGurk, *Latin Gospel Books from A.D. 400 to A.D. 800* (1961), no. 32; L. Webster and J. Backhouse, *The Making of England: Anglo-Saxon Art and Culture AD 600–900* (London, 1991), no. 1.

3. For reproductions and discussion, see F. Wormald, 'The Miniatures in the Gospels of St Augustine, Corpus Christi College, Cambridge, MS 286', repr. in *Francis Wormald: Collected Writings, I, Studies in Medieval Art from the Sixth to the Twelfth Centuries*, eds J.J.G. Alexander, T.J. Brown and J. Gibbs (Oxford, 1984), pp. 13–35; ills 1, 2, 7–24;

and Webster and Backhouse, *The Making of England*, no. 1.
4. *CLA*, II, no. 230; McGurk, *Latin Gospel Books*, no. 32.
5. *HE*, I, 26: 'In hac ergo et ipsi primo conuenire psallere orare missas facere praedicare et baptizare coeperunt . . .', pp. 76, 77.
6. *HE*, I, 29: 'et per eos generaliter uniuersa, quae ad cultum erant ac ministerium ecclesiae necessaria, uasa uidelicet sacra et uestimenta altarium, ornamenta quoque ecclesiarum et sacerdotalia uel clericilia indumenta, sanctorum etiam apostolorum ac martyrum reliquias, necnon et codices plurimos' (eds Colgrave and Mynors, pp. 104, 105).
7. I discuss these corrections, and those in O, below.
8. For details, see N.R. Ker, *Catalogue of Manuscripts Containing Anglo-Saxon* (Oxford, 1957; reissued with supplement, 1990), no. 54.
9. On the former possibility, see Lowe, *CLA*, II, no. 230; and on the latter, M.R. James, *The Ancient Libraries of Canterbury and Dover* (Cambridge, 1903), pp. lxviii–lxix, and Ker, *Catalogue*, no. 290.
10. Ed. Charles Hardwick, *Historia monasterii S. Augustini Cantuariensis by Thomas of Elham, fomerly Monk and Treasurer of that Foundation* (London, 1858), pp. 96–7. Elmham's list is discussed by James, *Ancient Libraries*, pp. lxiii–lxix, and J. Chapman, *Notes on the Early History of the Vulgate Gospels* (Oxford, 1908), pp. 181–3. See also Mildred Budny, ch. 11 above.
11. Trans. James, *Ancient Libraries*, p. lxv.
12. Cambridge, Trinity Hall, 1. The diagram is reproduced in Sir William Dugdale's *Monasticon Anglicanum: A New Edition*, eds J. Caley, H. Ellis and B. Bandinel (London, 1817), between pp. 120 and 121, and, in colour, in Richard Gameson, *St Augustine of Canterbury* (Canterbury, 1997), p. 36.
13. BL, Cotton Vespasian A. i: *CLA*, II, no. 193; Ker, *Catalogue*, pp. 266–7, no. 203; Alexander, *Manuscripts*, pp. 55–6, no. 29; also Richard Gameson, ch. 13 below. Facsimile: *The Vespasian Psalter*, eds D.H. Wright and A. Campbell, EEMF 14 (Copenhagen, 1967).
14. See Mildred Budny, ch. 11 above.
15. *Historia monasterii*, ed. Hardwick, p. 99. On the interpretation of Elmham's words, see C. Plummer, *Venerabilis Baedae Opera Historica*, 2 vols (Oxford, 1896), II, pp. 56–7, and cf. Chapman, *Notes*, p. 182 and n. 1. We might compare the traditions which associated Bede directly with a number of ancient manuscripts of his works and which led to a spurious 'de manu Bedae' being added to several of them, thereby increasing their value as relics.
16. It is worth noting that Bertha, daughter of King Charibert of Paris, married Æthelberht of Kent some ten or fifteen years before Augustine's arrival. She was of course a Christian and was accompanied by Bishop Liudhard, as her personal chaplain, who must have possessed a copy of the gospels and service books for use at St Martin's. It is to my mind not inconceivable that he had a gospel book which had originated in Rome.
17. See especially Chapman's assessment, which was coloured by his view that the two gospel books had been copied more or less at the same time (*Notes*, pp. 210–13).
18. Berger, *Histoire de la Vulgate pendant les Premières Siècles du Moyen Âge* (Paris, 1893), pp. 35–6; H.J. White, 'The Vulgate', in *A Dictionary of the Bible*, ed. J. Hastings, 5 vols (London, 1898–1904), IV, pp. 873–89, at p. 887; Wordsworth and White, *Nouum Testamentum*, I. 705–6; and Chapman, *Notes*, pp. 183–8.

19. *CLA*, II, no. 197; McGurk, *Latin Gospel Books*, no. 26.
20. J: Cividale, Museo Archeologico Nationale, s.n. + Prague, Knihovna Metropolitní Kapitoly Cim. 1 + Venice, Biblioteca di S. Marco, s.n.: *CLA*, III, no. 285; McGurk, *Latin Gospel Books*, no. 94. See also Fischer, *Lateinische Bibelhandschriften im frühen Mittelalter*, Vetus Latina: Aus der Geschichte der lateinischen Bibel 11 (Freiburg, 1985), pp. 54–5.
21. Florence, Biblioteca Medicea Laurenziana, Amiatino 1 (before 716): *CLA*, III, no. 299; and BL, Cotton Nero D. iv (*s*. vii[ex]): *CLA*, II, no. 187. On the Northumbrian gospel text, see T.J. Brown in *Evangeliorum Quattuor Codex Lindisfarnensis. Musei Britannici Codex Cottonianus Nero D. iv*, eds T.D. Kendrick et al., 2 vols (Olten/Lausanne, 1956–60), II, pp. 47–58; C.D. Verey in *The Durham Gospels*, eds C.D. Verey, T.J. Brown and E. Coatsworth, EEMF 20 (Copenhagen, 1980), pp. 68–76, and 'The Gospel Texts at Lindisfarne at the Time of St Cuthbert', in *St Cuthbert, his Cult and his Community to AD 1200*, eds G. Bonner, D. Rollason and C. Stancliffe (Woodbridge, 1989), pp. 143–50.
22. Fischer, *Beiträge*, pp. 224–39.
23. Fulda, Hessische Landesbibliothek, Bonifatianus 1 (F [Jf]): *CLA*, VIII, no. 1196.
24. BL, Add. 24142 (H or θ[H] [Oh]).
25. D [Hd] Book of Armagh: Dublin, Trinity College 52 (Armagh, *c.* AD 807): *CLA*, II, no. 270; E [Be] BL, Egerton 609 (later in Tours, s. ix[2/4]); L [Hl] Lichfield Gospels: Lichfield, Cathedral Library s.n. (West Midlands or Wales, s. viii[1]): *CLA*, II, no. 159; Q [Hq] Book of Kells: Dublin, Trinity College 58 (?Iona, s. viii/ix): *CLA*, II, no. 274; R [Hr] MacRegol Gospels: BodL, Auct. D. 2 29 (?Birr, *c.* AD 822). See B. Fischer, *Beiträge zur Geschichte der lateinischen Bibeltexte*, Vetus Latina: Aus der Geschichte der lateinischen Bibel 12 (Freiburg, 1986), pp. 206–7, 227–30, and *Lateinische Bibelhandschriften*, pp. 29–30. Controversy still surrounds the precise origins and textual classification of the members of this group. The textual affiliations of the Lichfield Gospels, for instance, seem to be largely independent of the other members.
26. One of the variants in O which Berger classified as 'Irish' was the addition *fiat uoluntas tua sicut in caelo et in terra* in Luke 11:2 (*Histoire de la Vulgate*, p. 35, n. 2). Wordsworth's and White's edition would later show that, while this Old Latin interpolation is indeed in several Irish and English manuscripts, it is also in Perugia, Biblioteca Capitolare, 1 (P [Jp]), copied in Italy in *s*. vi[2] (see n. 31, below). Fischer's work now reveals that it is in almost a dozen other Italian manuscripts, including Z.
27. Such is the *s.* vi Milan, Biblioteca Ambrosiana, C. 39 inf. (M [Jm]), though its liturgical marginalia suggest an origin in the north, perhaps Aquileia (*CLA*, III, no. 313; McGurk, *Latin Gospel Books*, no. 95; Fischer, *Beiträge*, pp. 55–6, 225).
28. Biblioteca Apostolica Vaticana, Vatic. lat. 7016: *CLA*, I, no. 51; McGurk, *Latin Gospel Books*, no. 134.
29. Ancona, Biblioteca Capitolare, s.n.: *CLA*, III, no. 278; McGurk, *Latin Gospel Books*, no. 92.
30. In Mark 10:48, for instance, the erroneous variant *multitudo* for *multi* has been recorded only in XO [i.e. Jx and Jo], Ja, and a handful of non-Italian manuscripts of *s*. viii or ix, including the *s*. viii[med] Durham, Cathedral Library, A. II. 16 [Nd].
31. Perugia, Biblioteca Capitolare, 1: *CLA*, IV, no. 407; McGurk, *Latin Gospel Books*, no. 100.
32. Split, Cathedrale, s.n.: *CLA*, IX, no. 1669; McGurk, *Latin Gospel Books*, no. 138.
33. But both also have some of those variants which are in X but *not* in O.

34. Respectively, Brescia, Biblioteca Queriniana, s.n., s. vi, perhaps from Ravenna (*CLA*, III, no. 281; McGurk, *Latin Gospel Books*, no. 93), and Lucca, Biblioteca Capitolare, 8.
35. *Notes*, p. 213.
36. The *s.* v manuscript is Js (Wordsworth's and White's S), in St Gallen, Stiftsbibliothek, 1395 pp. 7–327, and other locations; it probably originated in northern Italy: *CLA*, VII, no. 984; McGurk, *Latin Gospel Books*, no. 122.
37. This phenomenon of main text/*capitula* incongruence is especially apparent in Bibles of *s.* ix and x, when the *capitula* series used in the early Alcuinian Bibles from Tours became far more widespread, and retained its textual integrity longer, than the Alcuinian Bible text itself.
38. See above, p. 289 and n. 13. The text, with an interlinear Old English gloss added in *s.* ix, is ed. S.M. Kuhn, *The Vespasian Psalter* (Ann Arbor, MI., 1965).
39. BodL, Selden Supra 30: *CLA*, II, no. 257; see further Gameson, ch. 13 below.
40. *HE*, IV, 2. See M. Lapidge, 'The School of Theodore and Hadrian', *ASE* 15 (1986), 45–72; Margaret Deansley, *The Pre-Conquest Church in England*, 2nd edn (London, 1963), pp. 104–59; N. Brooks, *The Early History of the Church of Canterbury. Christ Church from 597 to 1066* (Leicester, 1984), pp. 70–6, 94–9.
41. Milan, Biblioteca Ambrosiana, M. 79, sup. (59v–66r and 67v–91r). See Lapidge, 'The School', pp. 57–62; B. Bischoff, 'Wendepunkte in der Geschichte der lateinischen Exegese im Frühmittelalter', in *Mittelalterliche Studien* I, 205–73, at 207–9. The glosses are now ed. by B. Bischoff and M. Lapidge, *Biblical Commentaries from the Canterbury School of Theodore and Hadrian* (Cambridge, 1995).
42. 'Theodore's Bible: the gospels', in *Archbishop Theodore: Commemorative Studies on his Life and Influence*, ed. M. Lapidge (Cambridge, 1995), pp. 255–9. There is much evidence for the Pentateuch; see R. Marsden, 'Theodore's Bible: the Pentateuch', ibid., pp. 236–54.
43. *HE*, IV, 17: 'praepositis sacrosanctis euangeliis' (eds Colgrave and Mynors, p. 384). See G. Henderson, *Losses and Lacunae in Early Insular Art*, University of York Medieval Monograph Series 3 (1982), p. 10.
44. *Aldhelm: the Poetic Works*, eds M. Lapidge and L. Rosier, with an appendix by N. Wright (Cambridge, 1985), p. 1. The dates are given by Lapidge and Rosier, who estimate that Aldhelm died in late 709 or early 710 (ibid., pp. 9–10).
45. Of the nineteen, in nine cases the Old Latin and Vulgate versions do not differ substantially; in three other cases there may be some Old Latin influence, and in three more it is fairly certain.
46. Stockholm, Kungliga Biblioteket, A. 135: *CLA*, XI, no. 1642. See McGurk, *Latin Gospel Books*, no. 111; Hunter Blair, *World of Bede*, pp. 226, 229; Fischer, *Lateinische Bibelhandschriften*, pp. 159, 170; Fischer, *Beiträge*, pp. 234, 298; Richard Gameson, ch. 13 below.
47. Aldhelm did not of course spend all his life in Canterbury.
48. *Beiträge*, p. 298.
49. The *membra disjecta* are Canterbury, Cathedral Library, Add. 16 and BodL Lat. bib. b. 2 (P): *CLA*, II, nos 214, 244. See P. McGurk, 'An Anglo-Saxon Bible Fragment of the Late Eighth Century', *Journal of the Courtauld and Warburg Institute* 25 (1962), 18–34. The most detailed study to date is M.O. Budny, 'London, British Library MS Royal 1. E. VI: the Anatomy of an Anglo-Saxon Bible Fragment' (unpubl. Ph.D. dissertation, London University, 1985); see also her comments in ch. 11 above.

50. A two-volume Bible which ended up at Christ Church, though it was probably not copied there; see R. Marsden, *The Text of the Old Testament in Anglo-Saxon England*, (Cambridge, 1995), pp. 321–78, at pp. 326–7.
51. See her contribution to this volume.
52. Berger noted the appearance of these 'Irish' variants (*Histoire de la Vulgate*, p. 35 and n. 1), including *demoliuntur* in Matthew 6:16. Many Irish-Northumbrian manuscripts do have this reading but certainly it was Jerome's, even though many Italian and Insular manuscripts have the Old Latin variant *exterminant*. The latter was added to O, as a gloss; see below, p. 303.
53. H.H. Glunz, *History of the Vulgate in England from Alcuin to Roger Bacon* (Cambridge, 1933), pp. 29–30.
54. *CLA*, I, no. 54.
55. *CLA*, IV, no. 408.
56. See her contribution to this volume.
57. Thomas of Elham reports that the second volume of the *Biblia Gregoriana* began with Jerome's prologue on Isaiah (*Historia monasterii*, ed. Hardwick, pp. 96–7).
58. *CLA*, II, no. 262; McGurk, *Latin Gospel Books*, no. 38. See also Mildred Budny, ch. 11 above.
59. See Verey, *Durham*, pp. 69–70, and cf. C.H. Turner, *Early Worcester MSS: Fragments of Four Books and a Charter of the Eighth Century Belonging to Worcester Cathedral* (Oxford, 1916), and Glunz, *History of the Vulgate*, pp. 29–30, who thought that the Worcester text was of the same type as in XO.
60. *CLA*, II, no. 245; McGurk, *Latin Gospel Books*, no. 34. The text of neither this nor the Worcester manuscript is included in Fischer's collations.
61. Durham, Cathedral Library, A. II. 17, fols 2–102 + Cambridge, Magdalene College, Pepys 2981 (19): *CLA*, II, no. 149. See R.A.B. Mynors, *Durham Cathedral Manuscripts to the End of the Twelfth Century* (Oxford, 1939), no. 3; McGurk, *Latin Gospel Books*, no. 13; Alexander, *Insular Manuscripts*, no. 10; Webster and Backhouse, *Making of England*, no. 81; and especially Verey, *Durham*, pp. 68–105, and 'The Gospel Texts', pp. 146–9.
62. *Durham*, p. 72. Verey suggests also a more remote connection with X.
63. Respectively, CCCC, 197B, fols 1–36, and BL, Cotton Otho C. v: *CLA*, II, no. 125. See Verey's 'A Northumbrian Text Family', in *The Bible as Book: The Manuscript Tradition*, eds J.L. Sharpe and K. van Kampen (London, 1997), pp. 105–122, at pp. 111–13. Also McGurk, *Latin Gospel Books*, no. 2; Alexander, *Insular Manuscripts*, no. 12; Webster and Backhouse, *Making of England*, nos 83a, b; M. Budny, *Insular, Anglo-Saxon, and Early Anglo-Norman Manuscript Art at Corpus Christi College, Cambridge: An Illustrated Catalogue* (Kalamazoo, 1997), no. 3.
64. *CLA*, II, no. 148a, b, c; a fragment of the volume is in Cambridge, Magdalene College Library, 2981 (18). See Alexander, *Insular Manuscripts*, no. 16.
65. Interestingly, and confusingly, the Book of Kells (Q[Hq]), whose origin is disputed, shares 90 per cent of Durham Gospels' O readings in John. Writing in 1980, Verey suggested that Q (in John at least) derives either from Durham itself, in a direct line with few intermediaries, or from an archetype shared with O (*Durham*, pp.72–3).
66. See Verey, 'Gospel Texts', pp. 148–9, and J. Backhouse, 'Birds, Beasts and Initials in Lindisfarne's Gospel Books', in *St Cuthbert*, eds Bonner et al., pp. 165–74, at 171–3.
67. 'Birds, Beasts', p. 173. For a summary of the problems associated with the Echternach Gospels (BnF, lat. 9389: *CLA*,

V, no. 578), which have connections (though not textual ones) with the Durham Gospels, see Verey, 'Gospel Texts', pp. 148–9. Most recently, Verey has reported a close connection between Echternach and Durham A. II. 16 in the text of Matthew 1–22.
68. See Mildred Budny, ch. 11 above.
69. See my '"Ask What I Am Called": The Anglo-Saxons and their Bibles', *The Bible as Book*, eds Sharpe and Van Kampen, pp. 145–96, at pp. 169–76.
70. BnF, lat. 281 + 298: *CLA*, V, no. 526; McGurk, *Latin Gospel Books*, no. 58; Alexander, *Insular Manuscripts*, no. 34; Webster and Backhouse, *Making of England*, no. 155. See also Gameson ch. 13 in this volume.
71. *CLA*, X, no. 156.
72. The recto of the leaf is badly damaged and much text is illegible.
73. St Petersburg, Public Library, O. v. I. 1 + Avranches, Bibliothèque municipale, 48, fols i, iii; 68, fols i, ii; 71, fols A, B: *CLA*, VI, no. 730.
74. See this volume, pp. 347–8.
75. Biblioteca Apostolica Vaticana, Barb. lat. 570: *CLA*, I, no. 63; McGurk, *Latin Gospel Books*, no. 137; Alexander, *Insular Manuscripts*, no. 36; Webster and Backhouse, *Making of England*, no. 160.
76. 'The Lindisfarne Scriptorium from the Late Seventh to the Early Ninth Century', in *St Cuthbert*, ed. Bonner et al., pp. 151–63, at p. 161.
77. Augsburg, Universitätsbibliothek, Oettingen-Wallerstein'sche Bibl. 1. 2. 4⁰ 2: *CLA*, VIII, no. 1215; and Maaseik, Sint Katerinenkerk s.n.: *CLA*, X, no. 1558. On the manuscripts in relation to Echternach, see Nancy Netzer, 'Willibrord's Scriptorium at Echternach and Its Relationship to Ireland and Lindisfarne, in *St Cuthbert*, eds Bonner et al., pp. 203–12, and her *Cultural Interplay in the Eighth Century: The Trier Gospels and the making of a scriptorium at Echternach* (Cambridge, 1994), pp. 13–16; and cf. Dáibhí Ó Cróinín, 'Is the Augsburg Gospel Codex a Northumbrian Manuscript?', in *St Cuthbert*, eds Bonner et al., pp. 189–201. Netzer believes that Augsburg and Maeseyck shared an exemplar.
78. Luke seems rather less faithful to the Augsburg–Maeseyck text than the other three gospels, but many of the apparent variations both here and in the other books may be due in large part to careless copying, which is a characteristic of Barberini.
79. I shall present a fuller analysis of the text in a forthcoming article.
80. An example is the addition of the whole of Matthew 16:12, originally omitted by homoeoteleuton.
81. Examples are *langorem* > *languorem* in Matthew 10:2; *uides* > *uidetis* in Mark 13:2; *adprehensum* > *apprehensum* in Mark 12:3. A number of alterations (including that in Matthew 10:2) are overlooked in Wordsworth's and White's critical apparatus. My analysis of correctors' scripts is based on the assessment of various palaeographers, notably Lowe, and observations of my own. It is of course notoriously hard to date corrections accurately and to differentiate between the different scribes involved.
82. That is, it is found in none of the extant manuscripts which have so far been collated. AY readings often occur in the Rushworth Gospels (R [Nr]) also.
83. However, alternative tenses of *uoco* are found in a few manuscripts, including *uocabatur* ('was called'). The more common *cognominabatur* is taken to be Jerome's version (translating a participle form of the Greek verb epikaleo), but the present-tense variation *cognominatur* occurs in Z and some other manuscripts.

84. For example, in Luke 1:59, a re-ordering of words by the corrector – *nomine patris sui zacharia* > *zacharias nomine patris eius* – departs from the version in AY (and most other witnesses) and aligns X with a very small number of manuscripts which include O, D, L and Epternach; the change of *zacharia* to *zacharias* is most unusual (almost all manuscripts having *zachariam*). In Mark 1:36, X's *persequutus* (shared with the original text of Z) was altered to *persecutus* but not to AY's (and O's) *secutus*; in Luke 10:32, X's original 'AY' reading *euentura* was altered to *uentura*; in John 3:4, *rursus* was not changed to AY's *iterato*; and, similarly, substantial additions in John 3:6 and 7:29 (the latter in a form exclusive to X) were left intact, though neither is in A or Y.
85. See Chapman, *Notes*, pp. 191–202.
86. As I noted above, Matthew is the only gospel in O which was not originally written *per cola et commata*.
87. For example, Matthew 6:16 *receperunt* > *quia receperunt*; Mark 10:14 *parulos* > *paruulos*; Luke 1:24 *ei* > *eius*. Often e/i or b/u confusion was involved, as in Luke 1:4 *ueruorum* > *uerborum*; 1:28 *habe* > *haue*; Matthew 5:4 *mitis* > *mites*; 5:32 *demissam* > *dimissam*.
88. For example, Mark 10:6 *faeminem* > *feminam*; Luke 1:12 *irruit* > *inruit*.
89. For example, Matthew 10:13 *domus* + *illa*.
90. ἔμπροσθεν τοῦ θυσιαστηρίου.
91. Alternatively, the abbreviation stands for *aliter*, 'elsewhere', with of course the same implication.
92. Milan, Biblioteca Ambrosiana, C. 39 inf., perhaps from Aquileia: *CLA*, III, 313.
93. BnF, lat. 9380, the 'Mesmes Bible', *c.* 800/05, Orléans. It may be noted that the *Codex Aureus*, often a textual maverick, lacks the addition.
94. Fischer, *Beiträge*, p. 225.
95. The sense in the full phrase is that hypocrites 'disfigure' or 'distort' their faces (*demoliuntur enim facies suas*) in order to give the impression that they are fasting.
96. Without doubt, others of the J group will be found to contain these additions. The end of Luke does not survive in X.
97. The earliest remaining Old Testament manuscript is Durham, Cathedral Library, B. IV. 6, fol. 169* (*CLA*, II, no. 153), a fragment of Maccabees from an Italian part-Bible, copied in *s.* vi and brought to Northumbria in the 670s or 680s. It was probably an exemplar for the *Codex Amiatinus*.

CHAPTER 13

The Earliest Books of Christian Kent

Richard Gameson

We can be entirely confident that when Augustine arrived in Kent in 597 he came bearing various books. And when Gregory dispatched reinforcements for the mission four years later, he sent with them, Bede tells us, the things that were necessary for the worship and ministry of the church, which included 'very many books'.[1] Writing in the mid-eighth century, Archbishop Egbert of York alluded to an antiphoner and a missal that, he believed, Gregory had given to Augustine.[2] As such formal Mass books were only just evolving *c*. 600, this is unlikely to have been true as such. The underlying premise, however – that Augustine must have had books containing the prayers, readings and directions for Mass throughout the year, in addition to a Roman calendar, martyrology, and hymnal – is undoubtedly sound; and there is evidence for the presence of a psalter containing a version of the 'Old Hymnal' in Canterbury at an early date.[3] A good case can also be made for thinking that Saint Augustine's Abbey soon came to possess a Late Antique Bible.[4] Whether or not this venerable two-volume copy was really the Bible of St Gregory as was believed in the later Middle Ages,[5] the great Pope certainly saw holy reading in general as a key component of monastic virtue,[6] and regarded literacy as a precondition for admission to holy orders;[7] and his views will undoubtedly have informed those of his missionaries. Gregory was also conscious of the church's responsibility for, and the necessity of communicating with the illiterate, a class not only to be found in pagan Anglo-Saxon England, but equally in Gaul and among the Lombards on his doorstep.[8] It is highly probable that Augustine brought with him at least one of Gregory's own works, namely the *Regula pastoralis*: it had an obvious relevance to the missionary's circumstances, and certainly in the late ninth century the text was believed to have been introduced to England by Augustine personally.[9] Above all, we can be confident that he imported gospel books and psalters, the *sine qua non* of the faith;

and both figure prominently among the volumes which were venerated at Saint Augustine's Abbey in the later Middle Ages as the books of Gregory and Augustine (cf. figs 11.9–10).[10]

Whatever he brought with him or subsequently received from Gregory, and whatever books he may have inherited from the circle of Queen Bertha and Bishop Liudhard at Canterbury,[11] Augustine and his followers will have rapidly needed more. Although book production and learning were not the *raisons d'être* of the missionaries, they were of key importance for the long-term success of their endeavour.[12] Extra gospel books and psalters were a minimum requirement as the church gradually consolidated its foothold in the south-east; and native converts destined for holy orders had to be able to read Latin. At Canterbury itself, the centre of operations, where a school was evidently in existence by the 630s and doubtless before,[13] the need for other texts is likely to have grown continuously. By the late seventh century, Bede tells us, students were flocking to the school which was then enjoying a renaissance under the learned Archbishop Theodore of Tarsus (668–90) and Abbot Hadrian of Saint Augustine's (d. 709/10).[14] The curriculum then embraced biblical exegesis, Roman law, computus, and musical chant as well as Latin and Greek; and the high quality of the teaching is reflected in the work of distinguished alumni, notably Aldhelm (d. 709/10), later abbot of Malmesbury, Ceolfrith (d. 716), future abbot of Wearmouth–Jarrow, and Albinus (d. 733/4), Hadrian's successor at Saint Augustine's, whom Bede described as a man of universal learning.[15] Such activity presupposed a substantial book collection, embracing a broad range of subject matter. Unfortunately, the volumes in question have all seemingly vanished. Nor can we easily reconstruct the library by analysing Theodore and Hadrian's writings. Their personal literary legacy is slim. Moreover, as Theodore was an old man when he came to England and seems to have travelled quite extensively when he got here, there is no guarantee that all the works reflected in the small quantity of extant writings associated with him were actually to be found at Canterbury.[16]

If the problems are severe for Canterbury, they are insuperable for other important early Kentish foundations, such as Dover, Folkestone, Lyminge, Minster-in-Sheppey, Reculver and Rochester,[17] as for most other centres in the south as a whole. Indeed, there is only one other Kentish house outside Canterbury for which we have both documentary evidence relating to book production, and a possibly attributable manuscript, namely Minster-in-Thanet. We are thus faced with a paradox. We know that early christian Kent had a reasonable number of books, imports from Italy and France as well as local products, and we can make intelligent guesses about some of the texts that are likely to have been represented; however, as the volumes themselves are almost all

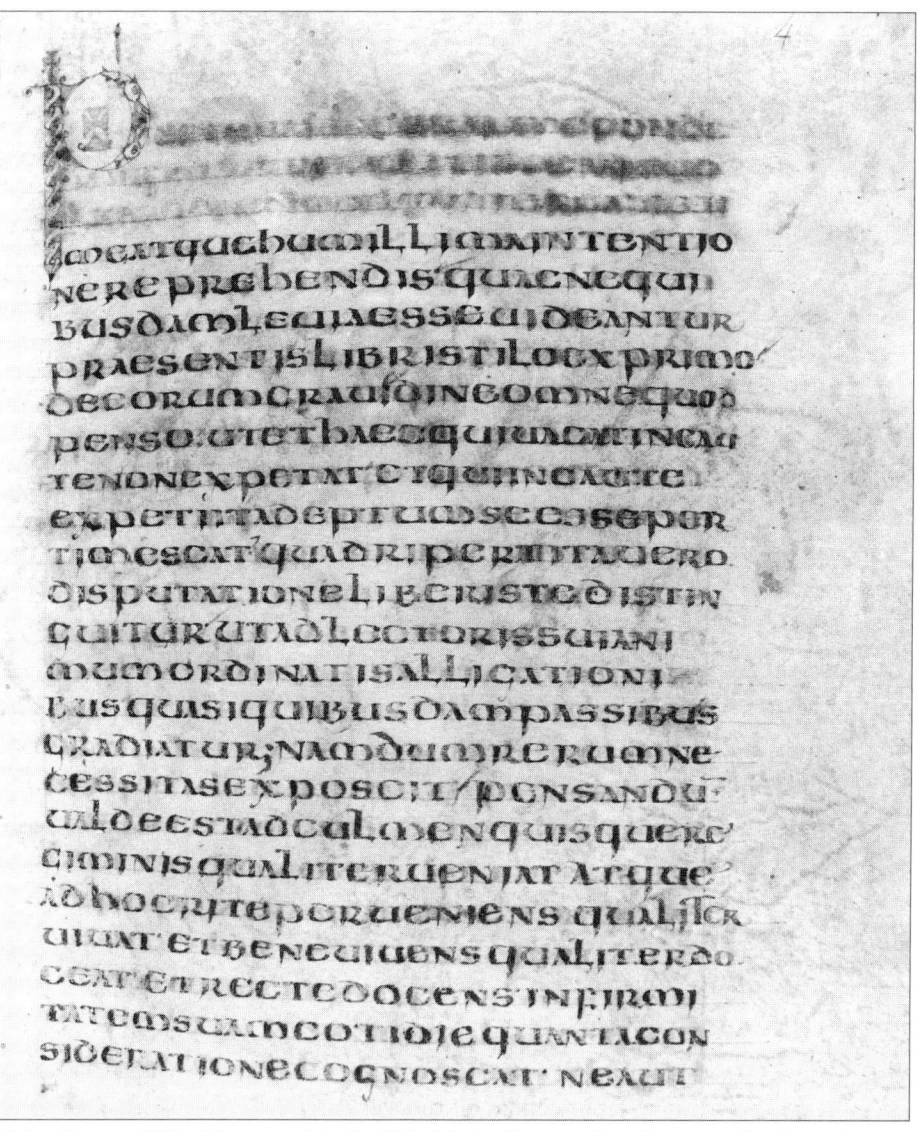

13.1. Troyes, Bibliothèque municipale, 504, fol. 4r. Gregory, Regula pastoralis. *Page size:* c. 290 × 230 mm. (Troyes, Bibl. mun.)

lost, any hopes of presenting even a semi-coherent account of them are vain, and our view of the evolution of Kentish scribal practices is obscured. The best we can do is examine the handful of relevant survivors, bearing in mind that each of these books is, merely by dint of having survived, highly exceptional. We shall consider them in approximate chronological order.[18]

Our first manuscript, it should be stated very clearly, is not in England and never has been. There are, as we have seen, good if circumstantial reasons for

13.2. Troyes, Bibliothèque municipale, 504, fol. 55r. (Troyes, Bibl. mun.)

believing that Augustine brought a copy of Gregory's *Regula pastoralis* to England with him; and in Troyes, Bibliothèque municipale, 504 we have a copy of the text that was probably written in Rome in the circle of the great Pope himself (figs 13.1–2).[19] Augustine's hypothetical copy might have resembled this one. A comparatively handsome volume of moderate size (288 × 230 mm, with a written area of 201 × 148 mm),[20] its construction is fairly typical for an Italian manuscript of its date. The quires are composed of six or occasionally five sheets (making twelve or ten folios respectively); and the parchment was arranged so

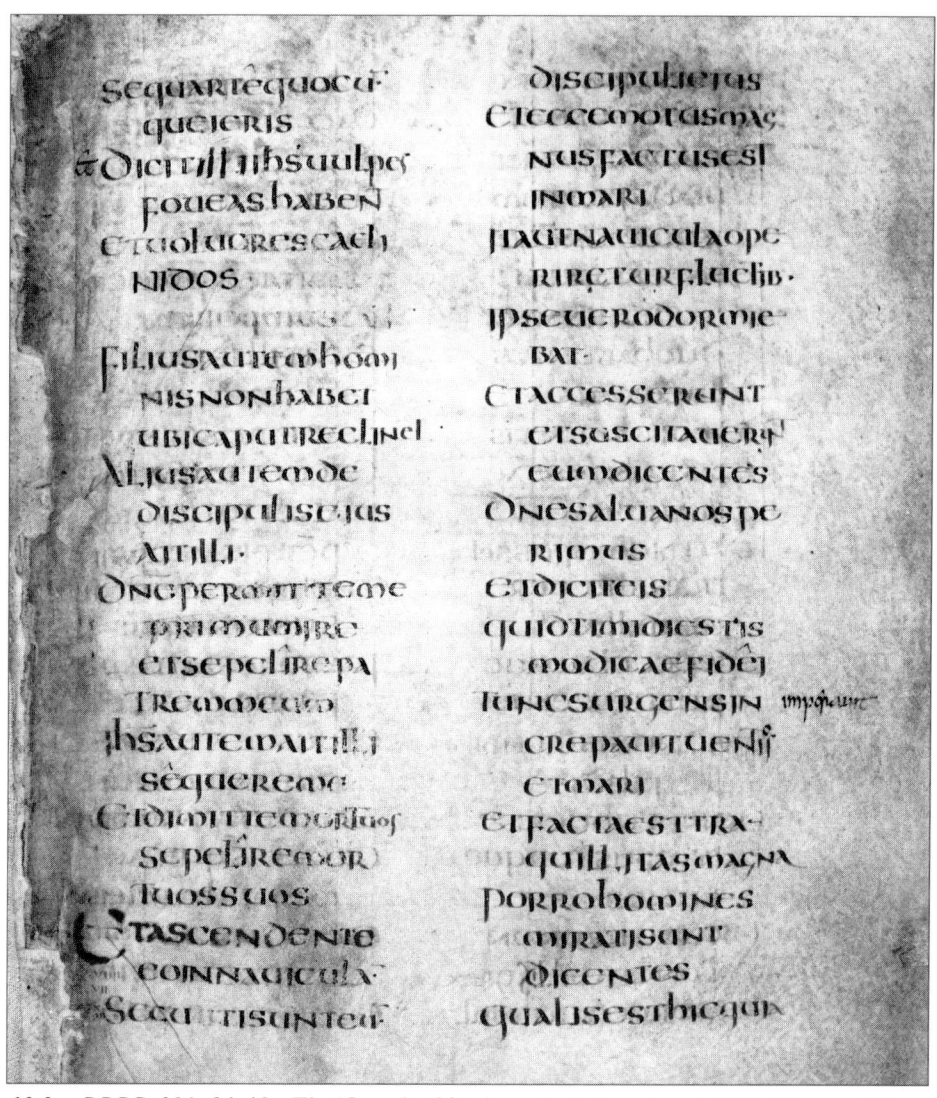

13.3. CCCC, 286, fol. 18r. The 'Gospels of St Augustine'. Page size: 245 × 180 mm. (The Master and Fellows of Corpus Christi College, Cambridge)

that hair sides faced hair, and flesh sides faced flesh throughout the quires, with a flesh side outermost. The prickings that were supplied to guide the ruling run through the written area; and the ruling was done on the flesh side of each bifolium, before folding.[21] The flesh side of the parchment did not take the ink well, and much of it has scaled off, a process which, to judge by retracings, had begun at an early date.[22] The main text is written, seemingly by a single scribe, in a fluid but square and squat uncial – the formal bookhand of Late Antiquity. There are no divisions between words, but the first line of each chapter is written in red and introduced by an enhanced initial; some of these initials are modestly decorated, particularly in Book III.[23] Scriptural citations are identified in the margins in an uncial hand contemporary with the original text. In addition, there are numerous contemporary corrections and insertions, often changing citations from an Old Latin version of the Bible to the corresponding Vulgate reading but also including more substantive, 'authorial' interventions; and it is these that seem to indicate that the volume was produced in Gregory's immediate milieu.[24]

An Italian manuscript which did come to England at an early date and whose Anglo-Saxon provenance was Saint Augustine's Abbey is the famous Gospels of St Augustine, CCCC, 286 (fig. 13.3; pls IV–V).[25] Its script points to a date in the second half of the sixth century, and is wholly compatible with an origin in Rome, a hypothesis which is strengthened by the remarkable treatment of St Peter in the imagery on the pictorial page following Mark's gospel (fol. 125r, pl. IV). The depiction of the way to the cross here is surprisingly long and drawn out, occupying all or part of the three bottom scenes. Why? Because normally one or more of these vignettes would also include the Denial of Peter which, most unusually, is entirely absent here.[26] Now, the centre most likely to have had reservations about depicting St Peter in an unfavourable light is undoubtedly Rome. One might also then expect the artist to have emphasised the positive side of Rome's patron saint in various ways, and this is exactly what we see. Peter is given unusual prominence and is depicted as a very vigorous figure at the arrest of Christ;[27] while in the foot-washing, he is seated not on a stool, but on a high-backed throne.[28] While neither point is unparalleled, their collocation here is striking; and this calculated depiction of Peter, added to the evidence of the script, makes a Roman origin not merely possible but probable.

The manuscript is a little smaller than the Troyes copy of the *Regula pastoralis* (242–50 × 182–8 mm); and the parchment is of a very modest quality, with a strong contrast between the hair and flesh sides of the membrane. The fact that the sheets were placed within the quires so that like faced like, with a flesh side outermost was therefore sensible (fig. 13.4). This was also, as we have seen, the case in Troyes 504; and it was, in fact, the most common arrangement among Italian manuscripts prior to the seventh century. The sheets were pricked and ruled before folding, the horizontal rulings being guided by a row of prickings running down the centre of the page, between the columns. Though written in *scriptura continua* like the *Regula pastoralis* manuscript, here the text was carefully laid out with lines of different lengths corresponding to the sense (*per cola et commata*)[29] to facilitate reading. The beginnings of the individual gospels did not receive much emphasis – the first line was merely written in red – and the same

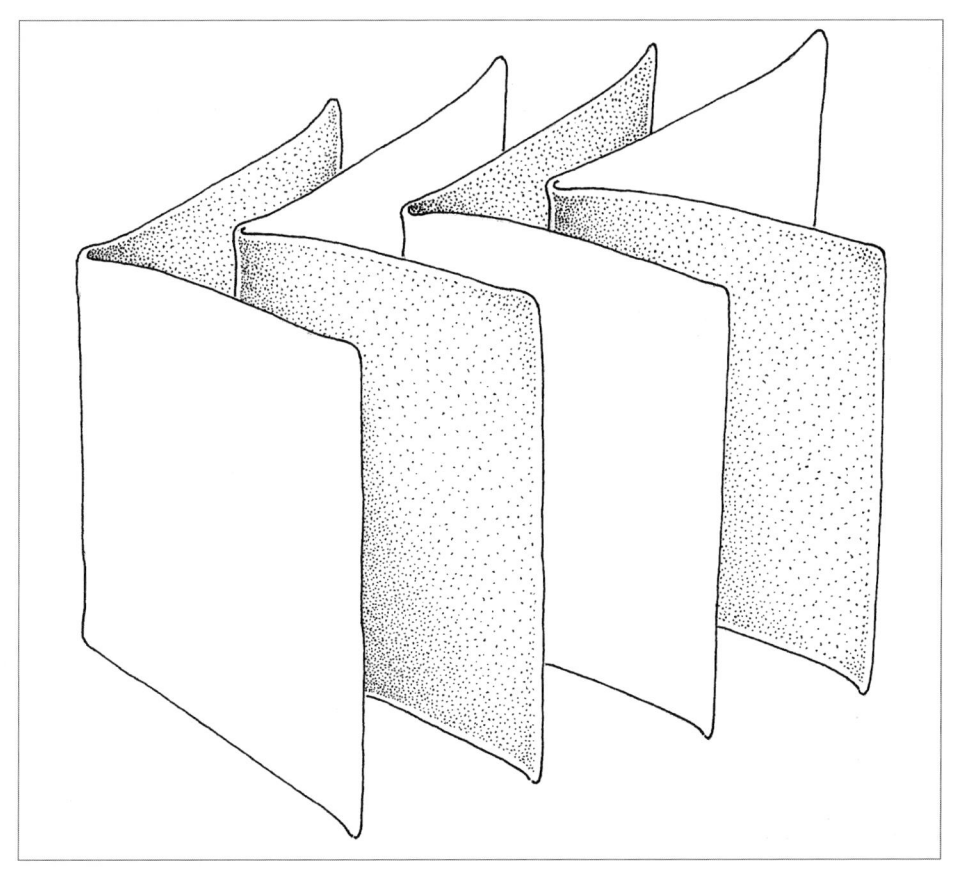

13.4. Makeup of a 'typical' quire in an early Italian manuscript. (Gameson)

restrained treatment was given to Matthew 1:18 ('*Christi autem generatio sic erat*': 'Moreover, the birth of Christ was thus'). On the other hand, a greater accent was placed at the end of texts: not only the *explicit* of a section but also the *incipit* for the one that followed were located at the end of the first section, generally written in rustic capitals. Both these points are typical of a book in the Late Antique tradition (and they still hold good in relation to some Italian gospel books produced up to two centuries after our one).[30]

At least two scribes were involved in the original writing of the Gospels of St Augustine, one being responsible for Matthew and Mark, a second for Luke and probably also John. Neither hand has much in common with the script of Troyes 504; but the scribe of Luke and John does have general resemblances to that of another broadly coeval uncial manuscript which has been attributed to Rome.[31] The scholar who has studied 'Roman uncial' most closely felt that Corpus Christi 286 itself belonged to this 'Roman' group.[32]

This is the oldest surviving Latin gospel book containing miniatures (pls IV–V). In its original state, it seems to have been decorated with four evangelist portraits – three preceding the relevant gospel texts, the fourth facing the relevant preface, not the gospel text – and two pictorial pages, one following Mark's gospel, the other after John's.[33] It probably also had ornamented canon tables. Two basic points worth stressing are that on the one hand the pictorial decoration does not seem to have been organized in an entirely regular way; while, on the other, the volume included considerably more imagery than virtually every other extant gospel book produced in the following three centuries. Our manuscript contains twenty-four narrative scenes in its surviving state, and the original total was probably seventy-two. Not until Ottonian manuscripts, produced some four hundred years later, does one find other gospel or pericopes books with narrative cycles on a comparable scale.

The evidence of later gospel books whose decoration echoes lost exemplars of an equivalent or even greater antiquity means we can be confident that there were other early copies with figural imagery. It is doubtful, however, that there were ever very many of them. Because the pictorial pages in our manuscript have been so widely reproduced, and because so many lost models have been hypothesized by modern scholars, it is easy to get the impression that Late Antique gospel books were generally decorated thus. In fact, precisely the reverse was true. It is quite clear from the corpus of surviving early gospel books that, however normal pictorial decoration – principally in the form of evangelist portraits – may have become by the ninth century, its use was not so widespread up to the seventh. In many early copies, including splendidly written ones, ornamentation was limited to modest calligraphic colophons and, perhaps, canon tables. The quire structures, not to mention the continuous texts, show that no decorated pages have been lost; and the individual gospels are merely heralded by rubrics in display script and simple decorated initials.

The Gospels of St Augustine was thus, by dint of its miniatures, a rarity even in its own day. Whether this was seen to make it especially suitable as equipment for a missionary coming to a pre-literate society is a nice question. If this were the case, it was on account of the book's greater symbolic value and its utility as an iconographic repository, and not because these particular images could have helped the evangelists in their work. Although, as is well known, Gregory appreciated the didactic value of visual imagery as a tool to be used by the clergy for instructing the *illiterati*,[34] the narrative scenes in our manuscript are much too small to have fulfilled such a role themselves. And before one gets too carried away with the wonders of this second-rate volume, we should stress that it was not by the standards of its day a particularly fine one. The primary and most highly regarded means of decorating books in Late Antiquity was not, of course,

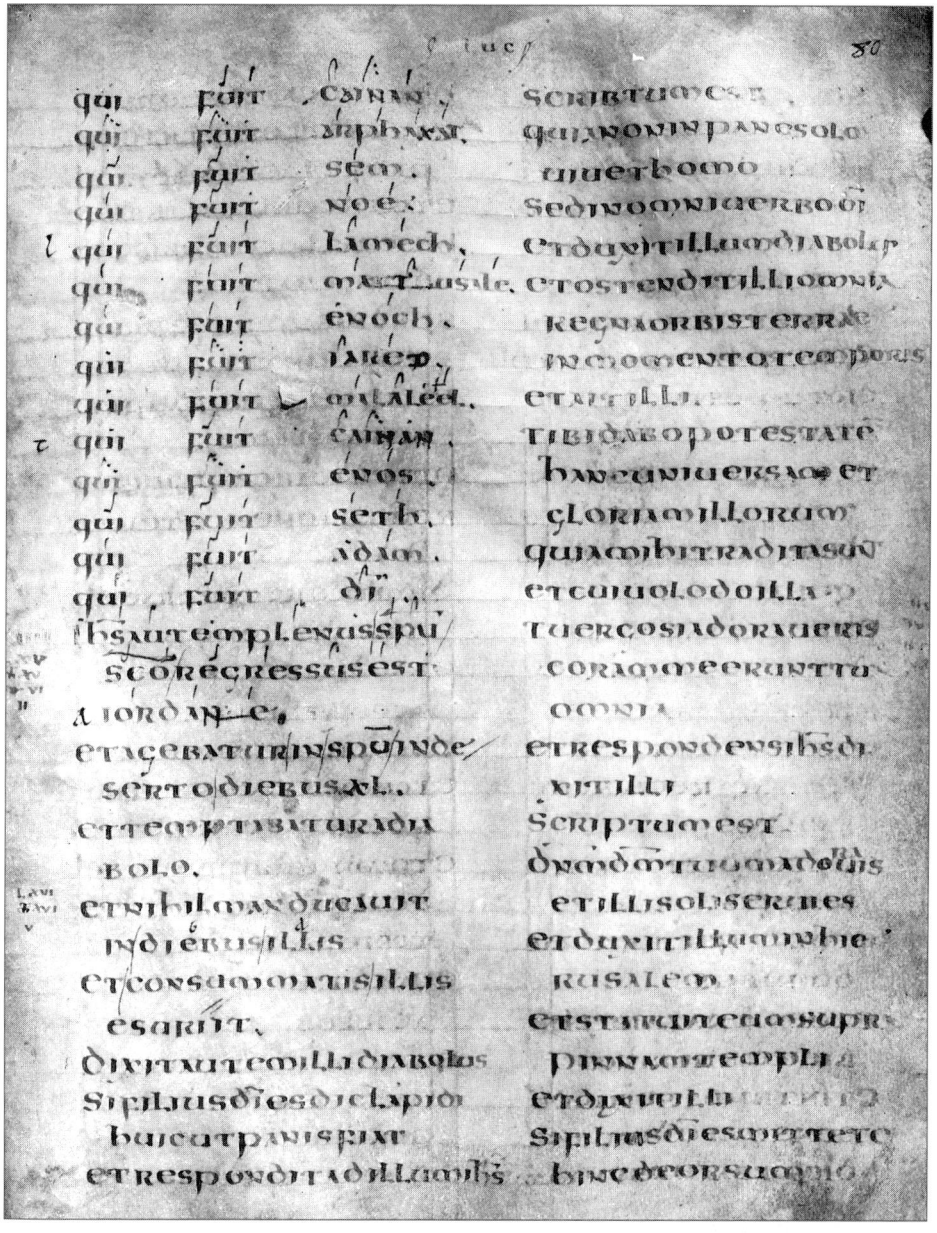

13.5. BodL, Auct. D. 2. 14, fol. 80r. Italian Gospel Book. Page size: 250 × 195 mm. (Bodleian Library, University of Oxford)

adding images to a few areas of them, but writing the entire text on purple parchment in letters of silver and gold. No fewer than six of the surviving Italian gospel books dating from before c. 800 were deluxe manuscripts of this sort.[35]

The Gospels of St Augustine bears various early additions in English hands, attesting to its continued use in this country up to the eleventh century and beyond. In the late seventh or eighth century, the period that concerns us here, titles were added to the narrative scenes, an attempt was made to restore the already decaying script, and the entire text was compared with that of another gospel book and altered accordingly. Specimen collation of the corrected readings suggests that this second volume belonged to the Italo-Northumbrian textual family best represented by the *Codex Amiatinus*.[36] Whether it was an Italian manuscript or a Northumbrian one is an interesting question, for although the former is more likely, at the date in question the latter possibility cannot be discounted. If Canterbury was indeed the home of our manuscript by this time, the work of textual revision itself would fit into the context of the school of Archishop Theodore and Abbot Hadrian.

A second Italian gospel book which was in England at an early date and is now in Oxford is also sometimes known as the Gospels of St Augustine, albeit with rather less good reason (fig. 13.5).[37] Probably slightly later in date than Corpus Christi 286, its eleventh-century provenance was possibly Bury St Edmunds, and it may have been at Lichfield in the eighth century. An unverifiable hint of some sort of connection with Kent, albeit quite possibly indirect, is provided by the affiliation of its text to that of a probably Kentish gospel book which dates from the second half of the eighth century; the unfortunate circumstance that the latter volume is now fragmentary in the extreme prevents a detailed assessment of the strength of the bond.[38] This Italian gospel book, too, bears a series of corrections and additions stretching from the eighth to the twelfth century, attesting to a long and varied history of use in this country. Wherever or however it first came to England, its main relevance in the present context is that it underlines some of the points we have made about early Italian manuscripts in general, and the exceptional features of Corpus Christi 286 in particular.

The quires are now regular quaternions, but the parchment is arranged within them exactly as it was in Troyes 504 and Corpus Christi 286 (i.e.: FH, HF; cf. fig. 13.4). The sheets were once again pricked open, not folded (the prickings now being within the outermost column), and they were ruled on each hair side. The text is written in uncials, seemingly by a single scribe, and is in *scriptura continua*. It is articulated with similar graphic devices to those used in Corpus Christi 286: Mark, Luke and John (but not Matthew, interestingly) are set out *per cola et commata*; sentences begin with a large capital, while the first lines of chapters are written in red. Once again little or no extra emphasis was given to the start of the individual gospels (the first line is written in red, the initial being slightly enhanced; in the case of Mark alone it is decorated with a simple zigzag line and surmounted by a cross);[39] conversely, the rubrics announcing the beginnings and ends of the gospels and prologues are visually more dramatic, being written in enlarged display capitals.[40] Typically, there is no pictorial decoration, nor was the book designed to have any. The text runs continuously from the end of one gospel on to the prologue, capitula, and text of the next.

Another Italian manuscript worth noting is Boulogne-sur-Mer, Bibliothèque municipale, 32, which probably dates from the later sixth century, and contains a selection of works by St Ambrose.[41] It is a modest sized volume of fairly square dimensions (245 × 220 mm), a little bigger than the Cambridge Gospels of St Augustine. Its quires are quaternions whose parchment is arranged with the flesh sides outermost, as in the other Italian manuscripts we have considered. The text is written without word separation in a squarish uncial that is distantly related to that of Troyes 504; while, as was the case in the other Italian books we have discussed, the beginnings of sections are presented in red. That the volume had a sojourn in England at an early date is suggested by the marginalia written in an eighth-century Anglo-Saxon minuscule that were added to a couple of pages. There is no positive evidence that the book was ever in Kent; however, its present location in Boulogne, geographically very close to Kent, many of whose manuscripts came from the medieval libraries of Saint-Bertin and Saint-Vaast which had frequent intercourse with Canterbury during the Anglo-Saxon period and beyond, provides a hint that this could have been the case. Be that as it may, the volume represents the sort of reading book – as opposed to service book – that Augustine and his followers are likely to have brought to England, and which will have formed the foundations of the earliest English libraries. The texts contained herein treat, among other themes, chastity, the forgiveness of sins, and the resurrection of the body.

One final sixth- or seventh-century continental manuscript which deserves mention is the copy of Arator's *Historia apostolica* (an interpretative, metrical version of the Acts of the Apostles) which survives only as a couple of offsets in the binding of BodL, e Mus. 66.[42] The host book was written at Saint Augustine's Abbey in the first half of the twelfth century and the binding is of late medieval date. Although the medieval provenance of the fragment was thus Saint Augustine's Abbey, and it *may* have arrived there shortly after it was written, we have no certain proof that it was even in England in the Anglo-Saxon period, so we should not make too much of it. Unlike the previous volumes which were all written in uncials, here a formal minuscule with some cursive elements was used. Lowe judged it to have been produced in northern Italy, but allowed that France was also a possibility. Whether or not this manuscript was in Canterbury at an early date, it usefully reminds us of several important points: that christian poetry and not just liturgical, pastoral and monastic reading books were brought into seventh-century England; that uncial was not the only imported script that

English converts were able to contemplate; and that France as well as Italy supplied southern England with books.[43] Indeed, in connection with this last point it is worth remarking that Augustine himself may have arrived in England with a few Frankish books, as well as Italian ones. The aid that Pope Gregory solicited for him from Frankish ecclesiastics and royalty might on occasion have included gifts of manuscripts; and the Frankish interpreters that the missionary recruited in Gaul could, if they were ecclesiastics, have brought some of their own books with them.

That the first generations of Christians in Kent made manuscripts can hardly be doubted, and that gospel books, psalters and liturgical texts were in the forefront of their output is highly likely; however, not one seventh-century Kentish book survives.[44] Whether anything is to be read into this is an open question: while it could be that the wealth of imports in the initial stages and the relative ease of communications with the continent meant that the number of local products was comparatively modest, the dearth of material could equally be – indeed is more probably – a simple accident of survival. (We do not, after all, have very much more from the eighth century, as we shall see.) Frustratingly, the one text we know for certain the missionaries did commit to writing in Kent before *c.* 616, namely King Æthelberht's law-code, has only come down to us in an early twelfth-century copy, and so sheds no light on the type of handwriting they used for such a document.[45] It is, nevertheless, quite clear that the Italians succeeded in transmitting the standard formal bookhand of their homeland to their English converts; and interestingly, our earliest witness to the practice of uncial in Kent, dating from 679, is not a book but a charter.

In contrast to its continental counterparts which are written in less formal scripts, King Hlothere's charter for Reculver is visually very imposing (fig. 13.6).[46] Whether uncial was used to make the document look impressive and assimilate it to a liturgical book or simply because this was the main hand then in use in the Kentish church is open to debate (Anglo-Saxon minuscule was certainly being used there for such documents by the earlier eighth century.)[47] The neat, squat uncial of the main body of Hlothere's charter (a less

13.6. *BL, Cotton Ch. Aug. II. 2. Charter of Hlothere (detail). (British Library)*

13.7. BL, Stowe Ch. 1. Charter of Wihtred. (British Library)

formal version of the script is used for the subscriptions) is broadly reminiscent of that in the Troyes 504 copy of Gregory's *Regula pastoralis* (figs 13.1–2). Although certain letter forms are different, the general matrix of the two scripts is closely comparable. One obvious point of contrast, however, is the treatment of the serifs (particularly noticeable on E, N, and T) which are now perceptibly triangular. Another is that the charter, unlike the manuscript, has discreet but nevertheless evident word separation. A possible source of inspiration for both developments is contemporary Insular script, the writing practised in Ireland and, under Irish influence, in much of Northumbria.[48]

Connections between Kent and Northumbria are attested in the seventh century at royal level at least;[49] and that such writing was known in late seventh-century Kent is shown by our next document, King Wihtred of Kent's charter for Lyminge (697 or 712), which is written in Insular script – an elegant hybrid of Insular half-uncial and formal minuscule (fig. 13.7).[50] It is interesting that, although belonging to a different script system, it was once again a very formal type of handwriting that was used. Apart from the numerous different letter forms observable here, seventh-century Insular writing departed from much contemporary continental work of a comparable formality in its more advanced word separation and more adventurous elaboration of initials.[51] Furthermore, Insular books were made in a slightly different manner from most continental ones: in the first place, the sheets of parchment generally all faced the same way throughout each quire so that a hair and a flesh side faced one another on most openings (i.e., HF, HF: cf. fig. 13.8); and secondly, the sheets were pricked and ruled with the quire folded, not open.

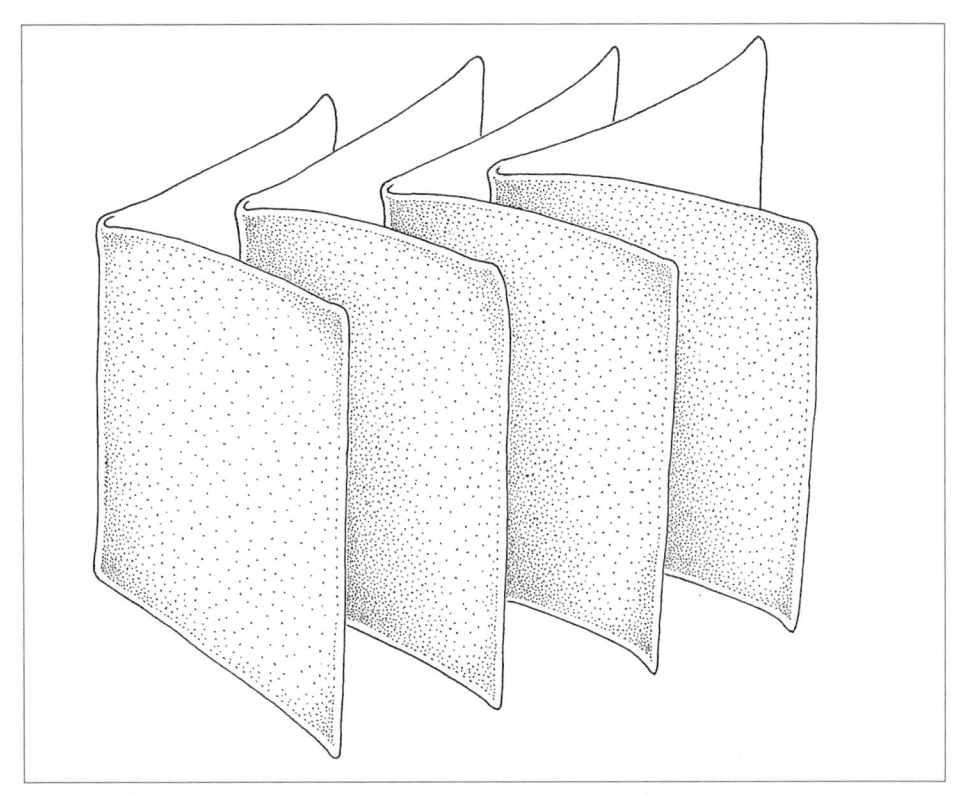

13.8. Makeup of a 'typical' quire in an 'Insular' manuscript. (Gameson)

Our first locally produced Kentish books (as opposed to charters) probably date from the second and third quarters of the eighth century. Although none of the three manuscripts in question is unequivocally located or dated, they are all of early Kentish provenance and they share sufficient features of script and/or decoration to suggest that they have a common geographical origin which is, therefore, likely to be identical with their shared provenance. Their common features are also sufficient to imply that they are fairly close in time to each other, and in one case there is some evidence to suggest a date shortly before or around the middle of the eighth century. These volumes are complemented by a couple of letters from St Boniface, the Anglo-Saxon missionary in Germany, to Abbess Eadburh of Minster-in-Thanet (d. 751) which reveal that she supplied him with manuscripts. In 735/6, for example, the missionary asked the abbess to make him a deluxe copy of the Epistles of St Peter, written in gold.[52] This celebrated letter not only reveals that luxury books were being produced in early eighth-century Kent, but also shows that women were involved in their manufacture.

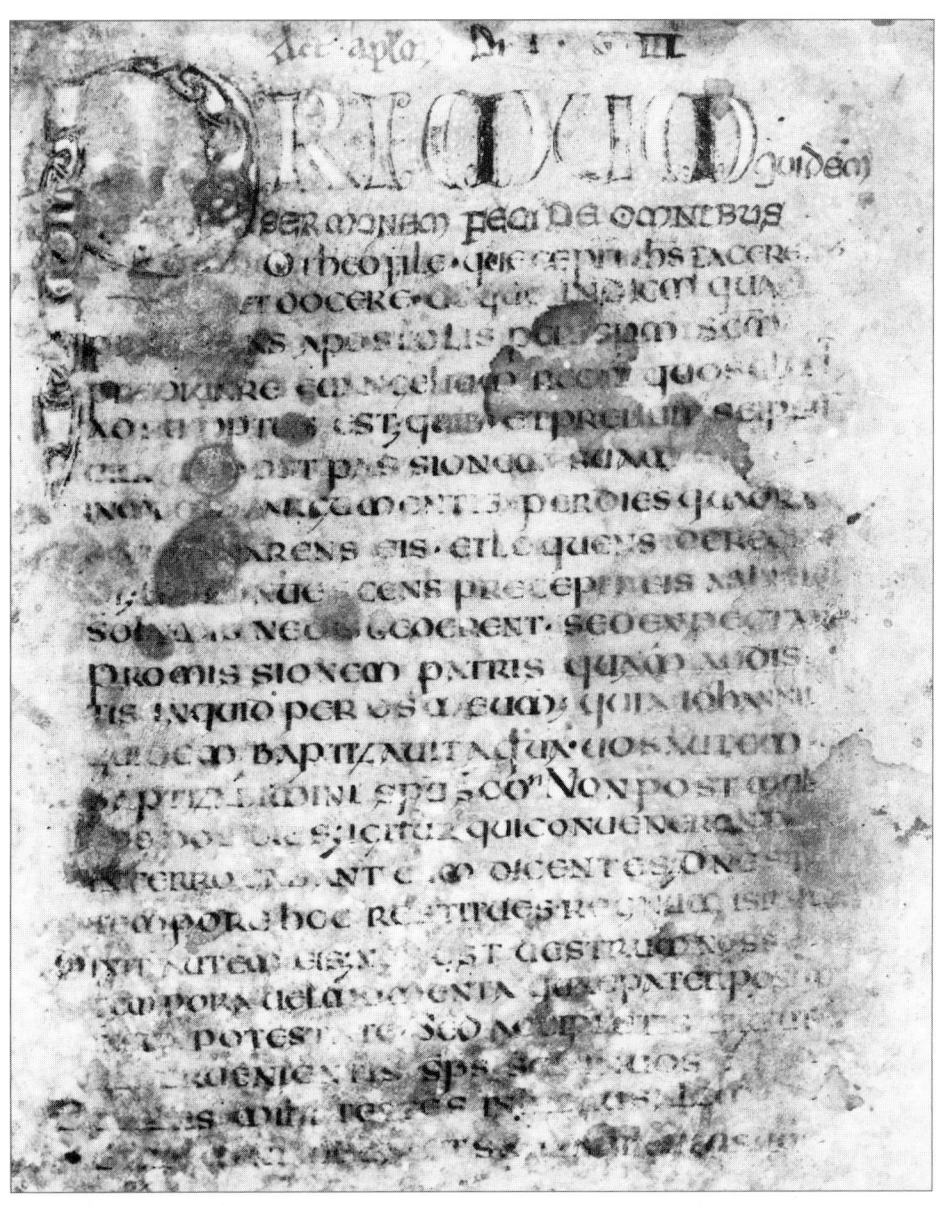

13.9. BodL, Selden Supra 30, p. 1. Acts of the Apostles. Page size: 229 × 176 mm. (Bodleian Library, University of Oxford)

The copy of the Acts of the Apostles now in Oxford (BodL, Selden Supra, 30), which is arguably the earliest of our eighth-century manuscripts, is not a deluxe volume (figs 13.9–10, 12).[53] It is, however, possible that it was written at Minster. Prayers that were added at an early date to page 70 are in the female form;[54] while the word 'Eadb' (conceivably a reference to Abbess Eadburh herself) was

13.10. BodL, Selden Supra 30, p. 41. Acts of the Apostles. (Bodleian Library, University of Oxford)

deeply incised in dry-point at the centre of the lower margin at page 47. Be that as it may, the medieval provenance of the volume was Saint Augustine's Abbey (which, incidentally, acquired many of the possessions of Minster, along with its relics and charters, when that community finally failed in the eleventh century).[55]

The manuscript is the work of two scribes, and its construction falls into two contrasting parts which exactly mirror their stints, suggesting that the scribes prepared their own quires (fig. 13.11). The fact that the first scribe's section ended with a blank leaf would seem to imply that they worked simultaneously. The arrangement of the parchment in the first section[56] was mainly but not entirely in the Insular manner (HF, HF). The quires were pricked with an awl after folding, the prickings being positioned in both margins; the way the sheets were ruled varied from quire to quire. In the second section, by contrast,[57] the parchment was consistently arranged in the Insular manner; the sheets were pricked with a knife after folding, the prickings now being located at the edge of the textblock; and the quires were ruled, made up, with direct rulings on to every other recto. Insular techniques predominate, but this book was evidently the product of a scriptorium which had not standardised its scribal procedures.

Although the manuscript was largely put together in the Insular way, its script is uncial of Kentish form. The hands of the two scribes are quite distinct. The first (figs 13.9–10) wrote a very regular, neat, carefully controlled uncial, reminiscent of that used in the Vespasian Psalter and for the prefaces of the *Codex Aureus* (manuscripts we shall examine shortly).[58] Word separation is generally clear if not always regular, and sentences are headed by an enlarged capital; larger, slightly embellished penwork initials distinguish the start of chapters. The second scribe, whose hand was less well controlled, wrote a quavery and rather larger version of the same script, with crude initials (fig. 13.12).[59] A few of the letters have a less formal, cursive feel, and some of them suggest that the scribe was familiar with a minuscule script. Though conceivably a continental form such as that of the Arator fragment at Oxford, several touches – particularly the 'a's – suggest it was more probably an Insular minuscule.

The Oxford manuscript of Acts thus shows us a scriptorium which had a flexible approach to constructing a manuscript – albeit favouring Insular over continental conventions – and included at least two scribes who practised a regional uncial. This, unsurprisingly, has grown further away from the version of the script found in earlier Italian models like the Gospels of St Augustine (fig. 13.3), but it has seemingly done so without reflecting contemporary continental uncial, and embodies instead discreet responses to types of script used elsewhere in the British Isles. Both scribes were extremely sparing with decoration. The glory of this book, like that of most fine Late Antique ones, is the unadulterated calligraphy of the best hand (that of scribe one). Decoration was confined to the beginning of the text, which was marked by a grander initial plus enlarged display script (fig. 13.9).[60] The work in question is now horribly damaged; but in so far as it can be made out, it bears little resemblance to Insular or even other Kentish illumination and is most strongly reminiscent of some eighth-century Frankish book decoration. If this be correct, it might strengthen

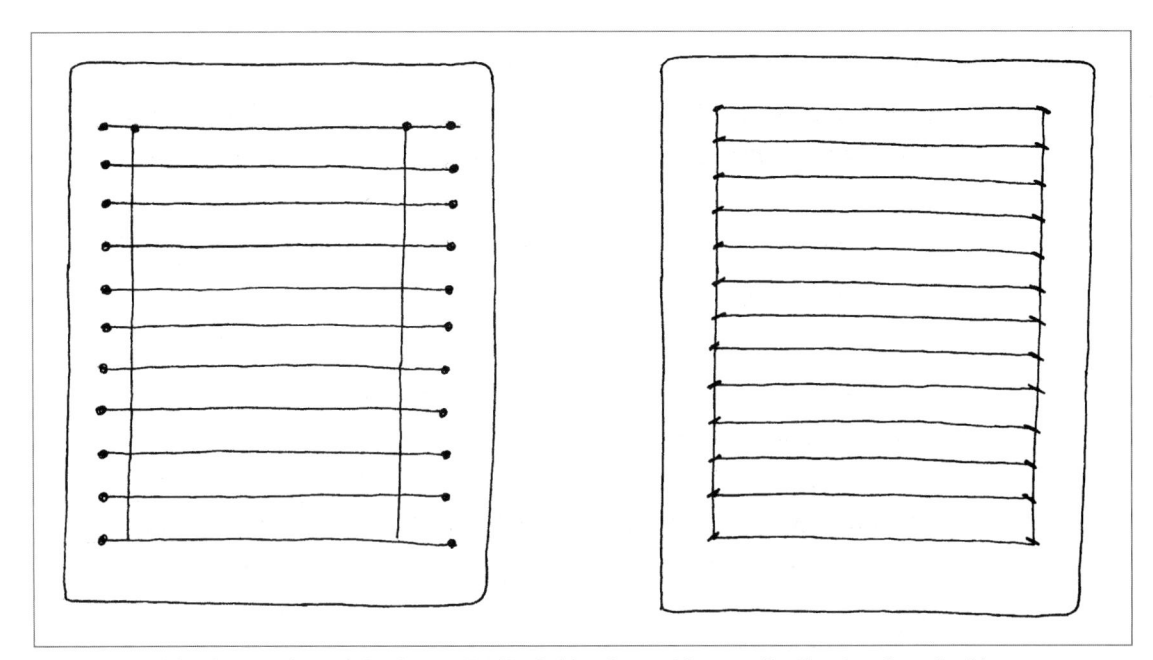

13.11. The pricking and ruling in BodL, Selden Supra 30: a. scribe 1's stint; b. scribe 2's stint. (Gameson)

the case for a Minster-in-Thanet origin for the manuscript: given that Mildred, its abbess from *c.* 700–*c.* 730, had been educated in the Merovingian monastery at Chelles (near Paris), Minster was probably the Kentish centre most likely to reflect Frankish scribal influence in the first half of the eighth century.[61]

Our next manuscript, the Vespasian Psalter (figs 13.13–14; pls VII–VIII), was probably described by Thomas of Elmham in the early fifteenth century as one of the books associated with Gregory and Augustine that were preserved at Saint Augustine's Abbey.[62] It had evidently been at Canterbury in the early eleventh century since at that time it received a supplement written by the celebrated Canterbury scribe, Eadui Basan.[63] As Eadui is known to have been based at Christ Church, there is at least a possibility that the volume was there and not at Saint Augustine's Abbey during the Anglo-Saxon period.

Measuring 235 × 180 mm, the Vespasian Psalter is a little larger than the Oxford copy of Acts we have just considered; and its parchment is of a much higher quality than the membrane of that manuscript.[64] Its structure is also rather different: the first nine quires of the psalm text are each composed of six sheets (ternions), thereafter quires of eight sheets were used (quaternions). The arrangement of hair and flesh sides does not follow any consistent pattern. The disposition of direct and transferred impressions shows that the sheets were

> ad hiemandū plurimi statuerunt consiliū
> nauigare siquomodo possent deueniente
> phenicem hiemare portū crete respicente
> ad affricū et adchor. Aspirante h' austro
> aestiman timantes propositū se tenere
> Cum sustulissent. de assos legabant creta
> Non post multum autem misit se contra
> ipsam uentus phenicus qui uocatur euro
> aquilo Cumq; arrepta esset nauis et non
> posset conari in uentū data nauis flatibus
> ferebamur Insulam h' quandam decurrent
> que uocatur cauda potuimus uix optinere
> scaffam qua sublata ad itoriis utebantur
> accingentes nauem timentes ne in syrte
> inciderent submisso uase sic ferebantur
> Ualide h' nobis tem pestate iactatis sequenti
> die iactū fecerunt Et tertia die suis manib;
> armamenta nauis proiecerunt Neq; sole h'
> neq; sideriB; apparentiB; per plures dies et
> tempestate non exigua imminente iam ab
> lata erat spes omnis salutis nostre Et cū
> multa ieiunatio fuisset Tunc stans paulus
> in medio eor dixit oportebat quidē Quiri
> audito me non tollere a creta lucriq; facere
> in iuriā hanc et iacturā Et nunc suadeo uobis

13.12. BodL, Selden Supra 30, p. 102. *Acts of the Apostles*. (Bodleian Library, University of Oxford)

pricked and ruled after folding; however, prickings appear only in the outer margin, not in both margins as was usual with the Insular system.[65] The scriptorium would thus seem to have used Insular methods of preparation, but so adapted them that the end result had a 'continental' appearance.

The main text (figs 13.13–14) is the work of a single scribe who wrote a superlative, characterful uncial, the form of which, with its neat triangular serifs, is patently related to that of the Oxford manuscript of Acts, particularly as practised

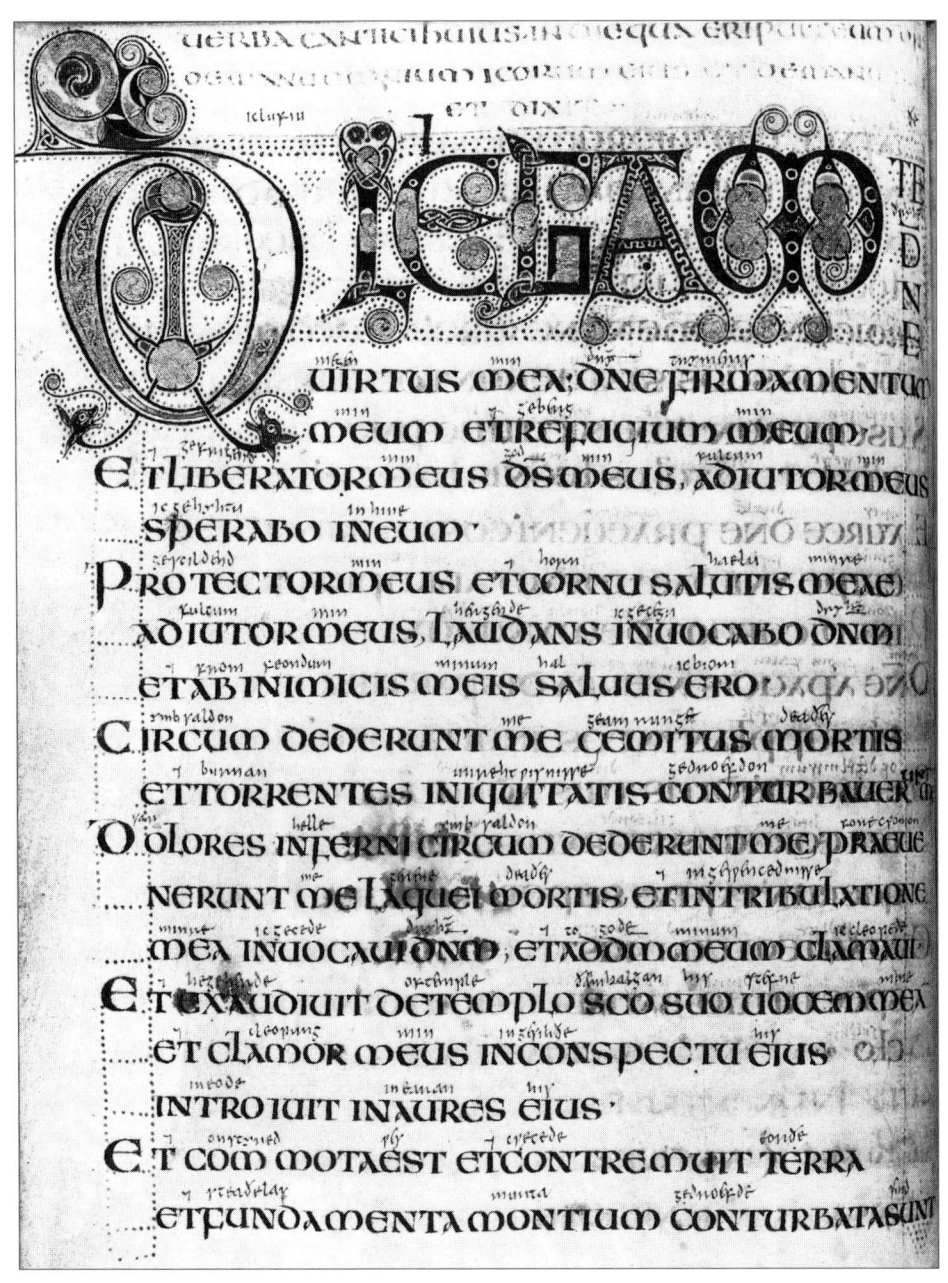

13.13. BL, Cotton Vespasian A. i, fol. 21v. The Vespasian Psalter: Psalm 17. Page size: 235 × 180 mm. (British Library)

by the first scribe (figs 13.9–10). Rustic capitals, an older Antique script, were used for the *tituli* to each psalm and for the prefatory texts;[66] while hybrid square capitals were deployed for the *explicit* to the psalter as a whole.[67] The psalter text is the *Romanum*, the version used at Rome and undoubtedly that which was brought to

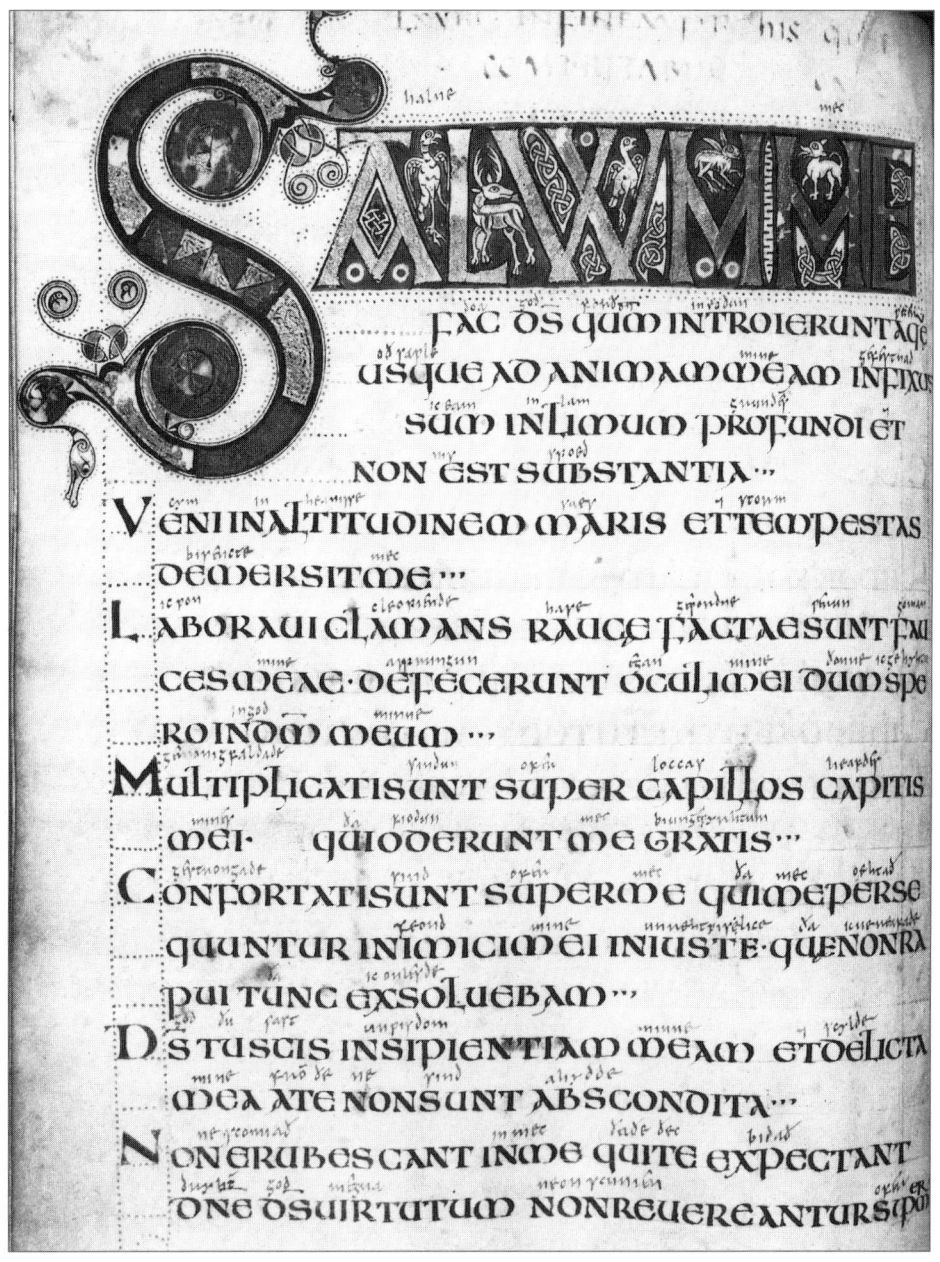

13.14. BL, Cotton Vespasian A. i, fol. 64v. The Vespasian Psalter: Psalm 68. (British Library)

Canterbury by St Augustine: in point of fact, this is the oldest *Romanum* psalter in existence. Textually its nearest relatives are two other early English psalters, a copy from Echternach, and one from Mondsee (Austria) – the closest being one of the English books, the so-called Blicking or Lothian Psalter.[68]

The volume is preceded by a large number of prefatory texts, including expositions of the Alleluia and Gloria as well as the *Origo psalmorum* (a text rarely found in subsequent Anglo-Saxon psalters, though common in continental ones); and it is probable that this unusually full collection of preliminary matter was compiled from several sources. The nine canticles that appear after the psalter accord with Roman usage; while the three hymns which follow them were excerpted from the 'Old Latin Hymnal', a collection that was current in monastic circles in the sixth century. Now we know that Saint Augustine's Abbey possessed a copy of this 'anthology' in the Middle Ages, contained in a now lost '*Psalterium Augustini quod sibi misit idem Gregorius*', for the volume in question was described in detail by Thomas of Elmham.[69] Whether or not this was really 'the psalter of Augustine which the same Gregory sent to him' as Elmham thought, the collection of hymns itself shows that it was indeed a very old manuscript, and it was precisely the sort of book that one would expect the missionary to have had. Whatever the possible relationship between this lost manuscript and the Vespasian Psalter, the compiler of the latter probably drew upon at least three earlier psalters when assembling this collection of ancillary texts, a circumstance which sheds a little indirect light both on the literary resources of early eighth-century Canterbury, and on contemporary attitudes towards such material.

Visually the Vespasian Psalter departs more markedly from Late Antique, contemporary Italian and even Frankish traditions than did the Oxford manuscript of Acts. The extent to which this reflects a general evolution, as opposed to differences in local taste, or distinctions in the functions of these particular books, or simply that a psalter was treated differently from a copy of Acts is debatable. However, it is clear that the Vespasian Psalter was altogether more luxuriously conceived than the copy of Acts; and it was certainly the particular character of the psalter text which defined the nature of its decorative programme. While the preliminary matter has no ornamentation, the psalms and canticles are articulated throughout by decoration. Verse initials, alternately red and blue, are placed in the margin within a continous ornamental border of red dots;[70] every psalm is headed by a decorated initial, adorned with unburnished gold leaf; while particularly elaborate ornamentation plus continuation lettering was used to distinguish the psalms of the eight-fold liturgical division (figs 13.13–14). Two of these initials (those to Psalms 26 and 52) are historiated, the first with David and Jonathan, the second with David saving a lamb from a lion (pls VII–VIII). Psalm 1 is now missing, but Thomas of Elmham's description reveals that its initial B included a representation of Samuel (and its subject was probably, therefore, Samuel anointing David). Another lost leaf, which formerly separated the psalter from the canticles, seems to have borne an ornamental

13.15. *Stockholm, Kungl. Bibliotek, A. 135, fol. 9v.* Codex Aureus, *portrait of Matthew. Page size: 390 × 320 mm. (Kungl. Bibliotek)*

'carpet page', the design of which (as the offset on the facing page reveals) was based around a large cross.[71] Given that this was a form of decoration that was prominent in Insular manuscripts, most spectacularly the Lindisfarne Gospels, its presence here suggests a response to a Northumbrian model.

There is one surviving miniature, probably originally a frontispiece, which shows King David composing the psalms surrounded by his scribes and musicians (pl. VII). It has been argued that the immediate model for the figures was an Italian illumination of the sixth century; and given the similarities between the composition and that in the earliest surviving illustrated Byzantine psalter, a work originating in an Italian centre under Byzantine influence, notably Ravenna, has been favoured.[72] However, a Byzantine model itself is not out of the question. Whatever the pictorial sources, what makes this page so powerful is the marriage of decoration and iconography. The draughtsmanship of the figures is undeniably gauche,[73] but they are skilfully painted, and they stand out because they are fully modelled while the grounds and the frame are rendered in unmodulated, single colours. At the same time, however, it is the masterful ornamentation of the frame which unifies and enhances the whole composition, which thereby succeeds in being decorative in a way that the portrait of Luke in the Gospels of St Augustine was not.

In fact, exactly the same point applies to the book as a whole: it was designed to be highly decorative. This may be the oldest *Romanum* psalter and it may be written in Antique scripts, but it is far from looking like a Roman book. If Kentish scribes had inherited uncial from the Italian missionaries and their manuscripts as the highest grade bookhand, by the eighth century they evidently regarded Insular initial decoration as comparably prestigious. It is true that, unlike his Insular counterparts (and his Frankish ones, for that matter), the decorator of the Vespasian Psalter made extensive use of gold, along with some silver. Yet if the use of the metal itself harked back to luxury Antique manuscripts, the context and way in which they were deployed here – adorning specific areas of initials and display script conceived under Insular influence – was altogether different. The precious metals do, of course, enhance the exquisite quality of the Vespasian Psalter (which thereby far exceeds contemporary Frankish decorated books in richness) but, in contrast to the gold and silver manuscripts of Antiquity, here the metals contribute to the visual variety of the page rather than to its stateliness. The point is most obvious at the major textual divisions, where gold and silver display script is set against bands or panels in contrasting colours (pl. VIII).[74] These small, multicoloured patchwork areas dominated by gold and silver pave the way for our next manuscript, wherein the process of reconceiving the aesthetic of the uncial page was taken a dramatic step further.

The *Codex Aureus*, a gospel book now in Stockholm, is the most opulent surviving English medieval manuscript, and is one of the most extraordinary books ever made (figs 13.15–19, 21).[75] The pages are alternately purple and white throughout the four gospels, and the text is written in a variety of inks including gold and silver. The script of the manuscript links it to the Oxford copy of Acts and to the Vespasian Psalter, while its artwork provides further evidence for connections with the latter volume (indeed one scholar thought that the

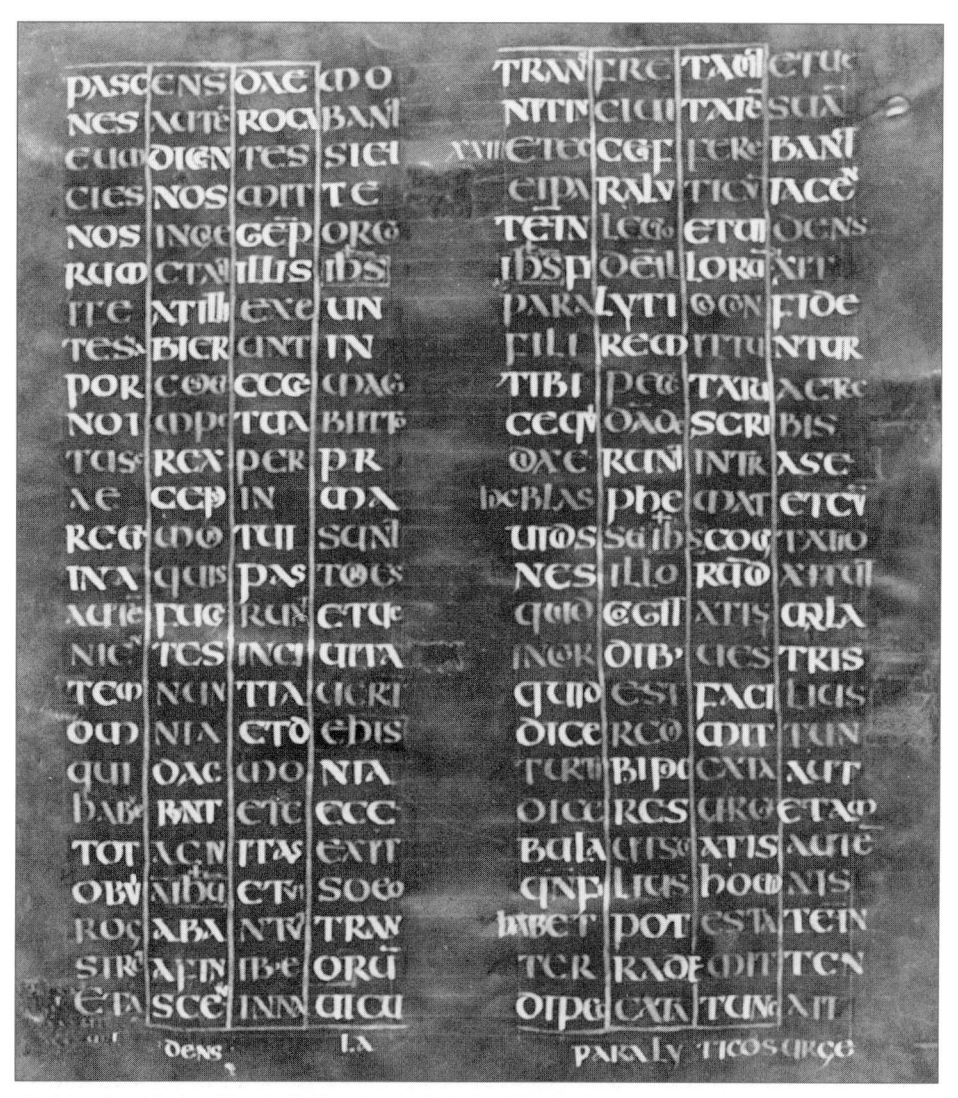

13.16. Stockholm, Kungl. Bibliotek, A. 135, fol. 22r. Codex Aureus, Matthew 8:31–9:6. (Kungl. Bibliotek)

two manuscripts had an artist in common).[76] Circumstantial evidence, considered below, suggests that the *Codex Aureus* was produced around the middle of the eighth century. By the second half of the ninth century it was certainly at Christ Church, but whether it was written there, as opposed to Saint Augustine's Abbey or Minster-in-Thanet is an open question. In each case there is slight evidence to suggest that the house *could* have produced the *Codex Aureus*, without actually proving that it did. Christ Church possessed, at least temporarily, a copy of Porfyrius's *Carmina figurata* which is a likely source of inspiration for some of the patterned pages in our manuscript; Saint Augustine's probably owned the

13.17. *Stockholm, Kungl. Bibliotek, A. 135, fol. 63r.* Codex Aureus, incipit *of Mark's gospel.* (Kungl. Bibliotek)

Gospels of St Augustine which is highly likely to have provided the model for its evangelist portraits; while thanks to Boniface's letter we know for certain that chrysography (writing in gold), a technique used throughout our manuscript and central to its conception, was practised at Minster-in-Thanet.[77]

The text of the *Codex Aureus* is not the Vulgate, but a hybrid characterized by the high density of Old Latin readings.[78] Collation of its text against that of the other surviving early gospel books suggests that none of its immediate relations is

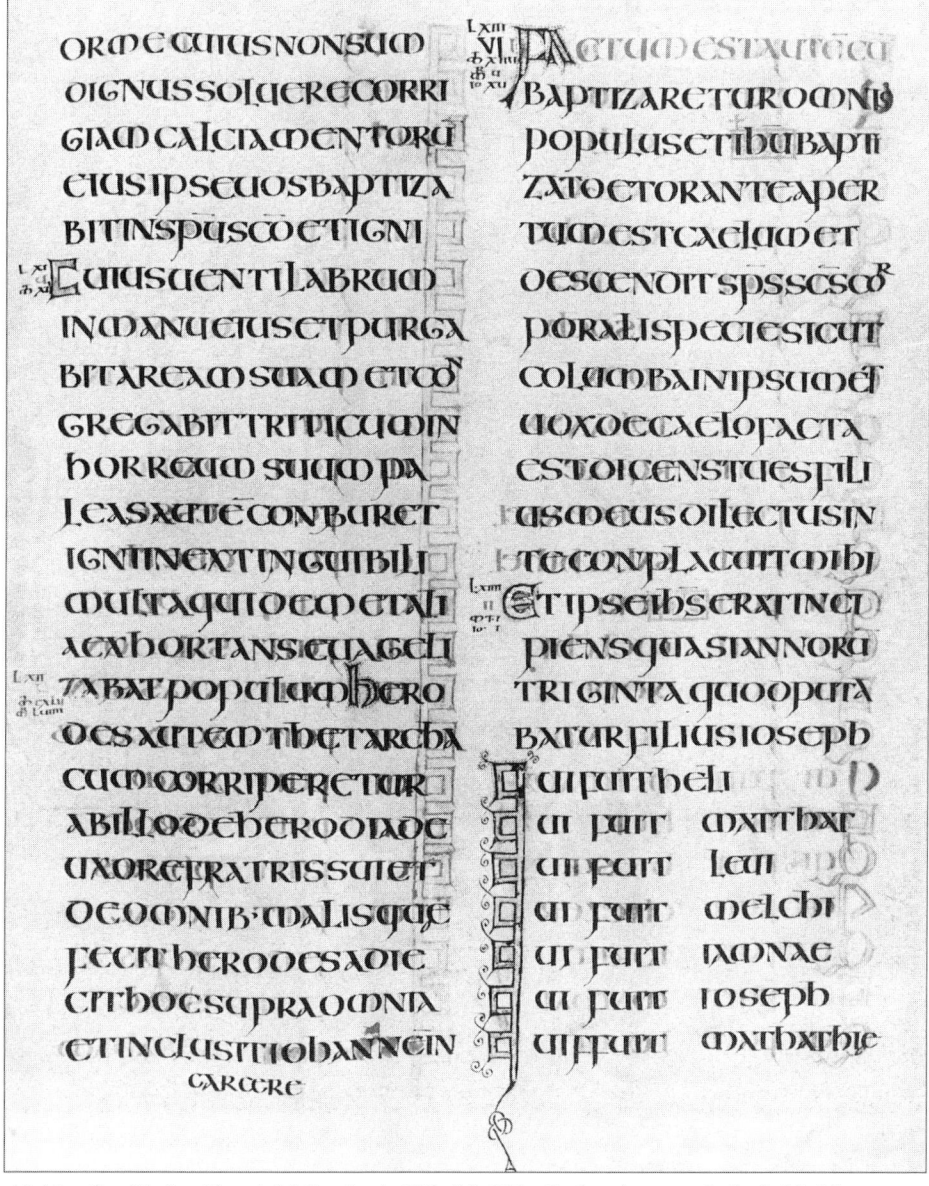

13.18. *Stockholm, Kungl. bibliotek, A. 135, fol. 104r. Codex Aureus, Luke 3:16–25.*
(Kungl. Bibliotek)

extant. On the other hand, several manuscripts do share sufficient numbers of variants to show that their text has an affinity to that of *Aureus*. The seven most important in this respect are a chronologically and geographically diffuse group. They include three early Italian manuscripts (two of which are also purple books),[79] two eighth-century volumes from Echternach (the Maeseyck and Augsburg Gospels),[80] one later eighth-century English book (the Barberini

Gospels),[81] and a French New Testament dating from the first half of the twelfth century.[82] The Gospels of St Augustine, it is worth stressing, is not among these volumes; and even the briefest comparison of its text suffices to show that it cannot have been the textual exemplar of the *Codex Aureus*.

The *Codex Aureus* is an exceptionally large manuscript. The folios now measure 395 × 320 mm, and each bifolium must orginally have been at least 400 × 650 mm. As it is unlikely that more than one good sheet of such a size could have been obtained from a single skin, the pelt of at least one hundred animals would have been needed to make the book. Not only is the *Codex Aureus* the largest gospel book from the English or Insular world, it is one of the very biggest from the early Middle Ages as a whole. Indeed, I am only aware of nine gospel books that exceed it in size; and the fact that of these one was made for King Charles the Bald, one for Henry II of Germany, and one for the Emperor Henry III speaks loud about the status of our book.[83] The *Codex Aureus* is also a very square manuscript: indeed the ruled area is almost exactly square (235 × 240 mm). This is one of several ways in which it evokes a Late Antique book.

As we have noted, half the gospel text is written on purple parchment, a material which was in itself a designation of outstanding worth (figs 13.16–17). It had regal and imperial overtones with christian symbolism intertwined. Purple manuscripts, luxury items even in Antiquity, were always rare. The colour expressed the supreme value of the text, and it is no accident that most of the small number of extant examples are gospel books. By dint of its many purple pages, the *Codex Aureus* is a member of a small, select group of books of the very highest luxury; moreover it is one of the largest of them. The alternation of purple and white pages, however, makes our manuscript unique. It also raised formidable practical problems. Clearly a conventional quire structure based on bifolia was out of the question: the alternation would break down in the middle. The facing pages at the centre of the quire, being two halves of the same bifolium, would inevitably be the same colour. Thus there was only one possible solution: the central leaf of each quire had to be a singleton. This radical scheme was adopted (fig. 13.20). The ruling was likewise a complex practical challenge. The changes in ink which created the designs on the patterned pages depended upon the rulings, and extra sets of vertical lines and other shapes had to be supplied to guide them.

No other manuscript with comparable patterned text pages survives from before the Carolingian period. On the other hand, there was a respectable tradition of acrostics in the early Middle Ages, and we know of the existence of a visual precedent. Around 325 Publilius Optatianus Porfyrius dedicated to the emperor Constantine a collection of verses which included acrostics and other

13.19. Stockholm, Kungl. Bibliotek, A. 135, fol. 150v. Codex Aureus, portrait of John. (Kungl. Bibliotek)

word games and which were set out in various shapes and designs. As ninth-century copies reveal, the collection included pages which bear a striking resemblance to a couple of those in the *Codex Aureus*.[84] Significantly, it is highly likely that a copy of this work was in Canterbury around the middle of the eighth century. A letter from Bishop Milred of Worcester written shortly after 754 mentions a volume of Porfyrius which was then in the possession of a certain Cuthbert, most probably to be identified with Cuthbert, archbishop of Canterbury 740–60.[85] Now, such a manuscript might have inspired not only the idea of creating patterns within the textblock, but also the basic concept of having alternately white and purple pages. The evidence for the latter is indirect but suggestive. The work of Porfyrius also lay behind the *De laudibus sanctae crucis*, a series of *carmina figurata* accompanied by prose explanations that were composed at the beginning of the ninth century by the Carolingian writer, Hrabanus Maurus (who, indeed, cites the Late Antique poet in his preface).[86] The finest extant copy of the *De laudibus*, written at Fulda in Hrabanus's lifetime and now in the Vatican,[87] presents the *carmina figurata* on purple painted pages (always a verso) with the relevant commentary on the accompanying recto on normal parchment, with the result that on twenty-six openings a purple page faces a white one. The similarity to the *Codex Aureus* is so striking, and such presentation is so unusual that one suspects this to have been a feature of the one source the two works almost certainly have in common, namely a Porfyrius manuscript. And the hypothesis that a copy of an extraordinary work that was dedicated to Constantine should have had a luxurious and unusual appearance hardly stretches one's credulity.

Three distinct types of uncials were used in the *Codex Aureus*: one for the gospel texts, another for the preliminary matter, and a third for the headings within the preliminary matter. The prefatory uncial is close to the script of the Vespasian Psalter and that of the first scribe of the Oxford manuscript of Acts. The gospel text uncial, though preserving some of the same features, is much larger, heavier and more stately; interestingly, at its most florid (in Luke and John; cf. fig. 13.18) it is distantly evocative of the uncial of the Troyes 504 copy of the

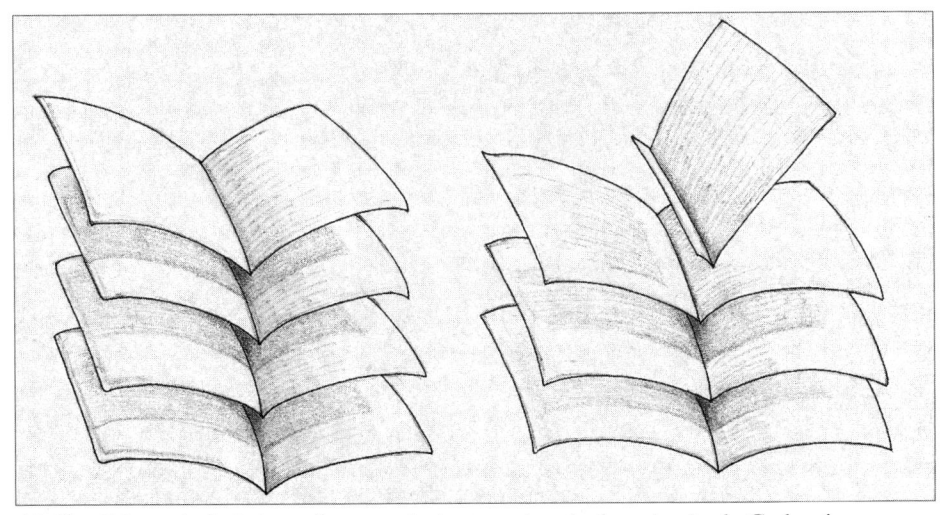

13.20. Schematic depictions of: a. a typical quaternion; b. the quires in the Codex Aureus. *(Gameson)*

Regula pastoralis (figs 13.1–2), suggesting that this scribe was familiar with a Roman manuscript written in a similar version of the script. The main text is written in *scriptura continua*, echoing the appearance of a Late Antique book. The two Italian gospel books that were in southern England by the eighth century, it will be remembered, had no word division; however they are appreciably easier to read than the *Codex Aureus*, since they are set out *per cola et commata* – with lines of different lengths reflecting sense units (figs 13.3, 5). In the *Codex Aureus*, by contrast, each column is a solid block of writing – something which was a necessary precondition of realizing the designs on the patterned pages, and which is likewise a feature of Porfyrius's poems. This manuscript was not designed with the convenience of the reader in mind.

Nor was it conceived for the convenience of the scribes: quite the reverse in fact. Writing the *Codex Aureus* was an extremely complicated task. Maintaining the very large uncial script was a challenge in itself, but the scribes also had to face the problem of using several types of ink with different properties on writing surfaces of differing textures. Moreover, many pages had to be produced in a piecemeal, disjointed fashion: adding the words required in one colour, while leaving the correct space for those that were subsequently to be supplied in another. The patterned pages were fiercely complicated to produce (fig. 13.16), and the scribes regularly had to compress their script or use superscript letters to keep their work on course. On fol. 16r, for example,[88] we can see the scribe adjusting the size of the golden letters to fit the available space within the cross pattern, and compressing his white ones to ensure they stopped immediately before the cross, as well as at the end of the column.

The main artwork, which is the work of at least two hands, comprises the canon tables, the evangelist portraits, and the chi-rho page. In addition, there are decorated initials to the general prefatory texts, as well as for the preface and capitula of John's gospel. By contrast, only a modest decorative emphasis was given to the gospel *incipits* of Matthew, Luke and John, with none at all for that of Mark (fig. 13.17). It is inconceivable that this extraordinarily deluxe manuscript did not originally have a magnificent decorated binding. This has long vanished, but a contemporary evocation of a jewelled binding is preserved in the depicted book held by the angel in the first evangelist portrait (fig. 13.15).[89] Although the Gospels of St Augustine was certainly not the exemplar for the text of the *Codex Aureus*, it is extremely likely that its portraits were the models for those in the later manuscript (pl. V; figs 13.15, 19).[90] Not only are the surviving images of closely similar type but, as we stressed earlier, Late Antique gospel books with such decoration were rare in the extreme, and it seems highly unlikely that there would have been two such rarities in the same place in England, let alone two whose evangelist portraits were closely similar. The eighth-century artist was far more skilful than his sixth-century predecessor, and it is interesting to note that his images selectively incorporate greater illusionism, and show much more subtlety in the use of paint than do those of the Late Antique exemplar. At the same time, the Anglo-Saxon has deliberately simplified the composition, removing the narrative scenes, and has made the figures themselves more stylised. The language of stylisation is closely comparable to that used in the Vespasian Psalter (pl. VII), particularly with regard to the draperies, but it is controlled and enhanced by the greater talent of this artist and by his keener understanding of human form and physiognomy. The result is more effectively human than in the Vespasian Psalter, and more monumental and focused than the Gospels of St Augustine. A Late Antique author contemplatively introducing his work, has been consciously transformed into a forceful icon of spirituality, directly confronting the beholder. There is also a small but significant iconographic change. The eighth-century evangelists, unlike the sixth-century one, are tonsured: in contrast to the situation in Late Antiquity, in the context of eighth-century Kent someone who could write was, by definition, a cleric.

Although, in contrast to the David page in the Vespasian Psalter, abstract ornament is almost excluded from the portrait pages in the *Codex Aureus*, it is present in the *Nouum opus*, the chi-rho, and above all in the decoration of the canon tables (fig. 13.21). Here the artistic vocabulary is dominated by Insular elements, such as spirals, interlace, and interlocking beasts, though Antique meander ornament also appears. The former are treated in a distinctive and slightly heavy-handed way, while the latter is realised with tellingly competent illusionism. As in the Vespasian Psalter, the decorated letters are arranged in panels, all the continuation lettering being of the same size, and extensive use is made of unburnished gold. The two Kentish books also share types of single strand wiry interlace, as well as the motif of complete beasts surrounded by double strand interlace.

Central to the aesthetic of the *Codex Aureus* (as in the Vespasian Psalter) is the tension between Late Antique models and values on the one hand, and indigenous Insular traits on the other. And this is not only the case in the artwork: exactly the same tension runs through the book as a whole. Although the text is written in uncials without word division in an archaic square format, the extensive adornment of every page with colour contrasts and patterns, not to mention the regular outlining of letters with red dots, clearly bespeaks Anglo-Saxon taste. Whereas in Porfyrius's work the letters that were emphasized within the text of the acrostic pages created meaningful phrases in their own right, those in the patterned pages of the *Codex Aureus* do not. Elaborate word games have

13.21. Stockholm, Kungl. Bibliotek, A. 135, fol. 6r. Codex Aureus, Canon II (cont.). (Kungl. Bibliotek)

been turned into elaborate visual games. The result is to superimpose the effect of a gold and garnet Kentish disc brooch (pl. IIIc)[91] on to the aesthetic of a luxurious Antique purple codex.

The circumstances that led to the making of this extraordinary manuscript in the mid-eighth century are, unfortunately, unrecorded; yet it is possible to see how it could have been a product of Archbishop Cuthbert's programme of ecclesiastical renewal.[92] More speculatively, one might wonder whether the

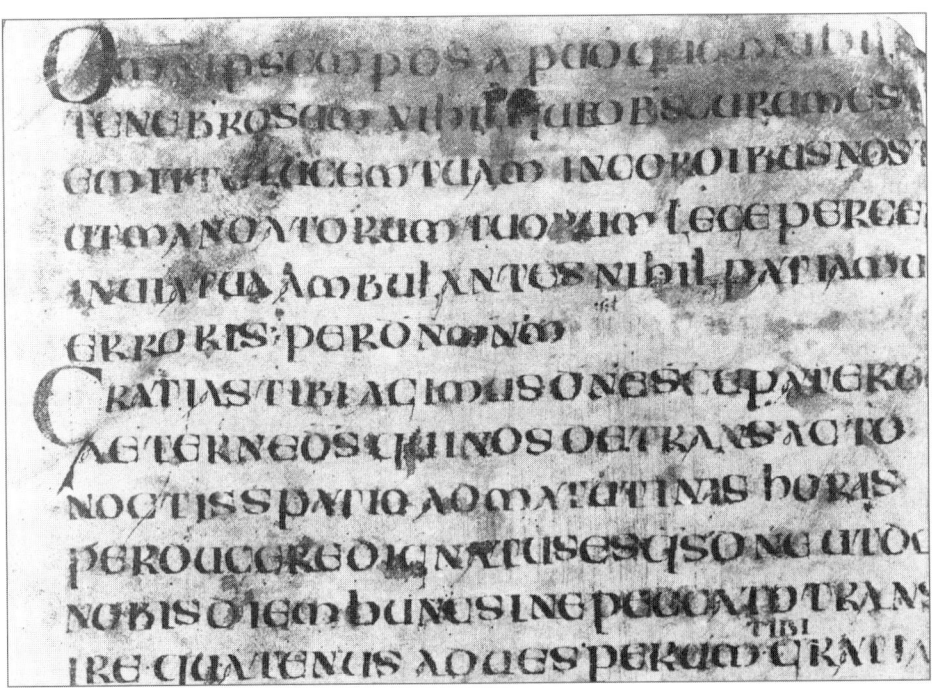

13.22. BL, Add. 37518, fol. 116r (detail). Fragment from a liturgical book. (British Library)

creation of an unsurpassably deluxe gospel book, inspired by a copy of the poems of the court poet of Constantine, written in magnificent uncials, with evangelist portraits based on those in the Gospels of St Augustine, could have been in part a response to the recent firm establishment of a rival archbishopric in the north of the country, of which Egbert (c. 732–66) was the first effective holder. Given that Egbert himself seems to have believed (erroneously) in the existence of liturgical books that Gregory the Great had sent to Augustine, a volume like the *Codex Aureus* was a forceful demonstration that the Kentish church had a continuous and living connection with the first Roman missionaries – kudos that the more recent northern see could not match.

Two other manuscripts, both now only fragments, are written in a script sufficiently similar to that of the books we have just examined to make an attribution to Kent a reasonable hypothesis. The first, now in the British Library, consists of a couple of sheets bearing prayers, which was perhaps originally part of a sacramentary (figs 13.22–3).[93] This preserves the work of three hands, all competent. The script of the second scribe is particularly close to some of that in the manuscripts we have just examined; while the expansive hand of the third shows that at least one other Kentish scribe could write uncial to the same grand scale as the scribes of the *Codex Aureus*.

The second set of fragments, divided between Avranches and St Petersburg, is the remnants of a gospel book (fig. 13.24).[94] Sufficient remains to show that it was originally a large and handsome volume, produced with great care: measuring at least 375 × 280 mm,[95] its size approached that of the *Codex Aureus*; and pairs of rulings were supplied for each line of writing to ensure maximum regularity of appearance. Although related in many points of detail to the earlier Kentish uncial, here the script has become more mannered and rectilinear with greatly extended ascenders and descenders. The effect, which is striking and very handsome, is increasingly distant from Late Antique and contemporary continental uncial. Overtly Insular features appear in the form of the red dots outlining the minor initials, and the serpentine decoration of a section initial.[96] On the other hand, rustic capitals and not a minuscule script were used to save space at the end of the page. This not only underlines the fact that the manuscript was a very formally conceived one, but also shows that the scriptorium responsible, while developing uncial in its own way, was well schooled in scribal traditions inherited from Late Antiquity. The text seems to be a fairly unexceptional Vulgate. It is chiefly notable for a couple of Insular spellings (which it has in common with, for instance, the Lichfield and Lindisfarne Gospels), and for the circumstance that the Avranches

13.23. BL, Add. 37518, fol. 117r (detail). Fragment from a liturgical book. (British Library)

> AIT PARALYTICO
> FILI DIMITTUNTUR
> TIBI PECCATA
> ERANT AUTEM ILLIC
> QUIDA DESCRIBIS
> SEDENTES ET COGI
> TANTES IN CORDIB; SUIS
> quid hic sic loquitur
> BLASPHEMAT
> quis potest dimittere
> PECCATA NISI SOLUS DS
> ~~...~~
> quia sic cogitarent
> INTRA SE
> DICIT ILLIS
> QUID ISTA COGITATIS
> IN CORDIB; UESTRIS
> quid facilius
> DICERE PARALYTICO
> DIMITTUNTUR TIBI
> PECCATA

> AN DICERE SURGE
> ET TOLLE GRAUATUM
> TUUM ET AMBULA
> UT AUTEM SCIATIS
> QUIA POTESTATE HABET
> FILIUS HOMINIS
> IN TERRA DIMITTENDI
> PECCATA
> AIT PARALYTICO
> TIBI DICO SURGE
> TOLLE GRABATU TUUM
> ET ~~VADE IN DOMUM TUAM~~
> ET SUBLATO GRABATO
> ABIIT CORAM OMNIB;
> ITA UT ADMIRARENTUR
> OMNES
> ET HONORIFICARENT
> DM DICENTES
> QUIA NUMQUAM
> SIC UIDIMUS
> EGRESSUS EST RVRSVS AD MAR

13.24. *Avranches, Bibliothèque municipale, 71, flyleaves. Gospel book fragment. (Avranches, Bibl. mun.)*

leaves at least share a number of readings with the Oxford Gospels of St Augustine – though, given the very limited sample of text, the significance of this should not be overstressed. In the absence of the rest of the manuscript, it is difficult to say much more. Nevertheless, one can observe that the point made in connection with the general appearance of the Vespasian Psalter and the *Codex Aureus* is here apparent in relation to the script alone – namely that the scribal vocabulary of Late Antique and continental manuscripts has been effectively mastered and adapted to form a distinctive new idiom.

The last manuscript of possible Kentish origin that we shall consider, the *Codex Bigotianus*, is also a gospel book (figs 13.25–7).[97] It is principally linked to our core volumes by its decoration, which is patently related to that of the Vespasian Psalter and the *Codex Aureus*. The script, a spacious, rounded uncial, which could be seen as a development of the majestic text uncial of the *Codex Aureus*, neither supports nor negates this affiliation: the closest parallel is provided by an older, probably Italian gospel book in Paris, which will be considered further below.[98] The layout of the *Codex Bigotianus* and its quire structure distances it somewhat from our core volumes, suggesting that, if it is a Kentish book, it originated in a different tradition from them. Its earliest known provenance (late medieval) was Fécamp in Normandy.[99]

Although not quite of the dimensions of the *Codex Aureus* and the Avranches-St Petersburg Gospels, the *Codex Bigotianus* is still a fairly big manuscript: despite brutal cropping[100] it still measures *c.* 350 × 255 mm, and is thus larger than the Lindisfarne Gospels, for instance. The parchment is smooth and even-

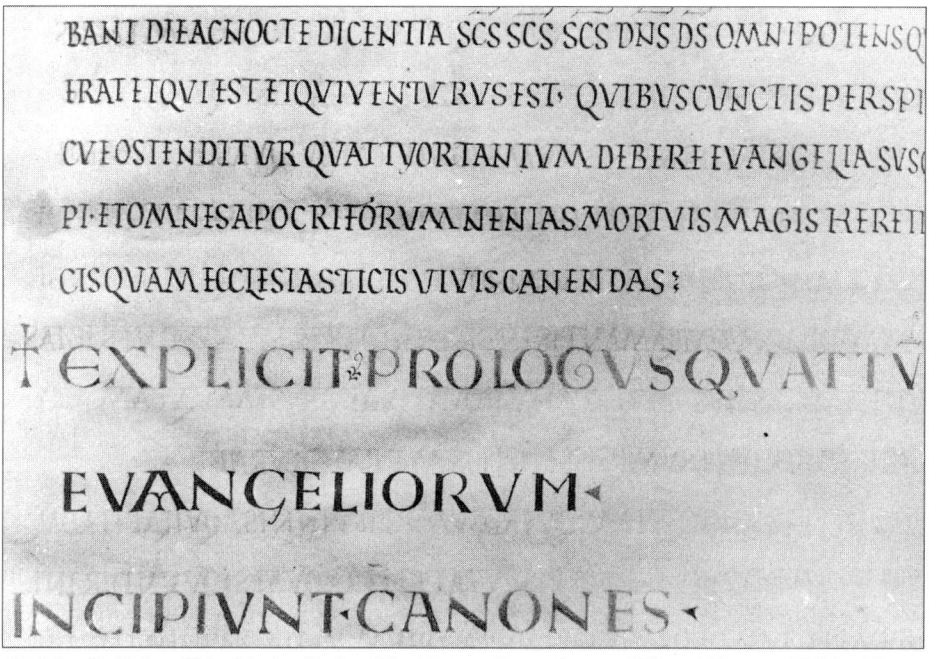

13.25. BnF, lat. 281, fol. 4v. Codex Bigotianus. Page size: c. 350 × 270 mm. (Bibliothèque nationale de France)

toned. Given that it is difficult to distinguish between the hair and flesh sides of the membrane, it is no surprise that there is little consistency in its arrangement. The quires are for the most part quinions (tens). The pages were pricked folded in the Insular manner, with a set of punctures in both margins on the outer edge of the textblock. In general, two sets of horizontal rulings (now very faint) were supplied for each line of writing.

Unlike the two early Italian gospel books, the *Codex Aureus* and the Avranches–St Petersburg Gospels all of whose texts are arranged two columns to the page, that of the *Codex Bigotianus* is presented in long lines, the resulting block being subdivided into paragraphs (each introduced by an enlarged initial).[101] Indeed, so wedded to a long line format was the scribe that he continued to use it even in the genealogy in Luke's gospel[102] where, in view of the fact that there are only three words per line (*qui fuit Heli*, etc. cf. fig. 13.5), many long-line manuscripts change to two columns.[103] Our scribe, by contrast, simply did his best to make the scanty available words fill the page, writing the '*qui fuit*'s at the left of the normal text area, then leaving a gap and supplying the proper names in the middle of the page.

Word division in the *Codex Bigotianus* is absolutely minimal; nevertheless it is there – a marginally bigger space was left between words than between the letters within a word, with a slightly larger gap being used at the beginnings of sentences. This seems, then, to be the work of someone who was used to inserting spaces between words but who here maintained *scriptura continua* for calculated effect. The aesthetic effect being sought – and which concessions to the needs of eighth-century readers have slightly disrupted – was presumably a solid block of letters evenly spaced across the writing area in the manner of an Antique book.

The general prefatory material and the prefaces to each gospel are written in oversized and idiosyncratic rustic capitals (fig. 13.26); square capitals were deployed for the first major explicits (fig. 13.25), an enlarged version of the already monumental text script being used thereafter. The gospel text is very spaciously written by a single scribe in a large, rounded and extraordinarily heavy uncial, which was produced by using a thick nib held absolutely parallel to the page (fig. 13.27). This script achieves its effect by sheer size and weight rather than by finesse of detail. Indeed, many of the downstrokes simply stop when they reach the baseline (i.e. they are not terminated by a serif or a sidestroke), a symptom of formidable pen control. Not all the letters are completely devoid of ornament, however, for triangular serifs appear on the cross-strokes of Es, Fs, and Ts, while the legs of the As are curiously formed from two very thin lines.[104] If they are both Kentish manuscripts and are broadly coeval, the *Codex Bigotianus* and the Avranches–St Petersburg Gospels represent the opposite extremes of

13.26. BnF, lat. 281, fol. 136r. Codex Bigotianus. *(Bibliothèque nationale de France)*

what Kentish uncial could become: one round and broad, the other rectilinear and mannered.

The uncial of the *Codex Bigotianus* could be seen as a distant descendant of the sort of broad, round uncial found in Milan, Biblioteca Ambrosiana C. 39 inf., a late sixth-century northern Italian manuscript;[105] and there are points of contact with the majestic text script of the *Codex Aureus*; while, as just noted, it has the triangular serifs characteristic of the Kentish books as a whole. The

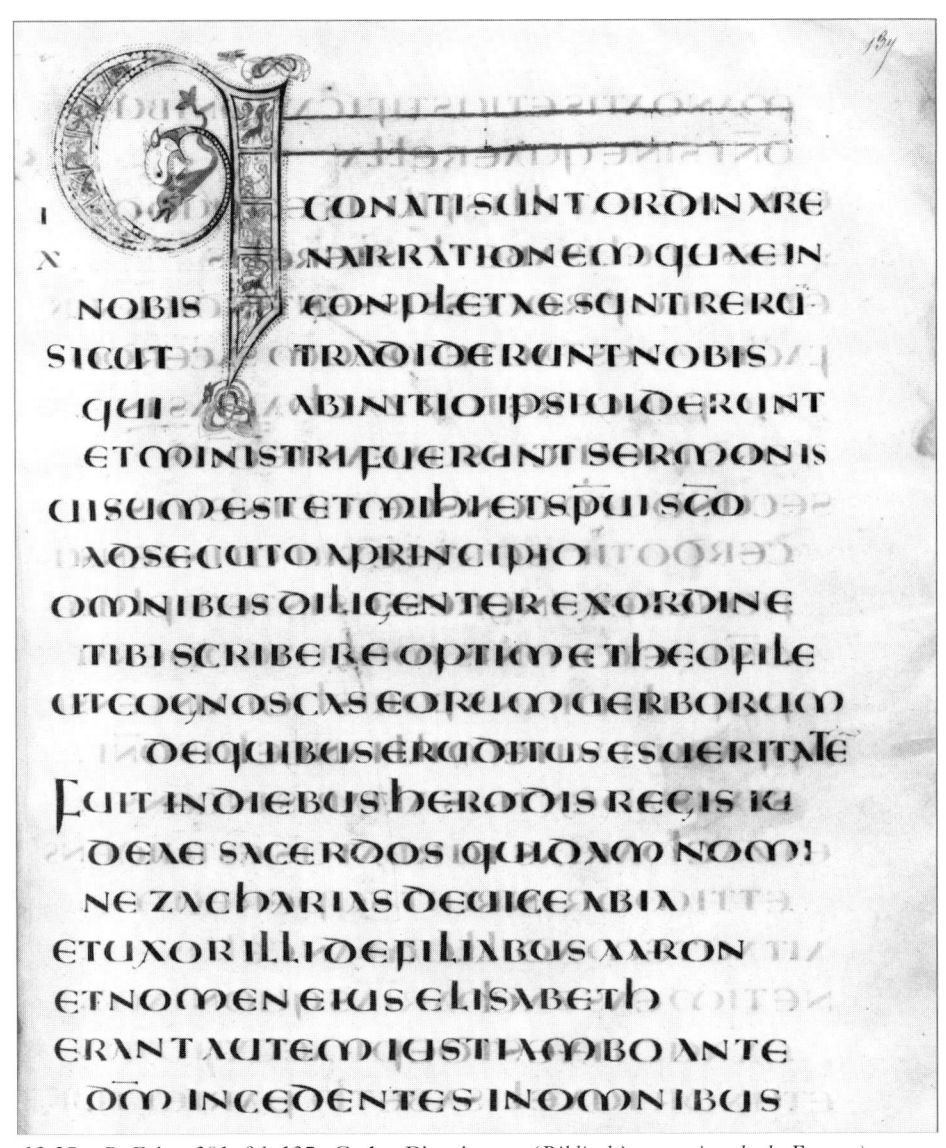

13.27. BnF, lat. 281, fol. 137r. Codex Bigotianus. (Bibliothèque nationale de France)

closest overall parallel, however, in terms of general aesthetic and dimensions, and also with regard to the detail of certain letters, is provided by Paris, Bibliothèque nationale de France, lat. 17226, a once handsome gospel book, probably of early eighth-century date and, to judge by the parchment, of Italian origin (fig. 13.28). Assuming lat. 17226 was indeed written in Italy, it clearly travelled north at an early date, for it bears corrections in an eighth-century northern French uncial, and contemporary French hands were also responsible for the extensive retracing of flaked letters; its later provenance was Notre

13.28. BnF, lat. 17226, fol. 15r. Gospel book. (Bibliothèque nationale de France)

Dame in Paris. There is also an intriguing hint that, between these two points, it may have travelled even further north – to England – for a small sketch in late Anglo-Saxon style was added to one folio.[106] Be that as it may, the main interest of the parallel is that it suggests that the script of the *Codex Bigotianus* could represent a response to Italian models which date from 150 years after the Gospels of St Augustine.

The text of *Bigotianus* is a conservative Vulgate with a comparatively small number of variants, the detail of its affiliations differing slightly from one gospel to the next. The groups of manuscripts with which it shares the largest numbers of variants are, in ascending order of importance: British-Insular, non-Northumbrian English, pre-Carolingian Frankish, Old Latin, and above all early Italian. The individual manuscripts with which it shares most variants include the Old Latin Vercelli Gospels, the Augsburg Gospels from Echternach, and the Cutbercht Gospels from Salzburg;[107] however the strongest presence is once again early Italian manuscripts, and interestingly, of the five books in question, no fewer than three are known to have been in England by the eighth century.[108] The manuscript whose text is closest in terms of the number of shared variants is the Oxford Gospels of St Augustine; nevertheless, the disagreements are sufficient to make a direct relationship unlikely.

The surviving decoration is limited to the *incipits* for the four gospels, all damaged to a greater or lesser extent (fig. 13.27). Each was introduced by an enlarged initial, subdivided into segments; the L for the first gospel is the grandest. In the initials for Matthew and Mark the segments were filled with simple interlace or foliate motifs, while slightly more intricate animals were used in Luke and John. In the case of Matthew, Luke and John the decorated initial was accompanied by a panel of continuation lettering, enhancing the overall effect; in Mark, on the other hand, it was simply followed by normal text. In further contrast to the other three initials, whose panels and outlines were originally filled with gold leaf,[109] there is no sign that Mark's I was ever similarly adorned. For what it is worth, we may note that the provision of a lesser visual emphasis for the *incipit* of Mark's gospel is something that *Bigotianus* shares with the *Codex Aureus*, in which Mark is the only gospel not to be introduced by a decorated initial. More significantly, not only the general conception but also the detail of individual motifs in *Bigotianus* link this work to the art of the Vespasian Psalter and the *Codex Aureus*. An individual, rather retrospective touch, reminiscent of Late Antique book decoration, is the dolphin which appears in the bowl of the initial Q to Luke's gospel.[110] This archaism, if such it be, is in character with the general appearance of the volume as a whole, and it inevitably makes one think of the dolphin that forms the first *Aliter* in the Troyes 504 copy of Gregory's *Regula pastoralis* (fig. 13.2). Compared with most of our other books, *Bigotianus* is very sparingly ornamented, and none of the text initials is enlivened with red dots; while such calligraphic embellishment of initials as occasionally appears (the A on fol. 146v of lat. 281, for example) has more in common with the penmanship of Troyes 504 than with any Kentish manuscript. If the script belongs to a baroque phase of Kentish uncial, the ruthless exclusion of ornament

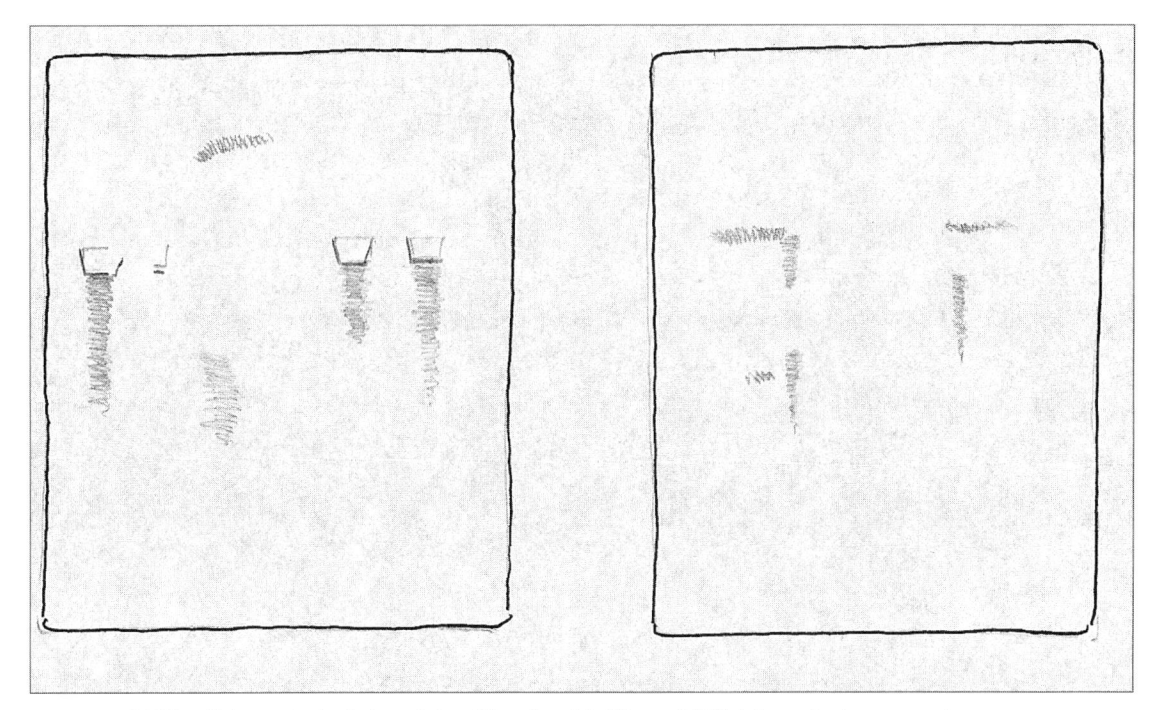

13.29. Schematic depiction of the offsets (on fols 86r and 137r) from the lost evangelist portraits in the Codex Bigotianus. *(Gameson)*

from it, like the studied preservation of *scriptura continua* in association with a long line format, suggests a deliberate attempt to regain an 'archaic' purity.

The start of the book is incomplete; nevertheless, it appears to have included canon tables since the rubric for them survives,[111] its position suggesting that they stood between the general prefaces and the preface to Matthew (fig. 13.25). In addition, the volume seems originally to have had evangelist portraits. Faint red offsets on the first page of Mark and Luke's gospels show that they were formerly faced by pictorial pages. Although shadowy and difficult to decipher in detail, the offsets from Mark reveal beyond reasonable doubt that the composition in question was framed by double columns and an arch (fig. 13.29). The general design would seem, therefore, to have resembled that used in the *Codex Aureus* and, even more closely, the Gospels of St Augustine.

Having surveyed our source material, such as it is, let us now in conclusion consider a couple of the general themes it raises.

First and foremost it is important to reiterate how pitifully little we have. At the most generous estimate, of the continental books imported into Kent, we now possess one or just possibly two gospel books, conceivably one library text, plus vestigial traces of one vanished poetry codex. We have no books produced in Kent from the seventh century, while from the eighth century prior to the period of Mercian dominance all that remains is one psalter, one copy of Acts, two nearly complete gospel books, a few pages from a third, plus perhaps a couple of leaves from a single service book. Although the strong showing of gospel books is doubtless a fair reflection of the fact that they were the most frequently copied and highly treasured volumes of the period, this unrepresentative handful of high-grade books is no basis for generalisations. As we noted at the outset, the appearance of early Kentish library books is entirely lost to us, as are such important themes as the emergence, form and use of Kentish minuscule bookhands.[112] Yet it should also be said that by contemporary English standards, this is actually a good haul. With the exception of Northumbria, the scriptoria and libraries of the other early Anglo-Saxon kingdoms have been even less fortunate and are even more obscure. The only other centres to which early books can be securely attributed are Lindisfarne and Wearmouth–Jarrow;[113] and as a result, the English comparanda for our manuscripts are strictly limited.

What then, given these weighty caveats, does our handful of unrepresentative Kentish books seem to show? They undoubtedly reflect something of the range of christian Kent's cultural contacts, and moreover shed some light on their relative importance. The primary debt, proclaimed by the uncial script, the use of purple parchment, the illusionistic figural decoration, not to mention textual affiliations, was to the Italian world. Moreover, our manuscripts reveal that Italian practices became living Kentish traditions which remained vigorous for 150 years. Conversely, much of the ornamental repertoire provides clear proof of the relationship between Kentish scriptoria and the Insular world, which also arguably exerted an influence on graphic articulation and even on the development of Kentish uncial. Yet this was a secondary strain, enriching and modifying rather than supplanting the Roman-derived core: Kentish scribes eschewed diminuendo, for instance; they resisted the distortion of letter forms in initials and display script; and they used the devices of Late Antiquity, namely precious metals, as much as the Insular welter of ornament to decorate and apotheosise text. Nevertheless the distinctive character of our manuscripts owes much to the interplay of these two traditions. The point is underlined by the contrast between the appearance of our books and that of the surviving examples produced at the other centre where Roman influence was strong, namely Wearmouth–Jarrow. The Kentish volumes seem very exotic in comparison with the austere, largely undecorated manuscripts from that Northumbrian centre, whose scriptorium at the end of the seventh century and the beginning of the eighth seems to have been more single-minded and conservative in its adherence to 'Roman' script and aesthetic values.

Echoes of Frankish books, by contrast, are far more elusive in our manuscripts, seemingly being limited to a few decorative motifs. In view of the facts that the very earliest books in Canterbury, those associated with Queen Bertha and Bishop Liudhard, were presumably Frankish, that a few Frankish manuscripts may have arrived with Augustine, that Frankia undoubtedly offered the nearest source of supply – indeed the dispatch of books from Chelles to England *c*. 700 is documented in the *Life of St Bertila*[114] – and that important women from Kent, such as Mildred of Thanet, went to centres in northern Gaul for their education, notably Chelles and Faremoutiers, one might have expected more. This is additionally the case given the stress that is sometimes placed on the Frankish influence on early Kentish political and religious life in the sixth and seventh centuries,[115] and the revalorisation of Frankish culture that has happened in recent years.[116] It is true that we cannot always distinguish between volumes written in Italy and Gaul on the grounds of script alone; and the standard corpus of early Latin manuscripts has been criticised on the grounds that its editor had a tendency to classify the best continental uncial as Italian, the lesser work as Frankish, thus minimising the achievement and importance of the latter. Yet, whatever the justice of this last point – and it is not universally accepted – Frankish book decoration *is* distinctive, and it does not appear to have had much impact in southern England. Granted that our Kentish books all date from the eighth century, they nevertheless seem to imply that Frankish scribal influence was limited, and to uphold the traditional view of a special relationship with Italian models. But then Augustine and his successors at Canterbury provided a living Roman tradition up to the mid-seventh century. The last Italian archbishop, Honorius, died in 653, and although he was followed by a West Saxon (Deusdedit, 655–64), relations with Rome and the papacy remained strong, and the next archbishop along with the contemporary abbot of Saint Augustine's were papal appointees. Thereafter Frankish models could not apparently compete either with the cachet of Italian ones of the past, or with the brilliance of Insular ones of the present.

Equally elusive is the influence of eastern mediterranean work. Apart from the debatable case of some of the imagery in the Vespasian Psalter, it seems to be limited to a few decorative motifs. One Greek-speaking archbishop and an uncertain quantity of imported luxury goods would seem to have spiced rather than determined the flavour of Kentish deluxe book production.

Yet although indebted to various sources, principally Italian and Insular, our books show that Kentish scribes and artists followed their own course, choosing and combining eclectically and introducing their own variations and features at every stage. In the construction of quires and the arrangement of parchment, for instance, they followed rigidly neither the continental nor the Insular norms; indeed the *Codex Aureus* reveals that they were prepared to depart from all known conventions if circumstances demanded it. Correspondingly, they gave more emphasis to explicits than was generally the case in Insular manuscripts, yet placed a greater stress on *incipits* than was found in continental ones. The Late Antique tradition favoured semi-naturalistic imagery; Insular scribes preferred abstract ornament; our calligraphers and illuminators achieved some of the most successful marriages of the two. In their finest products, Insular scribes turned certain words into beautiful but virtually illegible symbols, whereas their Italian conterparts preserved them as vehicles, albeit sometimes majestic ones, for verbal communication. The best Kentish books combine both traditions, preserving a purity of script, but enhancing it visually with greater and more skilful use of ornament. Moreover, in the case of the *Codex Aureus*, the entire text, though written in largely unornamented uncials, is elevated to the status of a symbol in an unparalleled and spectacular way.

This leads to our final point, which is the very high quality of our manuscripts. They were almost all well written in a more distinguished uncial than, and on parchment of superior quality to, that used for high-grade books on the other side of the Channel. Our three Kentish (or possibly Kentish) gospel books were all of exceptionally large size; and the realisation, script, and decoration of the Vespasian Psalter and the *Codex Aureus* can truly be described as superlative. Indeed, the Vespasian Psalter and the *Codex Aureus* are incontestably the finest and most opulent surviving books to have been produced anywhere in western Europe around the middle of the eighth century. They have a complexity and sophistication, a quality of artistry, and (with their precious metals) a luxuriousness that overshadows all the extant contemporary material from Northumbria, Gaul, and Italy. Comparison with such famous works as the Lichfield, Gundohinus, Flavigny, and San Vincenzo Gospels makes the point.[117] Although under the influence of the scholarly Bede, it is tempting to see the cultural history of the Kentish church in the eighth century in terms of a gradual but steady decline from the heights of Theodore and Hadrian's day, these manuscripts tell a very different story. Bede never saw them; but writing in the year Bede died (735), St Boniface, who was indomitable in pursuing the exact books he wanted, be they in Northumbria or Rome, turned to Kent for the one and only deluxe volume we know he commissioned. The fact that in the generation after our manuscripts were produced it required the efforts of Charlemagne, king of the Franks and emperor of the Romans, to achieve something comparable (and even so, the earlier court school manuscripts of the so-called Ada group are of a lesser overall quality and sophistication) highlights the magnitude of the achievement of our Kentish scribes and artists, and the strengths of the ecclesio-political regime and of the christian faith that supported them.[118]

APPENDIX I

EARLY MANUSCRIPTS THAT ARE SOMETIMES ASSOCIATED WITH KENT BUT WITHOUT SUFFICIENT CAUSE

Brief note should here be made of four eighth-century manuscripts that I would not myself attribute to Kent, but for which such an attribution has sometimes been advanced (nos 1–3, 5); and of one (no. 4) that is very difficult to localise but for which a south east English, even Kentish origin is not impossible. They are treated in alphabetical order of their present location.

1 CCCC, 173 (part ii: fols 57–83).

This much-used copy of Sedulius's *Carmen paschale* and other works is now bound with the Parker Chronicle ('A'). As originally produced, it was written for the most part in a cursive, spiky Insular minuscule with a more formal set minuscule for display script (fol. 59r); however, the general effect is now rather distorted owing to the fact that large areas of the text were rewritten in the earlier tenth century in square minuscule. It was modestly decorated in an Insular style which is easier to parallel in Southumbrian manuscripts than Northumbrian ones but is decidedly 'provincial'. The book thus has nothing in common palaeographically, and very little in common artistically with our core manuscripts; and its earliest known Anglo-Saxon provenance was probably Winchester.

CLA, II, no. 123; Ker, *Catalogue*, no. 40; R.I. Page, 'The Study of Latin Texts in late Anglo-Saxon England II: the evidence of English glosses' in *Latin and the Vernacular Languages in Early Medieval Britain*, ed. N. Brooks (Leicester, 1982), pp. 141–65, esp. pp. 154–60 with pl. on p. 155; Budny, *Insular, Anglo-Saxon, and Early Anglo-Norman Manuscript Art*, I, no. 4.

2 New York, Pierpont Morgan Library, M 776.

The so-called Blickling or Lothian Psalter is the closest relative textually of the Vespasian Psalter, with which it also shares a few decorative motifs (its most important decorated pages have been removed). The fact that the manuscript is written in Insular half-uncial does not automatically disqualify it from a Kentish origin given that, as we have seen, this script was practised there by the end of the seventh century. However, there is no positive evidence in support of the theory: neither the textual nor the artistic connections are particularly strong; the late medieval provenance of the book was Lincoln, while the script of the glosses suggests that it was in Wessex in the ninth century.

CLA, XI, no. 1661; Ker, *Catalogue*, no. 287; Collins, *Anglo-Saxon Manuscripts in America*, no. 10 with pl. 11; W.M. Voekle, *Medieval and Renaissance Manuscripts* (New York, 1974), no. 1; Alexander, *Insular Manuscripts*, cat. 31; J. Crick, 'The Case for a West Saxon Minuscule', *ASE*, 26 (1997), 63–79, esp. 68–70, 74–5.

3 BodL, Hatton 48.

The attribution to Kent of this manuscript, the oldest extant copy of the *Regula S. Benedicti*, has been based on the general aspect of the script. However, although certainly closer to Kentish uncial than to the Wearmouth–Jarrow versions, the writing is not sufficiently similar to that of our core witnesses to justify the localisation – particularly given that the earliest known provenance of the volume was Worcester.

CLA, II, no. 240; D. Wright, 'Some Notes on English Uncial', *Traditio*, 17 (1961), 441–56, at 449–50; facsimile: *The Rule of St Benedict*, ed. D.H. Farmer, EEMF, 15 (Copenhagen, 1968).

4 BnF, lat. 9561.

Although this copy of Pseudo-Isidore's *De ordine creaturarum* and Gregory the Great's *Regula pastoralis* has never been explicitly attributed to Kent, it nevertheless deserves to be mentioned in the present context (fig. 13.30, cf. 1.8). The earliest known provenance of the manuscript is Saint-Bertin, as an erased late medieval *ex libris* attests. Working backwards, it was evidently in an Anglo-Saxon milieu in the tenth century when a few glosses in Old English were entered on fols 33v–42r; and production in an English or English-influenced milieu is indicated by the ornamentation of the major initials – enlarged penwork letters with spiral terminals – and by the use of red dots to surround every sentence capital. Furthermore, the parchment seems to have the superior quality of that of some Anglo-Saxon books; and while the script – a very squat, square uncial (presumably thus conceived to save space) – is, on the whole, difficult to place, the scribe very occasionally 'drops' into an Insular minuscule (e.g. fol. 14v). All things considered, it seems probable that the book is of English origin; and the very restrained use of Insular ornament, the choice of uncial as the main bookhand, and the subsequent Saint-Bertin provenance might be held to favour a southern, specifically Kentish, origin. Moreover, on the brief occasions when the scribe wrote on a larger scale (generally in the continuation lettering after an initial, e.g. fol. 50r), the script undeniably resembles that of the *Codex Aureus*. Nevertheless, the case falls so far short of proof, and the manuscript has, in general, so little in common with better authenticated Kentish manuscripts, that it seems best to do no more than draw attention here to its possible relevance to our subject.

13.30. BnF, lat. 9561, fol. 50r. Gregory the Great, Regula pastoralis. *(Bibliothèque nationale de France)*

Chatelain, *Uncialis Scriptura*, pl. XLVIII; *CLA*, V, no. 590; Lowe, *English Uncial*, pl. XXXV; Avril and Stirnemann, *Manuscrits enluminés*, no. 5.

5   Vatican City, Biblioteca Apostolica Vaticana, Barberini lat. 570.
Attributions of this enigmatic and understudied gospel book (the Barberini Gospels) to southern England, occasionally explicitly to Canterbury, flit through

some of the more recent literature – alongside, it should be said, various other hypotheses. The case for an origin in Kent seems to be based on the fact that it has a notable textual affinity to the *Codex Aureus*, and on the circumstance that some of the script and ornament is comparable to that found in some slightly later (early ninth-century) Kentish books. In the absence of detailed study, any comment is necessarily premature. Nevertheless, given that the textual connections with *Aureus* are too distant to imply any direct association between the volumes; that the scribal stint in question does not indicate a connection with Kent in particular as opposed to 'greater Mercia' as a whole, while other stints clearly point away from the south; that the relevant decoration is similarly generically Southumbrian rather than Kentish; and that the provenance of the book is entirely unknown, it seems unlikely that an attribution to Kent (or any other centre) could ever be satisfactorily demonstrated. Whatever the truth, the manuscript has nothing in common with our core volumes, and seems rather to belong to the generation of books listed in Appendix II.

CLA, I, no. 63; McGurk, *Latin Gospel Books*, no. 137; Alexander, *Insular Manuscripts*, cat. 36; Webster and Backhouse (eds), *Making of England*, no. 160; Netzer, *Cultural Interplay*, esp. 13–17, 120; Budny, *Insular, Anglo-Saxon and Early Anglo-Norman Manuscript Art*, I, pp. 79, 90.

APPENDIX II
MANUSCRIPTS ASSOCIATED WITH KENT, S. VIII^{EX}–IX^1

For the sake of completeness, it is appropriate to list here the handful of extant manuscripts with a Kentish connection (differing in strength from case to case) that were produced between s. viii^{ex} and ix^1, i.e. in the generations immediately after the period we have surveyed. It is a striking fact that while all the earlier volumes which we have discussed were written in uncials, not one of these later books is. Whether these later manuscripts shed much light on the previous history of Insular half-uncial, Insular minuscule and hybrid minuscules as bookhands in Kent is a moot point. For each manuscript I give: shelf mark, content, script type, probable date, indication of the nature of its connection with Kent, and summary bibliography. The general scribal context has recently been discussed by M.P. Brown, *The Book of Cerne: Prayer, Patronage and Power in Ninth-Century England* (London, 1996), pp. 162–72.

1 CCCC, 144, fols. i+1–64.
Glossary; Insular half-uncial; ix^{in}. The manuscript bears a medieval *ex libris* of Saint Augustine's Abbey.
CLA, II, no. 122; Ker, *Catalogue*, no. 36; Webster and Backhouse (eds), *Making of England*, no. 63.

2 BL, Cotton Tiberius C. ii.

Bede, *Historia ecclesiastica*; set minuscule; ix¹. It is linked to Kent by its scribal similarities to Canterbury charters.

CLA, II, no. 191; Ker, *Catalogue*, no. 198; Alexander, *Insular Manuscripts*, no. 33; J. Morrish, 'Dated and Datable Manuscripts copied in England during the Ninth Century', *Medieval Studies*, 50 (1988), 512–38, at 528–9; Webster and Backhouse (eds), *Making of England*, no. 170.

3 BL, Royal 1 E. vi, + *membra disjecta*.

Bible fragment; set minuscule; ix¹. It bears a medieval *ex libris* of Saint Augustine's Abbey.

CLA, II, nos 214, 245, 262; Alexander, *Insular Manuscripts*, cat. 32; Morrish, 'Dated and Datable', p. 529; Webster and Backhouse (eds), *Making of England*, no. 171. See also Mildred Budny and Richard Marsden, chs 11–12 above, with pl. VI and figs 11.3–5, 7.

4 BnF, lat. 10861.

Vitae sanctorum; Insular minuscule; ix^in. It is linked to Kent by its scribal similarities to Christ Church charters.

Alexander, *Insular Manuscripts*, cat. 67; Avril and Stirnemann, *Manuscrits enluminés*, no. 11; M.P. Brown, 'Paris, BN lat. 10861 and the Scriptorium of Christ Church, Canterbury', *ASE*, 15 (1986), 119–37; Backhouse and Webster (eds), *Making of England*, no. 168.

NOTES

1. *HE*, I, 29, p. 104.
2. '*Hoc autem jejunium idem beatus Gregorius, per praefatum legatum, in antiphonario suo et missali, in plena ebdomada post Pentecosten Anglorum aecclesiae celebrandum destinauit.*': *Dialogus Egberti*, printed in *Councils and Ecclesiastical Documents Relating to Great Britain and Ireland*, eds A.W. Haddan and W. Stubbs, 3 vols (Oxford, 1869–79), III, pp. 403–13, at 412. Cf. H. Ashworth, 'Did Augustine bring the 'Gregorianum' to England?', *Ephemerides Liturgicae*, 72 (1958), 39–43.
3. Cf. Thomas of Elmham, *Historia Monasterii S. Augustini Cantuariensis*, ed. C. Hardwick, RS (London, 1858), 97; with H. Gneuss, *Hymnar und Hymnen im englischen Mittelalter* (Munich, 1968), pp. 17–19, 33. The most recent discussion of the liturgy of early Anglo-Saxon England in general, with references to earlier literature, is Y. Hen, 'The Liturgy of St Willibrord', *ASE*, 26 (1997).
4. See Mildred Budny, ch. 11 above.
5. Thomas of Elmham's account of the books begins, '*In primis habetur in librario Biblia Gregoriana in duobus uoluminibus quorum primum habet rubricam in primo folio De Capitulis Libri Geneseos*': *Historia Monasterii S. Augustini*, ed. Hardwick, 96; cf. also M.R. James, *The Ancient Libraries of Canterbury and Dover* (Cambridge, 1903), pp. lxiv, 500.
6. *S. Gregorii Magni, Registrum Epistolarum*, ed. D. Norberg, 2 vols, *CCSL* 140–140A (Turnhout, 1982), III, 3.
7. *Registrum Epistolarum*, ed. Norberg, II, 31, p. 118. Gregory's views on education as a whole are discussed by P. Riché, *Education et culture dans l'Occident barbare, 6e–8e*

siècles (Paris, 1962), pp. 187–200; also R. Markus, *Gregory the Great and his World* (Cambridge, 1997), pp. 34–40. On the changing role of books, and perception of them in Gregory's time see A. Petrucci, 'La concezione cristiana del libro', *Studi medievali*, 3rd series, 14 (1973), 961–84; trans. as 'The Christian Concept of the Book in the Sixth and Seventh Centuries' in his *Writers and Readers in Medieval Italy*, trans. C.M. Radding (New Haven and London, 1995), pp. 19–42. Gregory described Augustine as full of the knowledge of holy scripture ('*sacrae scripturae scientia repletus*'), e.g. *Registrum epistolarum*, ed. Norberg, XI, 37, p. 930.

8. *Registrum epistolarum*, ed. Norberg, IV, 4, p. 220; IX, 209; and XI, 10. On the illiteracy of the Lombards see A. Petrucci, 'Il problema longobardo', *Studi medievali*, 3rd series, 14 (1973), 984–1002; trans. in his *Writers and Readers*, pp. 43–58.

9. *Teste* Alfred's metrical preface to his translation of the work: *The Anglo-Saxon Poetic Records*, eds G. Krapp and E.V.K. Dobbie, 6 vols (London and New York, 1931–42), VI: *The Anglo-Saxon Minor Poems*, p. 110. For early English copies see *CLA*, II, nos 188, 229, 264; V, no. 590 (on which see further Appendix I, no. 4, below).

10. James, *Ancient Libraries*, pp. lxiii–lxix, 500.

11. Which must have included psalter, gospel book and some liturgical texts – the basic works outlined in connection with Augustine himself. Moreover, if there is anything more than courtesy in Gregory's description of Bertha as '*Litteris docta*' (*Registrum epistolarum*, ed. Norberg, I, 11), they may have included more.

12. Cf. P. Chaplais, 'Who Introduced Charters into England? The Case for Augustine', *Prisca Munimenta, Studies presented to A.E.J. Hollaender*, ed. F. Ranger (London, 1973), 88–107, esp. 89–99.

13. Cf. *HE*, III, 18.

14. *HE*, IV, 2. Cf. M. Lapidge, 'The School of Theodore and Hadrian', *ASE*, 15 (1986), 45–72; repr. in his *Anglo-Latin Literature 600–899* (London and Rio Grande, 1996), pp. 141–68; N. Brooks, *The Early History of the Church of Canterbury* (Leicester, 1984), pp. 94–9.

15. *HE*, preface; and cf. V, 20.

16. For the possibility that the surviving manuscripts of Tatwine's Grammar reflect an original manuscript with Old English annotations possibly made at Canterbury see V. Law, 'The Latin and Old English glossess in the *Ars Tatwini*', *ASE*, 6 (1977), 77–90; and 'The Transmission of the *Ars Bonifacii* and the *Ars Tatuini*', *Revue d'histoire des textes*, 9 (1979), 281–8.

17. The early history of these houses is conveniently synopsised in M. Deanesly, *The Pre-Conquest Church in England*, 2nd edn (London, 1963), pp. 202–5; see also W. Page (ed.), *The Victoria History of the County of Kent*, II (London, 1926), *passim*.

18. For a complementary account of the probable script history of seventh-century England based on inference from known contacts, and from Late Antique and contemporary continental practices see D.N. Dumville, 'The Importation of Mediterranean Manuscripts into Theodore's England', in M. Lapidge (ed.), *Archbishop Theodore* (Cambridge, 1995), pp. 96–119, at pp. 96–106.

19. *CLA*, VI, no. 838; A. Petrucci, 'L'Onciale Romana', *Studi medievali*, 12 (1972), 75–131, esp. 76–85, with pl. I. For further reproductions see: L. Moret-Payen, *Les plus beaux manuscrits et les plus belles reliures de la Bibliothèque de Troyes* (Troyes, 1935), p. 49 with pl. I; C. Nordenfalk, *Die spätantiken Zierbuchstaben*, 2 vols (Stockholm, 1970), II, pls VII, 68; J. Glenisson (ed.), *Le Livre au moyen âge* (Paris, 1988), p. 52; M.B. Parkes, *Pause and*

Effect: An Introduction to the History of Punctuation in the West (Aldershot, 1992), pl. 6; by far the best plate, A. Chatelain, *Uncialis Scriptura*, 2 vols (Paris, 1910), I, pl. XXXIX.

20. It has even been trimmed since the 'modern' foliation was added.
21. *Teste* Lowe; as every leaf is now entirely coated on both sides with a fine ?fabric mesh, the details of the pricking and ruling, not to mention the quality of the parchment, are now impossible to discern.
22. Occasionally (e.g. fol. 166v) almost nothing is left. It was presumably because of this, as well as the extreme thinness of some of the leaves that the decision was taken to coat the leaves, as mentioned in the previous note.
23. Particularly fols 4r (the start of the text proper), 55r, 65r, 75v, 78r, 81v, 83v, 87r, 89v, 102v, 108v, 130r. See further C. Nordenfalk, 'Before the Book of Durrow', *Acta Archaeologica*, 18 (1947), 141–74, esp. 151–9.
24. R.W. Clement, 'Two Contemporary Gregorian Editions of Pope Gregory the Great's *Regula Pastoralis* in Troyes 504', *Scriptorium*, 39 (1985), 89–97.
25. *CLA*, II, no. 126; F. Wormald, *The Miniatures in the Gospels of St Augustine* (Cambridge, 1954); Petrucci, 'L'Onciale Romana', esp. pp. 107–8, 110–11; M.O. Budny, *Insular, Anglo-Saxon and Early Anglo-Norman Manuscript Art at Corpus Christi College, Cambridge: an illustrated catalogue*, 2 vols (Kalamazoo, 1997), I, no. 1; R.G. Gameson, *The Gospels of St Augustine of Canterbury* (forthcoming). It is collated in *Nouum Testamentum Domini Nostri Iesu Christi Latine secundum editionem sancti Hieronymi*, ed. J. Wordsworth, H.J. White, H. Sparks and A. Adams, 3 vols (Oxford, 1889–1954), I: *Quattuor Euangelia*, as 'X'. This should be used in conjunction with the corrections in H. Glunz, *History of the Vulgate in England from Alcuin to Roger Bacon* (Cambridge, 1933), Appendix a, pp. 294–304.

26. Compare G. Schiller, *Iconography of Christian Art*, 2 vols (London, 1971–2), II, pls 186–88, 196–201, 206.
27. Compare Schiller, *Iconography*, II, pls 166, 168–75.
28. Compare Schiller, *Iconography*, II, pls 117–18, 120–30.
29. I.e. by clause and phrase.
30. For example, Vatican City, Biblioteca Apostolica Vaticana, lat. 7016 of s. viii[ex]; and BL, Add. 5463 of viii[med].
31. Vatican City, Biblioteca Apostolica Vaticana, Reg. lat. 267 (part i): *CLA*, I, no. 104a (where it is hesitatingly attributed to France); Petrucci, 'L'Onciale Romana', p. 97, with pl. IX.
32. Petrucci, 'L'Onciale Romana', pp. 76–85. Although it must be said that he seems to have known the manuscript only from reproductions and a microfilm, and his assessment of the script seems to have been slightly confused by the later corrections and rewritings.
33. Although only one pictorial page and one portrait remains, the existence of others is attested by offsets.
34. Or the *idioti* and *ignorantes*, to use his own words: *Registrum epistolarum*, ed. Norberg, IX, 209 and XI, 10. From the copious literature devoted to these letters see, for example, L.G. Duggan, 'Was Art Really the Book of the Illiterate', *Word and Image*, 5 (1989), 227–51.
35. Brescia, Biblioteca Queriniana, s.n.: *CLA*, III, no. 281; P. McGurk, *Latin Gospel Books from A.D. 400 to A.D. 800* (Brussels, 1961), no. 93; *Charlemagne: Oeuvre, rayonnement et survivance*, Council of Europe exh. cat. (Aachen, 1965), no. 388. Naples, Biblioteca Nazionale, lat. 3: *CLA*, III, no. 399; McGurk, *Latin Gospel Books*, no. 99.

Sarrezzano, Biblioteca Parrochiale, s.n. (= fragments from two purple gospel books, bound together): *CLA*, IV, nos 436a, b; McGurk, *Latin Gospel Books*, nos 102–3. Trent, Museo Nazionale, s.n. etc.: *CLA*, IV, no. 437; McGurk, *Latin Gospel Books*, no. 104.
Verona, Biblioteca Capitolare, VI (6): *CLA*, IV, no. 481; McGurk, *Latin Gospel Books*, no. 109; G. Turrini, *Millenium Scriptorii Veronensis dal iv° al xv° secolo* (Verona, 1967), fp; G. Zivelonghi and C. Adami, *I Codici Liturgici della Cattedrale di Verona* (Verona, 1987), pp. 66–7.

36. Florence, Biblioteca Medicea-Laurenziana, Amiatino 1: CLA III, no. 299; Alexander, *Insular Manuscripts*, cat. 7; R. Marsden, *The Text of the Old Testament in Anglo-Saxon England* (Cambridge, 1995), pp. 85–90, 98–201. Further on the corrections to the Gospels of St Augustine, see Richard Marsden, ch. 12 above.

37. BodL, Auct. D. 2. 14: *CLA*, II, no. 230; E. A. Lowe, *English Uncial* (Oxford, 1960), pl. 4. The text is collated as 'O' in *Nouum Testamentum*, ed. J. Wordsworth and H.J. White, I. As it survives, the manuscript contains Mark 4:14–John 21:15. See further the discussion by Richard Marsden, ch. 12 above.

38. The Avranches–St Petersburg Gospels: see n. 94 below.

39. The start of Matthew is lost: see n. 37.

40. For a colour illustration of fol. 130r (showing the end of the capitula and the beginning of the Gospel of St John) see R.G. Gameson, *St Augustine of Canterbury* (Canterbury, 1997), p. 28, no. 13.

41. *CLA*, VI, no. 735 (where surely dated too early); N.R. Ker, *Catalogue of Manuscripts Containing Anglo-Saxon* (Oxford, 1957), no. 6*, p. lxiii; Petrucci, 'L'Onciale Romana', pp. 112–13, n. 112. It contains Ambrose, *Apologia David de Psalmo L, De Joseph, De patriarchis, De paenitentia, De excessu fratris*, and *Epistolae*.

42. SC 3655; *CLA*, S, no. 1740 (the plate has more definition and is easier to read than the original); cf. also N.R. Ker and E.A. Lowe, 'A New Fragment of Arator in the Bodleian', *Speculum*, 19 (1944) 351–2, repr. in E.A. Lowe, *Palaeographical Papers*, ed. L. Bieler, 2 vols (Oxford, 1972), I, pp. 345–7 with pls 59–60. On the s. xii volume see J.J.G. Alexander and O. Pächt, *Illuminated Manuscripts in the Bodleian Library Oxford*, 3 vols (Oxford, 1966–73), III, no. 87, with pl. viii.

43. CCCC, 304 (Juvencus, *Libri euangeliorum*; Italy or Spain, *s.* viii[1]), was in England by the late Anglo-Saxon period and at Christ Church by the time of the xii[2] library catalogue; however, there is no evidence that it arrived before the Viking Age. Accordingly, it is noted rather than discussed here. It is written in a confident but untidy uncial with very high ascenders; the beginnings of individual books are introduced by enlarged decorated initials; and the start of the volume (1r–4v) is written in framed, coloured display script. See *CLA*, II, no. 127.

44. Although the very first books written in Kent (by the missionaries or those they trained) may have been virtually indistinguishable from contemporary Italian products in terms of script, it is nevertheless probable that even at that very early stage parchment produced from English animals would be distinguishable from Italian membrane, and hence that we would have been able to identify such a manuscript had it survived.

45. Rochester, Cathedral Library, A. 3. 5, part i, fols 1r–3v (deposited in Strood, Record Office as DRc/R1). Facsimile: *The Textus Roffensis*, ed. P. Sawyer, 2 vols, EEMF, 7, 11 (Copenhagen, 1957–62).

46. BL, Cott. Ch. Aug. II.2: A. Bruckner and R. Marichal (eds), *Chartae Latinae*

Antiquiores (Olten and Lausanne, 1954–) [henceforth *ChLA*], III, no. 182; Lowe, *English Uncial*, pl. XXI; colour: Gameson, *St Augustine*, p. 31, no. 26. see further: P. Sawyer, *Anglo-Saxon Charters: an annotated list and bibliography* (London, 1968), no. 8; *English Historical Documents* I, ed. D. Whitelock, 2nd edn (London, 1979), p. 482; P. Chaplais, 'Some Early Anglo-Saxon Diplomas on Single Sheets: originals or copies?', in *Prisca Munimenta*, ed. Ranger, pp. 63–87, esp. pp. 65–78; and P. Wormald, 'Bede and the Conversion of England: The Charter Evidence' (Jarrow Lecture, 1984), pp. 3–9.

47. See *ChLA* III, no. 190 (BL, Cott. Aug. II. 91); see also nos 195, 221 (Cott. Ch. viii. 34 and Stowe Ch. 3). Note should also be made of no. 189 (Wihtred of Kent for Lyminge, 700 or 715), which is written in a formal minuscule; and no. 185 (the letter of Bishop Wealdhere of London, datable 704x5) which is written in cursive minuscule. The status of the latter as an original document, which was doubted by Bruckner, is upheld by P. Chaplais, 'The Letter from Bishop Wealdhere of London to Archbishop Brihtwold of Canterbury: the earliest original "letter close" extant in the West', *Medieval Scribes, Manuscripts and Libraries, Essays presented to N.R. Ker*, eds M.B. Parkes and A.G. Watson (London, 1978), pp. 3–23.

48. For surveys of which see T.J. Brown, 'Tradition, Imitation and Invention in Insular Handwriting of the Seventh and Eighth Centuries', in his *A Palaeographer's View*, eds J. Bately, M.P. Brown and J. Roberts (London, 1993), pp. 179–200; and 'The Irish Element in the Insular System of Scripts to c. A.D. 850', in H. Lowen (ed.), *Iren und europa im früheren Mittelalter*, 2 vols (Stuttgart, 1982), I, pp. 101–19, repr. in his *A Palaeographer's View*, pp. 201–20.

49. B. Yorke, *Kings and Kingdoms of Early Anglo-Saxon England* (London, 1990), pp. 25–44; and in more detail, K.P. Witney, *The Kingdom of Kent* (Chichester, 1982), esp. pp. 126–8, 133, 158–9.

50. BL, Stowe Ch. 1: *ChLA*, III, no. 220; Sawyer, 19; Chaplais, 'Who Introduced Charters into England?', 102–5 (who judges it more probably the work of a Northumbrian in Kent than of a 'Kentish pupil of a Northumbrian writing master').

51. The most obvious exception is the work associated with Luxeuil: the relevant manuscripts are listed in *CLA*, VI, pp. xvi–xvii; see also D. Ganz, 'Luxeuil Prophets and Merovingian Missionary Strategies', *Beinecke Studies in Early Manuscripts: Yale University Library Gazette Supplement*, 66 (1991), 105–17, at 115–16, n. 8. Insular minuscule is fundamentally more legible than Luxeuil minuscule.

52. *Die Briefe des Heiligen Bonifatius und Lullus*, ed. M. Tangl, MGH epistolae selectae I (Berlin, 1916), no. 35; see also no. 30.

53. *CLA*, II, no. 257; Lowe, *English Uncial*, pl. XXV; Gameson, *St Augustine*, p. 33, no. 29. It is collated as 'O' in *Nouum Testamentum* II: *Actus Apostolorum – Apocalypsis Iohannis*, eds Wordsworth, White, Sparks and Adams (see pp. vii and xiv). The text lacks 14: 27–15: 32.

54. The hand in question wrote a quavery, degenerate uncial. The first prayer begins, 'Domine Deus omnipotens rex angelorum et creator animarum et omnium creaturarum libera me de multitudine iniquitatum mearum et ne despice me indignam famulam . . .'.

55. The shelf mark, 'D.I G.III' is written on p. 1. For a summary of the history of Minster see *Charters of St Augustine's Abbey, Canterbury and Minster-in-Thanet*, ed. S.E. Kelly (London, 1995), pp. xxv–xxxi, esp. pp. xxx–xxxi for its final

stages and the absorption of its resources by Saint Augustine's. Further on Saint Augustine's Abbey in the eleventh century see Richard Emms in this volume.

56. Pp. 1–70 (p. 70 being originally blank) = Qq. I–V; the first rectos of the quires occur on pp. 1, 17, 33, 49, 65, but it should be noted that a leaf is missing at the start of Q. V (i.e. between pp. 64 and 65).

57. Pp. 71–108 = Qq. VI–VIII; the first rectos of the quires fall on pp. 71, 87, 99, the last quire being piecemeal and complicated.

58. Reproduced: Lowe, *English Uncial*, pl. XXVa; *CLA*, II, no. 257; and Gameson, *St Augustine*, p. 33. The Italian background to this script type is discussed in relation to the Vespasian Psalter by D. Wright (see n. 62 below).

59. Reproduced: Lowe, *English Uncial*, pl. XXVb.

60. P. 1. The display script completes the first word (*Primum*). The colours are now very faint, but red, yellow and dark grey/black were used.

61. For the probable dates of Mildred's abbacy see *Charters of St Augustine's Abbey*, ed. Kelly, pp. xxv–xxvi. Goscelin's *Vita Mildrethae*, ch. 14, includes the picturesque detail of Mildred writing a psalter while at Chelles and sending it back to her mother with some of her own hair attached as a plea for help. The text is printed in D.W. Rollason, *The Mildrith Legend: A Study in Early Medieval Hagiography in England* (Leicester, 1982), Appendix c, pp. 105–43, at p. 126. The section in question may be translated: 'Meanwhile through divine inspiration she was writing a little psalter with her maidenly hand, the neatness and skill of which she knew would make it pleasing to her mother, Domneva. She placed her flowing locks, which had been ripped out with bloodthirsty malice, as a relic – like the tokens or signs of a martyr – in the upper margin of the little book, choosing this offering (through divine providence) as a messenger to her mother. At the same time, she set forth in words and tearful writings to what extent she suffered, not so much for her life which, removed from tribulations, rested peacefully in the Lord, as for the virginal crown dearer than life, which was being imperilled amongst the darts of Satan.'

62. BL, Cotton Vespasian A. i: *CLA*, II, no. 193. Facsimile: *The Vespasian Psalter*, ed. D. Wright, EEMF, 14 (Copenhagen, 1967). Elmham's description is analysed in detail at pp. 37–41. The most recent discussion of the nature of the interlinear gloss added in *s*. ix (which has dogged the question of the origin and provenance of the manuscript since the arguments of S. Kuhn, 'From Canterbury to Lichfield', *Speculum*, 23 (1948), 591–629) is P. Pulsiano, 'The Originality of the Old English Gloss of the Vespasian Psalter and its Relation to the Gloss of the Junius Psalter', *ASE*, 25 (1996), 37–62. Given the political dominance of Mercia in the eighth century, the presence of Mercians at Canterbury, and the similarity of 'Mercian' and 'Kentish' scribal work in the ninth century, there is nothing inexplicable about a gloss with Mercian features being copied in Kent.

63. T.A.M. Bishop, *English Caroline Minuscule* (Oxford, 1971), nos 24–5; cf. T.A. Heslop, 'The Production of *de luxe* Manuscripts and the Patronage of King Cnut and Queen Emma', *ASE*, 19 (1990), 151–95, esp. 173–6; D.N. Dumville, *English Caroline Script and Monastic History* (Woodbridge, 1993), pp. 126–8.

64. Though there are inevitably a few holes, it is even and creamy in tone with little distinction between the hair and the flesh sides of the leaves.

65. The ruling would seem, then, to have been

done with a T-square (*Vespasian Psalter*, ed. Wright, p. 18). There is at least one Northumbrian parallel for this, the *s.* viii gospel book, BL, Royal 1 B. vii: see R.G. Gameson, 'The Royal 1 B. vii Gospels and English Book Production in the Seventh and Eighth Centuries', *The Early Medieval Bible: Its Production, Decoration and Use*, ed. R.G. Gameson (Cambridge, 1994), pp. 24–52, at p. 29.

66. Fols 4r–11v, with a different hand responsible for those on 2v–3v: *Vespasian Psalter*, ed. Wright, pp. 59–60.

67. Fol. 140v: cf. *Vespasian Psalter*, ed. Wright, pp. 60–1. Compare the monumental display script in the *Codex Bigotianus*.

68. *Vespasian Psalter*, ed. Wright, pp. 45–7. The Blicking/Lothian Psalter: New York, Pierpont Morgan Library, M 776: *CLA*, XI, no. 1661; R. Collins, *Anglo-Saxon Vernacular Manuscripts in America* (New York, 1976), no. 10; Alexander, *Insular Manuscripts*, cat. 31.
The Salaberga Psalter: Berlin, Staatsbibliothek, Hamilton 553: *CLA*, VIII, no. 1048; Alexander, *Insular Manuscripts*, cat. 14. I have not been able to consult *Psalterium Salabergae*, ed. D. Ó Cróinín (Munich, 1994).
Montpellier, Bibliothèque universitaire, H 509: *CLA*, VI, no. 795; *Charlemagne*, no. 450; P.E. Schramm and F. Mütherich, *Denkmale der deutschen Könige und Kaiser. Ein Beitrag zur Herrschergeschichte von Karl dem Grossen bis Friedrich II, 768–1250*, 2nd edn (Munich, 1981), no. 7; Fried (ed.), *794: Karl der Grosse*, no. V/1, pp. 117–18.
Stuttgart, Landesbibliothek, Bibl. fol. 12: *CLA*, IX, no. 1353; Alexander, *Insular Manuscripts*, cat. 28; L. Webster and J. Backhouse (eds), *The Making of England* (London, 1991), no. 128; N. Netzer, 'Cultural Amalgamation in the Decoration of the Stuttgart Merovingian Psalter', in *From the Isles of the North: Early Medieval Art in Ireland and Britain*, ed. C. Bourke (Belfast, 1995), pp. 119–25.

69. Thomas of Elmham, *Historia Monasterii S. Augustini*, ed. Hardwick, 97; cf. Gneuss, *Hymnar und Hymnen*, pp. 16–17, 33–4; and I. Milfull, *The Hymns of the Anglo-Saxon Church* (Cambridge, 1996), pp. 1–4.

70. Occasionally the border itself is made to terminate in a beast head or interlace motif (e.g. fols 23v, 38v, 128v).

71. *Vespasian Psalter*, ed. Wright, pp. 15–16, with pl. IV.

72. *Vespasian Psalter*, ed. Wright, pp. 68–80; Moscow, Historical Museum, MS 129; facsimile: M.V. Scepkina, *Miniatjury Khludovskoi Psaltiri* (Moscow, 1977).

73. The rendering of David and Jonathan in the initial on fol. 31r is the clumsiest work in the book.

74. Fols 31r, 53r, 79v, 115v: the first two are reproduced in colour in Gameson, *St Augustine*, p. 32.

75. Stockholm, Kungliga Bibliotek, A. 135: *CLA*, XI, no. 1642; Lowe, *English Uncial*, pl. XXVIII; *Charlemagne*, no. 397; Alexander, *Insular Manuscripts*, cat. 30. The text is printed as *Codex Aureus siue Quattuor Euangelia ante Hieronymum Latine translata*, ed. J. Belsheim (Oslo, 1878). See further R.G. Gameson, '*Codex Aureus Cantuariensis*', *L'étude de la Bible d'Isidore à Rémi d'Auxerre*', eds F. Dolbeau, M. Dulaey and M. Gorman (Paris, forthcoming); and *Codex Aureus*, ed. R.G. Gameson, EEMF, 28 (Copenhagen, forthcoming).

76. C. Nordenfalk, *Celtic and Anglo-Saxon Painting* (London, 1977), p. 103.

77. See n. 52 above.

78. The point can be appreciated most easily from the collations at the front of *Codex Aureus*, ed. Belsheim, pp. xxiii–lvi. For brief observations on its text see B. Fischer, *Lateinische Bibelhandschriften im frühen Mittelalter*, Vetus Latina, 11

(Freiburg, 1985), 159, 170; also his *Beiträge sur Geschichte der lateinische Bibeltexte*, Vetus Latina, 12 (Freiburg, 1985), 234, 298.

79. *Codex Veronensis* (s. v): Verona, Biblioteca Capitolare, VI (6) (G. Turrini, *Millenium Scriptorii Veronensis dal IVº al XVº Secolo* (Verona, 1967), fp.; and A. Piazzi (ed.), *Biblioteca Capitolare Verona* (Fiesole, 1994), no. 1).
 Codex Brixianus (s. vi): Brescia, Biblioteca Civica Queriniana, s.n. (*CLA*, III, no. 281; H.J. Vogels, *Codicum Novi Testamenti Specimina* (Bonn, 1929), pl. 37).
 Codex Valerianus (s. vi–vii): Munich, Bayerische Staatsbibliothek, Clm 6224 (*CLA*, IX, no. 1249; K. Bierbrauer, *Die vorkarolingischen und karolingischen Handschriften der Bayerischen Staatsbibliothek*, 2 vols (Wiesbaden, 1990), I, cat. 3).

80. Maeseyck, Church of St Catherine, s.n.: *CLA*, X, no. 1558; Alexander, *Insular Manuscripts*, cat. 23.
 Augsburg, Universitätsbibliothek, I. 2. 4º2: *CLA*, VIII, no. 1215. The gospel books associated with early Echternach are discussed in detail in N. Netzer, *Cultural Interplay in the Eighth Century: The Trier Gospels and the Making of a Scriptorium at Echternach* (Cambridge, 1994).

81. Vatican City, Biblioteca Apostolica Vaticana, Barb. lat. 570: *CLA*, I, no. 63; Alexander, *Insular Manuscripts*, cat. 36; Webster and Backhouse (eds), *Making of England*, no. 160. See also Appendix I below.

82. BnF, lat. 254: S. Berger, *Histoire de la Vulgate pendant les Premiers Siècles du Moyen Age* (Paris, 1893), pp. 74–5; W. Cahn, *Romanesque Manuscripts*, 2 vols (London, 1996), II, cat. 31.

83. The *Codex Aureus* of St Emmeram: Munich, Bayerische Staatsbibliothek, Clm 14000 (K. Bierbrauer, *Die vorkarolingischen und karolingischen Handschriften der Bayerischen Staatsbibliothek*, 2 vols (Wiesbaden, 1990), I, no. 248; II, pls vi, 521–30; facsimile: *Der Codex Aureus der Bayerischen Staatsbibliothek in München*, ed. G. Leidinger (Munich, 1921–5)).
 The Pericopes Book of Henry II: Munich, Bayerische Staatsbibliothek, Clm 4452. Facsimile: *Das Perikopenbuch Heinrichs II, Clm 4452 der Bayerischen Staatsbibliothek, München*, eds F. Mütherich and K. Dachs (Frankfurt-am-Main, 1994); more accessible is H. Fillitz, R. Kahsnitz, and U. Kuder, *Zierde für ewige Zeit: Das Perikopenbuch Heinrichs II* (Munich, 1994).
 The Speyer Gospels of Henry III: El Escorial, Real Biblioteca, Vitr. 17: A. Boeckler, *Das Goldene Evangelienbuch Heinrich III* (Berlin, 1933).

84. As pointed out by C. Nordenfalk, 'A Note on the Stockholm Codex Aureus', *Libri Aurei* (= *Nordisk Tidskrift för Bok- och Biblioteksväsen* 38/4) (Stockholm, 1951), 1–11. Relevant copies are BnF, lat. 2421 (illustrated by Nordenfalk) and Berne, Burgerbibliothek, 212 (*Charlemagne*, no. 362; J. König, *Die Heiratsurkunde der kaiserin Theophanu* (Göttingen, 1972), no. 45). Further on Porfyrius see Nordenfalk, *Spätantiken Zierbuchstaben*, I, pp. 57–62.

85. '*librum pyrpyri metri ideo non misi quia gutbertus episc[opus] adhuc reddere distulit*': Boniface, ep. 112, ed. Tangl, p. 245. See further P. Sims-Williams, *Religion and Literature in Western England 600–800* (Cambridge, 1990), pp. 328–32.

86. *Hrabani Mauri Carmina*, ed. H. Dümmler, MGH Poetae aevi carolini II (Berlin, 1884), 154–63; M. Perrin, *Hraban Maur, De laudibus sanctae crucis* (Paris, 1988).

87. Vatican City, Biblioteca Apostolica Vaticana, Reg. lat. 124: A. Wilmart, *Bibliotheca Apostolica Vaticana, Codices Reginenses Latini*, 2 vols (Vatican City,

1937–45), I, pp. 293–4; H.-G. Müller, *Hrabanus Maurus, De laudibus sanctae crucis: Studien zur Überlieferung und Geistesgeschichte mit dem Faksimile-Textabdruck aus Codex Reg. lat. 124 der vatikanischen Bibliothek* (Düsseldorf *et alibi*, 1973). The status and function of this manuscript remains controversial: for a convenient summary see M. Perrin, 'La représentation figurée de César-Louis le Pieux chez Raban Maur en 835: Religion et idéologie', *Frankia*, 24/1 (1997), 39–64, at 56–8.
88. Nordenfalk, *Celtic and Anglo-Saxon Painting*, pl. 33.
89. Fol. 9v: Nordenfalk, *Celtic and Anglo-Saxon Painting*, pl. 36.
90. Wormald, *Miniatures in the Gospels of St Augustine*, pp. 7–11, compared the images with a range of later Anglo-Saxon examples, but hesitated to admit a direct connection. Subsequent writers (e.g. Alexander, *Insular Manuscripts*, pp. 56–7, and Budny, *Insular, Anglo-Saxon and Anglo-Norman Manuscript Art*, I, p. 6) have been more positive.
91. R. Jessup, *Anglo-Saxon Jewellery* (London, 1950), colour fp. and pls XXII–XXVII; Webster and Backhouse (eds), *Making of England*, nos 31–2; Gameson, *St Augustine*, p. 30, nos 19–23; M. Pinder, 'Anglo-Saxon Garnet Cloisonné Composite Disc Brooches: some aspects of their construction', *JBAA*, 148 (1995), 6–28.
92. See further Gameson, 'Codex Aureus Cantuariensis'.
93. BL, Add. 37518, fols 116–17: *CLA*, II, no. 176 (all three hands illustrated); Lowe, *English Uncial*, pl. XXIV. For the host book see P. Périn and L.-Ch. Feffer (eds), *La Neustrie: Les pays au nord de la Loire de Dagobert à Charles le Chauve* (Rouen, 1985), no. 90.
94. Avranches, Bibliothèque municipale, 48 (fols i–ii), 66 (fols i–ii), and 71 (fols A–B) + St Petersburg, Public Library, Lat. O. v. I. 1: *CLA*, VI, no. 730; A. Wilmart, 'Débris d'un manuscrit des Evangiles à Avranches et Leningrad', *Revue Biblique*, 38 (1929), 396–404; Lowe, *English Uncial*, pl. XXIX; O.A. Dobias-Rozdestvenskaja and W.W. Bakhtine, *Les anciens manuscrits latins de la Bibliothèque Publique Saltykov-Scedrin de Leningrad* (Paris, 1991), no. 25; M. Dosdat, *L'enluminure romane au Mont Saint-Michel x^e–xiie siècles* (Rennes, 1991), p. 22; and *eadem*, *Le livre saint en Normandie* (Avranches, 1995), no. 1.
95. The size of the most complete, surviving leaf (Avranches, 66); its written area is 274 × 215 mm.
96. St Petersburg, Lat. O. v. I. 1, fol. 2r: Lowe, *English Uncial*, pl. XXIX (b).
97. BnF, lat. 281 + 298: *CLA*, V, no. 526; J. Mallon, R. Marichal and C. Perrat, *L'Ecriture latine de la capitale romaine à la minuscule* (Paris, 1939), pl. XXXIX, no. 59; Lowe, *English Uncial*, pls XXX–XXXI; McGurk, *Latin Gospel Books*, no. 58; Alexander, *Insular Manuscripts*, cat. 34. Colour plates: Gameson, *St Augustine*, p. 34, no. 28. While lat. 281 is in generally good condition, lat. 298 is badly damaged and stained, strips of parchment having been cut from its lower margins.
98. BnF, lat. 17226: *CLA*, V, no. 667.
99. *Teste* the *s*. xv *ex libris* inscription on fol. 1v of lat. 298.
100. It has lost the tip of the initial L of *Liber* on fol. 7r of lat. 281, for instance.
101. Whose script form is the same as the rest of the text.
102. Lat. 281, fols 148r–9v.
103. For example, BnF, n. a. l. 1587 (the St Gatien Gospels). Moreover, some two-column manuscripts, like BnF, lat. 254, fit two columns of genealogy on to each of their normal columns.
104. Almost the only other thin line is the cross stroke of X (a fine leaf or vine motif was

supplied to isolate overruns). Occasionally to save space at the end of a page (e.g. lat. 281, fol. 44r) or for corrections, the scribe resorted to a slightly thinner version of the script.
105. *CLA*, III, no. 313; Chatelain, *Uncialis Scriptura*, pl. XVII.
106. Avril and Stirnemann, *Manuscrits enluminés*, no. 18, pl. VI. It is, of course, possible that this was done by an Anglo-Saxon abroad.
107. Vercelli, Biblioteca Capitolare, s.n.: *CLA*, IV, no. 467.
Augsburg, Universitätsbibliothek, Oettingen-Wallerstein'sche Bibliotek, I. 2. 4°2: *CLA*, VIII, no. 1215.
Vienna, Österreichische Nationalbibliothek, lat. 1224: *CLA*, X, no. 1500; *Charlemagne*, no. 452; E. Irblich, *Karl der Grosse und die Wissenschaft* (Vienna, 1993); S.E. von Daum Tholl, 'The Cutbercht Gospels and the Earliest Writing Center at Salzburg', in *Making the Medieval Book: Techniques of Production*, ed. L.L. Brownrigg (Los Altos, 1995), pp. 17–33.
Also Madrid, Biblioteca de la Universidad, 31 (*s. x*).
108. In ascending order of importance: CCCC, 286 (see n. 25 above); BL, Harley 1775 (*CLA*, II, no. 197); Würzburg, Universitätsbibliothek, M. p. th. f. 68 (the 'Burchard Gospels': *CLA*, IX, no. 1423B); Split (Spalato) Kathedrale, s.n. (*CLA*, XI, no. 1669); BodL, Auct. D. 2. 14 (see n. 37 above).
109. Traces of gold still remain on fol. 137r.
110. Lat. 281, fol. 137r.
111. I.e. between fols 4 and 5 of Lat. 281. Fol. 4v ends, *'Explicit prologus quattuor/ euangeliorum/ Incipiunt canones'* written in display capitals.
112. There is a tiny correction in minuscule in the *Codex Aureus* (fol. 115r), which clearly postdates *s.* viii[med]. See further in general Appendix II.
113. For overviews of which see M.B. Parkes, 'The Scriptorium of Wearmouth–Jarrow' (Jarrow Lecture, 1982); and M.P. Brown, 'The Lindisfarne Scriptorium from the late seventh to the early ninth century', *St Cuthbert, his cult and his community to A.D. 1200*, eds G. Bonner et al., (Woodbridge, 1989), pp. 151–63.
114. *Vita Bertilae Abbatissae Calensis*, ch. 6, ed. W. Levison, MGH Script. rerum Meroving. 6 (Hannover and Leipzig, 1993), 95–109, at 106–7. The passage in question may be translated as follows. 'And since [Bertila] acted with these and similar exemplary customs, the christian faith of her brothers and sisters was strengthened by the example of her piety; and also all the poor and the pilgrims were consoled by her generous munificence; and so great a harvest did the Lord amass through her for the salvation of souls that those believers from the cross-channel regions of the Saxon kingdom also begged her (through other believers who had been dispatched) to send them some of her disciples for the purpose of erudite and holy instruction (with which they had heard she was marvellously endowed) and in order also to construct communities for men and women in that region. This religious request for the health of souls she did not reject: rather, with the advice of the elders and the encouragement of the brothers, with gracious spirit and with great care, she sent thither chosen personnel and very devoted men with both relics of the saints and with many volumes of books, so that through her the harvest of souls increased in that people, too, and was multiplied by the grace of God.'
115. For example, I. Wood, *The Merovingian North Sea* (Alingsås, 1984).
116. Cf., for example, R. McKitterick, *Books, Scribes and Learning in the Frankish Kingdoms 6th–9th Centuries* (Aldershot, 1994), esp. pp. 317–19, 375–85.

117. Lichfield Cathedral, 1: *CLA*, II, no. 159; Alexander, *Insular Manuscripts*, cat. 21.
Autun, Bibliothèque municipale 3 (S 2): *CLA*, VI, no. 716; L. Nees, *The Gundohinus Gospels* (Cambridge, Mass., 1987).
Autun, Bibliothèque municipale 4 (S 3): *CLA*, VI, no. 717a; G. Lanoë et al., *Manuscrits d'Autun* (Autun, 1995), pp. 14, 49.
BL, Add. 5463: *CLA*, II, no. 162; *Charlemagne*, no. 390; A.G. Watson, *Catalogue of Dated and Datable Manuscripts c. 700–1600 in the Department of Manuscripts, The British Library*, 2 vols (London, 1979), I, no. 3; II, pl. 3; A. Theile (ed.), 794: *Karl der Grosse im Frankfurt am Main* (Sigmaringen, 1994), no. IV/19, p. 90.

118. I am grateful to the following libraries and their staff for enabling me to examine the manuscripts on which this study is based, and for granting permission to reproduce photographs of them: Boulogne-sur-Mer, Bibliothèque municipale; Cambridge, Corpus Christi College; London, British Library; Oxford, Bodleian Library; Paris, Bibliothèque nationale de France; Troyes, Bibliothèque municipale; and Vatican City, Biblioteca Apostolica Vaticana. In addition, I wish to record my thanks to the British Academy for a grant from the Neil Ker Fund which subsidised a period of study in Rome in 1998.

CHAPTER 14

In Gregory's Shadow? The Pre-Conquest Cult of St Augustine

Alan Thacker

According to the *Ecclesiastical History*, when Augustine died, probably in 604, his body was placed next to the still unfinished funerary church of SS Peter and Paul which the bishop had himself established outside the walls of Canterbury. As soon as the church was dedicated, the body was brought inside and interred in the north *porticus*, where all Augustine's successors were buried until the 660s. There in the early eighth century at a centrally placed altar dedicated to Pope Gregory, the 'deeds' of the early archbishops (the word used is *agendae*) were celebrated in the liturgy every Saturday by a priest of the abbey church.[1]

Bede's account of Augustine's death and interment could be – and indeed usually is – read as the making of a saint. Technically, of course, Augustine's body was translated, an action which in the seventh and early eighth centuries marked the formal inauguration of a cult by the community hosting the ceremony.[2] But caution is needed here: Bede expressly speaks as if Augustine's original interment was intended *ab initio* to be purely temporary, while a final and more appropriate resting place was being prepared. Any analysis of the early status of Augustine's tomb needs to take account of the interments in the north *porticus* as a group. The physical appearance and arrangement of that group have an important bearing on the question of whether or not they may be considered as shrines. Most unusually we are well informed about the original interments: we have both an eleventh-century description of the opening of the hitherto undisturbed tombs, and the physical remains of three of them: those of Laurence (d. 619), Mellitus (d. 624), and Justus (d. 627 x 31). The written record, Goscelin's history of the translations of the early archbishops, was composed in 1091 when the archbishops' remains were removed from the shortly to be demolished north *porticus* into the eastern limb of the new Norman church. It is very detailed and circumstantial and tallies with the archaeological record in

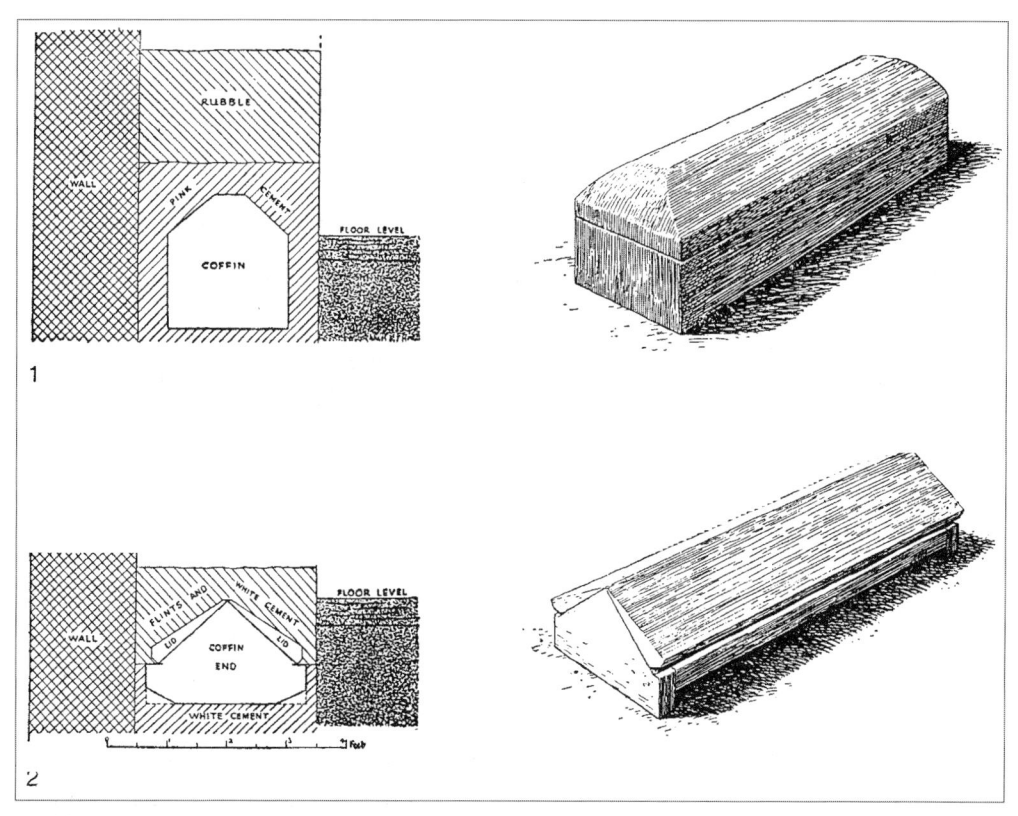

14.1. Tombs of Archbishops Laurentius and Justus (after W. St J. Hope 1917).

various important ways, so we may be sure that we are genuinely well informed about these burials.[3]

The early tombs were, in fact, very strange. Each comprised a wooden coffin placed in a pit and preserved in concrete which had been poured over it in a semi-liquid state and left to harden (fig. 14.1). The coffin cover protruded above ground level and at some stage, not necessarily at the original interment, the structure was further heightened by the addition of a platform of tile and rubble bonded together by mortar.[4] By the early eleventh century these monuments were also adorned with columns and arches, perhaps placed over them to form some kind of ciborium or canopy of honour.[5]

The archiepiscopal tombs were packed tightly into the small *porticus* (figs 14.2, 3). Augustine's monument (no. 1 on fig. 14.2) lay in the south-east corner, immediately to the south of the altar of St Gregory. The altar itself, very curiously, was built over an unmarked tomb, hidden in a cavity beneath the pavement, the unidentified inhabitant of which was christened 'Deo Notus' ('Known to God') by those responsible for the translations of 1091. To the north of the altar, in the north-east corner of the *porticus*, lay Augustine's successor Laurence, and then in an anticlockwise direction Mellitus, Justus in the north-west corner, Honorius (d. 653), projecting from the west wall, and Deusdedit (d. 664) in the south-west corner (nos 2–6 on fig. 14.2). The space on the south wall between Augustine and Deusdedit was occupied by the entrance into the *porticus* from the main body of the church.[6]

By the eleventh century Augustine's tomb, alone of the six original monuments, had an altar at the western end, and was adorned with sculpture including images of angels and the Lord in Majesty. It was almost certainly painted. The saint rested on a floor of polished purple tiles, facing eastwards with his feet against the east wall of the *porticus* and his head against the western altar. He was clothed in full pontificals, including chasuble, alb, stole, staff, and sandals. A sweet smell issuing from the grave when it was opened in 1091 indicated that the body had been embalmed, or at least anointed with spiced unguents.[7] We also know that by the early eighth century the tomb had an epitaph, for it is recorded by Bede:

> Here rests the reverend Augustine, first archbishop of Canterbury; sent hither by Blessed Gregory, pontiff of the city of Rome, and suffused by God with the power to work miracles, he led King Æthelberht and his people from the

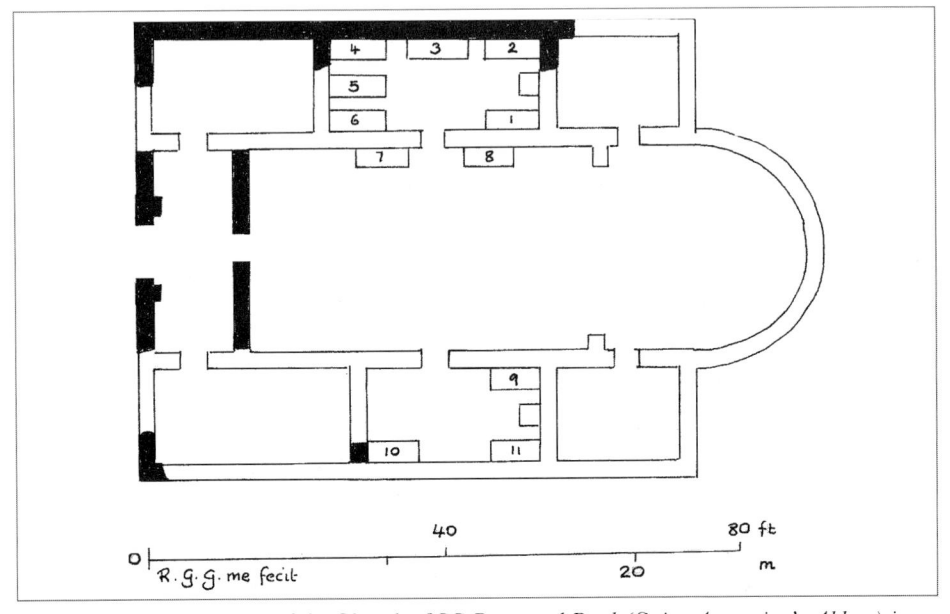

14.2. Reconstructed plan of the Church of SS Peter and Paul (Saint Augustine's Abbey) in the early seventh century, showing the episcopal and royal tombs. 1. Augustine; 2. Laurentius; 3. Mellitus; 4. Justus; 5. Honorius; 6. Deusdedit; 7. ? Berhtwald; 8. Theodore; 9. Liudhard; 10. Bertha; 11. Æthelberht. (Gameson)

14.3. View of the excavated remains of the north porticus *of SS Peter and Paul. (Gameson)*

worship of idols to the faith of Christ, and having fulfilled his days in office in peace, died on the seventh day before the Kalends of June [26 May] while the same king was still reigning.[8]

It is not clear whether these arrangements represented an enshrinement. For the clothing and anointing of the body we have little analogous contemporary evidence, although it seems likely that Cuthbert of Lindisfarne's body was similarly treated at its first interment some eighty years later.[9] The monument and its five fellows are even more difficult to place. As far as I am aware, there are no exact parallels to the cement-enshrouded tombs. We might expect Italy – Rome or perhaps Naples – to provide the closest analogies. But although north and central Italy had a tradition of brick, stone-built and rock-cut graves with plastered interiors, I know of none very like the burials at Canterbury.[10] Perhaps the now lost graves of the late sixth- and early seventh-century popes at St Peter's, including that of Gregory himself before the *secretarium*, could have provided the answer. It has been conjectured that they were in sarcophagi, buried with just their covers protruding above the ground. Like Augustine's tomb, they were identified by epitaphs, fixed to a nearby wall or column.[11] At Canterbury, the sealing in concrete with the lid protruding, indeed built-up, perhaps suggests an attempt to recreate these or similar arrangements in so far as local resources allowed. It also, of course, rendered access to the bodies very difficult, and may hence be related to contemporary papal prohibitions of the disturbance of the dead, and especially of the holy dead.[12]

Another possible link with Rome is provided by the columns and arches over the archbishops' tombs. If they were indeed early and if they did indeed represent primitive ciboria, then they are likely to have been inspired by the great canopies over the altar tombs of the apostles and of other saints in the major basilicas of Rome. We know that Gregory the Great when he redesigned the sanctuary at St Peter's erected a new ciborium adorned with precious metals over the tomb and the altar above it. We also know that his disciple and successor Honorius I (625–38) placed similar ciboria over the altar tombs of the extramural cemeterial basilicas of Sant' Agnese and San Pancrazio.[13] So such structures were fashionable in Gregorian circles in Rome in the early seventh century. If in Canterbury the early archbishops were indeed honoured in death with local renderings of the papal ciboria then it seems likely that their tombs were intended as shrines. But the analogy is not exact: although an altar was eventually attached to Augustine's tomb there is no evidence that it was early, and none of the others were in any sense altar tombs. Nor would there have been much space for such ciboria in the small *porticus*. On balance I incline reluctantly to the view that the structures described by Goscelin were less dramatic, less ritually charged.

In a more general way, the whole arrangement of the burials in the north *porticus* may look back to contemporary Italian, and more particularly Roman, tradition.[14] Since the later fifth century almost every pope had been buried at St Peter's, and special places – essentially communal mausolea like the north *porticus* at Canterbury – had been developed to receive their remains. The earliest of these was the sacristy (*secretarium*), a building at the south-east (entrance) end of the Vatican basilica in which Popes Leo the Great (443–61) and Benedict I (575–9) were buried.[15] Another was the adjacent vestibule or *porticus*, in front of the *secretarium* itself and connected with the western *porticus* of the atrium, built against the entrance front of the basilica. Simplicius (468–83), Gelasius I (492–6), Symmachus (498–514), John III (561–74), and Gregory himself are known to have been laid to rest there. Very probably the tombs of most other sixth- and seventh-century popes, whose exact location within St Peter's has not been recorded, were in or near this area.[16] The only exceptions are those who were buried within the basilica, in the outer south aisle near the place to be occupied from the ninth century by the oratory of St Gregory. Boniface IV (608–15) and perhaps Pelagius I (556–61) and Boniface III (607) were buried in that location, which was to become known as the *porticus pontificum*.[17]

In the earlier seventh century, then, when the archbishops of Canterbury were being buried in the north *porticus* of their cemeterial monastery, the papal tombs were mostly placed together in or near the narrow vestibule in front of the sacristy, where they offered an image of the popes as doorkeepers to St Peter, analogous to that of Peter himself as doorkeeper in heaven. When the location of the archiepiscopal tombs was established, not long after 604, there may have been especial interest in and experimentation with papal burial at St Peter's, with interments being made in a new site inside the basilica. Whether inside or out, however, the special annexe or enclosure containing the tombs seems to have been called at Rome, as at Canterbury, a *porticus*.[18]

By the late sixth century these arrangements were influencing other centres – in particular, the burials of the archbishops of Ravenna. After a long period of dispersed interments, the remains of the archbishops were concentrated at the extramural basilica of Sant' Apollinare in Classe. Archbishop John II Romanus (d. 595) was buried in a structure flanking the western portico, a position similar to that of the papal *secretarium*. His seventh-century successors were all buried in the *ardica*, apparently the western portico itself. Like the papal tombs they too were identified by epitaphs fixed to the wall above.[19]

It is easy to see that the arrangements at Canterbury are not so very different. Like the communities at the Vatican and Ravenna, that at Canterbury sought to bury its pontiffs in a specific dedicated location, attached to the basilica but not actually within the main ritual space. We know that Bede, and presumably therefore the community at Saint Augustine's, considered the north *porticus* to be outside the church, because Bede expressly states that when it was full, Archbishops Theodore (669–90) and Berctuald (692–731), who lay next to its entrance (fig. 14.2, nos 7–8), were buried 'in the church itself' (*in ipsa ecclesia*).[20]

These analogies suggest that in the first instance the early archiepiscopal burials, including Augustine's, were envisaged as honoured graves appropriate to high ecclesiastics rather than as shrines. Two other factors support this conclusion. First, the cramped space of the *porticus* already alluded to. The space between Augustine's tomb and the neighbouring altar of St Gregory – less than three feet – made little provision for access to the tomb itself, and the filling of the entire *porticus* with tombs suggests an official mausoleum rather than a shrine. Secondly, the absence of any later translation or elevation implies that there was relatively little activity at the tombs themselves. We know they had not been disturbed because in the late eleventh century Goscelin expressly stated that Augustine had lain in the *porticus* with his immediate successors, unmoved since the day of his deposition.[21] The only known attempt to honour them by translation occurred very late, in the abbacy of Ælfmær in the early eleventh century.[22]

It should be added at this point that Laurence, Mellitus, and Justus (but not Augustine himself) were commemorated as saints in the Stowe missal, a text which in its extant version seems to have been written down at the end of the eighth century but which probably represents the form of the mass as it evolved in Ireland in the seventh. The three English bishops occur in the section of the canon beginning *Memento etiam domine* which in the Gregorian missal commemorates the dead, and which in Stowe is elaborated with a list of patriarchs, prophets, apostles, martyrs and confessors. That list is probably early: apart from a single addition it contains no saint who died later than the early seventh century. Here, then, is good evidence that, in Ireland at least, some of the companions of Augustine were regarded as saints from the eighth century if not earlier.[23] Their inclusion, however, may have little to do with Canterbury tradition. It can be no coincidence surely that these were the three bishops named in a letter, partly recorded in Bede, to the bishops and abbots of Ireland.[24] Although to our eyes the letter itself untactfully laments the Irish failure to observe Roman customs, it may have appealed to Irish *Romani*, thereby securing the addition of the bishops to the list. Certainly, later tradition represents Laurence as having good relations with the Irish.[25]

It is quite clear that in the seventh and early eighth centuries, the saintly role that might reasonably have been assigned to Augustine (and which was indeed later assigned to him) – that of England's apostle – was in fact taken by Pope Gregory the Great. I have discussed this subject at length elsewhere and so will not dwell on it here.[26] Suffice it to say that, during this period, veneration of Gregory as a holy pastor and in particular as the apostolic evangelist of England appears to have developed in England itself and to a lesser extent in Rome, and to have reached its apogee between 704 and the 730s with the compilation at Whitby of a *Life* of the Pope and the publication of Bede's long encomium at the beginning of Book II of the *Ecclesiastical History*. I have argued that the principal agent of this development was Archbishop Theodore (669–90). Among the many changes which he introduced into the organization and spiritual life of the English church was a reshaping of the role of the bishop based at Canterbury. According to Gregory's plan, the former Roman province of Britannia was to have two metropolitans, the southern based initially at Canterbury but ultimately in London, the other based at York.[27] The scheme, however, was not fully implemented. The southern province was never moved to London and the northern fell into abeyance after Paulinus of York's flight in 633. When Theodore arrived in 669, the very existence of the church established by the mission was endangered.[28] Theodore may well have felt that in these circumstances a revised plan centred on his personal authority was necessary. At all events, by 679 he had so come to ignore the Gregorian plan as to style himself 'archbishop of the island of Britain'.[29] As such, he was perhaps claiming the kind of status assigned to certain eastern archbishops who were heads of the church throughout an entire imperial province. The archbishop of

Alexandria, for example, could approve and consecrate all bishops made within the six Egyptian ecclesiastical provinces over which he presided.[30] To use an anachronistic comparison, his position was not unlike that of the archiepiscopal head of what is now called an 'autocephalous church' (such as Greece).

If Theodore was, as I would maintain, seeking to interpret his role in such terms, then almost certainly he was not particularly interested in promoting the cult of a predecessor like Augustine who was identified primarily with the see and province of Canterbury. By encouraging instead the cult of Gregory he was associating himself with a figure who could be presented as the apostle of the English as a whole – of the Northumbrians as much as the men of Kent and the south-east – and who could hence be used to underpin his authority outside the southern province. This strategy seems to have been successful. The Northumbrian élite identified with Gregory, the apostolic figure who admired and sought to save the Anglian slave boys in Rome.[31] Theodore developed a close relationship with the important royal monastery of Whitby and both there and at York altars dedicated to Gregory were established.[32] Paulinus (d. 644), the Roman missionary who became first bishop of the Northumbrians, was revered as a saint, despite his withdrawal to Kent after his patron King Edwin's defeat and death in 633.[33] Augustine, however, was not generally regarded: although his feast day was apparently recorded by Bede in his martyrology, he was omitted from the calendar compiled for the Northumbrian *peregrinus* Willibrord around 700, and was still not included in the York calendar in the later eighth century. When in the 780s or 790s Alcuin composed his poem eulogizing the saints, bishops and kings of York, he made Paulinus a central figure and did not even mention Augustine.[34]

Almost certainly, it was divisions within the ecclesiastical and political establishment of Northumbria which permitted Theodore to undermine the Gregorian plan for a northern metropolitan. The archbishop was empowered by a widespread desire to cut the Northumbrian bishop Wilfrid (d. 709) down to size by dividing his great see, a wish shared by King Ecgfrith (670–85) and the monasteries of Whitby, and perhaps Lindisfarne.[35] Augustine had no place in that scenario, and it is unlikely that his cult received much attention then or indeed at any time during Theodore's long pontificate.

Such considerations helped to shape the portrait of Augustine in the *Historia ecclesiastica*. Bede undoubtedly approved of Theodore's decision to divide the Northumbrian see, and records without criticism his subversion of the Gregorian plan.[36] Moreover, his principal informant on the early history of the church, and indeed one of those instrumental in prevailing upon him to write the *History*, was Albinus, abbot (709x10–32) of Saint Augustine's or, as it was then still known, the monastery of SS Peter and Paul. Albinus, as Bede carefully tells us in his preface addressed to King Ceolwulf, had been a student at the school of Canterbury and was a pupil of Theodore and his coadjutor, Abbot Hadrian (669/70–708).[37]

It is often argued that Bede's account of Augustine and the mission was shaped by Canterbury tradition, sober and austere, uninterested in tomb cults, and relatively sparse in colour and incident. I suspect, however, that more to the point are the priorities of Canterbury in the later seventh and early eighth centuries, priorities with which Bede himself had considerable sympathy.

Although as I have already said, Bede in his martyrology records the deposition of Augustine, 'first bishop of the English', his account of the Roman mission is focused upon Gregory rather than Augustine. It includes a number of papal documents in which (inevitably) Gregory is seen as the initiator and organizer and Augustine as the pupil, seeking out his mentor for instruction and advice. The *Libellus responsionum* in particular highlights Augustine's dependency upon the Pope.[38] Other texts seem to have been included expressly to diminish the archbishop. In one letter Gregory notes that Augustine has been performing miracles in his evangelizing of the English, but warns him not to be elated by their number: it is not necessarily the elect who work miracles, and in any case those vouchsafed to Augustine had been to effect the conversion of the English not to demonstrate his personal sanctity.[39]

It is, famously, Gregory whom Bede describes as apostle of the English and whom he praises at length in a position of especial prominence at the beginning of Book II of the *History*. Gregory too is expressly named as the sender of Paulinus, ultimately the evangelist of Northumbria.[40] After the warmth of Bede's eulogy of the Pope, comes the story of Augustine's meeting with the British bishops and teachers. Although Augustine is presented as on the righteous side, indeed is allowed a miracle to justify his cause, he is scarcely presented sympathetically. His discourtesy in failing to rise at the arrival of the British is recorded by Bede without comment, but is (it seems to me) indirectly condemned by Bede's praise of the wise and holy hermit whom the British consult and who advises them to judge Augustine's cause by his personal behaviour.[41] In any case, Augustine's attitude is in pointed contrast to Gregory's magnanimity in seeking to accommodate local custom, as recorded in the *Responsiones* and in the letter to Mellitus recommending the conversion of pagan cemeteries to christian use.[42] Indeed, it is not only in comparison with Gregory that Augustine cuts a poor figure: those who are treated with considerably greater warmth in the *Historia ecclesiastica* include Aidan of Lindisfarne (635–51), whose personal holiness and ability to work miracles is stressed, Paulinus, whose personal appearance and delicate relations with the Northumbrian King Edwin (616–33) are recorded in approving detail, and – more surprisingly – Mellitus, who is described by a tried and tested hagiographical *topos* ('noble in birth, but nobler in spirit') and who is depicted performing a miracle ascribed to his personal standing as an intercessor.[43]

I am, then, with those who detect a certain reserve in Bede's treatment of Augustine. Although that reserve may well reflect a patriotic desire to ensure that the evangelist of Kent did not rival the founding fathers of Northumbrian Christianity (namely Gregory, Paulinus, and Aidan), it may also derive from a certain indifference to Augustine's memory in Canterbury itself, arising in part from Theodore's enthusiasm for the Gregorian cult. It is significant, for example, that the community at Canterbury had apparently not troubled to record the year of Augustine's death, that despite Gregory's reference to the bishop's many miracles while alive only one such story survives, and that there are no posthumous miracles at all. In such circumstances it is perhaps possible that the story of the second meeting with the British bishops (whatever its source) could have been mediated to Bede via Canterbury, unadorned and without justification of the central protagonist. Bede himself could have added the telling qualifications – such as the description of the hermit as holy and wise. There is no need to suppose that he derived the story directly from a British source, or to deny its potentially unfavourable presentation of Augustine. At the time when it was being transmitted, Augustine's cult (if there was one) appears to have been of the most limited local interest.

All this, however, was to change within a generation. In the early 730s the Northumbrian prince Ecgberht (d. 766) became bishop of York and the see's metropolitan status was revived.[44] By then, clearly, Theodore's successors at Canterbury had abandoned their pretensions to archiepiscopal control over the whole of Britannia, and as a result their attention was focused much more upon Canterbury. Most probably it was then that a start was made to cultivate Canterbury's own saints. In particular, St Augustine's stock as founder of the see and co-founder with Æthelberht of the monastery, seems to have risen. In 747 at the council of Clofeshoh, held under the presidency of Archbishop Cuthbert of Canterbury, Augustine was honoured together with Gregory as the first christian teacher of the English. His feast day (26 May) was, like Gregory's, to be kept by churches and monasteries throughout the southern province, and his name was to be invoked after Gregory's in the litanies.[45]

The provisions of Clofeshoh mark an important stage in the development of Augustine's cult at least as a liturgical phenomenon. Before that the only surviving record of the feast seems to be Bede's martyrology. Thereafter, Augustine was included in the Old English martyrology, a late ninth-century Mercian text, which describes him as the bishop who first brought baptism to the English people and refers its readers to Bede's account in the *Ecclesiastical History*.[46] By the early ninth century, indeed, the cult was sufficiently developed in Canterbury for the monastery of SS Peter and Paul to be referred to as the *familia* of St Augustine and for gifts to the community to be in honour of or to obtain the intercession of the saint. The monastery was known, it seems, as that which sheltered the body of St Augustine. These developments may well reflect the favour which the West Saxon kings (themselves perhaps of Kentish descent) showed the monastery after they became rulers of Kent in 825.[47]

Augustine's feast seems to have remained a liturgically significant and well-known day: the *Anglo-Saxon Chronicle*, for example, records that in 946 King Edmund was murdered on St Augustine's 'mass-day',[48] and it occurs in all the surviving Anglo-Saxon calendars and in numerous litanies.[49] The saint was apparently held in high honour by both Athelstan (925–39) and Cnut (1016–35),[50] and his cult seems to have reached its full pre-Conquest liturgical development under the reformers at Canterbury and Winchester in the late tenth and early eleventh centuries. Bishop Æthelwold of Winchester (963–84) in particular had a strong interest in saints of the golden age of the English church, especially those who appeared in the *Historia ecclesiastica*, and he may have helped to stimulate interest in Augustine. Significantly, Wulfstan, the precentor of Old Minster, who flourished in the late tenth century and was responsible for a *Life of Æthelwold*, was the author of three hymns in honour of St Augustine.[51] At all events, there seems to have been an increased interest in the cult at the abbey itself, where according to its later historians, in 978 Archbishop Dunstan rededicated the church, presumably after a major building campaign, in honour of SS Peter and Paul and St Augustine.[52] That there was strong interest in Augustine in Canterbury at this time is borne out by books such as the Bosworth Psalter, written between 988 and 1012 and now taken to be a product of Saint Augustine's (though the issue is not perhaps completely settled). The calendar which prefaces the psalter[53] includes not only the feast of Augustine, recorded in capitals as of especial note, but also the feast days of Laurence, Mellitus, Justus and Deusdedit.[54] A slightly later calendar produced at Christ Church between 1012 and 1023 and evidently concerned primarily with its own saints still includes Augustine although the other early archbishops are all omitted.[55]

At Saint Augustine's itself the community seems indeed to have been on the point of translating the early archbishops. According to Goscelin, Abbot Ælfmær (1006–1023 x 7), had this in mind when he removed the columns and arches above the tombs.[56] Nevertheless, little was done. Ælfmær's successor, Abbot Ælfstan (1023x7–1045/6), contented himself with an especially grand celebration of the saint's day, which included a lavish feast for those attending the ceremonies.[57] In 1030[58] he acquired the relics of the seventh-century saint Mildreth from the defunct minster of Thanet, placing them in a shrine before the high altar and clearly treating them as the principal relics in the abbey church.[59] The abandonment of the translation of Augustine and his companions and the special honour paid to Mildreth suggests that, as earlier, the cult of Augustine was primarily liturgical, and that there was still no significant tomb cult.

That too is confirmed by Goscelin's account of the saint's miracles, compiled at the time of the 1091 translation.[60] Apart from a story of the theft of a pall covering the tomb 'at the time of the Danish invasions',[61] they all seem to date from the eleventh century, often emphasizing the proper observance of the feast day whatever the location or however difficult the circumstances in which the subject might find himself. Interest in the tomb itself is implicit, for example, in Goscelin's story of a cure effected upon a crippled Englishman (*vir Saxonicus*) called Leodegar, at the *Sancta Sanctorum*, the archbishops' burial place, by means of a vision in which Augustine, Laurence, and Mellitus manifested themselves in splendour and were subsequently seen to disappear into their graves. Such interest, however, appears to have been a late development: the miracle in question dates at the earliest from the reign of Cnut.[62]

In the late eleventh century St Augustine was credited with apostolic status at his abbey. Indeed, he had usurped from Gregory the Great the title *apostolus anglorum*, being so described in Goscelin's *Life* and *Miracles* and in a sacramentary produced at Saint Augustine's *c*. 1100.[63] In fact, this designation pre-dates the 1090s: it occurs, for example, in a benediction in a Christ Church pontifical of the late tenth century.[64] A similar epithet, *doctor anglorum*, is found in a vernacular homily on the saint, perhaps produced at Saint Augustine's in the early eleventh century when the cult was being elaborated there.[65] By contrast, in other texts from Christ Church, (apart from the pontifical just mentioned), Augustine was generally termed *archiepiscopus anglorum*.[66] The adoption of the apostolic title represents, of course, a further upgrading of Augustine's standing vis-à-vis Gregory. The sharp distinction, however, between the single certain pre-Conquest record of its use and Goscelin's heavy emphasis upon it suggests that that upgrading was developed more fully in the changed circumstances and more controversial atmosphere of Canterbury in the late eleventh century.[67]

The liturgical evidence suggests that the reformers were the main agents in the promotion of Augustine's cult in the late tenth and early eleventh centuries. In particular, the only early missals to preserve propers for a mass on his feast day emanate from Winchester or Canterbury.[68] Significantly too the only pontificals to include blessings for the day are probably from Christ Church.[69] Worcester produced its own liturgical texts honouring Augustine, including collects for his feast recorded in the eleventh-century breviary known as Wulfstan's portiforium,[70] and the archbishop also features in a metrical calendar compiled in the 990s at Oswald of Worcester's great monastery of Ramsey, where he is designated *Anglorum praesul*.[71]

In sum, it would seem that by the eleventh century, although Augustine's day was widely known and the saint himself regularly invoked in the litanies, commemoration of his feast with special prayers and masses was still very patchy and probably confined to the main centres of reform – to Canterbury, Winchester, Worcester, and perhaps Ramsey. It is interesting, for example, that only one fragmentary and anonymous homily survives. We might have expected Augustine to feature in the homilies and hagiography of Ælfric or in texts such as the legendary which formed one of Ælfric's main sources; in fact, however, no *Life* or similar text was compiled until Goscelin's *Vita* in the late eleventh century.[72]

Lastly, I shall look briefly at the evidence of the dedications. A few monastic buildings were clearly dedicated to the saint in the late tenth and eleventh centuries. In addition to Dunstan's dedication at Canterbury itself, Abbot Æthelwin of Athelney built a tower at his own abbey in Augustine's honour, in the belief that he had himself been saved from peril at sea by calling on the saint.[73] Some thirty or so ancient churches also bear dedications to a St Augustine, but it is not always possible to say whether the saint in question is the bishop of Canterbury or Hippo. In several cases, where the church was served by Augustinian canons it seems likely that the titular was in fact the saint of Hippo. In others, such as the four Augustinian dedications of parish churches in Kent, the Canterbury saint is much more likely.[74] In few if any instances, however, is it possible to say whether these dedications pre-date the translation of 1091. At present we may note that three at least seem relatively early: London, Norwich, and Leicester. They were recorded as extant by Goscelin in the late eleventh century, and there was no suggestion that they were new then.[75] Of those, perhaps the most interesting is that of St Augustine *ad portam* in the city of London, a foundation which stood at the entrance to St Paul's churchyard and was apparently aligned with a group of other potentially early churches: St Paul's itself, St Gregory, and St Martin's, Ludgate Hill.[76] That may be a genuinely early dedication at one of the churches first established by the Roman missionaries.

I have suggested that the tombs of the early archbishops need to be considered as a group, that the available evidence suggests that they were intended as honoured burials, in the tradition of the Roman missionaries' Italian homeland, rather than as shrines. It is not difficult to envisage the north *porticus* as intended to evoke the contemporary arrangements at Rome (or indeed Ravenna) even if the execution of the work was carried out by Kentish or Gallic craftsmen. Although there may have been an incipient cult – that certainly is suggested by the inclusion of Laurence, Mellitus, and Justus in an early Irish version of the canon of the mass – it was never highly developed, and above all, I suspect, never much centred on the tombs. Even when the cult was elaborated, at Saint Augustine's in the ninth century and at both Saint Augustine's and Christ Church in the late tenth and early eleventh, its focus was primarily the liturgy rather than wonders at the tomb. It was not really until after the Conquest, and more especially the translation of 1091, that the cults were fully established in a physical sense – in shrines located at altars around the east end of the new Norman church. It was then too that Augustine came into his own as *apostolus anglorum*. Paradoxically, it was the Normans who did most to promote Augustine and his early companions as saints and as founders of English Christianity.

NOTES

1. Bede, *HE*, II, 3.
2. A.T. Thacker, 'Making of a Saint', in *Local Saints and Local Churches*, eds R. Sharpe and A.T. Thacker (Oxford, forthcoming).
3. Goscelin, *Historia Translationis Sancti Augustini*, in *Acta Sanctorum*, May VI, eds G. Henschenius and D. Papebroch (Brussels, 1688), pp. 411–43.
4. W. St John Hope, 'Recent Discoveries in the Abbey Church of St. Austin at Canterbury', *Archaeologia*, 66 (1915), 376–400, esp. 390–9, and in *Arch Cant*, 32 (1917), 1–26; H.M. and J. Taylor, *Anglo-Saxon Architecture*, 3 vols (Cambridge, 1965–78), I, pp. 134–43; R. Gem, 'The Anglo-Saxon and Norman Churches', *St. Augustine's Abbey*, ed. *idem* (London, 1997), pp. 90–122, at pp. 100–1.
5. 'Augustinensis Abbas Almarus quasi quodam voto et praesagio futurae translationis, arcus et columnas, super sanctorum corpora Romana elegantia solemniter aedificatos, abstulit; quantumque audebat, viam exsurgendi illis paravit: de ipsis vero columnis et arcubus monasterii sui claustrum exornavit': Goscelin, *Hist. Trans.* p. 432, II, cap. 1.1.
6. Ibid., p. 416, I, caps 2.17–18.
7. Ibid., pp. 413–14, 416, 420, I, caps 2.3, 2.9, 2.17, 5.29.
8. Bede, *HE*, II, 3.
9. A.T. Thacker, 'Lindisfarne and the Origins of the Cult of St. Cuthbert', in *St. Cuthbert, His Cult and His Community*, eds G. Bonner, D.W. Rollason, C. Stancliffe (Woodbridge, 1989), pp. 103–22.
10. H. Blake, 'Sepolture', *Archeologico Medievale*, 10 (1983), 175–97. I am grateful to Dr Guy Halsall for this reference. Cf. R. Hodges, *San Vincenzo al Volturno*, 2 vols (Archaeological Monographs of the British School at Rome, 7, 9) (1993–5), I, 61, 63, 97–100, 123–90; II, 98–118.
11. J.-Ch. Picard, 'Étude sur l'emplacement des tombes des papes du IIe au Xe siècle', *Melanges d'archéologie et d'histoire. École Française de Rome*, 81 (1969), 725–82, esp. 755–64, 778–9; *Liber Pontificalis*, ed. L. Duchesne, Bibliothèque des Écoles Françaises d'Athènes et de Rome, 2nd series 3, 3 vols, 2nd edn (Paris, 1955–7), I, pp. 312–14; Bede, *HE*, II, 1.
12. For example, especially Gregory the Great: *Registrum Epistolarum*, ed. P. Ewald, MGH, *Epistulae*, I (Berlin, 1887), pp. iv, 30.
13. *Liber Pontificalis*, I, pp. 312, 323–4.
14. For very similar conclusions, reached independently, see É. Ó Carragáin, 'The Term *Porticus* and *Imitatio Romae* in Early Anglo-Saxon England', in *Text and Gloss: Studies in Insular Language and Literature*, eds Helen Conrad-O'Briain, Anne Marie Darcy and John Scattergood (Dublin,

1999), pp. 13–34. I am grateful to Professor Ó Carragáin for sending me a copy of his article in advance of publication.

15. Picard, 'Étude sur l'emplacement', 757–60, 773; M. Borgolte, *Petrusnachfolge und Kaiserimitation: die Grablegen der Papste, ihre Genese und Traditionsbildung*, Veröffentlichungen des Max-Planck-Instituts fur Geschichte, 95 (Göttingen, 1989), 49–71, 76, 88–93, Abbildung 7.

16. Picard, 'Étude sur l'emplacement', 760–4, 773–4; Borgolte, *Petrusnachfolge*, pp. 72–93, Abbildung 7.

17. Picard, 'Étude sur le'emplacement', 762–4; Borgolte, *Petrusnachfolge*, pp. 76–7, Abbildung 7.

18. This point is brought out very clearly by Ó Carragáin, 'Term *Porticus* and *Imitatio Romae*', esp. pp. 15–22, 26–7.

19. J.-Ch. Picard, *Le Souvenir des Évêques: Sepultures, Listes Episcopales, et Culte des Évêques en Italie du Nord des Origines au X*^e *Siècle* (École Française de Rome, 1988), esp. pp. 180–9; Borgolte, *Petrusnachfolge*, p. 87.

20. Bede, *HE*, II, 3.

21. Goscelin, *Hist. Trans.*, p. 414, I, cap. 1.10: 'Unde et ubi, sicut primitus ipse cum beatis collegis suis a die dormitionis est conditus, eodem loco et eodem modo immotissimus est inventus.'

22. Ibid., p. 432, II, cap.1.1.

23. Dublin, Royal Irish Academy, D II 3, fols 12–67; *The Stowe Missal*, ed. G.F. Warner, 2 vols, HBS 31–2 (London, 1906–15), II, pp. xxvi–xxxii, 14–15; J.F. Kenney, *Sources for the Early History of Ireland* (Columbia, 1929), pp. 691–9.

24. Bede, *HE*, II, 4.

25. C. Plummer, *Venerabilis Baedae Opera Historica*, 2 vols (Oxford, 1896), II, p. 83; A.W. Haddan and W. Stubbs, *Councils and Ecclesiastical Documents*, 3 vols (Oxford, 1869–78), III, pp. 61–2.

26. For what follows see A.T. Thacker, 'Memorializing Gregory the Great: The Origins and Transmission of a Papal Cult in the Seventh and Early Eighth Centuries', *Early Medieval Europe*, 7.i (1998), 59–84.

27. Bede, *HE*, I, 29.

28. Only three bishops remained, and one of those was a simoniac: H.M. Mayr-Harting, *The Coming of Christianity to Anglo-Saxon England*, 3rd edn (London, 1991), p. 130.

29. Bede, *HE*, IV, 17. The surviving papal letters and original documents from the earlier seventh century, transcribed by Bede, suggest that this may have been the first use of the title archbishop in England, and that Theodore's predecessors were styled bishop and metropolitan. In this paper, however, the conventional title has been retained.

30. *Works of Joseph Bingham*, ed. R. Bingham, 10 vols (Oxford, 1855), I, p. 94, 171, 201–3, 206–7; *Dictionnaire d' archéologie chrétienne et de liturgie*, eds F. Cabrol and H. Leclercq, 15 vols (Paris, 1907–52), 1, part 2, cols 2732–3. Cf. Isidore of Seville, *Etymologiae*, VII, xii, 6–10, ed. W.M. Lindsay, 2 vols (Oxford, 1911), I, p. 299.

31. Bede, *HE*, II, 1.

32. Thacker, 'Memorializing Gregory', esp. 75–8; Bede, *HE*, II, 20; *The Earliest Life of Gregory the Great*, ed. B. Colgrave (Kansas, 1968), cap. 19.

33. A. Wilmart, 'Un témoin anglo-saxon du calendrier métrique d' York', *Revue Bénédictine*, 46 (1934), 41–69; Alcuin, *Bishops, Kings and Saints of York*, ed. P. Godman (Oxford, 1982), pp. xlix, 14–18, 22; *Earliest Life*, caps 15–17; Bede, *HE*, II, 9, 12, 16–18, 20; III, 14; *Calendar of St. Willibrord*, ed. H.A. Wilson, HBS 55 (London, 1918), 12 (*Pauli episcopi in Cantia*); H. Quentin, *Les martyrologes historiques du moyen âge* (Paris, 1908), p. 55.

34. *Calendar of Willibrord*, pl. V, p. 7; Quentin, *Les martyologes*, p. 51.

35. Mayr-Harting, *Coming of Christianity*, pp. 130–9. For Whitby's attitude see A.T. Thacker, 'Monks, Preaching and Pastoral Care', in *Pastoral Care Before the Parish*, eds J. Blair and R. Sharpe (Leicester, 1992), pp. 137–70, at pp. 149–50. There is no record of Lindisfarne's attitude in 678, but by 687 they were definitely hostile: W. Goffart, *Narrators of Barbarian History* (Princeton, 1988), pp. 291–2; Thacker, 'Origins of Cult of St. Cuthbert', 116, 120.
36. Bede, *HE*, III, 29; IV, 1, 3; A.T. Thacker, 'Bede and the Irish', in *Beda Venerabilis: Historian, Monk and Northumbrian*, ed. L.A.R. Houwen and A.A. MacDonald (Groningen, 1996), pp. 31–59, at pp. 46–7.
37. Bede, *HE*, preface.
38. Ibid., I, 27. See also Rob Meens, ch. 8 above.
39. Bede, *HE*, I, 31.
40. Ibid., I, 31; V, 24.
41. Ibid., II, 2. Cf. Mayr-Harting, *Coming of Christianity*, p. 72; and Clare Stancliffe, ch. 6 above.
42. Bede, *HE*, I, 27, 30.
43. Ibid., II, 7, 9, 16; III, 5.
44. *Venerabilis Baedae Opera Historica*, ed. C. Plummer, 2 vols (Oxford, 1896), *Continuatio*, I, p. 361.
45. Haddan and Stubbs, *Councils*, III, p. 368; Catherine Cubitt, *Anglo-Saxon Church Councils, c.650–c.850* (London, 1995), pp. 125–52, esp. p. 151.
46. *Das altenglische Martyrologium* ed. G. Kotzor, Bayerische Akademie der Wissenschaften, phil.-hist. Klasse, Abh. 88, 2 vols (Munich, 1981), II, p. 109; trans. G. Herzfeld, *Old English Martyrology* (old series), 116 (1900), p. 87.
47. S. Kelly, *Charters of St. Augustine's Abbey, Canterbury, and Minster-in-Thanet*, Anglo-Saxon Charters, IV (Oxford, 1995), pp. xiii–xiv, 60–3 (no. 15), 70–4 (no. 17), 74–7 (no. 18), 79–82 (no. 20), 97–9 (no. 25). On the Kentish origins of Ecgberht of Wessex, see A. Scharer, 'The Writing of History at King Alfred's Court', *Early Medieval Europe*, 5.ii (1996), 177–206, at 183–4.
48. *Two Saxon Chronicles Parallel*, eds C. Plummer and J. Earle, 2 vols (Oxford, 1892–9), I, p. 112.
49. Cf. A.T. Thacker, 'Saint Making and Relic Collecting by Oswald and His Communities', in *Saint Oswald of Worcester: Life and Influence*, ed. N. Brooks and C. Cubitt (London, 1996), pp. 244–68, at p. 267.
50. Goscelin, *Miracula Sancti Augustini*, in *Acta Sanctorum*, May VI, ed. Henschenius and Papebroch, pp. 397–411, at 399–400, I, caps 9, 11.
51. *Hymns of the Anglo-Saxon Church*, ed. Inge B. Milfull (Cambridge, 1996), pp. 320–5; Wulfstan of Worcester, *Life of Æthelwold*, ed. M. Lapidge (Oxford, 1991), esp. pp. xxxvii–xxxix.
52. William Thorne, *Historiae Anglicanae Scriptores X*, ed. R. Twysden (London, 1652), col. 1780; Thomas of Elmham, *Historiae Monasterii Sancti Augustini Cantuariensis*, ed. C. Hardwick, RS (London, 1858), p. 22.
53. It is physically distinct from, and a little later than, the psalter itself: *Bosworth Psalter*, eds F.A. Gasquet and E. Bishop (London, 1908), pp. 3, 5. I am grateful to Dr Gameson for drawing my attention to this point.
54. BL, Add. 37517; *Bosworth Psalter*, pp. 15–74; P.M. Korhammer, 'Origin of Bosworth Psalter', *ASE*, 2 (1973), 173–87; N. Orchard, 'Bosworth Psalter and St. Augustine's Missal', in *Canterbury and the Norman Conquest*, eds R. Eales and R. Sharpe (London, 1995), pp. 87–94; *English Kalendars Before 1100*, ed. F. Wormald, HBS 72 (London, 1934), 57–69.
55. BL, Arundel 155, fols 2–7v.
56. Goscelin, *Hist. Trans.* p. 432, II, cap. 1.1. Above, n. 4.

57. Goscelin, *Miracula S. Aug.*, p. 406, III, cap. 37.
58. For the date see R. Sharpe, 'The Date of St. Mildreth's Translation from Minster-in-Thanet to Canterbury', *Medieval Studies* 53 (1991), 349–54.
59. Goscelin, *Translatio S. Mildrethae*, ed. D.W. Rollason, *Medieval Studies*, 48 (1986), 139–210; idem, *Historia Trans.*, p. 432, II, cap. 1.1.
60. Goscelin, *Miracula S. Augustini*, pp. 397–411.
61. Ibid., p. 397.
62. Ibid., pp. 397–8. Cf. the statement in Archbishop Eadsige's grant of Littlebourne (?1047) that the archbishop placed the *libellus* recording his gift on the tomb of St Augustine: Kelly, *Charters of St. Augustine's*, pp. 131–2, no. 37. But see below, at n. 64.
63. Goscelin, *Vita Sancti Augustini*, in *Acta Sanctorum*, May VI, eds Henschenius and Papebroch, pp. 375–95, at 377, cap. I; idem, *Miracula S. Augustini*, p. 411; CCCC, 270; *The Missal of St. Augustine's, Canterbury*, ed. M. Rule (Cambridge, 1896), p. 90. Cf. idem, *Historia Trans.*, p. 413, I, cap. 1.1; *Miracula S. Augustini*, pp. 399–400, I, caps 7–8, 14.
64. BnF, MS lat. 943, fol. 131v; J. Rosenthal, 'The Pontifical of St. Dunstan', in *St. Dunstan: His Life, Times and Cult*, eds N. Ramsay, M. Sparks and T. Tatton-Brown (Woodbridge, 1992), pp. 143–63, at p. 149. Prof. Richard Sharpe, in a paper given at the conference in Canterbury in September 1997, suggested that a further occurrence of the title apostle, in Archbishop Eadsige's grant of Littlebourne to Saint Augustine's (?1047), was perhaps a forgery, made after the translation of 1091. Cf. Kelly, *Charters of St. Augustine's*, pp. 131–2, no. 37.
65. CCCC, 162, p. 153; N. Ker, *Catalogue of Manuscripts Containing Anglo-Saxon* (Oxford, 1957), 56.
66. Rosenthal, 'Pontifical', 149; Korhammer, 'Bosworth Psalter', 178.
67. R. Sharpe, 'The Setting of St. Augustine's Translation in 1091', in *Canterbury and the Norman Conquest*, eds R. Eales and R. Sharpe, pp. 1–13.
68. i.e. Le Havre, Bibliothèque municipale, 330; *The Missal of the New Minster, Winchester*, ed. D.H. Turner, HBS 93 (London, 1962), esp. 98–9; CCCC, 270, fol. 92v.; *Missal of St. Augustine's*, pp. xi, 90; Rouen, Bibliothèque municipale, Y.6 (274); *The Missal of Robert of Jumièges*, ed. H.A. Wilson, HBS 11 (London, 1896), esp. xxviii–xxix, 177.
69. That is BnF, lat. 943; BL, Add. 57337. See Rosenthal, 'Pontifical', 148–9; 'Liturgical Books in Anglo-Saxon England and Their Old English Terminology', in *Learning and Literature in Anglo-Saxon England Studies Presented to Peter Clemoes on the Occasion of His Sixty-Fifth Birthday*, eds M. Lapidge and H. Gneuss (Cambridge, 1985), pp. 91–142, at p. 132.
70. *The Portiforium of St. Wulfstan*, ed. A. Hughes, HBS 89–90, 2 vols (London, 1959–60), I, 125.
71. M. Lapidge, 'A Tenth-Century Metrical Calendar from Ramsey', *Revue Bénédictine*, 94 (1984), 326–69, esp. p. 364.
72. For the text see above, at n. 63. For discussion of the work see Fiona Gameson, ch. 15 below.
73. Goscelin, *Miracula S. Augustini*, p. 400, I, cap. 14.
74. F. Arnold-Foster, *Studies in Church Dedications*, 3 vols (London, 1899), I, pp. 310–22; III, 3, p. 340.
75. Goscelin, *Historia Trans.*, p. 429, I, caps 8.51–3.
76. T. Tatton-Brown, 'The Topography of Anglo-Saxon London', *Antiquity*, 60 (1986), 21–8, at 22–3.

CHAPTER 15

Goscelin's *Life* of Augustine of Canterbury

Fiona Gameson

This is your portion for Christ, this your inheritance, this your native land removed to heaven! O native star of Rome, our patriarch in this realm! You have harvested this land for the Lord, you have harvested it and made it your own; whatever piety this land brings forth, whatever bears flowers, whatever bears fruit, you are the cultivator, you are the sower, you are the planter; everything is yours in the Lord. Whatever holy things are produced, you are the founder, you are the director, you are the leader; everything upon which you laboured with the Lord looks back to you, follows you and crowns you: you will be able to trust in the work of your hands; you are blessed and it will be well with you. Kings, nobles, leading men, the nation, follow you; they sing your praises as protector and first father.[1]

This fulsome panegyric with which Goscelin of Saint-Bertin draws to a close the first chapter of the *Historia Maior Sancti Augustini* which he wrote at Canterbury at the end of the eleventh century is, to the modern reader, paradoxically both too much and too little.[2] In his lyrical apostrophe to the saint he raises him above the rank of missionary to a heathen people to a position equal to, or surpassing that of the first apostles of the church,[3] as though he were Christ's direct emissary to the benighted English.[4] However, along with this elevation goes a singular lack of any personal detail or human touch which would make the saint seem a living, historical figure. At one level, this is a reflection of the genre within which Goscelin is working since it is the role of the divine emissary which is of paramount importance; and even if he had known more about the real Augustine, he would doubtless only have revealed it to his audience with a suitable gilding – the ornamentation of saintly glamour.[5] Indeed, when he does attempt a physical description of Augustine, it is almost certainly, as we shall see, less indebted to reality than to literary and hagiographic ideals.

At another level, however, the lack of personal detail is a direct reflection of the limitations of Goscelin's knowledge. For it would appear that he knew next to nothing about the man Augustine, other than what could be learned from the account in Bede's *Historia ecclesiastica*, despite the fact that he lived and worked among, and was commissioned to write this *Vita* by the monks of Augustine's own foundation – the abbey which bore his name. Indeed, despite his fulsome treatment of the mission as a whole, Goscelin is not only sparing in relation to personal details about Augustine, but also, more remarkably, is virtually silent concerning any great deeds and miracles the saint might have wrought in Canterbury itself. Very little in the way of documentary or even anecdotal evidence recounting the saint's life, death and, in particular, his immediate *post mortem* miracles,[6] and almost nothing relating to his residence in Canterbury would thus seem to have been preserved at Saint Augustine's Abbey in the late eleventh century. Moreover, although the sources behind some of the non-Bedan material he includes are debatable, such clues as are available for the matter in question point away from, rather than towards Saint Augustine's Abbey itself. We should resist deducing from this that Augustine lacked charisma.[7] More relevant, perhaps, was the circumstance that the newly introduced religion foundered in Kent soon after his death upon the demise of King Æthelberht,[8] – not to mention the subsequent disruption to the abbey and its traditions during the Viking invasions. The most important factor, however, was the extraordinary reverence accorded to Gregory, which overshadowed the memory of Augustine and coloured Bede's version of the mission.[9]

The debt that Goscelin's *Vita* owes to Bede's account is undoubtedly enormous – about half of the fifty-three chapters recount material drawn from the *Historia ecclesiastica*, albeit vastly extended and elaborated with rhetorical flourishes, invented speeches, and authorial comments. The familiar landmarks appear along the 'road' beginning with the papal encounter with the fair-haired boys in the market place at Rome and the accompanying puns; the initial intention of Gregory to act as missionary himself which is thwarted by events so that Augustine is sent in his place; and the near-collapse of the enterprise as Augustine and his band lose heart in southern Gaul and he is sent back to Rome, only to be encouraged once more by Gregory who supplies him with letters of introduction. Similarly, we learn thereafter of the arrival of the missionaries at Thanet, and the cordial encounter between Augustine and Æthelberht; the establishment of the saint and his band in Canterbury; the baptism of Æthelberht and the conversion of Kent; Augustine's request for reinforcements; his far from successful encounters with the leaders of the British church ending in their rejection of him and his cursing of them; and finally his death in Canterbury at some unspecified time, having consecrated Laurentius as his successor.[10] Goscelin even follows Bede so far as to perpetuate the mistaken idea that shortly after his arrival in England, Augustine returned to Arles where he was ordained archbishop of the English by Archbishop Etherius.[11]

Yet this is not to say that Goscelin's *Vita* is merely a recasting of the material supplied by Bede: far from it. He was, after all, a professional hagiographer who already had a number of substantial works to his credit, and a shortage of concrete biographical information was not going to hamper his ability to construct a suitably exalted and ornate monument to honour this worthy subject.[12] Indeed, while the basic landmarks of the story may be the same as in the *Historia ecclesiastica*, Goscelin has profoundly altered the account in numerous more or less striking ways.

One of the more subtle alterations to the part of the narrative that is largely based upon Bede (chapters 4–30 of the *Vita*) is Goscelin's use of Pope Gregory's correspondence. At first sight it is easy to believe that the hagiographer was merely copying straight from Bede's account where many such letters are transcribed; and indeed this must be true in at least one case since the Pope's letter of exhortation to the missionaries as they waited faint-heartedly in southern Gaul, was not preserved in the *Register* of Gregory's letters, but is only found in Bede's *Historia ecclesiastica*.[13] Yet on some occasions Goscelin seems consciously to have rejected material in Bede, while on others he instead turned straight to the *Register* to supply suitable documents which were not to be found in his principal source. The first of these stratagems – the omission of Bedan material – is understandable from the point of view of creating an independent life of the saint. Thus Goscelin omits the letter written to Vergilius of Arles, instructing the latter to welcome Augustine should he come to him with queries or complaints about other bishops (Bede, *HE*, I, 28), possibly because there was no record of such a meeting, but more probably because this only detracted from the main thrust of the *Vita*, namely Augustine's conversion of the English. Altogether more notable is the fact that Goscelin omits the lengthy *Libellus responsionum* (Bede, *HE*, I, 27),[14] merely referring in passing to the fact that along with new personnel and many other things that were necessary for his ministry, Pope Gregory also sent clear answers to various questions. Interestingly, while Goscelin is usually silent about his sources, here he specifically invites the reader to turn to Bede for more information (Goscelin, chapter 25). This suggests that while he clearly perceived that the inclusion of the *Libellus responsionum* would be detrimental to the picture of Augustine he was trying to create, he was equally aware that any educated person would have been struck by its absence – hence this oblique reference. In choosing to omit the *Libellus responsionum*, Goscelin made a wise, if bold decision, since its presence would not only have disrupted the narrative flow, but would also have greatly increased the importance of Gregory at the expense of Augustine – as is the case in the *Historia ecclesiastica*.

As to those occasions where Goscelin inserts letters that are not found in Bede's version of the story but which are drawn from the *Register*, we can only speculate upon his motives. Certainly Gregory's letter to Eulogius, patriarch of Alexandria (Goscelin, chapter 39),[15] is a glowing testimonial to the success of Augustine's mission, and moreover shows papal approval of the saint's endeavours. On the other hand, the letter to Queen Bertha (Goscelin, chapter 30),[16] which appears as a companion to the one to King Æthelberht (chapter 29) – only this latter was transcribed by Bede – is essentially irrelevant to Augustine; and it was perhaps included primarily to enhance the reputation of the local royal family whose remains were, after all, also buried and venerated in Saint Augustine's Abbey (cf. fig. 14.2). There is one instance where Goscelin's skill in presenting Augustine in the best possible light might seem to have faltered as a result of his enthusiasm for using papal documents: instead of omitting Gregory's letter to Augustine warning against the sin of pride, not only does he follow Bede's example and include it, but he in fact quotes it in its entirety whereas Bede had only used an excerpt (Bede, I, 31; Goscelin, chapter 28).[17] This extended treatment of the sin of pride that could arise from the performance of miracles, justified though it might be by the existence of the Gregorian letter, may strike us as strange, even ill-advised, considering how much emphasis Goscelin places upon such incidents in his *Vita*. Yet we must remember that a saint's sanctity was judged by his miracles, and even if he might not feel pride in them himself, his devotees certainly should.[18] Moreover, this letter from the revered, saintly Pope Gregory is unshakable contemporary evidence for their existence.

It is when Goscelin is no longer drawing upon the sober account of Bede that he is able to allow his hagiographic skills to come into play and to provide the miracles which mark out the man as a saint. Bede, it is true, alludes to miracles performed by Augustine and his companions (as, incidentally, does Pope Gregory in his letter to Eulogius); however, the only miraculous occurrence he actually described was Augustine's healing of a blind man in the presence of the leaders of the British church, who had themselves failed to restore his sight (Bede, II, 2; Goscelin, chapter 33). Goscelin is less reticent! Interestingly, only one of the miracles he relates in the *Vita* appears to have any association with Canterbury (and then only by inference), underlining the circumstance noted above that few, if any records of such early wonders seem to have been kept at the abbey. Further support is lent to this contention by the circumstance that the events recounted in

PRIVILEGIVM ATHELBERTI REGIS PRIMI

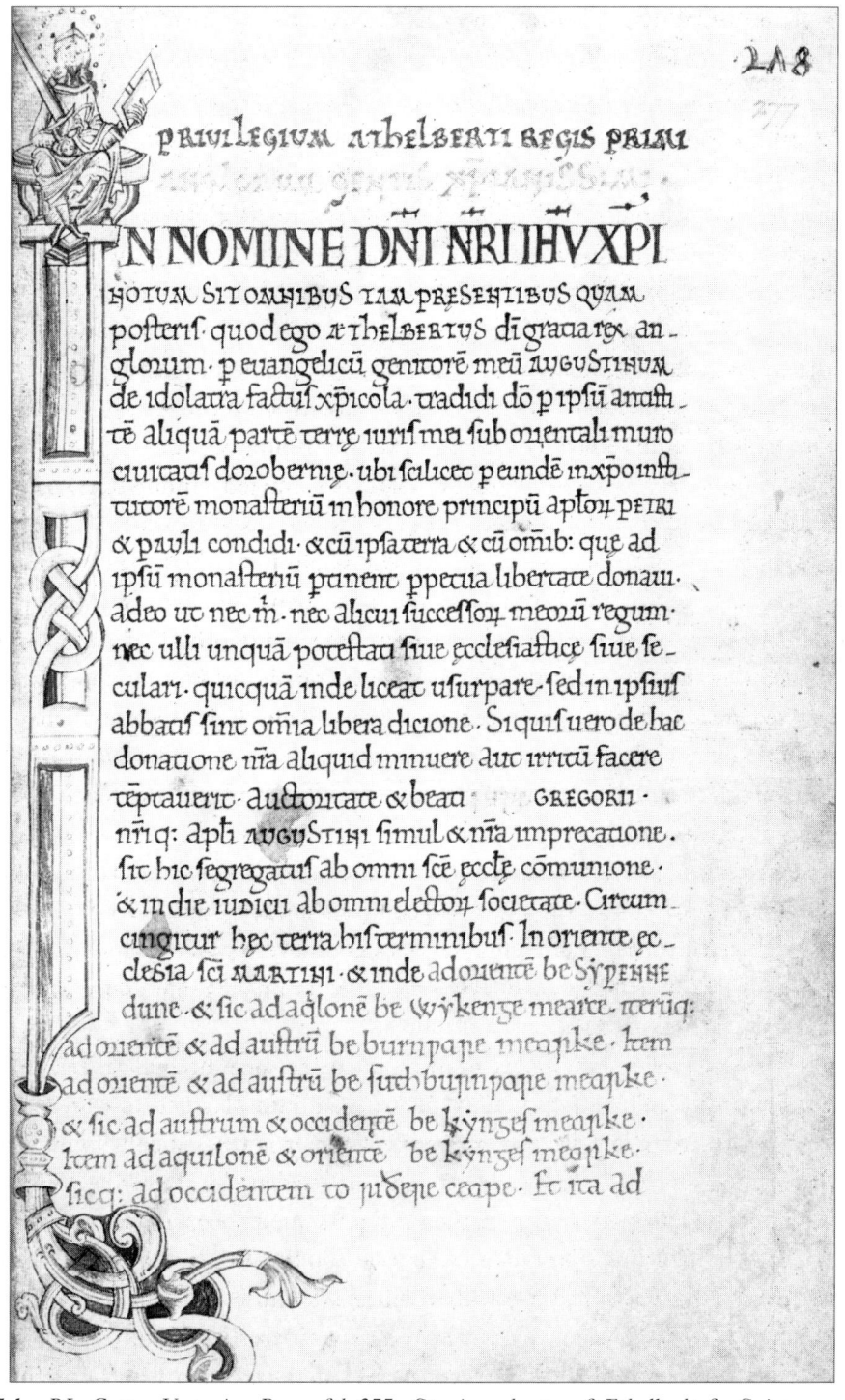

IN NOMINE DNI NRI IHV XPI

Notum sit omnibus tam presentibus quam posteris. quod ego æthelbertus di gratia rex anglorum. p euangelicū genitorē meū augustinum de idolatria factus xpicola. tradidi dō p ipsū antisti_te aliquā parte terre iuris mei sub orientali muro ciuitatis dorobernię. ubi scilicet p eundē in xpo insti_tutorē monasteriū in honore principū aptoȝ petri & pauli condidi. & cū ipsa terra & cū oĩbus: que ad ipsū monasteriū pinent ppetua libertate donaui. adeo ut nec m̃. nec alicui successoȝ meorū regum. nec ulli unquā potestati siue ecclesiastice siue se_culari. quicquā inde liceat usurpare. sed in ipsius abbatis sint oĩa libera dicione. Si quis uero de hac donatione m̃a aliquid minuere aut irritū facere teptauerit. auctoritate & beati   GREGORII. ñ̃ i q: apli AVGVSTINI simul & m̃a imprecatione. sit hic segregatus ab omni scē eccle comunione. & in die iudicii ab omni electoȝ societate. Circum cingitur hec terra bis terminibus. In oriente ec_clesia sci MARTINI. & inde ad orientē be Sypenne_dune. & sic ad aqlonē be Wykenge mearce. iteruq: ad orientē & ad austrū be burnpaþe meaþke. Item ad orientē & ad austrū be such burnpaþe meaþke. & sic ad austrum & occidentē be kynges meaþke. Item ad aquilonē & orientē be kynges meaþke. sicq: ad occidentem to ƿiðeȝe ceaþe. Et ita ad

15.1. BL, Cotton Vespasian B. xx, fol. 277r. Spurious charter of Æthelberht for Saint Augustine's (historiated with an image of King Æthelberht). It appears in an early twelfth-century manuscript that was made at Saint Augustine's Abbey, and contains Goscelin's Life of Augustine and other works. (British Library)

his separate work on Augustine's miracles, the *Miracula*, almost all date from 'modern times', namely the eleventh century. From where then, we may reasonably wonder, was he able to gather the otherwise unattested signs of divine power he included in the *Vita*? Such evidence as the stories provide suggests that they come from different sources, as we shall see, and is compatible with them having been garnered by Goscelin himself. Be that as it may, they bear the stamp of his artistry: of the five non-Bedan miracles recounted, four appear in matching pairs with a marked symmetry of structure. Although an arrangement over which Goscelin doubtless took pains, this hardly contributes to their credibility in modern eyes.

The first of the sequences in question is set in the environs of Angers, as Augustine and his companions travel through Gaul (chapters 10–13). Having been chased out of the town by a group of hostile women, the holy band are led by Augustine's staff to a spot where, nourished by a divine fountain springing forth from the earth, and illumined by a heavenly light of exceeding brightness, they spend the night in safety. The inhabitants are, naturally, drawn to the site of the unearthly light and there find, inscribed in the earth, the name of Augustine and his mission. Instantly filled with remorse, they build a church dedicated to his name from which women are strictly excluded. To illustrate the power of the saint, even when not personally present, Goscelin then relates the story of a certain importunate noble woman who tried to enter the said church, ostensibly to make an offering of a candle to the saint, with dire consequences:

> But scarcely had she touched the forbidden boundary and the sacred threshold, when her intestines ruptured and the innermost parts of her stomach poured on to the earth, and the unhappy woman rushed forth and died. And when the dead woman had been taken outside, this terrifyingly taught all those who had not believed anything to believe! (chapter 12)

Further to authenticate his story of the incident at Angers (rather than to counter any hint of misogyny on Augustine's part), Goscelin introduces the episode by saying:

> Many very honourable men from Angers, coming to Saint Augustine's in Canterbury, were greatly amazed that here, where he rests in his body, all women may enter legally and freely, whereas there it is not possible for them to have the benefit of that freedom. To those who wonder, the brothers answer: obviously those who drove out the holy man are deservedly driven out of his church; but those who, on the other hand, received him, ought to be received by him himself. (chapter 9)

Not the least remarkable aspect of this fabulous story is the location itself: for the extant letters of introduction from Gregory to possible hosts, which are the mainspring for our knowledge of Augustine's journey through Gaul, do not include one to the church of Angers.[19] So, we may well ask, why of all the places in Gaul through which Augustine probably did pass or might have passed *en route* to Thanet, is the one location about which Goscelin has a story the otherwise undocumented Angers? Certainty is elusive; however, it is striking, and possibly not a coincidence, that this is one of the continental towns in which we know Goscelin himself had a personal contact. Prior to his move to Canterbury, he had spent a lengthy period in the west of England in the circle of Bishop Herman of Sherborne (d. 1078), during which he had come to know the community of Wilton extremely well, and had possibly been its chaplain. Apart from writing a *Vita* of its noble patron, St Edith, he had also become the spiritual friend and adviser of one of the nuns, a certain Eve. He wrote his *Liber Confortatorius* for her in the early 1080s, by which time she had left Wilton to become a recluse – at Saint-Laurent-du-Tertre at Angers.[20]

This episode at the very outset of Augustine's mission is balanced stylistically by one towards the end of Goscelin's account. According to the *Vita* but no other source, Augustine makes an extended progress through the west of England (chapters 41–6), where he meets with some exceedingly fierce opposition:

> There an unholy people, blinded by darkness and detesting divine light, not only refused to listen to the life-giving proofs, but raved against the holy men of God with an entire tempest of ridicule and insults, driving them afar off from their lands. Nor is it to be believed that their unbridled audacity restrained their fists. (chapter 41)

No indeed, for Augustine is set upon forthwith and further humiliated by yet more natives,[21] who, however, are then smitten by a mysterious, all-consuming, invisible fire which makes their bodies burn unbearably. Realizing that this is a punishment for their attack on the saint, they flock to him and beg for baptism – which brings them instant relief (chapter 42). Having thus effected another mass conversion, Augustine travels on, but becomes lost in an arid waste where, as an answer to his prayers, a heavenly fountain springs out of the ground where he places his staff (reminiscent of Angers). A church was built to commemorate this spot, which forever after, we are told, was known as 'Cernel' (chapters 43–4). In the case of Angers, Goscelin fortified his account with one subsequent miracle (the tale of the hapless woman whose presumption to enter the church caused her fatal rupture); correspondingly here we learn that years later a sick priest from the local monastery was told by Augustine (who appeared to him in a dream) to bathe in the water of this fountain, and was forthwith cured (chapter 45). Although the sequence of events in Dorset is not identical to that in Angers, there are nevertheless striking parallels: the presence in both accounts of initially hostile, then remorseful natives; the sudden appearance of curative fountains; and the building of commemorative churches in which a later miracle is claimed to have taken place. Concerning Goscelin's source for the events at Cerne, while the details remain elusive, it is worth remembering that the writer had spent many years of his life in this part of the country. He may thus himself have heard the tale, or retained local contacts who might have supplied such anecdotes. Likewise, it is possible that familiarity with local tradition lies behind the spurious etymology he includes for the name 'Cernel': this he said derived from the Latin *'cernendus'* (seen) and the hebrew 'hel' (God) (chapter 44).[22] Be that as it may, just as his reference to the surprise of the visiting worthies from Angers at the presence of women at Augustine's tomb in Canterbury helps to authenticate the miraculous events in Gaul, so his 'factual' explanation of the name of Cerne validates the miracles in the wilds of England.

These two miracles frame, as it were, another matched pair of otherwise unattested episodes which occur on Augustine's journeys to and from York. It was Pope Gregory's intention, as he made clear in a letter to Augustine, that there should be two metropolitan sees, London and York;[23] however, in reality, the first phase of the mission never left the south. It was not until Paulinus went to the court of Edwin of Northumbria (d. 633), accompanying the Kentish christian princess, Æthelburh, that the faith was carried north; it did not really take root until the efforts of the Irish missionaries under Oswald (d. 642); and the northern archbishopric was not definitively established until 735. In striking contrast to historical reality, Goscelin has Augustine himself travelling to York where he is reputed to have baptized over 10,000 people (exactly the figure given by Gregory with reference to Kent at Christmas 597).[24] Goscelin thereby bolsters Canterbury's claims to supremacy over the see of York – a live issue in the late eleventh century.[25] It is debatable whether Saint Augustine's Abbey would have especially wished to help the cathedral on this point, given that relations between the two foundations were far from easy at this time; however, it was obviously relevant to Goscelin's case to present Augustine as the unquestioned initiator and superior of the church of all England. On his way both to and from the north he performs miracles of healing – first on a blind, paralysed beggar (chapter 36), and later on a leper (chapter 40). On both occasions the reader's attention is focused on the fact that such healings echo biblical events, and that Augustine is acting in direct succession to Christ and the apostles, especially Peter. Thus the point that was originally made in the opening chapter of the *Vita*, that Augustine is not merely a missionary but the chosen emissary of the Lord, is underlined once again.

The first of these miracles, that of the healing of the blind paralytic, is closely modelled upon the incident recounted in Luke 18:35–43, even to its taking place on the approach to a town – Christ entering Jericho, Augustine entering York. In both we have the same realistic image of the destitute man lying by the roadside, his becoming aware of the passing of a crowd because of the noise and, on learning the cause, shouting out for aid from the holy man. As the parallel is crucial to the resonance of the tale, Goscelin makes it explicit:

> the most merciful father, remembering how the Lord cured the blind man in the gospel, summoned the ill man to him.

Immediately afterwards he develops a comparison between Augustine and the prince of the apostles:

> And with the voice of the key-bearer of the Lord, Peter, whom he emulated with whole-hearted devotion as a fatherly instructor, he said: 'Silver and gold have I none, but what I have, I give to you; rise up whole, in the name of the lord, Jesus Christ'. (chapter 36)[26]

As for the second episode, the healing of the leprous man as Augustine leaves York, direct reference is again made to similar healings in the scriptures, though interestingly this time comparison is made with an Old Testament incident, the cleansing of Naaman by Elisha (II Kings 5:10–14). Naaman had to bathe seven times in the Jordan to be healed whereas, Goscelin comments, Augustine's curing of this leper was much more expeditious.

The final manifestation of Augustine's miraculous powers that Goscelin relates in the *Vita* is the only such occurrence seemingly associated with Canterbury – even so the exact location is somewhat vague.[27] We are told that after extensive travelling throughout England, Augustine returns 'to his perpetual home and dwelling-place of Canterbury' (chapter 46), whereafter a miracle is narrated which surpasses all the preceding displays of saintly power. For the petitioner this time has not one, nor two, but three afflictions, being crippled, deaf, and dumb! Goscelin takes the opportunity to indulge in some verbal display:

> Indeed Augustine, showing pity, released [him from] this misery by pious prayer, and in the grace of the Trinity drove off the threefold affliction with

threefold curing. His steps are given direction, his tongue is set free, his ears reopened. The man who had been ill in three ways gave thanks for his threefold health. He walks, he runs, he speaks, he hears unobstructedly, fully, clearly. (chapter 47)

However, concomitant with being a recipient of such divine grace, there is a moral responsibility to behave fittingly – as is soon made apparent. When the young man becomes disruptive in church and acts with such shamelessness and lack of respect that he scandalizes everyone, he is re-smitten even more grievously than before, in that now he can speak only gibberish, hear only foul stories, and he keeps running towards precipices! Understandably then repentant for his sin and folly, the young man is restored to health once again by Augustine. As in the parallel case of Ste Foi of Conques, whose most famous miracle was returning the eyes to a blinded man and then removing and restoring his sight on several occasions according to his behaviour, this is a salutary lesson not to misuse the divine grace channelled by the holy figure.[28]

We have yet to consider the one miracle performed by Augustine whose source is not in doubt, being also found in Bede (II, 2) – namely his healing of the blind man in competition with the British bishops. In comparison with all the previous examples, where the miracle was central to the story, this is but one small part of a lengthy and complex episode which has more bearing upon Augustine's role as papal missionary and head of the church in England than as a miracle-worker. When facing the challenge of having to recount Augustine's interaction with the British church, we can see Goscelin struggling to manipulate the problematic legacy left to him by Bede. The latter devotes considerable space at the beginning of his *Historia ecclesiastica* to the Britons and their church (I, 4–22) and he dwells upon the heresies that, as much as the onslaughts of the Anglo-Saxon invaders, led to the final downfall of that nation. He concludes his catalogue of their iniquities with the harsh judgement:

To other unspeakable crimes, which Gildas their own historian describes in doleful words, was added this crime, that they never preached the faith to the Saxons or Angles who inhabited Britain with them. Nevertheless God in his goodness did not reject the people whom he foreknew, but he had appointed much worthier heralds of the truth to bring this people to the faith. (I, 22)

Goscelin, for his part, naturally saw no reason to dwell on the early church in Britain and summarized its history in four sentences, concluding:

But at length they were corrupted by luxury and arrogance, while they preferred vices to the yoke of the Lord and, being wiped out by the sword of the gentiles, and with only a few of them remaining, they were driven out of almost their entire native land, and were confined to the wooded and waste places. (chapter 32)

The version of the encounter that Bede presents is lengthy and complicated, with perceptible fluctuations in tone and emphasis:[29] the Britons, though in the wrong, are sometimes shown in a favourable light; while Augustine, though in the right, could be perceived as fatally flawed at a crucial juncture. Goscelin needed to create a version which was more even and relentlessly pro-Augustine. The basic flow of events is fundamentally similar in both accounts; however, the eleventh-century hagiographer manipulated the eighth-century record in various ways. For instance, he seems to stress his hero's mildness from the outset, possibly to counter any suggestion that the Roman missionary could have been haughty. Thus we are told that when first meeting with the British, Augustine introduces his arguments, 'with persuasive words of fatherly sweetness, and with totally heart-felt charity' (chapter 32). Goscelin places his personal stamp upon the narrative most obviously through verbiage and invented detail. Thus he turns Bede's pithy 'After a long dispute they were unwilling, in spite of the prayers, exhortations, and rebukes of Augustine and his companions to give their assent, preferring their own traditions to those in which all the churches throughout the world agree in Christ' (II, 2) into a lengthy and detailed rehearsal of all the arguments used on both sides. Similarly he gives a full and very dramatic description of the healing of the blind man by which Augustine makes plain to even the most doubtful Briton that his way has divine approval.

Another more subtle but perhaps more significant alteration made by Goscelin is that he presents Augustine's adversaries as considerably more intransigent and unreasonable than they appear in Bede's account. From the very first we learn: 'Yet the more mildly the Britons were asked, the more fiercely did they refuse . . . by no moderation of reason were they deflected' (chapter 32). When they arrive at the second meeting and Augustine does not stand up to greet them:

Then indeed they bristled with anger, indignation, scorn, repudiation, arguments and disputes. Nor could their barbaric fury be mitigated by any gentleness on Father Augustine's part. Not only would they not suffer to hear him, but truly they tried to refute and rebut all of his preaching. (chapter 35)

It was not possible for Goscelin to change history which had been authoritatively recorded by Bede in his widely distributed 'classic' account;[30] however, he could give his hero the benefit of presenting the facts in such a light that his shortcomings would seem insignificant – perhaps even positive traits – when compared to the obvious faults of his opponents. Goscelin's authorial comment upon the difficult episode is clear and unequivocal:

> Neither in sitting down nor in standing up is the man of God to be known, but in his gentleness of heart and his brotherly love, since it is possible to discover both the most merciful man sitting, and the most savage standing. Moreover, it might be considered unfitting to church law that by standing up he should inflame such wild and wrong-headed people, whom rather he should correct by censuring. (chapter 35)

While this episode, with which the hagiographer wrestled, *had* to be included because of its presence in the *Historia ecclesiastica*, one non-Bedan incident that Goscelin chose to relate does not, intriguingly, shed much light on Augustine at all. Before turning to the sorrowful yet glorious recital of the saint's final days we are given a mini-narrative devoted to Livinus, bishop and martyr. It is evident from the outset that the source for this was a *Vita Livini*, for having explained that Augustine had paid a visit to 'the most religious king of Ireland, Colomann' (chapter 48), it is not this remarkable, (though completely fictitious) far-flung episcopal visit which is highlighted, but rather the circumstance that while he was there Augustine baptized the boy Livinus, with the king, queen and nobles standing sponsors. The rest of the chapter is effectively a *Vita* of this young Irishman and his holy companions – with angelic apparitions, miraculous crossing of the sea dry-shod, and so on – while Augustine is only mentioned as someone from whom Livinus would receive instruction. Moreover, although Augustine was a spur and an inspiration to this young martyr in the making, Goscelin does not make very much of this. Why then, we might wonder, does he here follow a subsidiary source to the virtual exclusion of his main subject – particularly since Livinus does not appear in English martyrologies, litanies or calendars? However, Livinus *was* culted in Flanders where, it was alleged, he had been martyred, and his relics rested at Saint Peter's, Ghent; and herein lies the probable explanation. Given that Goscelin was a native of Flanders and had been a monk at Saint-Bertin, his inclusion of this largely gratuitous account of a local saint is perhaps explicable in terms of his own background and interests.[31]

If the treatment of Livinus seems largely irrelevant, or at best tangential, the very next chapter, by contrast, appears to present an exceptionally intimate view of Augustine – it purports to give an eyewitness portrait of the saint himself. Yet it is worth remembering that for a hagiographer like Goscelin the facts of real significance were the subject's spiritual activities as missionary, evangelist, miracle-worker and his pattern of christian living, not his mere physical appearance and other ephemeral matters.[32] And, on closer inspection, these details are not all that they may seem, even though they are presented in a disarmingly ingenuous manner. While Bede did present a physical portrait of the Roman missionary Paulinus – information which was accessible to him because of the latter's association with Northumbria[33] – he had no such personal details to relate about Augustine. Bede learnt of Paulinus's appearance from a 'trustworthy abbot', who had in turn received it from an old man, who had himself been baptized by the missionary. The supposed origin and transmission of the information that Goscelin has about Augustine is remarkably similar. He presents his account as a story that had been told by an old man, which had been faithfully handed down through his family, and which related his grandfather's first-hand encounter with, and baptism by Augustine, culminating in the description of the saint himself. With such a carefully preserved and documented oral tradition, the ensuing portrait would seem to be well authenticated and eminently convincing. Augustine, we are told, was distinguished by his nobility and uprightness of stature so that he towered above ordinary men, and by his open expression which inspired both love and respect. We even learn of the callouses upon his feet which, as an apostolic pilgrim, he had incurred through constant walking, often barefooted, as he took his mission to the provinces. Yet all is not as it seems: whatever the veracity of this tradition, which had doubtless been treasured at Saint Augustine's Abbey, various details suggest it has been heavily doctored by Goscelin himself. At one point, for instance, Augustine is likened for nobility of bearing to the biblical figure of King Saul. This is not an immediately obvious comparison, and it is a very improbable one for an early Anglo-Saxon convert to have made. It is, however, one that is highly likely to have come into the mind of someone who had just been reading the end of Book I of the *Historia ecclesiastica* – as we know Goscelin was doing at precisely this time – for there, placed between the description of Augustine's establishment of the see of Canterbury and the record of the saint's encounter with the British bishops, Bede likens the Anglo-Saxon king, Æthelfrith of Northumbria, to Saul (I, 34). Shortly thereafter Goscelin uses the intriguing phrase, '*frons fenestrata*' (literally 'a forehead furnished with windows') (chapter 49), to describe Augustine's open and frank countenance. Again, clearly this is the expression of a well-read hagiographer, not a sixth-century Anglo-Saxon. Goscelin was not the first to use this striking idea of the human face or soul 'furnished with windows' and thus being transparent and open to others: for the similar '*pectora fenestrata*' ('a windowed breast') appears in the introduction to the third book of Vitruvius's *De architectura*, where the author reported Socrates's thoughts about the desirability for openness in human affairs.[34] Now, this work was exceedingly rare in Anglo-Saxon and early post-Conquest England, and only one English manuscript of this period has come down to us. It is all the more interesting that the volume in question has been associated with the library of Saint Augustine's Abbey, and that it is old enough to have been consulted by Goscelin, supplying him with a flamboyant phrase with weighty overtones.[35]

The death of Augustine, as presented by Goscelin, is in keeping with the life he has tried to construct for him – a model of saintliness to inspire devotion and emulation among lesser Christians. Whereas Bede provided a brief factual account of Augustine's death and burial before continuing his story of the church in the south-east as a whole, the saint's end is necessarily the culmination of Goscelin's independent work. The hagiographer, unhampered by the lack of additional historical material, portrayed the events as they *should* have been. Thus, after telling us – following Bede – that the missionary, not wishing to leave his newly founded church unprotected and vulnerable, appointed Laurentius as his successor, Goscelin continues, with less specific authority, to relate how, as his last hours approached, Augustine was gripped by an intensified longing for heavenly things and an abhorrence of earthly ones. He then invents and describes the saint's end, or rather apotheosis, in typically grandiloquent style:

> Why should my narration shrink from describing his departure from this present light in lengthy circumlocution? At last, the most victorious athlete of the Lord arrived from the extended race of life at the heavenly reward and the long desired prizes of the eternal kingdom. Now with indescribable rejoicing and the sweet-scented sacrifice of thanks he was opened through illness to the promptings of the Lord. Then, deeply moved with fatherly affection, he exhorted not only the king and the leaders, but equally the clergy and the people to serve the Lord in fear and to continue unwaveringly in the faith of Christ which had been divinely entrusted to them, rather than in the foul profanities of devilish sacrifices; and to cling to the one, true and living God, with faith and perpetual love; and diligently to observe those things which he had commanded through his anointed bishop and the servants of the Lord. Thus came the end of the storms of this world, and the dawn of eternal happiness shone forth. And when he had blessed the king, and strengthened in Christ the infant church of his own creation, leaving behind for all pledges of everlasting love and proofs of a blessed life, among the tearful anguish of his holy friends and disciples, with blessed Laurentius standing by with a crowd of the people, he set down the burden of the flesh and was taken into heaven with

a triumph of celestial virtues and glory, being met and received by all inestimably, and with everlasting joy. O with what great solemnity was all of heaven adorned and crowned – that is, at the arrival of so distinguished a citizen! The ethereal squadrons surrounded the palm-bearing victor, the apostles invited their apostolic comrade to their seats, the empurpled camps of the martyrs encouraged the one bearing the sign of martyrdom, the splendid ranks of confessors and the venerable host of priests embraced the famous archbishop, and the shining band of virgins serenaded their virginal leader in sweet hymns . . . (chapter 51)

With Augustine's soul rapturously received into heaven, the 'precious pearl of his body' was, Goscelin tells us, placed in the church of the monastery that he himself had founded, and which was later to bear his name (chapter 52).[36] To the information in Bede's terse account Goscelin adds the reasonable conjecture that this was done in the presence of King Æthelberht and a great gathering of the people. Subsequently Augustine was joined there by the bodies of his successors who had come with the mission from Rome – whose lives Goscelin recounted at lesser length[37] – and, five centuries later, by that of St Mildreth of Thanet (whose *Vita* Goscelin also wrote).[38] Goscelin concludes his account of Augustine by recording the epitaph which was later placed adjacent to his resting place.

Stepping back from the details and considering Goscelin's presentation of Augustine as a whole, it is difficult to separate the man from the myth, the seventh-century evangelist from the eleventh-century icon and this was doubtless his express intention. Whereas Bede presented a narrative of the mission, slanted in favour of Gregory, which was based around a series of documents that incorporated information about Augustine, Goscelin expanded the historical facts and enriched them with other incidents centring upon Augustine to create a self-contained *Vita* that relates the missionary's own story and projects his sanctity. Goscelin was an effective hagiographer, skilful in crafting suitable vehicles for the interests and aspirations of the community in which he worked. At Wilton he had elevated and authenticated the Anglo-Saxon patron of that monastery, Edith, and her mother, Wulfthryth, so that their cults might flourish in the post-Conquest world.[39] At Saint Augustine's, Canterbury, just as the rebuilding of the abbey church advertised the importance of the beleaguered community, so his *Vitae* both honoured and promoted the saints who were not only central to its identity but were part of its actual spirituality.[40] If the rather obscure, though locally revered Mildreth of Thanet – whose relics along with the lands of her erstwhile monastery had come into the possession of Saint Augustine's after 1030 – merited an ornate and eulogistic *Vita* expressing her sanctity, how much more deserving of one was the saint who had not only established the abbey itself, but who had actually brought the christian faith to England? Whereas the scant facts of St Mildreth's life had to be extended by lengthy consideration of her royal and saintly pedigree, as well as the circumstances surrounding the foundation of the monastery with which she had been associated, and the rather meagre examples of her miraculous visionary powers related in grandiloquent prose with frequent allusions to scripture, Goscelin had much more material, factual or otherwise, to draw upon for his account of St Augustine. The resulting synthesis of historical material drawn from Bede and Gregory with anecdotal evidence from the west of England, Flanders and Angers, augmented with biblical parallels and resounding language, created within the genre a dynamic portrait. Here was a man who had confronted hostility and brought about remorse, who had achieved the conversion of a pagan people, who had argued eloquently and orthodoxly with unbelieving kings and erring bishops, and who in every word and deed had shown himself to be the direct successor of Christ and St Peter. Here, indeed, was a saint and, moreover, one who should command the respect not only of the members of the abbey he had founded, but also, in theory, of every Englishman and Christian!

The historical Augustine was an impressive figure who dedicated the last years of his life to a difficult mission.[41] He may have been sent on a venture that Gregory had reputedly wished to undertake himself, but he had proven himself more than equal to this extremely daunting task – he had borne most of the burden, and personally deserves most of the credit for its successes. Augustine may have received less than his due share of praise during the preceding centuries – not least because of the devotion of the Anglo-Saxons and above all of Bede to Pope Gregory – but in his *Vita* Goscelin had (at least for the monks of Saint Augustine's Abbey) finally put the record straight. Whether or not we agree with William of Malmesbury's generous assessment of Goscelin that 'in the celebration of the English saints he was second to none since Bede',[42] it is hard to fault his efforts in publicising and celebrating this previously undervalued figure, the missionary who was truly the 'Apostle of the English'.[43]

NOTES

1. The text followed here is perforce that of the edition found in *PL*, 80, cols 43–94. Where the meaning of a particular phrase was of crucial importance, it has been checked against the earliest manuscript of the work, BL, Cotton Vesp. B. xx (dating from the beginning of the twelfth century) and also the later copy BL, Harley 105 (from the mid- to third quarter of the twelfth century). This exercise showed, incidentally, that the *PL* text was broadly reliable, though erroneous and occasionally seriously misleading readings did occur. Interpretation was not made easier by

having to decipher the text with a reading machine using a nearly illegible photocopy of the notoriously poorly printed *PL* version. The promised edition of this and other works of Goscelin by R. Sharpe will undoubtedly make this work more accessible.

2. See the discussion of Goscelin's life in *The Life of King Edward who Rests at Westminster*, ed. F. Barlow (London and Edinburgh, 1962), pp. 91–111.

3. See references to Augustine as 'Apostle of the English' in Alan Thacker's contribution, ch. 14 above. In the oldest manuscript collection of Goscelin's texts treating Augustine and others, BL, Cotton Vesp. B. xx (cf. fig. 15.1), the contemporary *incipit* to the *Historia minor* (fol. 5r) reads '*Incipit libellus de adventu beatissimi Anglorum apostolorum Augustini sociorumque eius in Brittaniam et de ipsius virtutibus*'. The later copy, Harley 105, has a similar *incipit*, introducing the volume as a whole (fol. 5v).

4. Much is made of the image of the light of the faith that Augustine brought: 'Augustine illuminated, with his moon-like torch, the gloomy world of the unbeliever and the dark chaos of the Ocean' (Goscelin, ch. 1).

5. Whereas Sulpicius Severus (d. *c.* 430) continually asserts the veracity of the stories in his *Vita Sancti Martini*, Goscelin, a more sophisticated hagiographer, does not even raise the possibility that what he is relating is not simply the truth.

6. Even in his separate work, the *Miracula*, there is a dearth of early material: most of the episodes that are recorded come from the eleventh century. If more material had been preserved up to the early eighth century it would presumably have been included among 'whatever seemed worth remembering' that was supplied by Albinus to Bede (*HE*, preface) – though as Alan Thacker points out (ch. 14 above), Theodore, who was Albinus's 'master', may have developed the cult of Gregory at the expense of Augustine.

7. The case for the charismatic dimension of Augustine's personality is put by I. Wood, 'Augustine and Aidan: bureaucrat and charismatic', *Saint Augustin de Cantorbéry à Arles*, ed. C. de Dreuille (Arles, forthcoming).

8. See Bede, II, 5–6.

9. See the discussions by Richard Gameson and Alan Thacker in chs 1 and 14 above. The Anglo-Saxon veneration of Gregory is treated by Anton Scharer in ch. 9 above.

10. The chronological order as represented here is that of Goscelin not Bede. The latter presents the papal encounter with the English slaves and its resulting evangelical inspiration in his encomium on Gregory which commemorates his death (II, 1), after describing the success of the mission.

11. Not only is it more probable that he was consecrated in Frankia during his initial journey to England, but it is certain that Etherius was bishop of Lyons and not of Arles as Bede thought (Bede, I, 26). For a succinct summary of the issues see J.M. Wallace-Hadrill, *Bede's Ecclesiastical History of the English People: a historical commentary* (Oxford, 1988), pp. 31–2, 38–9, 42.

12. See the list of his works in R. Sharpe, *A Handlist of the Latin Writers of Great Britain and Ireland before 1540* (Turnhout, 1997), pp. 151-4.

13. Bede, I, 23; Goscelin, ch. 7. See Gregorius Magnus, *Registrum epistularum*, ed. D. Norberg, 2 vols (Turnhout, 1982), VI, 53, with apparatus.

14. For a discussion of this dossier and its content see Richard Gameson and Rob Meens, chs 1 and 8 above.

15. Gregory, *Reg. ep.*, VIII, 30.

16. Gregory, *Reg. ep.*, XI, 35.

17. Gregory, *Reg. ep.*, XI, 36.

18. A popular perception of miracles, as expressed by an earlier English author writing about no less a figure than Gregory himself, is relevant in this context: 'Miracles are granted for the destruction of the idols of unbelieving pagans, or sometimes to confirm the weak faith of believers; most of all, they are granted to those who instruct the pagans, and so, the more gloriously and frequently they are manifested in those lands, the more convincing they become as teachers.' See *The Earliest Life of Gregory the Great*, ch. 4, ed. and trans. B. Colgrave (Kansas, 1968), p. 79.
19. Among the letters Gregory supplied to the reinforcements of 601 is one addressed to seven Frankish bishops, including Licinus of Angers (Gregory, *Reg. ep.*, XI, 41); but this does not necessarily imply that Augustine had visited the town.
20. See *The Life of King Edward*, ed. Barlow, pp. 93–100; also S.J. Ridyard, *The Royal Saints of Anglo-Saxon England* (Cambridge, 1988), p. 39.
21. It would appear that the belligerent natives hung fish tails on the saint and his companions!
22. See E. Ekwall, *The Concise Oxford Dictionary of Place-names*, 4th edn (Oxford, 1960), p. 93, where it is suggested the name derives from the Welsh for 'rock'.
23. Gregory, *Reg. ep.*, XI, 39.
24. This is taken from Gregory's letter to Eulogius, patriarch of Alexandria, which does not appear in Bede: *Reg. ep.*, VIII, 30.
25. For a brief but authoritative overview of the primacy dispute see Hugh the Chanter, *The History of the Church of York 1066–1127*, ed. C. Johnson, rev. by M. Brett, C.N.L. Brooke and M. Winterbottom (Oxford, 1990), pp. xxx–xlv.
26. Acts 3:6. At a time when the institutional church was condemning simony with renewed vigour and individuals were seeking to live a *vita apostolica*, these words placed in the mouth of Augustine may have had additional resonance.
27. Several, though by no means all of the incidents recounted in the *Miracula* are localized to Canterbury and the neighbouring villages.
28. See *Liber miraculorum sancte Fidis*, I, 1: *The Book of Sainte Foy*, trans. P. Sheingorn (Philadelphia, 1995), pp. 43–51.
29. See the discussion by Clare Stancliffe, ch. 6 above.
30. For a succinct discussion of the popularity of Bede's work between 1066 and 1130 see R.G. Gameson, *The Manuscripts of Early Norman England c. 1066–1130* (London, 1999), pp. 32–7.
31. It would appear that not just the *Vita* but the very existence of Livinus is spurious. He is probably to be identified with the eighth-century English missionary to the continent, Lebuinus or Liafwine (both Livinus and Lebuinus share 12 November as their feast day): see H. Thurston and D. Attwater (eds), *Butler's Lives of the Saints*, 4 vols (London, 1954), IV, 12 November . Texts relating to Livinus are inventoried by the Bollandists in *Bibliotheca Hagiographica Latina Antiquae et Mediae Aetatis* (Brussels, 1901), nos 4960–3; those for Lebuinus are nos 4811–14.
32. See, *inter alia*, M. Lapidge, 'The Saintly Life in Anglo-Saxon England', in M. Godden and M. Lapidge (eds), *The Cambridge Companion to Old English Literature* (Cambridge, 1991), pp. 243–63.
33. See Bede, II, 16.
34. Vitruvius, *De architectura*, ed. and trans. F. Granger, 2 vols (Cambridge, Mass., 1931–4), III, preface.
35. For the manuscript transmission in general of the *De architectura* see L.D. Reynolds (ed.) *Texts and Transmission* (Oxford, 1983),

pp. 440–45, esp. p. 443. The text was clearly very rare in Anglo-Saxon England. There is only one copy of pre-Conquest date which is possibly of English origin: now part A (fols 2–82 + 1 unnumbered blank) of the composite volume, BL, Cotton Cleo. D. i; the first scribe has an English hand (the others have northern French or Flemish ones). The late medieval provenance of this and the following part of the volume was Saint Augustine's Abbey. It is worth noting that this work does not appear in the lost (?), early twelfth-century library catalogue of Saint-Bertin: see G. Becker, *Catalogi Bibliothecarum Antiqui* (Bonn, 1885), no. 77.

36. For the history and development of the abbey, see the contribution of Richard Emms, ch. 16 below.

37. See *Vitae SS. Laurentii, Melliti, Iusti, Honorii, Deusdedit,* also in BL, Cotton Vesp. B. xx, and Harley 105, but unedited.

38. Edited in D.W. Rollason, *The Mildrith Legend: a study in early medieval hagiography in England* (Leicester, 1982), pp. 105–43.

39. See 'La Légende de Ste Edith en prose et vers par le moine Goscelin', ed. A. Wilmart, *Analecta Bollandiana*, 56 (1938), pp. 5–101, 265–307; see also Ridyard, *The Royal Saints,* pp. 38–44, 140–75.

40. See further R. Sharpe, 'The Setting of St Augustine's Translation, 1091', in R. Eales and R. Sharpe (eds), *Canterbury and the Norman Conquest: churches, saints and scholars, 1066–1109* (London, 1995), pp. 1–13.

41. See Richard Gameson, ch. 1 above.

42. William of Malmesbury, *Gesta regum Anglorum,* IV, 344, eds R.A.B. Mynors, R.M. Thomson, and M. Winterbottom (Oxford, 1998), p. 592.

43. I would like to express my warmest appreciation of the editor's patience, encouragement and invaluable assistance during the writing of this chapter which was undertaken at a very late stage in the preparation of this volume.

CHAPTER 16

The Early History of Saint Augustine's Abbey, Canterbury

Richard Emms

FROM THE BEGINNINGS TO THE DEATH OF ALBINUS (C. 732)

This chapter explores aspects of the history of Saint Augustine's Abbey, Canterbury, from its foundation up to the year 1100 (fig. 16.1). It should be said at the outset that the available sources do not allow a continuous history to be written. The references, based on Canterbury tradition, incorporated in Bede's *Historia ecclesiastica* and the copies of the Anglo-Saxon charters found in later cartularies and chronicles are fundamental material; nevertheless they leave many gaps. No saints' lives associated with the abbey (apart from Old English fragments relating to St Mildreth) survive from before the Conquest. It was not until the end of the eleventh century that the experienced hagiographer Goscelin produced a corpus of such material and although he used the conventions of hagiography with great skill, he was clearly working from a meagre factual basis; consequently any information about the early figures which cannot be verified from other sources, notably Bede, should be treated with great caution. When reporting events of his own time, however, such as the translation of the relics of the saints into the new Romanesque church, Goscelin becomes a primary authority of great importance. The later chroniclers of the abbey, Thomas Sprott (late thirteenth century), William Thorne (late fourteenth century) and Thomas of Elmham (early fifteenth century) are secondary authorities for our period, which was far distant from their own; moreover, they often used sources which had been altered to promote the interests of the abbey in its disputes with the archbishops. Fascinating though it is, the historical tradition of Saint Augustine's embodied in their work misleads more often than helps us in relation to the pre-Conquest period. The destruction of the early buildings of the abbey in successive reconstructions, above all in the late eleventh century, has obscured the

16.1. General view of the remains of the abbey church of Saint Augustine's, looking east. (Gameson)

details of their forms; and although excellent work has been done based on the excavated remains, the absence of full archaeological reports of the excavations carried out at the site in the first half of the twentieth century makes their interpretation problematical. Fuller investigation of comparative material, particularly from Winchester and Worcester might, it is true, yield information of value for the early history of Saint Augustine's: however, such work lies beyond the scope of this brief and necessarily selective survey, the emphasis of which inevitably reflect the vagaries of the sources.[1]

There can be no doubt that the church of SS Peter and Paul (which, with the additional churches dedicated to St Mary and to St Pancras, later came to be known as Saint Augustine's) was founded by Augustine himself. Bede wrote in his *Historia ecclesiastica*, 'He [Augustine] also founded a monastery not far from the city, in which Æthelberht, encouraged by him, built from its foundations the church of the apostles St Peter and St Paul and endowed it with various gifts, so that the bodies of Augustine himself and all the bishops of Canterbury and kings of Kent might be placed in it.'[2] This statement, based on information supplied by Albinus, abbot of Saint Augustine's (d. 732) is convincing. On this point, at least, there is no good reason for doubting the accuracy of the Canterbury tradition. The attribution of the actual building of the church to King Æthelberht of Kent, who provided the necessary resources, shows that he should be regarded as co-founder. Although the date of the foundation remains uncertain, it is unlikely to have been in the earliest years of the mission and was probably not before the return from Rome in 601/2 of the priest Peter, who was its first abbot. However, we know that the church of SS Peter and Paul was not completed until after Augustine had died (604x9), as the consecration was carried out by Laurentius, his successor as archbishop of Canterbury.[3]

The reason for the foundation of the church of SS Peter and Paul given by Bede was to provide a burial church both for the kings of Kent and for the bishops of Canterbury (fig. 16.2; cf. fig. 14.2). Burials within the city walls were still regarded, as in Roman times, as inappropriate. It is possible that, in establishing a burial church outside the walls of the city, King Æthelberht was influenced by Merovingian practice. St Geneviève, at that time dedicated to SS Peter and Paul, was the royal burial church outside the walls of Paris. He may well have been familiar with such arrangements, not least because of his Merovingian wife, Bertha.[4] Bede did not mention a monastic function for the new church, but perhaps he took it for granted that Augustine and his followers would keep a monastic rule. It has also been suggested that they were influenced by arrangements in Rome, where monks joined secular clergy for the main daytime offices, but took responsibility for short offices during the day as well as for

16.2. Excavated north porticus of the abbey church of SS Peter and Paul, showing the sites of three (arch)episcopal tombs. (Gameson)

nocturns.[5] Be that as it may, it is likely that in the early years the new cathedral and monastery in Canterbury worked closely together; and it is probable that both Merovingian practice and the arrangements between churches in Rome influenced the nature of the new foundation.

The church of SS Peter and Paul was located in relation to the existing late Roman cemetery outside the city walls; it lay between the Roman church which is presumed to have occupied the site of the later cathedral on the one hand and on the other, the church of St Martin, used by Queen Bertha, her chaplain Bishop Liudhard and such Christians as there were in Canterbury before the arrival of Augustine's mission (cf. pl. II).[6] Though situated in relation to existing monuments, SS Peter and Paul was both the first church building to be constructed *de novo* as a result of the Augustinian mission, and the first English 'minster' to be established. The identity of those who actually built this highly significant church is undocumented but the most likely hypothesis is that King Æthelberht engaged Frankish workmen with experience of building in stone. The building comprised a rectangular nave surrounded on the north and south sides by a series of side chambers (*porticus*) and terminating at the east end in a rounded apse. The *porticus* were used for the burial of the bishops from Augustine himself onwards (later in the seventh century, archbishops) and for the burial of the members of the Kentish royal house, beginning, of course, with King Æthelberht. A few years after completion of the church of SS Peter and Paul, King Eadbald, Æthelberht's son and successor (616–40), who had returned to the christian faith after a period of apostasy, sponsored further building work, constructing the church of St Mary immediately to the east of the original basilica. Although the only archaeological evidence for this building is the lower part of the west wall of the nave, it is likely that St Mary's was similar in design to SS Peter and Paul, though smaller in scale. This church became the burial place for some abbots of the foundation. We can be confident that in addition to the churches, a number of small, domestic buildings must have been constructed in these early years, but no traces of these structures, which were probably of wood, have been found. The other surviving early remains, indeed the best preserved, are from the enigmatic church of St Pancras: either built *de novo* or reconstructed in the seventh century, it provided the monastery with three churches in alignment, an arrangement which could be paralleled in Gaul and was subsequently used elsewhere in England.[7]

There can be no doubt that King Æthelberht and his successors in the first half of the seventh century supplied their new monastic foundation with substantial estates. Charters purporting to show these are, as is well known, forgeries from around the end of the eleventh century (cf. fig. 15.1). However, the fact that the abbey did, by the time of Domesday Book, hold large estates in east Kent, such as Sturry, Chislet and Northbourne, without written title, suggests that the lands in question were very early grants.[8] It would have been impossible to acquire such substantial holdings in later Anglo-Saxon times, and still more after the Conquest, without leaving some traces in charters. The kings of Kent clearly provided Saint Augustine's with a solid economic base, which helped the community to survive in the difficult times of the late eighth and ninth centuries and made its later achievements possible.[9]

Little can be said of the half century between 620 and 670. The names of the abbots from this period are known, but not what they did to develop the young community.[10] Thereafter the situation changes. When Nathanael, the sixth abbot, died in 667 there followed a vacancy, during part of which Benedict Biscop, best known for his founding of Wearmouth and Jarrow, may have directed the monastery. Then Hadrian, companion of Archbishop Theodore, arrived (probably in 670), to begin an abbacy which lasted nearly forty years. He was a Greek-speaking North African who had fled to Naples at an early date and become known to both the Byzantine emperor, Constans II (641–68) and to the Pope, Vitalian (657–72). He might himself have been sent to England as archbishop of Canterbury had he not instead recommended his older and more experienced friend, Theodore, for the position in his place.[11] However, Bede tells us, Vitalian insisted that Hadrian should accompany Theodore to England. The two made a most effective team, providing leadership in the English church and developing a famous school in Canterbury. While this doubtless enhanced the literary resources and prestige of Saint Augustine's, the practical effects of such activity for the day-to-day life and running of the abbey remain unclear. Cathedral and abbey must have co-operated closely; but questions such as whether classes were held on both sites are unanswerable. The cultural life of the abbey was enriched by Hadrian's presence; no doubt books were both imported and copied in the abbey, but the surviving evidence is slight.

The grant of exemption from episcopal control made to the abbey by Pope Agatho in 679 x 80 is agreed to have a genuine basis; this could be understood as recognition of Hadrian's eminence and ability.[12] The *Textus S. Adriani* referred to by later Saint Augustine's writers as an authoritative source has unfortunately been lost, but the first strata of English additions to the Gospels of St Augustine, which probably date from the late seventh or early eighth century, may provide some first-hand evidence of the school's activities.[13] After the death of Archbishop Theodore (690), Hadrian was the senior figure in the school, a role which he may have passed on to his disciple and successor as abbot of Saint Augustine's, Albinus (d. 732). Bede's high opinion of the latter's intellectual abilities suggest that he carried on the school successfully; and, if this were so, it seems reasonable to presume that it was now centred more on the abbey than on the cathedral. In encouraging Bede to write his *Historia ecclesiastica* and in passing him both written and oral information, Albinus was the first Saint Augustine's monk known to have strong historical interests. The oldest existing book that was probably produced in Canterbury, the Vespasian Psalter, may date from the end of Albinus's abbacy (pls VII–VIII; figs 13.13–14). If the assumption is correct, this small but luxurious psalter attests to the existence of a scriptorium with very high standards, and the compilation of the prefatory texts from a range of at least three sources sheds a little light on the editorial activities of the Canterbury school.[14]

From Albinus to c. 942

Around the middle of the eighth century Saint Augustine's lost its role as the burial church for the archbishops. This seems clear even though most of the details, which depend on much later partisan sources, are open to question. The Saint Augustine's historical tradition, as recorded by William Thorne at the end of the fourteenth century, regarded the change as a 'vulpine fraud' carried through at the instigation of Archbishop Cuthbert (d. 760), who instructed his household to say nothing of his final illness and subsequent death until his body was buried in the newly built church of St John the Baptist adjoining the cathedral. William Thorne, still angry (some 650 years later) at the turn of events, told how Abbot Aldhun and his monks, on hearing of the death of Archbishop Cuthbert, came to claim the body for burial at Saint Augustine's only to find that they were too late: the archbishop's body had already been buried in the new church belonging to the cathedral.[15] Thereafter, the only archbishop to be buried at Saint Augustine's was Iaenberht (d. 792), a former abbot who, disapproving of the change of site, tried in vain to revive the old custom.

What lay behind this change? Certainly burial customs were altering and by the mid-eighth century the objections to burials inside the city likely to have been put forward by sixth-century Italian churchmen would have ceased to carry weight. Further, it is possible that the earlier close co-operation between cathedral and monastery was breaking down in the face of changing circumstances. The broader context was that the power of Mercia was threatening the independence of the kingdom of Kent – something reflected in the appointment of Mercians to the archbishopric – which may have led in turn to a more competitive relationship between the two major ecclesiastical institutions in Canterbury. It may even have been the case (*pace* the later chroniclers) that 150 years after its foundation Saint Augustine's had come to see itself as a monastic church rather than as a burial church and was prepared to allow the custom to lapse. The demise of the Kentish royal family in the 760s certainly ensured that there were no more kings to be buried there.[16]

It is difficult to estimate the effects of rule from outside Kent, first Mercian, then West Saxon, on Saint Augustine's. Charters indicate that some grants of land were made during the hundred years after the 760s, but of course neither the Mercian nor West Saxon royal houses took the interest in Saint Augustine's that had been shown by the kings of Kent.[17] On the other hand, the Kentish nobility continued to provide landed endowments; and the result was that up to the time of Domesday Book at least, Saint Augustine's held no land outside the county of Kent. Indeed the great majority of its holdings were in the east of the county.[18]

It was during the ninth century that the name Saint Augustine's came to be employed frequently for the community, the first recorded use being in a charter of 826.[19] The reasons for this are not clear: one may suggest that it was a side effect of the development of the cult of St Augustine, something which appears to have been taking place during the eighth century.[20] Certainly the designation Saint Augustine's readily distinguished the abbey from the many other churches dedicated either to St Peter or to SS Peter and Paul.[21]

That cultural activity continued to flourish at Saint Augustine's into the ninth century is shown by the production there of a fine Bible, a fragment of which remains in BL, Royal 1.E. vi (pl. VI; figs 11.3–5). Even though the context for this project is obscure, it nevertheless attests to a scriptorium of high standards that both used the venerable models at its disposal and was alive to contemporary developments.[22] Yet, if literary activity survived longer at Saint Augustine's than elsewhere, it was not immune to the pressures of the times, the most obvious being the Viking invasions. Saint Augustine's is likely to have suffered from Viking raids, as for instance when Canterbury was attacked in 851. Even if the abbey was wealthy enough to buy off such assaults, thus escaping destruction, its position outside the walls made it vulnerable and certainly more so than Christ Church. Nevertheless, although we know next to nothing about the nature and activities of the community during this time, the unbroken list of abbots through the later ninth and early tenth centuries has generally been taken to indicate continuity of the community through this most difficult period for English monasteries. This deduction still stands, even though the names and dates of abbots have been altered over the years by later Saint Augustine's writers trying to solve the chronological problems they posed.[23] The suggestion that there was a peculiarly close connection between the personnel of cathedral and abbey during these years cannot be proved, though it may be that adverse circumstances drove them together. The significance of the term 'priest-abbot' used in the ninth-century charters remains uncertain. At least there is no record of refoundation in the tenth century, so it can be concluded that, in spite of the problems, the community maintained a continuous existence.[24]

By the time of King Æthelstan (d. 939) when we have slightly more source material, the abbey was not merely existing but was also receiving a share in the profits of the mint at Canterbury. The king's law-code issued at Grately (926 × 30) contains a well-known reference to the seven moneyers at Canterbury, four of whom appertained to the king, two to the bishop and one to the abbot of Saint Augustine's.[25] No other abbot was mentioned, which suggests a special position for Saint Augustine's. From the same period we have evidence of scribal activity at the abbey in the form of a charter entered into a formerly blank space in the Gospels of St Augustine (fig. 16.3). This copy of a mid-ninth century Old English charter granting food-rent from land in Brabourne to the community of Saint Augustine is likely to have been placed in the gospel book to strengthen the sanctions against the current owner who may have been in dispute with the abbey.[26] Such hints give the impression of a community which was well established and fairly vigorous even before the rise of the tenth-century reform movement which was responsible for reviving many other southern foundations.

FROM C. 942 TO THE ACCESSION OF ABBOT ÆLFSTAN (1023 × 7)

If Saint Augustine's Abbey, Canterbury was one of very few, or even the only monastic community to enjoy continuity of existence through the ninth and tenth centuries, it might have been expected to play a leading part in the revival of Benedictine monasticism that affected southern England in the mid-tenth century. Earlier monasteries that had ceased to exist at some point in the ninth century were revived; occasionally changes were rapid as when in the 960s Bishop Æthelwold expelled the secular canons from the Old and New Minsters, Winchester, to replace them with

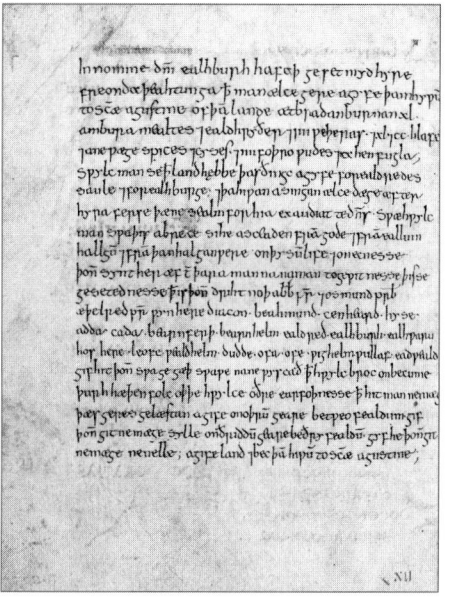

16.3. *CCCC, 286, fol. 74v. Charter added to the 'Gospels of St Augustine'. (Mildred Budny & The Master and Fellows of Corpus Christi College, Cambridge)*

reformed Benedictine monks.[27] As is the case with the great majority of pre-Conquest English monasteries, there is no record of any such revolutionary actions at Saint Augustine's. The changes that took place within the community were presumably gradual – and hence almost imperceptible to us – as its aims came into line with the ideals of the tenth-century reformers described in the *Regularis Concordia*.[28] It might have been expected that when he became archbishop (*c.* 959–88), Dunstan, the elder statesman of the reformers, would have played a part in the reform of Saint Augustine's; however, it is questionable whether he had much to do with the reform of the cathedral, and the one record of him visiting the abbey, an occasion on which he saw a vision in the church of St Mary, made no reference to reform.[29] Yet he was credited with the rededication of 978, when the dedication to St Augustine, already used at times over the previous 150 years, was confirmed.[30]

There is, however, fairly plentiful internal evidence for prosperity and spiritual fervour during this period. A western extension to the church of SS Peter and Paul, including a narthex and forecourt, was made, presumably in the years before 978.[31] Traces of an early, possibly tenth-century cloister, have also been found – although in the absence of a full excavation report this evidence cannot be used with confidence.[32] Surviving manuscripts reveal that the scriptorium of Saint Augustine's was extremely active from the mid-tenth century and the hands of some forty scribes have been identified in the extant volumes.[33] However, some of the books in question are intimately connected with Benedictine monasticism – notably a copy of the Rule of St Benedict and related documents, which is now BL, Harley 5431 (fig. 16.4) – suggesting that Saint Augustine's was fully committed to Benedictine ideals at the time of its production.[34] Thus even though documentary references shed little light on the changing nature of the community in the tenth century, architectural and scribal evidence suggests that it was active, prosperous and essentially Benedictine. Royal support for monastic

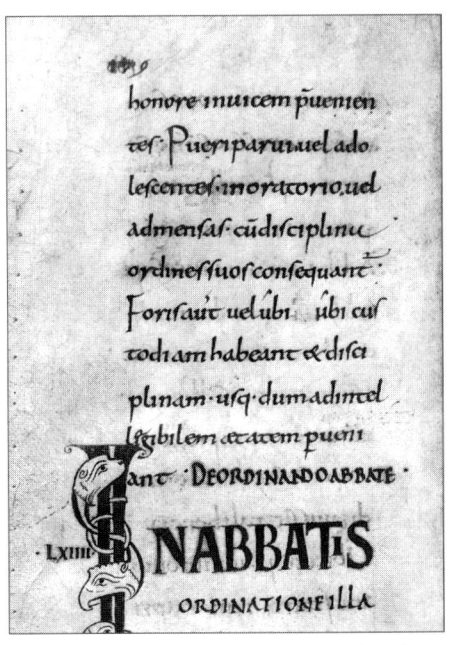

16.4. *BL, Harley 5431, fol. 85v (detail). Later tenth-century Saint Augustine's Abbey copy of the* Rule of St Benedict. *(British Library)*

reform, strong in the heartlands of Wessex, was much weaker in Canterbury, and Saint Augustine's may have been left to reform itself using the resources of its own community.

The renewed Danish attacks during the reign of King Æthelred provided a severe test for reformed monasteries. The heavy costs of buying off the Danes on various occasions meant that resources were tight. In September 1011 the Danish army besieged Canterbury and entered the city through the treachery of Ælfmær, who is generally identified with the abbot of that name. Since the *Anglo-Saxon Chronicle* recorded that the Danes allowed Abbot Ælfmær to escape, it has often been suggested that he bought the safety of his monastery at a cost of letting the Danes into the city.[35] However, there are problems with this interpretation. First, since Saint Augustine's lay outside the walls, the abbot was not well placed to let the Danes into the city itself. Secondly, writing in the twelfth century, John of Worcester added that the Ælfmær who betrayed the city was an archdeacon, not the abbot of the same name; and this sounds convincing as he would have lived inside the walls and would thus have been better placed to facilitate the Danish entry.[36] Yet, whatever the truth of the matter, Abbot Ælfmær must have made a deal with the Danes, otherwise the destruction of Saint Augustine's, outside the walls and defenceless, would have been inevitable. The monks did not commit the affair to the collective memory of the community, preferring to believe that their patron saint had saved them, effectively closing the matter to historical enquiry. William Thorne attributed the survival of the monastery to a miracle in which the pall covering the tomb of St Augustine clung so strongly to the Dane who tried to carry it away that it could not be moved until the thief had confessed his guilt.[37] Thus the details of what happened have been unfortunately lost to us, as have the effects on the community of this Danish attack.

From Abbot Ælfstan to c. 1100

There can be no doubt that Ælfstan, who became abbot of Saint Augustine's around the mid-1020s was a man of outstanding ability and determination who left the abbey stronger and wealthier as a result of his activities. His acquisition of the remains of St Mildreth, the site of the former abbey of Minster-in-Thanet, and its estates was an achievement of great importance which added significantly to the spiritual and economic resources of the abbey.

Our information comes from Goscelin of Saint-Bertin, the best known hagiographer of the late eleventh century, who after staying at various abbeys writing the lives of their saints, spent the last twenty or so years of his life at

Saint Augustine's. In the 1090s he wrote a *Life of St Mildreth*, an account of the translation of her relics, and a refutation of the claim of the canons of the newly founded house of St Gregory to hold these relics. Goscelin's partisan approach and his extensive use of the conventions of hagiography have to be kept in mind when evaluating his evidence, but when such allowances have been made, his account of the translation contains some valuable and reliable details.[38]

Goscelin carefully set the scene for the translation by listing the rulers of the time, perhaps following the example of Luke's Gospel (3:1). Not all of these were correct; however, his dating of the translation itself to 18 May 1030 is convincing.[39] Whitsunday, when Abbot Ælfstan went to Minster to celebrate the feast was on 17 May that year. It was during that night, following the conventions of *furta sacra*, that the relics were removed from the tomb, and it was therefore Monday 18 May when the abbot and his party triumphantly arrived in Canterbury bearing the prized relics, with the monks shouting: '*Mildretha nobis venit beata; beata venit nobis Mildretha*'. Goscelin included some vivid details in his story: early on the Monday morning the abbot and his party pursued by angry islanders who had discovered the theft, just managed to reach the ferry at Sarre to return to the mainland before being caught.[40] While there may be general parallels to such a story in other earlier saints' lives, it is quite possible that stories like this one – reflecting contemporary perception of events – were preserved in the memory of the community at Saint Augustine's more than sixty years later. Other documentary evidence relating to the acquisition of St Mildreth and her property is of less value. The writ of King Cnut purporting to grant the body of St Mildreth with all her land is not authentic in its present form, and it is open to question whether it reflects the substance of a genuine document issued by him.[41]

Abbot Ælfstan's success in acquiring the lands and relics of St Mildreth was not matched by success in a further ambitious project – to gain an interest in the port of Sandwich for his abbey. A charter presented on a contemporary single sheet told the story vividly, though from a point of view hostile to Ælfstan.[42] King Harold Harefoot had taken over Sandwich from Christ Church, and Ælfstan had succeeded by means of his crafty devices and his gold and silver in acquiring from the king's steward the third penny of the toll at Sandwich. When King Harold was lying ill at Oxford, the cathedral community sent a messenger seeking the restitution of this valuable port. The king swore that the alienation was not the result of his instructions, and it became clear that Abbot Ælfstan had been scheming 'behind the scenes'. When the king had ordered that all his rights at Sandwich should be restored to Christ Church, Ælfstan asked the archbishop of Canterbury, Eadsige, to support his attempt to regain the third penny. Surprisingly the archbishop agreed, but the community of Christ Church would

16.5. Abbey church of Saint Augustine's, looking west. (Gameson)

not consider supporting him. Ælfstan, who would not accept defeat, then asked permission to build a wharf in Sandwich opposite 'St. Mildreth's field' on the island of Thanet. The Christ Church community again refused, after which Ælfstan sent workers to build a harbour at Ebbsfleet on the island across the water from Sandwich. In spite of heroic efforts, the project was finally abandoned, presumably because the movement of gravel by the sea made the plan impracticable. For his part, the Christ Church writer was convinced that the undertaking was against the will of Christ. This incident provides remarkable insight into Ælfstan's character, and shows to what lengths an abbot could go to add to the wealth of his abbey. It is not surprising that, after this great effort, Ælfstan retired from his abbey in 1045 because of infirmity; Wulfric was consecrated abbot in his place.[43]

Wulfric was also a man of ability and vision. He was one of two English abbots who attended the council of Reims on 1049 'so that they might inform the king of whatever was decided in the interests of Christendom'.[44] Goscelin claimed that Abbot Wulfric was given a seat next to the abbot of Monte Cassino,[45] however, Anselm of Reims' description of the order in which the abbots sat, placed Wulfric fifteenth.[46] So this is an instance in which Goscelin can be seen bending the facts, perhaps following the traditions of the community, in order to increase the prestige of Saint Augustine's. Wulfric took advantage of this opportunity to speak to the Pope about his plans for enlarging the buildings of his abbey and duly received the latter's blessing on them. His plan was ambitious: he intended to join up the churches of SS Peter and Paul and St Mary by means of a rotunda, perhaps with a tower above (fig. 16.5).[47] The line of separate churches at Saint Augustine's (now four in number with the addition of a church to the west of SS Peter and Paul in the eleventh century), was looking outdated by the middle of the century when much larger church buildings were becoming fashionable, particularly on the continent. It is not clear why Wulfric's plan was not brought to completion. He was abbot until his death in 1061, twelve years after the council of Reims. So it was not that he did not have the time, and the community was certainly not short of resources. Perhaps opinion in the abbey turned against the development after it had been started; alternatively, the example of the huge new church being built for Westminster Abbey under the aegis of Edward the Confessor may have persuaded Wulfric that his idea was too conservative and that a complete rebuilding on a grand scale would be better. Perhaps he lost faith in his plan, but did not dare destroy the old buildings in order to build a great church. Certainly, Wulfric's death was ascribed by Goscelin to the displeasure of the Virgin Mary at the partial destruction of her church.[48] The dedication of this building appears to have made it even more sacred than the original church of SS Peter and Paul.

In 1061 Æthelsige, a monk of St Swithun's, Winchester, was chosen by the king to succeed Wulfric, whose building project he left well alone.[49] Goscelin related that Æthelsige went on a mission to Rome in 1063, and was there granted the privilege of wearing mitre and sandals, thus making his abbey exempt from episcopal control.[50] While such a grant was not impossible, it would have been extremely surprising at the time, given that the abbot of Cluny, for example, was not granted this right until 1088.[51] The story appears to fit better into the period of conflict around 1090 than into the 1060s when relations between Archbishop Stigand and Saint Augustine's were cordial. The statement in the *Liber Eliensis* that Stigand held Saint Augustine's does not find support in local sources.[52] William Thorne described with evident approval the gift of a large cross by Stigand to the abbey in 1064;[53] for Saint Augustine's, at least, his patronage appears to have been benign.

The *Liber Eliensis* also described how the abbots of Ely, Glastonbury and Saint Augustine's each took four months of the year working for the king as 'Chancellor'. No other evidence for such a system has been found and modern scholars have not been able to account satisfactorily for this passage.[54] Certainly abbots were expected on particular occasions to do business for the king, but the Ely writer was claiming far more than that. He was of course writing more than a hundred years later and this information cannot be taken at face value. On the other hand, it is worth noting that a twelfth-century Ely writer saw nothing incongruous in crediting such an important role to the pre-Conquest abbots of Saint Augustine's. As a whole, the career of Æthelsige remains enigmatic. After the Conquest his position was compromised by his association with Stigand: he may have been involved in opposition to King William I and so fled to Denmark.[55] A writ of William I, dated 14 July 1077, referred archly to him as '*abbas Alsinus fugitivus meus*,' accusing him of giving away land or allowing it to be alienated through carelessness, fear or greed.[56] We cannot tell why the Conqueror referred to him as 'my fugitive' nor whether there was substance in the accusations. If he was the Ælfsige who became abbot of Ramsey in 1080, the king must have forgiven him by then.[57]

It is not definitely known when Æthelsige left his post, but it is certain that in 1070 Scotland, a monk of the abbey of Mont Saint-Michel in Normandy, was chosen by the king as abbot of Saint Augustine's.[58] Although he was not formally installed by Archbishop Lanfranc until 1071–2, he may have taken charge of the abbey from 1070, perhaps to deal with pressing problems.[59] Scotland turned out to be a firm and effective ruler who recovered lost lands, and undertook a complete rebuilding of the abbey church. This involved the gradual demolition of the earlier line of churches (except St Pancras) as well as the partly built rotunda started by Wulfric, all to be replaced by a new fully Romanesque church. By the time of Scotland's death in 1087, the new structure comprised choir and ambulatory (with crypt below) and a significant portion of the nave.[60] Although criticised by later Saint Augustine's writers as being too subservient to Lanfranc, Scotland was a capable and successful abbot, a worthy successor to the last three abbots of Anglo-Saxon times.[61] Whether his policies were in any way to blame for the violent disturbances that took place after his death is a matter for conjecture.

The subsequent imposition of Wido by Lanfranc was strongly resisted by the monks of Saint Augustine's, almost all of whom left the abbey church in protest when the archbishop brought in the abbot elect to install him. They believed (with some justification) that their right of choosing their own abbot went back to the seventh century. This does not altogether explain the outbreaks of violence and the intense animosity against Wido which, for instance, led the monk Columbanus to admit to Lanfranc that he would kill his abbot if he could. Perhaps the demolition of the old buildings contributed to feelings of insecurity among some older monks. The involvement of citizens (no doubt encouraged by some of the monks) in the attempt to kill Wido after the death of Lanfranc remains unexplained. It would be surprising if they were motivated by the desire to uphold the ancient rights of a long-established community. However, this is not the occasion to re-examine this remarkable story, which incidentally finds no place in the records of Saint Augustine's itself.[62] It was a low point in the life of the community which later generations did not care to remember.

The rebuilding of the abbey church, which was completed in the early twelfth century, may be taken to mark the end of the early history of Saint Augustine's Abbey. The magnificent translation of the relics of St Augustine and of other saints into the new church in September 1091, coming as it did so soon after the troubles of 1087–9, must have done a great deal to rebuild the morale of the shattered community, and to imbue the twenty-four monks who had been introduced from Christ Church with the spirit of Saint Augustine's.[63] The writings of Goscelin, providing a stylish and up-to-date series of local saints' lives, played an important part in reconstructing the identity of the community, making its members aware of their glorious past. Soon after 1100, the scene was set for the next 400 years of Saint Augustine's existence as a great abbey, when it won its battle against the archbishops for exemption; however, as time went on it became a place of local rather than of national importance.

The early history of the abbey remained important to its later writers, culminating in the outstanding work of Thomas of Elmham in the early fifteenth century. He has some claim to be regarded as a founder of modern Anglo-Saxon studies, since he slipped almost imperceptibly from promoting the rights of his house to an interest in the early period of its history for its own sake.[64] It remains puzzling that a community which depended heavily on promoting its earliest traditions preserved so little early material relating to Augustine himself. Albinus passed information about Augustine and his mission to Bede, but why did he not write a life of Augustine at a time when a life of Gregory the Great was written in Northumbria?[65] The perceived importance of Gregory, which seems to have stifled the early development of a cult of St Augustine was doubtless a factor, as too was the existence of some account in Bede's authoritative *Historia ecclesiastica*. However, part of the explanation may also lie in the way that the community thought, at a time when oral tradition was more immediate and important than the written word. The emergence of Augustine in the later eleventh century as '*apostolus Anglorum*' was not solely due to the genius of Goscelin and events of the time.[66] It must have been the result of devotion to the saint in the community over the previous 500 years: not indeed articulated in prose, but genuine all the same. Other abbeys acquired relics of saints from elsewhere, but at Saint Augustine's their founder remained among them and continued to provide them with inspiration and support. So certain of this were they that for many years they felt no need to write about his life.

NOTES

1. For further discussion of historical interests at Saint Augustine's see my article: 'The historical traditions of St. Augustine's Abbey, Canterbury' in *Canterbury and the Norman Conquest*, eds R. Eales and R Sharpe (London, 1995), pp. 159–68. In writing this present article which, particularly for the earlier period, draws heavily on the work of others, I am most grateful to all who have discussed the history of Saint Augustine's with me over the years. My particular thanks go to Richard Gameson for all his helpful suggestions as editor.
2. *HE*, I, 33.
3. S.E. Kelly, 'The Pre-Conquest History and Archive of Saint Augustine's Abbey, Canterbury', unpublished Ph.D. dissertation (Cambridge, 1986), p. 3. I am most grateful to Susan Kelly for giving me a copy of the dissertation, the only full and scholarly treatment of the pre-Conquest history of Saint Augustine's. I follow her practice in using the name Saint Augustine's throughout the history of the abbey.
4. Kelly, 'Pre-Conquest History', pp. 20–2.
5. N.P. Brooks, *The Early History of the Church of Canterbury* (Leicester, 1984), pp. 91–2.
6. For full discussion see Kelly, 'Pre-Conquest History', pp. 11–17.
7. For more details see R. Gem, 'Reconstructions of St. Augustine's Abbey, Canterbury in the Anglo-Saxon Period', in *St. Dunstan: His Life, Times and Cult*, eds N. Ramsay, M. Sparks and T. Tatton-Brown (Woodbridge, 1992), pp. 59–63, which should be read in conjunction with the discussion of Eric Cambridge, ch. 10 in the present volume.
8. For texts of the forged charters see *Charters of St. Augustine's Abbey Canterbury and Minster-in-Thanet*, ed. S.E. Kelly (London, 1995), nos 3, 5.
9. For fuller details see Kelly, 'Pre-Conquest History', pp. 64–74.
10. For discussion of the dates of abbots see Kelly, *Charters*, Appendix 4.
11. Michael Lapidge has described Abbot Hadrian's life and career fully in *Biblical Commentaries from the Canterbury School of Theodore and Hadrian*, eds B. Bischoff and M. Lapidge (Cambridge, 1994), chs 3 and 4.
12. *Cartularium Saxonicum*, ed. W. de Gray Birch, 3 vols (London, 1885–93), no. 38; W. Levison, *England and the Continent in the Eighth Century* (Oxford, 1946), pp. 187–90.
13. Kelly, *Charters*, pp. xxxvi–xxxvii. Gospels of St Augustine: CCCC, 286. Richard Gameson's forthcoming study will shed further light on this point. See further chs 12 and 13 above.
14. The Vespasian Psalter: BL, Cotton Vespasian A i, on which see further ch. 13 above. The quest for the books associated with the school of Theodore and Hadrian has been going on at least since the time of Archbishop Matthew Parker in s. xvi. For the problems of identifying such manuscripts, see D. Dumville, 'The Importation of Mediterranean Manuscripts into Theodore's England', in *Archbishop Theodore*, ed. M. Lapidge. (Cambridge, 1995), pp. 96–119.
15. W. Thorne, *De rebus gestis abbatum S. Augustini Cantuariae*, in *Historiae anglicanae scriptores decem*, ed. R. Twysden, (London, 1652), cols 1772–4; *William Thorne's Chronicle of St. Augustine's Abbey, Canterbury*, now rendered into English by A.H. Davis (Oxford, 1934), pp. 26–8.
16. For fuller discussion see Brooks, *Church of Canterbury*, pp. 81–3; Kelly, *Charters*, p. xv.

17. See Kelly, 'Pre-Conquest History', pp. 75–80.
18. See Kelly, *Charters*, pp. cvi–vii for further discussion of this point.
19. Kelly, *Charters*, no. 17.
20. See the contribution of Alan Thacker to the present volume (ch. 14).
21. Kelly, 'Pre-Conquest History', pp. 27–9.
22. See the contribution of Mildred Budny to the present volume (ch. 11).
23. Susan Kelly first made this important point; see her *Charters*, p. xvii.
24. Brooks, *Church of Canterbury*, pp. 162–4; Kelly, 'Pre-Conquest History', pp. 45–6.
25. *Die Gesetze der Angelsachsen*, ed. F. Liebermann, 3 vols (Halle, 1903–16), I, 159; *English Historical Documents, I, c. 500–1042*, ed. D. Whitelock, 2nd edn (London, 1979), p. 420; see comment in Kelly, 'Pre-Conquest History', pp. 46–7.
26. D. Dumville, 'English Square Minuscule Script: the background and earliest phases', *ASE*, 16 (1987), 147–79, esp. 169–73.
27. For a discussion of tenth-century monasticism see *inter alia*, A. Gransden, 'Tradition and Continuity in Late Anglo-Saxon Monasticism', *JEH*, 40 (1989), 159–207.
28. The most recent edition is *Die Regularis Concordia und ihre altenglische interlinearversion*, ed. L. Kornexl (Munich, 1993).
29. *Memorials of St. Dunstan*, ed. W. Stubbs, RS 63 (London, 1874), pp. 48–9.
30. Thorne, *De rebus gestis abbatum S. Augustini Cantuariae*, col. 1780.
31. C.R. Peers and A.W. Clapham, 'St. Augustine's Abbey Church, Canterbury, before the Norman Conquest, *Archaeologia*, 77 (1927), 201–17.
32. A.W. Clapham, 'A Note on the Layout of the Cloister at St. Austin's Abbey, Canterbury', *Arch. Cant*, 46 (1934), 191–4. See the comments on problems of interpretation by R. Cramp 'Monastic Sites', in *The Archaeology of Anglo-Saxon England*, ed. D. Wilson, (London, 1976), pp. 248–9.
33. T.A.M. Bishop, 'Manuscripts connected with St. Augustine's Abbey, Canterbury', in *Transactions of the Cambridge Bibliographical Society*, 2 (1957), 323–36; 3 (1960), 93–5; and 4 (1963), 412–3. See also, for the most recent work on these manuscripts, H.A. McKee, 'St. Augustine's Abbey, Canterbury: Book production in the tenth and eleventh centuries', unpublished Ph.D. dissertation (Cambridge, 1997). I am most grateful to Helen McKee for providing me with a copy of her dissertation.
34. For details and bibliography see E. Temple, *Anglo-Saxon Manuscripts, 900–1066* (London, 1976), no. 38.
35. *Anglo-Saxon Chronicle s.a.* 1011 in *The Anglo-Saxon Chronicle*, a revised translation, eds D. Whitelock, D.C. Douglas and S.I. Tucker (London, 1961), p. 91.
36. *The Chronicle of John of Worcester*, vol. II, eds R. Darlington and P. McGurk, (Oxford, 1995), pp. 466–70.
37. Thorne, *De rebus gestis abbatum S. Augustini Cantuariae*, col. 1782.
38. D.W. Rollason, 'Goscelin's account of the Translation and Miracles of St. Mildrith: (BHL 5961–4) an edition with notes', *Medieval Studies*, 48 (1986), 139–210; M. Colker, 'A Hagiographic Polemic', *Medieval Studies*, 39 (1977), 60–108.
39. For the date of the translation see R. Sharpe, 'The Date of St. Mildreth's translation from Minster-in-Thanet to Canterbury', *Medieval Studies*, 53 (1991), 349–54.
40. Rollason, 'Goscelin's St. Mildrith', pp. 173–4.
41. F. Harmer, *Anglo-Saxon Writs* (Manchester, 1952), no. 37.

42. BL, Cotton Augustus ii 90; printed with translation in *Anglo-Saxon Charters*, ed. A. Robertson (Cambridge, 1939), pp. 174–9.
43. *Anglo-Saxon Chronicle* E s.a. 1045, eds Whitelock et al., p. 109.
44. *Anglo-Saxon Chronicle* E s.a. 1049, eds Whitelock et al., p. 112.
45. Goscelin, *Historia Translationis Sancti Augustini: PL*, CXLV, cols 31–3. The abbreviated version of the '*Historia translationis*' in *PL* covers all my references. For a full edition of this work consult *Acta Sanctorum Maii* VI, eds G. Henschenius and D. Papebroch (Antwerp, 1688), 411–36. Richard Sharpe's forthcoming edition of *Goscelin's Canterbury Lives* will be a great boon.
46. Anselm of Reims, *Historia dedicationis ecclesie S. Remigii: PL*, CXLII, col. 1431.
47. Gem, 'Reconstructions of St. Augustine's Abbey', pp. 67–71.
48. Goscelin, *Historia translationis: PL*, CLV, col. 33.
49. *Anglo-Saxon Chronicle* E, eds Whitelock et al., pp. 135–6.
50. Goscelin, *Historia translationis: PL*, CLV, cols 33–4.
51. Pope Urban II, *Ep. 9: PL*, CLI, cols 291–3.
52. *Liber Eliensis*, ed. E. Blake (London, 1962), p. 168.
53. Thorne, *De rebus gestis abbatum S. Augustini Cantuariae*, cols 1785–6.
54. *Liber Eliensis*, ed. Blake, pp. 146–7. See the comment of S. Keynes, *The Diplomas of King Æthelred the Unready 978–1016*, (Cambridge, 1980), pp. 150–1.
55. Thomas of Elmham, *Historia Monasterii S. Augustini Cantuariensis*, ed. C. Hardwick, RS 8 (London, 1858), p. 28.
56. *Regesta Regum Anglo-Normannorum: the Acta of William I* (1066–87), ed. D. Bates (Oxford, 1998), no. 83.
57. *The Heads of Religious Houses: England and Wales 940–1216*, eds D. Knowles, C.N.L. Brooke and V.C.M. London (Cambridge, 1972), p. 62.
58. Orderic Vitalis, *Ecclesiastical History*, ed. M. Chibnall, 6 vols (Oxford, 1969), II, 248.
59. '*Acta Lanfranci*' in *Two of the Saxon Chronicles Parallel*, eds J. Earle and C. Plummer, 2 vols (Oxford, 1892–8), I, 288.
60. Goscelin, *Historia translationis: PL*, CLV, col. 34.
61. Thorne, *De rebus gestis abbatum S. Augustini Cantuariae*, col. 1791.
62. '*Acta Lanfranci*', eds Earle and Plummer, I, pp. 288–92.
63. The dramatic nature of the translations of September 1091 is brought out by R. Sharpe, 'The setting of St. Augustine's translation, 1091', in *Canterbury and the Norman Conquest*, eds Eales and Sharpe, pp. 1–13.
64. For more details about Thomas of Elmham as antiquary see A. Gransden, 'Antiquarian Studies in Fifteenth-century England', *Antiquaries Journal*, 60 (1980), 74–81; see also my 'Historical Traditions of St. Augustine's Abbey', pp. 166–8.
65. *The earliest life of Gregory the Great by an anonymous monk of Whitby*, ed. and trans. B. Colgrave (Lawrence, Kansas, 1968).
66. Richard Sharpe, speaking at the conference, put forward the view that this phrase was not used earlier than by Goscelin; see further the contribution of Alan Thacker to the present volume. Further on Goscelin's *Vita Augustini* see Fiona Gameson, ch. 15 above.

General Index

Adalhard, abbot of Tours 245
Adam of Bremen 153
Ælfmaer, abbot of Saint Augustine's 384, 419–21
Ælfnoth, priest 164
Ælfric, homilist 386
Ælfsige of Ramsey 423
Æthelberht, king of Kent 8, 15–17, 18–19, 21–3, 26, 27, 29, 30–3, 34, 35, 39, 40, 43, 44, 54, 70–1, 123, 133, 136–7, 145 n. 76, 150 n. 176, 159, 160, 161, 162, 165, 167, 174, 189, 209, 223, 226, 272, 324, 392, 411, 413
Æthelburh of Barking 190
Æthelburh of Kent and Northumbria 16, 29, 159, 169 n. 18, 398
Æthelfrith, king of Northumbria 36, 108, 124–5, 167, 403
Æthelred, king of England 419
Æthelred, king of Mercia 163, 188, 190
Æthelsige, abbot of Saint Augustine's 422–3
Æthelweard, chronicler 169 n. 20
Æthelwin, abbot of Athelney 386
Æthelwold, bishop of Winchester 384, 417
Agatho, Pope 414
Agilbert, bishop of Wessex 160
Agiulf, deacon 72–3, 74
Aidan of Lindisfarne 3, 166, 382, 383
Aix-en-Provence 11, 68
Albinus, abbot of St Augustine's 1, 3, 118, 126, 127, 128, 129, 272, 314, 381–2, 411, 414–15, 424
Alcuin 58, 194, 381
Aldfrith, king of Northumbria 169 n. 17
Aldhelm of Malmesbury 110, 128, 130, 132, 190, 294, 314
Alfred the Great 187, 195–6
Allen, Thomas 258
Amandus, St 91, 136
Ambrose, St 323
Amiens 135
Angers 41, 207, 396–7
Anglo-Saxon Chronicle 14, 56, 196, 359, 384, 419
Anselm of Reims 421
Antoninus Pius, column of 247
Arator 323

Ari Thorgilsson 164
Arles 11, 12, 13, 21, 41, 68, 114, 393
Arras 135
Aschheim 99
Asser 195–6
Asthal, Oxon. 96
Athelney 386
Athelstan, king of England 384, 417
Augsburg 99
Augst-Basel 99
Augustine of Canterbury *Lege librum, o piger*
Augustine of Hippo 249, 386
Authari, king of the Lombards 92
Autun 11

Bangor-is-Coed 5, 35 6, 108, 109, 116, 125–6, 128
Bardney, Lincs. 128, 163, 188
Barking, Essex 190–1
Bassa 208
Bayeux Tapestry 270
Beauvais 135
Béccánn, hermit 131
Bede 1–40, 41–2, 50–4, 76, 79, 102, 107–8, 110, 112, 118, 124–33, 152–5, 161–2, 165, 166–8, 175, 190, 191, 193–4, 211, 213, 248, 272, 288, 293, 294, 307 n. 15, 314, 358, 374, 379, 380, 381–2, 383, 392–4, 400–2, 403, 404, 405, 410, 411, 415, 424
Benedict, St 91, 196
Benedict, St, Rule of 31, 360, 418
Benedict I, Pope 378
Benedict Biscop 414
Benedictus Levita 179
Benouville 53
Benty Grange 90
Benty Grange helmet 92, 165
Berctuald, archbishop 379
Bertha, queen of Kent 5, 7, 12, 15, 16–17, 22, 31, 54, 61, 70–4, 87, 160, 174, 209, 213, 224, 226, 307 n. 16, 314, 357, 364 n. 11, 394, 412, 413
Bertila of Chelles 357, 372 n. 114
Biblia Gregoriana 237–73, 296, 313
boats 52–3, 59–60, 62

Boniface, St 23, 26, 29, 58, 59–60, 89, 91–2, 159, 178, 194, 326, 338, 358
Boniface III, Pope 378
Boniface IV, Pope 378
Boniface V, Pope 29, 159, 169 n. 18
Boulogne (Gessoriacum) 14, 51, 135
Brabourne 417
Bradwell-on-Sea, Essex 204, 208, 215, 217
Breedon, Leics. 103
Brocmail 125, 126–7
Brunhild, queen of Franks 10, 13, 14, 45, 61, 68, 69, 74–5, 76–8, 80, 109, 150 n. 169, 160
Burchard of Worms 180
burial customs 20, 86–103
Bury St Edmunds 288, 322

Cadoc, St 36
Cadwallon, king of Gwynedd 109–10, 139
Caedwalla, king of Wessex 162, 163, 191
Caesarius of Arles 111, 120, 142 n. 20
Cambrai 135
Candidus, *vicedominus* 7, 68, 69, 75
Canterbury 15, 20–1, 54, 56, 57, 115, 118, 160, 193, 211–12, 272, 286, 288, 293, 296, 301, 305, 313, 330, 333, 380, 384, 385, 386, 399
   Christ Church 33, 118, 174, 207, 269, 270, 337, 384, 387, 398, 416, 420–1, 424
   Saint Augustine's 9, 32, 33–4, 37–8, 237, 252, 288–9, 293, 295, 313–14, 323, 328, 334 337, 374–9, 383–4, 387, 392, 394, 396, 398, 405, 410–24
   St Gregory 420
   St John the Baptist 415
   St Martin's 17, 21, 72, 102, 118, 144 n. 71, 174, 213, 217, 288, 413
   St Mary 205, 208, 209, 411, 413, 418, 422
   St Pancras 204, 205, 206, 211, 213–16, 217, 219, 220–1, 411
   SS Peter and Paul 202, 203, 205–6, 207, 208, 209, 210, 215, 217, 226, 374, 411–13, 418, 422; *see also* Saint Augustine's
carmina figurata 341–2, 344–5
Cassiodorus 296
Cedd, St 26, 166, 208–9
Centwine, king of Wessex 163
Ceolfrid of Wearmouth–Jarrow 192, 248–9, 314
Ceolwulf, king of Northumbria 172 n. 85, 382
Cerne 397–8
Chad, St 110, 288
Châlon 41
Charibert I, king of Franks 12, 16, 54, 70, 71–2, 307 n. 16
Charlemagne 92, 358
Charles Martel 91
Chelles 357
Chertsey 191

Chessell Down, Isle of Wight 158
Chester, battle of 36, 109, 125, 126–7, 129
childbirth 175–82
Childebert I, king of Franks 71
Childebert II, king of Franks 74, 75, 76, 77, 80
Childeric, king of Franks 157–8
Chilperic I, king of Franks 16, 71, 76
Chlothar II, king of Franks 13, 69, 74, 76, 77, 78, 80, 99, 136
Clofesho 194, 383
Clovis, king of Franks 91, 136
Cluny 422
Cnut, king of Denmark and England 384, 420
Codex Aureus see Index of Manuscripts: Stockholm, Kungl. Bibliotek, A. 135
Codex Bigotianus see Index of Manuscripts: BnF, lat. 281 + 298
Codex Grandior 296
Coifi, priest 153, 154
coinage 54–5, 57, 59, 61, 157, 158
Colmán 133, 149 n. 158
Cologne 87, 181
Colomann, king of Ireland 402
Columbanus of Bobbio and Luxeuil 91, 92, 111, 113–14, 116, 131, 132, 133, 134, 150 n. 169, 160, 178
Columbanus of Canterbury 423
Constance 88, 99
Constans II, emperor 414
Constantine I, emperor 31, 44, 340, 342, 346
Constantinople 271
Constantius of Lyon 4, 112, 113
Corbinian, St 91
Coroticus 139
Cotton, Robert 254, 286, 297
crosses, gold foil 93, 95
crosses, pectoral 92
Cummean, penitential of 120
Cummian, computist 131
Cuthbert, archbishop of Canterbury 194, 341, 345, 377, 383, 415
Cuthbert, St, coffin of 92
Cynegils, king of Wessex 162
Cyriacus, monk 43

Dagan, bishop 113
Dagobert I, king of Franks 99, 103, 136
Damasus, Pope 239
Daniel, bishop of Winchester 23, 159
Desiderius, bishop of Auxerre 75
Deusdedit of Canterbury 357, 376, 384
Dinoot, abbot of Bangor 124, 126–8
disc brooch, kentish 345
Domesday Book 414, 416
Dorestad 57, 58
Dover 51, 314
Dunningen 101
Dunstan, St 384, 418

Eadbald, king of Kent 26, 31, 34, 54, 165, 169 n. 18, 171 n. 58, 208, 209, 413
Eadburh, abbess of Minster 326, 327
Eadsige, archbishop of Canterbury 390 nn. 62, 64, 420
Eadui Basan, scribe 330
Ealdwulf, king of East Anglia 162
Earkonwald, bishop of London 190, 191
Ebbsfleet 14, 421
Eccles, Kent 118, 119, 174
Ecgberht, king of Kent 208
Ecgberht alter 108
Ecgfrith, king of Northumbria 169 n. 17, 381
Echternach 299, 333, 339
Edith of Wilton 397, 405
Edmund, king and martyr 384
Edward the Confessor 422
Edwin, king of Northumbria 16, 21–2, 29, 31, 109, 139, 154, 157, 159, 162, 188, 381, 382, 398
Egbert, archbishop of York 194, 313, 346, 383
Egil Skalla-Grimsson 164
Emmeram, St 91, 99, 101
Eorcengota, St 164
Eorconberht, king of Kent 20, 32, 162, 164, 210
Eormenric, king of Kent 15
Epiphanius of Cyprus 249
Erasmus of Rotterdam 182
Escomb, Co. Durham 102
Etherius of Arles 393
Eulogius, bishop of Alexandria 12, 21, 394
Eusebius of Caesarea 239
Eustasius of Luxeuil 92
Eve of Wilton 397

Faremoutier-en-Brie 164, 357
Farnham 191
Faversham 119
Fécamp 349
Felix, bishop of East Anglia 160
Finglesham buckle 155
fish tails 408 n. 21
Foi, Ste, of Conques 400
Folkestone 314
Fordwich 56
founder-graves 96–102
Foxley, Wilts. 102
Frankfurt-am-Main 92
Franks Casket 167
Fredegar, *Chronicle of* 70, 74, 75, 76, 77, 78, 170 n. 27
Fredegund, queen of Franks 13, 74, 75, 76, 77, 80
Fridolin, St 103
Friedberg 93
Frithuric, *princeps* 103
Frithuwald, sub-king of Surrey 191

Friya 20
Fulda 92, 342

Gallus, St 92
Gap 46
Gelasius I, Pope 378
genealogies 155
Geraint, king of Dumnonia 110, 130
Germanus of Auxerre 4, 111, 112, 131
Ghent 402
Gilbert, W.S. 9
Gildas 4, 52, 110, 116–17, 127, 133, 139, 400
Goodmanham 153, 154
Goscelin of Saint-Bertin/Canterbury 3, 38, 374, 378, 379, 384, 386, 391–406, 410, 419–20, 421, 424
Gospels of St Augustine *see* Index of Manuscripts: CCCC, 286; BodL Auct. D. 2. 14
Gratian 181–2
Gregory I, pope 3, 6–14, 17, 20, 21, 24–32, 34, 36, 37, 39, 41–7, 68–70, 74, 75–7, 79–80, 108–9, 111–15, 121–4, 130, 131, 132, 133, 136–7, 140, 150 n. 169, 159, 160, 162, 165, 174–7, 187–96, 226, 251, 258, 271, 288, 313, 320, 324, 346, 378, 380, 381, 382, 383, 385, 392, 393–4, 398, 406, 424
Gregory II, Pope 3
Gregory of Tours 12, 16, 52, 70, 71, 72, 74, 76, 77, 88, 91
Grobbendonk 102
Gruibingen 99
Gundulf, bishop of Rochester 38
Guntram, king of Franks 13, 16, 74

Hadrian of Canterbury 9, 288, 293–4, 314, 322, 358, 382, 414–15
Hamwih *see* Southampton
Harald Bluetooth, king of Denmark 23
Hare, Robert 258
Harold Harefoot, king of England 420
Hatfield, Synod of 294
Helgi inn Magri 164
hell 167
Hengest (and Horsa) 14, 155
Hérard, bishop of Tours 179
Herman, bishop of Sherborne 397
Herrsching 99–100
Hilarius, Pope 249
Hilda of Whitby 190
Hildilith, abbess of Barking 190
Hlothere, king of Kent 324
Hodilred *see* Æthelred
Honorius I, Pope 25, 212, 225, 227, 378
Honorius of Canterbury 357, 376
Hospito, duke 43
Hrabanus Maurus 342
Huosi, family of 100

Iaenberht of Canterbury 415
icon 18, 247, 271
Ingoberga, wife of Charibert I 12, 16, 70, 71, 72, 74
Ipswich 55–6, 58
Isaac of Langres 179
L'Isle Jourdain 217
Ivo of Chartres 180–1

James I, king of England 248
Jerome 237, 239, 242, 249, 290
John II Romanus, archbishop of Ravenna 379
John III, Pope 378
John the Deacon 256
John of Worcester 419
Jonas of Bobbio 178
Jonas of Orléans 179
Juliana Anicia, princess 247
Julius Caesar 4
Justus 28, 70, 78, 113, 374, 376, 379, 384

Kornwestheim 101

Landnámabók 164
Lanfranc of Bec 180, 423
Lauchheim 95
Laurentius of Canterbury 24, 37, 68, 113, 123, 143 n. 41, 171 n. 58, 208, 231 n. 54, 374, 375–6, 379, 384, 392, 404, 411
Lavoye 85
Le Mans 72
Leander of Seville 112
Leicester 386
Leland, John 257
Leo I, Pope 111, 378
Leodegar, cripple 385
Lérins 10–11, 68
Leuthere, bishop of Wessex 160
Libellus responsionum 24–8, 120, 175–8, 393–4
Liber Eliensis 422–3
Lichfield 288, 322
Licinus, bishop of Angers 408 n. 19
Liège 298
Lillebonne 51
Lincoln 360
Lindisfarne 190, 298, 356, 381, 389 n. 35
Lindisfarne Gospels *see* Index of Manuscripts: BL, Cott. Nero D. iv
Littlebourne 390 n. 62
Liudger, St, Life of 56
Liudhard, bishop 16, 18, 22, 70, 79, 87, 118, 120, 160, 174, 307 n. 16, 314, 357, 412
Liudhard medalet 18, 79
Livinus, St 402
London 30, 31, 34, 39, 54, 56, 58, 59, 115, 137, 138, 196, 209, 386, 398
Louis the Pious 195
Lucca 291

Lul, bishop of Mainz 194
Lullingstone 118
Lumley, John Lord 258
Luxeuil 114, 367 n. 50
Lyminge 203, 208, 314, 325
Lyon 11, 41, 217, 233 n. 128

Maastricht 135
Mâcon, Synod of 149 n. 154
Malmesbury 128, 129, 294
Margate 118
Marseille 11, 41, 68
Martin of Tours, St 12, 72, 98, 101
Maserfelth 128
Maximian of Ravenna 265
Mellitus 28, 44, 68, 78, 113, 143 n. 41, 165, 208, 211–12, 230 n. 54, 374, 376, 379, 382, 384
menstruation 175–82
Metz 41, 88
Mildreth of Thanet 330, 357, 368 n. 61, 384–5, 405–6, 410, 419–20
Milred, bishop of Worcester 341
Minster-in-Sheppey 203, 208, 209, 314
Minster-in-Thanet 288, 314, 326–7, 337–8, 384, 419
Mondsee 333
Morken 102
Mount Sinai 247
Moutier-Grandval 103

Nazeingbury, Essex 102
Nicholas I, Pope 179–80
Norwich 386
Nothelm 178, 191
Nydam boat 53, 62

Odin *see* Wodin
Oeric, son of Hengist 155
Offa, king of Mercia 249
Old English martyrology 195, 383
Orléans 290
Osthryth of Northumbria and Mercia 188
Oswald, king of Northumbria 32, 128, 157, 164, 172 nn. 66, 90, 188, 398
Oswestry 128
Oswine, king of Northumbria 166
Oswiu, king of Northumbria 153, 160, 188
Oxford 420

paganism 19–20, 84–90, 153–5, 161–5, 176–7
parchment, purple 243–4, 268, 338, 340
Paris 16, 41, 70, 72, 78, 181, 249, 353, 412
Parker, Matthew 254, 273, 285, 297
Patrick, St 117, 139
Paucapalea 181
Paulinus of York and Rochester 16, 28, 31, 190, 380, 381, 382, 398, 403
Pavia 113

Peada, king of Middle Angles 162
Pehthelm, bishop of Whithorn 128–9
Pelagius I, Pope 378
Pelagius II, Pope 18
Penda, king of Mercia 31, 32, 162, 163
penitentials 177–82
Perugia 220, 295
Peter of Dover 70, 78
Pfullingen 99
Pirmin 91
Pliny the Elder 127
Poreč 220
Porfyrius 337, 340–1, 343, 344
ports 14, 51–2, 53–61
Praetextatus, bishop of Rouen 76
Procopius 53
Protadius, bishop 68

Quentovic 14, 57–8, 59, 61, 62

Radbod of Frisia 167
Rædwald, king of East Anglia 22, 54, 162, 164
Ramsey 385, 386
Ravenna 217, 218, 221, 222, 223, 224, 225, 265, 309 n. 34, 336, 379, 386
Reculver 202, 204, 205, 206, 207, 208, 209, 210, 215, 217, 218, 219, 221–3, 226, 314, 324
Regensburg 96, 99, 100–1
Regino of Prüm 180
Regularis Concordia 418
Reichenau 91, 103
Reims, Council of 421, 422
Richborough 14–15, 51, 118
Rochester 31, 34, 39, 203, 204–5, 208, 209, 210, 314
Rome 6, 8, 21, 23–4, 58, 72, 111, 117, 120, 137, 160, 171 n. 53, 178, 179–80, 188–9, 191, 211–12, 217, 221–2, 223, 224, 225, 235 n. 127, 239, 249, 316, 318, 332, 377–8, 380, 381, 386, 391, 392, 412, 422
    San Andreas in Clivo Scauri 8, 191
    San Lorenzo fuori le Mura 18
    San Pancrazio 378
    San Petro 377–9
    Sant'Agnese 378
    Lateran 33, 212
Rouen 41, 52, 54, 58, 135
Roundway Down 90, 159
Royal Bible *see* Index of Manuscripts: BL, Royal 1 E. vi
Rufinianus 28
Rufinus of Bologna 181
Rupert, St 91

Säckingen 103
Saebbi, king of Essex 163
Sæbert, king of Essex 22, 162
St Albans 122
Saint-Bertin 323, 360
Saint-Denis 87, 217
St Gallen 103
Saint-Imier 103
Saint-Mitre-les-Remparts 217
Saint-Osyth, Essex 146 n. 90
Saint-Quentin 99
Saint-Ursanne 103
Saint-Vaast 323
Samson, St, Life of 116
Sandwich 56, 57, 420–1
Sardinia 6, 43
Sarre 420
Scotland, abbot of Saint Augustine's 37, 423
Ségéne, abbot of Iona 131
sexual intercourse 28, 175–82
Sherborne 294
Sidonius Apollinaris 53
Sigehere, king of Essex 163, 172 n. 78
Sigibert, king of East Anglia 30, 54, 163
Sigibert, king of Essex 26, 153, 166
Sigibert I, king of Franks 16, 74, 76
Simplicius, Pope 378
Sixtus (unknown martyr) 5, 27, 121, 123, 174
Sixtus II, Pope 174
Snorri Sturluson 84
Socrates 404
Southampton (Hamwih) 57, 58, 59, 60
Speyer 99
Stephen of Ripon 61
Stigand, archbishop of Canterbury 422, 423
Stonor 14
Stowe Missal *see* Index of Manuscripts: Dublin, Royal Irish Academy, D. II. 3
Strasbourg 99
Sullivan, A. 9
Sulpicius Severus 72, 407 n. 4
Sutcliffe, Matthew 248
Sutton Hoo 96
Sutton Hoo ship burial 29, 54, 57, 61, 155, 156–8
Swallowcliffe Down 90
Syagrius, bishop of Autun 11–12, 69, 75, 76, 77, 150 n. 169, 160
Symmachus, Pope 378

Tatwine 364 n. 16
Thanet 14–15, 50, 288, 397; *see also* Minster-in-Thanet
Theodebert II, king of Franks 10, 13, 61, 68, 69, 74, 75, 76, 78, 79, 108
Theodelinda of Bavaria and Lombardy 92, 271
Theoderic II, king of Franks 10, 13, 61, 68, 69, 74–5, 78, 79, 108
Theodo, duke of Bavaria 91
Theodore of Tarsus, archbishop of Canterbury 3, 9, 31, 37, 57, 110, 128, 175, 177–9, 194,

288, 293–4, 314, 322, 358, 379, 380–2, 414–15
Theodosius I, emperor 44
Theodulf of Orélans 261
Theudebald, duke 91
Thomas Becket 38
Thomas of Elmham 237, 251–5, 257, 262, 263, 272, 288–9, 293, 295, 297, 330, 334, 410, 424
Thomas Sprott 272, 410
Thor 20, 84, 164
Thwaites, Edward 39
Tiw / Tiu 20, 84
Toulon 41
Tournai 135
Tours 11, 12, 60–1, 68, 72, 73–4, 245, 261, 263, 309 n. 37
Trajan, emperor 195

Uppsala 153

Venantius Fortunatus 71
Vendel 157
Vergilius of Arles 393
Vermand 135
Vespasian Psalter *see* Index of Manuscripts: BL, Cott. Vesp. A. i
Victor of Capua 290
Victorius of Aquitaine 117, 132
Vienne 11, 46, 68, 218, 235 n. 128
Vindonissa-Windisch 99
Vitalian, Pope 414
Vitruvius 403–4
Vortigern, king of Britons 4, 155

Walcheren/Domburg 55–6, 59
Wanley, Hunfrey 248
Wantsum Channel 14, 50
Wealdhere, bishop of London 367 n. 47
Wearmouth–Jarrow 192–3, 248–9, 294, 356, 360, 414

Werferth, bishop of Worcester 195
Westminster 422
Whitby 188, 381
Whitby *Life of Gregory the Great* 3, 6, 41, 188, 189–90, 193, 196, 380, 424
Whitby, synod of 110, 128, 129, 148 nn. 143, 158
Wido, abbot of Saint Augustine's 37, 423–4
Wihtred, king of Kent 172 n. 77, 325
Wilfrid, St 57, 58, 61–2, 148 n. 143, 169 n. 16, 381
Wilfrid, St, Life of 61–2, 122
William I, king of England 423
William of Malmesbury 406
William Thorne 32, 39, 410, 415, 419, 422
Willibald 29, 58, 59–60
Willibrord, St 190, 299, 381
Wilton 397, 405
Winchester 57, 384, 385, 386, 411, 417–18, 422
Winchester, Old Minster 102
Wine, bishop of the West Saxons 110
Winster Moor 90
Woden / Odin 19, 20, 84, 155, 156, 164, 167, 189
Worcester 249, 360, 385, 386, 411
Wulfhere, king of Mercia 163
Wulfric, abbot of St Augustine's 421–2
Wulfstan of Winchester 384
Wulfstan of Worcester, St 385
Wulfthryth of Wilton 405

Yeavering 20, 102, 153, 154
York 30, 56, 58, 59, 115, 137, 138, 380, 381, 398, 399

Zabarda, duke 43
Zacharias, Pope 89
Zofingen 99
Zurich 96
Zurzach 98–9

Index of Manuscripts

Ancona, Biblioteca Capitolare, s.n.: 291
Augsburg, Universitätsbibliothek, 1 2 4º 2: 299, 339, 354
Autun, Bibliothèque municipale, 3 (S2): 358
   4 (S3): 358
Avranches, Bibliothèque municipale, 48 (i, iii) + 68 (i, ii) + 71 (A, B): 298, 322, 347–9, 350–1

Bamberg, Staatliche Bibliothek, Misc. Bibl. 1: 245
Berlin, Staatsbibliothek, Hamilton 553: 333
Berne, Burgerbibliothek, 212: 370 n. 84
Boulogne-sur-Mer, Bibliothèque municipale, 32: 323
Brescia, Biblioteca Queriniana, s.n.: 292, 321, 339
Brussels, Bibliothèque Royale Albert 1er, II.436: 298
   18723: 247

Cambridge University Library, Ll. 1. 10: 266
Cambridge, CCC, 144: 362
   162: 385
   173, pt ii: 359
   189: 272–3
   197B: 252–3, 272, 297
   270: 385
   286: 29, 252, 270, 272, 285–96, 298–306, 317–22, 323, 329, 336, 337–8, 340, 343–4, 346, 354, 355, 417
   304: 366 n. 43
   391: 385
Cambridge, Magdalene College, Pepys 2981(18): 310 n. 64
   Pepys 2981(19): 296–7
Cambridge, Trinity College, R. 17. 1: 269
Cambridge, Trinity Hall, 1: 39, 250, 251, 258
Canterbury Cathedral Library and Archives, Add. 16: 237, 238, 255, 258

Dublin, Royal Irish Academy, D. II. 3: 379–80
Dublin, Trinity College, 52: 290–1
   58: 85, 290–1, 303, 310 n. 65
   360: 257

Durham Cathedral Library, A. II. 16: 297, 308 n. 30
   A. II. 17: 296–7
   B. IV. 6: 312 n. 97

El Escorial, Real Biblioteca, Vitr. 17: 340
Erevan, Matenadaran, 2374 (olim 229): 265

Florence, Biblioteca Medicea-Laurenziana, Amiatino 1: 192, 249, 264, 290, 295, 296, 312 n. 97, 322
Fulda, Hessische Landesbibliothek, Bonifatianus 1: 290

Le Havre, Bibliothèque municipale, 330: 385
Lichfield Cathedral, 1: 85, 290–1, 347, 358
London, BL, Add. 5111: 264
   Add. 5463: 358
   Add. 10546: 261
   Add. 24142: 261
   Add. 37472 (1): 269–70
   Add. 37517: 384
   Add. 37518: 346
   Add. 37777: 249, 262
   Add. 45025: 249
   Add. 57337: 385
   Arundel 155: 384
   Cott. Ch. Aug. II. 2: 324–5
   Cott. Ch. Aug. II. 29: 190–1
   Cott. Ch. Aug. II. 91: 367 n. 47
   Cott. Claud. B. iv: 269
   Cott. Cleo. D. i: 409 n. 35
   Cott. Nero D. iv: 290, 335, 347, 349
   Cott. Otho A. i: 194
   Cott. Otho B. vi: 268
   Cott. Otho C. v: 253, 272, 297
   Cott. Tib. C. ii: 363
   Cott. Vesp. A. i: 243, 251–2, 257, 289, 293, 329, 330–6, 342, 344, 349, 357, 358, 359, 415
   Cott. Vesp. B. xx: 38, 395, 406 n. 1, 407 n. 3
   Egerton 609: 290–1, 303
   Harley 105: 406 n. 1, 407, n. 3
   Harley 1775: 290, 291, 292, 295
   Harley 5431: 418

Harley 6018: 277 n. 40
Loan 81: 249
Royal 1 B. vii: 369 n. 65
Royal 1 E. vi: 237–48, 255–60, 264–8, 270–3,
   289, 295–6, 363, 416
Royal 1 E. vii + viii: 295
Royal 7 C. xii: 253
Stowe Ch. 1: 325
Stowe Ch. 3: 367 n. 47
London, Victoria and Albert Museum, 661:
   269–70
Los Angeles, J.P. Getty Museum, 9: 268
Lucca, Biblioteca Capitolare, 8: 292

Madrid, Biblioteca de la Universidad, 31: 372 n.
   107
Maeseyck, Church of St Catherine, s.n.: 299,
   339
Milan, Biblioteca Ambrosiana, C. 39 inf.: 303,
   308 n. 27, 351
   M. 79 sup.: 293
Montpellier, Bibliothèque universitaire, H 509:
   333
Monza, Biblioteca Capitolare, G 1: 264
Moscow, Historical Museum, 129: 369 n. 72
Mount Athos, Lavra, A. 23: 264
Munich, Bayerische Staatsbibliothek, Clm
   4452: 340
   Clm 6224: 339
   Clm 14000: 340

Nancy, Cathédrale, Trésor, s.n.: 245
Naples, Biblioteca Nazionale, lat. 3: 321
New Haven, Yale University, Beinecke Library,
   516: 192
New York, Pierpont Morgan Library, M 521:
   269–70
   M 724: 269–70
   M 776: 333, 359–60

Oxford, BodL, Auct.D. 2. 14: 260, 285–96,
   298–9, 301–6, 322–3, 348, 354
   Auct. D. 2. 29: 290–1, 311 n. 82
   e Mus. 66: 323–4, 329
   Hatton 48: 360
   Lat. Bibl. b. 2 (P): 237, 238–9, 255–6, 258
   Lat. Bibl. d. 1 (P): 259–60, 262, 270–1, 296
   Selden Supra 30: 293, 327–30, 331–2, 334,
   342

Paris, Bibliothèque Mazarine, 5: 263
Paris, BnF, lat. 254: 340, 371 n. 103
   lat. 281 + 298: 292, 297–8, 349–55
   lat. 943: 385
   lat. 2421: 370 n. 84

lat. 9380: 303
lat. 9389: 297
lat. 9561: 38, 360–1
lat. 10837: 190
lat. 10861: 363
lat. 17226: 349, 352–3
n.a.l. 1587: 371 n. 103
n.a.l. 1596: 192
suppl. gr. 1286: 244
Perugia, Biblioteca Capitolare, 1: 291, 308 n. 26
   2: 295
Prague, Knihovna Metropolitní Kapitoly, Cim.
   1: 260, 290
Prague, Universitní Knihovna, Roudnice VI.
   Fe. 50: 298

Rochester Cathedral Library, A. 3. 5: 324
Rossano, Biblioteca Arcivescovile, s.n.: 244
Rouen, Bibliothèque municipale, Y. 6: 385

St Gallen, Stiftsbibliothek, 75: 264
   1395: 292
St Petersburg, Public Library, Lat. O. v. I. 1:
   298, 322, 347–9
   Lat. Q. v. I. 18: 193
Sarrezzano, Biblioteca Parrochiale, s.n.: 321
Split Cathedral, s.n.: 291, 354
Stockholm, Kungl. Bibliotek, A. 135: 294–5,
   312 n. 93, 329, 336–46, 347, 349, 350,
   351, 354, 358, 360
Stuttgart, Landesbibliothek, Bibl. fol. 12: 333

Trent, Museo Nazionale, s.n.: 321
Troyes, Bibliothèque municipale, 504: 315–18,
   319, 322, 323, 325, 342–3, 354

Vatican City, Biblioteca Apostolica Vaticana,
   Barb.lat. 570: 298–9, 339–40, 361–2
   Reg. lat. 124: 342
   Reg. lat. 267: 365 n. 31
   Vat. lat. 7016: 291
   Vat. lat. 7223: 295
Vercelli, Biblioteca Capitolare, s.n.: 354
Verona, Biblioteca Capitolare, VI (6): 321,
   339
Vienna, Österreichische Nationalbibliothek, lat.
   847: 264
   lat. 1224: 354
   med. gr. 1: 247
   theol. gr. 31: 244, 268

Worcester Cathedral Library, Add. 1: 259–60,
   262, 270–1, 296
Würzburg, Universitätsbibliothek, M. p. th. f.
   68: 354